A LIBRARY OF LITERARY CRITICISM

Leonard S. Klein
General Editor

A Library
of Literary Criticism

VOLUME I

A-J

Frederick Ungar Publishing Co., New York

MODERN FRENCH LITERATURE

Compiled and edited by

DEBRA POPKIN

MICHAEL POPKIN

Library of Congress Cataloging in Publication Data

Main entry under title:

Modern French literature.

Includes index.
CONTENTS: v. 1. A-J.—v. 2. K-Z.
1. French literature—20th century—History
and criticism—Addresses, essays, lectures.
I. Popkin, Debra.   II. Popkin, Michael.
PQ306.M57   840'.009'14   76-15655
ISBN 0-8044-3256-2

INTRODUCTION

The Nobel Prize in Literature has gone to more French writers than to those of any other country. Proust died before he could be nominated, and Aragon and Malraux have still not won the award. But the French prize winners do include Sartre, Camus, and Gide, and perhaps the general excellence of French literature in the twentieth century is the most reasonable explanation for the Nobel committee's choices. After all, the same preference exists on college campuses throughout America, where freshmen taking a survey course in Humanities or World Literature usually read many more modern French writers than modern American writers. A survey of modern drama, for example, might possibly include no American playwright other than Eugene O'Neill, but could hardly bypass Jean Giraudoux, Jean Anouilh, Eugène Ionesco, and that transplanted Irishman Samuel Beckett, not to mention the theories of Antonin Artaud and their partial embodiment in the plays of Jean Genet. The fiction and criticism written today by such important figures as Alain Robbe-Grillet and Roland Barthes are having an enormous impact on the way college literature courses are taught, and poets such as Apollinaire and Valéry are being increasingly studied for both their poetry and their theoretical writings.

This collection of criticism is meant for both students and general readers who would like a concise introduction to the most important modern French writers before plunging into the enormous sea of material available in bookstores and libraries. The writers included are not a gallery of personal favorites, but the ones who are most read, taught, and written about today in France, the United States, and Britain. The list of writers to be included and the amount of space devoted to each writer were established largely through a detailed survey of every critical article and full-length study on French literature published during the past ten years. In addition to the annual foreign language bibliography published by the Modern Language Association, the more complete *French XX* (formerly *French VII*) bibliography, edited by Douglas W.

Alden, was an invaluable aid in making this collection as objective as possible. The *French XX* bibliography was also our single most important reference tool for locating the significant critical material on French literature published since World War II. This annual bibliography is the best place to find complete references to far more criticism than could be excerpted here. For criticism published before World War II, the two standard bibliographies by Thième and by Talvert and Place provide a partial listing of criticism on major authors. For further criticism on an individual writer, the readers should investigate the most recent full-length study of that writer, represented wherever possible in this book.

The critical excerpts reprinted in these volumes, arranged in chronological order for each author, include the books, essays, and reviews most frequently referred to and quoted in discussions of modern French literature. Any excerpt is, by definition, taken out of context, and it is hoped that readers will track down the original source for themselves whenever a viewpoint strikes a spark. For every author, an attempt was made to quote one of the earliest reviews; contrary to popular myth, greatness was usually recognized when it first reared its head. An attempt was also made to present the broadest spectrum possible of critical responses—in the case of controversial writers, the conflicting opinions do not add up to a "balanced" appraisal but rather indicate the potential reactions that any reader might experience. Certain viewpoints represented here strike us as totally wrong-headed, but none strikes us as uninteresting or unsupported. In short, our intention was not to tell a reader precisely what to think about modern French writers, but rather to present a source book of stimulating suggestions.

In his essay on the Académie Française Matthew Arnold quotes Sainte-Beuve as saying, "In France the first consideration for us is not whether we are amused and pleased by a work of art or mind, nor is it whether we are touched by it. What we seek above all to learn is, whether *we were right* in being amused with it, and in applauding it, and in being moved by it." Arnold agrees that "a Frenchman has, to a considerable degree, what one may call a conscience in intellectual matters; he has an active belief that there is a right and a wrong to them." Such generalizations seem less valid now than they once were, but they apply to much of the criticism in this work. Even today criticism in France often has the moral function it had for nineteenth-century critics like Arnold and Sainte-Beuve, and which it has seldom had in England and America in the twentieth century. Marxism or Catholicism is not an "extra-literary" matter to French critics like Sartre or Mauriac, who thus use tools that most English-language critics would shun. The most recent development in structuralist literary criticism, which sees a literary work primarily as a meaningful system of signs, and therefore removes the moral imperative not only from criticism but also from literature. Structuralism may well relegate traditional critics like Albert Thibaudet and Gustave Lanson to the attic in the future, as some of its proponents like to assert, but meanwhile readers will find relatively little mention of "signifiers" and "signified" in these pages—not out of any wish to exclude structuralism but rather out of a preference for viewpoints that can be succinctly expressed in several hundred words. The few selections that seem close to incomprehensible are included only to give some idea of a crucially important book or essay—which is, readers may rest assured, equally perplexing in its entirety.

Matthew Arnold concludes his essay "The Literary Influence of Academies" by rejecting such an institution as inappropriate to England, but not before citing an impressive list of advantages, foremost among them the loss of "provinciality." French writers and critics nevertheless manage to be surprisingly provincial, as the selections in these volumes indicate. There are innumerable references to Baudelaire and Proust, who along with Kafka and Dostoyevski have created what French critics take to be the modern sensibility. There are surprisingly few references to such seminal authors as James Joyce and T. S. Eliot, and references to English and American writers who lived before the twentieth century are usually limited to Shakespeare and Poe (in Baudelaire's translation). No English or American student of literature could know as little about Voltaire or Rabelais as the French seem to know about Milton and Chaucer.

French literary figures live in an atmosphere of annual awards and constant attention that exists in no other country. The yearly Prix Goncourt for fiction, whether won (Proust), lost (Céline) or refused (Gracq) is discussed not merely at length but seemingly forever, quite unlike America's National Book Awards and Pulitzer Prizes, which barely rate newspaper coverage. One's impression while reading through the diaries of twentieth-century French writers, who constantly describe their meetings with one another, is of a world smaller than eighteenth-century London. One of the most striking facts about the writers represented here is that most of them know or knew one another, and spent their careers editing one another, reviewing one another, and exchanging ideas with one another. More than the other volumes in Ungar's Library of Literary Criticism series, *Modern French Literature* features important writers discussing the lives and work of their colleagues. In this connection, it is suprising how perceptive and lucid writers like Breton and Aragon are when engaged in literary criticism: in France even the surrealists know how to write clearly when they want to.

The orientation of this collection is, however, intentionally non-provincial. Alongside such Parisians as Russian-born Nathalie Sarraute and Romain Gary, Rumanian-born Eugène Ionesco, and American-born Julien Green, the reader will find a good number of French-language writers from Africa, the Caribbean, and Canada, as well as Belgium and Switzerland (the nationality of writers from a French-speaking country other than France is designated at the beginning of those writers' sections). While other books, especially from France, tend to reserve a supplementary chapter for anyone who writes French but prefers to reside outside the hexagon, this work features not only the well-known Senghor and Césaire but many other black French writers, as well as several French Canadian writers, whose importance is just now beginning to be recognized. What may seem like a disproportionately large amount of space was allotted to the more difficult writers, especially the New Novelists, in an effort to provide as full an introduction as possible for the uninitiated reader. One further criterion for inclusion and allotment of space was the availability in English translation of a writer's work.

Some of the best cultural journals in the history of the world were published in France during this century. Two of them, *Les nouvelles littéraires* and *La nouvelle revue française*, are still in existence, but recent years have taken a heavy toll on the others. Of the defunct periodicals, special mention should be made of *Les lettres françaises*, an exception to any generalization about French provinciality. *Les nouvelles littéraires*, which has been in existence for fifty years, is the best way for contemporary readers to keep in close touch with French culture. *Le Figaro littéraire* is the only important French periodical not represented here, because permission to reprint material could not be negotiated. *La nouvelle revue française* and its publisher, Éditions Gallimard, are so important in the history of twentieth-century French literature that this collection would have been inconceivable without their support and generosity. So many of the writers discussed here have been published by Gallimard, and actually worked for the company in an editorial capacity, that one can understand why Violette Leduc writes of the "proper white Gallimard cover with the red title" as the "young blood of literature." The story goes that one Goncourt juror voted every year for the novel submitted by Gallimard without reading it, on the grounds that "if Gaston Gallimard published it, it must be good." The story may be apocryphal, but the juror was rarely wrong.

The emphasis in this introduction has been on French criticism, because more than half the material in these volumes is by French critics, most of it translated for the first time. Some of the critical writings represented here of even such widely translated writers as Gide, Sartre, and Camus have never appeared in English before. All translations made for this work from the French, as well as from Spanish and Italian sources, have been done by the editors and are marked by a dagger at the end of the credit line. Readers will also find selections by the leading American and English authorities on French literature, as well as some surprising selections by such creative writers as Dylan Thomas, Ernest Hemingway, and Richard Wright, who are not generally associated with French literature. We have also included a sampling of criticism by important European writers such as Gorki, Hesse, Goytisolo, and Pasolini to indicate the breadth of response to the major twentieth-century French writers. Hundreds of sources, both scholarly and popular, were consulted in an effort to make the choice of material on each author as varied as possible. Even specialists on a particular writer should find some provocative material here that is new to them.

The Works Mentioned section, which comes after the critical selections in each volume, lists all the French works discussed in the critical excerpts, including poems and stories. In every case a literal translation of the French title is given in the text, and the title of the published translation, if any, is provided in the bibliography. Thus, Proust's masterpiece is referred to in the text as *In Search of Lost Time*, not the more beautiful but less accurate *Remembrance of Things Past*. The listing of Authors as Critics, near the beginning of each volume, should be used in conjunction with the Index to Critics at the end of Volume II, to locate all the pages on which Paul Claudel, for example, writes about his contemporaries. The Cross-Reference Index to Authors, which precedes the Index to Critics, pinpoints where the reader may find additional discussion (not passing mention) of a writer included in these volumes in another writer's section.

We would like to thank Leonard S. Klein, the General Editor of A Library of Literary Criticism, for his interest, concern, and advice during every stage of the three-year preparation of the manuscript, and Professor Justin O'Brien for his continuing inspiration. Professor Leon Roudiez of Columbia University and Professor André Martinet of the Sorbonne made helpful suggestions during the planning of this work; Professors John Guernelli, Violet Horvath, and Marshall Schneider of Baruch College and Professor Joseph Lowin of Touro College were kind enough to help with translation problems.

D. P.
M. P.

AUTHORS INCLUDED

VOLUME I

Achard, Marcel
    (pseud. of Marcel Auguste
    Ferréol)
Adamov, Arthur
Alain
    (pseud. of Émile-Auguste
    Chartier)
Alain-Fournier
    (pseud. of Henri-Alban
    Fournier)
Alexis, Jacques-Stéphen
Anouilh, Jean
Apollinaire, Guillaume
    (pseud. of Wilhelm Apollinaris
    de Kostrowitsky)
Aragon, Louis
Arland, Marcel
Arrabal, Fernando
Artaud, Antonin
Audiberti, Jacques
Aymé, Marcel
Barbusse, Henri
Barrès, Maurice
Barthes, Roland
Bataille, Georges
Bazin, Hervé
    (pseud. of Jean Pierre Marie
    Hervé-Bazin)
Beauvoir, Simone de
Beckett, Samuel
Benda, Julien
Bergson, Henri
Bernanos, Georges

Bernard, Jean-Jacques
Beti, Mongo
    (pseud. of Alexandre Biyidi)
Bhêly-Quénum, Olympe
Billetdoux, François
Blais, Marie-Claire
Blanchot, Maurice
Bloy, Léon
Bonnefoy, Yves
Breton, André
Brieux, Eugène
Butor, Michel
Camara, Laye
Camus, Albert
Cayrol, Jean
Céline, Louis-Ferdinand
    (pseud. of Louis-Ferdinand
    Destouches)
Cendrars, Blaise
    (pseud. of Frédéric Sauser)
Césaire, Aimé
Char, René
Claudel, Paul
Cocteau, Jean
Colette, Sidonie Gabrielle
Courteline, Georges
    (pseud. of Georges Moinaux)
Crommelynck, Fernand
Curel, François de
Dadié, Bernard Binlin
Damas, Léon-Gontran
Desnos, Robert
Dib, Mohammed

VOLUME II

Péret, Benjamin
Pieyre de Mandiargues, André
Pinget, Robert
Ponge, Francis
Porto-Riche, Georges de
Prévert, Jacques
Proust, Marcel
Queneau, Raymond
Radiguet, Raymond
Ramuz, Charles-Ferdinand
Régnier, Henri de
Reverdy, Pierre
Ricardou, Jean
Ringuet
     (pseud. of Philippe Panneton)
Robbe-Grillet, Alain
Roblès, Emmanuel
Rolland, Romain
Romains, Jules
     (pseud. of Louis Farigoule)
Rostand, Edmond
Roumain, Jacques
Roussel, Raymond
Roy, Gabrielle
Sagan, Françoise
     (pseud. of Françoise Quoirez)
Saint-Exupéry, Antoine de
Saint-John Perse
     (pseud. of Marie-René-Alexis
       Saint-Léger Léger)
Salacrou, Armand

Sarment, Jean
     (pseud. of Jean Bellemère)
Sarraute, Nathalie
Sartre, Jean-Paul
Sembène, Ousmane
Senghor, Léopold Sédar
Simenon, Georges
Simon, Claude
Sollers, Philippe
Soupault, Philippe
Supervielle, Jules
Tardieu, Jean
Thoby-Marcelin, Philippe
Tournier, Michel
Tzara, Tristan
     (pseud. of Sami Rosenstock)
Vailland, Roger
Valéry, Paul
Vauthier, Jean
Vercors
     (pseud. of Jean Bruller)
Verhaeren, Émile
Vian, Boris
Vildrac, Charles
     (pseud. of Charles Messager)
Weil, Simone
Yacine, Kateb
Yourcenar, Marguerite
     (pseud. of Marguerite de
      Crayencour)

AUTHORS BY COUNTRY

For all authors not listed here, France is to be understood as the nationality. See Introduction for more details.

ALGERIA

Dib, Mohammed
Feraoun, Mouloud
Mammeri, Mouloud

Roblès, Emmanuel
Yacine, Kateb

BELGIUM

Crommelynck, Fernand
Ghelderode, Michel de
Maeterlinck, Maurice
Mallet-Joris, Françoise

Michaux, Henri
Simenon, Georges
Verhaeren, Émile

CAMEROON

Beti, Mongo

Oyono, Ferdinand

CANADA

Blais, Marie-Claire
Hébert, Anne
Langevin, André

Nelligan, Émile
Ringuet
Roy, Gabrielle

DAHOMEY

Bhêly-Quénum, Olympe

FRENCH GUIANA

Damas, Léon-Gontran

GUINEA

Camara, Laye

HAITI

Alexis, Jacques-Stéphen
Marcelin, Pierre

Roumain, Jacques
Thoby-Marcelin, Philippe

IVORY COAST

Dadié, Bernard Binlin

MARTINIQUE

Césaire, Aimé

Maran, René

SENEGAL

Diop, Briago
Diop, David
Kane, Cheikh Hamidou

Sembène, Ousmane
Senghor, Léopold Sédar

SWITZERLAND

Cendrars, Blaise
Pinget, Robert

Ramuz, Charles-Ferdinand

TUNISIA

Memmi, Albert

AUTHORS AS CRITICS

The following is a listing of authors included in this book who are also quoted as critics on their colleagues. See the Index to Critics, which begins on p. 567 of Volume II, for complete details.

Achard, Marcel
Adamov, Arthur
Alain
Alain-Fournier
Alexis, Jacques-Stéphen
Anouilh, Jean
Apollinaire, Guillaume
Aragon, Louis
Arland, Marcel
Artaud, Antonin
Aymé, Marcel
Barbusse, Henri
Barrès, Maurice
Barthes, Roland
Bataille, Georges
Beauvoir, Simone de
Beckett, Samuel
Benda, Julien
Bernanos, Georges
Beti, Mongo
Bhêly-Quénum, Olympe
Billetdoux, François
Blanchot, Maurice
Bonnefoy, Yves
Breton, André
Butor, Michel
Camus, Albert
Cendrars, Blaise
Claudel, Paul
Cocteau, Jean

Colette, Sidonie Gabrielle
Diop, David
Drieu la Rochelle, Pierre
Duhamel, Georges
Éluard, Paul
Emmanuel, Pierre
Fargue, Léon-Paul
Feraoun, Mouloud
France, Anatole
Gascar, Pierre
Genet, Jean
Gide, André
Gracq, Julien
Green, Julien
Huysmans, Joris-Karl
Ionesco, Eugène
Jacob, Max
Jammes, Francis
Jouhandeau, Marcel
Jouve, Pierre Jean
Larbaud, Valery
Le Clézio, J. M. G.
Leduc, Violette
Leiris, Michel
Lenormand, Henri-René
Mallet-Joris, Françoise
Malraux, André
Marcel, Gabriel
Martin du Gard, Roger
Mauriac, Claude

PERIODICALS USED

Where no abbreviation is indicated, the periodical references are used in full.

	Action française (Paris)
Adam	Adam International Review (London)
AfricaR	Africa Report (New York)
AfrF	African Forum (New York)
AgN	L'âge nouveau (Paris)
APL	Les annales politiques et littéraires (Paris)
	L'arc (Aix-en-Provence)
	Arts (Paris)
	Arts et loisirs (Paris)
	Atlas (New York)
AUMLA	AUMLA: Journal of the Australasian Universities Language and Literature Association (James Cook University, Queensland)
AJFS	Australian Journal of French Studies (Clayton, Victoria)
BerkR	The Berkeley Review (Berkeley)
BO	Black Orpheus (Ibadan, Nigeria)
	Black World (Chicago)
BFN	The Book Find News (New York)
BkWd	Book World (Washington, D.C.)
BA	Books Abroad (Norman, Okla.)
CRB	Cahiers de la Compagnie Madeleine Renaud–Jean-Louis Barrault (Paris)
CSais	Cahiers des saisons (Paris)
CdC	Cahiers du cinéma (Paris)
CS	Cahiers du Sud (Marseille)
CIS	Cahiers internationaux de symbolisme (Geneva)
CanL	Canadian Literature (Vancouver)
ChelR	Chelsea Review (New York)
ChiR	The Chicago Review (Chicago)
	Chrysalis (Boston)
CE	College English (Chicago)
	The Colosseum (London)
ColF	The Columbia Forum (New York)

Cmty	Commentary (New York)
Com	Commonweal (New York)
CompD	Comparative Drama (Kalamazoo, Mich.)
	Confluences (Lyon, later Paris)
	Congo-Afrique (later, Zaïre-Afrique, Kinshasa)
	La connaissance (Paris)
CL	Contemporary Literature (Madison, Wisc.)
	Corriere della sera (Milan)
	The Criterion (London)
CQ	The Critical Quarterly (Manchester)
	Critique (Paris)
CA	Cuadernos americanos (Mexico City)
DR	The Dalhousie Review (Halifax, N. S.)
	The Dial (Chicago, later New York)
DV	Le disque vert (Brussels)
	Dissent (New York)
	Drama (London)
	Empreintes (Brussels)
Enc	Encounter (London)
EngR	The English Review (London)
	Esprit (Paris)
ECr	L'esprit créateur (Lawrence, Kan.)
	Esquire (New York)
	Études (Paris)
EL	L'Europa letteraria (Rome)
	Europe (Paris)
	L'Europe nouvelle (Paris)
	L'express (Paris)
	Les feuilles libres (Paris)
	Flair (New York)
	Fontaine (Paris)
FR	The French Review (Chapel Hill, N.C.)
FS	French Studies (Oxford)
GR	Le grande revue (Paris)
	Gringoire (Paris)
	Haïti-Journal (Port-au-Prince)
Harper's	Harper's Magazine (New York)
	Hémisphères (Brooklyn)
	L'Herne (Paris)
	The Hibbert Journal (London)
	Horizon (London)
HdR	The Hudson Review (New York)
	L'humanité (Paris)
	Icare (Paris)
	L'illustration (Paris)
JP	The Journal of Philosophy (New York)
	The Journal of Politics (Gainesville, Fla.)

JNALA	Journal of the New African Literature and the Arts (New York)
KFLQ	Kentucky Foreign Language Quarterly (Lexington)
	Lectures (Montreal)
	Les lettres (Paris)
LetF	Les lettres françaises (Paris)
LetN	Les lettres nouvelles (Paris)
LL	Life and Letters (London)
List	The Listener (London)
LdF	Livres de France (Paris)
MagL	Magazine littéraire (Paris)
	Makerere Journal (Kampala, Uganda)
	Les marges (Paris)
	Marginales (Brussels)
MdF	Mercure de France (Paris)
MD	Modern Drama (Toronto)
MLJ	The Modern Language Journal (New York)
MLN	Modern Language Notes (Baltimore)
MLQ	The Modern Language Quarterly (Seattle)
ML	Modern Languages (London)
	Le monde (Paris)
	The Monist (La Salle, Ill.)
Nation	The Nation (New York)
	La Nef (Paris)
NEW	The New English Weekly (London)
NLr	The New Leader (New York)
NR	The New Republic (Washington, D.C.)
NSo	New Society (London)
NS	New Statesman (London)
NSN	New Statesman and Nation (London)
NYHT	New York Herald Tribune Book Section (New York)
NYP	The New York Post (New York)
NYR	The New York Review of Books (New York)
NYT	The New York Times Book Review (New York)
NYTd	The New York Times, daily (New York)
NY	The New Yorker (New York)
NC	The Nineteenth Century (later, The Nineteenth Century and After, London)
NorthAR	The North American Review (New York)
NO	Le nouvel observateur (Paris)
NRF	La nouvelle revue français (Paris)
NL	Les nouvelles littéraires (Paris)
Obs	The Observer (London)
	L'Occident (Paris)
	Paris-Théâtre (Paris)
PR	Partisan Review (New Brunswick, N.J.)
	Paru (Monaco)

PMLA	PMLA: Publications of the Modern Language Association of America (New York)
	Poésie (Paris)
	Poetry (Chicago)
	Le point (Paris)
	Le point (Souillac, France)
PCP	Points et contrepoints (Paris)
PA	Présence africaine (Paris)
PFr	Présence francophone (Sherbrooke, Quebec)
	Preuves (Paris)
QR	Quarterly Review (London)
QL	La quinzaine littéraire (Paris)
	Renascence (Milwaukee, Wis.)
Reporter	The Reporter (New York)
	La révolution surréaliste (Paris)
RUL	La revue de l'Université Laval (Quebec)
RdP	La revue de Paris (Paris)
	Revue de l'Amérique latine (Paris)
RDM	La revue des deux mondes (Paris)
RLM	La revue des lettres modernes (Paris)
RevS	La revue du siècle (Lyon)
RevE	La revue européenne (Paris)
RGB	Revue générale belge (Brussels)
RH	La revue hebdomadaire (Paris)
RevN	La revue nouvelle (Brussels)
RevU	La revue universelle (Paris)
RU	Revue universitaire (Paris)
	Rivista d'Italia (Rome)
RR	Romanic Review (New York)
SatN	Saturday Night (Toronto)
SR	Saturday Review (New York)
SR (London)	The Saturday Review of Politics, Literature, Science, and Art (London)
SwR	The Sewanee Review (Sewanee, Tenn.)
	Sic (Paris)
	Simoun (Oran, Algeria)
	Société des amis de Georges Bernanos: Bulletin périodique (Paris)
SoR	The Southern Review (Baton Rouge, La.)
Spec	The Spectator (London)
SSF	Studies in Short Fiction (Newberry, S.C.)
	Sur (Buenos Aires)
	The Symposium (Concord, N.H.)
	Synthèses (Brussels)
TR	La table ronde (Paris)
TamR	The Tamarack Review (Toronto)
TelQ	Tel quel (Paris)
	Le temps (Paris)

TM	Les temps modernes (Paris)
TP	Temps présent (Paris)
	Tendances (Paris)
TSLL	Texas Studies in Literature and Language (Austin)
TA	Theatre Arts (New York)
	Le thyrse (Brussels)
TT	Time and Tide (London)
Times	The Times (London)
TLS	TLS: The Times Literary Supplement (London)
TSW	Toronto Star Weekly (Toronto)
	Transition (Paris)
TDR	Tulane Drama Review (New Orleans, later New York, as TDR: The Drama Review)
UTQ	The University of Toronto Quarterly (Toronto)
	Vendredi (Paris)
	Vers et prose (Paris)
VL	Vie et langage (Paris)
	View (New York)
YFS	Yale French Studies (New Haven, Conn.)
YR	The Yale Review (New Haven, Conn.)

ACHARD, MARCEL (1899–1974)

On seeing *Malborough Goes to War!*, I could not keep from thinking of Shakespeare and of Musset. Only this was of the year 1925, quite close to us, and visibly a play written after the war; although, according to the stage directions, the action was taking place "in an eighteenth century of the imagination."

And in truth the whole thing was a fantasy, an enchanting one, rather than something which could properly be called a play. . . .

As I have said, it is a post-war play. Malborough is the perfect general of war poetry—of Siegfried Sassoon and Wilfred Owen—glorious to history and posterity, but incompetent, wire-pulling and cowardly. He cannot direct an army, he cannot use a map. Circumstances, a clever front of bluster and swagger, and his clear understanding of the importance of women, are useful to him and serve to lift him to a pedestal. . . .

Of women there are two. Lady Malborough, a coquette, though not excessively so; disloyal, but hardly more so than the next woman; as inconstant as the rest, but not much more so; hardly capable of love; changeful in response to every impression, every opinion in the light of which she must play her role. . . .

And there is Bettina, beloved of the four officers, who would willingly marry all four of them if she were permitted. And above all there is, everywhere, an atmosphere of poignant mockery, veiling a sentiment, exquisite and very delicate.

There is also in this fantasy, in all these audacities and contrasts, a very sure technique, equal to any requirements, a technique which makes no slips. And this amazing technique, these contrasts, these audacities, this cynicism, and this poetry which is there despite them all, bring us to a few reflections on this modern art which some extol, and some despise, and others seem disposed to treat as merely farcical.

Paul Ranson Morand. *RR*. July–Sept., 1926,
pp. 350–52

1

The five acts [of *Next to My Blonde*] depict the history of a family, but in reverse chronological order. . . . Achard's aim is the same as [J. B.] Priestley's [in *Time and the Conways*]: to give the viewer, who trustingly or downright enthusiastically contemplates a little world, a heightened awareness of the dreadful disappointments that time, as if in ambush, prepares for the unsuspecting. But it is doubtful whether such an effect, which works well enough for the transposition of a single act in Priestley's play, can succeed when the playwright reverses the order of five acts. In *Next to My Blonde* the distances are too great, the references get lost, and the calculated effects grow weaker. . . .

Achard is a sparkling writer, whose great secret has always been that he does not take himself too seriously, even when he sighs and cries. . . . There was all the more need for a light, brilliant, airy tone in a play like this, which has much more difficulty than his others in achieving fanciful effects, since it draws on elements from the most common, trite, and—except for a tragic moment—banal reality. I recall having read in a French review that the public should derive from this play nothing less than the "pleasure of the gods." In other words, we can witness the life of a poor family, its plans and its illusions, as if watching a puppet show—the family as plaything of indifferent or hostile gods (which, after all, if you think about it, was the idea underlying Sophoclean tragedy). But it is certainly hard to find a trace of greatness in a subject so modest that it cannot support any such aims. [April 23, 1947]

Silvio d'Amico. Palcoscenico del dopoguerra (Torino,
Edizioni Radio Italiana, 1952), Vol. I, pp. 196–98†

With *Do You Want to Play with Me?* a dramatist was born, who had instinctively found his timing, his range, and his style. He showed himself to be a very subtle creator of whimsy, in the tradition of Musset; a bantering ironist, brought up in the school of Jules Laforgue; and his own brand of moralist, but one nevertheless in the tradition of Bernard Shaw. . . .

[In Achard's plays] nothing irreparable happens. The women are little angelic monsters who scratch. The lovers are afraid to become tender; they declare their love in pirouettes, and they part on a riddle. And the world goes on; there are toothaches and kicks in the rear, cuckolds by the dozens, and, as in life, a great many fools, and truth comes out of the mouths of fools. . . .

Achard's plays have the fluidity of songs, the wise yet unstudied vigor of popular speech: its sudden spurts of poetry, its flights of illuminations and its returns down to earth. People full of tenderness and weakness populate his plays, frail people who radiate genuine warmth, with their reticence as well as their secret plans. . . .

Few works are closer to us than those of Achard, who touches us by the ever-veiled sparkle of his style. It is the fine firm style of a French writer, one so appropriate to the theater that it does not even seem to be a style.

Michel Aubriant. *Paris-Théâtre*. March, 1953,

pp. 11, 13†

Achard has created a type, reminiscent of the charming figures in the Commedia dell'Arte: the dreamy Pierrot who worships precisely the wrong woman and who gains the sympathy of the audience by his persistent naïveté, a kind of stupefying charm. Achard's heroes fumble and stumble to a happy end; their virtues are, incongruously enough, a plentiful lack of wit, excessive credulity, lack of sex appeal, exasperating garrulity—and yet they triumph. Why? They are imbued with an indefatigable optimism, with which the spectator can identify himself, perhaps against his own will.

The intrigues of the plays follow the traditional pattern of the vaudeville triangle: two men love the same woman. In the first act she loves one, in the second the other, and in the third she goes back to number one. The humor of the situation consists essentially of the author's attitude that life cannot be taken too seriously. . . .

Almost thirty years [after *Jean from the Moon*], Achard wrote *Sweet Potato*, a play that proved the outstanding success of the last two theatrical seasons in Paris. When adapted for Broadway by Irwin Shaw, it failed to receive any critical acclaim whatsoever, showing once again the distance between French and American humor. . . .

In the United States, the concept of cuckoldry is too alien to be comical. We long for a symbiosis between sex, love, and happiness, and we take our pursuit very seriously. The French believe in pleasure rather than in happiness, Gallic humor is more realistic, albeit a little cynical: pleasure may stem from someone else's "courage," love is a naughty game played without rules in which the best man may lose.

Paul Mankin. *YFS*. Summer, 1959, pp. 34–35, 38

Usually Marcel Achard is more successful in creating plots than in portraying characters. [In *The Stupid Girl*] the reverse is true: in the least-polished plot of any of his plays, he offers us one of his finest characterizations. . . .

Because of his likeable natural naïveté and a no-less-likeable misunderstanding of the detective-story drama—a form that he is attempting here for the first time—Achard missed all the fine opportunities for suspense his subject offered him. He even is slow in giving us the keys to this mystery; this slowness would be irritating if it did not show his tender ingenuousness. . . .

[Josépha's] spontaneity makes her so noble, almost in spite of herself, that after having foolishly accused herself without seeming ridiculous, she can accuse her employers without seeming nasty. There is no trace in her of that threatened, brittle, uneasy purity so dear to Anouilh. Her own purity consists of having accepted her impurities from birth, with an aggressive confidence in life. . . .

The Stupid Girl, Josépha, assumed such a strong life of her own that she inspired an ending from Achard very unlike his usual dénouements. After some heartrending farewells to the investigator, she yields, without enthusiasm but also without bitterness, to the licentious advances of the most idiotic of the republican guards. The ending is so real it makes you want to cry with anger; and it is tragic. We have forgotten the laughter of the beginning of the play. Whether he intended to or not, the king of comedy leaves us close to tears.

Bertrand Poirot-Delpech. *Le monde*. Sept. 24, 1960,

p. 12†

The secret of the life and survival of a dramatic work lies in the invention of a character who crystallizes a particular psychological mechanism. Jef, called Jean from the Moon [in *Jean from the Moon*], is such a character—and among the most remarkable of them, since you never stop asking yourself questions about him: Does he know? Does he not know? Is he stupid, naïve, innocent, credulous, a little foolish, or completely idiotic? Out of what therefore is his love created? Is it voluntary blindness, an almost heroic delicacy, a tremendous fear of losing a person who remains indispensable to him, or an almost diabolical shrewdness? Who is this Jef with his nice smile, who is this good-natured, peaceful man who one might think is sure of himself and of everything! . . .

One can go on and on with this game of hypotheses. There is enough material to sustain it. So many possibilities are suggested by Jef. Achard provoked these questions thirty-five years ago; and the public has not stopped asking them. The play has remained very young and very much alive, because it has that eternal quality—it extends the tradition of Marivaux into our century.

I was moreover pleased to note that what gave me the keenest pleasure was not just the famous scenes, which, through memory, the film [of *Jean from the Moon*], recitals, and records, have become anthology pieces. It was not just those scenes but the rediscovery of all the rest of the work that was such a pleasure. [May 26, 1967]

Jean-Jacques Gautier. *Théâtre d'aujourd'hui*
(Paris, Julliard, 1972), pp. 242–44†

ADAMOV, ARTHUR (1908–1970)

There is so much to say about *The Invasion*! First, about the subject itself, which is so subtle, which seems to be hidden in the innermost corners of the dialogue, and which remains almost recessed from the action. Then about the extraordinary skill with which this subject is emphasized. . . .

Paradoxically, it is essential for you [Adamov] to bring into the foreground an absence: that of the deceased, whose thoughts dominate and subjugate, bind together and then divide, the actors of the drama. It is essential that you persuade us, the spectators, that these thoughts are of the highest importance for all humanity. [The deceased wrote] a work that he left unfinished, on sheets of paper scattered like the leaves of the Sibyl, a work whose very illegible writing the dead man's devoted friends try in different ways to decipher. These sheets of paper will finally become the victim of a puff of wind that scatters them, the plaything of a careless child. And that is the secret subject of this drama—this active posthumous presence, which, after some attempts at survival, becomes progressively and then totally annihilated.

André Gide. In Arthur Adamov, *La parodie,*
L'invasion (Paris, Charlot, 1950), pp. 9–10†

It would be vain to outline the "plot" of an Adamov play or analyze the "psychology" of the characters, for these terms—at least in their conventional meanings—simply do not apply to the "invented universe" which Adamov brings to the theatre. Even the complete printed texts of the plays, with the detailed notes on mise-en-scène, are more like musical scores than traditional "literary" or "psychological" dramas; they can be "read" by anyone with the necessary skill and imagination, but they cannot be fully grasped apart from actual performance. . . .

The Invasion might be called "the play about absurd fidelity." For the heterogeneous little group of people brought together in the promiscuity of a single room, the room itself encumbered with too much furniture and with disorderly piles of manuscript, the most oppressive presence is an absence—that of the author, now dead, of these countless manuscript sheets, with their almost illegible markings. Do these papers contain a vital, irreplaceable message of salvation for humanity? Or is the effort of those characters who are seeking to decipher a message based upon a pathetic illusion? There is no answer to this question, and one recalls Kafka's *The Castle*, in which K. carries on an endless, frustrating quest for something which remains elusive and enigmatic.

The characters in *The Invasion* suffer, like those in *Parody*, from solitude and the failure of communication: they talk, they struggle, but their language, like their lives, remains opaque. . . .

The "invasion" of the title is an ambiguous term: it refers to the infiltration of "disorder" in the lives of the characters, but also, no doubt, to the influence of the idea that the manuscript left by a man now dead might contain a meaning for the living, if only it could be deciphered. But in the action of the play, the disorder gradually encroaches on this other "invasion." Indeed, one may wonder at the end, was not the manuscript, with its enigma, simply another manifestation, or even the agent, of the all-pervasive disorder? For in Adamov's world, solitude and disorder are the rule, and "it is not man's lot to find the road that would lead him to the goal."

Carlos Lynes, Jr. YFS. Winter, 1954–55, pp. 50–52

Ping Pong [is] one of the masterpieces of the Theatre of the Absurd. . . . *Ping Pong*, like Adamov's first play, *Parody*, is concerned with the futility of human endeavor. But while *Parody* merely asserted that whatever you do, in the end you die, *Ping Pong* provides a powerful and closely integrated argument to back that proposition—it also shows *how* so much of human endeavor becomes futile, and *why*. It is in losing themselves to a *thing*, a machine that promises them power, money, influence over the woman they desire, that Victor and Arthur waste their lives in the futile pursuit of shadows. By making a machine, a means to an end, an end in itself, they pervert all those values of their lives that are genuine ends in themselves—their creative instinct, their capacity to love, their sense of being part of a community. *Ping Pong* is a powerful image of the alienation of man through the worship of a false objective, the deification of a machine, an ambition, or an ideology.

The pinball machine in *Ping Pong* is more than just a machine; it is the centerpiece of an organization and of a body of thought. The moment the objective—the improvement of pinball machines—becomes an ideal, it embodies itself in an organization with its own struggles for power, its own intrigues and politics, its own tactics and strategies. As such it becomes a matter of life and death for all who serve the ideal. A number of the characters in the play are destroyed in the service of the organization, or in its internal struggle for power. All this is conducted with the utmost fervor, seriousness, and intensity. And what is it all about? A childish game, a pinball machine—nothing. But are most of the objectives men devote their lives to in the real world—the world of business, politics, the arts, or scholarship—essentially different from Arthur's and Victor's dominating obsession? It is the power and beauty of *Ping Pong* that it very graphically raises this very question. Adamov

achieves the difficult feat of elevating the pinball machine to a convincing image of the objectives of *all* human endeavor. He does so by the
poetic intensity with which he invests his characters when they talk
about the most absurd aspects of that absurd apparatus with a conviction and obsessive concentration that sound utterly true.

Martin Esslin. *The Theatre of the Absurd*
(Garden City, N.Y., Doubleday, 1961), pp. 65–67

Like Ionesco, Adamov came to the theater as a voice of protest, and his
first play *Parody* is an attempt to embody in a crude and *visible* manner
the themes of solitude and absence of communication suggested by the
most common of everyday scenes. Like the other "police state" plays,
Parody is an outgrowth of a close personal contact with Artaud the man
and with his radical criticism of the conventional theater. In spite of
Adamov's later skepticism regarding the value of Artaud's ideas, it is
quite clear that the author of *The Theater and Its Double* has exercised
an enormous influence on him. Adamov follows Artaud in his rejection
of psychology, in his acceptance of the basic idea of a "theater of
cruelty," and in his utilization of the theater above all as a space to be
occupied. . . .

Particularly in the police state plays [*Parody, The Great and Small
Maneuver, The Direction of the March*, and *All against All*], but also
to some extent in the others of the same period, [Adamov] rejected
plot more completely than has either Beckett or Ionesco, spurned
characterization, and relegated dialogue to a minor role in his universe
where characters rarely say what they mean, and never succeed in really
communicating with each other. Instead of crackling and exploding
dramatically, as does Ionesco's language, instead of dropping "like
leaves, like sand," in an intense lyric overflow as does Beckett's,
Adamov's dialogue simply drags along. Stressing the visible resources of
the stage, he reminds us that drama is more than literature and that a
play is only a play when it is presented on the boards before spectators.
But the same may be said of ballet and pantomime, and it has been
Adamov's error to deny certain essentials that distinguish drama from
other genres in order to stress the importance of an element that is
equally essential. . . .

Adamov may involve our intellect, never our emotions. The coldness of his early theater already betrays the future admirer of Brecht,
and perhaps reveals better than the works of Brecht himself the famous
alienation technique that the master of epic theater espoused.

Leonard Cabell Pronko. *Avant-Garde: The Experimental
Theater in France* (Berkeley, University of California
Press, 1962), pp. 132, 139–40

Paolo Paoli shows the development in France of a state of mind that made World War I possible. In order to present this story Adamov has taken over a stage technique perfected by Bertolt Brecht in *The Preventable Rise of Arturo Ui*. Each of the twelve scenes is preceded by a short "movie show" of pictures and extracts from newspapers, magazines, and speeches of the pre-World War I period. These provide an ironic contrast with the action that follows and serve to put that action into its proper historical focus. Adamov himself states that the purpose of the technique is to remind the audience how war was slowly but inevitably being prepared underneath the veneer of carefree and euphoric living. The tragedy of the political events described in the screen projections is underlined by an accompaniment of contemporary popular songs, which slowly change to military marches as the play progresses.

The idea is excellent, but the actual story of Paolo Paoli is simply dull. In turning from the general to the specific, Adamov has paradoxically lost the knack of telling a story in dramatic terms. The specific petty chicaneries of Paolo Paoli as he trades in butterfly bodies may be symbolic of a materialism that sacrifices esthetic values for commercial considerations, but they are not interesting in themselves. The continuous vacillation from faithfulness to adultery of Paoli's half-Catholic, half-Protestant, Franco-German wife may be symbolic of a moral degeneration which, when raised to the social level, leads inevitably to war, but it is merely dull in itself.

George E. Wellwarth. *The Theater of Protest and Paradox* (New York, New York University Press, 1964), pp. 31–32

Today . . . the Ionesco-Adamov-Beckett trinity has lost its meaning. . . . Adamov defected: after having written a few plays comparable to those of Ionesco, situated in what he himself calls the no-man's-land of the theatre of the absurd, he repudiated the genre and moved in the direction of a Brechtian theatre. He thus set himself up as the head of a new "critical" drama, whose objective is the portrayal of a collective destiny, clearly situated in history. . . .

The Politics of Garbage is perhaps Adamov's most modern play—not so much in form (the trial of a white South African who has killed a black man is presented through traditional flashbacks) as in his use of an object psychosis, which does not naïvely explain the protagonist's racism but is structurally parallel to it. Little is said during the trial to indicate that one is the cause of the other; there is simply a constant criss-cross of the two themes—an obsession with the refuse of the world (cigarette butts, old torn-up tickets, kitchen peelings, and so on) and a fear of the expansion of the black population. It is not until the play is over that the spectator sees the significant relationship between the two and realizes that the racist murderer grasps the accumulation of civilization's refuse and the multiplication or political rise of the blacks in one act of consciousness, feeling equally and identically threatened by them both. Without foundering in a demonstrative discourse, the play is a gripping metaphor of one vision of the modern world, in which a proliferation of refuse and a proliferation of human beings leads to the same terror.

Jacques Guicharnaud, with June Guicharnaud.
Modern French Theatre from Giraudoux to Genet,
rev. ed. (New Haven, Conn., Yale University Press,
1967), pp. 197, 201–2

The difficulty of composition which characterized Adamov's first attempts to write for the theatre was radically overcome when he wrote *Professor Taranne.* This work, the nearly verbatim transposition of a dream, took only two days to shape into its present form. Among his early plays, *Professor Taranne* is almost the only one which Adamov now feels was a good play, because he made no effort to allegorize its elements. Everything that happens to Professor Taranne in the play happened to Adamov in his dream, with the single exception that when the Professor cries, "I am Professor Taranne," Adamov had cried in his dream, "I am the author of *Parody!*"

It is by no means clear whether Professor Taranne is a free agent confronted with a monstrous conspiracy of circumstances bent upon his destruction or whether he is a fraud by some inner compulsion, who is at last exposed for what he really is. That he is alone is undoubted. He shares in no meaningful community with anyone. Despite his claims for his university standing, and perhaps because of them, he is revealed as an individual in the radical sense of having no relationships through which he can gain a reflection of his own self-understanding. His claims and those of his accusers are equally reasonable and absurd. . . . In the face of an apparently absurd world, he opts to enact his guilt, thus becoming guilty existentially. This final gesture of guilt-acceptance grants a kind of tragic stature to Taranne. We are left with an image of isolated man whose only means of asserting his identity is a gesture, and in this case a gesture by which he intensifies his isolation and guilt.

Richard E. Sherrell. *The Human Image: Avant-Garde
and Christian* (Richmond, Va., John Knox, 1969),
pp. 123, 127–28

Adamov was a great individualist because of his face and his manners, because of the kind of life he liked, because of his violent stripping away of nonessentials in his work, and because of the healthy exaggeration to which he let his thoughts lead him. . . .

This great individualist was also a great rebel. The evolution of his work could be cited: from practically his first book, *The Confession*, with its often atrocious masochism; from his first plays, *Parody* and *The Invasion*, which were the beginning of all the things that are now praised as "new theater." As Adamov went on in a life that never stopped being tragic for him, he kept growing more aware of the fundamental injustice that resides in capitalist society. And his personal drama receded more and more into the background when he was faced with the universal drama of oppression, which makes innocent victims of so many people. Each of his recent works categorically takes a position against the powers of exploitation, against the chief power of evil, which masquerades as a torch bearer. For these reasons, this writer, spurned by bourgeois moralists, will earn the recognition of men everywhere, and I do not think I am mistaken in praising the lesson he gives to many pseudo-revolutionaries.

Adamov's tormented genius is just as totally, profoundly, and magnificently Russian as that of the greatest poets and novelists of his native land.

André Pieyre de Mandiargues. LetF. March 25, 1970,
pp. 4–5†

ALAIN (1868–1951)

In one of the biggest *lycées* of Paris, Alain teaches philosophy. Or rather he is supposed by a benevolent administration (which really knows better) to be teaching philosophy. But Alain is no philosopher. He is a *sage*. He teaches life—or rather, since that is really impossible, he teaches his conception of life. . . .

Alain is not a philosopher. In the tangle of human feelings, he gropes for a way. He has no system, he explains nothing, he holds no solution. He feels and he thinks. He believes in thought, he believes in the nobility of human nature. He is conscious of the evil also that is in men's thoughts and in their feelings. He is not a very religious man. He rather feels, on the whole, that the gods—whatever gods there be—are taking a rather mean advantage of mankind. He would be rather inclined, out of a sort of impulse towards revenge, to say that there are no gods. But Alain himself was once the pupil of a great philosopher (so Alain thinks), Jules Lagneau, and this man believed in God. Consequently Alain rather feels that there must be something in the idea. And was not that, after all, Montaigne's attitude? It is a very good attitude for an essayist, as an essayist is, essentially, a man who, rather tentatively, tries to find his way into the heart of things, but who does not pretend quite to know the way.

> Denis Saurat. Foreword to Alain,
> *Mars; or, The Truth about War* (London,
> Jonathan Cape, 1930), pp. 21, 23

It is unfortunate that Alain should be introduced to the English public by [*Mars; or, The Truth about War*], little essays on a subject which —unlike aesthetics and religion, on which he has written a number of books usually referred to by thinkers who praise him—is comparatively amenable to analysis. War is a phenomenon with economic and social causes, and there is already a considerable literature upon it in economics and social psychology; anyone who writes about war with any hope of saying something important must take this literature into consideration, and must certainly be prepared to elaborate fully his ideas. Beside [Wilfred] Trotter's *Instincts of the Herd in Peace and War*—I compare it to a book which is also a psychological study, tentative and speculative—Alain's essays appear thin, pontifical in their brevity, and literary in the worst sense of that word.

Alain hates war, thinks it not inevitable, and considers its cure to be the reduction of the power of the state, which he considers at best a necessary evil. He considers the conflict of interests to be "only the occasion" for war, its cause is "the passions." The conflict of interests and the passions are talked of as if they were individual as well as social phenomena; which they are at any point is not quite clear; and their relation to the war-waging state is not developed. An individualistic psychology—Alain tells us that Descartes has said the last word on the passions—is scarcely the instrument with which to analyze a group phenomenon like war.

> Felix Morrow. *Nation*. Nov. 5, 1930, p. 500

Reading *History of My Thoughts*, one realizes very quickly that Alain would have done better to call this book "History of My Intellectual Exercises." . . .

Alain does not like either to plummet to the depths or scale the heights; what he does like more than anything else are good exercises. He teaches that philosophy consists of "exercising doubt to the point at which universal skepticism becomes truth." The history of his ideas is the history of the selections he made from other people's ideas, to nourish a solid humanism, but one lacking boldness. . . .

The merit of Alain's purposely restrained philosophy is that it forms a tableau depicting man's beauties, adding all the colors that can enliven and enrich that tableau. Surely this is one of the reasons for Alain's success, and one of the most legitimate reasons. But one may also wonder whether such a task does not amount to gathering the flowers of humanity to store them in a prison, or at best to put them into vases in a classroom. As for making an original philosophy out of all the philosophical flowers gathered elsewhere, that is another matter. For this, one would need qualities which Alain not only lacks—but which would become faults in him if he had them.

Alain once wrote that no writer has been more betrayed than Hegel. The fate of all great philosophers is to be betrayed. But there are traitors of great ability, who become great philosophers in their own right. A master is a disciple who turned out badly in his own master's terms. But Alain has only students, not disciples, because he has never been a master, but only a professor.

André Rousseaux. Littérature du vingtième siècle
(Paris, Éditions Albin Michel, 1938),
Vol. I, pp. 55–60†

In every one of Alain's *propos* [short essays], despite the apparent accumulation of thoughts and images along the way, a single idea or proposition generally is introduced, expanded, and resolved. Many times Alain expresses his controlling idea at the very beginning, often seeking to astonish, charm, or captivate the reader. The approach is intentionally surprising, to be sure, but Alain never weakens, no matter what paradoxical or strange phrases he chooses as he goes along. There he is, according to one of his favorite images, on his little boat, even far from shore, happy to struggle and to teach the doctrine of will. The whole remainder of each *propos* serves to convert the idea, which at first glance had seemed unrealistic, into a commonplace. The final line, as in seventeenth-century sonnets, is almost always carefully polished, beautiful, and detached. . . .

Scarcely anyone could fail to notice the musicality and harmony of Alain's style. Who would deny that he possesses a fine vocabulary, stripped of jargon and mannerisms? Perhaps, through the influence of his profession as educator, he was too easily oratorical, although he wished to repress eloquence.

Henri Mondor. Alain (Paris, Gallimard, 1953),
pp. 125–26†

Alain . . . created the genre he called the *propos* to discipline his style and his ideas. The *propos* is a short essay in a spoken style—two pages written on small-sized letter paper, says Alain—which begins with a short item of apparently minimal importance and expands it into a generalization. Alain disdained objections and proofs; he distrusted professional philosophers, preferring poets and novelists, who are more firmly rooted in concrete reality. Alain's first *propos*, written for a daily newspaper in Rouen, took current events as their starting point. Later he based his *propos* on details from his own personal experiences, but also on Stendhal and Balzac, to whom he devoted two studies (1935 and 1937) in the form of *propos*. . . .

System of the Fine Arts and *Propos on Literature* seem to be simply collections of unconnected *propos*. Despite appearances, these books yield a coherent theory of artistic creation: a work of art undoubtedly arises from the passions, but in art the passions are surmounted and directed by thought, and by the resistance of the form itself. The hardness of marble, the rules of versification, the natural form and colors of the plants that can be combined in a garden, the true incident that serves as a point of departure for a novel—all those factors discipline an artist's imagination, which in its turn purifies the passions of his audience. The artist profits from fortunate accidents, and the work of art acquires its beauty *during* the process of creation, *not* at the moment of conception. The outlines of Alain's doctrine resemble the ideas Valéry had formulated about poetic creation.

Alain also published *Propos on Education*, which shows an extreme distrust of children. Alain's influence was primarily exerted orally, like that of Socrates, to whom Alain's fanatical disciples like to compare him.

Jacques Nathan. *Histoire de la littérature*
contemporaine (Paris, Fernand Nathan, 1954),
pp. 236–38†

In the long series of *propos*, Alain has his favorite subjects. He is interested in every manner of thing and speaks impartially of grooming horses and love's passions, the byways of politics, the painter's art, war, and God. But he buttresses each subject with a set of central ideas that serve as a framework for his thought and to which he constantly refers as the basis for a well-aimed thrust. Is he repetitious? Undeniably. "They say I repeat myself," wrote Voltaire. "Well, I shall continue to repeat myself until they mend their ways!" Alain, however, repeats himself in order to correct *himself*, in order to state more forcefully or with more poetry what he considers essential. . . .

A treatise on happiness was extracted from the mass of the *propos*.

There was nothing wrong with the idea. The *Propos on Happiness* rescued a goodly number of readers from despairs for which no real evils could satisfactorily account. In isolation, however, these *propos* on the conduct of life took on the air of recipes. They are more beautiful when seen as part of a huge landscape of ideas. Saturated in ancient myth, inbued with Christianity, they blossom forth. Alain's numerous remarks on appearances make us see more clearly how imagination dupes us and how, for instance, it is false to say that we think of our deaths with fear—for such a thought has no object: we cannot think of ourselves as other than alive. That the pain of the imagined accident is almost always worse than that caused by the actual accident, that the sick man's suffering is different from that of the man in good health—and of a kind the latter cannot possibly imagine—these are all nails to be driven deep, for they contribute to peace of mind. [1963]

André Maurois. *From Proust to Camus* (Garden
City, N.Y., Doubleday, 1966), pp. 105, 107–8

Alain built a corpus of classical morality, and he was able to make that corpus intelligible and concrete, able to enrich it with a thousand charming, ingenious, or imperious examples. The paradox is to see heroism, a virtue inherited from Plato and Corneille, play so great a role in the first half of a century like ours; our century is pleasure-loving or impassioned, indifferent or confused, but it is a century that has usually rejected heroism. Alain still belonged to the era of Péguy. . . .

One may well ask what is Alain's place in twentieth-century literature. He was universal in his own way; he interested and pleased readers; but the abundance of his work does him a disservice. Since each essay was so short, Alain seems long because he repeats himself. His students have told us that he stammered. He did not accept such hesitations in his prose, and he built himself a trenchant language by using an heroic method: he refused to correct himself. . . . He dipped his pen too often into the inkwell of the précieux writers. To be sure, he gave new strength to commonplaces or banal ideas, by organizing them differently. But he did enjoy sculpting his style, as he himself admitted. . . . One can detect a certain twist in his mind that led this philosophical laborer to wish to seem airy and nonchalant. . . . There are thus reasons to fear that so fine a thinker will be misunderstood in the future; yet, how can anyone imagine that some day his books will be forgotten by students? Less admired, perhaps; but certainly never useless. One cannot think of Alain without thinking of his benevolence; one cannot think of benevolence without realizing that it has a definite purpose.

Roger Nimier. *Journées de lecture*
(Paris, Gallimard, 1965), pp. 20, 24–25†

Alain's understanding of the crucial role of the passions sets him apart from most modern philosophers and psychologists, who spend little time either on the passions or on wisdom. Their lack of concern for these topics is undoubtedly due to excessive specialization. But perhaps specialization is itself only the screen covering modern man's real metaphysics—nihilism. For if we no longer have the right to speak of universal values, either in politics, in art, in ethics, or in philosophy, what criteria remain to enable us to know ourselves? Who will make distinctions between what protects and what kills, what creates and what destroys—who will differentiate wisdom from passion? Alain, even though an atheist, enables us to make this differentiation, and he remains a guide for us. Despite his narrowness—and sometimes because of it—he offers wisdom and salvation to each of us: a wisdom that flows from the clearest and liveliest sources in philosophy and literature; a salvation that, without being religious in the full meaning of the word, has at least the merit of establishing a fully secular morality—in other words, a universal morality.

Olivier Reboul. *L'homme et ses passions d'après Alain*
(Tunis, Presses Universitaires de France, 1968),
Vol. II, p. 269†

1968 is the centenary of one of the most unjustly neglected figures in modern French thought: Alain. He was a member of an astonishingly distinguished literary generation, being born in the same year—1868— as Claudel, only one year before Gide, and only three years before Proust and Valéry, both born in 1871. Perhaps it is in part this very *embarras de richesses* that has prevented critics from doing equal justice to all these great figures, though there are certainly other reasons as well for the relative neglect of Alain. One is a reaction, probably only temporary, against the respect, amounting almost to veneration, with which he was treated in his lifetime by his pupils and *disciples*. In a sense, too, he has suffered from the mastery with which he straddled the fields of literature and philosophy, being considered by many literary critics as a "philosophical" figure and by many philosophers as a "literary" one— particularly since his philosophical viewpoint, with its emphasis on traditional ethical values, is no longer very fashionable. Nor, in an age of moral relativism, is the authoritative tone, occasionally even the dogmatic tone, in which he expresses his conviction that these values are still the right ones. It is commonly stated or implied that Alain stands outside the main stream of contemporary thought, and on the surface there appears to be some justification for this attitude . . .

Yet to dismiss Alain as an "out-dated" thinker is to do him a gross injustice, and to underestimate the timelessness of his views on a wide range of issues which remain as relevant to us in 1968 as they were to the men of his generation. We can find in his writings on religion, for instance, a most interesting foreshadowing of recent attempts to reinterpret religious thought in mythological and symbolic terms, and in relation to basic human psychological needs. His aesthetic theories too are strikingly contemporary in their emphasis on the creative role of materials and formal structures rather than intellectual concepts in the shaping of works of art. In the field of politics, this supposedly old-fashioned French radical speaks to us with a new voice as we reread his reflections on the dangers of the overconcentration of power in the hands of any government, even a democratic one, and on the ordinary citizen's responsibility to criticize his government's excesses and dissent openly from its policies when they show signs of deviating from the path of wise and humane conduct.

Judith Robinson. *AJFS*. Sept.–Dec., 1968, pp. 235–36

Alain used the common noun, *propos*, a word rich in meanings, to define his newspaper articles; in so doing he created a unique literary genre as distinctive as the essay Montaigne had created. Basically, the French word *propos* means spoken words, or words exchanged in the course of a conversation. It therefore suggests something relatively informal and social. Furthermore, it contains the notion of proposing; Alain's *propos* are propositions which the reader is invited, and indeed urged, to examine. The overlapping meanings of the word itself indicate in a general way the rhythm and tonality of Alain's *propos*. Short aphoristic pieces of fifty or sixty lines, they move along easily and wittily.

Alain made it a principle never to rewrite or modify what he had once written down. Years later he recalled how he wrote the *propos*: each evening he would sit down before two sheets of paper, knowing before he started that the last line would be written on the bottom of the second page, and that within the confines of those two pages he would write a piece which, if he succeeded, would have "movement, air, and elevation." He also knew that he would make no corrections, erasures, or changes; since the piece would be published the next day, he did not have time for the niceties of anguished composition. He saw the bottom of the second page approach, and ruthlessly suppressed every idea that was not germane to his theme. "The final barrier approached as other ideas began to appear; they were repressed; but, and I don't know how, they succeeded in filling out the principal idea. . . . The result was a kind of poetry and strength."

The urgent necessity of meeting a journalistic deadline taught Alain another lesson: he learned the importance of exercising the will. There is, he realized, only one way for a man to create anything, whether it be the writing of an article, the making of a chair, or the planting of a garden, and that is simply to do it. Here we approach the heart of Alain's message on happiness: there is no happiness except what a man creates for himself by exercising his will.

Robert D. Cottrell. Introduction to *Alain on Happiness* (New York, Frederick Ungar, 1973), pp. xiv–xv

ALAIN-FOURNIER (1886–1914)

[*Big Meaulnes*] is certainly the most delightful and best-told story for anyone who reads with his heart as well as his eyes, a story, moreover, that touches the imagination as deeply as it touches the heart.

Do you remember your first emotions as a reader (reading some of Dickens's novels, for example) when we were not allowed to read whatever we wanted to and still had a mysterious enthusiasm untouched within us? We followed the adventures of a hero whom we thought of as our own brother, for all young people belong to the same family when they are pursuing a dream. I felt these same emotions again while following the adventures of Big Meaulnes. . . .

Big Meaulnes also represents the poet—but do not be frightened by the novel's symbolic meaning. Never was a symbolist work more naïvely simple and more within the grasp of all simple hearts. Alain-Fournier should not be upset that I praise him for a quality—simplicity—so many others consider to be a fault, for they fail to understand that a *perfect* symbolist work must be within the reach of the whole reading public, if I may use such a vulgar term. Is there any masterpiece that does not contain its symbol, in other words its drop of eternity?

Big Meaulnes is a country schoolboy who comes to live with the Seurels; the teacher's son is a younger boy who, in the eyes of his parents and neighbors, is not very remarkable, but who possesses a fine inner life. And Big Meaulnes leads young Seurel into an adventure. The poor little narrator, whose knee is not perfect, who walks with difficulty, will be the guardian angel watching over Meaulnes's surprising adventure, which is so perfectly human and so sadly beautiful.

Rachilde. *MdF*. Dec. 16, 1913, pp. 783–84†

In [*Big Meaulnes*] there is an air of fantasy that does not much appeal to me; the unreality of that fantasy is all the more inappropriate because this fairy tale, which should have taken place in a dreamworld, beyond time, supposedly belongs to real, contemporary life. I know that Gérard de Nerval has written exquisite works in this genre; his example is a dangerous one to follow. Still, there are very lovely details in this book, and the most charming of them occur when the author, awakening from his dreams, is willing to look at the inhabitants of his village with a clear-sighted irony, or look at the countryside with a soul moved by the beauty of things. [Dec. 24, 1913]

Gustave Lanson. In Jean Bastaire, Alain-Fournier;
ou, La tentation de l'enfance (Paris, Plon, 1964),
p. 166†

Among the most enchanting of all [novels of childhood] I would place *Big Meaulnes*. Alain-Fournier leapt into being (from a literary point of view) in 1913 with this strange romantic little novel. . . . Over every page of *Big Meaulnes* there slips and trembles the light that never was on sea or land. The heroes are two lads of fifteen and seventeen; and rarely has any author rendered more delicately the prestige of the big boy for the little boy, and the chivalrous half-mystic hero-worship in which he walks enveloped. The mystery, the beauty, the wonderfulness of the poet's world transfigure the homely story, which is merely that of a schoolboy of seventeen who runs away from school, who misses his way and gets caught up in the whirl of a large country wedding at a quaint half-ruined manor-house whose name he does not know. Never again can the lad find that manor or that beautiful girl who was the bridegroom's sister, with whom he has fallen in love.

Mary Duclaux. Twentieth-Century French Writers
(London, W. Collins Sons, 1919), pp. 250–51

The event in Alain-Fournier's life that inspired *Big Meaulnes* . . . is so delicate, so fragile, that I scarcely dare to touch it with words; I am afraid of breaking it to pieces by retelling it. And yet its repercussions on Alain-Fournier's whole emotional and even intellectual life were immense. . . .

The fact is simply that one day in Paris, on the Cours-la-Reine, he saw a marvelously beautiful girl, whom he followed and whose name and address he somehow obtained. The next time he saw her, he finally approached her, although she seemed extremely reserved. Miraculously, he received a few words from her in reply that led him to believe that he was not totally scorned. But he felt that this strange apparition was making an effort to cut off the conversation by telling him, "We must leave one another. We have been mad."

The years that passed after this meeting did not erase the strong impression Alain-Fournier had received; on the contrary, that impression grew constantly deeper.

The girl had left Paris; Alain-Fournier had a great deal of difficulty discovering any trace of her; when he finally succeeded, long afterward, it was only to learn, to his great despair, that she was married.

As someone who was Alain-Fournier's friend from his adolescence until his death, I can say that this modest incident was the most important event in his life, and that until the end of his life the memory of that incident inspired fervor, sadness, and ecstasy in him.

Jacques Rivière. *NRF*. Dec., 1922, pp. 657–58†

Alain-Fournier disliked intellectual abstractions; he moved in the sphere of the intangible. Yet he was an acute critic with the most precise knowledge of the subtle course of his own mind. Although receptive to outside influences, he only admitted such as were akin to his own temperament. He knew from an early period his exact aim, and the exact equipment he possessed for attaining it, although he was not at first sure of the path by which it was to be reached. The letters written to [Jacques] Rivière from school days on to maturity—besides being one side of a most notable record of friendship—form a fascinating document of the sensitively self-conscious evolution of an original artist and are a real contribution to the psychology of art.

The posthumous volume of Fournier's fragments is entitled, in accordance with the headings of some of them, *Miracles*, and that title chances to indicate the nature of his work. In a supreme masterpiece of literature which describes and symbolises what are called "miracles," it is told how the divine artist may turn simple water into wine, or make a little everyday bread suffice to feed a multitude. Such always is the miracle of the finest art, stupendous only in its simplicity. . . . Alain-Fournier put forth no magnificent effort. He remained true to his early maxim of the unity of life and art. It is possible to say that there is nothing in *Big Meaulnes* from one end to the other but the trivial details of real life as its author had known life. Only they had fallen slowly from childhood on a peculiarly sensitive and vibrant organism, and when at last they were transformed into art a miracle was achieved and the water had become wine.

Havelock Ellis. Introduction to Alain-Fournier,
The Wanderer (Boston, Houghton Mifflin, 1928),
pp. xxvii-xxvix

Reading the four thick volumes of *Correspondence between Jacques Rivière and Alain-Fournier* I was startled by the inordinate space given over to literature, criticism, textual analysis, style, and ideas. What a miracle that *Big Meaulnes* could have been created under such deplorable conditions! The only explanation for Alain-Fournier's isolation and his sudden escape into his own world, a world cleansed of every literary miasma, is that his childhood had remained intact. There are brief moments, however, in these letters that reveal that the young writer had already, perhaps unconsciously, come into contact with his own genius. The letters written from La Chapelle-d'Angillon show his fondness for the soil and for the simple folk who live off the land. Aunt Julie's store, so carefully described at the beginning of the novel's third section, was reconstructed with the help of direct memories; this description has no visible link to the "mysterious domain"—which, in contrast, is pure fiction. But the fusion between dream and reality is absolute, just as the characters of Meaulnes and François Seurel constantly fit together to make a whole, each one illuminating the other and in turn illuminated by the other.

This contrast is the general theme of a narrative that contains both legend and memory. The miraculous, which seems quite natural to the child because he discovers it by chance, regains its true mystery when seen through the mists of the past, which transfigure it. [1929]

> Yves-Gérard Le Dantec. In *Hommage à
> Alain-Fournier* (Paris, Librairie Gallimard, 1930),
> p. 74†

It is a commonplace of criticism that when a writer is young he writes— *faute de mieux*—about himself; and the odds are that Alain-Fournier divided himself up, unequally, between his three chief male characters [in *Big Meaulnes*]: Meaulnes, Frantz de Galais, and François Seurel. Frantz, with his fatal charm and his romantic good looks, represents the fascinations of the negative principle. He is the disturber of habit, the harlequin, the joker, the trouble-maker, the grain of poison that stimulates the human organism to higher activity. François Seurel, on the other hand, is the child who is always left behind when the others run out into the garden or the playground—the companion faithful unto death—Kurvenal to Tristan, Sancho Panza to Don Quixote—the "true, sick-hearted slave" in Housman's poem. As for Meaulnes himself, with his pride, his silence, and his single-minded devotion to an ideal, he is what another French writer, speaking of a very different character, has called a "resigned adventurer": that is, one who never tries to resist his fate, or complains when it brings him grief instead of joy. . . .

If he had lived, Alain-Fournier would certainly have written other books (he had already planned a second novel); and I think it probable that he would have outgrown the phase of adolescent melancholy and frustration which produced his first book. For all its narrative power, and the extraordinary atmosphere of excitement which pervades it—not to speak of its moments of gaiety and light-heartedness—*Big Meaulnes* is a terribly sad book. It is not in the least depressing, because the final impression it leaves is strangely, almost uniquely, beautiful; but it would be idle to pretend that it is not sad.

Edward Sackville-West. *List.* Feb. 12, 1948, p. 269

Of the critics who have attacked *Big Meaulnes*, little need be said except that where they are not perverse, they are merely obtuse, and that sometimes they are both. Henry de Montherlant, for example, has dismissed the book as "insignificant" and tedious, and this is quite understandable when one appreciates that in his philosophy, women are simply instruments of pleasure, and the words "pure love" merely a meaningless jingle.

This criticism of Montherlant's has been repeated *ad nauseam* by the School of Half-Hearties and Pseudo-Intellectuals who dismiss *Big Meaulnes* as "escapist" literature. Such "criticism" must not be allowed to pass unchallenged. . . . All art, being at one remove from reality, whatever its form or content, is escapism of a sort.

[Gustave] Lanson's rejection of the novel as a ridiculous and fantastic jumble is an expression of the "pigeon-hole" mentality at its worst. Because he cannot readily attach to *Big Meaulnes* a definite label, "love-story," "pure fantasy," "realistic," "symbolist," or even "tragical-comical-historical-pastoral," he loses patience with the novel and tosses it aside. The fault is with the "pigeon-hole" system, not with the novel. . . .

Perhaps it is too early to describe *Big Meaulnes* as immortal, but in a sense it can already be considered an established classic, because the forty years of change which separate us from the world before 1914 can only now be crossed by those works which have special claims for survival. *Big Meaulnes* has crossed this gap and is still widely read today, since the theme of human happiness can never be dismissed as irrelevant. [1953]

Robert Gibson. *The Quest of Alain-Fournier*
(New Haven, Conn., Yale University Press, 1954),
pp. 270–73

In adopting Seurel's point of view, Alain-Fournier wishes to express the attitude of his childhood. He says he is aiming at simplicity. This simplicity is artificial. A child's impressions may be "simple," in the sense of being innocent and naïve. But as soon as he tries to express these impressions, he will become either flowery or awkward. Alain-Fournier has to be artificial, in a favorable sense of the word, in order to write from Seurel's point of view. In his own terms, he has to convey child-hood without childishness. The presence of Meaulnes does not mean that Seurel will not be "himself." It will simply prevent him from center-ing the story in himself, as was the case in Alain-Fournier's previous literary attempts.

From a strictly literary point of view, this is one of the aspects in which *Big Meaulnes* is superior to [Nerval's] *Sylvie*. From the descrip-tions of Nerval, there emanates the same stale odor as from Rimbaud's "Buffet." *Sylvie* and *Big Meaulnes* were conceived in opposite ways. Alain-Fournier starts from Seurel and directs the reader toward Meaulnes whom, in experience, he could not quite reach. Nerval was able to reach *his* "Meaulnes," but the Meaulnes he reached was mad. . . .

In spite of the similarity between the two works, it would be wrong to assume an influence of Nerval on Fournier. The idea of the "strange festival" may have originated in the reading of *Sylvie*. But then, this festival has been organized by Frantz; it is part of the pseudoromantic world of Frantz, in the same way that the grocery store of Uncle Floren-tin belongs to Seurel's world. Meaulnes has to progress beyond their two worlds; he has to pass these two tests. It is in this passing of tests, of trials, that Meaulnes is a hero in a familiar sense.

Robert Champigny. *Portrait of a Symbolist Hero*
(Bloomington, Indiana University Press, 1954),
pp. 22–23

The dream atmosphere [in *Big Meaulnes*] is enhanced because we see everything through the eyes of Meaulnes, whose childlike nature is more susceptible to accepting it than we would be ourselves. Moreover, the character of Yvonne, to a certain extent, adds to the dream. There is something very immaterial about her. This gentle, beautiful creature, associated as she is with the faraway sound of music, and floating along lakes in a climate much more reminiscent of summer than the middle of winter, is the stuff of which dreams are made.

However, the "marvelous," so important a word in *Big Meaulnes*, does not represent something fantastic, completely outside human ex-perience. The alliance of the dream world with a lived past permits the "marvelous" elements of the book to be closely bound up with concrete reality, because it is these very concrete things that Alain-Fournier as a child used to find wonderful—the countryside, the lives of the people he knew (e.g. his grandparents); and of those he did not know (e.g. the local château people). This presupposes the transformation of ordinary things into wonderful ones through the imagination of a child. In later life, ordinary things are transformed by the presence of love. The two chief elements of the "strange festival"—childhood and love—combine thus, to produce the third, the "marvelous." . . .

Perhaps Alain-Fournier's great achievement is to have succeeded in incorporating Meaulnes's dream into real life with the minimum of jarring elements, so that the incursion into the dream world follows naturally from real-life events and links up with them once more afterwards, with perfect continuity. . . .

Meaulnes's misery is caused largely by his inability to dissociate real life from his dream life. Escape from reality permits him to live in a dream. The essential quality of Meaulnes's dream is that it must remain a dream.

Marian Giles Jones. *A Critical Commentary on Alain-Fournier's "Le Grand Meaulnes"* (New York, St. Martin's, 1968), pp, 48–49, 61

ALEXIS, JACQUES-STÉPHEN (1922–1961)

HAITI

[In *Comrade General Sun*] Alexis tells the story of Hilarion and Claire-Heureuse, who are poor blacks in Haiti in the prewar years. The novel is primarily a love story, for Hilarion and Claire-Heureuse love each other, love the joy of the sun and the peacefulness of conversations and the beach; they love life. But the novel is also a story of poverty and hatred, for the protagonists are hungry; Hilarion has stolen in order to eat. He has been locked up, beaten, and humiliated, and he has come out of prison a communist. . . .

This long, sumptuously colored romantic chronicle, which combines evocations of Caribbean family life and political demands, and which uses the resources of the art of the popular tale and the richness, preciosity, and naïveté of the Creole dialect, reveals the power of a literature that is nourished by the folklore, the language, and the passions of a country that is still innocent of "western" literature. In this respect, Alexis's novel seems much more promising than, for example, Aimé Césaire's poetry, which is all too full of surrealist memories and is too Europeanized. . . .

Throughout *Comrade General Sun* there run a force and a lyric freedom that unify the love story, the exoticism, and the political message. The message thus appears as a necessary metamorphosis of the storyteller's sensibility, not as the result of a deliberate choice among several ways of telling the story. Alexis's achievement is that he does not in any way give the impression of having written the novel out of his convictions as a Haitian communist; instead, his work suggests that there is no other way to speak about the Caribbean people today. Passages as different as Paco's death and his immediate assumption of a symbolic function, scenes of labor in the sugar-cane fields, and the love of the young couple all become simultaneous moments—the colorful, violent, and tender scenes of a single painting illuminated by the rays of "Comrade Sun," who is the great joyful source of strength for the men tied to poverty and to hope for their land.

François Nourissier. NRF. Oct., 1955, pp. 787–88†

In the Blink of an Eye revives the sentimental theme, made fashionable by Hugo and Alexandre Dumas *fils*, of the fallen woman who is redeemed by love. But the story of the woman's fall is very long in Alexis's novel. The details about La Nina Estrellita's "profession" and her vices recall the climate of crudeness that reigns in Zola's *Nana*. And yet, despite the evidence of La Nina's moral debasement, she is the woman whom El Caucho has chosen. Around this couple there is an indefinable halo which indicates the similarity of their souls and which is the sign of the eternal promises inscribed in their flesh. . . .

Is *In the Blink of an Eye* Jacques Alexis's best novel? Perhaps so, if one shares the novelist's own conviction. In any case, this novel is the book in which he accomplished his mission. The characterization of El Caucho is indeed the culmination of an undertaking begun with Hilarion. . . . El Caucho is a true proletarian. He does not have to be trained: his training has been completed. He is the worker who is conscious of his role in society and of his importance in the struggle that is being waged. . . .

Yet the character of El Caucho does not entirely account for Alexis's preference for this novel. In *In the Blink of an Eye* he not only accomplished his mission but he also liberated himself [from his obsession with the bourgeoisie]. *Comrade General Sun* is overloaded with criticism of society. It is the story of a revolt against God and against the capitalistic organization of man's work. The description of the strikes that stand out in the narrative and the murders that are committed has the appearance of protest writing. And the moral of *The Musical Trees*, whereby the earth takes revenge and triumphs over the greed of the authorities, has no other meaning than its protest.

In the Blink of an Eye, on the other hand, calmly asserts refusal by creating a universe outside the bounds of bourgeois virtue and the demands of conventional morality. The milieu in which the novel takes place, the atmosphere of vice, perversion, and obscenity in which it is clothed, is itself a defiance of the bourgeoisie. But that is not all. La Nina's rehabilitation is a symbol, as is El Caucho's natural chivalry.

This book is a vision that contrasts with the portrait drawn elsewhere by the novelist of a bourgeois society in which everything is borrowed, falsely enlightening, and obscurely corrupt.

Ghislain Gouraige. *Histoire de la littérature haïtienne*
Port-au-Prince, Imprimerie H. A. Théodore, 1960),
pp. 293–97†

As a novelist Alexis is similar to the unanimist Jules Romains. Like the author of *Men of Good Will,* Alexis wished to express life in all its multiplicity and movement during an era of his country's history. A panorama of Haitian life from 1934 to 1942 is presented in *Comrade General Sun* and *The Musical Trees.*

Alexis does not construct his works around a single plot. . . . The life of Hilarion and that of Gonaïbo [the hero of *The Musical Trees*] are only secondary to an immense documentary fresco composed of descriptions, portraits, various peasant scenes, and psychological analyses. The danger of this style is quite evident: it diffuses the reader's interest.

Like Voltaire and Anatole France, Alexis has made his ideas explicit in his various works. It is easy to discover his political and social thoughts and his religious ideas in his writing.

In politics he leans toward communism. His liking for Pierre Roumel and Doctor Jean-Michel and for his hero Hilarion, who has been indoctrinated by these two militants, is clear. The message left by the dying Hilarion leaves no doubt about this point.

It must be added that Alexis is profoundly nationalist. The narrative of *The Musical Trees* is in itself enough proof of Alexis's nationalism. He also seems anti-bourgeois—which is explained by his socialism. His depictions of Port-au-Prince society are often satirical. On the other hand, Alexis loves the common people: he commiserates with their poverty and defends their customs and traditions.

It cannot be said that Alexis is indifferent to religion. He favors a national Catholic clergy and also the Catholic Church. But he would like Haitian priests to be more attentive to the voices of the native land and to the voices of the ancestors. Thus, people came to believe that he was urging the Haitian clergy to practice an impossible "mixture" [of Christianity and voodooism]. . . .

He chooses images that are sometimes realistic, sometimes ethereal, sometimes grandiose, and sometimes pretty. It is evident that Alexis possesses an extraordinary, marvelous imagination, a gift that had never been granted to a Haitian novelist before him.

Manuel illustré d'histoire de la littérature haïtienne
(Port-au-Prince, Éditions Henri Deschamps, 1961),
pp. 487–88†

Jacques Alexis was born on April 22, 1922, in the city of Gonaives. He studied medicine in Paris. His admiration for Jacques Roumain is well known. A writer and a political militant, Alexis was the cofounder in 1959 of a Haitian communist party, the Entente Populaire. To carry out a secret mission, he landed surreptitiously on the northwest coast of Haiti. There he was spotted, seized, and executed. That was in April, 1961.

Direct political activity was not the only field on which Jacques Alexis struggled. He also fought on the literary battlefield for the development of his country. A struggle for development was indeed the way in which he conceived of his mission as a novelist. . . .

The novel *The Musical Trees* is an analysis of the situation in Haiti in 1941–42. At that time the rural world of the Haitian peasants was under attack on two fronts, economic and religious: an American rubber company was setting up a plantation on land stolen from the peasants, and the Catholics were campaigning against the voodoo religion. This intertwining, this overlapping, this intersecting of events, provides the author with an opportunity to develop his views on the role of the Catholic religion in the development of rural Haiti. What, in Jacques Alexis's opinion, is the role played by the Catholic religion? His negative attitude toward the Church is very close to that of Jacques Roumain. Indeed, Roumain himself is present in the novel under the name Pierre Roumel, a journalist defending the peasants' cause. When Alexis attacks the Church, he uses almost the same arguments Roumain used.

Claude Souffrant. *Europe*. Jan., 1971, pp. 34–35†

Alexis took advantage of his exile in France to continue his medical studies. He specialized in neurology. His innate restlessness led him to frequent the numerous intellectual circles that blossomed in Paris right after the war. He got to know Césaire, Senghor, and all the exponents of Negritude. He was drawn to existentialism. He became friendly with Aragon and the most advanced of the progressive intellectuals. He immersed himself in social realism, which dates back to Zola and Anatole France; he discovered socialist realism, Gorki and Ehrenburg. A need, an impulse, a new passion then arose, and took form through these new aesthetic prisms. Between his busy hours at the hospital, Alexis the neurologist wanted to write, to re-create the distant image of his fatherland by harmonizing the flow of images that beseiged his mind despite the years of exile and separation. . . .

Alexis's first two novels, as well as his collection of stories [*Romancero in the Stars*], explored the unlimited field of traditions, legends, and beliefs of rural life in Haiti. "If the zombi stories are legends," insists Alexis, "happy are those whose legends are so great and alive!" Thus, the artist's imagination and the multicolored marvels of social reality intertwine to the point at which it is difficult to distinguish one from the other. Then a new dimension of realism is born: "magic realism," which suffuses Alexis's literary works. His characters seem to spring from the most authentic tableaux in Haitian primitive painting. They arise from real life as well. Their lives are shaped by the lush tropical vegetation, the tribulations of peasant life, the mysteries and rites of voodoo, and the serene desire for improvement characteristic of the Haitian people.

Gérard Pierre-Charles. Europe. Jan., 1971,
pp. 67–68†

ANOUILH, JEAN (1910–   )

Should the play and the heroine really be called *The Untamed Girl*? Anouilh's titles are not good enough for his plays, which overpower their labels. Indeed, would it be possible for anyone to give titles to these works dominated by compelling central figures, by heroes who are prevented from following the course of their lives by the same anguish, heroes who are not so much rebellious as unadaptable, characters who swim against the current, lovers of obstacles who prefer their personal drama, their private misfortune, to a benevolent destiny? Anouilh, at twenty-six, is of the age of bold creation, of sacrifices enthusiastically accepted, an age when one does not hesitate to choose a mission over happiness, even if that mission may be imaginary.

Following *Traveler without Luggage* and *There Was a Prisoner*, Jean Anouilh [in *The Untamed Girl*] has chosen a woman as the mirror of his poignant refusals, thus adding power to his portrayal of characters who stand apart, for women are endowed, more than men, with a social consciousness, and their nature and roles demand that they adapt in relation to everything, that they approach all steep slopes and obstacles indirectly. Creating obstacles and nothing but obstacles, like his heroine Thérèse, Anouilh overdoes ingenuity and makes his theme less believable by making a woman in love sacrifice love in favor of a higher principle.

Not that I consider such a choice to be impossible! It would not be the first time that a woman thought she could purify and magnify her love by renouncing it, and felt that possessing and rejecting could be part of the same act of love. But the fact that Thérèse flees happiness to return to the very milieu she deeply despises indicates a temperament and an ideology that are not very feminine. . . .

Let us not forget that there are some fine things in Anouilh's play. There is no doubt that he strikes deep and untapped chords in us, that he is knowledgeable in illuminating emotions. Does this writer soliloquize rather than present dialogue? Are his images sometimes weak? Yes, but a tone one can recognize from the first exchanges on stage, a power and ease in handling stagecraft, enable Anouilh to surpass the dramatists of his generation; the attractions of fresh intellectual content are quite sufficient to conquer, to erase, what from time to time gives us the impression of weakness. [Jan. 16, 1938]

Colette. *Œuvres complètes* (Paris, Le Fleuron, 1949), Vol. X, pp. 493–94, 496†

[Anouilh's heroines] are thin, small, and dark, with bulging foreheads and unruly hair, and are often compared with "little goats," "little rats," or "little snakes." While having generally bitter regrets that they were not born boys, they are jealous of those beautiful feminine creatures who are made-up, well dressed, and well groomed—the ones sought after by men—and they imitate these women awkwardly and unconvincingly when they try to please. Antigone [in *Antigone*], Thérèse [in *The Untamed Girl*], Jeannette [in *Romeo and Jeannette*], and Eurydice [in *Eurydice*] are girls rather than women, in the sense in which high-school students say "girls." They climb trees and they fight, their chests are flat, the calves of their legs are as strong as rope, their stomachs are hard and dark. We cannot imagine them as wives or mothers. Their sexual ambiguity, an attribute of adolescence, strictly determines their destinies. . . .

[Anouilh's plays] imply a conception of love that would find its highest image in a kind of boyish friendship or coed scouting—a demanding and confused conception, and one that excludes women, that is, feminine women. . . . The flesh is not absent from these characters' concerns or from the thoughts of their companions: they desire one another and embrace each other. . . . But none of these characters seems to view sexual communion as the goal, as the very aim of their love, or even as love's safeguard. Quite unlike the heroes of D. H. Lawrence, they do not think of sexual union as a privileged moment or as the only form of true communication between two human beings. On the contrary, whatever the desires of Anouilh's characters may be, they display a certain repugnance, mixed with fear, for physical realities, for bedrooms, beds, and physical acts.

Hubert Gignoux. *Jean Anouilh* (Paris, Éditions du Temps Présent, 1946), pp. 69, 71–73†

A sensation being bruited, I went last week to see M. Anouilh's new play, *Poor Bitos; or, the Masquerade Dinner-Party*, which has split Paris into two camps—those who dislike it, and those who detest it. Mere dislike is the Right-Wing reaction, while active loathing issues from the Left: both camps, needless to say, are packing the theater. Far more than *Antigone, Poor Bitos* is Anouilh's political manifesto. It is a cruel, discordant work, as bitterly imagined as written, in a mood as violent as that of a neurotic schoolboy locked up in a dormitory while his class-mates frolic in the sun; and its conclusion lies somewhere between "A plague on both your houses" and "I'll be revenged on the whole pack of you." It is the blackest by far of Anouilh's plays. It is also the most cunningly constructed, a dirty act done with the utmost art, a torture-chamber designed by a master builder.

In shape it resembles a fox-hunt, except that the fox in this in-stance has envenomed teeth. A truer similitude, perhaps, would be the slow tearing of wings from a wasp. . . .

As an essay in political thought, the play is imitative and negligible. As a study of human character, it is hysterical and often foul-mouthed. As a piece of dramatic architecture, it is, as I have said, exquisitely gripping. But it fascinates me most in another aspect: as an exercise in self-revelation. Whose side is the author on? The question has agitated Paris ever since the play opened a fortnight ago. To be sure, M. Anouilh's aristos are heartless sadists; but I have little doubt that his real enemy is Bitos, in whose wounds no knife is let unturned. This despised provincial upstart is drawn with an ugly, obsessive passion, almost as if he were a ghost that the haunted author were struggling to exorcise. The name Bitos called up an odd echo. I found myself thinking of the derisive nickname, "Anouilh le Miteux" [Anouilh the poverty stricken, literally "full of mites"], that Jouvet bestowed on the young upstart from Bordeaux; scruffy Anouilh, at whose work the maestro laughed, saying that it reeked of old socks. In every Anouilh play there is mockery, and in many there is hatred; but in this one I smell self-hatred. [1956]

Kenneth Tynan. Curtains (New York, Atheneum,
1961), pp. 395–96

In *The Lark*, of course, the theme of love is absent, but the eventual refusal of life by Joan of Arc . . . is motivated in much the same way as elsewhere in Anouilh. What leads her to withdraw her recantation and face death is her realization that acceptance of life means acceptance of the lesser, trivial and miserable satisfactions of life—"the little shreds of happiness" as Antigone [in *Antigone*] calls them—as well as betrayal of her own ideal of her mission and of her voices.

For life taints all that it touches, and the shock of this discovery to Anouilh's heroes (and heroines) is the spring of their fastidious gesture of refusal as they grow up into a world of corruption and hypocrisy. . . . Confronted with this, they sheer off and refuse the responsibility of living altogether, preferring to adopt the child's open and unruly defiance and refusal to understand; and in their thirst for purity they envision only two ways of escape, the first being unrealizable—a return to the innocence of childhood—and the second being death. . . .

There is of course one way in which *The Lark* steps outside the range of the ordinary "Black Play" [one category of Anouilh's plays] situation. Joan's death has a wider triumphant meaning than that of Antigone, which was so much for her own sake alone. Hence the brilliant theatrical device of the ending of the play, with its pronouncement, true in the *deepest* historical sense despite what actually happened— "Joan of Arc is a story that ends well." . . .

We should be wary of seeking signs and messages in [Anouilh's] work or attaching labels to him where they do not apply; particularly so in a play like *The Lark*, where the heroine's sacrifice is not made in lonely isolation, like Antigone's, but in the name of humanity. This time, the enemy is the Church and not society—as a whole or in part— or the State; yet, like these, the Church is worldly and the disparity between its moral tenets and Joan's quest for perfection is the same conflict as before but in another form. Joan's compassion can moreover be traced in Thérèse Tarde [in *The Untamed Girl*], who found she had to associate herself with the rest of humanity in the shadow of her past.

Merlin Thomas and Simon Lee. Introduction to
Jean Anouilh, *L'alouette* (New York,
Appleton-Century-Crofts, 1957), pp. 24–25, 27–28

One feels in *Antigone* an even more frantic desire [than in Anouilh's other plays] for a purity that is impossible in this world. Therefore, Antigone will choose to die to find that purity. Beyond this refinement of the archetypal Anouilh heroine, *Antigone* would not have brought much new, had there not been the character of Creon.

Antigone has the freedom to reject this world, and she does so with ecstasy . . . the ecstasy of revolt. But this revolt is only a rejection, a negation. [Arthur] Koestler, himself a rebel, has honestly pointed out the difference between the rebel and the revolutionary. Both set themselves apart from an existing order. But the revolutionary wants to blow up a structure in order to establish one he considers better. There is something positive and constructive in his attitude. The rebel, according to Koestler, struggles unceasingly against a world which does not accept him and which he wants to destroy only to achieve the ideal of unbridled individualism. This is the burning quest of anarchists and libertarians, a quest whose futility and sterility need no detailed explanation. Whatever he may do or say, man is part of the human situation; he must assume the burden of the condition common to all mankind. The rebel is a person who refuses to understand, like Antigone; and we cannot accept those who knowingly will not understand. If they are young brats, the solution is a spanking; if they are anarchists, the execution squad. One cannot and must not constantly say "no." Because he did not accept this fact of life, Anouilh's theater was slowly asphyxiating itself—until he created the character of Creon. . . .

The Sartrean image of "dirty hands" is perfectly applicable to Creon, who speaks in a language close to that of Hoederer [the hero of Sartre's play *Dirty Hands*]. True courage can be found in accepting life and its ugliness.

Jean-Pierre Lassalle. *Jean Anouilh; ou, La vaine révolte* (Rodez, Éditions Subervie, 1958), pp. 26–27†

Sophocles' Antigone is intransigent and proud; so is Anouilh's, but she is *bent* toward childhood. She is therefore stubborn and obstinate rather than willful. She is "little Antigone," as she likes to call herself.

She is altogether "little" because she remains *attached to her past*. Sophocles' heroine looks toward her future as a woman, toward her fulfillment as a human being. . . . Anouilh's heroine, he tells us, is twenty years old. The whole opening scene of the tragedy shows her seeking refuge in her little-girl past, which is represented by her nurse. . . . She is also a little girl when contemplating nature in the morning. . . . She is especially a little girl when she carries out her act . . . of burying Polynices: her "insignia," indeed her symbol, is the shovel, abandoned on the field, which will betray her, the shovel of the sand castles of her childhood, the "very old and rusty" shovel, which has not been used for a long time and which, like the nurse, represents attachment to a time that has irrevocably ended. . . .

While the Greek Antigone considers the order of the gods as the highest value, Anouilh's Antigone places the highest value on the *order of childhood*. She insists upon it with her little gestures and her little deeds, which come up against the prohibitions of "grown-up people."

In place of the kingdom of the gods [Anouilh] has substituted that of childhood, and it is for this realm alone that Antigone will finally fight. Creon, here not the proud man but the skeptic, will in effect destroy the girl's firm belief in the gods and her love for Polynices; he will prove how absurdly automatic are the religious rites and how worthless was the young man.

Robert de Luppé. *Jean Anouilh* (Paris, Éditions Universitaires, 1959), pp. 58–60†

Anouilh's universe is certainly one of the most coherent and one of the most poetic that anyone of his generation has created for us. . . . In [*Invitation to the Chateau*] Anouilh did not even bother with any detailed descriptions of his characters, thereby taking advantage of a luxury that only the writers of the Italian *commedia dell'arte* could indulge in: all the characters in *Invitation to the Chateau* are the familiar figures of Anouilh's universe.

Closely related to the comedy of intrigue of the great French playwrights of the eighteenth century, this play is nothing but a series of entrances, exits, and misunderstandings. It is almost like a ballet, controlled in every detail and in the course of which comic invention, which never gets winded, leads the viewer from surprise to surprise. The dialogue is both lively and witty, with one line melting into the next. It is sometimes full of bitterness, but soon wild happenings gain the upper hand and the overall lightness established at the beginning is maintained, without faltering, until the final denouement.

Perhaps never as much as in this divertissement has Anouilh given free rein to his virtuosity. Combining the themes of a "black play" with the rhythm of a "pink play" [two of the categories used by Anouilh in grouping his plays], having systematic fun with the techniques of classical comedy, mingling the everyday and the artificial to create something truer than nature, Anouilh has, in *Invitation to the Chateau*, written a play that will remain in the memories of viewers as a masterpiece of imagination and humanity.

André Barsacq. *CRB*. May, 1959, pp. 35–36†

In [Anouilh's] later plays, money continues to be an obstacle in some instances, and the cause of much evil in others, but the problem of love is stated in more fundamental terms. Difference in background no longer rends the couple apart, but certain weaknesses inherent in love make it impossible for the hero to accept such a union.

For Eurydice [in *Eurydice*] everything could be so simple, if only Orpheus would stop thinking and accept things as they are; if he would let his hands love her, and speak no more. This superficial love of hand for body and body for hand—nothing more than a contact of surfaces—is what the people of Anouilh's world call happiness. Orpheus cannot accept such happiness, for he realizes what Eurydice and all those who lean toward the simple and easy cannot realize: that "life is not a matter of gestures." For the hero, life must be lived deeply, on levels other than the purely physical. To realize that each man is alone and can never understand another is a painful discovery. And herein lies one of the inherent weaknesses of love, as Anouilh pictures it: love's original sin, which condemns it irremediably to failure. Love for his characters is only a touching of surfaces. In spite of his desire to vanquish the sense of solitude which pervades the life of every thinking being, Orpheus realizes that the couple is inevitably two. . . . The couple may establish a physical contact, but the pleasure it brings is only an illusion and one finds himself alone again. . . .

[The] desire of the lover to lose himself in the beloved constitutes a second weakness in love as Anouilh depicts it, for it involves a loss of the authentic self. In his efforts to understand or please the other, the lover must make certain compromises with himself. . . . Even Orpheus . . . must give up a certain part of himself for Eurydice.

There is yet another weakness: love threatens to become a habit and the couple seek each other because they are accustomed to one another—caught within the net they have woven. The relationship loses its spontaneity and becomes nothing more than the gestures of love. . . .

[In Anouilh's tragedies] life is love's irreconcilable enemy, with its piling-up of habit and compromise—its destruction of spontaneity. The longer we live, the further we go from that kingdom in which Antigone takes her stand.

Leonard Cabell Pronko. The World of Jean Anouilh
(Berkeley, University of California Press, 1961),
pp. 82–83, 86

The characters of Jean Anouilh's plays are latter-day romantics whose inability or refusal to adjust to their social *milieu*, and consequently to life itself, is the direct cause of their alienation. . . . Anouilh has divided his earlier plays into two categories, the "pink plays" and the "black plays," the only difference between the two being that in the former the tone is lighter and the end seldom tragic. In both groups, however, there are the same flights from reality and the same emphasis on the sordidness of the everyday world.

The world as Anouilh sees it is materialistic, a world in which there are only haves and have-nots. In this world social and economic distinctions are of utmost importance, and a character can seldom move from one social or financial group to another without serious results. The world of the author of *The Untamed Girl* is a vulgar world, a world of egotists and hypocrites who are interested in their own welfare and who care about others only in proportion to their financial value. Into this world, in each play, steps a young idealist whose quest in this world for an absolute, be it absolute purity or absolute love, is doomed to failure before the action actually starts.

These young idealists, because of their origins, resemble the heroes of many of the nineteenth-century romantic plays. Like [Hugo's Hernani, Ruy Blas, and [Dumas *père*'s] Antony, Anouilh's characters

—Thérèse in *The Untamed Girl*, Frantz in *The Ermine*, Marc in *Jezabel*, Georges in *Rendezvous at Senlis*, and Diane in *Invitation to the Chateau*—have a malediction weighing upon them, a malediction brought about by their origins.

Robert Emmet Jones. *The Alienated Hero in Modern French Drama* (Athens, University of Georgia Press, 1962), pp. 58–59

Regardless of [Anouilh's] method of writing, regardless of the force with which the creatures have lived and asserted themselves in his mind, one thing is certain: by the time they reach the stage, they are closer to caricatures than to real people. And it is not simply because Anouilh is a theatricalist that this is so. Pirandello, Thornton Wilder, Salacrou—to name but a few practitioners of the same aesthetic—sometimes found it more effective to unleash quite realistic people within their play worlds. Even Giraudoux, despite an occasional pasteboard prop for poetic or intellectual display, created stage people that seem more human than many of Anouilh's caricatures. The latter's rationale, then, would seem to be a personal and arbitrary one.

Why caricatures in the first place, one wonders. In an interview in 1951, after once again stressing that he had always considered theatre a game of the intellect, Anouilh said quite simply, "Isn't caricaturing the most important game of the intellect?" An unconventional theory, to say the least . . . before the footlights Anouilh's remark does have a certain validity. The dictionary defines a caricature as a picture or description "ludicrously exaggerating the peculiarities or defects of persons or things." Then every stage character, we should say, tends somewhat toward caricature: as there is rarely enough time during a play to represent a whole personality, whatever we may think we mean by "whole personality," dramatists must settle on presenting only those facets of a man vital to the situation at hand, and may even exaggerate these for the sake of clarity. . . .

Rather than compose his character about a number of significant traits, Anouilh simply pounces on one or two trivial traits, draws them out, and parades a disfigured and often ridiculous creature before the public. His distinctiveness lies in his intention: he deliberately flattens characters into caricatures.

John Harvey. *Anouilh: A Study in Theatrics* (New Haven, Conn., Yale University Press, 1964), pp. 29–31

Whereas [T. S. Eliot's] *Murder in the Cathedral* is a study in inner conflict, spirituality, and the nature of martyrdom written by a deeply

religious person, *Becket* focuses on human relationships and the absurdity of man's lot on earth. For Anouilh, man's only satisfaction can
result from the manner in which he plays out the role allotted to him by
destiny—only then does his life take on structure and validity.

The painful soul-searching that Eliot's Archbishop must undergo
is spared Anouilh's Becket, for he has known from the beginning that, by
his very nature, he is denied any choice. The temptations of his former
life of pleasure and his friendship with Henry may intensify the conflict,
but they cannot influence Becket's course of action. When Henry names
him Archbishop, Becket's decision is made for him; his only alternative
is to defend to the best of his abilities the honor which has been for-
tuitously thrust upon him.

Unlike the conflict of Eliot's Becket, the struggle of Anouilh's hero
is far removed from the realm of martyrdom. He is not plagued by
doubt nor does he experience any revelation, for he does not see his task
in terms of divine commandment, but merely in terms of his duty as a
human being. Anouilh's Becket is denied the spiritual tranquility granted
those who sacrifice themselves to the will of God, for he knows that it is
always *his* will which he is exerting, that it is always *his* sense of duty
which he is fulfilling. The burden of life falls squarely upon his shoulders. He will also meet his death peacefully, not in the knowledge that he
has faithfully served God, but in the knowledge that he has faithfully
served his own sense of duty and has done his job wholeheartedly. . . .

With the same seriousness of purpose as Eliot, Anouilh has nevertheless created in his loosely and informally structured play a world
which allows of comedy, digression and gaiety. He does not shy away
from puns, slang and even indecent language. It is as though Anouilh
used laughter as a weapon to allay the misery, injustice, and absurdity of
life.

Bettina L. Knapp and Alba della Fazia. Introduction
to Jean Anouilh, *Becket; ou, L'honneur de Dieu*
(New York, Appleton-Century-Crofts, 1969),
pp. xiii–xv

If in [Anouilh's] "black plays" society triumphs over the absolute
ideal and compels the heroes to seek a tragic form of escape, in the "pink
plays" Anouilh's characters escape black reality through fantasy, illusion, and changing personality. It is as if the author felt that the world,
with its fiendish problems, lacked and needed the sense of humor that he
attempted to provide in "pink" situations. . . .

Thieves' Carnival despite a few dark moments is essentially a
"pink" fantasy. . . . The fanciful nature of this play provides Anouilh
with a vehicle through which to demonstrate his concern with the rela-

tivity of truth, for thieves can be honest men and honest men thieves, bored women can be tricksters and clarinet players detectives, according to how they wish to appear and how others care to look at them. The multiplicity of the human personality underlies the instability of "truth": man is too complex, possesses too many conflicting personalities, ever to become a peaceful unity.

Alba della Fazia. Jean Anouilh (New York,
Twayne, 1969), pp. 68–69

I experienced an immense pleasure last night. I said to myself several times that it must have been like this in 1926, at the opening of Giraudoux's *Siegfried*, or in 1937, at the opening of Anouilh's *Traveler without Luggage*, and that everyone must have heaved the same sigh of contentment. I had thought beforehand that maybe Anouilh was a little too old now, but *Dear Antoine* is a play of wild youth, even in its faults, which are those of a young writer trying to say too much. . . .

Anouilh says somewhere in *Dear Antoine* . . . that the theater is a situation, characters who talk, and then an intermission when sweets are sold. In this play the situation is simple. Antoine, a "great dramatist," has died in 1913 in an isolated villa in Bavaria, 1,800 meters in altitude. He had asked a notary to bring together several close friends and relatives for the reading of his will. They arrive dead-tired from the trip, at a house they have never been to before. They have given in to Antoine's final whim out of love, curiosity, or idleness. . . .

You will discover the "sweets" *after* the intermission, as you see how a play grows out of a play. You will get to know this Antoine, so amazingly talented, a sort of Edmond Rostand who would have discovered Pirandellianism before Pirandello himself, who would have invented the famous scene between Geneviève and Siegfried before Giraudoux had a chance, who would have dreamed of writing *The Cherry Orchard* before Chekhov. You will note in passing that this dear Antoine also had a big flop, an adaptation of Kleist's *Katherine of Heilbronn*, just as Anouilh failed with the same play three years ago at the Théâtre Montparnasse.

This is a prodigiously narcissistic play, if you will, full of self-indulgent dialogue—but denounced as soon as it is uttered, deactivated with a smile, a shrug, an original witticism announced as such. How can we resist it! Anouilh takes us by the hand and tells us a secret, half smiling and half in tears. Out of this confidence arises a delicate, discreet, insidious and subtle emotional reaction.

François-Régis Bastide. NL. Oct. 16, 1969, p. 13†

What is *Don't Wake the Lady*? It is the study of a character, a producer-director-actor, a cross between [Georges] Pitoëff and [Louis]

Jouvet. It is the portrait of a family of actors, struggling with its past, its illusions, its dreams, and its lies—struggling with itself. Furthermore, it is another new portrait of Anouilh by Anouilh, following *Dear Antoine* and *The Goldfish*. But above all, above all, it is a play for the theater written by a man of the theater, the one man who probably knows best what the theater is and the one who undoubtedly loves the theater more than anyone because the theater is his very soul: he has been molded out of it. It is therefore a play about the theater written with as much love as ferocity.

A comedy, says the playbill. Yes, a comedy in Anouilh's manner, that is, one that moves from the wildest buffoonery, from the most energetic humor, to serious drama, even tragedy. In this tragicomedy, in this serious burlesque, Anouilh makes use of theater in its entirety, all theatrical forms and all forms of the theater. Farce, melodrama, of course; but also all the other kinds of plays that are regularly performed —or rather rehearsed—from the ultra-Russian to *Hamlet* by way of Scandinavian drama. . . .

He also adds the prompter, the commentator; and then a scene that had been tender and melancholy becomes cynical, cruel, and base, like life seen from the other end, when one finally has lost all hope of deceiving oneself. . . .

At times Anouilh falls into jokes that are too facile or ones he has already used in other works. And I am a little upset by this, because with a little pruning, a few cuts, which would have been so easy to make, we would have a real masterpiece that would constantly delight us by its mastery, its dazzling virtuosity, its warm sincerity, and its succession of moving confessions.

But my reservations and regrets are really of little weight, because a few over-long passages cannot detract from the altogether exceptional quality of this play. We can feel, behind all the fantasy and beyond all the skill and all the fine humor of the play, a sadness, a grief, a serious-ness, a kind of profound discomfort, an inability to be satisfied with what gives pleasure and joy to others, all of which constitutes the great-ness of this troubled soul and this suffering heart. [Oct. 23, 1970]

Jean-Jacques Gautier. *Théâtre d'aujourd'hui*
(Paris, Julliard, 1972), pp. 350–52†

Anouilh is a romantic idealist whose idealism plagues him. He yearns for purity, nobility, moral courage, glory, but discerns little but pet-tiness, chicanery, deception and vice. Life riles him because it isn't consistent; he abhors the bulk of humanity because it professes virtues it doesn't practice. There is something comic in this and a great measure of "fun," but though he is able to laugh at it, it upsets his vitals. He is a sentimentalist become bitter because everything he beholds, everything that has happened to him since he first conceived of the loveliness of experience—especially in matters of love—has proved false and vain.

Oh, if it were only not so, Anouilh's plays seem to wail—beauty not despoiled, grandeur not debased, purity not debauched. But since it is not so, we must make the best of it in humankind's shabby fashion, bedecking ourselves in social courtesies, official pomp and at best in common-sense compromise. Once in a long while some splendid gesture or leap of the soul, like a lark in the sky, momentarily redeems us.

This makes Anouilh both a conservative and a cynic. He will not budge from his safe position—"agin" everything except the Ideal. He endures life with a grimace of disgust, a salty chuckle, an ache of regret, and above all with sharp-edged *practical shrewdness*. The latter feature produces his formidable stage craftsmanship.

The Waltz of the Toreadors is an acidulous bonbon, a despondent farce. Within its coruscating invention, its delightful trickery, its rib-tickling skepticism, there also dwells something subtly tender, softly sighing. The colors of Vuillard and Bonnard surround it; a fragrance of old-time corruption, elegance and bourgeois crassness, decorum and dissoluteness emanates from it. An echo of sweet romance as the French from 1875 to 1900 dreamed of it—a kind of domestic or village romance—wafts through it.

Harold Clurman. *Nation.* Oct. 8, 1973, p. 349

APOLLINAIRE, GUILLAUME (1880–1918)

Nothing is more reminiscent of a shop selling second-hand goods than this collection of verse published by Guillaume Apollinaire, with a simple yet mysterious title—*Alcohols*. I say second-hand goods because in this hovel a mass of heterogeneous objects can be seen; some of them have value, but none of them represents the dealer's own craft. This is one of the characteristics of second-hand trade: it resells; it does not create. . . .

Apollinaire certainly brings a mixture of candor and guile to the writing of his poems. It would perhaps be polite to seem amazed by this mixture; I think, however, that one should always distinguish a combination of literary eloquence and the jargon heard in large commercial ports from the inspired delirium communicated to us by the symbolists. . . .

Apollinaire seems to have taken it upon himself to perpetuate the legacy of every weakness left by dead literary schools. As a stroke of originality, he removed all punctuation marks from the proofs of his book, so that, among these two hundred pages, one would look in vain for a single comma. By being so thorough, however, Apollinaire has missed a fine opportunity to puzzle his readers. He should have retained at least a pair of commas and a single semicolon, hidden them in the midst of the text, and promised, in his preface, a prize to any reader clever enough to discover these punctuation marks and indicate their location.

Georges Duhamel. MdF. June 16, 1913,
pp. 800–801†

Apollinaire is a strange and even somewhat mysterious figure. I like him very much; I have a great deal of affection for him, as I have for [André] Billy. Yet sometimes Apollinaire strikes me as having something ambivalent, something of the adventurer about him. He told me the other day that he does not yet feel "free" with me, since he needs to know people very well. I do know that he is very intelligent, searching, and secretive; knowledgeable about strange customs, unusual books, little-known things; very cosmopolitan. I told him once, a few years ago, when he published *The Heresiarch and Co.*, "You use all those elements to write your books." He denied it, especially regarding his poetry, which, he claims, contains the most of himself.

Apollinaire the man is very simple, not at all snobbish. At home he goes about in short sleeves without a collar, and he helps Marie Laurencin prepare and serve dinner.

I certainly have a great liking for Apollinaire. I like him as a man, and I like him as a writer. As a poet, he is very strange, and his "Anecdotal Life" series in the *Mercure de France*, is written in a simple yet extremely subtle style. What a peculiar figure! I get the feeling he has many hidden facets. . . . Billy says Apollinaire is, above all, a weak man, who can be led into almost anything. [July 9, 1913]

Paul Léautaud. Journal littéraire (Paris,
Mercure de France, 1956), Vol. III, p. 99†

Apollinaire's poetry [in *Alcohols*] has an astonishing, incommensurable intimacy, reminiscent of Verlaine but a Verlaine polished by coming into contact with society, disencumbered of a certain childish or effeminate quality, yet still ready to confess and weep. One day Verlaine wept in prison: "Tell me, what have *you* done/With your youth?" All the despair of that cry *de profundis* has been regathered in the lines in which Apollinaire cried, when he, too, was in prison. (He had been imprisoned in 1911 under an unfounded suspicion that he was involved in the theft of the Mona Lisa.) [Apollinaire wrote:] "Guillaume what has become of you . . ./One day/One day I was waiting for myself/I said to myself Guillaume it is time for you to come/So that I may finally know who I am."

Indeed, it is not easy to know who this man is: perhaps one can call him a symbolist, but does that term suit the sadness, the anxiety, the friendship, and the sensibility that inspire his poems? . . .

His poems have the calm sound of crystal, as well as a mocking yet infinitely sad tone. As a refrain we keep hearing the words "Remember, remember"—remember innumerable little things that are beautiful only because they are part of the past: "Next to the gleaming past tomorrow is colorless." This line is disconcerting in the work of a man who is still young, an Americanized European of our century. . . .

His entire life revolves around memories. The sad resonance of things experienced, surrounding the forsaken man—this is the fundamental tone of Apollinaire's poetry, a tone that always resides in his poetry, whatever his subject may be. Always this purely interior tone, which governs the entire shape of objects and transforms them into immaterial phantoms, into memories. [Jan. 30, 1914]

Karel Čapek. *RLM*. Autumn, 1963, pp. 142–43†

[The critic] Rachilde tells us that at the first performance of [Jarry's] *King Ubu* hostilities erupted—"fiery hostilities: old against young, young against old, young against young." Why has Apollinaire's surrealist drama [*The Breasts of Tiresias*], first performed on June 24, 1917, managed to reawaken all these hostilities a generation later? The notion of pursuing parallels between the two plays could only have come to critics' minds because of the controversies both works created. The names of Aristophanes and Rabelais were brought up with equally little justification.

Without detracting from its satirical and moral significance, I would suggest that if one wants to link Apollinaire's play with another drama, the choice should be *The Playboy of the Western World* by John Millington Synge, about whom the writer of *The Breasts of Tiresias* himself said: "From his realism, of an always unexpected perfection, there arises a poetry so strong that I am not surprised if it shocked people." *The Breasts of Tiresias* struck me as a good-humored play; it was a pleasure to laugh at it without thinking any further. Nevertheless, I know that Apollinaire is aware of the secret of modern humor, something deeper and more tragic than what we find in *The Breasts of Tiresias*; he must have intentionally not used that modern humor in this play.

I might as well say that the play, in its choice of means, does not display the same infallible judgment as does Jarry's masterpiece. Nevertheless, Apollinaire's play questions again the nature of the New Spirit, whose immense proportions Apollinaire has somewhat sensed. [1917]

André Breton. Les pas perdus (Paris, Éditions de la
Nouvelle Revue Française, 1924), pp. 43–44

Guillaume Apollinaire had been a witness at my wedding in the church of Saint-Merry on July 13, 1909. He returned there in 1919 . . . and after his second visit he sang about the church in "The Musician of Saint-Merry." . . .

I think that Apollinaire's returns to previous sources of inspiration are important because they explain a whole side of his work; I do not think I need to give additional examples. Only long-standing close friends of this great poet know the extent of these returns; I leave to others the task of writing detailed footnotes. . . .

An examination of this phenomenon, constantly recurring in my friend's works, would lead one to discover its origin: a facility, or rather a necessity he felt, not to appropriate but to transform an event born of others and with which he was associated, to transform it into either his own actions or his own words. This explains why Apollinaire was perhaps the first poet able to write unbothered by the noise created by the conversations of his friends, and even strangers, those unwelcome visitors who crowded his house. . . .

When Apollinaire was interrupted in what, before the Parnassian school, was called "meditation," he would seize the most banal and the most trivial statement—if the statement were incongruous, it could be a lucky find for the "new spirit"!—and, without embellishing what he heard, without betraying the *revelation* it contained, he would use the statement as a new point of departure.

André Salmon. NRF. Nov., 1920, pp. 682–83†

I have just reread *The Heresiarch and Co.*, generally considered Apollinaire's prose masterpiece. In my opinion, his masterpiece is *The Poet Assassinated*. Here he most felicitously gives free rein to his lyrical verve; here his philosophy of life, his concept of the poet and of himself, find their strongest and freshest expression. Nevertheless, *The Heresiarch and Co.*, despite the passing of time, still inspires the same sense of revelation it did ten years ago, and some of the stories in it have a wholeness and perfection not attained in Apollinaire's subsequent works. Even in the short stories of a purely anecdotal interest, such as "Honoré Subrac's Disappearance" and "The Sailor from Amsterdam," Apollinaire's original art and charm turn these baroque anecdotes into what the writer wanted them to be: *philters of fantasy*, stimulants for the imagination, drugs. . . .

Apollinaire's definition of "good taste" was a collection of conventions and prejudices, residues of obsolete civilizations against which his instinctual and primitive nature rebelled; in this rebellion lay his genius. . . .

The article [by Duhamel] in the *Mercure de France* about *Alcohols* deeply saddened Guillaume. He asked me if I did not think it proper for him to send representatives to the author of the article and challenge him to a duel. Apollinaire's notion of honor was always ready to be translated into action. [1923]

André Billy. *Intimités littéraires* (Paris, Flammarion, 1932), pp. 184–85, 204†

Picaresque literature has a burlesque style to which the world has now returned for sustenance, after centuries of neglecting a style that was once highly cultivated. This literature and style influenced Apollinaire as barbarously and as magnificently as the intoxication produced by an old wine. . . .

From the time he had translated picaresque Spanish literature and had rewritten picaresque French literature, he always retained the freedom of the man who writes seated at a table facing the fields where the first roosters sing.

"An infinite faculty for desiring things, a great uneasiness of mind, a tyrannical curiosity, an immense passion for understanding—those are the secrets of his personality," his good friend [Jean] Royère told me in confidence. . . .

His fiction, while plunging into unfathomable depths of modernism, also retains something of the medieval tales. The pride of medieval France appears in his stories. Apollinaire is not one of those who just needs a moonlit night for inspiration, rather than literary ancestors.

Perhaps he is a troubadour, blessed with bold lyrical gifts, who has imbibed from the same castle fountains at which the famous troubadours of old stopped to drink.

Ramón Gómez de la Serna. *Ismos* (Madrid, Biblioteca Nueva, 1931), p. 38†

The last time we saw [Apollinaire] was after he had come back to Paris from the war. He had been badly wounded in the head and had had a piece of his skull removed. He looked very wonderful with his bleu horizon [uniform] and his bandaged head. He lunched with us and we all talked a long time together. He was tired and his heavy head nodded. He was very serious almost solemn. We went away shortly after, we were working with the American Fund for French Wounded, and never saw him again. Later Olga Picasso, the wife of Picasso, told us that the night of the armistice Guillaume Apollinaire died, that they were with him that whole evening and it was warm and the windows were open and the crowd passing were shouting, à bas Guillaume, down with [Kaiser] William and as every one always called Guillaume Apollinaire Guillaume, even in his death agony it troubled him.

He had really been heroic. As a foreigner, his mother was a pole, his father possibly an italian, it was not at all necessary that he should volunteer to fight. He was a man full of habit, accustomed to a literary life and the delights of the table, and in spite of everything he volunteered. He went into the artillery first. Every one advised this as it was less dangerous and easier than the infantry, but after a while he could not bear this half protection and he changed into the infantry and was wounded in a charge. He was a long time in hospital, recovered a little, it was at this time that we saw him, and finally died on the day of the armistice.

The death of Guillaume Apollinaire at this time made a very serious difference to all his friends apart from their sorrow at his death. It was the moment just after the war when many things had changed and people naturally fell apart. Guillaume would have been a bond of union, he always had a quality of keeping people together, and now that he was gone everybody ceased to be friends.

Gertrude Stein. *The Autobiography of Alice B. Toklas*
(New York, Random House, 1933), pp. 59–60

[Apollinaire] possessed the inborn gift of calling forth, by the juxtaposition of the most simple, unassuming vocables, spiritual entities beyond the grasp of our senses. Profoundly sensitive to the mysterious affinities between words, he was able by their association to evoke the most extraordinarily delicate shades of feeling. There is to his words a miraculous ring that a Mallarmé might have envied. Nevertheless these associations of words were not, as in the case of Mallarmé, the result of conscious, systematic effort. They came in the course of the rhythmic development of the sentences as these unfolded themselves spontaneously. His sentences may not have any strict, definite signification; often they do not seem designed to give any clear statement of a particular idea or fact; they unroll and spread by virtue of an internal force, being engendered, as it were, automatically, as they slowly but irresistibly progress and grow. . . .

Apollinaire, however, did not trust the spontaneous verbal development of his subconscious mind to the extent of giving to the public the crude and unpolished product of his automatic divagations. He never entirely lost control of his reveries; he always took care to direct the flux of images surging up from the depths of his personality into predefined and well-marked channels. Moreover, he obviously touched up and corrected his first drafts, using the resources of a thoroughly conscious intelligence in order to make his sketches into consummate works of art. This process is typically illustrative of Guillaume Apollinaire's literary position: though inclined, on principle, to give free rein to the instinctive mystic forces lying within him, he always felt reluctant to go to the very extremities implied by his own premises, and he would unobtrusively reintroduce an element of organizing intelligence in order to elaborate the data of his subconscious Ego. His works thus gained undeniably in external, artistic beauty; but to the more uncompromising poets, who were to come later, it seemed that he had stopped short of the full realization of his program. They assumed the duty of pursuing further the course that he had daringly initiated.

Georges Lemaitre. *From Cubism to Surrealism in French Literature* (Cambridge, Mass., Harvard University Press, 1941), pp. 112–14

I knew [Apollinaire] in a pale blue uniform, his head shaven, one temple marked by a scar like a starfish. An arrangement of bandages and leather made him a kind of turban or little helmet. One might have thought that this little helmet hid a microphone by means of which he heard what others cannot hear and secretly surveyed an exquisite world. He would transcribe its messages. Some of his poems do not even translate its code. We would often see him listening in. He would lower his eyelids, hum, dip his pen. A drop of ink hung upon it. This drop would tremble and fall. It would star the paper. *Alcohols, Calligrams*—so many cyphers of a secret code.

François Villon and Guillaume Apollinaire are the only two I know of who steer a steady course through the limping measures of which poetry is made, and which is not suspected even by those who think they are producing poetry because they write verse.

The rare word (and he certainly used it) lost, between Apollinaire's fingers, its picturesqueness. The commonplace word became unusual. And he would set those amethysts, moonstones, emeralds, cornelians, agates which he uses, wherever they came from, like a basket-maker plaiting a chair on the pavement. One cannot imagine a craftsman more modest, more alert than this soldier in blue. . . .

Others will analyse Apollinaire, his magic, based as it should be, on the virtue of herbs. He used to collect herbs from the Seine to the Rhine. The concoctions he made, stirring them with a spoon in a mess-tin on a spirit lamp, bear witness to the attraction exercised upon his episcopal self by sacrileges of every kind. One can imagine him equally well on his knees, serving the mass of the regimental chaplain, as presiding at some black mass, removing shell splinters from a wound, as sticking needles into a wax figure. On the Spanish Inquisitor's seat as at the stake. He is both Duke Alexander and Lorenzaccio. [1947]

Jean Cocteau. The Difficulty of Being (New York,
Coward-McCann, 1967), pp. 102, 107

Apollinaire was never an enemy of mine. I have never spoken ill of Apollinaire. . . . So don't listen to gossip! Today people credit me with influencing him, but what do I care? I had sung about the Eiffel Tower. He sang about the Eiffel Tower. And many others have sung about it since. Neither those others nor Apollinaire nor I invented the Tower; it was Eiffel, after all, who conceived and constructed it to win a bet and to shock other engineers. . . .

The Eiffel Tower's time had come. It was the French radio antenna. It told all the ships on the high seas what time it was. Why shouldn't it tell poets what time it was? . . .

I suggested to him the title for *Alcohols*; he preferred the title *Eaux-de-vie* [Spirits], which he considered more symbolic and which he retained right through the final proofs of the Mercure de France edition. When he returned those proofs, however, and gave his approval to print, he changed the title and also removed all punctuation.

After he returned from the front and had his operation, as I have already said, Apollinaire was no longer the same. He became vain, childish, moody, impatient, proud, jealous. . . . Never again, except for a few reappearances of his old spark, did I see him lively and full of laughter, as he was before. He was worried, filled with apprehension about the future, and he believed in his bad omens. At that time, through André Billy's instigation, he entered the Censorship Office, the lowest depths for a creative mind such as his!

Blaise Cendrars. Blaise Cendrars vous parle
(Paris, Denoël, 1952), pp. 219, 221, 244–45†

[*The Cubist Painters*] stands as the monument to Apollinaire's championing of cubism and immediately reveals the unsystematic but penetrating nature of his criticism. Beyond a doubt he succeeds in picking the major cubists: Picasso, Braque, [Jean] Metzinger, [Albert] Gleizes, Marie Laurencin, Gris, Léger, [Francis] Picabia, Marcel Duchamp, and [Raymond] Duchamp-Villon. One could take exception only to Marie Laurencin, whose talents are agreeable but severely limited and scarcely cubist, and perhaps Picabia, who did not fully live up to the promise he showed in 1913. . . .

The famous fourfold classification of cubism inserted in the proofs of his book was in reality Apollinaire's attempt to reconcile his wide-ranging aesthetic enthusiasms. It was not a success. Scientific, physical, orphic, and instinctive cubism did not denote four distinct strands in the development of the new movement. The first two have become "analytic" and "synthetic" cubism (though no nomenclature is universal); orphism falls outside the movement; "instinctive" was the dubious catchall heading for Marie Laurencin and others—even Rousseau, one supposes, if Apollinaire had dared. Nevertheless, the attempted classification shows considerable boldness for the year 1913. . . .

In Apollinaire's declamations we feel some of the precariousness of cubism's early researches into the shifting appearances of things, yet his confidence helped establish the movement. Such confidence came partly from his facility with words, his ability to construct a provisionally habitable edifice out of untested materials. Thus, while the cubists produced a magnificent collection of paintings defying the entire tradition of post-Renaissance art, Apollinaire was the first to transform their ideas from incoherence into persuasive intelligibility.

Roger Shattuck. The Banquet Years (New York,
Harcourt, Brace, 1958), pp. 218–19

[*The Cubist Painters*] is a curious volume, much of it written in the turgid, pseudo-metaphysical style that Apollinaire seems to have been the first to consider essential to a discussion of *avant-garde* art but which has since become all too familiar to readers of prefaces to art books and introductions to exhibitions by contemporary artists. *The Cubist Painters* achieved a first, small reprinting only in 1922, and a second only in 1950, but it has always had a fame far greater than its sales. Widely referred to as "the first book on Cubism" (which it is not: [Albert] Gleizes and [Jean] Metzinger had published their *On Cubism* a year earlier), it is chiefly *The Cubist Painters*—or, more precisely, its reputation—that has given Apollinaire himself a considerable reputation as an art critic. . . . "Leader of the school of Cubism," and "Perhaps the greatest critic of our century" are only two of the honorary titles recently conferred on him by writers on modern art. . . .

Today Apollinaire's status as a poet, for example, can be discussed freely and without danger, whereas to question his competency to be "leader of the school of Cubism" is a perilous enterprise. It seems not to be widely known that several of the very painters about whom Apollinaire wrote in *The Cubist Painters* are, to put it mildly, skeptical on this point. . . .

[According to Braque], "Apollinaire's art writings are those of a poet, attracted to the new painting by sympathy for Picasso, myself and other personalities; also, he was a little proud to be part of something new. He never wrote penetratingly about our art, as did for example

Reverdy. I'm afraid we kept encouraging Apollinaire to write about us as he did so that our names would be kept before at least part of the public."

Francis Steegmuller. *Apollinaire: Poet among the Painters* (New York, Farrar, Straus, 1963), pp. 139–41

Of all Apollinaire's pronouncements ["The New Spirit and the Poets"] is the most important, and vital for an understanding of his attitude to his art and to life generally. It is really a credo summing up all that he has been trying to formulate and embody throughout his life, and a most manifest example of his real single-mindedness of purpose. "Days go by I remain."

It is interesting to note that Apollinaire's "new spirit," which if he had lived he would probably have had the influence to impose as the major movement in post-war literature, lies at the opposite extreme in every way from the wave of Existentialism that dominated French ways of thinking after the Second World War. Undoubtedly the reasons for this lie not in literary or philosophical influences but in Apollinaire's own personality. Energy, optimism, irony, laughter, fantasy, common-sense, and a transcendent idealism, these are all his personal attributes. And he is harnessing them here in an attempt to re-create a new role for poetry in a changing world. . . .

Through the miracle of science, he has seen the inside of his own head. To rival that achievement poetry must be prepared to make use of new discoveries both in the infinitely great universe within ourselves—that is, the analysis of the subconscious and of dreams—or in the infinitely great universes around us in space. It can borrow from the techniques of the cinema and the gramophone, or from the visual arts. It can hoist itself on to the shoulders of prophesy, or stoop to pick up a mere handkerchief. It can present itself in a great guffaw of laughter, and most of all in the devastating, eye-opening shock of surprise. . . .

[Apollinaire] had begun his lecture on a sober note cataloguing the national and traditional characteristics that form the base for his rocketing new spirit. As he follows its soaring trajectory he is transported by vibrant enthusiasm and the lecture takes on the tone of an inspired sermon. He actually ends his declaration of faith in the tones of a prophet.

Margaret Davies. *Apollinaire* (New York, St. Martin's, 1964), pp. 289–91

[Apollinaire] listened to the songs of the streets and of the woods, and trained himself carefully, methodically, to speak to himself in the lines of verse, in strophes of this kind on his walks. . . .

As a result of this practice, Apollinaire's prosody, departing from that of the romantics which was based on syllable count, returns to the much older prosody which regards the line of verse as a unit of utterance. . . .

It follows that the suppression of punctuation in *Alcohols* is the direct consequence of this state of things. Whereas punctuation is indispensable in the broken, crannied versification of a Hugo, the internal silences in the lines often being longer than those which separate the lines, the introduction of punctuation marks in the first strophe of "The Song of the Badly Loved" is not only futile but harmful. . . .

Of course the advantages of punctuation in the control not only of grammar but of intonation are tremendous and so obvious that the radical solution adopted by Apollinaire and by so many poets after him—total suppression—is necessarily provisional, so many opportunities being accessible when we combine the two systems; but it has had an eminent value as a manifesto, a proclamation, and has obliged us to become aware once again of what punctuation really was, of its value and its function, as well as of what verse was, and its arrangement on the page. If we can today explore the entire realm which extends from Apollinaire's non-punctuation to the punctuation of classical prose, it is indeed to him that we owe the fact, and the experiments which he conducted in this realm deserve the closest study. [1965]

Michel Butor. Inventory (New York,
Simon and Schuster, 1968), pp. 191, 194

"The Musician of Saint-Merry" is a complex poem, although not in the sense that Mallarmé's are. I mention this poet for two reasons: first, because he is Apollinaire's immediate antecedent: second, because his work is the touchstone for all modern French, even universal poetry. In the case of Mallarmé, obscurity is inseparable from the poem; his poetic method, he said several times, is that of *transposition*, and it consists of replacing perceived reality with a word which without specifically naming that reality elicits another, equivalent, reality. The poet does not name the swan or the white female bather: he creates *an idea* of whiteness that combines feminine flesh, water, and the plumes of the bird.

Apollinaire also begins with an anecdote, one or another reality, but he does not erase it: he separates it into fragments that he brings together according to a new order: this shock, or confrontation, is the poem—the true reality. Mallarmé proposes to abolish the object, to the benefit of the language, abolish language to benefit the idea, which in turn resolves into an absolute which is identical to nothingness. Thus, his poem does not present things to us, but words, or more exactly, rhythmic signs. Apollinaire intends to destroy and reconstruct the object through language; the word continues to be a means of allowing us to see things in their instantaneous vivacity. There is no transposition of reality, rather, transfiguration. Mallarmé's method approximates music, Apollinaire's, painting, especially the cubist esthetic. [1965]

Octavio Paz. *ECr.* Winter, 1970, p. 278

Apollinaire's lyrical acceptance of World War I and his role in it of artillery sergeant and infantry lieutenant was in keeping with his character and ideas. He had foreseen a blood purge of nations since his adolescence; he knew the dangers of the antipoetic forces loose in the technological age; and he had felt early in his life the world's need for the hegemony of French art to save it from barbarism.

He was always one to be in the forefront of every movement he endorsed. His early poetry had been among the most medieval and Decadent, his anarchistic tracts the most violent, his anticlerical stories the most satirical, his Rhenish lyrics the most Romantic, his pornographic writings the most erotic, his Symbolism the most messianic, his Futurism the most destructive, and his "poem-conversations" the most modern of our times; it was natural that his war poetry was to become among the most heroic. He knew the secret of giving himself fully to a cause; and his main weapon, in war as in peace, was his personal example, his myth. The shift from errant poet to knight-errant poet was correspondingly easy. The soldier had been a leading symbol of poetic adventure in *Alcohols*, and the simplified and intensified life in wartime with its easy blacks and whites and great surface reserves of emotion waiting to be exploited gave extra significance to his favorite verbs *sing, dance, look, love, weep,* and *die.* He knew that mere photographic reporting of love and life grew charged with emotion when it came from under a bombardment on the front; his hundreds of poetic dispatches to friends and periodicals used the simplified, impressionistic cosmopolitanism of his prewar muse to keep ahead of exploding events. . . .

At their best—in "The Night of April 1915," for example—[his war poems] present a unique appreciation of life and love in the most harrowing situations. . . . At their worst, they comprise the excessively conceptual, patriotic *war poems* of forgotten anthologies.

Scott Bates. *Guillaume Apollinaire* (New York, Twayne, 1967), pp. 138–40

[In 1903] Apollinaire composed "The Song of the Badly Loved," which many consider his greatest poem and one of the masterpieces of French lyric poetry. Inspired by Annie [Playden, the English governess]'s rejection of his love in London, where he pursued her after the return from Neu-Glück [in the Rhineland], it contains all the shades of the poet's ambivalent feelings from deep desire and despair to the most virulent hostility. Much of its power comes from the tension between the opposing principles of continuity and discontinuity in the structure. The octosyllabic five-line stanzas with their *a b a b a* rhyme scheme flow along smoothly, carrying the song of the poet's lost love through the subtly shifting moods. At least *within* each section. The sections themselves, however, stand out like separate, distinct blocks which by their juxtaposition produce a series of unexpected breaks in the flow, as though Stravinsky were driving wedges into Debussy. . . .

One has only to recall the single, fixed décor of the most celebrated French love poem of the nineteenth century, Lamartine's "The Lake," to appreciate the tremendous diversity of material in "The Song of the Badly Loved." Disparate blocks of imagination jostle each other between the two terminal points which pin down the poem in reality. Discontinuity of course is a risky technique which can easily become the enemy of coherence. The problem for Apollinaire was to create an effect of disorder reflecting the turbulence of the poet-lover's distraught soul while imposing enough order to make the poem aesthetically valid. Hence the necessity for a compromise with the devices of continuity: the regular verse form, the more or less symmetrical architecture (avoiding at all costs the coldly mathematical), the transitional stanzas uniting certain but by no means all of the sections. Thanks to these compromises the lyric sentiment is at once multifaceted and single. Projected into the vastness of history and legend it retains at the same time all the intimacy of the subjective self. Much of the power of "The Song of the Badly Loved" derives from the delicate balance it achieves between "Order" and "Adventure," the Apollonian and the Dionysian.

LeRoy C. Breunig. *Guillaume Apollinaire*
(New York, Columbia University Press, 1969),
pp. 18, 23

ARAGON, LOUIS (1897–   )

What I find attractive about Aragon is that he has prodigious gifts, the sort of grace in expressing himself that only one writer in any generation possesses, and a poetic imagination that is direct, immediate, and spontaneous. . . . What disturbs me about Aragon is everything systematic he adds to what comes spontaneously to him. Make no mistake: this anarchist, through the very intensity with which he is haunted by a compulsion to break every law and to scoff at every accepted value, becomes a sort of philosopher or priest. . . .

For Aragon, Dada has been a means of demonstrating, of making claims, instead of creating. Aragon, who attacks every pretension so cruelly, who is able to ridicule every pretension so well, should nevertheless be aware that denial can also be pretentious, and that true naturalness and freedom consist of letting oneself flow along with life, without even trying to make overall judgments; the most independent writer is the one who accepts his readers as they are. . . .

I would like simply to point out to Aragon that as a writer there is a danger worse than death to which his system is leading him—the danger of growing old in revolt. For anyone who fears ridicule, there is nothing worse. If Aragon does not yield to some tenderness in himself, some of the naïveté and simplicity he persists in repressing, if he does not decide to let the smile within him replace the harsh laughter he cultivates, he risks not only losing all his gifts (although he will pretend to be easily consolable) but also becoming proclaimed a great pontiff by the literary world of the cafés, by the clan of literary failures (this would undoubtedly seem less amusing to him).

My qualms abate, however, when I realize that he is still at an age when a writer can waste his talent by choosing to have faith in something other than himself. Despite everything, Aragon began with too much talent not to let the moment come when he will feel—more than any metaphysical concern—the need to express himself, to become graspable, touchable, judgeable. A writer has to become that modest. . . . There is a time to make fun of others, and a time to let others make fun of you.

Jacques Rivière. NRF. April, 1923, pp. 700–703†

We may well wonder whether Aragon, a thinker, an inexorable logician, has ever been a surrealist except occasionally, and out of curiosity. What he prizes above everything is revolt; he joined the revolts of the dadaists, of the surrealists, and of the communists. Satirical and cynical, but a city dweller who needs society in order to flout it, he might have taken up the Voltairean tradition (read his *Anicet; or, The Panorama*); no less easily, by merely following the aggressive, corrosive bent of his thought, he might have wielded that "demoralizing" power which Flaubert once dreamed of assuming, and at the same time left behind him a brilliant poetry of despair.

For a long time, his fear of being snugly placed somewhere in a world irretrievably given over to stupidity, more or less close to those whom he abhors, as well as his love for disorder and his refusal to be interested in anything except his revulsions and hatreds, imprisoned him

within a circle of blasphemies and monotonous vociferations. His thirst
for scandal has been quenched successively by erotic fury and scatology;
he has played rather well the part of the man with the knife between his
teeth. According to Gabriel Bounoure, Aragon "realized that the most
effective cleansing was cleansing by filth—the diversion of a great sewer
into the Augean stables." The danger of this undertaking—as Rimbaud
could testify—is that it is difficult to cleanse oneself of so much dirt
later on. [1933]

Marcel Raymond. *From Baudelaire to Surrealism*
(London, Methuen, 1970), pp. 273–74

From Surrealism to Socialist Realism is a long step, and Aragon did not
achieve it easily. But while his work since 1930 does spring from a
fundamental reorientation of his whole being, involving a literary rebirth, his new work is not wholly a denial of his early work. . . . His
whole concern with creating a modern mythology and a new repertory
of poetic images arose from an extraordinarily keen observation of
commonplace reality. His writing, even at its most extravagant, was
always remarkably faithful to the form, the texture, the color of experienced things, and vividly reflected the fine gradations of sense impressions. But in his study of human behavior he came to recognize more
and more the importance of the social compulsions that motivate people
and determine the patterns of everyday life. The struggle for livelihood,
the disparities in economic and social privilege, the functioning of political institutions, the special conditions of modern industry and urban life,
and above all the specter of war hovering over the horizon—these, as
subject-matter, as meat for literature, for poetic treatment, came to
occupy him increasingly. His early anti-militarism forms a direct link
with his present work, whose theme is concerned with war and whose
aim is to reveal, through a panoramic picture of French society, the
intricate combination of forces that produced the World War and the
manner in which those forces molded the lives of people at different
social levels. . . .

The Good Neighborhoods, a sequel to The Bells of Basel, is the
second in a projected series that bears the general title, *The Real World*.
This epic differs from Jules Romains's *Men of Good Will* and from
Roger Martin du Gard's *The Thibaults*, which cover much the same
ground, in that it is written from a definite philosophical, political, and
esthetic point of view. Aragon rejects the theory that art can be, or ever
has been, objective. He writes, or aims to write, from the point of view
of the many who today live in want, insecurity, and fear, at the mercy of
cyclical depressions, and under the constant menace of war. Aragon
thus addresses his writings, no longer to a small coterie of highbrows,

but to the masses of common people, to those who work, produce, and build. He believes, with André Malraux, that it is the function of art to help men to live.

Haakon M. Chevalier. Introduction to Louis Aragon,
Residential Quarter (New York, Harcourt, Brace,
1938), pp. viii–ix

[His trip to Russia in 1930] led to Aragon's break with the group he had helped to found, of which, with Breton and Éluard, he was one of the acknowledged mainstays. Did his departure have a general meaning for surrealism, or should it be regarded as no more than a phenomenon of individual significance? Often, in the texts dealing with surrealism, and hence merely repeating an idea whose source is Breton, Aragon is said to have followed the same path as [Pierre] Naville to a position of "political opportunism." Both had, in effect, broken with surrealism to join the Communist Party, but according to methods and in periods that were entirely different. Naville openly put the question, not of simply joining the Communist Party, which would have had a merely formal significance, but of a shift to means of revolutionary action which would have led *the entire movement* to Marxist policy, then represented by the Third International. And at that time his determined adversary was Aragon, who qualified political action as "dishonoring."

Aragon himself *individually* took the step which has always separated surrealism from political action, from Marxism; that is, he *renounced* surrealism to become a communist. And since for several months his attitude was not at all defined, the surrealists soon came to regard it as a maneuver of intimidation in order to induce them to come out in favor of the literary policy of the Communist Party. They could see nothing else in the Communist Party's demands in their regard than an abjuration and a submission to the literature of propaganda.

More important still, Naville's evolution and Aragon's did not occur at the same period. Aragon merely followed the current that with increasing power swept the advanced intellectuals of every nation toward the USSR, at a time when this adherence no longer occasioned any disadvantage for those who adopted it, quite the contrary. The surrealists did not choose to regard Aragon's move as a development, but as a palinode, "a betrayal" which they were to censure him for bitterly down through the years. [1944]

Maurice Nadeau. *The History of Surrealism*
(New York, Macmillan, 1965), pp. 181–82

[World War II] gave back to Aragon the world in which words have a real meaning, even the tritest of the words that describe human experiences. He was like a traveler returning after years to his own countryside, in which everything is familiar and yet has a different value, being seen with different eyes. That explains the effect, in his best poems, of a complex situation reduced, after years, to a statement as simple as that of the old Scotch ballads. He was the Border minstrel of this war.

Even Aragon's principal fault becomes a virtue in his wartime poetry. He writes easily, with apparently endless powers of invention, but sometimes also with deliberate negligence, with a willingness to follow the rhyme or the image wherever they lead him, with a tendency to repeat himself where he would refuse to copy others. He has a power of concentration that shames those of us who need quiet and leisure for their best work, or any work at all. Aragon works anywhere, at any hour and in any company. . . .

For the poetry he wrote during the war, his special gift was necessary. There was no time for self-questioning, for writhing in the pains of composition; there was not much time to write at all, except for a man like Aragon who could do his work in barracks, in trains, in waiting rooms, or on the beach at Dunkerque. Unlike less naturally gifted poets, he was able to set down his impressions and emotions as they came, so that his six volumes of wartime poetry became a month-by-month record of the struggle: the boredom and loneliness of the "phony war"; the grotesque horror of the German invasion, like Breughel's conception of hell; the utter weight of defeat, under which Aragon was among the first to stand erect; then the impulse for reëxamining French history, to find the real strength of the nation; and the growing power of the Resistance, which at first he merely suggested in his poems, but later mirrored frankly, so that his work was forbidden by the Vichy censors and he turned to writing ballads of combat to be printed in the underground newspapers or smuggled across the border and published in Switzerland; and at last the frantic joy of "Paris, Paris, of herself liberated"—all of it is there, in Aragon's verse.

Malcolm Cowley. In Hannah Josephson and Malcolm
Cowley, eds., *Aragon: Poet of the French Resistance*
(New York, Duell, Sloan and Pearce, 1945), pp. 6–8

[The English collection *Aragon: Poet of the French Resistance*] is a bright-eyed, prosaic collaboration to exalt a traitor to modern poetry, Louis Aragon. Naïvely, Waldo Frank, who contributes a brief personal reminiscence of Aragon before the latter's conversion to banality, manages to admit that even when Aragon was a brand-new Surrealist he showed signs of that lush patriotism speaking its crudest pitch in the phrase, "La Belle France." This, the academic version of French patriotism, along with other bourgeois trademarks, was wrecked by the Surrealists, Dadaists, and other moderns, when the esthetic revolution was staged after the beginning of this century. The truth is that only as Aragon *remains a Surrealist*, i.e., a poet capable of original invention, is it possible to read him without disgust.

The 25 poems printed here attest that Aragon showed his literary support of the French nation during the Second World War by converting the tradition of French poetry into a sort of army food-ration: a concentrated mélange of effects from Villon to Rimbaud and the former Aragon, including a sizeable assortment of anonymous clichés. In this respect, the reader's anticipation is oddly stimulated as to what the next line may produce. The national alexandrine becomes a kind of citation for heroism, whose pattern is detailed with lines that may sound like T. S. Eliot, Kenneth Fearing, Wilfred Owen, and even the kind of verse that newspapers print "direct from the front." Needless to say, nothing in Aragon challenges the masters. I think that of these 25 poems, perhaps only one, "Elsa at the Mirror," remains wholly unflawed by some vulgarity, infelicity, or crêpe-paper cockade. . . .

In this book, Malcolm Cowley calls Aragon a "folk poet." This means merely that he can be read by literate elements of the French proletariat and middle class as a sentimentalist brave enough to sing the Marseillaise even as the Germans march through the Paris streets. But Aragon did not need to write verse to help resist the Germans; he was personally active and wrote stories and pamphlets. No, the 25 poems are, as we say in America, "pure gravy." In effect, that is. Virtually, they formed a "necessary" conversion of esthetic principle aligning itself with the conception of art previously animated in Aragon by Stalinism, a political philosophy which means esthetically a pandering to the cultural limitations of the proletariat, the middle class, and the reactionary intelligentsia.

Parker Tyler. View. Jan., 1946, pp. 16–17

When does [Aragon] find the time to write? *The Communists*, Volume 1, published May 5, 1949; *The Communists*, Volume 2, published October 14, 1949; *The Communists*, Volume 3, published March 15, 1950; *The Communists*, Volume 4, published October 12, 1950. To be sure, Dickens and Balzac also produced a great deal of work—shelves full—but I wonder if what they did was as *extraordinary* as the feat this uncanny man is now performing . . . this writer whose days are as long as yours or mine, twenty-four hours, and whose days are filled with other tasks—proceedings, boring visitors, telephone calls, duties, meetings, committees, board meetings, tasks of every variety—this writer who always makes himself available and receptive to others but who in the midst of everything still finds time to write a monumental novel as well as poems, articles, speeches, and letters. . . .

The Communists is never a *simplistic* book. Nor is the world presented in it as some kind of big, confused stew, as a mixture of absurd accidents and circumstances—and neither are the people. Of course, Aragon is not *objective*; he lacks the kind of objectivity that puts the whole world in the same sack and every person in the same basket. But when Aragon gazes at people, he is marvelously accurate and attentive, and he does not falsify the lighting in order to darken one person or put a halo around another. This very honest book has a fairness of tone that reflects a fairness of heart and soul. Aragon makes human contact with even the most abject of his characters.

Claude Roy. Aragon (Paris, Éditions Pierre Seghers,
1951), pp. 18–19, 88†

A.P.: [By the close of World War I] did Aragon already have the fascinating and original mind revealed later in *The Peasant of Paris*?

A.B.: Yes, he did. As for those tastes of his that could have put him in opposition to Soupault and to me as well, he very quickly put a damper on them. I can still remember him as an extraordinary walking companion. When one walked through parts of Paris with him—even the most colorless places—the experience was greatly enhanced by his magical-novelistic gift for stories, a gift that never failed and that came to him at any street corner or shop window. Even before *The Peasant of Paris*, a book like *Anicet* gave an idea of these riches. No one was more skilled than Aragon in detecting the unusual in all of its forms; no one else could have been led to such intoxicating reveries about the hidden life of the city. . . .

His memory was equal to any task, and long after reading them he could outline the plots of innumerable novels. The mobility of his mind was incomparable, but this mobility may have led to his rather considerable laxity in his opinions and also a certain susceptibility to impressions. Extremely warm, he devoted himself wholeheartedly to his friends. The only danger he risked came from his excessive desire to please. He *sparkled!*

A.P.: Was he already a rebel in some manner?

A.B.: There was not much rebellion in him at that time. He had a taste for subversion and made a show of it, almost out of affectation, but in reality he cheerfully endured the impositions of the war and his professional (medical) training. . . .

In 1923, in [the journal] *Littérature*, Aragon was already advocating "scandal for the sake of scandal." Even in surrealist circles, a statement like that seemed indefensible and was sharply criticized. No matter how great an influence he exercised at that time, even his friends were able to detect a *verbal* excess in him. One has to imagine Aragon as he was then, torn between the natural gifts which made him shine and which he enjoyed displaying, and the attempts he made to adopt the temperament and the viewpoint—basically more somber—of the surrealists.

André Breton. *Entretiens* [*avec André Parinaud*]
(Paris, Gallimard, 1952), pp. 38–39, 96†

Aragon's Communists are saints. A Communist in his novels always has the right instincts and is never wrong. Whatever the professed "realism" of this worker's world, Aragon, a bourgeois himself, becomes extravagantly lyrical whenever he enters its sphere. His worker has something in common with the "good savage" of the eighteenth century. He is strong, sane, inarticulate and naïve, but canny, with laughing, childlike eyes and an inexhaustible store of common sense.

Aragon's first novels are directed to the bourgeoisie—his readers— more than to the proletariat. In *The Communists* he is addressing the proletariat, to whose existing legend he is adding a new page. The fictional chronicle he writes is shamelessly partial and its fictional value almost nil. And yet, as is not very apparent in *The Communists*, Aragon is a born novelist. He knows how to tell an ample, living story, full of color and movement; he is able to sustain unusual and strongly differentiated characterizations; his satire is often pungent. In addition, a holdover perhaps from his surrealist years, he has a fertile imagination that often carries him into the realm of pure fantasy. One can detect in Aragon a poet whose senses are alive to form and color, in particular to the charm of feminine beauty and fashion. One can detect the romantic writer of melodrama—and melodrama can make exciting reading. Unfortunately all these potentialities are hampered by Aragon's over-simplified Marxist dogma. He has an answer to all the questions of his time. This allows him to order his novels unhesitatingly according to a consistent point of view. But his novels lose in depth and honesty what they gain in certainty. As far as Aragon is concerned, the point of view in itself justifies the existence of his novels; the result cannot be expected to sustain the interest of the impartial reader who wants to read a novel for the novel's sake, not as a document.

Germaine Brée and Margaret Guiton. *An Age of
Fiction: The French Novel from Gide to Camus*
(New Brunswick, N.J., Rutgers University Press,
1957), pp. 87–88

In the great fresco of *The Communists* Aragon has taken the national drama of the "phony war," the defeat, and the Occupation, and has made it live again. He has depicted the behavior of different social classes, parties, and individuals during the torment. He has shown the painful path that some people took to arrive at an accurate conception of their duty to the nation. He has exalted the struggle of Communists during the war for the liberty of the people and the salvation of France. The young people of today, who were not old enough then to understand that tragic period, so important for an understanding of all contemporary history, find in Aragon's monumental work a prodigious tableau of strength and vitality. . . .

Struggle is what solves problems. Struggle enables us to surmount difficulties. *The Communists*, as much an historical work as a work of the imagination, offers vibrant proof of the need for struggle. That is why our entire Party and all progressive opinion have placed such high value on this masterly work by our friend Aragon. . . .

It is true that small minds, embarrassed to find themselves moved by [*Holy Week*], have insinuated that the revolutionary writer has put his flag in his pocket, has turned his back on the problems of today. As if pamphlets and satires, poetry linked to events, and articles about current topics were the only genres permitted a Communist writer; as if the historical novel or personal lyricism were forbidden to him! The founders of scientific socialism have fought against the ridiculous idea, the simplistic and dogmatic idea, that any "inclination" always has to be "explicitly formulated." [1959]

Maurice Thorez. Œuvres choisies (Paris, Éditions
Sociales, 1965), Vol. III, pp. 123–24†

To understand [*Holy Week*] and its author, we must remember that Aragon was a member of the French Communist Party for 35 years; that he was elected a deputy and then a member of the Central Committee; that, as director of the weekly *Les lettres françaises*, he combined a campaign to seduce the younger "uncommitted" writers with a most aggressive and fanatical defense of the cult of Stalinism and the aesthetics of [Andrei] Zhdanov [Stalin's cultural policy-maker], to a degree unparalleled by any other known writer, justifying the most obviously monstrous political trials, insulting the victims of these proceedings, and slandering those who protested against them. . . .

Aragon's militant orthodoxy was of an extremist and truly provocative nature, like the anti-Semitism of Céline; and in the end he linked this cult of Stalinism with a vulgar chauvinism, insisting, at the close of the war, that no German should be permitted to own a painting by a French artist and, of course, clamoring for the annexation of the Rhineland by France. As to his alleged "Socialist Realism Movement": except for his own series of novels *The Communists*, and some unreadable books put out by a few party hacks like [Pierre] Daix or [André] Stil, such a movement never existed in France. . . .

The truth is that no work by Aragon (who, incidentally, has not used his first name as a writer for many years), least of all *Holy Week*, can be understood without understanding the influence of the surrealist movement on his prose and the role played by dreams and the magic of language. If, in the name of Zhdanovist doctrine, Aragon sought to prevent his juniors—and even French Communist painters!—from engaging, as he did, in free experimentation, we must interpret this as proof of a bottomless egotism which expresses itself through his addiction to monologue and an urge to dominate. For if, by some vast misfortune, France had at that time fallen under the power of the Communist Party which Aragon served in the role of leading intellectual inquisitor, there would have remained, towering over the dull mass of those elected to carry out literary orthodoxy, only one writer not yet enslaved by his media and who still retained stature; and that one would have been Aragon. . . .

Holy Week . . . is a great poet's novel, and a veritable resurrection of a writer who had, several times in the past, stooped to the worst type of proselytic writing and the most odious sort of polemical journalism.

François Bondy. *NR*. Dec. 25, 1961, p. 17

Louis XVIII is rushing toward the frontier, and Napoleon is returning. That is the subject [of *Holy Week*], and it could have been treated as an historical fresco—either a cloak-and-dagger novel or a satirical tale in which a gouty king, no longer protected by foreign armies, has to flee. The treatment Aragon gave this subject is a mark of his genius.

Dazzling erudition was needed to write *Holy Week*; but that erudition is hidden. What we see are landscapes, cities, roads, a springtime that is born and a winter that lingers, villages suddenly awakened by a "great gust of wind," rain, mud. What we see, above all, is a whole world, from Paris to the frontier, "the world . . . so much richer and more terrible than we thought . . . the world full of turning points and beacons, abysses, life." Indeed, there are two worlds, equally vivid and touching, but for opposite reasons: one world continuing and enduring in spite of everything, the other world striving to come into being; a past which is not caricatured, and a future which is barely perceptible and in which one can scarcely believe. And through all this, mingling with everything, is the "divine and profound music of love." . . .

I used to envy those people who, many years ago, bought a brand-new book by chance one evening; they opened the book when they arrived home, without knowing what they were going to read, vaguely curious—and that book was [Stendhal's] *The Charterhouse of Parma*. I no longer envy them. A few years ago I bought a book, leafed through it here and there, and finally read it, a book which had just been published and which no one had yet said a word about, and it was *Holy Week.*

José Cabanis. *Europe.* Feb.–March, 1967, pp. 160–61 †

[In 1945–46] I saw concentrated in Aragon the whole new force of defiant love and poetic transformation: poetry with the last barrier between it and the world of action broken down: poetry resuming the magical processes, the power over change, the ability to embody all the violences of reality, which Rimbaud had wanted, but overcoming the final check which had made those powers and glories seem to Rimbaud a snare and a delusion. It seemed that he had made possible the achievement of poetry as action. Not as a substitute for action; not as something adulterated and made impure by an effort to subserve the needs of history and thereby taking its directives from the outside. But as a force, which while busy with a world of practical purposes, remained integrally poetry, operating by its own laws, needs, purposes. Here indeed seemed revolutionary poetry which was able to preserve its integrity because in all its involvement with circumstance it was never satisfied by any criterion save that of true human unity, the concrete universal. . . .

The implication with action had its pure moments, especially during the war, but the balance wasn't so simply maintained as it seemed to me in 1945–46. With such an impetuous character the equal union of poetry-action could not but tend to work out as poetry serving action. In so far as a conscious drive took over from the deep impulse of love that had issued in *Heartbreak* and *Elsa's Eyes*, the stress could not but be on the needs of the situation politically considered. And so the pure union of love weakened before the power-drive, the overwhelming demand for success in a good cause which justified the use of poetry as a means. And this element of unbalance linked with the stormy mixture of gay frank friendliness and suspicious angers; the power-drive got into the political tactics of literature and in turn affected the poet, who edited [the newspaper] *Ce soir* for years, as well as carrying on multiple political activities and becoming a member of the Central Committee of the French CP.

I make this analysis with some misgivings, as it concerns a part of Aragon which I never personally encountered; but the point seems necessary to make, if one is to explain the extent to which Aragon became an explicit politician, and the various conflicts (for instance with Sartre) that helped to break down the united front which was Aragon's deepest hope and dream. [1968]

Jack Lindsay. *Meetings with Poets* (New York, Frederick Ungar, 1969), pp. 182–83

On November 6, 1928, Aragon met Elsa Triolet, who was to transform him completely as a man and as a writer.

The lyrical portion of this work ceaselessly revolves around this *extraordinary* event: Aragon's being born to a second life at the age of thirty. From *Heartbreak* (although, indeed, the first poem Elsa appears in was published in 1931 in *Persecuted Persecutor*) to *The Rooms,* Aragon's volumes of poetry form a constellation around the presence of Elsa, a presence that illuminates the poet's actions, thoughts, and words. And—an exceptional feature in the history of poets and their muses—it is not only the woman who inspires Aragon but the woman-novelist as well, each of whose works is a revelation to him. That is why Aragon's fiction and poetry must be read side by side with the works of Elsa Triolet. . . .

It is acknowledged (even in the mass-circulation women's magazines) that Aragon is the *poet of love,* but above all he is the *poet of woman*: the central theme of his poetry and fiction is the definition and celebration of woman's role in the future, renewed society. From the revelation that Elsa's love was for him, he derives an ethic valid for all men: through this trial of purification that is love, pass all great human feelings, and they emerge heightened, purified.

To love mankind, one must have loved a woman and have been freed of one's egotism: therefore, the act of loving becomes the point of departure for all social faith, because only woman can give a meaning to life. To communicate this conviction, tested through the concrete experiences of life, Aragon tirelessly repeats that everything in him "can be summarized by the name of Elsa," who was the inspiration for his political action in the Resistance and the Party, and the inspiration for his works.

Bernard Lecherbonnier. Aragon (Paris, Bordas, 1971), pp. 143, 149†

Anicet [in *Anicet*] had dreamed of systematizing life, the Peasant of Paris [in *The Peasant of Paris*] had dreamed of a new order, the Communist [in *The Communists*] believed that changing the methods of distribution would bring about this new order and that Socialist Realism would both reflect this order and contribute to it. But the promises proved illusory, and [in *The Moment of Truth*] Aragon expresses for the first time a hostile attitude toward Socialist Realism. Socialist Realism puts the cart before the horse, states Aragon, since it places upon the artist the burden of changing the world. In order to make the rules of Socialist Realism worth-while, it is necessary to change not the brain of the novelist, but the world. The writers might in all fairness reproach the politicians for not having produced the positive heroes they need as models for their novels, instead of being reproached by them for not furnishing the people with heroes to emulate. . . .

Aragon's progressive disillusionment with Marxism is again reflected [in *Blanche; or, Forgetfulness*], as he remarks that he was one of those who firmly believed that it was enough to change the economic basis of society to make theft, murder, and unhappy love disappear. This was because the idea we have of things does not necessarily take into account the complexity of life. In *Blanche; or, Forgetfulness*, Aragon writes that he has spent his life trying to imagine the world other than it is, but to no avail. . . .

His novel, writes Aragon, is a meditation on life that is formed at the level of his awareness of the world, at the level of language. It is an enormous semantic unity that makes life possible for him and which he finds indispensable. A novel is language organized by him, an entity that permits him to live. Thus, in *Blanche; or, Forgetfulness*, the cycle started in 1919 is completed. To palliate the despair occasioned by the horrors of war and the bankruptcy of modern civilization, the Surrealist Aragon had proposed the magic of words and love. When, almost fifty years later, he cries out—"How can we bear the world as it is?"—the answer is still supplied by literary creativity and love.

Lucille F. Becker. *Louis Aragon* (New York, Twayne, 1971), pp. 107, 110–11

ARLAND, MARCEL (1899–   )

Where the Heart Is Divided is the best book Marcel Arland has published to date. Its artistic merits are no greater than those of *The Souls in Purgatory*, for example; but in this work nothing comes between the author and the central issue of all his books—the meaning of destiny. It can be said that Arland has not written a line that does not form part of an answer to one of the following two questions: "What is life?" and "How can I, how should I, direct my life?" Such questions, when they penetrate, can lead the mind either to a metaphysical attitude or to a religious attitude. Arland is permeated with but not convinced by Christianity. He accepts the negations of Christianity without difficulty; but he does not accept its affirmations. This position explains the tone and the thought of the three meditations [that comprise *Where the Heart Is Divided*]—meditations quite naturally dominated by the idea of death. . . .

Suburban landscapes, office-workers or laborers in the trains, a woman, the author, figures and designs without any *particular* importance—all are linked to one another like the sections of a symphony. They blend in perfect harmony: the grave, humane, sometimes poignant tone of meditation does not diminish, and each of the three sections of the book exerts its own power. Arland's intentions in *The Souls in Purgatory* were not unrelated to those of *Where the Heart Is Divided,* but short stories do not lend themselves as readily as essays to an undertaking of this sort, and the individual lives of the characters necessarily limited the intellectual argument. In *Where the Heart Is Divided,* however, since no pursuit of fictional technique intervenes, Arland achieves great purity.

André Malraux. NRF. Feb., 1928, pp. 250–51†

Antares comes as a moment of happy abandon in the work of Marcel Arland—less because of the style, which reaches a remarkable precision and serves Arland's purposes marvelously, than because of a pervasive grace that enlivens this novel. For once the author of *Order* reflects on the people he has known without bitterness and without anguish. This serenity contributes a great deal, in my opinion, to the charm of *Antares.*

Two women, a nun, and a few children; a cemetery with its white tombstones and pearls scattered by time at the feet of its crosses; and a house in the distance, outside the town—these elements have enabled Marcel Arland to create the clearest, lightest atmosphere imaginable. Every line in this novel bears the halo of airy poetry. The whole work is somewhat reminiscent—*mutatis mutandis*—of the best passages in [Alain-Fournier's] *Big Meaulnes,* the celebration at the chateau, for example. But in *Antares* the enchantment is closer to nature; the trees and the sky play a role at least as important as that of the real people— to the extent that they are real, that we ourselves are real. This world is shown to us through the eyes of a child, who contributes quite a bit to pushing back the narrow frontier separating dreams from reality. . . .

Antares is a novel of peace and silence, but a silence filled with more life, more light, thoughts, and overtones of all sorts, than many tumultuous works.

Marc Bernard. Europe. Dec. 15, 1932, p. 620†

When I read a story by Marcel Arland, I always feel that I am being initiated into a better life. I feel the gust of pure air, receive a lesson in harmony, and think of the coming of the elect.

And yet, Arland is not a simplistic novelist who believes only in goodness and seeks only to edify the reader. In *The Most Beautiful of Our Days,* the characters are humble people, dressed in heavy wool, who speak a rough language and struggle with the difficulties of life. They partake of the earth with all their senses. Their idyll is accompanied by fear, torment, and gradual deterioration. Their "most beautiful days" are often devoid of tranquillity.

But as realistic as his approach and details may be, Arland is above all the companion of men's souls. He seeks that fineness and density which is revealed in all people at certain moments; these are the times when Arland's vision is aroused, when his pen traces someone's life story.

Since he is a great artist and is uncompromising in his integrity, he does not attempt to prove anything; he does not preach. Man as he is seems to be reason enough for Arland to be a humanitarian. In this respect, Arland is almost the only writer among us who has not compromised, the only one who has not made part of his vocabulary the various "isms" that political parties have thrust on us.

It pleases me that we are offered such an example by someone who is neither a loafer nor an aesthete nor a calculating and ambitious man, but one who knows, through experience, that culture nourishes people, that work elevates them, that art is a source of joy.

> Jacques de Lacretelle. *L'heure qui change* (Geneva,
> Éditions du Milieu du Monde, 1941), pp. 89–90†

From his first efforts, the author of *The Souls in Purgatory* showed that he was one of the greatest storytellers of his generation. . . . Only Jules Supervielle and Marcel Aymé can be compared to him in this talent. . . .

Perhaps the writer whom this exemplary Frenchman most resembles is Maksim Gorki, because of the straightforwardness of his method and because of the power of the revelation to which his method leads. The revelation is accompanied by no commentary because it has no consequences. In Arland's search for sensitive areas—suddenly a character cries out in pain; this cry throws our notions of existence and destiny into confusion; and then the crisis is over—the reader does not find the convulsive sobs or the wringing of hands that conclude the contemplations of the great Russian writers. Arland's work is not governed by a religion of suffering. With a writer like Arland, Sonia would not grovel before Raskolnikov; such a gesture would seem medieval to Arland. The horror of man's fate on earth, but brightened by a Western smile, which brings decency to despair and moderation to madness— such is the substance of these tales suffused with a wonderful and patient gentleness. Man is stripped bare in them, but he is not skinned alive.

> Robert Poulet. *La lanterne magique* (Paris,
> Nouvelles Éditions Debresse, 1956), pp. 95–96†

In articles in the *NRF* and later in books of criticism, Arland, whether evaluating his contemporaries or writers of the past, has long been dedicated to knowledge and understanding. . . . In his finest book of criticism, *The Gift of Writing*, Arland defined his constant preoccupation: "I asked each of the writers I approached: How did you accept the gift of writing that was given to you? What is the authenticity of your works? What is there about them that is living and lasting?"

The advantage of such an inquiry can be seen: Constant, Diderot, and Marivaux take on a new existence. When requested to answer basic questions, these writers come down from the library shelves where they have been too long put away by the critics. They breathe in front of us, with their imperfections, their hesitations, and, suddenly, those flashes of genius which justify our admiration. This is Arland's fundamental method—to force the artist to answer specific questions: How have you modified the image of man as it was conceived in your era? For what purpose did you create that imaginary world which overshadows any man's actual biography? . . .

As for contemporary writers, including beginners, Arland untiringly asks them the same questions: What do you want to express? Does what you write measure up to your dreams? In what way do you think your writings modify the image of man you have inherited? How do you live in your creation, and how does your creation live in you?

People talk about Arland's "strictness." They forget that before being strict with other writers, Arland is first strict with himself; they forget that his strictness represents the acuteness of his interest in literature. Few writers have helped as many beginners as Arland. This is well known but not talked about much. To understand Arland's contribution, one has to see him at work in the editor's office of the *NRF*, to which he sacrifices his time, and at which he performs a sacred function.

Jean Duvignaud. Arland (Paris, Éditions Gallimard,
1962), pp. 65–66†

[In *The Great Pardon* Arland] has drawn upon the experiences of a lifetime to conjure up a long procession of characters reflecting many aspects of love. Love indeed, or its absence, is the prime mover of their lives. They belong to all classes of society: aristocracy, bourgeoisie, peasants and humble workers, et al. Several are lawyers, medical doctors, teachers, and businessmen. Their adventures in love take place in various provinces: Île de France, Brittany, Provence, Auvergne, Normandy, and Alsace in particular, and in Paris, of course.

The author is able to evoke the atmosphere of a given region: local people, landscapes, churches, monuments, religious life, superstitions, folklore. His language is most apt in describing the beauties of nature, and the emotions of the heart and the senses. He emphasizes too much, it seems to me, the Freudian aspects of love and erotic obsessions. . . .

We suspect that Arland has wished to rid himself in one volume of all the memories he has gathered through a long life of introspection and keen observation. He displays genuine ability to tolerate faults in others and a desire to understand, if not condone, the most objectionable deeds of characters whom he hopes to see again (at least, so he implies) in another world. Altogether, *The Great Pardon* has much to attract, and to irritate, several classes of devotees of contemporary French literature. His style and language are varied, rich in descriptive power, and above all correct, a rare quality in our days of facile and careless writing.

Pierre Courtines. *BA*. Summer, 1966, p. 294

Arland, currently editor of *La nouvelle revue française*, showed in his first stories . . . his affiliation with the American story and short novel of the later nineteenth century. The guiding theme of his entire production up to this time, consisting in large part of novellae, stories, and essays, is the human endeavor to work out a *modus vivendi* both with the ego and with the world outside. It seems a simple matter, but in Arland's narratives it proves to be an infinitely difficult assignment. . . . The most mature work of this author is doubtless the novel *Order* which was distinguished with the Prix Goncourt. Here Arland combines the continuity of a novel of development with the portrayal of character of a Radiguet, whose *The Devil in the Flesh* had appeared six years previously, or of a Stendhal. . . .

Order is the novel of the development of an individual intent upon using his arrogant Stendhalesque drives to secure for himself a place outside of tradition, mores, and decency. Fate destroys Gilbert's amoral escapades. The proximity of *The Red and the Black* is striking, but Arland does not regard his hero, as did Stendhal, with pride and love. . . . In this novel of development, which is simultaneously a novel of fate, we have—to boot—a novel of bourgeois morality. Gilbert Villars violates the rules, he becomes a foreign body in the bourgeois organism and is rejected. Hardly another author of the twentieth century has understood Stendhal and has simultaneously overcome Stendhal as did Arland. That establishes the significance of *Order*.

Winfried Engler. *The French Novel from Eighteen Hundred to the Present* (New York, Frederick Ungar, 1969), pp. 130–31

ARRABAL, FERNANDO (1932–   )

Arrabal, this young man of Spanish origin writing in French, brings to the theater an original voice, which can lead to the creation of valuable plays. He works through the perspective opened up by Beckett, which can be defined, essentially, as a thorough application of a formula such as "the theater means something other than what is revealed." Arrabal's plays often make worthwhile reading because of their direct poetry, their pretended naïveté that reveals terrifying depths, the well-handled and provocative situations, whose apparent absurdity is set off by savage humor. . . .

[The director, Jean-Marie] Serreau seems to have striven for a variety of effects in his production [of *Picnic on the Battlefield*], possibly to avoid calling attention to a structure that, in Arrabal's plays, is still a little fragile, despite his formidable talents. The play begins with a penetrating dramatic vision, which . . . is paradoxical and challenging. But this brilliant situation is hardly developed at all. Arrabal no doubt feels that action, in the traditional sense, is perhaps dead. In the plays of today's major dramatists, however, it is replaced by a heightening of tension, a movement through various points of view that are inevitably interwoven, thus necessitating a highly complex organization. I hope that, without losing his integrity, Arrabal will apply his very considerable talent to tackling these more difficult problems. I do think that, starting today, he has to be recognized as one of the hopes of the French theater, which does not have all that many.

Jacques Scherer. LetN. May 13, 1959, pp. 41–42†

Arrabal's works are not merely a reflection of influences or a reminder of illustrious predecessors. First of all, most of his gentle heroes are murderers or accomplices in murder and physical torture. In *The Tricycle*, Climando and his friend, the lethargic Apal, assassinate "the man with the banknotes." In *The Labyrinth*, Étienne leaves his fellow prisoner to die of thirst. In *The Condemned Man's Bicycle*, Viloro asks Tasla to throw him a kiss every time Paso, whom she pulls over in his cage to be tortured, is whipped. Fidio and Lilbé have killed a child in *Orison*. Fando kills Lis in *Fando and Lis*. Emanou, in *The Automobile Graveyard*, says he has killed people. "Not many," and only to do them a favor when he sees they're in bad trouble; but then he is an image of Christ. . . .

The characters are all adolescents or adults: they prove it by their sexual capacities. But they have the mentality of children. When they try to make conversation and proudly show off their intelligence, they talk in platitudes or meaningless phrases, either going into raptures over what the other says or rejecting it with the innocent bad faith of a child who makes no distinction between reality and play. They live in a world in which urinating is extraordinarily interesting—at any rate, of prime importance, as well as the places and privileged objects such an obsession implies. Basically, they are exhibitionists or voyeurs, often both; at the same time, they can be unexpectedly prudish. Although murderers who, once they commit a crime, lose all interest in it, or who from the depths of their innocence judge that it is good, they can show great consideration and spontaneous tenderness for others, and forget it just as quickly. . . .

The ambiguity of the metaphor of childhood sometimes comes off rather well. The "automobile graveyard," in the play of that name, successfully and synthetically represents both the junkyards in which children play and the projection of such games in the universe of adult sexuality. In other plays, anger—childish to begin with—smoothly leads to its necessary conclusion: the adult gesture of murder. Because of the characters' childish oscillation, innocence and goodness are like the dead evoked by Ulysses: we see them clearly, but when we want to grasp them they disappear. A lost paradise? Rather, a missing paradise.

Jacques Guicharnaud. YFS. Spring–Summer, 1962,
pp. 116–18

Once again I unfortunately am forced to display my reserve when faced with one of the avant-garde writers who pretend to be filling the void left by those playwrights who either have died or have, it seems, nothing left to say. . . . What struck me perhaps most of all [about *The Automobile Graveyard*] is the manifest disparity between the writer's ambitiousness and the elaborate stage machinery put at his disposal, on the one hand, and the extraordinary meagerness of the text, on the other hand.

When I speak of the text, moreover, I am referring only to the times when it could be heard. There were many moments when the uproar and howling were such that it was impossible to grasp a word. I said the uproar, but a much stronger term should be found to describe the paroxysm of noise inflicted upon us: several times, the viewer might have thought he was in a forge or a repair shop. . . .

The Théâtre des Arts was completely transformed so that it could house the shells of automobiles, some of which are hung from the ceiling and then lowered, for no particular reason, and disassembled. The job of the stage crew in *The Automobile Graveyard* is undoubtedly more demanding and more exhausting than that of the actors, although the actors do have to perform frantic gymnastics, taking turns throwing each other on the floor; this to the amused fright of the public, which finds itself pushed back by a stage that is oversized and menacing. I was subjected to having one of the actors land in my lap.

But in the end, why all this? What does this automobile graveyard mean? It is a symbol, of course, of a decaying world; but, with all the good will in the world, I cannot figure out how the play translates that symbol in an adequate way, this death agony of civilization to which I am, I might add, as sensitive as Arrabal can be.

Gabriel Marcel. NL. Dec. 28, 1967, p. 13†

[*The Architect and the Emperor of Assyria*] is the story of an impossible friendship. Like the characters of Beckett, Arrabal's try to trick themselves out of their terrible solitude, and through silences or threats of departure, they torture each other without being able to tear themselves away from one another. The vague impulses toward revolt against his monarch shown by the architect stretch out the action or interrupt it. But like [Beckett's] Estragon or Clov, he never goes so far as to leave his companion in suffering. . . .

In its virtuosity *The Architect and the Emperor of Assyria* is the freest demonstration of Arrabal's concept of Theater of Panic. Didacticism make *The Coronation* dull. In that play the games never reach the level of fantasy, the joy of creation, which carries away the characters in *The Architect and the Emperor of Assyria*. Giafar is merely an allegorical figure, an idealized image of Arrabal. In the character of the emperor, carnal and impure life asserts itself in the theater, which, as Peter Brook said, must accept showing "excrement and heaven." Anything pornographic or scatological in the play derives not from a desire to be provocative but rather from a fidelity to the sublime and grotesque web of dreams that is man. *The Architect and the Emperor of Assyria* expresses an affection which will not let itself be fooled and which would be destroyed by crudeness or excessive humor.

How can one explain the appearance of this thundering and painful celebration? The year 1966 marked the triumph of the "grotesque" at the Théâtre des Nations. [Jerzy] Grotowski's group and the Living Theater both threw into confusion all traditional notions of the role of the actor. The actors for *The Architect and the Emperor of Assyria* need to have had a training without any "specialization," a background enabling them to cope with all the techniques of physical and oral expression. There is no doubt that Arrabal found new freedom after seeing the plays performed by the American and Polish ensembles.

Bernard Gille. Fernando Arrabal (Paris, Seghers,
1970), pp. 91, 97–98†

Four years ago Fernando Arrabal, who has lived in France since 1955, revisited his native Spain, was arrested and charged with blasphemy and calumny, and spent 24 days in jail. During his imprisonment he observed political prisoners "guilty" of crimes of opinion. From this experience he wrote *And They Put Handcuffs on the Flowers*, a harrowing and disturbing work of art. . . .

Steel bars clang. An ear-punishing horn bleats. The theater is a prison. Three men are confined inside a cell. One has been made mute by his imprisonment. He paces the cell, squaring the corners, his hand tremblingly fixed to his mouth as if in search of a voice. The others are on the edge of madness.

The three remember and fantasize. They leave their cell to become other characters or themselves in fantasy. There are occasional "love dreams" and flashes of bitter humor, but mostly the prisoners enact nightmares of psychological bestiality, physical torture and sexual abuse. Before long we have not only an excruciating picture of the prisoners but also a history of this prison's depravity; and an indictment of a dictatorial nation.

The play's structure is loose and episodic, and the narrative is further interrupted by ritualistic announcements blandly recited by an actor dressed as a girl. Harsh prison noises collide with church music. . . .

The title of the play, according to Arrabal, was a statement made by García Lorca in despair just before he was murdered. The most haunting image in the play is not the handcuffed flowers, but the condemned man whose face is masked with a dog muzzle, forcing his mouth to remain open, while prohibiting even a cry of pain or protest at execution.

In the past, Arrabal's plays have seemed dryly intellectual and self-consciously poetic, but this time he has forsaken mannerisms. The evening is discomforting, almost unbearable. Some people will be offended, even disgusted. But it is powerful—the playwright's own unmuzzled cry in favor of freedom.

Mel Gussow. NYTd. Oct. 19, 1971, p. 53

Having seen and disliked Alexandro Jodorowsky's screen adaptation of an early Arrabal play, *Fando and Lis*, and having duly noted the symbols of horror, the rituals of disgust, the obligatory and unfelt eroticism, and the pervasive allegory, I was in no way prepared for Fernando Arrabal's own first film, *Long Live Death*, in which those elements reappear—but charged now with an intensity and a complex vitality that I have not seen equalled in recent cinema, especially not in any recent cinema of the absurd. . . . Though no perfect movie, it seems to me inescapably a major work.

Its hero . . . a young boy, is also named Fando, and its story closely parallels the early life history of Fernando Arrabal, whose mother betrayed her leftist husband to the Fascists during the Spanish civil war— and who taught her son that his father was dead, whereas in fact he was miserably imprisoned. Fando searches for his father and never finds him, as Arrabal never found his, but he remembers him and imagines his fate—and in a series of harsh monochrome fantasy passages, memory and imagination largely define the unique life of the film. . . .

The enemy in *Long Live Death* seems not so much the Fascist state or its police, as the women who fear it and collaborate with it: the mother, an aunt, a grandmother, all in black, like ministers of death, and yet in mourning for the suffering caused by their own ministry. The mourning is genuine, as is the cruelty—and it is Arrabal's great distinction not to undercut the one by the other, but rather to hold each in balance so that no contradictory impulse is lost on us. . . .

Near the end of *Long Live Death* it is discovered that Fando has tuberculosis (as Arrabal had), and he is taken to a hospital ship and eventually operated on. From his recovery room he is abducted by a mysterious little girl, also in black, who keeps a pet turkey and whom he has known and casually tormented all through the film. A captive now of his own sweet bitter fate he is wheeled off into a part of the gorgeous arid landscape that is the film's locale. And boy, and girl, and great improbable bird enter a configuration that outlasts the generations and is not explained but is somehow understood as an emblem of unending torture and delight.

Roger Greenspun. *NYTd*. Oct. 26, 1971, p. 50

ARTAUD, ANTONIN (1896–1948)

The story of the Cenci family [which Artaud used for his *The Cenci*] is indeed one of the eternal—not to say immutable—dreams, like that of Oedipus and that of Lear. Shelley says of the Cenci in the preface to his version that they existed in tradition before they appeared in any tragedy on the stage. The daughter who is raped by her father, who kills him, and who does not feel guilty, but whom society puts to death—this story has resonances in all of us. A crime committed last year showed with what ferocity these things take place; so do not say that you know nothing about such subjects. There are two or three moments in Artaud's play when we recognize a frightening or painful or sensitive face that is our own, a face that has elicited internal moans from us on a thousand occasions when we contemplated it. . . . This theater is not calculated to please: Artaud constantly plays against the audience and wins. The spectator is constantly troubled and sometimes wounded by the sharpest kind of tension. . . .

Artaud's Cenci is a "guilty madman," less erotic than destructive and demonic, too self-aware and not enough of a "bestial sumptuary" to be a true creature of the Renaissance. But this mad blasphemer of God, an atheist in the manner of Sade, whose pride in doing evil and whose spirit of revenge undeniably result from paranoia, still displays enough genuine pain and defiance to move us during his torture. It is only regrettable that the man is so exactly defined from a psychiatric point of view that the power of "destiny" is thereby diminished. The tragic element, as soon as it surfaces, is pushed back upon itself and weakened.

Pierre Jean Jouve. *NRF.* June, 1935, pp. 912–13†

Antonin Artaud's work is only beginning to be known. It took the scandal of his internment in a mental institution and his recent release to draw attention to the man who is, for some, the greatest living poet and, for some others, the *only* living poet. Why the only poet? Because he is the only one who wants his work to disturb men and be "like an open door leading them where they would never have agreed to go, a door that simply opens onto reality."

"What is the importance of a book that cannot at least once transport us beyond all other books?" Nietzsche wrote earlier. The greatest poets have in common the fact that they strive all their lives to exceed what is in their grasp. Artaud went so far on this path that he wound up totally alone. . . .

Despite all the very real persecutions Artaud had to suffer from both men and nameless forces that pursued him and tracked him down, his work has not stopped growing. Artaud's latest books do not perhaps offer the implacable architecture of those that first brought him to attention. But if the art, in the usual sense, is diminished, Artaud has diminished it to make room for a rarer light. . . .

What is also striking in Artaud's latest works is the total reinvention of form, the verbal discovery, a sort of phonetic miracle that is constantly renewed. Sentences not only grate inhumanly, break and come apart; they also rise to incantation and return to poetry through a new path—the path of a rediscovered assonance that makes one forget about rhyme.

In a man who has never separated thought from art and life, one could have expected an evolution of ideas incarnated in language in an immediate and corporeal manner. For Artaud now, everything is suspect except the body, the only value that is not deceptive.

Arthur Adamov. *Paru.* April, 1947, pp. 7, 10–12†

His mouth, like the whole of Artaud, preyed upon itself. His spine was bent like a bow. His lean arms with their long hands, like two twisted forked trunks, seemed to be trying to plough up his belly.

His voice, rising up from his innermost caverns, bounded towards his head with such rare force that it was dashed against the sounding board of his forehead. It was both sonorous and hollow, strong yet immediately muted. He was essentially an aristocrat. Artaud was a prince. . . .

He was an engrossing man. Obviously I devoured "The Theater and the Plague" and "The Theater of Cruelty" together with the other articles that the N.R.F. had just assembled and published under the title of *The Theater and Its Double. The Theater and Its Double* is far and away the most important thing that has been written about the theatre in the twentieth century. . . .

Artaud was a poet first and foremost. He was a wonderful writer, as everyone knows; but he was also an actor. And it was in the character of a poet that he always played. [1949]

Jean-Louis Barrault. *Reflections on the Theatre* (London, Rockliff, 1951), pp. 49–50

I like those articles [in the journal *La révolution surréaliste*, edited by Artaud in 1925], especially those in which Artaud's presence is most strongly felt. Once again I appreciate, in terms of his destiny, the great role played by suffering in motivating his almost total negation—which was also our negation, but he was the most suitable and the most ardent person to formulate it.

Nevertheless, although I entirely shared the spirit that gave rise to these articles—they were, moreover, the fruit of long discussions among several of us—and although I had few reservations to make about their content, it did not take me very long to become worried about the atmosphere that they created. Because of the very fact that these articles appeared one after another in so short a time, and because this highly polemical activity necessarily tended to assume more importance than all our other activities, I had the impression that, without really knowing it, we had caught a fever and the air around us had become too thin. I can better understand the reasons for my resistance to him, which was then still obscure to me, when I consider it more closely today. Artaud's path, partly liberating and partly mystical, was not entirely my own, and I came to consider it more an impasse than a path (and I was not the only one who did). Artaud led me into a region that has always seemed to me an abstract place, a hall of mirrors. I always find something "verbal" there, even if the words in question are very noble and beautiful. It is a place of gaps and ellipses where I feel I lose communication with the innumerable things that, in spite of everything, please me and keep me on this earth. It is too frequently forgotten that surrealism had a great deal of *love* in it, and it furiously condemned precisely those things that can harm love.

Finally, I distrusted a certain paroxysm toward which Artaud was unquestionably heading—and toward which Desnos must have been heading on a different level—and it seemed to me that we were expending energy for which we would never be able to compensate in the future. To put it another way, I could easily see that the machine was running at full speed, but I could no longer see how it was going to continue to find fuel.

André Breton. *Entretiens* [*avec André Parinaud*]
(Paris, Gallimard, 1952), pp. 109–10†

Artaud's defect was not simply that he was neither a poet nor a dramatist, but that he was neither a god nor a demon: he was a simple actor and director, or rather stage manager. His magic and alchemical theater can be reduced to stage management, a few lighting tricks, and a few props. He was a stage manager without a theater and a director without a text, possibly because the author Artaud had dreamed of did not exist at the time. Artaud would have so magnificently directed such an author's plays that every boulevard theater and every realist-socialist-Brechtian theater would have been forever compromised, devalued, and negated.

Since theatrical mediocrity continues to reign—bourgeois or anti-bourgeois, supposedly realist but, basically, insufficiently real—the reason is partly that Artaud was not a great poet of the theater. He certainly did have an excessive messianic ambition (we can have an inkling only of the paths, not of the solutions he would have proposed), incompatible with his intellectual power. Before anyone can go beyond culture, one must first have assimilated culture. Alas, his theories of cruelty, his knowledge of the ritual theater of the Far East, his knowledge of Tibetan and Hindu metaphysics, in which he thought he could find salvation for the West—all of this really seems to have been amassed by chance. There was, nevertheless, something profoundly worthy in Artaud—his devouring flame, so authentic that it did in fact devour him. . . .

Artaud also exemplified the fact that all the precise solutions in the world are not as valuable as ardor, life, and the desperate struggle of the spirit itself. As for "solutions," they lead to systems—the same crushing systems that Artaud rejected.

Eugène Ionesco. CRB. May, 1958, pp. 133–34†

Artaud's little book on the theatre [The Theater and Its Double] is by a man in love and banking everything on his love. He wills this love to give a meaning to life and he wills by this love to counterattack in the society where he is desperate. What he says is often wrong-headed and he often contradicts himself, but he also sees and says important truths with bright simplicity. . . .

It is in the context of theatre as effectual action that Artaud comes to his celebrated assault on literary plays, his refusal to use text to direct from. . . . There is an aspect of the action of speech that he quite neglects and that makes his attack far too sweeping. Words have interpersonal effect, they get under the skin, and not only by their tone but especially by their syntax and style: the mood, voice and person of sentences, the coordination and subordination of clauses. The personalities of men are largely their speech habits, and in the drama of personalities the thing-language that Artaud is after is not sufficient; we need text, but a text not of ideas and thoughts, but of syntactical relations. Artaud polemically condemns Racine as literary, but he surely knew that Racine's theatre did not depend on the content of those speeches, but on the clash of personalities in them, and especially on the coup de théâtre of the sudden entrances and the carefully prepared big scenes. Coup de théâtre is theatre as action. If the old slow preparation makes us impatient, the fault may be ours.

Artaud neglects these obvious things because he has, I am afraid, one basically wrong idea: he says that the art of theatre aims at utilizing a space and the things in the space; and therefore he makes quite absolute claims for the staging. But this is too general; for the theatre-relation is what someone looks at and is affected by, not a space with things and sounds, but persons behaving in their places. Theatre is actors acting on us. So the chief thing is neither interpreting the text nor the staging, but the blocking-and-timing (conceived as one space-time solid): it is the directedness of the points of view, the confrontation of personalities, the on-going process of the plot.

Paul Goodman. Nation. Nov. 29, 1958, pp. 412–14

Artaud was associated with both the Dadaists and the Surrealists early in his career, and he shares their loathing of traditional art, of modern industrial life, and of Western civilization. But he turns these negative attitudes into positive acts, transforming the nihilism, sterility, and buffoonery of his predecessors into profoundly revolutionary theory.

Artaud's revolt is so radical, and so deadly serious, that it leads him into messianic conclusions. A Romantic who tolerates no boundaries, a prophet of rebellion who preaches "extreme action, pushed beyond all limits," Artaud demands nothing less than a total transformation of the existing structure. And this revolution will begin in the theatre.

For the theatre, to Artaud, is not simply a place where audiences are entertained, instructed, or irritated; it is the very pulse of civilization itself. And one sign that Western civilization is decaying is that its theatre has enshrined such "lazy, unserviceable notions" as "art." In place of these notions, Artaud wants to substitute what he calls *culture*. Western art is essentially divorced from the people and disperses them, but culture brings men together. Art is an excrescence; culture is functional. Art is the expression of one man; culture is the expression of all. For this reason, Artaud is drawn to primitive countries like Mexico, where "things are made for use. And the world is in perpetual exaltation." . . .

Artaud's idea of culture is based on primitive ritual which he hopes to reintroduce into civilized life. Like all messianic thinkers, he is trying to bring about change through a revolution in the religious consciousness. The religions of the West, however, are unacceptable, since they have emptied life of its magical content, and killed the instinctual side of man—killed, that is to say, his divinity. . . . Like the Surrealists, then, Artaud would like to build a theatre of myths. . . . These myths, however, will come neither from the Greco-Roman nor from the Christian tradition, for the traditional myths, though once vital, have now become exhausted and tame, like the civilizations from which they sprang. . . .

The primary function of Artaud's theatre, then, is the exorcism of fantasies. Similar to the Great Mysteries—the Orphic and Eleusinian rites—it is based on sacrifice and revolves around crime; but in exteriorizing the spectator's desire for crime, it acts as a catharsis, and drains the violence.

Robert Brustein. *The Theatre of Revolt* (Boston, Little, Brown, 1964), pp. 366–68, 370

[When I met him in 1946] Artaud had achieved something very rare: he had succeeded in giving a meaning to *his* life and, by the same token, to *life*. One could not remain insensitive to this. Everything he said seemed, at the moment he said it, so evident and so true. He was this truth to such a degree that one accepted him, totally. . . .

I had just arrived at Ivry late in the morning, when a journalist from I don't remember which newspaper came to ask Artaud the following question: "What is your definition of black humor?" Artaud asked him to sit down but did not answer. He spoke rather lengthily with me, took out a notebook, wrote a few pages, and the journalist waited. Artaud's meal was brought in to him, he ate it, remained silent for a long while, and the journalist was still waiting. Then he took his enormous penknife, and, after finding the right place under his hair, he held the point against it (this was his usual custom because he said it relieved him of certain pains). Suddenly, and with a rapid gesture, he stuck the knife straight into the table which was near him. "You asked me, Sir, for my definition of black humor. Well, here it is, black humor is this!" And the journalist left.

Paule Thévenin. TDR. Spring, 1965, pp. 103–5

Artaud felt that writing and achieving recognition as a writer were the sole means he had of struggling against the menace of "the collapse of the soul at its centre." He struggled against it by expressing it totally, letting it do all the havoc it could, and making it the distinctive feature of his personality. One is led to say that in contemporary society the only way of asserting one's full individuality without restriction is to achieve success as an artist. Since Artaud could not make his mark in the republic of letters as a master of form, he was driven to push to the limit what [Jacques] Rivière [editor of *La nouvelle revue française*] termed the "animal operation of the mind," venturing in all possible directions until he reached the very boundaries of the meaningless. Given his condition, the fatal result was that the disease corroding his mind was purposely aggravated. By putting his illness at the service of his pen he was forced to enter a closed circuit where mental turmoil produced verbal turmoil which, in turn, augmented mental turmoil every time the current was turned on.

In short, by falling under the spell of literature, by becoming involved in the question of literary form (and its negation, a no less literary problem) Artaud betrayed himself and the truth he carried within him. Artaud's human situation was an absolute one. It defied expression, and the only solution it permitted was, perhaps, a religious one, a passage to another order of reality. It was this that he frenziedly searched for all his life through writing. But obviously writing could not lead him there.

Nicola Chiaromonte. Enc. August, 1967, p. 45

If one can isolate any single incident as most important in the formation of Artaud's dramatic ideas, it is without doubt the Balinese dance performance at the Colonial Exposition in Paris in 1931. . . . The oriental theater not only imparted a certain spirit to the dramatic concepts of Artaud, but actually provided him with certain definite models for the structure of plays as well as the structure of the theater itself. . . .

Artaud's attraction to the oriental theater is usually dated from his attendance at the Cambodian dances in front of the reconstruction of the temple of Angkor in Marseilles in 1922, the attraction then being precipitated into concepts following the 1931 Balinese experience. However, it would appear that Artaud had already brought to [Charles] Dullin's Théâtre de l'Atelier in late 1921 the germ of a style and concepts which were akin to the oriental, and Dullin's own great interest in the oriental theater no doubt underscored Artaud's enthusiasm and prepared him for the 1922 Cambodian experience. . . .

It should be pointed out that Artaud never sought to bring the oriental mystique intact onto the western stage. He realized that if the occidental theater was to be renewed, it had rather to find again its own archetypes upon which it might construct a primal dramatic language. It was necessary to dig deep into one's own tradition, not cut across the surface to purloin the tradition of another culture.

Eric Sellin. *The Dramatic Concepts of Antonin Artaud* (Chicago, University of Chicago Press, 1968), pp. 49–53

Today the enterprises stemming from Artaud and inspired by his writing are, it is true, unfaithful to his idea of the theater. The unrestrained absolutism of the prophet of Cruelty could not fail to attract men who were in love with theatrical revolution; their productions, once they were performed, could not fail to appear as caricatures and mockeries of Artaud's aims. This is true if only because Artaud's vision of the theater is closely linked to a vision of the world, while the directors who claim to "do Artaud" today are artificially separating his theatrical "message" —and that word is inaccurate—from his complete contribution. But with that in mind, we still have no reason for stating categorically that there is no hope of ever achieving Artaud's conception of the theater. . . .

[The director] Victor Garcia stated in 1968 that it is not enough simply to read Artaud; instead, Artaud must be lived. This is a perfectly intelligent attitude. The two methods undoubtedly give life to each other —and the firm refusal to sanctify Artaud's writings can only be approved. The danger was precisely that his major texts would be made into a sort of bible of theatrical modernism, would be referred to as if they were laws carved on tablets, both too sacred to be deformed and impracticable in their purity. It is fortunate that, on the contrary, directors have not been afraid to take liberties with Artaud's words. This is a legitimate form of treason: not because Artaud's words are inapplicable and unrealizable in concrete form but because his principal strength is that he constitutes an inexhaustible seed, whose varied fruits we are seeing today. . . .

Even though the theater is one of the keystones of Artaud's thought, we should never lose sight of the fact that his theatrical aims can only be understood and implemented in the context of a complete reconstruction of man and the world. The quest being pursued is an ontological one. The only people who have the right to betray Artaud are those who never neglect the "totalitarian" dimension of his thoughts about the theater.

Alain Virmaux. MagL. Feb., 1972, pp. 16–17†

AUDIBERTI, JACQUES (1899–1965)

Audiberti . . . has an immense and splendid vocabulary in his grasp; the thousand million images God has thrown into our air have all fallen into Audiberti's hat. His writing is an awesome carnival at which the confetti threatens to bury the universe. Yet, this gift does not stop Audiberti from being down-to-earth, and he never loses his understanding of the world, because he possesses courage, love, and pity. His is a bantering pity, as delicate as that of the elephant who feels the blade of grass under his feet as if it were a needle in his heart, a pity that knows the thousands of nuances of the most subtle kinds of ferocity. . . .

With each succeeding book, Audiberti's style has become more expansive, simpler, and firmer. . . . Now he amplifies his gestures, finds the right rhythm, and strikes with longer and surer thrusts. . . .

Céline does not mind exhausting himself, twisting himself, and expressing himself down to the last drop. Giono also lets himself go completely. . . . Certainly, they are all flirting with very serious dangers. Giono sometimes falls into preaching, often for pages and pages. Audiberti can be macaronic as a result of first taking a portrait, a country scene, a totally wild idea and then fiddling with possible and impossible suggestions and then rearranging it again into the hundred thousand images that make it disordered; as a result of extending his subject in every direction, Audiberti ends up by pumping all meaning from it.

If you like, Audiberti, Céline, and Giono are long-haired poets growing a bit bald. But they can permit themselves these follies, because they have the irreplaceable and indestructible wisdom of sure talent.

Pierre Drieu la Rochelle. NRF. Sept., 1942,
pp. 360–62†

Everyone and everything betrays the Princess [in Evil Is in the Air], and she discovers to her horror that the world has fallen prey to evil.

She thus stops resisting; she yields to evil with the same strength she used to sustain innocence. But she does not really act out of despair; her motive is a desire to consummate evil, or rather a frantic attempt to consume it and thereby hasten its disappearance from the world. Alas! Evil is infinite, like goodness, and the Princess's plan is certainly bad; but at least her anger is not feeble, nor is her plan, and the viewer cannot help liking her, while condemning her at the same time.

The boundlessness of evil is, I believe, the theme of *Evil Is in the Air*, a play that sometimes reminded me of Albert Camus's *Caligula*, although it has a completely different tone. Princess Alarica may be quite well described as a female Caligula. But to speak of the theme is to limit quite wrongly a work whose value lies in the variety, freedom, and freshness of its lyricism. Audiberti's strong temperament combined with verbal richness and agility make the best parts of this play a true delight. All these qualities are healthy, fleshy, based on the most natural and valid assumptions. When she speaks of physical love, for example, Alarica has a few epithets that hit the mark. And when her shame and grief burst out, what a torrent, what a blast, what images! [June, 1947]

> Francis Ambrière. *La galerie dramatique* (Paris,
> Éditions Corrêa, 1949), pp. 202–3†

It is an easy matter to damn the author of *Race of Men* as so in love with words that coherence and meaning are lost. In a later poem, "Monument with Words," and in a long essay of 1942, *The New Origin*, [Audiberti] confesses his infatuation with words, not only for their connotation but for their sound. Poetically this is not really vicious, for Audiberti's abundance of vocabulary, his combinations of strictly classical terms with technical, rare, exotic, or popular words, offer the element of surprise, that element which Apollinaire once called the mainspring of the modern poetic spirit. Perhaps they better aid the writer to carry out his purpose, the contemporary aspect of man with the multitude of new and traditional details which claim his attention, his multiple relationships with realities and chiefly the stratifications of his thought.

Audiberti's poems, especially those which are long, contain a great diversity of tone, the serious passage suddenly offers a little oasis of comical, ironic, or erotic development and then returns to more sober tonality. This is certainly contrary to the idea of literary form as the expression of unity, yet it is perhaps more true to life and is not without savor. The mind which sees sculpture on doorways as clusters of tonsils or a horse butcher's sign as a Pegasus castrated up to the neck and which endows a bridge or a subway with such strong sexual symbolism avoids boredom. The curious manner in which the idea is no sooner expressed than it is borne forth in many directions, the recurrence of the theme seemingly engulfed in the flood, the dual notes of revolt and ecstasy, and especially the visionary strength of the lines make their author appear as having reached one of the extremes of possible poetic originality.

Kenneth Cornell. YFS. 2, 2, 1949, p. 102

The Greeks used to tell chatterers, "Put an ox on your tongue." Audiberti would do well to put at least a sheep on his. What a favor anyone could do for him by showing him the way to slow down his torrential flow of words, to harness his overactive imagination, to introduce "pauses"—moments of reflection and choice—into the unchecked effervescence of his mind!

[In *The Gardens and the Rivers*] the author of *Carnage* did not invent difficulties. He took the first subject that occurred to him, a simple background, commonplace characters, the technique of Flaubert (as modified by Joyce and Céline) and he began from there, with the playfulness of a fox terrier out for a walk. . . .

The novel has a theatrical setting because Audiberti has a thorough knowledge of that milieu; and also because the theater of Jean-Désiré Lazerm [the hero] and his colleagues provides a very appropriate excuse for Audiberti to insert two or three of his "dramatic sketches." Except for this framework, the novel proceeds randomly, by whatever way Audiberti's staggering creative breath propels it. . . . And "staggering" should be taken literally. . . .

Despite his explosive words and subversive technique, Audiberti is no revolutionary. His most violent protests against the order of the world or against social conventions do not prevent the reader from recognizing his Mediterranean optimism—the intimate and complete satisfaction of those who have seen the heart's kindnesses and life's sweetness shine in the sun since birth. The misfortune and ugliness to which Jean-Désiré is subjected at no time go so far as to shake the foundations of the universe. Fate's threats do not preclude the sidewalk café, the patch of vineyards, the hill planted with olive trees, from the top of which the eye can see the shifting smile of the sea.

Robert Poulet. La lanterne magique (Paris,
Nouvelles Éditions Debresse, 1956), pp. 188–90†

Sex is for Audiberti a manifestation of Paganism. It is *natural*: neither good or bad, but ineluctable. Evil arises from its transformation in society into something artificial and therefore perverted. This state of affairs brings about a double evil: the evil that is implicit in repression and perversion themselves, and the evil that comes when as a result of this the too long repressed force of sex inevitably breaks out with cyclonic savagery. In this latter form, Audiberti's sex is analogous to Artaud's plague—the heedless emotional whirlwind that takes the human being back into the long-abandoned racial subconsciousness, his only true reality.

Audiberti's most explicit statement of this theme and at the same time far and away his best play is *The Black Feast*. This play is of particular importance to students of the *avant-garde* drama as being what must surely be the most successful and faithful dramatization of the theories of Antonin Artaud. *The Black Feast* takes place in a wild and mountainous region of southern France, where Félicien, the hero of the piece, is the local doctor. Félicien's one desire is to win the love of a woman. But this is precisely the one thing that always eludes him. As the unnatural repression builds up in him, Félicien becomes a sort of perverted superman figure, a symbol of the masculine drive, the motor force behind men's actions, hemmed in by the restrictions imposed on its free outpouring by the laws of civilized society. Audiberti sees Félicien as Superman Bound—and bound so effectively that his ineluctable force can emerge only in a horribly twisted form, maliciously revenging itself on the culture that has fettered it. . . .

Not only does Audiberti use the [Artaud's] "plague" (in the form of the destructive beast) as his binding theme, but he also follows Artaud's specifications for involving the spectators in the vortex of emotion. Just before the "beast" is led in to be killed, Audiberti has the following stage direction: "Brouhaha. The ground shakes under the audience's seats. Green leaves fly through the auditorium. At the back of the stage a hairy, sallow face floats by. It will be quite easy to bring about this rapid apparition."

George E. Wellwarth. TSLL. Autumn, 1962, pp. 336–38

The main key to Audiberti's work, the one that puts you in contact with his motives and gives you access to his secret treasure chests, is the knowledge that his nature is that of a poet. "I have lost the state of innocence," he said, undoubtedly wishing to express some regret over having chosen the roles of a novelist and playwright in favor of his initial sacred mission [as a poet]. Such self-reproach is unjustifiable. Audiberti has always remained what he was from the beginning—an exceptionally talented magician who steals everyday reality so that he can return it to us in a burning and hallucinatory form. He naturally begins by casting a spell on language, the essential means of communication between men, and by pulverizing words in his own way so that, once they have been tamed to his rhythm, he can give them a new structure and effectiveness. . . .

Although he defines himself as a man of the nineteenth century and aligns himself with the "classicism" of the Parnassian poets and Hugo, Audiberti's poetry tells us by its very substance that it is postsurrealist. Even if it does not show any obvious traces of surrealism, it nonetheless has profited from surrealism's existence. . . .

In his odes, sonnets, rondos, and songs, all the stanzas sparkle from the unheard-of richness with which they are crammed. The glory and misery of man are mingled with the fury of the elements, the power of the earth, and the violence of desire. It is a world in perpetual fusion, one re-created from its origins. . . .

The solidity of Audiberti's poetic structures supports that famous "eloquence" which some call a "verbal torrent" but which many agree is the recognizable mark of Audiberti's genius.

André Deslandes. Audiberti (Paris, Gallimard,
1964), pp. 55, 57–58†

Audiberti himself once declared that a play is a literary genre like any other and does not depend on being performed. While he gradually discovered the exigences of performance and tried to comply with them, he remained primarily a manipulator of language. In fact his joy in writing words was so narcissistic that when one of his last plays, *The Ant in the Body*, was performed in 1962 at the Comédie Française, some of the Parisian critics were still accusing him of verbalism and of writing gibberish.

Yet Audiberti's technique is more than logorrhea. In most of his adventure-comedies the poet's imagination is given free rein. Indeed, it draws on all the sources (farce, Boulevard, melodrama) and goes off in all directions. Audiberti does not disdain apparently facile effects. . . . The final horrors of *The Falcon* [and] Turenne's clownery with the cannonball in *The Ant in the Body* are so many quasi-surrealist or terrifying extensions of situations otherwise parodic and simple.

The effect of Audiberti's imagination—uncontrolled in regard to the quality or quantity of its products and at its most inventive in the matter of events or deliriously colorful language—is to disclose a monstrous reality behind all the jesting or beneath the absurdity of a preposterous adventure. For his drama is built on the relations between a surface life and deeply hidden primitive forces. The surface, whether contemporary or historical, consists of a chaos of events that is made to appear funny by a use of comical images, puns, and distortions of syntax. But that tumultuous and sparkling verbal flow both contains and reveals hidden forces. . . .

Doubtless a good example of poetry *of* the theatre, Audiberti's works are also and unfortunately too often an example of poetry *in* the theatre. While the verbal delirium evokes the richness of a threatening or threatened reality, it sometimes ends by turning in on itself, evoking, in its complacency, neither the absurd nor the mysterious: all that is left are words—and obscurity. Although the onslaught of curious images, mixing the familiar with the fantastic, and the variations of the variations on a central theme communicate the writer's joy of freedom and give the plays their poetic atmosphere and their savor, often the verbal techniques attract more attention than they should, become wearisome in their useless abundance, and somehow make the mask opaque instead of contributing to its transparency.

Jacques Guicharnaud, with June Guicharnaud.
Modern French Theatre from Giraudoux to Genet,
rev. ed. (New Haven, Conn., Yale University Press,
1967), pp. 162–64

[*The Falcon*] is constructed very traditionally. All the dramatic conventions are used; Audiberti's genius consists in finding the material for such conventions in a mere trifle, a word, a pirouette, an enormous outburst of laughter, a lyrical tirade, a whiff of pure poetry. Trumpets blow when they should. The guards are at their posts. The clowns juggle, as in a medieval mystery play; the lines are striking, as in a drama by Victor Hugo. It is not the Middle Ages, and the playwright is not Hugo: Audiberti straddles the centuries and proclaims, from atop the ramparts of Antibes [his native town], that he is the *pagan* Claudel of our century.

People have pointed out too many times that Audiberti is talkative, harsh, and immoderate. It should be added that he is also simple, clear, quick, and instinctive. When his virgin [heroine] is happy, she says: "I am as happy as a cherry." When the baron feels taken in by his wife's hypocritical sweetness, he says: "I have been bitten by your saliva." . . .

Above all else, there is Audiberti's strange mythology, his belief in a savage god, in a divine Eros, in an "ab-human" human race, as he puts it; and this religion seems strangely modern today, as if it had just come into being. . . . [Audiberti's] woman-god is the Falcon, who leads us to see "good and evil constantly struggling" within man.

François-Régis Bastide. *NL.* June 26, 1969, p. 13†

AYMÉ, MARCEL (1902–1967)

Marcel Aymé is a peculiar novelist. Possessing talents that make him lean at times toward realism and at times toward pure fantasy, he approaches one mode, runs away toward the other, and finally takes intermediate paths that belong only to him. This does not always prevent him from getting lost, at least in my opinion. But the remarkable authority he has acquired over his public survives his tentativeness. One senses the presence of Aymé even when his method is uncertain. Thus, *The Green Mare*, a novel whose incoherence at times seems tedious, remains one of his greatest successes. If you ask those who speak highly of it what kind of pleasure it gives them, their answer at first is confused. But their very real ecstasy makes up for their lack of coherent arguments. And you understand that they are grateful to Aymé for having put them in this state merely by the trick of a style in which everything is baroque, in which every word furnishes a new surprise. They like Aymé insofar as he makes them forget reality. . . .

The ridicule in his jokes does not mean that Aymé has no compassion. One feels that he pities some of his characters for lending themselves to so much laughter. Through his pen these puppets become representatives of human misery. This is perhaps where their surest attraction lies. Attending a Punch and Judy show restores to the mature man some of his child's soul. Two stages of life meet.

Robert Bourget-Pailleron. *RDM*. April 1, 1938,
pp. 686–88†

Clérambard is neither a subtle psychological study, an intellectual parlor game, nor a comedy of absurdity, an area into which some of our dramatists have followed the Americans. Aymé's humor combines great energy and great simplicity in comic invention: a main character whose madness creates a series of increasingly extravagant situations all around him; yet a character who never, for all his improbability, lacks truth and human significance. The dramatist was very daring to choose as his theme a Franciscan love of the meek, the sinful, and our brothers the animals, and to provoke almost continual laughter in his audience by vividly showing the effects of that kind of love in the modern world. If I may say so, Aymé has written a comedy about saintliness, and he has succeeded in making saintliness comical without ever losing its saintliness.

Thierry Maulnier. *RdP*. April, 1950, p. 147†

Immediately after the liberation of France in 1944, that country proceeded to purge itself of the elements that had collaborated with the
enemy. Many accounts were settled, some political and some purely
personal, as denunciations and trials multiplied. Anyone who had played
a part, no matter how slight, in the Resistance automatically became a
hero; and the Communists attempted to monopolize patriotism.

In *Uranus* Marcel Aymé, the keenest satirist writing in France
today, has chosen a small town devastated by Allied bombing as the
scene of that insidious reign of terror known as the "purification."
Classes from the bombed-out school meet in cafés, reciting Racine to
the accompaniment of the tinkle of glasses being washed for the apéritif
hour, and young lovers meet among the ruins and discuss their parents'
attempts to whitewash black-market activities. . . .

The modest and retiring Marcel Aymé, whose gifts as a humorous
storyteller class him among the greatest in that Gallic tradition, satirizes
the foibles of his time much as Molière, Daumier and Anatole France
once did. In *Travelingue* . . . he ticked off the epoch of the Popular
Front before it had died; in *The Road of the Students* he immortalized
the black market while it was still flourishing; and here he has said the
last word on the post-war Great Whitewash.

Such novels are worthy to stand beside Anatole France's *The
Crainquebille Affair* and *The Revolt of the Angels*. For anyone with
normal curiosity and a sense of humor it would be impossible to read
the initial paragraph of *Uranus* without continuing.

Justin O'Brien. *NYT*. May 14, 1950, p. 4

The Heads of Others does not deal with justice during the post-World
War II purges. Quite to the contrary, the justice that is briefly cross-
examined [in this play] is that of the Occupation. . . . But it is impossible to get rid of the idea that in writing his play, Marcel Aymé was
thinking at least in part about the administering of justice right after the
Liberation. At the very least, the sentences pronounced at that time,
which seemed excessive to him, could only have reinforced his fundamental antagonism toward the death penalty. . . .

The first act is in a style that is comic but terrifying, the kind of
comedy perhaps best suited to get to the heart of the problem. Aymé is
particularly at ease in this style. What could be more stinging than to
create irresponsible and inconsequential personalities for those characters whose function is precisely to shed light on other people's responsibilities? . . .

The second act begins very strongly with the entrance of two hired
killers, former Gestapo agents, who, as they prepare to execute their
victim, start a violent discussion about the respective advantages of

secular versus religious education for their children and finally wind up locked up in a closet by the victim, who has been reprieved. Because of the vividness of the characters, the humor of the gap between what they are saying and the situation, and the verbal brilliance, this scene is worthy of inclusion in anthologies.

Immediately afterward, the viewer's interest is scattered. The most diffuse targets—the magistrature, corruption of the State, morals, the after-effects of the Occupation and the Liberation, and so forth—receive such a frantic bombardment from the author that everything crumbles, including the play. . . . The satire comes clattering down to the level of cabaret revues, whose facile techniques the play had occasionally appropriated earlier. It borrows their irritating, hasty, total mockery of authorities, constituted bodies, and powers—a mockery that is always warmly received by a segment of the public, which finds in such mockery an explanation and a confused revenge against all its past and present problems.

Jacques Carat. Preuves. March, 1952, p. 58†

Aymé's real world is rather strictly limited and seems almost too easy to grasp. When the reader has finished chuckling over the incongruities of the man who passes through walls [in "The Walker-through-Walls"] or the green mare [in *The Green Mare*] with strange erotic powers in her eyes, he becomes more and more conscious that in Aymé two areas of reality remain constant. They make a strange pair. Children (particularly those caught between adolescence and adulthood) and sexual desire—these are the chief stays of Aymé's fictional world. They are for the most part purely incidental, the backdrop upon which he develops what appear to be more obvious themes. The psychology of marriage is one of them; political actuality is another. The most apparent side is, of course, the rollicking libertinage reminiscent of Rabelais and Boccaccio. Most of the fantastic—the playing with time, the change of personality and physical appearance, the arrival of fairy-land denizens—is connected with these more obvious themes. But the school boy and school girl on the one hand, and physical desire on the other give us the occasional flash of sober reality we need. The fantasy is possible and more delightful because of them, the satire is more biting because of them; they are unwittingly the sounding board of Aymé's subtle cruelty. . . .

His satire seeks out the same reference point—the only proper reference point for satire. Whether he is telling us of pixies, snake-ladies, green mares, passers-through-walls, multiple transformations or politicians, he is showing us the basic stupidity of the social man when compared with the potential beauty and composure of the untrammeled

man. The fantasy of his points of departure is not more fantastic, he
seems to say, than what we all accept as the realities of social living.
From his subtly destructive pen escape only those two unspoiled realities
—childhood and frank physical desire. Their interreaction would seem
to be his ultimate truth.

                                              J. Robert Loy. *FR*. Dec., 1954, pp. 116–17

A distinguishing characteristic of Marcel Aymé, when set beside other
contemporary novelists in France, is the fact that he neither comes from
nor has ever been assimilated to the Paris bourgeoisie. Throughout his
literary career he has remained an unreconstructed Jura peasant. . . . He
is most at home within the microcosm of the small provincial village,
where peasants, animals and small-scale local powers achieve a healthy,
if somewhat uninspiring, pattern of existence. This is the setting of his
early novels and of his charming fairy stories for children, *The Tales of
the Perched Cat*—the adventures of two little peasant girls and their
remarkable animal friends. When, as in his later novels, the scene removes to Paris, Aymé becomes suspicious; and when the scene is further
complicated by political events, suspicion turns into downright misanthropy. Old-fashioned French individualist that he is, Aymé seems to
be judging the complexities and corruptions of contemporary political
society in terms of the simplicity and balance of tiny peasant communi-
ties. This point of view, however limited in scope, can be extremely
refreshing, as is already apparent in Aymé's first successful novel, *The
Green Mare*. . . .

    A man in full possession of his five senses, he, like his green mare,
is gifted with a direct, almost physical flair for the elementary and
generally unacknowledged motives of human behavior. He has a fertile
and salty imagination. The supernatural, a frequent element in Aymé's
early novels and his later stories, has none of the dreamlike, otherworldly qualities of the surrealists but is firmly planted in the terrestrial
logic of everyday events. Finally, and most important, Aymé is a novelist who can make his reader laugh out loud.

    These qualities—the functional plot, the concrete fantasy, a
healthy taste for life and a highly developed sense of the ridiculous—are
singularly lacking, if not deliberately suppressed, in the contemporary
French novel. Aymé's sudden emergence in 1933 is thus something like
a violent irruption of Sancho Panza upon a literary scene crowded with
intellectuals, poets, prophets, and anguished rebels.

                                          Germaine Brée and Margaret Guiton. *An Age of
                                         Fiction: The French Novel from Gide to Camus*
                                          (New Brunswick, N.J., Rutgers University Press,
                                                                        1957), pp. 89, 91

In [*The Green Mare*] the libido governs men. It is a tyrannical mistress, a binding destiny. Everything depends on it, opinions as well as quarrels. Friendship and hatred are only pretexts—balloons thrown to the peasants so that they can deceive others. The libido alone is living reality, the true force people obey. Human passions are only the reflections of man's sensual dispositions. . . .

   The Green Mare is the Gallic epic of the countryside. The heroes and heroines of this novel are not fastidious. The boys pounce upon the girls without wondering whether they have the right to do so or whether they run the risk of being beaten by a jealous husband. Flesh, for them, is not sad, and they are lucky enough not to have read any books. The girls let themselves be pushed into ditches without making any great fuss about it. . . . Everything takes place with an animallike lack of awareness, with a serene obscenity.

Pol Vandromme. Marcel Aymé (Paris, Gallimard,
1960), pp. 74–75†

Aymé's sense of the comic may appear at first, on the most obvious level, to apply to the language. Like all great humorists, he has a gift for language and likes to play with words; like Rabelais, he is fond of the repetitive process, of lists and alliterations; like Voltaire, he blends into mock-serious descriptions diverse heterogeneous elements which cast a sudden startling light upon the scene; like Proust, he uses associations and comparisons; like Queneau, he coins new, amusing words. He does not reject certain easy technical devices such as tongue-in-cheek parentheses and footnotes. This indulgence in verbal invention and certain devices of style is in no way so pronounced, however, as that found in the works of Rabelais, Queneau and others: in most of Aymé's novels, for instance, one would not find more than a sprinkling of coined words or unconventional spellings.

   Aymé, then, is not essentially a writer who juggles with language or with figures of speech. He is primarily a man of imagination. Freely he creates new situations, new worlds where the laws of our cosmos are abrogated or suspended. There, his creatures move about with an imperturbable logic of their own, forcing our assent. We are freed from our hidebound concepts of time and space, cause and effect; and we can appraise characters and events with a fresh outlook. Like La Fontaine, Aymé composes fables and apologues; like Swift and Lewis Carroll, he is the inventor of surrealistic new worlds.

   Thirdly, Aymé is a novelist of mores. Like Balzac, Stendhal, Proust, and many others, he observes the human comedy and describes man in society. He is not a sociologist, however; what gives many of his works their documentary value is that he possesses a remarkably keen eye and ear for significant traits.

Dorothy R. Brodin. *The Comic World of
Marcel Aymé* (Paris, Nouvelles Éditions Debresse,
1964), pp. 155–56

Aymé's style is indeed one of the unifying elements of all his works. The writer constantly remains faithful to the clarity he defended in *Intellectual Comfort*. Aymé tells a story without superfluous detours. If he tells a rustic tale . . . he has the peasants speak the language of the soil, with all its charm, and even all its grammatical oddities. If he describes a district in Montmartre, as in *The Walker-through-Walls*, he has the native Parisian speak. . . . By introducing spoken language in the heart of his work, Aymé shows the influence exerted on him by Louis-Ferdinand Céline. . . .

Like Céline, Aymé sometimes gives the impression that he is incapable of controlling his rancor, his hatred, or at least his intolerance of certain people and institutions. Therefore, his frankness, or rather his excess of sincerity, sometimes overflows into platitudes or even leads to grossness. . . .

Aymé says what he thinks without being concerned about society, for he knows that such a concern would inevitably contain a defense mechanism, a justification, a lack of sincerity. Aymé is just as nonchalantly sincere as some of the heroes of his novels, such as Honoré Haudouin in *The Green Mare* and Professor Wattrin in *Uranus*. Furthermore, because of his great care for the form of his tales, because of the great pains he takes with the choice, the sound, the handling, and the arrangement of all the components of his sentences, Aymé is undoubtedly a great stylist.

Jean-Louis Dumont. *Marcel Aymé et le merveilleux*
(Paris, Nouvelles Éditions Debresse, 1967),
pp. 181–83†

BARBUSSE, HENRI (1873–1935)

I cannot say that [*Fire*] by Henri Barbusse shows no talent. It is full of the well-known, predictable kind of talent whose nature and tradition were established by the novels of Émile Zola. . . . The photographic exactness of some of the details masks the unreality of the whole.

[*Fire*] also has passion, which is sometimes a virtue in works of art. But Barbusse's passion is an ugly kind: it is anger. . . . Barbusse yields completely to his anger . . . he carefully gathers the anger of his comrades as well as his own. . . . Talent is also used at the expense of truth and beauty. This anger, which is uncontrollably spread everywhere, gives the work an ugly color, a ghastly color. This hypocritical syrup is not the whole truth. . . .

It is an ambitious plan to want to reconstruct a true picture of the Great War by this method. The sufferings of the French infantryman are many, and Barbusse . . . has not exhausted them. Nevertheless, he does not include anything of the scent of the precious flowers that remain amidst these trials: he omits the virtues that ennoble the humblest of men, even the most depraved, the gaiety that reacts against the weight of circumstances and rejuvenates even those who are already bent with age, and everything can make suffering men joke and laugh like children. . . . He does his best to destroy the vigorous motives that enabled the men to bear their trials—love of country and hatred of the enemy—by proposing to replace them with ancient ideologies that no longer kindle men's hearts. . . .

Although he claims to be offering a true picture, reality is beyond him, and what he gives us instead is an angry work of propaganda.

Le Biffin [Charles Maurras]. *Action française.*
March 30, 1917, p. 1; March 31, 1917, p. 1†

We Others consists of forty-five very short stories—divided into three groups: "Fate," "The Madness of Love," and "Pity"—almost all of which have some kind of comic tone. Yet this book expresses a total and uncompromising conviction that it is impossible to believe in the goodness of life. Barbusse is now on such intimate terms with the truth and uses analysis so skillfully that he no longer needs to shut himself up inside himself, as in *The Supplicants*, or to work unceasingly on the complete dissection of a single object, as in *The Inferno*, in order to savor the unpleasant smell of the truth. He has only to walk through society, to glean its petty events; he has only to let his lively storyteller's pen take its course; immediately the truth emerges from the events and people. The truth takes away their composure, stigmatizes them, and gives them lepers' garbs. . . .

The reader feels he is associating with men skinned alive, with exposed souls.

Henri Hertz. *Henri Barbusse* (Paris, Éditions du
Carnet-Critique, 1920), p. 32†

[In *Light*] Barbusse treats one of the most important themes of contemporary France—the mental awakening of the average Frenchman, the insignificant office worker or petit bourgeois who gradually comes to a precise understanding of social realities and turns into a revolutionary. Long before Vichy brought to light the sickness gnawing away at France, which almost caused France's death—namely, the egotism, incompetence, and ignorance of the ruling class, which can no longer ensure the progress or the greatness of the nation—Barbusse showed that salvation resides in the creation of a true democracy, in the revolutionary struggle for a new social regime founded on the abolition of economic privileges and injustice. . . .

A new certainty is born, which will grow. Barbusse no longer surrounds himself with a squadron [as in *Fire*]; in *Light* it is an army, an army of the humble and the victimized, to whom he brings a clear-sighted faith and a promise of regeneration, in the great dawn rising from the East—the Russian Revolution.

[After writing *Light*], Barbusse began a long mission of preaching, which continued until his death. Each of his works accompanied, clarified, or added to his militant action. He made appeals, addressed meetings, presided at congresses; during this uninterrupted whirlwind of concerns and struggles, he still managed to edit the literary page of *L'humanité*, to launch periodicals—*Clarté* first, then *Monde*—and despite enormous political tasks, enough to consume any other man's energies, Barbusse still wrote stories of striking significance, wrote great books, pamphlets, prefaces, and manifestos, and published numerous studies of the Soviet Union and the Balkan states. [Sept. 6, 1945]

Jean Fréville. *Henri Barbusse* (Paris,
Éditions Sociales, 1946), pp. 32–34†

Light is a social-thesis novel, a war novel (an antimilitarist novel), and at the same time a moral, philosophical, and political confession of a petit-bourgeois intellectual. . . .

The book is clearly divided in three parts, connected to each other by the protagonist, Simon Paulin, some sort of employee around whom we see first the milieu of a provincial city, Viviers, then the life of drafted soldiers in the barracks and on the front. Finally, we see the emotional crisis of Simon Paulin, seriously wounded on the battlefield, nursed in the hospital, and back home in Viviers with his wife. . . .

During an attack Simon Paulin, hit by a bullet, faints on the battlefield between the French and German lines; out of exhaustion and fever, he becomes delirious and has apocalyptic visions of past and future wars. . . . During the feverish crisis he experiences, his ideas and opinions are scourged of secular prejudices and clarified into a revolutionary consciousness. . . .

When Paulin awakens from his phantasmagoric dreams, in a hospital, he sees life differently. One day, his wife calls for him and brings him back to Viviers, and he is supposed to "pick up his life" where he left off. But he finds everything changed because he sees "things as they really are." He feels he has come not to the end but to the beginning. In his interior monologues and conversations with his wife, he formulates his new knowledge, his socialist credo, which soon puts him in opposition to everything which he formerly believed in and which still holds sway in Viviers and elsewhere. . . . He has lost his religious faith but has gained freedom; he feels liberated. From the front, from the hospital, he has brought back the need for truth, a critical spirit directed at religion and all its prejudices, and at the old social order.

Vladimír Brett. *Henri Barbusse: Sa marche vers
la clarté* (Prague, Éditions de l'Académie
Tchécoslovaque des Sciences, 1963), pp. 147,
152–53†

Read simply as a novel, in isolation of what came before and after, *The Inferno* is rather forbidding, thick with the cobwebs of an earlier mannerism, but seen as a bridge between the torments of decadence and the simplicities of Revolution, *The Inferno* becomes of great interest. It contains all Barbusse's old disgust with the ways of God and of a majority of men, but the assault is made with a new ferocity and a new precision. . . . Looking back on this book [Barbusse] said that he felt he had never been more extreme in his opinions than he was here, by which he meant particularly the attacks he makes on Christian belief, at any rate where it distracts us from present suffering and injustice, and on the concept of aggressive nationalism. . . . He exposes with force the conjuring trick of our emotions, whereby we can cause the present moment to vanish between regret for the past and hope for the future. In *The Inferno* Barbusse rivets his attention finally on the possibilities of the here and now, and rejects the ephemeral and self-indulgent policies of the heart for the more enduring ones of the intelligence.

There is a sound reason then why this novel should contain a lot of what one critic called "exasperated sensuality." . . . Fifty years ago [Barbusse's perversities] were thought capable of undermining the war effort; in 1917 there was a public reading from *The Inferno* in the Chambre des Députés, because its apparently fortuitous conjunction of internationalist and secularist propaganda with so many scenes of sexual deviation was a handy card for the warlords to play in their attempt to discredit the very successful anti-war effort of *Fire*. . . .

In *The Inferno* . . . Barbusse seems to pile perversion on perversion when he causes all these goings-on to take place in a single hotel room, where they are observed by a sensitive young man through a hole in the wall. Yet . . . this narrator is more a seer than a voyeur, he wants evidence rather than kicks. . . . To take a room in a fictional hotel of course is to book into a microcosm, and what Barbusse's young man sees is intended to be the final truth about the great majority of people who live by the body. . . . *The Inferno* is intended to show the fraud of basing our life on an emotional involvement with another individual, for such a relationship will oscillate between expectation and regret.

TLS. Nov. 17, 1966, p. 1044

[The Goncourt Prize] in December, 1916, brought crucial support to [*Fire*] a work that profoundly portrayed the aspirations of soldiers, who too often have been misrepresented by features and attitudes given them and projected on them by those who stayed behind.

In this work, however, war is demythologized. Mud and blood cover the images of false heroism. A hell is brought into view, the hell that is the daily lot of condemned multitudes. Through their infinite suffering, they gradually develop a philosophy. Their eyes are opened. The truth about life and death proves to be blinding. A whole world is condemned: not only the political, economic, and military oligarchies that set people against each other but also the shameful love of military glory that takes hold of even the purest hearts and absolves this kind of killing because of the glory of dying in war, as if people should love fires because of the fearlessness of firemen.

God, too, the God of organized religion, is put on trial. The aviator flying above the lines hears prayers rising from both sides toward the silence of heaven. Faced with this immense damnation, should one despair? No. The future lies in the unity of those who have suffered, in enlightened men like Karl Liebknecht who is mentioned by the dying Corporal Bertrand, who resembles Henri Barbusse like a brother.

In the last lines of *Fire* a timid ray of light breaks through the darkness above the trenches as if to provide evidence that the sun exists.

Pierre Paraf. Europe. Jan., 1969, pp. 9–10†

BARRÈS, MAURICE (1862–1923)

All of Maurice Barrès's works strike me as an inspiring struggle with death. In this struggle he displays the kind of heroism Roland [in *The Song of Roland*] showed at Roncevaux when he refused to sound his horn. The knight counted on his courage alone. Barrès does not want help from anybody, and he puts his trust in the weapons he has forged for himself by his *cultivation of the ego*. Following the philosophical essays of Kant, Fichte, and Hegel, and the lyricism of the great romantics, in our time it is Barrès who has made the most formidable effort on behalf of individualism. He claims to extract the universe and human life from individualism. What he has done, in reality, is to show once again individualism's beauty and its errors, its greatness and its impotence.

He shows the beauty of individualism by strengthening the inner life. The inner life becomes extinguished too often in each of us. It is essential to revive it. Without it, we are nothing but the playthings of events. Through our inner lives we are sheltered from circumstances and better prepared to resist the blows of the outer world. At a time when people readily deny the power of the will, the strength of energy, and even the human individual, Barrès magnificently praises energy and will. What a difference in tone from that of the pantheistic poets! Finally, he has enlarged the definition of individualism to include piety in the memory of our dead and the love of our native land. For Barrès, we are ourselves only when we are suffused with and steeped in the traditions of our race, and our life can be beautiful and complete only if it continues these traditions. The same thought will lay the foundations of the destiny of the generations that are to follow ours.

But individualism, however broad and however noble one conceives of it, brings with it egotism and pride, and through them unrest. . . . Pride and egotism are fatally engendered by the quest for sensations. Leonardo is supposed to have said: "The more sensations there are, the more torment." And [Thomas a Kempis's] *The Imitation of Christ* teaches us that we find peace of mind by resisting passions, not by yielding to them. Barrès is completely unaware of this peace of mind. His work is nothing but a cry of desire and unrest. Never has he found serenity. [Dec., 1903]

Henry Bordeaux. Deux méditations sur la mort
(Paris, E. Sansot, 1905), pp. 49–51†

In 1888—he was then twenty-six—the young Lorrainer Maurice Barrès astonished Paris as the high priest of a new cult—*le culte du Moi* (Ego-worship). Such is the collective title of his first three novels, *Under the Eyes of the Barbarians, A Free Man, The Garden of Bérénice.* Novels? It is impossible to tag any label on these strange concoctions, which the author himself calls "ideologies." A minimum of fact, a certain element of psycho-picturesque description, symbols, reflections, meditations—a farrago of Ignatius de Loyola, Stendhal, Heine, and not a few others: the result is wilful, absurd, exasperating to a degree, yet with undeniable powers of fascination. It belongs to that esoteric literature which is so dear to very young people. The element of conscious mystification is not lacking either—as in the symbolic poetry of Mallarmé . . . or, in more recent years, Post-Impressionist Art.

Maurice Barrès became a power among a widening circle of initiated. But there was sense and energy in the man, in spite of his affectations. His "cult of the Ego" is no passive worship: it implies the cultivation as well as the adoration of the Ego. And, different in this respect from certain developments of Nietzscheism, it is made ethically palatable through its respect for other individualities. It is corrected by the Kantian reverence for human personality, or simply by the golden rule.

Albert Léon Guérard. Five Masters of French
Romance (London, T. Fisher Unwin, 1916),
pp. 216–18

There is nothing more appropriate in tone, more delicate, or more skillful in Barrès's work than *In the Service of Germany*. Because of the smoothness of the narration, the delicacy of the touch, the skill with which the nature or attitude of a character is indicated in a single stroke, and the clarity, the balance, and the polish of the episodes, it can be compared to the best works of Alphonse Daudet. It has the artistry of *Monday Tales*, without Daudet's Dickensian sentimentality and abrupt irony. In *In the Service of Germany* one has the pleasure of seeing all the results obtained not by the obscure and unconscious powers of genius but by a flexible intelligence that is extremely acute and at ease with itself. The principal problem for Barrès in constructing the book was the blending of two necessarily distinct subjects, one of which could have destroyed the effects of the other: the story of an Alsatian among Germans, and that of a young bourgeois in the barracks among brutal soldiers. Barrès did his best to minimize this problem, but he did not resolve it completely. And this structural problem stood in the way of the success of the book.

Barrès's great popular triumph came with *Colette Baudoche*, which was published at a more propitious time. . . . The book is shorter and somewhat less artistically successful than *In the Service of Germany*. One finds in it the same perfection in the narration, an attractive, Flemish-like clarity in its episodes, and a bantering grace reminiscent of La Fontaine in its mockery of men from the other side of the Rhine. . . . Although the character of the German professor is treated superficially, this defect does not diminish the value of the book very much, since it is called *Colette Baudoche*, not *Frédéric Asmus*. It is enough for Asmus to give Barrès the opportunity to reveal the soul of a maiden from Metz, so that she can then symbolically represent all of Lorraine.

Like *In the Service of Germany*, *Colette Baudoche* is a book of intelligence and awareness. Perhaps it has a touch of exaggeration. . . . Let us say that Barrès wrote *Colette Baudoche* in the manner of a French administrator wearing the blue military uniform in reconquered Lorraine.

Albert Thibaudet. *La vie de Maurice Barrès*
(Paris, Librairie Gallimard, 1921), pp. 268–69†

Almost alone in his generation Barrès knew the value of sounds, the color of words, the cadence of phrases; he created images capable of moving the senses and astonishing the mind; saying nothing he constantly invented new pleasures and new pains. More than any other man of his age Barrès had the gift of seeing in language a reservoir of forces and of knowing how to use it. If his sonorous sentences are sometimes hollow, one may say that they are so after the fashion of crowns, and deck a royal void. They show that their master lacked neither desire nor strength, but only that cleverness or littleness necessary to cross the low and narrow doors of the treasures of the world.

Freeing literature from servitude, humble and material cares, Barrès restored the prestige formerly given it in France by the great Classics, with their intellectual nobility, by the Romantics, with their apostolic ambition. He did more: his renunciation, not entirely devoid of egoism or of grandeur, continued the Symbolist crusade against the external world. Barrès divined the most intimate suffering of his time and its most essential need: like the Symbolists he turned toward an art of creation, of liberation, where the mind would dominate the flesh, where the artist would be a magician, not copying the prestidigitations of science, but on the contrary strong enough to escape that obsession of cleverness, industry, progress, which weighs upon us like a nightmare, and deceives us.

Bernard Faÿ. *Since Victor Hugo* (Boston,
Little, Brown, 1927), pp. 108–9

Barrès, a lover of resonance, begins and ends [*The Sacred Hill*] on a note of Ciceronian grandeur, and throughout he rises above the vulgarity of his peasants to ambitious passages of rhetoric. But his stylization is grounded upon a very realistic plot, even admitting of lapses into episodes which look dangerously like "comic relief." The grandiose appears sporadically, to be dropped when the events are not *per se* of a grandiose nature. . . .

Barrès, in his juxtaposition of differing elements, comes nearer to a Shakespearean than a Racinian tragedy. The clowns, the drunkards, the porters who proclaim their vulgar selves about the periphery of the dignified characters in a Shakespearean drama have their counterpart in Barrès's villagers; they would be eliminated or subdued to fit an artistically tyrannous framework in Racine or Pater. One gets less the sense of breadth than of a broken framework. Barrès began with a set of actual characters, building his book about a situation which did arise in Lorraine, engrafting upon this recalcitrant tale the oratorical manner which he prefers. With this manner, however, one may be so much in sympathy that he cannot concede the readiness with which the author permits it to subside.

The oratory itself rises to volume, it is conveyed in long rhythms and in interruptions of rhythm, in delicately spaced phrasings. . . . But it is often constructed of ideas which are more musical than vigorous. . . .

[*The Sacred Hill*] is not likely to win wide favor with the American public. To people raised among no religions or many religions, the central theme of *The Sacred Hill*, the psychology of heresy, can supply little categorical excitement. We may be impressed with the author's treatment of his subject, but we do not meet him halfway by prior engrossments in this subject.

Kenneth Burke. *NYHT*. Nov. 10, 1929, p. 4

[Barrès was] a great writer. One must repeat untiringly that a great writer is as far removed and as different from "good" writers and "distinguished" writers as from people who do not write at all. One must repeat untiringly that a great writer is never great by his form alone, but rather by what he puts into that form—in other words, by what he is. "There are no great writers; there are only great men," said André Suarès, a great writer himself.

What was Barrès? A man with an extremely penetrating mind, a man nature had consecrated to the role of observer and artist. But he loved greatness; he had to become more powerful; he did so through his country and even through religion. Through them, he expanded the idea he wanted to have of himself, and he also increased his importance in society. "To serve is also to serve oneself," wrote someone I know well. The service to the fatherland and to lofty causes nourished Barrès's authentic nobility and at the same time satisfied the need he had for approval.

He became the prisoner of the exemplary figure he had striven to become. The prolongation of World War I fixed him in this role a little longer than was necessary. When, after peace had come, he wanted to relax a little (by writing *A Garden on the Orontes*), he was made to feel that he would be considered a traitor if he ever took it into his head to become natural again. He sighed, and resumed his pose once more. His last photographs show the admirable mask of a man ravaged by boredom: he no longer had much time left; what had he done about happiness? Fame and duty are not all. "There has perhaps been too much will in my life," he said. . . . He died bereft, in theory of a heart attack, in reality of constraint, worn out before his time by constraint, by the chains with which he had loaded himself down. . . . Today we call for national figures, who could be the voice of established order, in its most valid aspects. Such a role will always tempt a noble soul, but we must see what that soul sacrifices to this role. [1933]

> Henry de Montherlant. Preface to *L'œuvre de*
> *Maurice Barrès* (Paris, Club de l'Honnête Homme,
> 1967), Vol. XI, pp. xvii–xviii†

In his old age, just as though to show that he could yet relax and play, play with the acquired and dearly bought wisdom of maturity, [Barrès] wrote in 1922 *A Garden on the Orontes*. A simple and wicked tale of the Crusaders, of a western lord who falls in love with an eastern lady, and how he comes to his death, and how perfect destiny is. A strange book after all the great efforts. But again a masterpiece, as though the dumb Middle Ages had become intelligent and bad, and had added to their effectiveness the naïveté, the ruse and the viciousness supposed to belong to our later ages. But who knows? We have no reason to think the Middle Ages, especially in Syria, were not as wicked as we can ever hope to be, and Barrès leaves us wondering what we would have done on the Orontes River. Destiny also is a work of art, and the real writer can tell how a good story should go so that the pattern of his imaginary events somehow harmonizes with that obscure but inevitable force that we can only suppose to be the will of God chastising our wickedness by means of the deceitfulness of very fair, of unbearably fair, ladies, especially eastern ladies.

Here is a true synthesis of Barrès; *The Garden of Bérénice* is *on the Orontes*, but also the knight is obviously an *uprooted* person who should have stayed on *The Sacred Hill*, or perhaps managed to bring back his eastern lady to Lorraine. Worse things have happened. Thus Barrès ends on an ironical note, and we are richer for it.

Denis Saurat. *Modern French Literature, 1870–1940*
(New York, G. P. Putnam's Sons, 1946), p. 79

The Cult of the Ego was only Barrès's first, superficial attempt to assert his profound personality—an attempt that was extended through exoticism, travels, and a love of the Orient, a love that he conceived as a pilgrimage to man's origins.

Barrès gradually forged for himself some sort of mythology of nature and grace, elements of which can be found later in Mauriac's metaphysics and in Montherlant's ethics. Barrès's effort was to reconcile the religion of Cybele with the religion of Christ: there was no call to Antiquity—Barrès was never much concerned with the Greeks and Romans—but rather a return to the old Gallic sources, to Celtic legends, to primitive cults. In a sense, Barrès's mythology was really an extension of his nationalism, an extension into prehistory, the time when the national subconscious was being forged.

The Sacred Hill was published in 1913; the general public found the story enigmatic, but enthusiasts of "Barrèsism" (the word had been in use since *A Free Man*) saw admirable symbols in it, and considered it Barrès's *magnum opus*. The first pages begin with the famous invocations, poetic stanzas in prose, to the "places where the spirit blows." Perhaps the lyrical flight of these pages leaves the reader thirsting for more. The very simple and beautiful symbol of the hill of Sion-Vaudémont, that flower of the history of Lorraine made into a heroic myth, masks the complexity of the legend. . . .

Whatever reservations we may have about the evocative powers and novelistic realities of *The Sacred Hill*, there is no work by Barrès that tells us more about his concept of Christianity—a concept summarized in the poetic dialogue between the Chapel and the Meadow. To the Meadow's claims to possess the "spirit of the land and of our most distant ancestors, freedom and inspiration," the Chapel responds by asserting itself as "rule, authority, bonds, a body of fixed thoughts and the ordained City of Souls."

Pierre de Boisdeffre. *Barrès parmi nous* (Paris,
Le Livre Contemporain, 1952), pp. 58–60†

If [Charles] Maurras repelled even his supporters, Barrès charmed even his opponents. An anti-semite who could always count Jews among his admirers, the high priest of nationalism who came to admire Clemenceau, the hater of socialism who could write condolingly to [Jean] Jaurès's daughter after his assassination could not but be an attractive figure. Some doubted his sincerity and others his wisdom, but all seemed to agree that the man who could become a member of the Académie Française at the age of forty-five must be something special, perhaps the new Alcibiades. Barrès died too early to be given the chance of going over to Sparta.

Barrès made his intellectual reputation with the idea of the *déraciné*—the rootless, cosmopolitan metic—and harnessed it to a mystical nationalism. Beyond this, his interest in political matters was limited, despite a political career in the Chamber which spanned over thirty years and several political labels. Nor is it perhaps altogether correct to put Barrès on the right. . . . Barrès did not object to socialism as such. For him, the important thing was that if a man was to be a socialist, he ought to be a French socialist if he is French, a national socialist in a specific sense. What attracts Barrès in [Pierre] Proudhon is not that Proudhon is on the left, but that he is a Burgundian, French, and therefore within the pale. Barrès's work is full of his feeling for Lorraine, yet one wonders what Lorraine really meant for him. The Lorraine he writes of is not the Lorraine of reality. . . .

Yet the mystique of Lorraine was, and remains, a powerful symbol in French political life. Barrès began it; Claudel eulogized it . . . De Gaulle, with deep sagacity, exploited it as Barrès did.

J. S. McClelland. *The French Right from de Maistre*
to Maurras (New York, Harper & Row, 1970),
pp. 143–44

Barrèsian ideas have had a mixed career, enjoying a certain multi-ideological success, from fascism to Gaullism. Not all these ideas, of course, originated with Barrès alone. Hippolyte Taine, Édouard Drumont, Georges Sorel, Charles Maurras, and a host of lesser writers propagated many of the same ideas. If fascism was not as successful in France in the 1920s and 1930s as it was in Italy, Germany, and elsewhere, it was not because fascist or proto-fascist ideas did not have distinct roots in French political and intellectual tradition. A generation before Mussolini and Hitler came to power, Barrès, along with others, anticipated a cluster of fascist values, sentiments, and doctrines. While, again, this does not mean that Barrès would have approved the Buchenwald atrocities, it does suggest that French conservative traditionalism, as expressed by one of its most influential representatives, was not always as far removed from fascist ideology as some have contended. Too often, historians of the French Right have made the mistake of rigidly divorcing conservatism from fascism in theory when in practice, that is historically, these movements interpenetrated one another in a very disconcerting way—disconcerting at least if one expects intellectual and political phenomena to be neatly compartmentalized and self-contained. As the Vichy era tragically displayed, the lines between those movements were often blurred and untidy. . . .

[Since World War II] French conservative theoreticians have argued that their credo was fundamentally opposed to fascism on ethical as well as nationalist grounds. If this be so, those among them who look back to Maurice Barrès as one of their masters would do well to reexamine certain Barrèsian concepts before repropagating them, including his concept of "moral" regeneration. . . . Some of the most callous aspects of Barrèsism were often rooted in certain "spiritual" values: a belief in brute force, animalistic combat, realism, racism, and energy. Perhaps most pervasive of all because it was more subtle and respectable, was Barrès's belief in psychic rootedness, a belief that provided him with the emotional security of a fixed personal identity but also limited his vision to parochial, antihumanitarian confines.

Robert Soucy. *Fascism in France: The Case of*
Maurice Barrès (Berkeley, University of California
Press, 1972), pp. 313–15

BARTHES, ROLAND (1915–   )

I am surprised that Marxism, a doctrine that constantly challenges ideologies, has never attempted to analyze ideologies precisely, has created nothing that could pass for a mere outline of a science of ideologies, has not even described their role in our daily lives. An astonishing gap (as if Marxism were no less frightening to Marxists themselves than it is to others, as if Marxists were afraid that they would find a nameless something that was new and terrifying). The importance of any book attempting to fill this gap is therefore the source of the attention we owe Roland Barthes' *Mythologies*. If we really care about the silent and constant deception going on inside us and outside us, a deception that forms the air we breathe and the breath of our words, how can we fail to be interested in an effort to correct our images, an effort to strip bare our unspoken thoughts?

I doubt, however, that Barthes's effort to correct things will please everyone. The outrage it will provoke and the nature of this outrage will not fail to teach us something. For two years, Barthes has been publishing rather short texts every month, usually in *Les lettres nouvelles*; in these texts he comments on a topical item chosen freely from among commonplace news stories. . . . His manner of approaching the smallest events—with which we fill our moments of emptiness with another emptiness—is itself very revealing. Barthes looks at minor events as if they were texts to study, as if these texts, which seem to be meaningless or whose meaning is obvious, had a hidden or more subtle meaning that needed to be brought to light. His technique stems in part from phenomenology and psychoanalysis. These two great methods, as different as they are from one another, have these characteristics in common: first, they are interested in everything—nothing takes precedence; second, they examine things while suspecting that these things have more meaning than is visible, believing that these things have other layers, an intricate system of latent meanings that must be revealed without disrupting the object, through a slow and patient approach whose movement must somehow reproduce the hidden meaning.

Maurice Blanchot. *NRF*. June, 1957, pp. 1066–68†

Roland Barthes's latest book, *On Racine*, is not a unified work but a collection of three studies that have already been published in various places, in which Racine's dramas seem to be less the theme of a systematic study than the pretext for very brilliant and suggestive variations. . . .

Some of Barthes's analyses are excellent, for example his discussion of the character of Phaedra as sometimes guilty, a condition based on tragedy in the literal sense, and sometimes jealous, a condition, based on social psychology and closely approximating bourgeois comedy. . . .

But it must be understood that all Barthes's detailed discussions are linked to a general philosophy, one in which a consideration of infra-conscious principles, on the one hand, and sociological conditioning, on the other hand, plays the greatest role. Thus, Barthes was led to squeeze Racine's theater between two theories. According to the first theory, the fundamental relationship between Racine's characters is that of authority, and the tragedy's eroticism stems from the fact that the most powerful wants to impose love on someone weaker who rejects it. . . . The other theory is that Racine's theater is dominated by the myth of the Father, in other words, a sacred, traditional, moral, and always constraining authority, in short a *legality* (which moreover can be just as well incarnated by a woman—Hermione, Agrippina—or in an institution—Port-Royal, the monarchy) against which an individual seeks to assert his autonomy. The ten pages in which Barthes takes apart the whole tragedy of *Andromache* and reconstructs it again to show how it is essentially a drama of *legality*, of the passage from an old order (oath, conjugal fidelity, nationalistic vendetta, and so forth) to a new order in which individuals will seek happiness by believing in the instant and in instinct is a good example of Barthes's dialectical virtuosity, which sometimes captivates us and sometimes makes us uneasy. But ultimately, beyond the fact that we need a little prodding here and there to make us accept this implicitly Sartrean exegesis of *Andromache* in which the words "tenderness," "duty," "dignity," and even "crime" seem to have no meaning any longer, at least one thing is astonishing: if legality were the mythical and psychological meaning of his tragedy, Racine hid it so well in his text that nobody ever realized it before now, not even Racine. [1963]

> Pierre-Henri Simon. *Diagnostic des lettres françaises contemporaines* (Brussels, La Renaissance du Livre, 1966), pp. 402–5†

The universal laws established by Mr. Barthes [in *On Racine*] concerning Racine's universe apply on the average to two or three of the eleven tragedies. The laws of physics, in spite of their uncertainty, seem to be more consistent in their application. Mr. Barthes transposes the "You cannot tell the truth about nature" of contemporary thought into "You cannot tell the truth about Racine," and from the "Anything can happen" of modern indeterminism he draws a sort of "You can say anything." He is right in that it is impossible even to conceive of what the whole, absolute, definitive truth about Racine might be, but he is wrong in that you cannot say just anything.

No, you cannot say just anything. Racine's words have a literal meaning which was obligatory for the spectators and readers of the seventeenth century, and which cannot be ignored without a game of chance being made of the language. . . . There is a Racinian truth, concerning which everyone can manage to agree. Relying especially on the certainties of language, on the implications of psychological coherence, on the demands of the genre's structure, the modest and patient scholar manages to spot pieces of evidence which in some measure determine zones of objectivity; it is from that point on, that he can— very prudently—attempt to make interpretations. . . .

I have spent long, often fruitless hours in studying this book. If I have done so, it is because it has seemed to me that the book is particularly dangerous. The obvious cleverness of its author, his intellectual imagination, his ideological prestidigitation, his dialectical tight-rope walking, his verbal illuminations—in a word, incontestable talent but talent gone astray—all this is not without glamor for certain types of readers. [1965]

> Raymond Picard. *New Criticism or New Fraud?* (Pullman, Washington State University Press, 1969), pp. 20–21, 27

Roland Barthes' views have been developed and extended in his two volumes of collected essays: *Mythologies* and *Critical Essays*. He explains in the earlier of the two books that "myth" like literature is a product of language and stands for the unconscious factors at work in a variety of social phenomena. He goes further in *Critical Essays*. Literature is described as a "system of meaning," but it is not the only system. There are a number of "extra-linguistic languages"—food, clothes, pictures, the cinema, fashion—which like literature reflect social attitudes.

Mythologies (published in 1957) is not primarily concerned with literature. Without the long closing essay on "Myth Today," we might have assumed from a first glance that the fifty short essays are purely occasional pieces dealing with topical subjects such as detergents, holidays, guide books, astrology, or "people in the news" like the Abbé Pierre, Billy Graham, and Poujade. We might even have suspected that an over-serious Frenchman was using these rather flimsy themes as an excuse for constructing a series of ponderous philosophical edifices. It is true that they are reprinted from different magazines, but behind them is a firm purpose which gives unity to the scattered essays. For Barthes makes a very determined effort to get down to "rock bottom," to uncover the "myths" at the root of activities which though sometimes trivial in themselves are symptomatic of the society in which we are living. These activities can be divided broadly into four groups: contemporary cults, publicity, literature, and *spectacles* (a word that in French includes virtually every kind of performance from straight plays to all-in wrestling). If they are not invariably convincing, his essays are for the most part extremely penetrating and often highly entertaining. . . .

Critical Essays probes further into some of the fundamental problems of literature, the function of criticism, and the relations between the two. . . . The task of criticism, he declares, is not to "discover in the work of the author under consideration something 'hidden' or 'profound' or 'secret' which has previously escaped notice." It lies in "*fitting together*, in the manner of a skilled cabinet-maker, the language of the day (Existentialism, Marxism, or psychoanalysis) and the language of the author, that is, the formal system of logical rules that he has evolved in the conditions of his time. . . .

The "formalist" approach explains the austerity or, more accurately, the aridity of some of the essays on individual authors.

Martin Turnell. Enc. Feb., 1966, pp. 32–35

What is generally taken for the French critical spirit is a highly developed taste for attacking intellectual dwarfs. . . . It is in fact largely gratuitous and incomprehensible except as a ritualistic act of self-congratulation. You would think from the hysterical sarcasm directed by some of the second-line new critics against the government and the press that they were being effectively persecuted, or at the very least that Frenchmen were being prevented from reading Roland Barthes and coerced into finding Pierre-Henri Simon of *Le monde* a more exciting critic of literature. Certainly the journalistic reaction to Barthes's *On Racine* was a particularly unpleasant and even violent display of philistinism, and, as we know, official hostility toward intellectual life does not have to become real persecution in order to be felt as oppressive. But the distinction between the two, which the French prefer to ignore, is a useful one to make, if only as an aid in determining proper strategies of resistance. Furthermore, some of the attacks on the new critics surely express intellectual insecurity more than ideological hostility: Barthes, Blanchot and [Jean-Pierre] Richard are by no means always easy to read, and they are at least as much a threat to intellectual vanity as they are to bourgeois institutions. . . .

The central piety of traditional criticism is a belief in the existence of an analyzable literary object. [Raymond] Picard, in his anti-new-critical pamphlet, *New Criticism or New Fraud?*, at least has the merit of explicitly, if somewhat simplemindedly, defending this belief. We can't, he argues, say just anything about Racine's plays: "There is a truth about Racine on which we can all agree." You wonder why this exegetic Utopia had not been reached before the new critics. Never mind; the objective aspects of literature which will lead us directly to interpretive unanimity are the certainties of language, the implications of psychological coherence and the structural imperatives of the tragic genre.

I won't insist on the obviously simplistic notions of linguistic meaning and psychological coherence which are the most glaring defects of this critical credo. More interesting, as Barthes points out in his answer to Picard (*Criticism and Truth*), is the question of the *kind* of interpretations sanctioned by an appeal to the supposedly objective criteria of a text's language and structure. . . . The central issue between Picard and Barthes (which both see, but which Picard is unable to argue effectively) is the *specificity* of literary language. To what extent are its structures different from those of other organizing systems, from, say, those of dreams or of myths? Barthes doesn't deny literature's specificity, but it could be said that, like other new critics in France, he neglects formal and textual particularities in order to repostulate them within a general theory of human signs.

Leo Bersani. *PR*. Spring, 1967, pp. 217–19

In *Criticism and Truth* Barthes replies to one objection that is frequently addressed to him: that his conception of criticism leads fatally to subjectivity in interpretation. He lists three sanctions that apply to criticism as he understands it. (1) It must take everything into account; it must find a place in a system of meanings for every detail. (2) It must proceed according to definite rules; however, they will be derived, not from a model of scientific reasoning in the usual sense, but from the logic (as yet only partly developed and understood) of symbolic language. Here linguistics will be powerfully aided by psychoanalysis, which already can provide some of the formulas by which polyvalent language may be unified—either from the analysis of persons, as practiced by Freud and others, or from the analysis of substances, as exemplified in the works of Gaston Bachelard and his disciples. Barthes mentions specifically the processes of substitution, omission, condensation, displacement, denegation. (3) It must move always in the same direction, assuming the same conditions accepted by the writer, and, in particular, this basic one, that *language*, not *the person speaking*, is the subject under consideration. If these three sanctions are observed, the critic is not by any means free to say "just anything." Bound by a kind of objectivity that fits his inquiry, he will trace out in a work long chains of transformations, developments of themes, and series of images.

Actually, criticism is only one of three activities that Barthes sees developing about literary works. It stands rather like a middle term between two other acts or disciplines. At the bottom, we have *lecture* or reading. When a text is merely read, the reader does not undertake to surround the original text or speech with a second text or speech; he desires the work, not his own language, as a means of doubling that of the author. On the second degree of the scale the critic accepts just this challenge, along with its risks, as he writes out the sense that he can give to the work. In the third place, Barthes sees the possibility of a science of literature, of a discipline that concerns itself not with the particular senses of literary works, but with their plurality of senses as a significant fact in itself, and with the logic of symbolic language. The model for this science is drawn from linguistics, specifically, from generative grammar. Just as generative grammar sets down the axioms, elements, and rules of combination for the construction of sentences in a language, so this science will state axioms, elements, and rules of combination for the construction of works, which are in a way like long and complicated sentences. Just as it is the business of such a grammar to state what the basis of *grammaticality* is in a language, it will be the business of the science of literature to describe the conditions of *acceptability* in combinations of symbolic speech. In a way this ambitious program picks up where Mallarmé and Valéry left off; I see in it the same enthusiasm for elements, functions, and rules of composition, but raised to a more abstract and systematic level of treatment.

Hugh M. Davidson. CL. Summer, 1968, pp. 373–74

To the two familiar concepts of language and style modern French critics have added a third—*écriture*, or "writing." . . . A mode of writing is arrived at by an act of choice. Not indeed a completely free choice. The writer chooses the social area within which he situates his work, but he chooses under the pressure of history and tradition. He cannot behave as though the whole gamut of possible modes is open to him in a non-temporal fashion. Much that once existed is out of reach; much that is available is contaminated with undesired associations. But a choice must be made, and when it is made it is a commitment to one aspect or another of the society of the time.

Barthes' argument, brief as it is, sketches the outline of a criticism that could be both literary in the strict sense—concerned with the literary use of language—and in a broader sense a humanistic study—concerned with human intention, with the choice of ends and means under the social and historical pressures in which men actually live. *Writing Degree Zero*, the brilliant essay of which it forms a part, also gives some summary illustrations of this criticism in action. It is to my mind the most impressive of Barthes' writings, some of which are certainly open to the objections that have so abundantly been brought against them. I cite it here not because it has any special pre-eminence in current critical theory, but because it is a striking example of a way of thinking about literature that has no analogue in English criticism. In England when we think of literary criticism as expanding into a humanist critique of culture in general we think of something that began with Matthew Arnold and has been going on with steadily decreasing momentum ever since.

Graham Hough. In Malcolm Bradbury and
David Palmer, eds., *Contemporary Criticism*
(New York, St. Martin's, 1970), pp. 39–40

Although very few contemporary critics formally claim membership in the "school" of "new criticism," the supporters of this criticism, taken as a whole, nevertheless propose some criteria that distinguish "new criticism" from so-called traditional criticism. Most importantly, the critic must *declare himself*. Forbidden is the dishonesty of a point of view that is not proclaimed, one lying behind the claim of objectivity. Barthes's vehemence on this subject can be heard in all its strength in *Mythologies* and can be found almost everywhere in his work, although perhaps without the same devastatingly witty brilliance. The critic worthy of the name therefore announces his position, his analytical method, and his ideology. . . .

We must insist on the fact that all of Barthes's work has a constant goal—the human meaning of all communication. The text to be ana-

lyzed can vary (advertising, painting, theater, food, fashion, or literature) and so can the methodology of the critic (Marxism, psychoanalysis, structuralism). This diversity has even led some of Barthes's critics
into error in evaluating his work. By willfully limiting their perspective,
these critics choose to see only the technical aspect of Barthes's work,
which they find abstract and dehumanized. Their overly restricted point
of view makes them miss an important truth about Barthes. From *Writing Degree Zero* to *The Empire of Signs* Barthes has been seeking the
connotation, the "secondary meaning," the irrevocably historical
meaning—and therefore the human meaning.

While Barthes's criticism has evolved in technique, his goal has
remained the same. Neither the thrust of his investigations, which have
always aimed at meaning, nor even, one might say, the object of those
investigations has changed, because sociological facts, too, have interested him from the beginning, just as much as strictly literary facts. We
can, however, see a methodological evolution. Without wanting to give
the word "evolution" a necessarily positive connotation, we merely note
that Barthes's work began under the aegis of psychoanalysis (Bache-
lardian, Freudian, or existential) before moving to an analytical technique that is more rigorously semeiological.

Guy de Mallac and Margaret Eberbach. Barthes
(Paris, Éditions Universitaires, 1971), pp. 10–11†

Barthes correctly describes structuralism as an endless activity of imitation founded not on the analogy of substances but on the analogy of
functions. And the final key language of structuralism is shelved in the
Library of Babel. The elegance and the terror of such a world view,
completely confined to discourse, is a veritable nightmare utopia composed out of nothing but impeccably organized writing; it is the subject
of Borges's work. When Barthes wishes to abolish the distinction between art and criticism he uses the word *writing* (*écriture*) to level the
difference between them (here again Borges' work comes to mind).
Thus writing illuminates writing, which in turn illuminates other writing
—to infinity. The sum total of all writing is silence, zero. The end of a
structuralist's job of work is, according to Barthes, silence, the silence
that comes with having reached the eschatalogical limit, said all there is
to say. [Claude] Lévi-Strauss too describes a work of his once written
as a dead being, a world in which he had very ardently lived but that
now excludes him from its intimacy.

In Barthes's case one is willing to accept Gérard Genette's view
(presented in a beautifully balanced essay in *Figures*) that what governs
the semiotic project is a nostalgia for objects and bodies whose solid
presence has the undeniable reality of Dr. Johnson's stone. Genette sees

Barthes longing for the silent quiddity of objects undisturbed by the intervening yammerings of language. There is, I think, no less a case for believing that Barthes and the structuralists long also for the zero calm of original primitivism and wholeness. The longing shores up the integrity of their faith in the irresistible metamorphic powers of language. For if one text might serve them all as a banner it is Ovid's *Metamorphoses*, that celebration of reality as ceaseless transformation and unhindered function for its own sake. Yet, Barthes, with [Michel] Foucault, Lévi-Strauss, and [Louis] Althusser, does have a stoically ironic and almost poetic vision of his own position that invigorates the solemnity of work done near an indefinitely postponed apocalypse.

Edward W. Said. In John K. Simon, ed.,
Modern French Criticism (Chicago, University of
Chicago Press, 1972), pp. 365–66

BATAILLE, GEORGES (1897–1962)

A work like Bataille's [*Inner Experience*] must be singled out as worthy of very special attention. I would not hesitate to call the book an essay in martyrdom (Bataille himself authorizes the label, because his book deals so often with agony). . . . He strips himself bare, he displays himself, and he is not a pleasant companion. Does the topic of human misery arise? Look, he says, at my ulcers and my wounds. And then he throws aside his clothing. But he is not trying to give vent to a poetic emotion. If he exhibits himself, it is to prove something. No sooner has he let us catch a glimpse of his wretched nakedness than he has covered himself again, and he involves us in an argument about Hegel's system or Descartes's *cogito*. And then the argument stops short and the man reappears. . . .

Some men could be called survivors. They have lost someone dear very early—a father, a friend, a mistress—and their lives are no longer anything but the dreary morning after that death. Bataille has survived the death of God. And if we reflect on the matter, it appears that our whole era has survived the same death that Bataille has lived through, suffered through, and survived. . . .

God is dead, but, even so, man has still not become an atheist. The silence of the transcendent being, joined with the persistence of modern man's religious need, is the great dilemma, today as yesterday. This is the problem that tormented Nietzsche, Heidegger, and Jaspers. This is Bataille's personal drama. [1943]

Jean-Paul Sartre. *Situations* (Paris, Gallimard, 1947),
Vol. I, pp. 133–34, 142†

Bataille scorns literary expression and one might observe with a certain malice that literary expression returns his sentiment. It is not artistic perfection that he seeks, and [*Hatred of Poetry*] is no more of a literary work from the standpoint of craftmanship than were its predecessors. As in the case of Pascal or Nietzsche its development allows of commentary and hastily formulated notation, as well as the sometimes obscure, sometimes illuminating expression of incommunicable subjective currents. Their value rarely resides in the image (the author has only a small quantity of these at his disposal which move constantly around the same theme), but rather in analogical suggestion. His fictions reject the narrative forms and are composed of elements thrown pell-mell together which hardly serve any purpose other than to bring to the level of clear awareness and render present by means of shifting approximations a substratum of permanent obsession. Bataille is not to be counted among those who reveal truth by the sheer quality of their writing.

Thus we are in the presence of a curious, disturbing figure whose distinctive features defy critical petrification. We should like to be able to imprison it behind the bars of a few definitions that would determine its place in our epoch and in the general movement of ideas. But we must content ourselves with reference points which, due to a movement of perpetual evolution, are themselves unstable. Freed from all intellectual and moral restraints and commanded by the strictest sense of honesty, Bataille rejects the various solutions proposed to the insoluble problem of the situation of modern man, and he constantly subjects those he himself has found and advocated to re-examination. He has nevertheless driven through the very heart of the eternal recurrence of his obsessions a firm axis: which is, the "feeling of being faced with a decisive combat from which nothing can now deter me." This combat, we divine, is the same in which Pascal, Sade, Rimbaud and Nietzsche were engaged. Only they threw themselves into it in all innocence, whereas Bataille knows that it can only end by his own defeat. He admits this and gaily, even, being impelled towards the impossible by a desire which has already made him master of many values that hold good for us all: rejection of the given world, revolt, the will towards universal communication, the conquest of total man—flesh and spirit, instinct, reason and intuition all intermingled—and the necessity for this total man to continue on his path, wherever it may lead. [1947]

Maurice Nadeau. Transition Forty-Eight. No. 4,
1948, pp. 111–12

Although Georges Bataille's *Story of the Eye* includes several named characters and the narrative of their erotic adventures, he certainly does not give us the story of Simone, Marcelle, or the narrator (as Sade could write the story of Justine or Juliette). *Story of the Eye* is actually the story of an object. How can an object have a story? No doubt it can pass from hand to hand . . . it can also pass from image to image, so that its story is that of a migration, the cycle of the avatars it traverses far from its original being, according to the tendency of a certain imagination which distorts yet does not discard it: this is the case with Bataille's book.

What happens to the Eye (and no longer to Marcelle, Simone, or the narrator) cannot be identified with ordinary fiction; the "adventures" of an object which simply changes owner derive from a novelistic imagination content to arrange reality; on the other hand, its "avatars," since they must be absolutely imaginary (and no longer simply "invented"), can be only the imagination itself: they are not its product but its substance. . . . The narrative is only a kind of flowing matter, a vehicle for the precious metaphoric substance: if we are in a park at night, it is so that a thread of moonlight can turn translucent the moist patch of Marcelle's sheet, which floats out the window of her room; if we are in Madrid, it is so that there can be a *corrida*, an offering of the bull's testicles, the enucleation of Granero's eye, and if in Seville, it is so that the sky there can express that yellowish liquid luminosity whose metaphoric nature we know by the rest of the chain. Even in the interior of each series, the narrative is a *form* whose constraint, fruitful on the same basis as the old metrical rules or the unities of tragedy, permits us to *extend* the terms of the metaphor beyond their constitutive virtuality. [1963]

Roland Barthes. *Critical Essays* (Evanston, Ill., Northwestern University Press, 1972), pp. 239, 243

The essays of Georges Bataille, which identify literature with evil, must seem strangely wrongheaded. They do few of the things that criticism is supposed to do: they do not explain much and they interpret even less; they disregard the formal structure of individual works, and their own structure looks haphazard and fragmentary. Finally, their strictures resemble the most outdated forms of ethical criticism, but they praise only immoral works. Bataille's approach to the written word is perverse, his scorn for the greater part of literature, narrow and uncompromising.

A bizarre terminology borrowed from Hegel, political science, ethnology, economics, and mysticism disconcerts the reader who does not readily grasp its relevance to literary problems. On the other hand, Bataille ignores the technical terms derived from rhetoric, poetics, and linguistics which have brought some measure of lucidity to modern critical discourse.

Such key words as "sovereignty," "evil," "transgression," "excess," and "consummation," with their connotation of barbaric ritual, bespeak Bataille's refusal of "civilization": to him, literature belongs outside the law, it challenges order. Through writing, modern man attempts a return to the primitive darkness of violence and eroticism. Literature must seek the antipodes of reason and culture, or sink into nothingness.

As a writer, and a critic, Bataille himself tried to be an outlaw: his underground, pornographic novels constitute an aggression against taste, morality, and the regular uses of language. His criticism defies all lawful theories of literature and chooses to explore the wilderness of violence. The field of rational criticism begins where Bataille's meditation on the written word ends, and the two approaches do not readily meet in a unified field. Bataille does not yield to synthesizing efforts. Between Bataille and most other critics (with the exception of such outsiders as Blanchot, [Pierre] Klossowski, and [Roger] Caillois), there lies a precipitous gap. Bataille's thought endangers all criticism. . . .

We cannot pin Bataille down; reading his essays is like wrestling with an elusive angel, or with an invader from a fourth dimension. To make matters worse, we are faced with Bataille's laughter, which punctuates his excursions into nonsense. Bataille laughs at himself and at the reader, signifying that man is the odd animal endowed with reason who can speak outside reason and still make a strange kind of sense—the only kind of sense that matters, perhaps, in view of man's tragic condition in a godless world.

Michel Beaujour. In John K. Simon, ed., Modern French Criticism (Chicago, University of Chicago Press, 1972), pp. 149–51

Bataille wrote in fragments as Nietzsche wrote in aphorisms, but the fragments are linked by a similarity of emotion rather than by structure or by an intellectual dialectic. In Bataille's work, the fragmentary mode of writing used by Pascal and Nietzsche came into its own. Pascal's notes were intended as a basis for a coherent apologia, and Nietzsche's for a systematic treatise. For them, the fragment was merely a temporary expedient; for Bataille, it was a deliberately chosen form, the only one suitable to his thought. Bataille did not wish either to demonstrate or to construct; he was not concerned with communicating knowledge or a system. He did not speculate on an experience in order to convert it into thought; he *was* his experience, and he had to express it in its entirety at the first attempt. Moreover, his experience was such that it could not take an intellectual form, because it was an awareness of that primordial unity which thought must inevitably destroy, because thought implies division. Bataille's inner experience was the experience of not knowing. . . .

One may legitimately wonder how Bataille was able to come down from the "sovereign experience" to the mundane world of revolutionary political thought? For Bataille has this interest as well, and he devoted a great many essays to the structures of fascism, communism, and capitalism; and he always made specific political choices. Although it is hard to reconcile these two sides of Bataille, it must be pointed out that in none of his work did Bataille look for shortcuts; he opened up the whole range of contemporary thought. He heralded contemporary thought by rejecting all counterfeits, all the meanings that humanism was content to accept. No one has better expressed the realization that everything that has been said is silent on what there is to say; no one has better cleared the ground.

> Gaëtan Picon. *Contemporary French Literature*
> (New York, Frederick Ungar, 1974),
> pp. 73, 75

BAZIN, HERVÉ (1911–   )

Viper in the Fist, the first novel by a young French writer, Hervé Bazin, is an awkward proposition from the critical point of view. It is extremely entertaining as farce, and the temptation is to let it go at that, but it has been festooned with literary awards—the Prix Apollinaire and the Prix des Lecteurs—whose respectability pushes one toward considering it as serious literature. As soon as one does so, however, it becomes apparent that it is concerned with ideas that are untenable and corrupt. So the critic is compelled to a two-faced performance, saying with one mouth, "This is very good fun," and with the other, "This is a fundamentally worthless book of a rather dangerous kind." M. Bazin is an abundantly gifted writer, with a mastery of comedy, who has invested his talent in making a statement that is not worth making about his own experience, and developing a theory of life from it that is manifestly false. The statement can be summarized as "Mummy was a bitch, and I had a horrid, horrid childhood." . . .

What gives Bazin's infantilism its interest is the singular transparency of its form and the directness with which it arrives at a new literary low point. There has probably never been a time before in the history of any culture when the idea of a grown man sitting down to build a work of art around the simple whimper "I hate Mummy" would have been received with anything but incredulous laughter. Bazin's performance is symptomatic; he is far from being alone. What makes him seem alone is his explicitness; most infantilist writing is screened by symbolism and generally clouded by rebel syntax into the bargain.

Anthony West. NY. May 26, 1951, p. 111

The characters of Hervé Bazin want to be totally and gratuitously what they are. As a rule, they are only weak or ill in order to struggle all the better. It is never the worn-out body that gives way, but the will. It is better to be abnormal than to be weak. This presumes, at the very least, that they have all their wits: the paradox is that even if they hurl their heads against the walls, they keep them very solidly planted on their shoulders.

Their common misery is the inability to admit that a thousand and one social barriers are interposed between what they *know* they are and what others believe that they are. Revolt—which enlarges them in their own eyes and saves them—often comes from this lack of power to achieve their potential, from this feeling of being imprisoned for life. The more others try, from the exterior, to crush them, the more energy they rediscover to foil the plots of others. The only way to overcome these indomitable characters would be to seem to share their points of view. Because of a failure to see clearly, their adversaries are always beaten. In making peace Folcoche, if not actually disarming him, would at least mislead Brasse-Bouillon, and this is what happens at the end of *Viper in the Fist*. But in taking the offensive again, in *The Death of the Little Horse*, she will give her son the definitive method of conquering her. The pride of the two protagonists is so great that each one is convinced that he can come out of the battle with a victory.

Constance Orglaise [in *Stand Up and Walk*], if she were healthy, would have been nothing but an insufferable girl who was too self-satisfied. Because she is sick, she draws her strength from her illness and finds energy in the weakness of others. . . . Her bitter compensation is knowingly to eliminate all metaphysical concerns from her attitude. She would not have the bad taste to do it diabolically because, not believing in God, she does not believe in the devil.

Pierre Cogny. Sept romanciers au-delà du roman
(Paris, A. G. Nizet, 1963), pp. 44–45†

Certainly, one of the elements that worked against Hervé Bazin [in *Viper in the Fist*] was his frankness. Let us agree that his book would have gained in persuasiveness if he had stripped it of some of its excesses of language. The narrator generally calls his mother the "old hag" and the "old bat," not usual phrases for an offspring speaking of his mother. He could have made a better point by more often using the sober "Madame Rezeau," a phrase that sounds awful enough coming from a son. This lack of restraint betrays the tempestuousness of his bitterness. In more than one place in his novel Bazin shows enough precocious mastery to have been able to lower his register if he had so desired. . . .

Bazin, in a contradictory manner, has sometimes acknowledged and sometimes denied that the two novels about the Rezeau family (*Viper in the Fist, The Death of the Little Horse*) are autobiographical. "Let's say twenty-five percent," he once conceded. But he also said, "Don't try to sort it out, because I can't do that myself." . . .

Bazin is, among contemporary novelists, one of the most sensitive and most attentive to the concerns of the present. (I can surely reveal that at the Académie Goncourt, in its discussions at the end of the year, this criterion of "problems of the present time" is the one that comes to members' lips most often and influences the choice of prize-winners.) Yet Bazin has never ceased to look in the same direction as when he began, with the same questioning and the same pity. This is what entitles us and obliges us to speak so much about *Viper in the Fist* whenever we seek to focus on his work as a whole. While this first novel of his is not his greatest, or his best written (which, in my opinion, is *Whom I Dare Love*), or his most innovative (which, I think, is *In the Name of the Son*), it is, nevertheless, an overture in which all his major themes are present.

Philippe Hériat. *RDM*. May, 1966, pp. 8, 11–12†

[*Matrimony* presents the] terrifying picture of the housewife who is turned into an infant by her daily habits and chores, of the mother who grows old herself and becomes weak as a result of playing her role, completely occupied with talking nonsense with her brats. What a fate for a nice girl, what a pitiable future! Bazin spares us nothing: the humiliations, the smudges, the sordid details of feminine life, the obsession with pregnancies, the myth of the pill, the tragedy of abortion. This book is an accumulation of ugly morbidities; it would be absolutely unbearable without the taut and lively style and without the sneering that is occasionally pushed into laughter. Is this therefore a defense of women? On the contrary! But unintentionally, by repeating that men are the victims of women (has not this been Bazin's theme since *Viper in the Fist*?), the writer has shown simply that both sexes are the victims of life.

The subject here is life, life "as it is," on its most mediocre level, that of the little households of shopkeepers, of unsuccessful lawyers, of nice guys who are very ordinary, the ones who populate our streets. And life is first of all marriage, that pitiful curve that extends from engagements without love to children's sicknesses, to marital quarrels, to shabby aging, passing through inevitable adultery: a swamp of foul water. Bazin's gaze makes things unclean, but unfortunately this comes from his lucidity. What he discovers with his bitter humor is absolutely true. . . . And yet this reading of life is a treason! Nothing shows the mystery of happiness better than this furious accusation. How can the flower of tenderness take root in such a desert? How can the sacred find a nest in so much vulgarity? And when Bazin is not looking, why does the exasperating baby Loulou assume the appearance of an angel? Bazin explores the opposite side of the coin. Fortunately, true life is elsewhere —on the side Bazin refuses to see. Therefore, this book, which is so true, is thoroughly false, because it is inhuman.

Jean Onimus. TR. May, 1968, pp. 113–14†

Why on earth are there so many nasty mamas in our literature . . . so many savage mothers, so many emasculating matriarchs who raise the same face, ripened by rancor, and the same murderous umbrella above our best pages? . . . Everyone knows that it is with such a monster that Hervé Bazin made a boisterous debut twenty-five years ago. Intact in our memories . . . the Folcoche of *Viper in the Fist* has become something that immortalizes a character in a novel: a type beyond psychology and pathology, a natural force, the symbol of a class, a point of reference, almost a common noun. . . . Although a half-century has elapsed [since the period described in *Viper in the Fist*]—a half-century about which we know almost nothing except that the widow Rezeau has spent it selling off meadowland and closing the rooms of the "Belle Angerie" one by one—here she is again [in *The Cry of the Screech Owl*] as she was in the most glorious days of her reign. . . .

In our collection of accounts of maternal deaths, all the striving for detachment established by [François] Mauriac, out of his sense of decency, by [Roger] Peyrefitte, out of a desire to provoke, or by Simone de Beauvoir, in the name of phenomenology, has now been demolished. It is difficult to believe that a son, even if he has suffered from a lack of love, could observe the dying agony of his own mother, as this one does, while munching sandwiches, with no more uneasiness than if he were watching a machine coming to a stop, without the least trembling of his pen, with much less emotion and style than in listening to the bell of his childhood ring for the last time. . . .

Once the screech owl has uttered its cry, the book falls back on the family chronicles that Bazin, notably in *Matrimony*, has made a popular specialty. All that matters now is for parents to learn how the young people of 1972 lose their innocence or just miss reform school. . . . The immediate sympathy that a vast public now feels for Hervé Bazin is certainly due primarily to his lack of a particular style, to his tone of a father who does what he can and who says so in ordinary language, in everyday language, to his refusal to put on airs and to write "literature" in the sense that the word is ordinarily understood—a difficult lie for an educated class of readers.

Bertrand Poirot-Delpech. *Le monde*. Oct. 6, 1972, p. 17†

BEAUVOIR, SIMONE DE (1908–   )

The characters in *The Guest* lack any "moral sense." They do not find good and evil in things. They do not believe that human life, by itself, makes any definite demands, or that it follows a self-contained law as trees or bees do. They consider the world (including society and their own bodies) as an "unfinished piece of work"—to use [Nicolas de] Malebranche's profound phrase—which they question with curiosity and treat in various ways.

It is not so much their actions which bring down censure on these characters. Books, after all, are full of adultery, perversion, and crime, and the critics have come across them before this. The smallest town has more than one *ménage à trois*. Such a "family" is still a family. But how is one to accept the fact that Pierre, Françoise, and Xavière are totally ignorant of the holy natural law of the couple and that they try in all honesty—and without, moreover, any hint of sexual complicity—to form a trio? The sinner is always accepted, even in the strictest societies, because he is part of the system and, as a sinner, does not question its principles. What one finds unbearable in Pierre and Françoise is their artless disavowal of morality, that air of candor and youth, that absolute lack of gravity, dizziness, and remorse. In brief, they think as they act and act as they think. . . .

True morality does not consist in following exterior rules or in respecting objective values: there are no ways to *be* just or to *be* saved. One would do better to pay less attention to the unusual situation of the three characters in *The Guest* and more to the good faith, the loyalty to promises, the respect for others, the generosity and the seriousness of the two principals [Pierre and Françoise]. For the value is there. It consists of actively being what we are by chance, of establishing that communication with others and with ourselves for which our temporal structure gives us the opportunity and of which our liberty is only the rough outline. [1945]

Maurice Merleau-Ponty. *Sense and Non-Sense* (Evanston, Ill., Northwestern University Press, 1964), pp. 38–40

Simone de Beauvoir! How this noble and likeable woman can disturb and irritate us! Her books seize our attention and charm us, but are difficult to evaluate. In her latest novel, *All Men Are Mortal*, she contrives outlandish situations yet, through her art, impresses them upon the reader's memory. She succeeds in giving physical presence and weight to a timeless character type; but although she achieves such a worthy success, when she tries too hard to understand these individuals, with whom she has made us so familiar through her very simple and personal manner of putting them into action, she awkwardly freezes them. . . . [Beauvoir's] good faith and integrity are the very qualities that prevent her from gaining control over certain situations. She is a victim of her moral virtues because she uses them toward aesthetic ends. . . .

Extremely gifted and courageous, Simone de Beauvoir sometimes has the sparks of a masculine genius and a gift for poetry that is as bewitching as a child's outburst of anger. But she bears the burden of the absurdities of both philosophy and scholarship: she is the sacrificial offering of existentialism.

Joë Bousquet. Critique. May, 1947, pp. 390–92†

There are so many things I want to say about [*The Second Sex*]. First, that it is a great book, a book that will be read long after most works which have been written on the subject will have been forgotten. Second, in its qualities of analysis, restrained eloquence, and the influence it is bound to have upon human thought and conduct, it ranks next to John Stuart Mill's *Subjection of Women* (1869). Third, one cannot help being impressed by the skill with which the author has avoided the pitfalls into which so many others have fallen in discussing such thoroughly misunderstood institutions, for example, as matriarchy. Fourth, the balance, good common sense, and profound insight of the author constitute a most refreshing and illuminating experience in an area in which the discussion is usually tendentious and biased. Fifth, the book is beautifully written in all senses of the word. And sixth, while the book could have been written by a man, it took a woman to do it. . . .

Woman, as the author points out, is brought up without ever being impressed with the necessity of taking charge of her own existence. Men have taken it over, and have oppressed women; as oppressors they cannot be expected to make a move of gratuitous generosity. It will be up to the women of the world fully to emancipate themselves. Some men will help, but for the present women will largely be forced to do the necessary work for themselves. Meanwhile, Simone de Beauvoir's *The Second Sex* may serve them not only as a breviary but also as a call to action.

Ashley Montagu. SR. Feb. 21, 1953, p. 29

Just as all the men [in *The Mandarins*] are alike, the women are varied and autonomous, simultaneously real and fictional. . . . As soon as a woman—whatever her character may be—steps into a narrative by Simone de Beauvoir, and as soon as the question of love is raised, everything becomes firmer and brighter. Simply from the narrative related by Anne—indeed, simply from those fragments in her account that concern her brief love affair in America with Lewis Brogan—one can extract one of the most striking love stories ever written by a woman. This story contains everything—the sudden and heart-rending revelation, the wonder of the first night, the great fire of happiness, the ashes of the separations, the anguish of the silences, the alternations between hope and doubt, the ambiguity of the reunions. . . . At the end of the novel, having lost her lover and feeling certain that neither her daughter nor her husband nor her friends need her any more, Anne comes very close to doubting that there is meaning in anything. Yet it is she who, through the passion for life she radiates, makes the novel pulsate. Nothing escapes her; she does not lie about anything. . . .

The novel's universe is one in which nobody else lies either. The women especially are ferociously honest; even the unbearable Nadine plans her evil deeds openly. The reader shudders to see Anne so willingly recognize the face she will have in ten years in the faces of other women; and also to see her recognize that saying so is a more subtle way of maintaining her self-esteem as a woman. It is certain that this particularly feminine keenness, toughness, and shrewdness constitute a great deal of the power of *The Mandarins*.

Dominique Aury. *NRF*. Dec., 1954, pp. 1082–84†

What a course has been traversed between *The Guest* and *The Mandarins*! . . . The remarkable fact is that the most recent novel has all the qualities generally found in a first novel: spontaneity, rich inner life, and many varied characters. One obtains from reading it the impression of vigor and youth, and at the same time the impression that an experience has been revealed in its totality, as happens in those first books in which the author tells everything.

Everything flows naturally, and everything seems matured in this novel. The reader may prefer *The Guest* because of its classical strictness and its philosophical basis, or *All Men Are Mortal* because of the originality of its theme and the existential anguish that emerges from it. But *The Mandarins* has much richer resonances. The multiplicity of the themes, the vigorous tone, and above all the emotional sensitivity revealed in Anne's story make this novel perhaps Beauvoir's masterpiece. It is undoubtedly not by chance that the heroine of the book, unlike Beauvoir's other heroines, is a married woman and a mother (and even soon to be a grandmother!). . . . She calmly accepts the limitations imposed by her sex. . . .

As different as they may be, all of Beauvoir's female characters accept their condition as women. . . . But until the great achievement of *The Mandarins*, there was still something cerebral and slightly artificial in the portrayal of these women, who had only a distant relationship to their creator. It was in *The Second Sex* that Beauvoir had put all of herself.

Geneviève Gennari. *Simone de Beauvoir* (Paris, Éditions Universitaires, 1958), pp. 76–77, 80†

André Gide, one of the writers who represented liberation to Simone de Beauvoir during her trying adolescence, poignantly attempted, or thought he attempted, to achieve sincerity toward himself (and, of course, toward the reader at the same time). [Beauvoir in *Memoirs of a Dutiful Daughter*] has succeeded in achieving this sincerity as if the task were child's play. As the title suggests, these memoirs are full of humor; and it is quite wonderful to see an extraordinary mind contemplating itself, in its development since childhood, with a sly lucidity and a total absence of both complacency and malice. . . .

The narrative unfolds through two simultaneous perspectives: that of the student who comes up against the contradictions of her bourgeois universe and tries, in a somewhat frenzied way, to "get other people interested in her soul"; and that of the writer who has reached full maturity and reflects back upon her past, not because she is narcissistic but because this past is characteristic of an age of transition and because one can better refer to one's own memories than to the memories of others. I am not saying that Beauvoir is not strongly egocentric; but her egocentrism somewhat resembles the sun: it casts its rays in all directions.

Béatrix Beck. *RdP*. Dec., 1958, p. 168†

The Blood of Others is no doubt, of all the Existentialist novels, the one to focus most sharply on the problem of involvement, giving it its neatest artistic formulation. The epigraph from *The Brothers Karamazov* sets the tone: "Everyone is responsible to everybody for everything." The novel, on the surface at least, appears to illustrate this dictum.

It also queries it. *The Blood of Others* is far from a simple demonstration. Concerned with the dense and shifting texture of existence, Simone de Beauvoir is aware that no situation can ever be entirely limpid or entirely imperative. The interest of the book stems in part from an implicit dialectical movement. The author develops an ethic of *engagement* [commitment] while concerned, on the psychological level, with the intertwined and often paralyzing strands of guilt, solidarity and alienation. Similarly the hero, in quest of a guiding truth, discovers that he has penetrated into a blind alley. If on the one hand the novel is a clear formulation of Existentialist ethics, it also presents in dramatic terms the most characteristic Existentialist ambiguities. . . .

The Blood of Others is not an easy book. The point of view, largely retrospective, implies a steady reassessment of past events and past attitudes. The language is often abstract. The fundamental outlook, when love is being considered, is remarkably austere. The characters, as well as the author, seem permanently afflicted with a Jansenist pessimism. . . . Yet the difficulty of the technique (the frequent unheralded switches of point of view), as well as the intransigent moral tone of the book, also prevent the main themes from degenerating into pedestrian thesis-literature. Moreover, the novel deals not merely with abstractions. *The Blood of Others* is among the few excellent books about the Occupation and the Resistance. Simone de Beauvoir succeeded not only in creating a number of touching scenes . . . but in dramatizing in a sustained manner the difficulty of living.

Victor Brombert. *The Intellectual Hero: Studies in
the French Novel, 1880–1955* (Philadelphia,
J. B. Lippincott, 1961), pp. 232–34

[*The Prime of Life*] is a book with a heroine—the narrator—and a hero—Sartre; and its central narrative is the story of their life together. Although it does not dwell, as a novel might, on the sexual *rapports* between its chief protagonists, it has much to say about human relationships and the connexion between the world of ideas and the world of personal experience. It is, in a way, a romantic story. During their early years together Sartre and Simone de Beauvoir were much separated, with Simone de Beauvoir in Marseille and Sartre in Laon or Berlin. But later, when she was working in Rouen and he at Le Havre, they could meet regularly and when Sartre found work in Paris they were able to take rooms in the same hotel. They never set up house together and a great deal of their time was spent in cafés (something hardly conceivable in any country but France). Simone de Beauvoir did all her writing at café tables, and it was in cafés—notably the Flore—that they held court after they became successful and before an even greater fame drove them into a more retired way of life.

Simone de Beauvoir explains that she and Sartre would have married if there had been a question of having children; as a childless couple, they could find no valid reason for compromising with their anti-bourgeois principles. She declares that she herself never felt any desire for children, but from the life she describes in her memoirs and the situations which recur in her novels, it is obvious that parental relationships in some transmuted form have had an important place in her experience. Sartre and she have together moulded more than one young person's life; and these young protégés and protégées were, in a sense, their children, just as their favourite cafés were their home.

Maurice Cranston. In John Cruickshank, ed.,
The Novelist as Philosopher (London, Oxford
University Press, 1962), pp. 179–80

Simone de Beauvoir's novels, like Sartre's, are kneaded out of metaphysics. She believes it is just as valid to write metaphysical novels as it is to write psychological novels, and that the novelist's job is to depict the emotional consequences of metaphysical experience. In *her* work however, philosophy serves only as leavening, as yeast; in Sartre's it is the dough itself. . . .

In her non-fiction Simone de Beauvoir intends to cut deep, and does. "I'm not interested in resorting to emotional appeals when I have the truth on my side." In her novels, on the other hand, she concentrates on nuance. "My non-fiction reflects my personal choices; my novels the state of wonderment the human condition—both as a whole and in its particulars—throws me into." Only a novel could allow her to sort out the multiple swirling significations of the changed world she awoke to in 1944. . . . She wrote *The Mandarins*. She wanted to depict intellectuals, a special breed "whom people advise novelists not to rub elbows with." But people are wrong; an intelligent man's experiences can be equally as interesting as those of an illiterate; and intellectuals are, after all, human beings with human feelings.

Many have talked about *The Mandarins* as a roman à clef, pointing out that Dubreuil and Henri are Sartre and Camus, and that Dubreuil's wife, Anne, is Simone de Beauvoir herself. But this is totally to misunderstand the nature of fiction. A novelist gives his characters certain traits of actual people, but he doesn't paint portraits. He transforms, he mixes, he shifts, he constructs. Dubreuil is an elderly man and very different from Sartre. Henri is like Camus in being young, dark-complected, and the editor of a newspaper, but "the similarity ends there." . . .

"All of the materials that I drew from memory, I broke up, twisted around, hammered out, exaggerated, combined, transposed, distorted, even sometimes made their opposite, and in each and every instance re-created. I hoped that people would take the book for what it is—not autobiography or reportage, but an evocation." That, indeed, is just what it is—the compelling evocation of a group, of a period, of a state of mind—and a great novel, one of the best of our time. [1965]

André Maurois. *From Proust to Camus: Profiles of*
Modern French Writers (Garden City, N.Y.,
Doubleday, 1966), pp. 329–30, 333–34

The more I read of Mlle. Beauvoir, the more I have the impression that I met her, under various manifestations, during my schooldays. No doubt there is one in every educational establishment. She was the one in the front row of the class whose high marks led you to hope for an original intelligence. Disappointed (quickly) of that, you still looked for a reliable academic mind. It turned out to be a mind capable of missing entire points, and incapable both of the precision of an artist and of the accuracy of a scholar. Not inspired enough to be slapdash, it was often slipshod. In the end, you were obliged to admit that the high marks reflected nothing but obedient work; that what seemed to be intellectual passion was only a sense of duty—plus, it might be, a devotion to the professor; that you were up against, in short, a plodder. . . .

The third and latest volume of her autobiography [*The Force of Things*] is Mlle. Beauvoir's most pedestrian plod yet. It covers the years—1944 to 1962—in which she was pretty much top of the class, thanks partly, it seems fair to guess, to her devotion to the professor but thanks also to the prevailing mystical belief that the tedious must be profound. Her method here is simply to amass. . . .

It is sheer heap. . . . In it, intellectual analysis and atmosphere are alike suffocated. The political vision is as banal as a leader-writer's: there are two power blocs in the world, and it is hard for a European intellectual to choose between them. Mlle. Beauvoir's account of her trip from a still austere France to the luxuries of Switzerland is less evocative than one stylish nail-paring from Colette's aged and arthritic hand —the baroque paean of gluttony, for instance, which (in *The Blue Lantern*) Colette made of *her* postwar visit to Geneva. . . .

Sense of style Mlle. Beauvoir seems to lack utterly. She claims "a certain rigour" for the style of this book—but that is almost as ironic as her fear of sounding pedantic if she finishes her sentences in conversation. So far is she from pedantry that in this book she does not get the middle of her sentences syntactically correct. . . .

Mlle. Beauvoir has often (though not so often as she might, had she exercised her intellect and imagination more ardently) been on the side of the angels; but the method by which she arrived there must often have been enough to make the angels weep.

Brigid Brophy. *NYT*. May 9, 1965, pp. 1, 24–25

In addition to working out the ethical implications of existentialist thought in action and in art, Simone de Beauvoir has brought to the movement an emphasis which is uniquely hers and which may stand ultimately as her most original contribution. She has expressed the *emotional* side of philosophical and moral issues with striking force. Her pursuit of personal happiness has led her to concentrate on the more immediate, less abstract facets of life. She frequently expresses a joy in living uncharacteristic of much of existentialist literature. . . . She has demanded that the capacity for joy be allowed to unfold in places where it was absent: in female sexuality, in oppressed minorities, and under-developed countries. In her monumental (and often incredibly dull) *The Second Sex* she elaborated an existential interpretation of women in the modern world based primarily on her concern with the self-other dilemma. In her autobiography she succinctly states her thesis thus: "Femininity is not an essence or a nature: it is a situation created by civilizations on the basis of certain psychological facts." The "female condition" is something she has sought to remedy by illustration in her writings and by example in her own life. . . .

In the best of her novels she evokes an emotional, sensible universe, where responsibility is *felt* rather than demonstrated. She is both easier to read and less profound than Sartre, her technique less radical, her characters either far more vivid than his or, when unsuccessfully created, totally wooden. In existentialist fiction, Simone de Beauvoir occupies a domain which is uniquely her own. In her concern with the relationship between sensibility and responsibility, best expressed in *The Guest* and *The Mandarins*, she has achieved an imaginative re-creation of the human situation in mid-century.

Rima Drell Reck. *Literature and Responsibility*
(Baton Rouge, Louisiana State University Press,
1969), pp. 88–89, 115

In *Old Age* Simone de Beauvoir has written an extraordinary, altogether engrossing, large work on growing old. I cannot take issue with it since in its sweep I have learned all that I know about the matter. Personal experience and observation are confirmed and enriched at every point by the learned intensity of the book and the generosity of the feelings. A fluent use of history and literature, the portraits of great and humble persons who were given long life, the lessons of philosophy and the power of social indignation—these come together in a prodigious outburst of energy and imagination. . . .

About our life today, *Old Age* is a fierce indictment of society's indifference and cruelty toward old people. The degradation, the hatred of the elderly are scarcely recognized and their plight, shrouded not so much in ignorance as in the determination to ignore, is harsh beyond all necessity. . . . The only way to give old age decency is, in the author's view, to give "value to the life of others, by means of love, friendship, indignation, compassion." The huge space between those privileged, either by talent or class, and the great body of mankind is at its most dishonorable and unjust in the case of the old. Millions of people are literally abandoned, "scrapped," as if while still breathing they were already dead, buried alive.

The ruins of time—a tragic, inescapable subject.

Elizabeth Hardwick. *NYT*. May 14, 1972, pp. 1, 42

The death of Simone de Beauvoir's mother is the most detailed of all the encounters with death [in her work]. It is the only death to which an entire book is devoted although it might be said that the memoirs are, in fact, about the death of Simone de Beauvoir. This book [*A Very Easy Death*], in which there is more mother and less I, is perhaps Simone de Beauvoir's best. Neither fiction nor memoir, *A Very Easy Death* is a *récit-reportage* [short-narrative–journalism] shorter in length and more tightly constructed than Simone de Beauvoir's other writings. . . .

The reader who is familiar with the three volumes of Simone de Beauvoir's memoirs is familiar, too, with the figure of Françoise de Beauvoir. Simone de Beauvoir portrays her mother as a rather attractive but silly woman, a willing victim of the Catholic milieu to which she belonged and enthusiastically adhered. The reader shares Simone de Beauvoir's resentment of the innumerable prejudices that clogged Françoise de Beauvoir's mind and heart and that restricted her capacity to feel and see. Simone de Beauvoir is quite explicit about her own preference for her non-conformist father. She was never very close to her mother, and one senses that her revolt against the despicable bourgeoisie is, in part, an outgrowth of her revolt against Françoise de Beauvoir. . . . [But] what she thought she felt about her mother does not coincide with what she feels during the long agony.

The pity, horror, and helplessness the reader of *A Very Easy Death* feels, corresponds both to the author's central emotion and to the underlying theme. No attempt is made at any moment in the main body of the *récit* to transcend the facts of dying or the sentiments, gestures, and words of the woman who is dying and the daughters who are watching her die. The irony of both the Dylan Thomas quotation which is used as an epigraph, "Do not go gentle into that good night," and of the title is continued throughout the book in a courageous desire to break through some of the simplistic left-wing ideology that often replaces intelligent analysis in her other books. When the bourgeois Catholic images which she had so firmly and so conveniently affixed to her mother are displaced, a human being begins to die, and Simone de Beauvoir begins to suffer for someone other than herself. Sartre is absent from all but two scenes in the *récit*, and this significant absence helps to explain Simone de Beauvoir's ability to sustain, for so long a time, an excruciating lucidity.

Elaine Marks. *Simone de Beauvoir: Encounters with Death* (New Brunswick, N.J., Rutgers University Press, 1973), pp. 100–102

Beauvoir distinguishes sharply between the nature of fiction and that of autobiography. She believes that a novel, however loosely constructed, ends up conveying a sense of an inevitable sequence of events. It cannot convey the sense of uncertainty, of limitless possibilities, of an unformed future which is characteristic of experience. On the other hand, she believes that in an autobiography she can present events in all their gratuitousness, their apparent meaninglessness, and thus remain closer to experience. "There is a danger," she recognizes, "that through this capricious profusion, the reader, unable to distinguish any clear image, will see only a jumble."

No reader would accuse the first volume of the autobiography, *Memoirs of a Dutiful Daughter,* of being "a jumble." It is one of Beauvoir's most rigorously composed books. She herself explains that if this volume has more unity than the others it is because her childhood and adolescence were guided by a clear and overriding goal: to become an adult. The last three volumes—*The Prime of Life, The Force of Things,* and especially *All Said and Done*—are in fact marked by the presence of gratuitous and seemingly meaningless details (lists of films she has seen, books she has read, records she has listened to) that annoy some readers but that, for others, convey to a remarkable degree the sense of contingency, the untidiness of life itself. . . .

More discursive and ruminative than the previous volumes, *All Said and Done* bears somewhat the same relationship to the complete autobiography that Montaigne's third and final book of essays bears to his entire *Essays*. Both authors seem ultimately to establish a curious kind of distance between the self and the world. Not that either loses interest in the surrounding world. On the contrary, in none of Montaigne's essays is the physical world with its clutter, its jumble of things and sensations more present than in the essays of the last book. And in none of Beauvoir's books is the everyday hum of life, the trivia of daily existence, more pervasively present than in *All Said and Done*.

Robert D. Cottrell. *Simone de Beauvoir* (New York, Frederick Ungar, 1975), pp. 133, 146

BECKETT, SAMUEL (1906–   )

It is easy, flippant, and correct to say that Mr. Samuel Beckett—whose first, very imitative novel, *More Pricks than Kicks*, I remember more by Joyce than chance—has not yet thrown off the influence of those writers who have made [the journal] *transition* their permanent resting-place. But Mr. Beckett, who is a great legpuller and an enemy of obviousness, would hate to be reviewed by the cash-register system that deals in the currency of petty facts and penny praises, so if I do not straightforwardly praise his new book *Murphy*, for its obvious qualities—of energy, hilarity, irony, and comic invention—then it is his fault: he should never try to sell his bluffs over the double counter. I must say that *Murphy* is difficult, serious, and wrong.

It is difficult because it is written in a style that attempts to make up for its general verbosity by the difficulty of the words and phrases it uses for the sake of particular economy, and because the story never quite knows whether it is being told objectively from the inside of its characters or subjectively from the outside. It is serious because it is, mainly, the study of a complex and oddly tragic character who cannot reconcile the unreality of the seen world with the reality of the unseen, and who, through scorn and neglect of "normal" society, drifts into the society of the certified abnormal in his search for "a little world." Murphy is the individual ostrich in the mass-produced desert.

I call the book wrong for many reasons. It is not rightly what it should be, that is, what Mr. Beckett intended it to be: a story about the conflict between the inside and the outsides of certain curious people. It fails in its purpose because the minds and the bodies of these characters are almost utterly without relations to each other. . . . Mr. Beckett supposes that he writes about the lowest strata of society, about the dispossessed and the regardless-of-possession, but he takes a most romantic view of it; he looks generously at the dregs, and makes every dirty, empty tankard wink at the brim; romantically he searches in the gutter for splendour and, in every fool and villain he finds, substitutes the gunpowder brain for the heart of gold.

And, lastly, Mr. Beckett's humour, for the book is packed with it even in the most serious sections and the most pathological discussions. Sometimes the humour is like that of an Irish comic journalist forced to write in an advanced Paris-American quarterly, sometimes like that of an old-fashioned music-hall character-comedian attempting to alter his

the same gesture. Joyce suddenly asked some such question as, "How could the idealist Hume write a history?" Beckett replied, "A history of representations." . . .

[Joyce] would ask the young man to read to him passages from [Fritz] Mauthner's *Beiträge zu Einer Kritik der Sprache*, in which the nominalistic view of language seemed something Joyce was looking for. Once or twice he dictated a bit of *Finnegans Wake* to Beckett, though dictation did not work very well for him; in the middle of one such session there was a knock at the door which Beckett didn't hear. Joyce said, "Come in," and Beckett wrote it down. Afterwards he read back what he had written and Joyce said, "What's that 'Come in'?" "Yes, you said that," said Beckett. Joyce thought for a moment, then said, "Let it stand." He was quite willing to accept coincidence as his collaborator. Beckett was fascinated and thwarted by Joyce's singular method.

Richard Ellmann. *James Joyce* (New York,
Oxford University Press, 1959), pp. 661–62

The stream of consciousness, so lively and going dramatically from image to image in Joyce, is [in Beckett's trilogy, *Molloy, Malone Dies,* and *The Unnamable*] a stream of imageless verbosity occasionally broken by a jab of obscene anger, but gray, gray, and it goes monotonously along in phrases usually about seven words long, like some regularly bumping old tram. This is, of course, not so much the stream of consciousness as the stream of solitude and provides the comedy of overhearing a man talking to himself. . . .

Why is Beckett interesting as a writer? As a contemporary phenomenon, he is one more negative protest against the world going to the slaughterhouse, one more protest on behalf of privacy, a voice for myopia. He is a modern Oblomov, fretful and apathetic, enclosed in private fantasy, dropping off into words instead of sleep. They are eloquent, cunning, unremitting words.

He is far from feeble, for there is a devil-like slyness in the half grin on the faces of his old men who can hit out with their crutches. What tedium! they exclaim—speaking not only of existence and human solitude—but, we suspect, of ourselves. His imagination has the Irish cruelty and self-destructiveness that Yeats once spoke of. Beckett's anti-novels, like all anti-novels, have to deal with small areas of experience because their pretension is to evoke the whole of life, *i.e.*, life unfixed by art; the result is that these verbose books are like long ironical, stinging footnotes in small print to some theme not formulated. But there is a flash of deep insight in the madness he evokes: it is strange that in a generation which has put all its stress on youth and achievement, he alone should have written about old age, loneliness and decrepitude, a subject which arouses perhaps our deepest repressed guilt and fears. He is the product of a civilization which has become suddenly old. He is a considerable, muttering, comic writer, and although he conveys unbearable pain, he also conveys the element of sardonic tenacity and danger that lies at the heart of the comic gift.

V. S. Pritchett. NS. April 2, 1960, p. 489

In *The Unnamable* we come as near to the core of the onion as it is possible to come, and discover of course that there is no core, no undividable unit of continuous personality. It is difficult to say just where or what the Unnamable is, because, as in the brothel scene of [Joyce's] *Ulysses*, his fluctuating moods create their own surroundings. One hypothesis is that he is sitting in a crouched posture with tears pouring out of his eyes, like some of the damned in Dante, or like the Heraclitus who became the weeping philosopher by contemplating the flowing of all things. Another is that he is in a jar outside a Paris restaurant opposite a horsemeat shop, suspended between life and death like the sibyl in Petronius who presides over [Eliot's] *The Waste Land*.

Ordinarily we are aware of a duality between mind and body, of the necessity of keeping the body still to let the mind work. If we sit quietly we become aware of bodily processes, notably the heartbeat and pulse, carrying on automatically and involuntarily. Some religious disciplines, such as yoga, go another stage, and try to keep the mind still to set some higher principle free. When this happens, the mind can be seen from the outside as a rushing current of thoughts and associations and memories and worries and images suggested by desire, pulsating automatically and with all the habit-energy of the ego behind it. Each monologue in [Beckett's] trilogy suggests a mind half-freed from its own automatism. It is detached enough to feel imprisoned and enslaved, and to have no confidence in any of its assertions, but immediately to deny or contradict or qualify or put forward another hypothesis to whatever it says. But it is particularly the monologue of *The Unnamable*, an endless, querulous, compulsive, impersonal babble, much the same in effect whether read in French or in English, and with no purpose except to keep going, that most clearly suggests a "stream of consciousness" from which real consciousness is somehow absent. *The Unnamable* could readily be called a tedious book, but its use of tedium is exuberant, and in this respect it resembles *Watt*.

Northrop Frye. HdR. Autumn, 1960, p. 447

There have been many writers who have risen to fame with works written in a language other than their own, but usually they are compelled by circumstances to write in a foreign language: the necessities of exile; a desire to break the connection with their country of origin for political or ideological reasons; or the wish to reach a world audience, which might induce the citizen of a small language community, a Rumanian or a Dutchman, to write in French or English. But Beckett was certainly not an exile in that sense, and his mother tongue is the accepted lingua franca of the twentieth century. He chose to write his masterpieces in French because he felt that he needed the discipline that the use of an acquired language would impose upon him. As he told a student writing a thesis on his work who asked him why he used French, "Because in French it is easier to write without style." In other words, while in his own language a writer may be tempted to indulge in virtuosity of style for its own sake, the use of another language may force him to divert the ingenuity that might be expended on mere embellishments of style in his own idiom to the utmost clarity and economy of expression. . . .

The fact that in his own translations the English language perfectly renders his meaning and intention shows that it is not just a surface quality that he prefers in French, but the challenge and discipline it presents to his powers of expression. . . . The danger of being carried along by the logic of language is clearly greater in one's mother tongue, with its unconsciously accepted meanings and associations. By writing in a foreign language, Beckett insures that his writing remains a constant struggle, a painful wrestling with the spirit of language itself. That is why he considers the radio plays and occasional pieces he has since written in English as a relaxation, a rest from this hard struggle with meaning and language. But accordingly he also attaches less importance to these works. They came too easily.

Martin Esslin. The Theatre of the Absurd
(Garden City, N.Y., Doubleday, 1961), pp. 8–9

The Unnamable suggests as its central meaning, beyond the persistent metaphysical questioning, the perhaps more interesting one of the relationships of the writer to his characters. What is mysterious about the world without is that it is indiscernible from the mysterious world within, and "voices" from a distance may be of one's own creation, an attempt to isolate the condition of finiteness and to understand it in relationship to something beyond it, without which it cannot have even a relative meaning. Thus the Murphys, Molloys, Morans, and Malones are manipulated for a time as surrogate sufferers of one's pain; this pain is projected outward so that it might be witnessed and understood. In the end, however, the dreamer cannot remain content with this. What must concern him is himself alone, and there remains only the blackness of self, "shorn of all its accidents"; here there is metaphysical chaos, no dimensions, no time, no relatives, no absolutes beyond the fluctuating absolute of the "I" which continues on but which finds no rest because there is no final answer. There are never less than two answers; one must always continue on.

Yet for all of this Beckett's characters do not despair, and though their world seems illogical and cruel there is none of the romantic, grim acceptance of "what is" one finds in facets of existentialism, but rather a paradoxical delight in the "black joy" this peculiar world affords. Beckett's situations are so absurd as to beggar parody, and his people realize this and exult in the fact. . . . In the world of the trilogy one always exists positively, in spite of or because of his recognition of the ultimate vanity and endless contradictions of human speculation, and of the fact that nothing can be rejected but that it must be reclaimed, nothing can be claimed but that it must be rejected.

J[oyce] C[arol] Oates. Renascence. Spring, 1962,
p. 164

Swift, Shaw, Yeats, Synge, Joyce—like these Beckett was born in Dublin. Like Swift, he went to Trinity College, an Anglo-Irish island within John Bull's other island. Like Joyce, Beckett preferred life in Paris, where, keeping himself to himself, he seems again the insulated man or, better, the man in pot or garbage can. Going to pot became his theme. As for Ireland: an Irishman seems one who, somewhere else, is where he was. When Beckett's works have an identifiable locality, it is commonly the streets, bogs, ditches, dumps, and madhouses of Dublin and the district to the south, or what Beckett calls the Molloy country, a region suitable for the action or inaction of Moran, Macmann, Watt, Rooney, and "them."

It may be that Godot, a created nothing, made his creator known, but Beckett the writer, not Beckett the man, whose life for us is another nothing—or almost. Interviews yield little, letters less. How can we know the potter from the pot? What little we know is this: that, shortly after his first communion, he found the Anglican church "irksome" and left it; that, having read modern languages at Trinity, he taught French in Dublin, English in Paris. There, in the late 1920s, he became Joyce's friend and, in the 1930s, a fugitive from his amorous daughter until they put her away. Even Peggy Guggenheim found Beckett odd. Hanging around with the transition [journal] crowd, he shared its devotion to surrealism, to the extent of translating several poems and essays of Breton and Éluard. At Vaucluse or thereabouts, during the war, he began to write in French. Some of his friends think that he is married.

William York Tindall. Samuel Beckett (New York,
Columbia University Press, 1964), pp. 3–4 how it is I quote and unquote by Samuel Beckett published by Grove Press translated from the French by the author Samuel Beckett

in French how it is is comment c'est which is a pun id est commencez which means begin in English no pun simply how it is otherwise not much probably lost in translation

begin beginning not so easy book is written how it is I quote unquote in words like this unpunctuated clumps of words with spaces white between then I guess you'd call them paragraphs I write it as I read it

word clumps no punctuation commas no periods colons no semi colons none of them ampersands and asterisks or even arse yes asterisks not one but now and then in caps I said in ARE YOU LISTENING capitals to make it quite clear CAPITALS and there it is how how it is is written technically considered

aesthetically considered

something wrong here. . . .

something undergraduate inert a neoclassicism in which one's early works are taken as the classics a laziness in which young urgencies become old rhetoric hermetic avantgardism unviolated by the outer word the world beyond the skin except the customary almost automatic glimpse of rural maybe Irish bliss which bothers Beckett like a mote of blue sky in his eye

this proud priest perfecting his forlorn ritual

the plays OKAY very the stage an altar anyway the radio plays EVEN BETTER the ear rebuilds the actors foist existence on the words I remember the wonderful lavender sandals of the messenger boy in a certain production of Godot and his mystical haircut BUT

in how it is where Joyce and Kafka intersect one misses now the one and now the other compare The Burrow compare Nighttown compare The Penal Colony and deplore the relative thinness the sterile stridency

question is the novel no longer a fit vessel for Beckett's noble sorrow and quote comedy of incapacity unquote Hugh Kenner

unanswered but good the end of review the END of meditating upon this mud and subprimate sadism NO MORE no more thinking upon it few books have I read I will not reread sooner SORRY but that is how it is [1964]

John Updike. *Assorted Prose* (New York, Alfred A. Knopf, 1965), pp. 314–15, 317–18

I really like what [Beckett's] done, of course, even though he has become too systematic. He's cleared the stage of its accessories, he's made no concessions to the audience, he knows how to write and knows how to think, only his plays seem to be moving towards gimmickry. It's as if *now* he was making concessions to *his* audience, the audience he formed. You sometimes get the feeling he's no longer trying to say what he has to say, but to find gimmicks that will leave the audience gasping. After the dustbins, it was the basins, then he buried his characters, and so on. It's a permanent succession of daring feats. . . .

Of course there's a basic sincerity. In his quest for new techniques, there's the expression of something he's trying to encompass or to reach. I have the feeling that, for the time being, he's becoming a formalist, not—obviously—in the sense that pedants or militants use the word. I think that right now he's most concerned with purely formal experiments, because he's already said the most important things he had to say, and said them several times, in *Waiting for Godot*, in *Endgame*, in *Happy Days*. [1966]

Eugène Ionesco. In Claude Bonnefoy, Conversations
with Eugène Ionesco (New York, Holt, Rinehart,
and Winston, 1971), p. 162

To be together in the world of Winnie and Willie [in *Happy Days*] does not mean to see one another, to be able to see each other. I have watched paralyzed patients in a hospital room, who for months could hear one another, even talked, but never saw each other, or could only see one another occasionally, when the pillows were arranged in a special way. Often, one patient could see another but was never seen by him. . . .

The world in which Winnie and Willie live seems, sometimes, to have no gaps, no empty places; it is tightly filled with voices, objects, memories. But all these voices, memories, objects are loose; they intermingle haphazardly, to no purpose, like necessary and unnecessary trifles crammed together in a big plastic bag.

In this tight Beckettian world the existentialist metaphor seems crystal clear for the first time: consciousness is a gap in existence, a bottomless pit. Beckett is very consistent in his choice of objects. Winnie takes a revolver out of her bag. In the second act the revolver lies on the mound, close by her. Why the revolver? The world of Winnie and Willie is a closed one, yet one can escape from it. One can leave it. But what for? In any case, the bell will ring. But before it rings, there is still so much happiness to be had. Our misery is always matched by our happiness. Winnie has been paralyzed up to her neck. Willie can still crawl. But Willie will not be able to crawl up to Winnie. He will, however, be able to look at her. A gap in existence will then be able to say to another gap in existence: "My Winnie."

The world of Beckett is precise and verifiable, subject to all rigors; even to realism. This kind of realism can be called infra-realism, or sub-realism. In a Beckett play, a wide generalization, the total and absolute human situation, always corresponds to a real, concrete individual situation. That situation can always be shown. It can be performed.

> Jan Kott. *TDR.* Spring, 1966, pp. 158–59

Beckett is more than an author, he is a poet. Above all, a profoundly sincere man, as sincere as he is secret. He cannot bear the symbols that are found in his work, the theories that are elaborated out of his writings. When I say "he cannot bear" I mean that he wants to ignore them, because I have never seen him in a rage. In any case, he refuses to be defined as a twentieth-century author, the head of an avant-garde. I think that he simply wants to be a man who knows how to observe and to understand. The universe that he describes is certainly his own, he lives it every day, and for him it is descriptive evidence itself.

One could work twenty hours a day with Beckett without ever seeing him relax or depart from his reserve. The best way to understand him is to read his works without looking for any philosophy other than a great human compassion. *Happy Days* is a marvellous love poem, the song of a woman who still wants to see and hear the man she loves. When I read the play for the first time I was overcome by it. I was reading everything that I had not dared to think since... since my first middle-aged wrinkle. And how quickly those wrinkles come!

It can seem cruel to play a Winnie, just as it can be cruel to cast any lucid glance on the human condition. It is true that no-one can go farther than *Happy Days*. At any rate, I do not think so.

I do not know what Beckett thinks of women, but I know that he understands them profoundly from the inside. If his plays manage to affect us and move us (and if they did not succeed in invading our sensibilities they would not be played throughout the entire world), it is because Beckett, in spite of his modesty, manages to express his immense compassion for all human life and because he is one of those exceptional men to whom love and lucidity are on the same level.

> Madeleine Renaud. In John Calder, ed., *Beckett at 60*
> (London, Calder and Boyars, 1967), pp. 82–83

If I wanted to try to pinpoint the essence of the unique exhilaration I feel when I read Beckett, I could explain it only with a statement that, if he ever read it, would undoubtedly make Beckett laugh uncontrollably. Try to imagine Beckett laughing uncontrollably; I'd like to hear about that! Therefore, I admit—and I do not care if God himself bursts out laughing!—that what gives Beckett's novels their incomparable character is that *they begin without ending.* Do you understand me? I mean that even the last word of every novel is the first. That every road begins where it ends. That every sentence is simultaneously both the beginning and the ending. . . .

I was told that André Breton, as he was being taken away in an ambulance from his house in Lot, said to those around him, "I am making a very bad exit." Are there any good exits? How can we finish? Beckett's music turns desperately around in circles, like a broken record when the needle gets stuck in a groove. The sentences grow longer, intersected by commas, they extend to three and four pages, then the last sentence, if it is the last, will run six pages (or I do not know how to count), I enter the sentence, I leap aboard. . . .

And now the Nobel Prize has been awarded to the author of *Waiting for Godot.* I feel as if I secretly had voted for him.

Aragon. *LetF*. Oct. 29–Nov. 4, 1969, pp. 3–4†

[Beckett's] dramatic works would not place him in the very front rank of twentieth-century writers, which is where his French novels situate him. For whereas the fiction pursues single-mindedly a path that leads to one goal, silence, the silence of the form which has exhausted itself, each of the plays is *sui generis*. Beckett himself admits that they are by-products, the amusement of a prodigiously gifted and inventive mind fascinated by media (the stage, the television, the cinema, and radio) which have periodically tempted him away from the arduous wrestling with fictional prose. His dramatic writings are therefore not systematic in the way his novels are. Usually he wrote them with a particular actor in mind (Patrick Magee in the case of *Krapp's Last Tape*, for example), or in response to an invitation, such as that extended by the BBC which led to *All that Fall*. . . .

Beckett is very concerned that the humour of his writing should come over in production. He doesn't of course want naïve playing for laughs, but he does want the humour implicit in the words and situations to be brought out. In the preface to the script of *Film* he specifies "climate of film comic and unreal. O should invite laughter throughout by his way of moving." Similarly, he intends that Vladimir's duck-waddle and Estragon's tussles with his boots [in *Waiting for Godot*] should be funny to watch. . . .

One of the shrewdest things ever written about Beckett's theatre was Jean Anouilh's comment that *Waiting for Godot* was like the *Thoughts* of Pascal performed by the Fratellini clowns. We do not usually associate the circus and metaphysics. Beckett has taught us to do so, and it is this which constitutes what is unique about the tone of his drama.

John Fletcher. In John Fletcher, ed., *Forces in
Modern French Drama* (New York,
Frederick Ungar, 1972), pp. 198, 202–3

However great the skill and austerity of Beckett's novels, their final effect is, both literally and deliberately, deadening. They are honed to such a fine point of bodiless desolation, so technically difficult, and so narrow in range, that it is doubtful they would be read by anyone except a few devotees and specialists were it not for the plays. . . .

In a curious way the first-person narrator of Beckett's novels seems consistently less personal and human than the figures on the stage into whom the same preoccupations are projected. This is not simply because the plays use live actors—after all, Beckett has done his best to overcome this disadvantage by burying them in urns, sand, and dustbins. Rather, it has to do with the quality of the writing. There is nothing in any of Beckett's prose or verse so sharp, immediate, and alive with suggestion as there is in his writing for the stage and radio. . . .

Even more than the narrators of the novels, Beckett's actors are aware of their false position as objects in a work of art and strenuously try to maintain their poise by pre-empting the audience's response. . . . It is, I suppose, yet another of Beckett's ways of keeping a decent distance between himself and what might otherwise seem statements of indecently personal intent. But however aware the characters may be of the roles they are playing, and however much they insist on puncturing the theatrical illusion for the audience, the fact that they are there on stage means that the desert of depression is, albeit reluctantly, peopled. The depression has moved out of the bodiless, claustrophobic, pointless world of mere language and assumed the qualifying substantiality of flesh and blood. In the novels Beckett's wit was self-regarding, concerned exclusively with its own learning and elegance. In the plays it ranges easily over the broader absurdity of the characters' gloom and bodily functions. It becomes human instead of literary.

A. Alvarez. *Samuel Beckett* (New York, Viking,
1973), pp. 75, 81–82, 94

Severe words have been spoken about "imitative form," an aesthetic fallacy which mimics the inexpressible by the unintelligible. But here we encounter Beckett the syntactician, whose beautiful sentences are never unintelligible, nor ever deficient in neo-classical linkage the one to the next, except when a sudden rage seizes the speaker, or a grimace of wilfulness passes across his face. (Men are prey to such episodes, that is understandable.) So like some Henry Moore sculpture, shaping the empty spaces which perforate it, a Beckett play or novel locates and shapes unreason, some unsubduable stuff which permeates the universe and is not to be abolished by refusal to think about it. . . .

Each time we confront a new Beckett work we are installed in some new world, a world where men wait, a world where women sink into the sand, a world where couples lie barely breathing in symmetrical entombment. We deduce the world's rules of order, and adduce pertinent memories of other orders. We must actively adduce such memories; the books and plays do not solicit analogy. Though *Lessness* recalls a sestina and *Waiting for Godot* a succession of music-hall turns, *Lessness* and *Waiting for Godot* do not protect themselves by hinting that nothing need unsettle, that some familiar paradigm is merely putting forth an instance. They are content to seem as strange as they are. Living with their strangeness, we gradually discover for ourselves how traditional they are. This is in part to guess that traditional procedures may have always served to shape voids, though never explicitly.

Hugh Kenner. *A Reader's Guide to Samuel Beckett*
(New York, Farrar, Straus and Giroux, 1973),
pp. 188–89

BENDA, JULIEN (1867–1956)

Félix [in *The Ordination*] sets out to write a great philosophical tome. Married to an intelligent and gentle woman who respects his work, and with a charming daughter, he is a happy man, living in the comfort of a peaceful home with two people to whom he gives very little of himself, saving his energies for his ideas. Suddenly he is struck by misfortune: his daughter, Suzanne, contracts a hip disease. Her illness is not only a great sorrow to him; it precipitates a complete inner revolution. God was punishing him, was chastising him, for his selfishness. While I do sympathize with his anguish, I do not understand his mystical revelation very well, or his repentance, or his feeling of rebellion. . . .

The conflict between love and intellectual pursuit strikes me as artificial. Any truly superior and level-headed man knows how to reconcile the intellect and the emotions, putting each in its proper place. . . . But when the child's health has improved enough for her mother to become calm again, Félix, astonishingly, does not regain enough peace of mind to return to the writing of his precious treatise. . . .

Felix finally becomes only a husband and a father. He has given up philosophy, concluding that it requires thorough asceticism; living alone is indispensable for the mind to triumph over love. But this is ridiculous! Ideas are not pagan idols. They do not demand mutilations and bloody sacrifices. Julien Benda's imagination has a dark and somewhat biblical bent. I think his conclusions must be challenged. But he does have a great deal of talent. [1912]

Paul Souday. *Les livres du temps* (Paris, Émile-Paul Frères, 1913), pp. 275–78†

M. Julien Benda has the formal beauty which the American critics lack, and a close affinity to them in point of view. He restricts himself, perhaps, to a narrower field of ideas, but within that field he manipulates the ideas with a very exceptional cogency and clarity. . . .

Almost the only person who has ever figured in England and attempted a task at all similar to that of M. Benda is Matthew Arnold. Matthew Arnold was intelligent, and by so much difference as the presence of one intelligent man makes, our age is inferior to that of Arnold. But what an advantage a man like M. Benda has over Arnold. It is not simply that he has a critical tradition behind him, and that Arnold is using a language which constantly tempts the user away from dispassionate exposition into sarcasm and diatribe, a language less fitting for criticism than the English of the eighteenth century. It is that the follies and stupidities of the French, no matter how base, express themselves in the form of ideas. . . .

T. S. Eliot. *The Sacred Wood* (London, Methuen, 1920), pp. 44–45

Against *La nouvelle revue française*, Julien Benda plays a lone and quite skilful hand; it may be that Schopenhauer had precondemned most of the Rue Madame writers [that is, *NRF* writers], where he says that when men won't put down their thought briefly and clearly the reader may rouse his suspicion. . . .

If Benda is not the rich loam in which a new literature may germinate he is at any rate a fine disinfectant. No foreigner has the patience, no foreigner wants to or will take the time to analyse a decadence which he, himself, can easily avoid; and if one has had any sort of Faith in France one can but be refreshed and delighted when in the midst of a rather depressing jungle one finds this clearing of common sense, this place open to wind and light.

[Rémy de] Gourmont in *The Book of Masks* had been faced with a different problem: that of establishing a whole new generation of writers; he did the work admirably with a method suited thereto; and since abused. To its abuse Benda is an excellent corrective. He is not on the other hand an upholder of the new pseudo-classic "movement," though classicists in search of support have leaned upon some of his writing.

Ezra Pound. *The Dial*. Oct., 1920, pp. 410–11

As soon as Julien Benda's early works appeared, they became known to the intellectual elite; his first novel, *The Ordination*, came close to winning the Prix Goncourt in 1912 (five votes for and five against). But Benda did not truly reach the general public until 1919, with the publication of *Belphegor*, "an essay on the aesthetics of French society today."

In the opening lines of this essay, he defines the "aesthetic aspirations" of French society in a single sentence: "French society today asks that works of art stir the emotions and the senses; no longer is any intellectual pleasure sought from works of art." Throughout this famous book, Benda scolds the "upper classes" for disdaining intelligence and reason. And yet the same "upper classes" made *Belphegor* a success!

What should one conclude? When our contemporaries embrace a book in which they are flogged, should we see this as a manifestation of masochism, or should we infer that Benda's survey and conclusions are overly pessimistic, are disproved by the success of the book? . . . The explanation for *Belphegor*'s success lies primarily in the book's intrinsic worth. . . . Benda is, in my opinion, the foremost essayist of our time.

Frédéric Lefèvre. *Entretien avec Julien Benda*
(Paris, "Le Livre," 1924), pp. 3–5†

I think M. Benda succeeds admirably in the purpose announced in his title [*Attempt at a Coherent Discourse on the Relationships between God and the World*] of rendering his discourse coherent. If once we accept his definitions, his corollaries follow. Clearly and bravely he disengages his idea of infinity from other properties usually assigned to the deity, such as power, omniscience, goodness, and tutelary functions in respect to life, or to some special human society. But coherence is not completeness, nor even a reasonable measure of descriptive truth; and certain considerations are omitted from M. Benda's view which are of such moment that, if they were included, they might transform the whole issue. Perhaps the chief of these omissions is that of an organ for thought. M. Benda throughout is engaged simply in clarifying his own ideas, and repeatedly disclaims any ulterior pretensions. He finds in the panorama of his thoughts an idea of infinite Being, or God, and proceeds to study the relation of that conception to all others. It is a task of critical analysis and religious confession: and nothing could be more legitimate and, to some of us, more interesting. But whence these various ideas, and whence the spell which the idea of infinite Being in particular casts over the meditative mind? Unless we can view these movements of thought in their natural setting and order of genesis, we shall be in danger of turning autobiography into cosmology and inwardness into folly.

George Santayana. *JP*. May 26, 1932, p. 284

Belphegor . . . may be singled out as the most successful of Benda's polemical essays. It was inevitable that the stimulus of *The Treason of the Intellectuals* should be largely negative. *Belphegor*, on the other hand —however rightly is a matter for later discussion—provided a rallying point for the neo-classical criticism of the post-war decade. Turning back from *The Treason of the Intellectuals* we find the same precision, the same propensity for synthetic organization, for methodological discrimination, as characterized the former, mobilized for the indictment of contemporary aesthetics. Based on documentation accumulated in the course of some twenty years' research, it is a discussion on what he would signal as the symptoms of aesthetic decadence, namely, an excessive predominance of impulsive and passional elements. . . .

Posing as an exponent of classical standards, the champion of hellenic values, professing to defend the "rights" of intelligence in an unfriendly world, Benda rarely evinces that equilibrium, that serenity of judgment to be expected of a classicist. His passionate onslaughts, his ideological fanaticism (his term) is hardly calculated to carry conviction even if he has, by sheer shock-tactics, managed to gain a hearing, and the respect of his audience. . . .

Despite the acuteness of his diagnoses, despite the confirmation they would seem to extend to the contentions of the [Charles] Maurras, the [Ernest] Seillères, the [Jacques] Maritains, Benda remains an isolated figure in the battle against the modern movement. Precisely because ultimately his work is, to borrow Babbitt's phrase, "a sweeping indictment of modernism by a modern." Sweeping, one might add, because his intransigeance, and with it his almost quixotic insistence on Isolation—not to mention his apparent misanthropy—would seem bred less of strength of conviction than of disposition, have its source less in reason than emotion.

John Kaestlin. *The Colosseum*. Dec., 1937, pp. 265, 267

In *The Youth of an Intellectual* Julien Benda offers us his most important book, the one that explains all his other works, by explaining the man who wrote them. But perhaps he should never have written this book, if he wanted readers to continue interpreting his other books according to the surface appearance he gave them. For the truth about Benda and his work is primarily unpleasant. This frightening truth can be stated in four words: Benda has no heart. . . .

All of Benda's life and work truly consists of having transformed his lack of heart into an advantage. Like the fox with no tail, Benda has worked steadfastly, and with a kind of frigid genius, at making his lack of heart look—if not like the human norm—at least like a manifestation of superiority. . . . His memoirs [*The Youth of an Intellectual*] do nothing but trace the development of this incomplete creature, this inhuman creature, from his earliest years. . . .

If Benda had any taste, he could never have undertaken this exposition of his intellectual self, to which he has devoted his entire life. Intellectual life should create a sense of its own modesty, which would dictate that any honorable intellectual should not open the door to his workroom to all comers, any more than an honorable woman would receive strangers in her bathroom. Benda, however, invites the whole universe to visit and scrutinize him in his cerebral laboratory, saying: There is one pure intellectual in the world, look at him—I am he.

André Rousseaux. *Littérature du vingtième siècle*
(Paris, Éditions Albin Michel, 1938), Vol. I,
pp. 95–97, 99†

No one but Julien Benda could have emphasized the true nature of French literature with as much severity and shrewdness—and it must be said that no one else could have done so with as much intelligence. Benda, in fact, rejects contemporary French literature [in *Byzantine France*] only in the name of intelligence. The clerks have committed treason and continue to do so. Literature no longer aims at the objective study of the human heart and mind, as it did in the heroic age of classicism. Writers today, led astray by romanticism, subjugated by the doctrine of art for art's sake, have failed to fulfill the mission of serving intelligence. Instead, they are enslaved to what Benda once called the god Belphegor, and now denounces as byzantinism—the worst of evils and the very evil that characterizes us. Our era (more precisely, the period immediately preceding ours) saw the triumph of "pure literature," and Benda cannot abide it. . . .

Both [Benda and Sartre] have the same goal—the destruction of "pure literature." It matters little that Benda advocates an intellectual literature and Sartre a social literature. Wrong reasons lead both men to wish to undermine all of literature. . . . "Pure literature" should not be condemned because two different sides desire its destruction in the name of opposing doctrines.

André Brincourt. *Desarroi de l'écriture* (Paris,
Jean Vigneau, 1947), pp. 135, 143†

I do not know anyone who ever claimed to be a disciple of Benda's; he is not *believed* by anyone. Nevertheless, everyone reads him, is interested in what he writes, is entertained by it, makes use of it. Everyone goes back to his writings and studies them. A critic writes ten consecutive essays to show that Benda is frivolous, that he makes condemnations with no evidence, that he is jealous and cannot bear the fame of any other writer, that he is ill-tempered and resentful, that the cleverness of his titles and the competence of his theses do not stop Benda's evidence from being inaccurate and his doctrines from being contradictory. Nevertheless, the critic does not tire of making his case against Benda, and no sooner is one demonstration concluded than the critic begins another one. As if there were some indefinable profit to be drawn from Benda; as if Benda, for want of a coherent philosophical doctrine, were at least able to construct a machine for inducing reflection.

Jean Paulhan. *Critique*. June, 1948, p. 512†

With all his discussions of the role of the pure intellectual, with all his theory of the "clerk," there are abundant proofs in Benda's work that he is far more of a man and far more interested in mankind than his clerkly or near-clerkly condition might seem to indicate. . . . His life and career are perhaps best symbolized in *The Ordination*, where Félix, who pursues ideas with panting love, succumbs, when faced with the illness and crippling of his daughter, to pity, as any mere human might do, abandons the life of intellect, and becomes only one of those who love. It is difficult to escape the impression, when *The Ordination* is read in the light of his autobiographical confessions, that very early in his life Benda had realized the truth about himself: that he was condemned to preach the clerkly life, to approach it in the course of his existence and to hold it before him as the ideal of living, but never quite to attain it in the fullness of its renunciation. For the clerk cannot be a man, and Benda is a man and not a monster.

As a man he demonstrates an individuality that is one of the most compelling of our time, the more so since its power is employed in the service of a philosophy and a moral code which have as their basis theories of anti-egoism, anti-individualism, universality, and abstraction, and especially since it stands in such sharp contrast to the search for security that fidelity to "the tradition" implies. His real complexity lies here, in the defense of doctrines in all fields of intellectuality that are basically timid and conservative by the instrumentality of a personality that is as hard, angular, and free as any our century can boast.

Robert J. Niess. *Julien Benda* (Ann Arbor,
University of Michigan Press, 1956), pp. 29–30

There is a greatness in being a man with only one thing to say, when what you say scandalizes conformists. A writer like Péguy achieved that kind of greatness. Why does not Benda reach it, despite a few pages here and there of inspired vehemence, like the pages that close *The Treason of the Intellectuals*? Why does his work produce the painful impression of what Baudelaire called the "senile sleep of decrepitude?" And yet the man is so intelligent, so alert! . . .

If one investigates the disappointment one feels in reading Benda, he will find that the real reason is Benda's aridness of soul and, so to speak, his self-concealment. He never surrenders to himself, never feels a sense of abandon, is precisely the opposite of an apostle. . . .

An apostle can be pardoned for repeating himself, because he speaks from an overabundance of feeling, from his overflowing faith. The polemicist Benda cannot be pardoned for the same fault, because he rages bitterly. Love has no more verbal resources than bitterness. Yet love can give worn-out expressions a luster that is always new, while resentment wears out even expressions that have never been used before. Resentment, by its very nature, keeps repeating itself endlessly.

Jean Sarocchi. *Julien Benda: Portrait d'un intellectual*
(Paris, A. G. Nizet, 1968), pp. 181, 189, 191†

BERGSON, HENRI (1859–1941)

Professor Henri Bergson is a young man, comparatively, as influential philosophers go, having been born at Paris in 1859. His career has been the routine one of a successful French professor. . . .

I have to confess that Bergson's originality is so profuse that many of his ideas baffle me entirely. Now, many men are profusely original in that no man can understand them: violently peculiar ways of looking at things are no great rarity. The rarity is when great peculiarity of vision is allied with great lucidity and unusual command of all the classic expository apparatus. Bergson's resources in the way of erudition are remarkable, and in the way of expression they are simply phenomenal. This is why in France, where the art of saying things well counts for so much and is so sure of appreciation, he has immediately taken so eminent a place in public esteem. Old-fashioned professors, whom his ideas quite fail to satisfy, nevertheless speak of his talent almost with bated breath, while the youngsters flock to him as to a master.

If anything can make hard things easy to follow, it is a style like Bergson's. A straightforward style, an American reviewer lately called it, failing to see that such straightforwardness means a flexibility of verbal resource that follows the thought without a crease or wrinkle, as elastic silk underclothing follows the movements of one's body. The lucidity of Bergson's way of putting things is what all readers are first struck by. It seduces you and bribes you in advance to become his disciple. It is a miracle, and he a real magician.

William James. *The Hibbert Journal*. April, 1909,
pp. 562–63

As a rule [Bergson] does not give reasons for his opinions, but relies on their inherent attractiveness, and on the charm of an excellent style. Like the advertisers of Oxo, he relies upon picturesque and varied statement, and an apparent explanation of many obscure facts. Analogies and similes, especially, form a very large part of the whole process by which he recommends his views to the reader. The number of similes for life to be found in his works exceeds the number in any poet known to me. Life, he says [in *Creative Evolution*], is like a shell bursting into fragments which are again shells. . . .

Of course a large part of Bergson's philosophy, probably the part to which most of its popularity is due, does not depend upon argument, and cannot be upset by argument. His imaginative picture of the world, regarded as a poetic effort, is in the main not capable of either proof or disproof. Shakespeare says life's but a walking shadow, Shelley says it is like a dome of many-colored glass, Bergson says it is a shell which bursts into parts that are again shells. If you like Bergson's image better, it is just as legitimate.

The good which Bergson hopes to see realized in the world is action for the sake of action. All pure contemplation he calls "dreaming," and condemns by a whole series of uncomplimentary epithets: static, Platonic, mathematical, logical, intellectual. Those who desire some prevision of the end which action is to achieve are told that an end foreseen would be nothing new, because desire, like memory, is identified with its object. Thus we are condemned, in action, to be the blind slaves of instinct: the life-force pushes us on from behind, restlessly and unceasingly. There is no room in this philosophy for the moment of contemplative insight when, rising above the animal life, we become conscious of the greater ends that redeem man from the life of the brutes. Those to whom activity without purpose seems a sufficient good will find in Bergson's books a pleasing picture of the universe. But those to whom action, if it is to be of any value, must be inspired by some vision, by some imaginative foreshadowing of a world less painful, less unjust, less full of strife than the world of our every-day life, those, in a word, whose action is built on contemplation, will find in this philosophy nothing of what they seek, and will not regret that there is no reason to think it true.

Bertrand Russell. *The Monist*. July, 1912, pp. 332, 346–47

A "philosophy," strictly speaking, is at the very least a body of thought that *holds together*; as a philosopher, therefore, Bergson contributes nothing at all. . . .

Anyone is free to believe that a talent for subtle expression is superior to a systematic mind, and that such a talent is the only thing that is great, beautiful, or important. But then all I ask is that Bergson's talent for subtle expression be honored *as such*, without any effort to pass him off as a constructive force by piling honors upon him. There is no harm in finding Bergson admirable precisely for the perpetual contradiction of his thought, for his essential fluidity, for his inability to give his ideas a clear form, for his fluctuations, for his inconsistency, for the fact that he is *always* inconsistent. But then if these are his merits, let us not hear about Bergson's "doctrine" or his "new philosophy" or his "method that will totally renovate philosophy"; let us not hear Bergson's philosophy praised for the "solidity of its construction" and its "austere beauty" ([Édouard] Le Roy) or called a philosophy "that will go down in history as one of the five or six greatest philosophies" (Péguy). . . .

[Bergsonians,] you are free to love, embrace, believe, feel, and live; you are free to be saints, heroes, and poets; you are free to experience intimate, instantaneous, and total communion with things—and all the fusions, effusions, and confusions the rest of us will never experience. Even better, *be* things, *be* motion, *be* life—you have the right to do all that; you can never be deprived of such sublime pleasures; the only error our ancestors ever made was to hide those pleasures from you. However, when you take it upon yourselves to utter even the shadow of an *idea*, then you have gone too far.

Julien Benda. *Le bergsonisme* (Paris, Mercure de France, 1913), pp. 98–100, 102†

Whatever one may think of Cartesian philosophy as a metaphysical *system* . . . when Descartes set forth his *method* he won an eternal place in history. Whatever one may think of Bergsonism as a metaphysical *system*, when Bergson brought forth his *method* he won an eternal place in history. . . .

Bergsonism certainly contains a relentlessness that does not exist in Cartesian philosophy. But perhaps Bergsonism had to make a sharper break with the past than Cartesian philosophy, because the break made by Bergsonism was more dangerous, more precarious—and more indispensable. Descartes ended our subjection to irrationality and disorder, but Bergson ended our subjection to ready-made ideas—and our subjection to ready-made ideas was infinitely greater than our subjection to disorder; we are infinitely closer to relapsing into ready-made ideas than we are to relapsing into disorder. And the consequences of ready-made ideas are infinitely more disastrous. Disorder may have its moments of usefulness, even have its moments of order. But in tired ideas there is neither grace nor potential life. Of all the bad things in the world, mechanical habits are the worst. Cartesian philosophy drove back only one of our habits, our habit of irrational thinking. Bergsonism undertook to drive back habit itself—all our physical and mental habits.

Charles Péguy. *Note sur M. Bergson et la philosophie bergsonienne* (Paris, Cahiers de la Quinzaine, 1914), pp. 85, 87–88†

Bergson is very far away from all "fashions," although he understands the essential intellectual currents of our time and has expressed himself about them. Anyone who has found Nietzsche profitable can also find value in Bergson. Like Nietzsche, he is a champion of life against doctrine; he fights for new ways of perception and fights against the hallowed dogmas of the Kantian school. Bergson denies to the understanding, to the intelligence operating with concepts and logic, the ability of real perception, of true apprehension of what is alive. And so, for Kant's disciples and for intellectualists of every kind, he is ipso facto dismissed as no more than a romantic and poet. He forgoes all claim to the provability and universal validity of logicoscientific work, not because he does not understand it and has not mastered it, but because his strongly artistically inclined nature urges him along the path of intuition, of empathy, and of supralogical, prophetic perception.

Let the professional philosophers decide how high they wish to rate Bergson as a thinker. For the rest of us, there is no reason to neglect Bergson's splendid books. They are so full of sagacity and liveliness, so fresh and personal, at the same time so admirably written and full of apt, lightning inspirations and similes that their reading alone must count as valuable and beneficial, even though for philosophers working scientifically they may contain dangers. [1916]

Hermann Hesse. *My Belief* (New York, Farrar, Straus and Giroux, 1974), p. 364

Bergson once said to me, "Perhaps genius consists essentially in coming into contact with some inner current and remaining in contact with it." At any rate, Bergson's own genius consists essentially in that, and his profound definition of genius seems to explain to me the perfection of his style of writing and the reason why his style bears so little resemblance to what we usually mean by the word "style." . . .

The author of a marvelous article on intellectual effort, Bergson has never had any goal in life but to renew that effort perpetually. Bergson's center of gravity always lies in the act of gathering his resources and withdrawing into his own deepest recesses. His effort to "probe the depths"—to use one of his own favorite expressions—is so total, so unselfish, and always so humble, that when he returns to the surface, through the action of writing down what he has discovered, his writing is smooth and peaceful, at no time appearing forced. His style is not that of a stylist and not that of an ideologue; it is rather the movement of thought itself, with its perpetual ebb and flow. The word disappears entirely in the meaning; each word does not exist individually, the way it would exist for a pure artist.

You might object to this assertion: what about the images, the metaphors for which Bergson is praised even by those who attack him for everything else? As it happens, Bergson's modesty and generosity can be best seen in his use of images and metaphors. Admirable in themselves, these images are moreover seen as a way of enlightening the reader, almost as a way of teaching a lesson. No great man has more constantly thought about his readers than Bergson; no great man has done more to make himself understood by his readers or done more to repress his secret desire to dazzle them. . . .

In Bergson's writing the image illuminates a thought that is difficult to grasp; the image never serves as a magnificent mask for the absence of thought. [Feb., 1922]

Charles Du Bos. *Journal, 1921–23* (Paris, Corrêa, 1946), pp. 58–59†

Bergsonians have reproached their adversaries for having given way, in calling Bergsonism an anti-intellectualist philosophy, to outrageous simplifications. No less outrageous is the simplification which claims that in employing this vocable one is quite plainly reproaching Bergson with having tried to philosophize without intelligence, yes, and even to "de-cerebrate" his unhappy disciples. Thus to deplore the lack of intelligence of the "intellectualists" is too easy a pleasure. [Albert] Thibaudet is right in pointing out that "the Bergsonism of pure instinct, Bergsonism as the enemy of thought, dada-Bergsonism, is a caricature about as exact as the Socrates of [Aristophanes'] *The Clouds* when he measures a flea's jump, or the Rousseau of *The Philosophers* when [Charles] Palissot makes him appear on the stage walking on all fours." . . .

I understand full well that [Bergson's] design was much less to institute a theory of knowledge than to criticize one method, in order to substitute for it another method—and to do so by the very movement of his research, as Diogenes did by walking. In that, there may have been some contingency in imposing the name "intellect" on the disapproved manner of operating, which one might equally well have imputed to "fabricating imagination" or to "spatializing analysis," for example. But . . . profound necessities, immanent in Bergsonian thought in its most individual aspect, have in reality suggested such a designation. Anti-intellectualism is not only an apparent sign, it is an essential characteristic of his thought. [1929]

Jacques Maritain. *Bergsonian Philosophy and Thomism* (New York, Philosophical Library, 1955), pp. 43–44

Many years ago Henri Bergson's *Creative Evolution* was one of the most widely discussed philosophical books in this country. The fame of the author spread from philosophical circles to the larger public, and he acquired something of the vogue enjoyed in more recent years by Professor Einstein. It is gratifying, after years of silence as far as the American public is concerned, to have his excellent treatise on morality and religion [*The Two Sources of Morality and Religion*], published three years ago in France, rendered into English. . . .

Professor Bergson's discussion of the nature and origin of morality and religion is always interesting and suggestive but not altogether convincing. It fails to convince at least this reviewer's mind because it finds two kinds of morality and two kinds of religion, a closed and open morality and a static and dynamic religion, and thus presents us with four different social forces, almost totally unrelated to each other. One is naturally skeptical toward explanations which thus separate hitherto unified concepts. . . .

It may seem presumptuous to criticize so great a master as Bergson. Yet it cannot be denied that this book, suggestive as it is, represents or seems to represent only an avocational interest in a great and perplexing subject. Failure to understand the paradoxes of religion and morality, particularly evident in his discussion of mysticism, thus leads him to make untenable distinctions between types of religion and morality.

Reinhold Niebuhr. *NYT.* April 28, 1935, pp. 3, 15

M. Bergson died last Saturday, January 4, at the age of eighty-one— died, it appears, without pain, from a congestion of the lungs. On Monday the great man's body was transferred from his home to the cemetery of Garches, in circumstances that were necessarily of the simplest and most moving. No funeral ceremony; no speeches; but those who were present were no doubt all the more quietly aware, in their meditations, of the exceptional loss we have suffered. About thirty people had assembled, in a drawing-room, round the coffin. I expressed the sympathy of the Académie Française to Mme. Bergson, and she asked me to thank you on her behalf. Immediately afterward the coffin was taken away, and at the door of the house we paid a last tribute to the greatest philosopher of our time.

He was the pride of our Society. Whether or not we were attracted by his metaphysics, whether or not we had followed him in the profound researches to which he devoted the whole of his life, and in the truly creative evolution of his thought, which became steadily bolder and more independent, we possessed in him the most authentic example of the highest intellectual virtues. In intellectual matters his name, universally known, stood for a sort of moral authority. France was able to appeal to that name and that authority in circumstances which I am sure you will recall. He had a large number of disciples who followed him with a fervor, almost a devotion, which no one coming after him in the world of ideas can at present flatter himself that he inspires. [1941]

Paul Valéry. *Masters and Friends* (Princeton, N.J.,
Princeton University Press, 1968), pp. 302–3

Never was a French philosopher, with the exception of Descartes, better entitled than Bergson to be studied, by the side of men of letters, as an integral part of a literary age. He was widely read, not only by the specialists, but by the cultivated public. His direct influence was felt in the circles of French, not to speak of European, thought and letters; and his work found itself in striking harmony with the artistic trend of the period. Lastly, he was himself an eminent writer, with a right to consideration of this ground alone. . . .

The image of the "stream of consciousness" has had an extraordinary fortune; it has invaded the world, not only of philosophy, but of literature and art. It is no less than a universally valid expression of man's central experience, which at one stroke establishes a new view of mental activity through all its channels. The natural unity and the fluidity of an unbroken flow, the course of which is only artificially divisible, were substituted for another image, a mosaic of parts laboriously adapted to one another by the engineering feat of a mechanical mind. Psychology, in its early stages, had seen its object in the light of the physical sciences; sense impressions were atoms, which a combining process would build into ideas. With the new image, the whole became the original, and the parts derivative. The intellect's function was to perceive the parts, and to erect upon that perception a systematic theory of their working; the function of intuition was to perceive the whole, and to reach in that contact an assurance that was at least half-mystical. That William James in America and Bergson in France developed this notion of the inner life at practically the same time, and independently of each other until they discovered their agreement, is common history. How that view met and confirmed the philosophical needs of the symbolist aesthetic is obvious enough. The novel was transformed within the span of one generation. The revelation in France of Freud and the subconscious followed the diffusion of Bergson's thought; and it was not long before the monumental work of Proust incorporated the one movement while illustrating the other.

L. Cazamian. *A History of French Literature*
(Oxford, Clarendon Press, 1955), pp. 405–6

The interest in "Bergsonism," already curtailed to a minimum, is destined to fade away entirely. And even though his insights and arguments will continue to effect their presence in philosophy, Bergson's characteristic biological and historical systems will come to be only engagingly interesting failures. Bergson's philosophy had a rocket-like beginning, and it blazed up, opening new and more expansive vistas than we could have hoped for; if we have seen the rocket exhaust itself and follow downward on a sad and ageless trajectory, it should not be too much of a disappointment. The contribution of Bergson is that he made a whole generation look up and see the possibility of a world large enough and tolerant enough to include the goods of varied viewpoints, varied endeavors, and varied types of men. A man's aspirations must always be counted more important than his achievements, otherwise no man is worth more than his tomb.

If the traditions of philosophy remain largely unaffected by "Bergsonism," they do not, I believe, remain impervious to Henri Bergson himself, for the man Bergson brought to philosophy an eloquence, an imagination, an expansiveness, and a concern for the value and uniqueness of men that is as rare as it is irreplaceable. If this much of the Bergsonian heritage is not worth carrying on, then, surely, philosophy itself is not worth carrying on.

Thomas Hanna. In Thomas Hanna, ed.,
The Bergsonian Heritage (New York,
Columbia University Press, 1962), pp. 30–31

BERNANOS, GEORGES (1888–1948)

Tomorrow the first book, the first novel, by a young writer, Georges Bernanos, will be in everyone's hands and Bernanos, the author of *Under the Sun of Satan*, will be famous. Today I say of him (as I once said of Marcel Proust) that a great intellectual and imaginative power has appeared in the firmament of French literature. But this time the power is one of synthesis and not one of analysis, and it is exercised in an area that to my knowledge has not yet been explored by the novel— the domain of spiritual life, of things and bodies governed by the soul.

Under the Sun of Satan is the compressed and dramatic story of the struggles of a saint against the spirit of evil. This saint's life bears some resemblance to the hagiography of the Curé of Ars [a nineteenth-century parish priest canonized in 1925]. This story is also analogous in some ways to the torments of the "dark night" described by Saint John of the Cross. From the point of view of current literature, this book's special importance is its unusual and powerful effort to reclaim the novel from a depiction of raw instincts and sentimental little love affairs and to use the novel for higher purposes. . . .

In *Under the Sun of Satan*, which develops a tragic crisis, the struggle between the Angel and the Demon, there are no theatrical effects. There is an actual meeting, on a road, between the hero of the book and the Evil One; there is a conversation with the Evil One, which is one of the most astonishing—I would say one of the most over-powering—passages in all of French literature. But everything is handled with reserve and sobriety. [April 7, 1926]

Léon Daudet. Société des amis de Georges Bernanos:
Bulletin périodique. Christmas, 1953, pp. 2–4†

Now here are my doubts or my objections [to *Under the Sun of Satan*]: one would think that your [Bernanos] hero is afraid of the devil, but no Christian—especially a saint—was ever afraid of the devil. . . .

My second objection is that although your power is great, for the moment it is confused. One does not get a clear impression of your hero: it seems as if you vacillated between two conceptions, each of which is alternately stressed. One conception is that of the emaciated *ascetic*, like the Curé of Ars; the other idea, which is all your own and which I find more interesting, is that of the *athlete* who has remained human, all too human, and who is unafraid to enter into hand-to-hand combat, as Saint Paul said, with the powers of darkness, putting all his cards on the table, even his eternal salvation. What is vitally important is to know whether such a combatant is driven by his love for God or by pride in his own strength; in your book it certainly seems that the second feeling is the stronger. The love for God and human souls appears in only a few passages—which, however, are very beautiful.

What I have just said should not be taken as critical observations but simply doubts, which a second reading may dispel. I will not put myself in the ridiculous position of most critics and claim to know more about what should have been accomplished than the writer who created the book, who lived in it and through it. My objections are no denigration of your admirable gifts as an artist and as a Christian. You show what tragedy, what dignity, what delicacy, and what depth can be added to our daily lives through the perspective of our eternal salvation or perdition, and through a glimpse of the invisible powers in whose service we are employed. [June 25, 1926]

Paul Claudel. Quoted in Albert Béguin, *Georges Bernanos* (Paris, Éditions du Seuil, 1949), pp. 65–66†

While reading *The Imposture* one feels, even more clearly than while reading *Under the Sun of Satan*, that each character set before us by Bernanos is subject to a destiny which does not stem from his own personality but which, on the contrary, begins at the very point at which his personality fades away. For Bernanos, the soul is not only the essential part of man; the soul is also what best expresses man. Nothing could do a greater disservice to *The Imposture* than a summary of the action: in this novel facts have only a secondary importance. What is of prime importance is a particular kind of conflict.

The real subject of *The Imposture* is the same as that of Bernanos's previous book: the study of Satan's power. *The Imposture* is composed in what I would call a musical way: I mean that the characters do not create the conflicts in the novel; instead, the conflicts give rise to the characters. This is why Bernanos continues to choose priests as protagonists, because they embody, with more force and clarity than any other human group, the feelings that Bernanos wishes to bring to light. . . .

Bernanos seeks not to analyze critical moments but to depict them. First he depicts the anguish of his character; then he makes the character act; suddenly, the character discovers that he has just made a significant gesture he had previously refused to make, has expressed something he had been hiding from himself. Then Satan steps in. Bernanos's methods are contrary to the usual techniques of the novel; his very conception of the novel is unlike that which meets with the most approval today—and Bernanos cannot be praised too highly for this. I believe that the lukewarm reception accorded both *Under the Sun of Satan* and *The Imposture*, despite merits that undeniably make Bernanos one of the best novelists of his generation, arises from the fact that this writer is not subject to reality as it is commonly perceived; he lives in a private world, created by himself.

André Malraux. *NRF*. March, 1928, pp. 406–7†

The Diary of a Country Priest . . . could only have been written within the Catholic tradition; it is realistic, imaginative, absorbing. Its theme is religion. I wonder if English readers, brought up to regard religion as a subject unfit for art, realise the extent and imaginative daring of French Catholic literature? . . . Among prose writers, Jouhandeau, [Abbé Henri] Bremond, Mauriac, half a dozen others. Bernanos I should class with Mauriac and perhaps a little below him. Here, English novelists offer no comparison at all; I have looked round for an English parallel to *The Diary of a Country Priest* and can find none. Protestantism perhaps tends to produce cranks rather than mystics, and the tendency is not favourable to art. . . .

Reading this book, with its spiritual preoccupations and its confession of heroic suffering, I was reminded forcibly of Léon Bloy. . . . M. Bernanos' *The Diary of a Country Priest* revives memories of [Bloy] partly by its subject—the solitude and inner drama of its central character, the insistence on poverty, suffering and evil—and partly by its failure to meet the supreme difficulties which a writer influenced by Bloy must overcome. Bloy was a poet and carried everything by imagination; M. Bernanos is a realist, he aims at exact psychology and at times we question the way in which his characters talk and behave. When he exaggerates, as he tends to, we are disturbed. Moreover, the diary form is lost in the long speeches of everyone with whom the priest talks, and in passages which belong to a narrative convention. Too much of the book, in fact, is undisguisedly written by a *novelist*, and the priest though "a bit of a poet" was certainly not a novelist. Nevertheless, despite these faults, which seem to me to reveal a fundamental coarseness of imagination, *The Diary of a Country Priest* is a book with remarkable qualities. . . . M. Bernanos is obviously a novelist of substantial talent; whether he could ever write a completely satisfying book, I doubt.

G. W. Stonier. *NSN*. Sept. 18, 1937, pp. 408–9

However silly it may be to write to an author, since his profession must always involve him in a flood of correspondence, I cannot refrain from doing so after having read *The Vast Cemeteries in the Moonlight*. Not that it is the first book of yours to touch me. *The Diary of a Country Priest* is in my opinion the best of them, at least of those I have read, and really a great book. But the fact that I have liked other books of yours gave me no reason for intruding upon you to say so. This last one, however, is a different matter. I have had an experience which corresponds to yours, although it was much shorter and was less profound; and although it was apparently—but only apparently—embraced in a different spirit. . . .

[After] a stay of about two months [in Spain] I no longer felt any inner compulsion to participate in a war which, instead of being what it had appeared when it began—a war of famished peasants against landed proprietors and their clerical supporters—had become a war between Russia on the one hand and Germany and Italy on the other.

I recognize the smell of civil war, the smell of blood and terror, which exhales from your book; I have breathed it too. I must admit that I neither saw nor heard of anything which quite equalled the ignominy of certain facts you relate, such as the murders of elderly peasants or the *Ballillas* [a Fascist corps] chasing old people and beating them with truncheons. But for all that, I heard quite enough. I was very nearly present at the execution of a priest. In the minutes of suspense I was asking myself whether I should simply look on or whether I should try to intervene and get myself shot as well. I still don't know which I would have done if a lucky chance had not prevented the execution. . . .

Having been in Spain, I now continually listen to and read all sorts of observations about Spain, but I could not point to a single person, except you alone, who has been exposed to the atmosphere of the civil war and has resisted it. What do I care that you are a royalist, a disciple of [Édouard] Drumont? You are incomparably nearer to me than my comrades of the Aragon militias—and yet I loved them. [1938]

> Simone Weil. *Seventy Letters* (London,
> Oxford University Press, 1965), pp. 105–6, 109

With Claudel now too old, Bernanos is the most powerful living Christian writer. Mauriac is also a Christian writer, but, in describing the soul's perversity, the weakness of the flesh, and the sins of the spirit, he confuses himself with his subject. . . .

Bernanos lives freely in the only living world, the world in which not only poets and saints but also true philosophers have lived—the world of vision, the world in which things are seen as they are, not as they appear. . . . The things of the "world here below" are never as vital as they are through the mystic's gaze. There would be no painters, poets, or musicians if there were no mystics. Artists are simply mystics who remain behind in the world of appearances and immediacy, mystics who are prisoners of the first phase of mysticism, but mystics all the same.

Bernanos is a mystic on both levels. I will admit that from time to time there is some weakening of mystical power and grace in him. Like Giono, his equal in inspiration and in power, he submits to the pernicious influence of France, and sometimes he falls into a kind of sentimental demagogy, a whining complacency. This Christian of good pedigree, this heir of Bloy, Villiers de l'Isle-Adam, [Jules] Barbey d'Aurevilly, and [Joseph] de Maistre falls into an incoherent delirium in which, surprised by the innovations of our century, he feels more hatred toward the unexpected and mysterious defenders of what he loves than toward his traditional enemies.

> Pierre Drieu la Rochelle. *Notes pour comprendre
> le siècle* (Paris, Gallimard, 1941), pp. 175–78†

Bernanos' refusal to compromise, however noble it may seem to us, nevertheless partakes of a certain sterile pride. This inspired soul, who was able to create saints, infusing into them his own breath, was also able to transmit some elements of his own deep nature to creatures molded by hate. . . .

That is enough to put us on our guard. In spite of Bernanos' advice and all his words of execration, men must stay in their native land and consent to work in the mud; the seeds sown by generations of democratic priests, at whom he scoffed, have to bear their fruit in the byways; simple Christians must be willing to dirty their hands in politics, they must wear themselves out laboring in the holds of the dismantled ship so they may repair all the leaks in them. Let us not yield to the easy temptation of placing the real nation on the level of Joan of Arc, the holy curate of Ars, and Péguy, so that we may have the right to kick aside the other France, as though it were a rotting boat. The real France is the one of which we are a part. We may be ashamed of it in this long period of waiting, but we still want to look into its ravaged face with love. That is the France to which we choose to remain loyal, not the excessively sublime image that Bernanos holds up above our reach through the centuries and into the heavens. [1948]

> François Mauriac. *Letters on Art and Literature*
> (New York, Philosophical Library, 1953), pp. 13–15

It was difficult for me to talk with Bernanos. Even his compliments were a problem: I did not know how to respond to them or how to reciprocate. He sent me a copy of *The Imposture* with a dedication I only showed to two people, and his praise was of great help to me later, during crises of doubt. . . .

Is it not shameful to write that twenty-three years after having received it I finally cut open the pages of *The Imposture*? I had never read it before. My conduct toward Bernanos was not what it should have been. He was kind and generous. I did not take the one step toward him that he had a right to expect, but he spoke about politics to me, and I immediately lost my footing. If he had spoken about religion instead, I do not for a moment doubt that he would have helped me, but perhaps he felt that he had said everything he had to say about that subject in his books. He had the strange quality that is called genius, the violent imbalance that always carries a person too far—in other words, to places others venture to later. He had neither the prudence and circumspection of X, nor the fondness for honors of Y, nor the cleverness of Z, who is merely clever. Bernanos had the blind courage of a charging bull.

All the faults of *The Imposture* do not diminish for me the captivation of its excesses themselves. The greatest of Bernanos's gifts was the sense of God and of sin. His Abbé Cénabre is ultimately frightening. Who before Bernanos had ever searched so deeply into the soul of a bad priest? All that said, I still find the content of the book ponderous. No matter how exciting Bernanos's psychological explanations may be, they are still reminiscent of the heavy furniture that only a very broad-shouldered man can move, and the reader cannot help but feel that he has lent a hand himself to the job of moving the furniture. The result is the fatigue one feels when reading Bernanos. But I do not want to give the impression of laughing at him; he is, in my eyes, one of the great ones. [March, 1950]

Julien Green. Journal, 1946–1950 (Paris,
Librairie Plon, 1951), pp. 346–47†

Dialogues of the Carmelites [is] the story of the Carmelite nuns of Compiègne who were guillotined during the French Revolution. Theirs is an old story, yet it is closer to us than France's 1940 defeat as seen by Sartre. I read it at one sitting, and for the first time in years felt the thrill of awe, the instinctive urge to pay tribute that a masterpiece awakens.

The beauty of this book, which makes Claudel's plays seem pale, is simple. Here the drama of fear—the essential drama of our time—is analyzed and mastered with inexorable logic: not with the pseudo-logic of modern naturalism but with the eternal accuracy of art. Bernanos does not describe appearances; he re-creates the feelings and actions of people who suffer in their individual ways the fatality of a history from which they must free themselves. For him the story, no matter how fearful, is a false prison; it cannot fetter the freedom through which man wins salvation. . . .

[What] might be a fresco from the Lives of the Saints . . . becomes a drama because of the presence among the novices of Blanche de la Force, a young aristocrat whose whole life has been dominated by fear and who sought refuge from the terrors of the world in the convent. Now in the cloister itself fear takes possession of her. It is a fear stronger and more sharply defined than any she has ever known. Cornered, compelled to face reality, she takes the martyr's vow with her companions. But no sooner has she spoken the words than she understands their real meaning, and flees. No human appeal can bring her back, for she has sunk into a disgrace more tenacious than fear itself. Yet on the day of the execution, as the "Veni Creator" ends on the last nun's lips, it rises again from the crowd, and Blanche in her turn comes forward to die. . . .

Bernanos has written the epic of fear for all time, and it is also an epic of freedom. Blanche de la Force ascends the scaffold not because she is moved by the example of others, but because she is free in the midst of her fear to take responsibility for it, and by so doing to master it, even though suffering it until the end.

Pierre Emmanuel. Com. April 7, 1950, pp. 680, 682

Bernanos the novelist, in relation to his characters, exercises not psychological analysis but a form of knowledge that bears a close resemblance to the knowledge with which he endows his priests. . . . It is not enough to say that Bernanos is the creator of the French priestly novel, in other words, the novel whose central character is a priest. One must go further and designate Bernanos himself as a "priestly novelist," that is, a novelist who, in relation to the creatures of his fictitious universe, performs functions similar to those of a priest. . . .

While the priest of Ambricourt [in *Diary of a Country Priest*] resembles the novelist Bernanos, the anti-priest Ouine [in *Mr. Ouine*] is the total inversion of Bernanos and could be taken as his portrayal of the psychological novelist. . . . Like other novels by Bernanos, *Mr. Ouine* was initially conceived as a satirical portrait, in this case of André Gide, and the protagonist's very name—*Ouine* is *oui-non*—alludes to the famous "open-mindedness" of Gide and to his refusal to make choices. Yet, clearly, Bernanos forgot his original model as he wrote the book—which cost him no less than ten years of anguished labor and whose final episodes he could not bring himself to confront for a long time—and Mr. Ouine began to resemble no one other than Bernanos himself—or rather what Bernanos would have been, as he well knew, if he had crossed the boundary he often approached: if he had given way to despair; if he had allowed love to wither away within him.

Albert Béguin. Bernanos par lui-même (Paris,
Éditions du Seuil, 1954), pp. 77–79†

Bernanos included himself among the poor and with every reason for he had brought up a large family of six children, and although his books were successful and sold well they for a long time brought him in hardly enough to live on. . . . To Bernanos poverty was not only natural but necessary. . . . Bernanos was proud of his service in the ranks of the poor in time of peace just as he was of his service in the ranks of the army in the time of war, since it seemed to him that only in the brotherhood of the poor did there remain any relic of the spirit of Christian chivalry, and of comradeship in arms.

Bernanos' method of work was closely bound up with this pride in his poverty. "We live on our work, and not on its accumulated income, we live and we work each day for that day, our work and our life are the same bread—*panem quotidianum.*" But honourable though it is such a rule of life had obvious disadvantages for a writer such as Bernanos. It meant that he had no time for reflection, little leisure to find out what he really wanted to write about. It meant that he could allow no time for his work to shape itself. His sensibility had always to be on the alert, always on edge, ready like a yapping house dog to jump out at the firstcomer, and liable to waste its mark and its bite on the butcher's boy when it should have been kept for the real burglar who comes quietly and by night. It meant in particular for Bernanos that he remained a pamphleteer when he might have become a political thinker, and that as a novelist he remained limited to the portrayal of a single state of mind from which he could never escape.

David Tylden-Wright. *The Image of France*
(London, Secker & Warburg, 1957), pp. 115–16

Charles Maurras wrote that there is no absolute assurance that France will survive for ever. There is a need for constant effort—this is the essence of civilization—to maintain a thing so fragile as a community of men. Bernanos' notion of France was, perhaps, less exclusive and intolerant than that of Maurras, but more spiritual and more truly mystical. In a sense, all his works, including his novels, deal with France; with the exception of *The Vast Cemeteries in the Moonlight*, they describe French events, take place on French soil and search out French problems. In another sense, however, they deal with the eternally human as reflected in France, in the French soul and history. His confidence in the destiny of France is Christian in inspiration, whereas the basic pessimism of Maurras strikes a late pagan tone, that of the dying Roman Empire. Bernanos refused to surrender to the monstrous forces he denounced because he stubbornly believed that Divine Providence rules the universe and that France, the finest fruit of man's achievement, has a supernatural backing. Thus his country was for him at once the guarantee of the ultimate survival of freedom in the world, *and* the sensitive instrument which measures mankind's state of spiritual integrity. . . .

Bernanos was not an aggressive nationalist like Maurras. With Maurras, nationalism was an ideology, a policy, a plan of action; with Bernanos, patriotism was a supernatural duty—a duty to remain human and linked to God, to continue living by bread and by faith. To be a patriot, for him, was as natural a task as to be religious and therefore essentially *open* towards others, not *closed* as the Maurrassian doctrine implies. Much has been said about "the civilizing mission of France," but it has been said by diplomats, professors, cultural organizations and textbooks, with the result that the expression has become a platitude; but Bernanos lived it as a reality. His vehemence against the *bienpensants* ["right-thinking"], Munich, the armistice, Vichy, against the abuses of the Liberation, cannot be understood except in the light of his horrified indignation that France was betraying itself. And his vivid hopes that his country would again resist, and resist better, against machines and robots, were born from the desire that by saving the world for freedom, France would redeem itself.

Thomas Molnar. *Bernanos: His Political Thought and Prophecy* (New York, Sheed and Ward, 1960), pp. 151–52, 154–55

Despite its failure as a novel—it is not fully successful as a mystery, nor does it really develop its stunning basic theme—*A Crime* is a fascinating work, for it revolves around the most enigmatic aspect of the Bernanosian "lie": the antagonist's thirst for the prophetic, life-giving role of the priest. More even than the "secret" of childhood, which in most lives does not survive the actual age of childhood, it is the mystery of the "child of grace" that obsesses the novelist's sterile and avid usurpers of life. In first killing, then impersonating the new curé of Mégère, the heroine of *A Crime* enacts, for the brief duration of her phantastic exploit, not only her mother's nostalgia for a lost Paradise but the evil dream of all the impostors who, inspired by a raging envy, seek to parody the priest's deep and vital communion with the mystery of creation through love, and presume to shape and direct human destinies. . . .

Bernanos' great drama of a counterfeit priestly vocation is found in *The Imposture* and *Joy*, the two novels which the writer deplored not having the time to recast into one and which really form an indivisible whole. . . .

Joy should have been Bernanos' greatest work. Its scope is extraordinary, encompassing as it does the journey of a spiritually gifted girl from her first joyful glimpse of Paradise; through a world of men who "prefer cold to hot" and whose perverse "thirst" for self-destruction the infinite spring of God's own love cannot redeem and quench save by spending itself to the last, to death; to her agony in the Garden of Olives, in which, in a final outflowing of the deepest springs of her life, she redeems Cénabre from the satanic abyss. As it stands, it is an uneven work, parts of which may justify Bernanos' own disappointed remark that it is a Magnificat that does not sing. But its best pages match the level of his masterpiece *The Diary of a Country Priest* both in evocative power and depth of vision.

Gerda Blumenthal. *The Poetic Imagination of
Georges Bernanos* (Baltimore, Johns Hopkins
University Press, 1965), pp. 67–68, 71, 93

The Diary of a Country Priest is the most famous, the most popular, and the most highly considered of Bernanos' novels. . . . No one else could have written it, and yet it is as different from *Under the Sun of Satan* as it is from *Mr. Ouine* or *A Bad Dream*. The soutane is there, on every page, but the features of those who wear it have radically changed. The themes are familiar, but the variations are new. *Under the Sun of Satan* is a sad book, and *Mr. Ouine* leads one to a precipice of despair. *The Diary of a Country Priest* is a happy book, for all its burden of sin and suffering, because Bernanos found happiness in writing it. . . .

A writer wishing to give the impression of the diurnal round, varying little from one day to another, will find the diary a convenient—perhaps a too convenient—form. Bernanos does not fall into such traps as are here laid out for him. In conveying monotony he does not weary the reader, and he registers all the time a gradual progress towards the climax of the book. There is the progress, hardly suspected, towards death; and there is a corresponding growth in spiritual wisdom as the lessons of experience are digested. The priest's old friend from the seminary, in whose arms he dies, is introduced to us at an early point; it is already made clear that he has left the active ministry and is living with a mistress. Moreover, in eschewing melodrama, Bernanos does not dispense with dramatic confrontations. . . .

Much of Bernanos' writing is a passionate monologue; *The Diary of a Country Priest* is a dialogue with himself, which he objectifies into a dialogue with other people.

Robert Speaight. *Georges Bernanos* (New York,
Liveright, 1974), pp. 146, 150, 152

BERNARD, JEAN-JACQUES (1888–1972)

The art [of indirect language] is perilous. It leads a dramatist to write plays that are forever the same, plays to which the public will become less and less responsive. What begins as a spontaneous inclination risks being transformed into a system. The writer will mechanically apply a method he has mastered and whose effectiveness he has tested. Beyond that, he will confine himself to a very narrow choice of subjects. He will refuse to present violent conflicts or unusual characters on stage, but will instead favor a slow pace and characters who are toned down, who have stray impulses instead of desires, and who have only embryonic passions. He will condemn himself to stories without events, to gray paintings, to impressions of veiled monotones. All this has its charm; but works so conceived are on a secondary level.

I do not doubt that Jean-Jacques Bernard knows these things very well. He has a natural inclination for this kind of dramatic conception. At the moment he does not dream of turning it into a system. Nevertheless, I believe he must beware. When I saw *Invitation to a Voyage* the other day, I understood how the dangers I have just described could arise. Some of the spectators did not know of the author, or at least had not seen any of his plays. These spectators were enthralled with the indirect dialogue, enveloped in dreams and full of resonance. They applauded the very subtle and original talent that was revealed to them. Those who were familiar with the playwright, those who had seen his previous plays, however, were less ready to admire this one and instead displayed a certain reserve. They could see what was artificial in the simplicity and the intentional bareness of these brief scenes. They felt that a system was in the making. . . . What will happen if he pursues this course and keeps writing plays just like this one?

I am expressing these fears because of the great hope I have for Jean-Jacques Bernard and because of my conviction that he is one of those who could help create the theater of tomorrow. I would like to see him aim higher and enlarge his scope. A play like *Invitation to a Voyage* confirms his reputation but does not increase it.

Pierre Brisson. APL. March 2, 1924, p. 229†

Jean-Jacques Bernard is not an isolated apparition. He is to be regarded as typical of a movement which is sensibly affecting most of the younger dramatists and which is having a very considerable influence on contemporary French acting and producing. His career, moreover, is admirably significant of the conditions now prevailing in Paris. His work is definitely of the younger school and it was first recognized by the smaller societies. But it is perhaps the most remarkable sign of the present vigorous theatrical times in Paris that the old-established houses are immediately ready to encourage any sane and promising development. . . . M. Jean-Jacques Bernard, proclaiming in 1922 that the theatre was above all an art of the unexpressed, was in 1924 admitted to the Théâtre de l'Odéon. The production at that theatre of *Invitation to a Voyage* was a signal triumph for the theory of silence. In the very citadel of the French literary tradition—a theatre in which heroes had for generations unpacked their hearts in Alexandrines without number—there was presented a play in which the hero not only failed to speak even a single word, but went so far as never to appear upon the stage. . . .

The Springtime of Others is a play in which the principal motive, though always actively present, is never once referred to explicitly. In *Martine*, produced by Les Campagnons de la Chimère in 1922, we have a play in which the theory of silence is applied to the presentment of the principal character. Martine, the most vital and comprehensible of the persons in the play, is the person who says least. Never once does she tell us explicitly what she is feeling and thinking. In spite of this—or rather because of it—she is more real to us, we divine and understand more of what is passing in her mind than we do of any of the others. The author obliges us to follow her thoughts and emotions from the things that are said to her. We are made to identify ourselves with that inarticulate figure as the people around her wound or solace her by the things they say or do. Every line is of importance in the play only so far as it touches Martine; we think only of its effect upon *her*; everything said or done increases our knowledge of this simple creature, who thus emerges alive and intimate from her environment.

John Palmer. *Studies in the Contemporary Theatre*
(London, Martin Secker, 1927), pp. 96, 104–5

M. Bernard is introduced [in the program for *Martine*] as the archexplainer of himself. He says: "The theatre, above all, is the art of the unexpressed. It is less according to the rejoinders themselves than by the effect of the rejoinders that the most profound sentiments ought to be revealed. In addition to the dialogue which is heard, it is necessary to bring out a subjacent dialogue and to render this intelligible to the audience. . . ."

Great artists should always be protected against themselves. What this very fine playwright means is that the theatre is a house of many mansions, one of which may properly be set aside for "the art of the unexpressed." As *Martine* proves, this can be a lovely little mansion, and in this line M. Bernard is easily the world's foremost painter and decorator. But just as all rooms in a house should not be alike, so it is nonsense to say that the theatre "above all" ought to be this, that, or the other thing. Long before M. Bernard "the logic of the theatre" did not admit sentiments which the situation did not demand. Or else we should find Goneril [in *King Lear*] interrupting her father's curse and telling the old man to put a sock in it. . . .

The theme of *Martine* is exquisitely suited not so much to the idiom as to the self-denying ordinance which M. Bernard has invented for and passed upon himself. But I have to say that in my opinion he has cheated. His theatre proclaims itself as relying not on dialogue which is heard, but upon subjacent dialogue which is not; its heard melodies may be sweet or sour, but those unheard ones are to be the ones that matter. Surely if this theory is to be at all valid it should be applied to people who have a power of expression which because of the dramatist's self-imposed discipline, they must not use? Silence is only golden because speech is silver, and dumbness is no virtue in a man who cannot speak. If, therefore, there were any serious theory of playwriting involved, the characters in this play must be capable not only of knowing what they are suffering, but of expressing that knowledge. Whereas the tragedy in this piece is the exact opposite, since it is the tragedy of dumb animals who do not need any theory of non-expression to explain their inability to talk.

James Agate. *Times*. May 28, 1933, p. 6

Bernard's concentration on pure emotion at the expense of the intellectual and reflective element in man indicates an impoverishment of the human material of the drama and a consequent lack of vitality in his work. As Silvio d'Amico says, there is a suggestion of decadence, "a refined decadence." The Unexpressed with Bernard is closely associated with an incompleteness of character, of which Marceline and Antoine of *The Unquiet Spirit* are extreme examples. There is a lack of equilibrium; the people are, as it were, overweighted emotionally, they have no serenity and are unequal to the demands of life. Bernard's characters tend to run away from life rather than struggle with it. His is an elegiac theatre of rêverie and escape. And it becomes clear that the essential factor missing in this "silent" drama is the human will as a positive force. . . .

The dramatic use of the Unexpressed, deriving as it does from emotion, either conscious or unconscious, involves a discounting of the human will. As with Racine, the fatality lies in the constitution of the personality. With Racine, however, the human will, though destined to be defeated, is a force to be reckoned with, and therefore dramatic. This is not the case with Bernard and the virtual elimination of so important

transcendental being, shows the extent to which the problematic individual's spirit tries to rationalize or to justify his downfall. . . . Is not the truly absurd or problematic man the one who, from the depths of his being, considers himself an absurdity, a meaningless being, yet who nevertheless clings to life with an unheard-of tenacity? In other words, however rational some of Ahouna's words may seem, they are less the result of a sober reflection on the overt world than the self-criticism of a psychological state mutilated by existential anxiety. It is in this anxiety that the real meaning and the motive of the hero's crime must be sought. And this crime, the murder of an innocent woman, can be considered here a gratuitous act. It has no other motivation than what can be furnished by a pathological neurosis.

Sunday O. Anozie. Sociologie du roman africain
(Paris, Éditions Aubier-Montaigne, 1970),
pp. 161–62, 164–65†

BILLETDOUX, FRANÇOIS (1927–   )

If I had to choose the best French play of the year, I would probably go for *Tchin-Tchin*, by a young writer named François Billetdoux, which I saw at a pocket theatre in Montparnasse. From the tiel and the locale, you might forgivably imagine it to be an experimental work of the kind that one associates with M. Ionesco and Samuel Beckett. In fact, it is a simple tragi-comedy, composed in a style that can only, if drably, be described as poetic realism.

The two main characters are a guarded young-middle-aged Englishwoman called Mrs. Puffy-Picq, whose husband has just left her, and Cesareo, a rueful Italian whose wife has just run off with Mr. Puffy-Picq. The Italian pays a nervous visit to the Englishwoman. Tentatively, they drink. They drink a lot; hence the title [a Chinese toast]. Gradually, hopelessly, they try to complete the classic pattern by falling in love themselves. It doesn't work; they mistrust each other too much, and, anyway, the equation doesn't balance. Yet by the end of the play they have achieved, after a series of violent ups and downs, something that approaches consolation. Neither of them will now collapse or commit suicide, though it is likely that both will go on drinking quite heavily. They remain, to the end, essentially comic characters, and that is what makes them moving; they will survive without sentimentality, suspecting that they may be fairly silly and not caring very much if they are.

The curtain falls on a note of true, hard-earned optimism, which I prefer to the facile pessimism of so much left-bank writing. . . . M.

Billetdoux is in his early thirties and has plenty of time to lure the younger French playwrights out of the blind alley into which Messrs. Beckett and Ionesco have beguiled them. To assert that all communication between human beings is impossible is rather like putting on a strait jacket and then complaining about the impossibility of shaking hands. If I understand him rightly, M. Billetdoux is saying that communication is desperate and rare, always difficult and seldom total; but possible, with whatever qualifications; possible, all the same. [1959]

Kenneth Tynan. Curtains (New York, Atheneum,
1961), pp. 421–22

The characters in François Billetdoux' plays utter the faint and anguished cries of men and women whose illusions have been shattered by the brutal forces of life which envelop them. Billetdoux introduces us to human beings searching to realize their dreams and aspirations, to fix and to hold on to something solid, and by so doing, to give themselves faith in living. But these intangibles in which his characters believe and which serve to propel them onward, are too abstract and too fleeting to be satisfying. A fundamental feeling of futility overcomes even those who seemingly inhabit a contented world in which religious and political questions are never baffling.

Billetdoux' theater is pessimistic. For his characters, living is a difficult struggle between how they wish to live and how they actually live. At times, he brightens his bleak world with light touches of humor. But his humor leaves a sting since it merely masks the dissatisfied yearnings which his creations cannot face and from which they constantly seek escape.

Billetdoux, a master of orthodox theatrical technique, fashions his plays with skill, leading us forward to climax and final dénouement. His style is taut and rapid, at once romantic and realistic; prosaic, yet with the counterforce of bold and tender images, frightening silences, periods of delirium. As his characters converse, their personalities are slowly revealed to us in all their grandeur and degradation. Billetdoux never manipulates his creations; he lets them glide and talk willy-nilly, responding to their inner compulsions. He tries to remain objective, an outsider peering in, a doctor studying a patient through a microscope, or a botanist fascinated by the thousands of small lines and hollows in a piece of vegetable. Yet, in spite of his efforts at detachment, Billetdoux still looks upon his characters with humanity and compassion.

Bettina L. Knapp. MD. Sept., 1964, p. 199

American audiences know Billetdoux's *Tchin-Tchin*, a rigorous, mathematical, and sober little play (despite its alcoholic content), with only two characters, which on Broadway was unfortunately blown up into a spectacular and burlesque star vehicle. Its theme was clearly defined, however, and from this first play to his later works, Billetdoux has raised questions about the relationship of the individual to society, his accomplishments in the outside world, and man's use of other men. . . .

The form of *How Is the World, Mister? It's Turning, Mister!* is extremely Brechtian. The characters move around in the world (from eastern Europe to the United States); the scenes are dated (from December 1944 to August 1945—the atomic bomb on Hiroshima and Nagasaki); the two "human" heroes are surrounded by mute figures (fellow prisoners, soldiers, civilians, customs officers, a wife, and so on) whose silence and pantomimes situate them on another level of scenic reality; and the scenes are interspersed with "meaningful" songs (a Nazi improvisation, a Jewish lament, a Negro spiritual, and a ballad in the manner of Boris Vian). But this truly Brechtian spectacle is primarily related to the German playwright's negative works, with the addition of a really French savor. The dialogue (only the two heroes speak, one a deported French soldier, the other an American prisoner) is midway between the language of Paul Raynal's 1914 soldiers in *Human Raw Material* (1935) and that of Louis-Ferdinand Céline. The subject matter itself is a common little Frenchman's cocky banter and gumption confronted by American pragmatism. . . .

Man can survive only by exploiting man or allowing himself to be exploited. Men love or hate one another for their exchange value. Thus, in contrast to the Marxists' "open" tragedy based on economy, Billetdoux has written a closed melodramatic epic based on a parallel explanation of the workings of society.

Jacques Guicharnaud, with June Guicharnaud.
Modern French Theatre from Giraudoux to Genet,
rev. ed. (New Haven, Yale University Press, 1967),
pp. 209–10

During the whole performance of [*Rintru Pa Trou Tar, Hin*]—an interminable rhapsody, an excessive hodgepodge, an overwhelming exercise in "messaphysics"—I kept wondering how many critics would have the courage to tell the truth the next day: that they were bored to death; that they had to expend the greatest effort to keep from sleeping; that their boredom was written on their faces; and, above all, that they didn't understand a single word and were honestly unable to say what the play was all about.

Is this the world of alcohol, of drugs, of more-or-less artificially induced dreams? Is this the psychiatrist's universe or the patient's? Where are we? Where do people talk this way, in what country? What is this gibberish, this mongrel language, this Chinese? In what kind of mind was this language of stomach rumbling developed, and to mean what? What are we being shown? A house that has exploded, an investigation, policemen, television reporters. What is Billetdoux trying to prove? That communication is impossible?—this is only too true when one is offered a vehicle for thought such as this. That each person has his own preoccupations and dramas? Is it a satire? Is it an attack? Against whom?—the police, governments, newspapers, radio, television, the innocent, the victims, the guilty, the "nutty"? I certainly do not know.

We swim in incoherence; we drown in absurdity; we choke on the tons of insanities we are fed—most of them not even in French. It is appalling. Faced with a play like this one by Billetdoux, I feel as if I were in the presence of the product of another species, another race, another form of humanity. [March 5, 1971]

Jean-Jacques Gautier. *Théâtre d'aujourd'hui* (Paris, Julliard, 1972), pp. 371–72†

François Billetdoux . . . is the only playwright of any stature to appear [in France] in recent years. He first attracted attention with his ironic study of two opposites drawn together through drink in *Tchin-Tchin* but it was the production of *Well, Go Along to Törpe's Place* in the Studio des Champs-Elysées (1961) which established him as a writer to watch. Here we meet the beautiful Madame Törpe in her Central European pensione where recently five of her clients have committed suicide. A police inspector arrives to investigate, only to discover that all her clients are hovering on the precipice of self-destruction, and that Madame is doing nothing about it. It is left to the inspector to argue the case for life. . . .

You Must Pass through the Clouds was produced by Jean-Louis Barrault in the Théâtre de France, 1964. Billetdoux describes this as a "bourgeois epic" in five movements. . . . It is a highly ambitious play, but the author has an excessive overflow of language and obscurity, and the play lacks, it seems to me, the precision of *Well, Go Along to Törpe's Place*; he is trying too hard to achieve effects, and the result is somewhat pretentious. Real achievement in art is simplicity; with *Silence, the Tree Is Still Moving* and even more so with *Rintru Pa Trou Tar, Hin!* Billetdoux seems to have fallen into confusion, and risks ending up with a coterie, impressed by his incoherence, rather than a public who cannot be fooled all the time.

Frederick Lumley. *New Trends in Twentieth Century Drama* (New York, Oxford University Press, 1972), pp. 363–64

BLAIS, MARIE-CLAIRE (1939–   )

CANADA

Miss Blais of Canada is said to claim that she finds comparison of herself with Miss Sagan of France invidious. Since she fails to announce with whom she might prefer to be grouped—like most writers of first novels she feels perhaps that she is *sui generis*—I retain the urge to classify her in that particular cult. She is surely one of the children who play at decadence. Certainly she bears no resemblance to the French-Canadian girls I myself knew when I was growing up in Quebec. If we stayed little girls for an incredible number of years, our French counterparts, isolated in their convents, were even more so. . . . We were on the whole notoriously unsophisticated. Now comes a new vintage French Canadian. The voice of television and of the beatnik and of the Latin Quarter is heard in the land. Even anachronistic Quebec responds by losing some of its parochial flavor. A home-grown product like Miss Blais becomes possible. . . .

The Beautiful Beast is a wild romance, compounded out of imagist poetry and youthful vapors. It is full of sighs and shudders and scornful laughs; it fairly crawls with the more obvious Freudian symbols. In New Yorkese, Miss Blais' characters are very sick indeed. They make the old fairy tales from which they are derived and in which it is currently fashionable to dig for nastiness look dreadfully wholesome. . . .

There is this to be said for Miss Blais. The faint fragrance of self-consciousness, the autobiographic actuality or the projected wish that makes the work of Françoise Sagan or of Yael Dayan embarrassing is missing here. The Beautiful Beast is made up out of whole bookish cloth. It can bear no resemblance to anyone's life, either literally or symbolically. Further, a certain poetic felicity and a merciful sense of brevity are at least partially saving graces.

Nora Magid. Com. Dec. 9, 1960, pp. 297–99

In *A Season in the Life of Emmanuel* [Blais] has made a definite new departure. The clairvoyant's crystal ball that revealed the diminished, remote and somewhat mysterious visions englobed in the early novels has been suddenly darkened and filled with the turbid and swirling sediment of the actual French Canadian world—with the squalor and the squirming life that swarms in the steep-roofed cement-covered houses of the little Canadian towns. . . . Though the material of *A Season in the Life of Emmanuel* is that of an actual milieu in all its prosaic and sordid detail, it is not presented prosaically nor even, in spite of its horrors, sordidly, but infused—and sometimes a little blurred—by the fantasies of adolescence, saturated with the terrors and appetites, the starving and stifled aspirations of these young people in their prisoned overpopulated world. . . .

I first read this book in manuscript and wondered whether it could ever be published in French Canada. . . . There has been, to be sure, in the local reviews some holding up of hands in horror at Marie-Claire Blais's unpleasant picture; but, on the whole, to one's astonishment, the reception of the book has been favorable. . . . [She] has in the past sometimes been the subject of exacerbated controversy; but one now gets the impression, in reading the reviews of Mlle. Blais's latest book, that her compatriots—who are now so zealous, in their struggle against the English-speaking ascendancy, to put forward their cultural claims— are becoming proud of this young writer.

Edmund Wilson. Introduction to Marie-Claire Blais,

A Season in the Life of Emmanuel (New York,

Farrar, Straus & Giroux, 1966), pp. vi–ix

It is worth noting that the structure of *The Day Is Dark*, a somewhat Gidean structure, is the same as that of *The Unsubmissive Woman*. In both Blais novels characters speak in turn, and each interior monologue forms a separate section of the book. The monologues add to or alter our feelings about the speakers created by the monologues of the other characters. In *The Day Is Dark* the characters' unbalance becomes evident even sooner than in *The Unsubmissive Woman*. . . .

Why are Blais's characters marked by misfortune and virtually fascinated by it? The answer is that they are all "unsubmissive." . . . What else is there to be said? They might be called metaphysical: they rebel against an eternal order of things (or at least against an order that has thus far been eternal)—the order of life, and therefore of time, and therefore of death. Very complex, secretive, and tormented, these characters have a romantic thirst for the absolute and the impossible. They want only to do good, and they lose their clear-sightedness in the process; they test their courage and do wrong, contrary to their intentions. With a shock of pain, they are made to face their imperfect and tragic condition —which is, moreover, governed by time. From the first page to the last of these short novels, death is an immortal bird spreading its black wings. [1966]

Yves Berger. Preface to Marie-Claire Blais,

L'insoumise (Paris, Éditions Bernard Grasset, 1971),

pp. 8–10†

Although the basic structures of fiction are still recognizable [in *The Day Is Dark* and *The Sacred Travelers*], they have been weakened and distorted to prevent any illusion of realistic dimension or true-to-life anecdote from distracting us from the author's intention. Without warning the narrative shifts from one character to another, chronology is jumbled, events are sometimes contradictory, and the fancied is never clearly separated from the real. By a series of interior monologues Mlle. Blais works along the lower levels of consciousness, and only rarely does she come to the surface.

The world of her revery is the somber, shadowy one of primitive urges and responses. The characters do not know why they exult in life or wish for death. Mysterious tropisms bring them into contact one with the other and cause them sorrowfully to part. Each obeys a force that resembles a tragic predestination, leading them in a lonely quest through life to their final destination. In *The Day is Dark* the prominence of the family as a unit suggests that the author is describing a house accursed by God. There is also a hint that she has in mind her generation—the last men on earth before the end of the world, "the time of assassins." Really nothing less than the mortal adventure itself is her theme and inspiration—the life of sorrow and symbolic gesture as apprehended by one sort of Christian consciousness.

To express her vision of life, Marie-Claire Blais lets her words pour forth in a rhapsodic torrent. In *The Sacred Travelers* they often form into verses, but everywhere they have the poetic qualities of image and cadence as they create laments and paeans, cries of love, lust, and hate for the wretched characters whose affliction is the sickness of life. The power of her writing is terrific.

Laurent LeSage. SR. April 29, 1967, p. 29

Four years ago the French-Canadian writer, Marie-Claire Blais wrote a remarkable novel, *A Season in the Life of Emmanuel*. I call it a novel for convenience, but more precisely the book is a Gothic romance. The empirical facts the story recites are offered not on their own account but as the appurtenances of dream, nightmare, fantasy. The child Emmanuel receives the gifts of time and place as if their only purpose were to sponsor the next acts of his inner life. Now Miss Blais has written another fiction [*The Manuscripts of Pauline Archange* and its continuation, *To Live! To Live!*] that emerges from the same context of feeling. The characters have different names, and there is a demonstrable change in the nature of the prime feeling, but the inner milieu is continuous with that of *A Season in the Life of Emmanuel.* . . .

If we think it wrong to call *A Season in the Life of Emmanuel* a novel, we must also give up calling [this volume] a novel, for it is a tale, something spoken and heard, a story recited from a great distance in the history of human feeling. Its formative terms are not, indeed, place and time, society, manners and morals, Quebec or today; it lives upon ancestral memories, natural laws, primitive needs. The world it invokes is indeed temporal, but haggard with the weight of centuries, and wise after the experience of death.

Denis Donoghue. NYT. July 12, 1970, p. 35

If in *The Unsubmissive Woman* Mlle. Blais indirectly explored the unrealized potential for good in the life of handsome, athletic, generous Paul Robinson, in [*David Sterne*] she investigates ugly tormented youth's capacity for evil and despair. The seminarian, Michel Rameau, is brilliant but frigidly rational. He believes that the only freedom in life lies in choosing one's own death. Sick and sensual David Sterne falls under his influence and together they conduct experiments in homosexuality, rape, theft and prostitution. These are cold and lonely experiments which provide no enjoyment, not even the satisfaction of revolt, not even a sense of solidarity in evil, for the two "friends" find no challenge in corruption and eventually grow callously indifferent to one another. Compared to the unrelieved, driven decadence of these two, Jean-Le Maigre's and Number Seven's dabbling in crime and perversion [in *A Season in the Life of Emmanuel*] seems robust and innocent fun. François Reine, the human torch and the most likable of the three, in turn falls under David Sterne's influence and, despairing of his feeble attempts to help the poor or to save or even reach David, finally chooses self-immolation.

In *David Sterne* Marie-Claire Blais is working close to the bottom of her murky imagination. Obsessed as always by the existence of evil and by what François Reine calls "the problem of lost souls," she engages the problem less in pursuit of a solution than as an observer on a one-way trip down the vortex of despair. She does not judge her miserable characters; she hardly attempts to account for their misery; she simply assumes it and tries to give it dramatic expression. In doing so she refuses the novelist's conventional all-seeing, all-knowing privileges and attitudes and presents her subject from the inside. So intense is her effort of sympathetic identification that her style, freeing itself from the rather mechanical control of *The Unsubmissive Woman*, breaks away into the lyric disarticulation of *The Day Is Dark*, though this time it carries much more violence and terror.

Philip Stratford. Marie-Claire Blais (Toronto,
Forum House, 1971), pp. 50–51

An almost standard Quebec vision of death is the vision of the dead baby (or dead babies): it's a fantasy often indulged in by mothers or grandmothers, and it's hard to tell whether they are torturing themselves with it or enjoying it, or both. Rose-Anna has this vision in [Gabrielle Roy's] *Secondhand Happiness*. . . . Grand-mère Antoinette in Blais' *A Season in the Life of Emmanuel* indulges in similar thoughts, though with more satisfaction. . . .

This obsession with death is not very cheering, but neither is it precisely morbid; it is simply an image which reflects a state of soul. What the image says is that the Quebec situation (or the Canadian situation) is dead or death-dealing, and therefore genuine knowledge of it must be knowledge of death. It is also an image of ultimate sterility and powerlessness, the final result of being a victim. . . .

The acquiescence in one's role as victim, the obsession with death [are the themes in] Marie-Claire Blais' *A Season in the Life of Emmanuel*. Again we find the poverty-stricken rural family, the mother drained by too-numerous babies, the coarse male figures who brutalize those weaker than themselves, the dying child, the daughter who elects to escape by becoming a nun. But the *willing* participation of the characters in the perpetuation of their own misery is here rendered explicitly. . . .

In such a world, pain is almost the only strong sensation available, and the characters take what pleasure they can from it. When Héloïse exchanges her convent and her family for a whorehouse, it isn't just a change from two authoritarian matriarchal institutions to a third: it's also a change from one kind of mortification of the flesh to another. And the author doesn't victimize her characters; she observes—through a nightmarish lens, to be sure—how they victimize themselves.

Margaret Atwood. *Survival* (Toronto, Anansi,
1972), pp. 223–26

Marie-Claire Blais's career was crowned in 1966 when she received the Prix Médicis for *A Season in the Life of Emmanuel*. . . . [The novel is] a veritable season in a hell in which poverty engenders vice, sickness, and death. *A Season in the Life of Emmanuel* is a brilliant achievement in which Blais pursues destiny in the manner of Bernanos and bares souls in the manner of Jouhandeau. It is a long cry of suffering and rebellion uttered by a procession of outcasts who have been brutalized by several centuries of submission. . . .

In *A Joualonais, His Joualonie* we are once again in Blais's fictional universe of unheroic heroes who are natural revolutionaries— more in words than in deeds—and who rebel against society, religion, and prevailing sexual mores. . . . These perverts are part of the world of hellish suffering, and Blais is its Hieronymus Bosch. Or, more accurately, the world of *A Joualonais, His Joualonie* is painted with the brush of [the Belgian artist James] Ensor.

The tragedy contains elements of farce. Misfortune comes close to buffoonery. Intellectuals, "gossipers from the thinking class," priests who "deflower children," shady members of the lower class, furious demonstrators—in the social tumult they all present only clownish faces, alternately sad and happy. Their constant scrambling is accompanied by the pervading mockery of *Joualon*, the popular French-Canadian speech, a cross between slang and patois, found in the city as well as in the country. Before this book Blais rarely used *Joualon*. . . . Blais is often criticized in Montreal literary circles for having spent more time in France and the United States during the past ten years than in Quebec. In *A Joualonais, His Joualone* she seems to be saying, with [her character] Eloi Papillon, "In this book my people should recognize themselves." It will consequently be more difficult for readers in France to follow her.

Jean Montalbetti. MagL. March, 1974, p. 29†

BLANCHOT, MAURICE (1907–   )

M. Blanchot does not remain faithful to his purpose. He had told us that he hopes that the meaning of *Aminadab* "vanishes as soon as one tries to understand it for itself." Very well, but in that case, why offer us a continual translation, a full commentary on its symbols? . . . I do not pretend to have grasped all the author's intentions and perhaps I have misunderstood a number of them. The fact that these intentions, even when obscure, were obvious, was enough to trouble me. I still think that with more effort or more intelligence I could have cleared them all up. In Kafka, the accidents link up in accordance with the necessities of the plot. In *The Trial*, for example, never for a moment do we lose sight of the fact that K. is struggling to defend his honourable character, his life. But why is Thomas [in *Aminadab*] struggling? He has no definite character, he has no purpose, he hardly interests us. And the events accumulate haphazardly. "As they do in life," someone may object. But life is not a novel, and the series of happenings without rhyme or reason that can be drawn from the novel turn our attention, in spite of ourselves, to the secret intentions of the author.

Why does Thomas lose his companion-in-chains and fall ill? Nothing in this upside-down world either prepares for or explains his illness. This means, then, that the reason for it lies outside this world, in the providential intentions of the author. Thus most of the time M. Blanchot is wasting his effort. He does not succeed in ensnaring the reader in the nightmarish world he is portraying. The reader escapes; he is outside—

outside with the author himself. He contemplates these dreams as he would a well-assembled machine.

He loses his footing only at rare moments. These moments are, moreover, enough to reveal in M. Blanchot a writer of quality. He is subtle and ingenious, at times profound. He has a love of words; he needs only to find his style. His venture into the fantastic is not without consequence, for it helps us to determine our bearings. Kafka could not be imitated; he remained on the horizon like a perpetual temptation. By having unwittingly imitated him, M. Blanchot delivers us from him. He brings his methods into the open. They are now catalogued, classified, fixed and useless, and no longer frightening or dizzying. [1943]

Jean-Paul Sartre. Literary and Philosophical Essays
(New York, Criterion, 1955), pp. 70–72

[In Blanchot's criticism] his metaphysical concern is so apparent and so unremitting that until some measure of justice has been done it, there can be no thought of lingering on the details of his critical techniques— it may, actually, be rendered almost superfluous to do so. From the outset we find ourselves beleaguered by anguish and nothingness in their reciprocally determined aggrandizement, by contradictions shackled irrevocably in the paradox, and we wonder, as Blanchot whirls us after him along the tortuous path which leads to ultimate insight (or ultimate bewilderment), whether aporistics, the science of the *discovery* of problems, must not indeed be viewed as the first and the only mental discipline. . . .

There is a remarkable absence of the comic sense in Blanchot's approach to literature. Not that any literary critic dealing with any author should seek to convulse the reader, but ambiguity, oscillation, paradox, how can they be divorced from wit, a wit which at times is the verbal equivalent of the chair displaced just as some dignitary is about to sit upon it? Peruse the list of his favored writers: to treat the quirks, sarcasms, parodies, banana skins of Kierkegaard, and Lautréamont, and Proust, and Bataille, and Raymond Queneau (Blanchot inevitably regards the fantastic or mythological novel as the true novel of the future) with no more than an occasional reference to "humour," "ironic," "comic," "absurd," and this last cannot be allowed to count, for the absurd, as the reader of Camus well knows, is nothing to laugh at—is close to being a *tour de force*. An interesting contrast is Kafka, the novelist of total frustration, of, as Sartre puts it, an impossible transcendence, who could not restrain his laughter while reading to his friends a chapter of *The Trial*.

Kenneth Douglas. YFS. Spring–Summer, 1947,
pp. 85, 88–89

The relationship between Kafka's fiction and Blanchot's in no way diminishes Blanchot's originality, because he continues the exploration and sheds light on his predecessor, instead of being satisfied, like so many others, with receiving light from Kafka. *The One Who Did Not Accompany Me* gives the impression, moreover, of Blanchot's moving on to something entirely new; consequently, the methods suitable for approaching Kafka's texts turn out to be almost unusable here. Blanchot's great triumph is to force us to borrow his language in order to speak about what he has created. . . .

He succeeds in evoking an attenuated double of reality, a double that explodes the weight and glory of our daily world as well as its precariousness. By showing us that it is possible to speak of a companion who, contrary to what we believed was necessary, did not accompany him, Blanchot somehow leads us into the antechamber of existence. This is why it is so difficult to summarize his text. It contains no action in the full sense of the word but only attempts unfolding in a space and time that lack some very important characteristics of our own.

The narrator has lost the firm surface of the world, and he is groping to find it again. His attempt can only be a return, because in any case his being is already there. Moreover, he says on many occasions that, during the whole course of his wandering, he is also elsewhere, and perfectly motionless. Part of him remains in this solid reality that has nevertheless escaped from him.

It would be useless to attempt to reduce this text to the description of a precise physiological or psychological condition. Nevertheless, it is clear that this text would have neither the same scope nor the same power if each of us were not capable of discovering parallels to our own experiences: insomnia, sickness, dizziness.

Michel Butor. *NRF*. Aug., 1953, pp. 331–32†

To the most serious-minded reader, I would recommend *The Last Man*, which could open his eyes to the "world we die in." But only after he has read this short book two or three times will the reader perceive the reason for taking up a book so arduous that at first he will be unable to enter into it. . . .

Three characters, each in his own way, come close to death. One of them, "the last man," finds himself near death before the other two: perhaps his entire life is a function of the death that enters into him. He does not have a definable concern about death himself, but the narrator watches him die, and for the narrator "the last man" is a reflection of the death that exists in him. In this man the narrator has the chance to observe and to contemplate death. . . .

It is hard to talk about *The Last Man*, because this book is so far beyond the limits within which most readers prefer to remain. But those who will undertake to read *The Last Man* will realize that it was in one man's power to dedicate his thought, in a book, to a movement that liberates him from his limits—at the risk of defying a danger. The writer is not the only one who needs the strength to confront that danger: Will the reader avoid this ultimate test? The extreme challenge of this book is to require us to confront head-on what this world and the existence we lead signify—their meaning and their non-meaning (only mental fatigue makes us separate the two).

Georges Bataille. *Critique*. Aug.–Sept., 1957,
pp. 676–77, 684†

Blanchot's work, says one of his few interpreters, offers no point of approach whatsoever. Today, twenty years after his first novel, he is still the most esoteric writer of contemporary France. There have appeared only three or four essays on his fiction; his novels remain untranslated. This is the more remarkable as Blanchot is also a prolific and well-known critic: besides his three novels, a number of *récits* [short narratives], and a dyad of short stories, he has published five thick volumes of criticism. But then his criticism has its difficulties too. . . .

The most puzzling as well as the most imaginative features of Blanchot's novels are linked to [his] dialectic of emanation, of strange intimacies and intimate estrangements. The distance between any two human beings in his novels is infinite and yet nothing. The magic of chance crystallizes and dissolves relationships. The shifts between familiarity and estrangement or, occasionally, life and death, are so quick and pervasive that they affect the very nature of the symbols used, and put the essence (the ontological status) of words in doubt. Blanchot is difficult to interpret because we can never say that *here* he reflects the world we know and *here* an imaginary world. He endows his symbols with a middle and unresolved quality, and he does this in part by a judicious use of the improbable, and an only exceptional use of the sheer fantastic. His latest *récits*, in fact, move purely in the realm of the improbable, and contain no fantastic incursions or overt breaches of the tenuous realism. The improbable, being a special case of chance, keeps the mind within the story, teasing it with the hope that all details together might solve the mystery, since no single event is quite absurd. But no resolution occurs, and the reader is obliged to take the mystery as an integral rather than resolved part of the whole; and since the whole is simply the novel, he thinks of the latter as the space in which a mystery is revealed, but *as* a mystery. . . .

Blanchot's personae never walk the straight line between two points: they seem imbued, physically and mentally, with a spirit of oblivion, and his novels strike us as being the most un-Aristotelian ever written—they are all *middle*. To be in Blanchot's world is to err: to follow something, to be involved in a maze of words or passageways, to encounter chance openings, to be attracted and distracted continually, to forget to remember, to remember to forget.

Geoffrey Hartman. In John Cruickshank, ed.,
The Novelist as Philosopher (London,
Oxford University Press, 1962), pp. 147, 150–51

We might call Blanchot the Mallarmé of the French novel, for he also is a writer in love with the absolute. His essays are long, meandering reflexions on language, its origins, its fundamental nature, and its possibilities. In a strange, esoteric fashion he links language with death, the essential and ultimate experience towards which all life tends. Language appears to him as a progression towards silence, the absolute speech. If Mallarmé's demon was that of analogy, Blanchot's is that of paradox. His thinking winds round and round upon itself until it seems that the essential antimonies of life and death, presence and absence, speech and silence resolve themselves into complete identity. In his criticism, he follows his metaphysical theme through other writers—English and German as well as French. In his creative pieces, he pursues it allegorically against a hallucinatory and fantastic background which recalls Kafka. *Aminadab*, which concerns a man who is seeking in a strange house the woman who has invited him there, would seem, for example, to depict humanity's groping efforts to orient itself in a world which it cannot understand. *The Almighty* gives a vision of mankind at the end of history, thus anticipating the author's later ruminations on the last man on earth, the last writer, the meaningless buzz that occurs after the last word has been uttered.

The novel, as Blanchot makes use of it, is therefore primarily an investigation of the language phenomenon—its form becomes its content, so to speak. And just as he conceives of the world as destroying the object it represents, he conceives of novels which destroy the novel in all of its conventional attributes. His own hero is always a phantomlike Everyman who has no story, no situation, and indeed no character. He is there only as a witness to an absurd creation, as an intelligence striving after meaning, as a soul overwhelmed by a tragic sense of existence. In Blanchot's creative works, which fit so exactly Sartre's definition of the anti-novel, we can see already at work the corrosive agents which younger novelists continue to apply to the traditional structures of fiction.

Laurent LeSage. *The French New Novel* (University
Park, Pa., Pennsylvania State University Press,
1962), pp. 61–62

We can set . . . all "criticism of signification" in opposition to Blanchot's discourse, a language moreover rather than a metalanguage, which is why Blanchot occupies an indeterminate place between criticism and literature. However, while refusing any semantic "solidification" with the work, Blanchot merely shows the empty shell, the void of meaning, and this is an enterprise whose very difficulty concerns the "criticism of signification" (and will perhaps concern it increasingly); we must not forget that nonmeaning is only a tendential object, a kind of philosophers' stone, perhaps a (lost or inaccessible) paradise of the intellect; to create meaning is very easy, our whole mass culture elaborates meaning all day long; to suspend meaning is already an infinitely more complicated enterprise—it is an "art"; but to "annihilate" meaning is a desperate project in proportion to its impossibility. Why? because what is "outside meaning" is infallibly absorbed (at a certain moment which the work has the power only to delay) into nonmeaning which itself is of course a meaning (under the name of the *absurd*): what could "signify" more than questions about meaning or the subversions of meaning, from Camus to Ionesco? Indeed, meaning can know only its contrary, which is not absence but opposition, so that any "nonmeaning" is always a "counter-meaning": there is no such thing as a zero degree of meaning. Blanchot's work, in criticism or fiction, therefore represents a kind of epic of meaning, an Adamite epic one might say, since it is the epic of the first man *before meaning*. [1963]

Roland Barthes. *Critical Essays* (Evanston, Ill., Northwestern University Press, 1972), pp. 271–72

Blanchot's works, whether novels or criticism, place us in a sort of hell—a hell, it is true, deprived of central heating. Fire is nonexistent there, and the coldness is severe. Perhaps what is most admirable in this intentionally frigid writing is its very coldness. This coldness is not only the coldness of thought that, like Jansenist thought, has reached the harshest barrenness, the humblest and at the same time the most uncompromising poverty. Blanchot's coldness is attributable even more to the calculated sparseness of a language that resists having any personal accent. "He needs only to find his style," Sartre once wrote of Blanchot. Nothing could be more inaccurate. Any stylistic frill or any individual stylistic mark would be excessive in Blanchot's writing. His language, like the other elements in his books, has to be reduced to the nakedness of a simple reptilian slither. All the qualities that make a style magical— according to Baudelaire, they are "intensity, sonority, clarity, vibration, depth, and resonance in space and in time"—all these qualities are carefully absent in Blanchot's works, except one, clarity, the least positive—because clarity, which plays such a great role in his style, consists, in his writing, of a simple general diffusion of light. Thus, the beauty of his language stems from the absence of almost all the usual beauties, from the fact that Blanchot forces language to be almost dull, colorless, flavorless, without timbre or warmth, thus succeeding in accurately expressing the negative aspects of a world stripped of appearances.

Blanchot's works are dreary, some of the saddest in any literature, and yet not tragic, not unhappy, but marked by an essential serenity, because unhappiness never appears in them as an event taking place in the present. It appears instead as the only explanation of a condition that is itself beyond unhappiness and in which clear-sightedness has established its exclusive reign forever.

Georges Poulet. Critique. June, 1966, pp. 496–97†

The "corridor separating two small rooms" is the central scene in Blanchot's writing. From *Thomas the Obscure* to *Waiting, Forgetting*, it seems that we remain in this corridor of a hotel, a hospital, or an apartment, leaving it only in order to return to it. This corridor is not a labyrinth and has no secrets; it leads from one door to another in no apparent order. These doors lead to rooms in which someone is lying in bed ill, in which someone is dying, in which people are dying. The corridor is the corridor of the immemorial vigil. Farther down the corridor perhaps is the door to the kitchen, where one can fill a glass with water. Outside lies the city, but the city is like the extension and the feverish complication of the room, and the city leads back to the room.

People are dying: there is no story by Blanchot in which people are not dying, not through a violent accident, but peacefully, through repetition. Death is at the heart of Blanchot's writing, and for Blanchot death is at the heart of all writing. If to write is to turn toward the uncharted terror, "to speak in the direction of the unknown," to enter the zone of strangeness, one can indeed conceive how writing is not so far from dying. The death "told" in Blanchot's fiction is the death of the other. But death is never only the death of the other; not because the survivor is reminded by that death of the fact that he too will die one day, but because death overflows the limits of the subject: "I" or "you" do not die, but "people" die. . . . When someone dies, he is not the only one who disappears; the world too wavers, because he has turned his blind eyes from it, and because it is forever excluded from his sight.

Françoise Collin. Maurice Blanchot et la question de
l'écriture (Paris, Gallimard, 1971), pp. 48–49†

Blanchot's first novel, *Thomas the Obscure*, was written somewhat in the style of Giraudoux, whom Blanchot the critic praised. But in

Animadab the influence of Giraudoux gave way to that of Kafka. Blanchot clearly did not regard language as an aesthetic exercise. And in his subsequent novels—*The Almighty, Death Sentence, The Last Man, Waiting, Forgetting*—which had an extraordinary tone of cold vehemence, an eloquence without eloquence, and a dispassionate shudder, Blanchot's style was neutral and impersonal. Rather than an individual or a writer, an anonymous witness speaks, conveying a truth that he sees as the only truth. It is a revelation that language has tried to express but which, in fact, it cannot express: the truth of the void, of absence, of nothingness, of death. This truth is perpetually waiting to be told but remains unsaid.

Everything in these works of Blanchot is situated in a strange, elusive, intermediate zone between life and death, in which life moves toward death but in which death cannot take place. This world between language and silence is like an almost mute downward slide, a movement that seems to lack motion and forever goes over the same ground. In his fiction Blanchot has presented the straining of language toward the "dangerous horizon where it seeks in vain to disappear"; he desires an inaccessible nonlanguage. He has commented on his quest in critical essays that have become more and more closely linked to his fiction, from *Literary Space* to *Infinite Conversation*.

The myth of Orpheus teaches us that we cannot look night in the face, that profundity is revealed only if it is concealed. But what good is this dissimulation, this constant fruitless searching for that which eludes us? The logic of the metaphysical experience (or mystical experience, but in a negative sense) has led Blanchot's work toward renunciation. Strangely enough, this tendency has been confirmed by a recent kind of revolutionary extremism, as if the unsaid were not only the forbidden area between life and death but also the area bourgeois civilization has forbidden to all of mankind, so that no one, for the moment, can speak for all men.

But the attempt to give a precise explanation of Blanchot's thought makes us run the risk of misrepresenting it. Blanchot's ideas can be grasped only in the way we appreciate music: by listening to it over and over again. The tenor of his thought always seems similar, but it eludes expression in words.

Gaëtan Picon. *Contemporary French Literature*
(New York, Frederick Ungar, 1974), pp. 67–68

BLOY, LÉON (1846–1917)

Ah, my poor friend, what a lofty and sad book [*The Man Who Revealed the Globe*] you have written about Christopher Columbus! . . . You have created a beautiful, an absolutely beautiful book; it is written in magnificent language that the Catholics would never be capable of finding—no, small chance of that!

The Devil who explodes in those unforgettable passages is splendidly horrifying and, I would add, disconcertingly and terrifyingly supernatural. I also strongly admire your magnificent angels of patience, the black seraphim. . . .

This book, which I want to read again, in small doses this time, seems to me tinged with a strange beauty created from an unappeased sadness, an inextinguishable rage for justice in the face of the perpetual infamy of mankind.

I cherish you for your holy rages, for your hatred that attacks the nauseating ignominy of this century; and from the professional point of view, I strongly admire your exalted art for the inventive oratorical style, the marvellously decisive adverbs, and the epithets that are so vigorous. [1884?]

Joris-Karl Huysmans. In Joseph Bollery, *Léon Bloy*
(Paris, Éditions Albin Michel, 1949), Vol. II, p. 93†

Alas! How fleeting is the purification of sewers! What good does it do to crush [the journalist] Albert Wolff if the mushroom's root, still under the slimy earth, will only send up a new venomous shoot on the next day? "I have contempt and disdain," said Victor Hugo. Léon Bloy has only one weapon—the broom. He cannot be asked to wield it like a sword, and he tirelessly uses it to sweep up the gutters.

A writer of pamphlets needs a style. Léon Bloy has a style. He gathered its first grains in the garden of [Jules] Barbey d'Aurevilly and the smaller garden of Huysmans. Barbey d'Aurevilly's fir tree has become, sown in Bloy's metaphor-filled soil, a powerful forest with lofty branches, and Huysmans's pungent carnation has become a bright field of magnificent poppies. Bloy is one of the greatest creators of images who ever walked the earth; these images hold his work together, the way a rock holds eroding earth together; these images give his thought the sharp silhouette of a mountain range. To be a very great writer, Bloy lacks only two ideas, because he already has one—the theological idea.

Bloy's genius is neither religious, nor philosophical, nor human, nor mystical; his genius is theological and Rabelaisian. His work seems to have been written by Saint Thomas Aquinas in collaboration with Gargantua. His books are scholastic and gigantic, eucharistic and scatological, idyllic and blasphemous. No Christian can accept them, but no atheist can take comfort in them. [1898]

Rémy de Gourmont. *Le deuxième livre des masques* (Paris, Mercure de France, 1920), pp. 48–50†

This apostle preaches in the desert; this talented man is almost unknown; Bloy himself never stops protesting against the conspiracy of silence that has inflicted years of extreme hardship upon him. The religious world is unaware of him or rejects him even more totally than the secular public, where he still has a few faithful readers among those who admire literary originality at any price. The very people who read Bloy with pleasure usually avoid speaking about him, and the ostracism of which Bloy complains so bitterly exists in fact. But Bloy also does not provide much encouragement: anyone who ventures to praise Bloy is almost infallibly rewarded, sooner or later, with a volley of insults. His readers prefer not to call themselves to his kind attention. . . .

But the very excess of Bloy's violence ultimately keeps him from being offensive. When one opens a book by Bloy, one is first offended to see living and dead men for whom one feels friendship or admiration vilified so crudely. Then one realizes that Bloy spares no one, that he impartially slanders the whole universe. He is not the champion of a particular cause, of a political or religious group, waging an abominable war on his adversaries: he is a monomaniac. Then one ceases to worry about whether Bloy is wrong or right; whether the man Bloy tears apart is really an imbecile and a scoundrel, or whether Bloy is indulging himself in an unjust and impudent attack. The names of his victims no longer matter. We read Bloy as if he had written two thousand years ago and were speaking to us of people who are completely forgotten today. . . .

Bloy is a mystical [counterpart to Molière's] Alceste [in *The Misanthrope*]; Bloy judges everything in terms of divine perfection. He has the soul of a martyr, and also the soul of an inquisitor. He certainly lacks kindness, tolerance, and politeness. But he has the excuse of having been very unhappy.

Paul Souday. *Les livres du Temps* (Paris, Émile-Paul Frères, 1913), pp. 127–28, 136†

I once wrote—and some people objected vigorously—that among Baudelaire, Barbey d'Aurevilly, Huysmans, and Bloy, the most Catholic of the four was Bloy. After an attentive study of his thought, I admit I expressed myself badly. He was incontestably the greatest *believer* of the four, but I now think . . . that he did not approach authentic Catholicism until toward the end of his life, after he had reached sixty. Nevertheless, his faith that Heaven looked on him with a special fondness was, for half a century, both ardent and constant. . . .

Bloy was, on the whole, a fifth-generation romantic, who adhered to Catholicism very early in life and for a long time used his own ideas, which he considered to be Catholic, as part of his ardent aspirations toward social power—aspirations that were justified, moreover, by his poetic gifts and his talent as a writer. But the dogmatic and moral discipline of the Roman Catholic Church (which he always claimed to accept with no reservations in theory, even though he at first took great liberties with them in practice) finally won him over totally. In his last years, therefore, he tacitly purified his doctrine, which for a long time had remained inaccessible to orthodoxy and even to common sense.

Ernest Seillière. *Léon Bloy: Psychologie d'un mystique*
(Paris, Éditions de la Nouvelle Revue Critique,
1936), pp. 8–10†

It is a waste of time criticizing Léon Bloy as a novelist: he hadn't the creative instinct—he was busy all the time being created himself, created by his own angers and hatreds and humiliations. Those who meet him first in this grotesque and ill-made novel [*The Woman Who Was Poor*] need go no further than the dedication to Brigand-Kaire, Ocean Captain, to feel the angry quality of his mind. "God keep you safe from fire and steel and contemporary literature and the malevolence of the evil dead." He was a religious man but without humility, a social reformer without disinterestedness; he hated the world as a saint might have done, but only because of what it did to him and not because of what it did to others. He never made the mistake by worldly standards of treating his enemies with tolerance—and in that he resembled the members of the literary cliques he most despised. Unlike his contemporary Péguy, he would never have risked damnation himself in order to save another soul, and though again and again we are surprised by sentences in his work of nobility or penetration, they are contradicted by the savage and selfish core of his intelligence. "I must stop now, my beloved," he wrote to his fiancée, "to go and suffer for another day"; he had prayed for suffering, and yet he never ceased to complain that he had been granted more of it than most men; it made him at the same time boastful and bitter. . . .

We read him with pleasure to just the extent that we share the hatred of life which prevented him from being a novelist or a mystic of the first order (he might have taken as his motto Gauguin's great phrase

—"Life being what it is, one dreams of revenge") and because of a certain indestructible honesty and self-knowledge which in the long run always enables him to turn his fury on himself.

Graham Greene. *Spec.* June 16, 1939, p. 1060

Claudel and Péguy, despite the attempts made to smother them under a misleading reputation, now appear as the two great renewers who, after a long period of intellectual mediocrity and aesthetic trifling, gave back to art its *true* value as knowledge—and no longer a magic Promethean knowledge but a confession of faith, prayer and truth. Today writers like Georges Bernanos and a number of the younger poets are finding the audience justly earned by their insight into events and their vigorous claim to reinstate all that has been disowned.

Léon Bloy, however, is still more or less unknown, and it is scarcely realised that he was one of those who had the clearest vision of the dreadful night descending upon the earth, and at the same time one of the most robustly positive of writers in this age of negations. For this lack of perception there are several reasons but no good ones.

In our present distress and, indeed, because of it, his work cannot fail to become intelligible and to meet a need. At the time when he was writing, his views on the history of mankind might seem exaggerated, and it is not at all surprising that an age of blind, earth-bound optimism saw in him a monster. A solitary voice upraised amid a general belief in the steady progress of the species and in the early advent of a golden age that was to put an end to centuries of instability, Bloy proclaimed that an abyss was about to open beneath the feet of mankind. With stubborn fury, for forty years, from 1877 to 1917, he did more than prophesy; he called down the wrath of God upon the paltry convictions and the precarious equilibrium of a complacent society which put its trust in science and bourgeois virtues, seeking the kind of tranquillity that comes from silencing one's soul and forgetting God.

We know now that his prophecies actually fell short of the reality; and we are dazzled by the spectacle of a human intelligence which, because it judged only from the standpoint of the Absolute, was able to form such a clear idea of the future course of history. [1944]

Albert Béguin. *Léon Bloy: A Study in Impatience*
(New York, Sheed and Ward, 1947), pp. 1–2

Bloy could not help writing with the full weight of his unique experience and prophetic intuition. The author of *Exegesis of Commonplaces*, aware of very remote reverberations in ordinary speech, almost never uses words with a flat literalism: his metaphors vibrate in a prophetic air. This is so even when the metaphor is apparently trivial or frivolous, like the endless zoological figures of speech which lie in wait for his personal enemies and literary rivals. . . .

Similarly the monotonous torrent of scatology, which made his name a scandal to the *bien-pensants* ["right-thinking"], has its significance in the general scheme. It expresses his humiliation at his exile and his contempt for the condition of fallen man as well as for those who believe that that condition is the natural and only possible one. . . .

By sheer passion Bloy succeeded where since the pre-Raphaelites so many wistful archaizers had failed: he wrote a medieval work about the nineteenth century [*Exegesis of Commonplaces*]. Yet integral and medieval though it is, and though it revives the symbolism of the Scriptures in the days of the symbolism of the decadents, the work is modern in one very important respect: it is, as well as being a *Summa*, an immense self-portrait. It is a poem in which the mystical interdependence of all life—the "reversibility of the Communion of Saints" extended—is always implied and therefore there are no absolute lines of demarcation between the personal, the historical, and the religious. Bloy's private agonies, the progress of the nineteenth century, the preparation for the Second Coming: these can be fused into one work because they are felt to be the same; *felt*, and in a very real way, for the agent of fusion is pain. Pain is the very stuff of history, religion, and consciousness itself.

Donat O'Donnell [Conor Cruise O'Brien]. *Maria Cross*
(New York, Oxford University Press, 1952),
pp. 219–22

Léon Bloy could never see anything except at the personal level; he described himself as being "antiswine," and all his most successful attacks were personal. He saw certain people as the prime examples of those human qualities he most hated, and immediately attacked without thought of consequences, or with enjoyment if he did think of them. The literary party described in his novel *The Desperate Man*, in which he violently attacked, under the most flimsy disguises, such influential people as Catulle Mendès, Francisque Sarcey, Aurélien Scholl, Jean Richepin, Alphonse Daudet, and others, is matched by the articles in which he tackled such people even more openly by their names. . . .

The whole of Bloy's polemical writing is a flow of unchecked fury at the modern world, modern Catholics and modern literary corruption. Obsessed as he was by the world's acceptance of false Christian virtues, Bloy let himself go completely and often passed all bounds of ordinary feeling. Death, for him, was no reason to restrain his violence; and it was after their deaths that many of his targets received their worst attacks. . . .

Bloy's polemical style is magnificent, though it breaks all the rules. His contorted sentences might be expected to mislead and bewilder the reader, his blatant exaggerations might be guaranteed to repel him, and his predilection for what one might call "lavatory-epithets" to revolt him. Yet the reader is swept along by a feeling of tortured urgency, a sense of frustrated hatred for all around the author. Bloy's violence is real. The man's personality appears in every word he wrote, and we are bludgeoned into following his hammering succession of insults, his rushing flow of fury.

Richard Griffiths. The Reactionary Revolution
(New York, Frederick Ungar, 1965), pp. 79–80, 84

The existence of *The Diary of Léon Bloy* did not become known until the publication of *The Thankless Mendicant* [the first of the eight volumes] in 1898. Bloy had been writing his diary since 1892. He does not reveal why he suddenly decided to present his life in slices to the public. Until then readers of the "pamphlet-writer" and the "co-signatory of God's Vengeance" had imagined Léon Bloy only through the character of Marchenoir [in *The Desperate Man*], whom, one could say, Bloy had created in his own image. And it is true that Bloy, who first revealed himself without a mask in *The Thankless Mendicant* . . . is certainly still the old Marchenoir, so closely was that "grandiloquent wretch" modeled on Bloy for the reader's benefit. And the reason for the originality of Bloy's diary is certainly that he wrote it with the same care as the pseudo-novels *The Desperate Man* and *The Woman Who Was Poor*; or the stories and fables for daily newspapers; or the prophecies of a visionary historian, *Salvation through the Jews* and *Napoleon's Soul.* . . .

Bloy clearly wanted to write the diary of a prophet. His oeuvre was ultimately limited by that ambition. He had had to force himself to give a fictional plot to *The Desperate Man*, to give that combination of soul and flesh the form of a poorly constructed novel. It was other people's idea that he write a novel—for his own good, so that he would win success more rapidly. Whatever the structure of that great Gothic book turned out to be, Bloy put into it all he knew, all he would ever know. With *The Woman Who Was Poor*, he attempted another novel, and the second time he had more success. Attacking his fellow writers less directly, or not attacking so many of them at once, he had a better reception from the reading public. But, all things considered, these two novels do not differ very much from his diary. *The Diary of Léon Bloy* is the spinal column of his complete works.

Stanislas Fumet. Léon Bloy: Captif de l'absolu
(Paris, Librairie Plon, 1967), pp. 95–96, 101†

BONNEFOY, YVES (1923–   )

Since [Valéry's] "The Young Fate," there has without a doubt been no poetic work that has displayed a greater—and more justified—ambition than Yves Bonnefoy's *On the Motion and Immobility of Douve.* . . .

The central image is the salamander. I get the impression that the poet spent a long time meditating and dreaming about the mythical significance of this "confined" and glowing creature, capable of the greatest immobility and also of the greatest motion; capable of moving unharmed because of its appearance (so closely does its color blend with the gray-brown of earth and walls), which makes both its motion and its immobility somehow untouchable; and imperishable at the moment when its frail body, according to myth, passes through flames, the "moment when the nearest flesh molts into knowledge." . . .

The allegory of the salamander is one of the keys to the poem. This allegory is mingled with and sometimes becomes indistinguishable from that of the phoenix, the mythical bird of the East that builds its own funeral pyre, burns all night in the flames, and dies to be reborn the next morning from its own ashes. Douve incorporates both allegories in herself, and that is Douve's whole story. . . . At the end of the poem, Douve is both the phoenix in the flames and a salamander on the hearthstone; Douve is already beyond the fire, which, instead of devouring her, separates her essence from its mortal dross to make that essence resemble a metal, henceforth indestructible. . . .

The only challenge worthy of a true poet has always been to seek to eliminate the boundaries between day and night, between life and death, between presence and absence. Bonnefoy, in my opinion, is the contemporary poet most capable of carrying out this ancient challenge.

Maurice Saillet. *LetN*. Nov., 1953,
pp. 1166, 1171–72†

I had to reread and reread this elusive book [*Yesterday Reigning Desert*], which kept slipping away from me on a first reading, to get some idea of it. I do not give up so easily, without making the effort required. In this case, I had to come to grips with obscurity. . . . The poet's intention to intrigue the reader and make him uneasy can be seen immediately, in the very title. . . .

The three words of the title perhaps take on their true meaning when they are applied to Delphi, "land called by memory," this site of religious ruins, where what reigned yesterday, and has today become a desert, belongs now only to memory. If this is the case, and if this solves the mystery, did this puzzle thrust on us deserve all the effort it took to solve it? It seems to me that to write as Bonnefoy does is to confine oneself intentionally to solitude—and to require so much from the reader that I myself admit having gotten a slight headache. But why should poetry not have its "suspense"? . . . Why should the admirers of obscure poetry be forbidden the kind of tense pleasure that good players find in chess, which demands just as much concentration. But that kind of pleasure can only be for the few, and everyone cannot share it. There is a further objection: How can anyone distinguish between a sincere, philosophical obscurity, like that of Bonnefoy, and an artificial obscurity; between a poet who offers a true nut to crack and one who offers only words?

To Bonnefoy's credit, it should be added—for the reader who is not discouraged by what I have just said—that Bonnefoy does not have any phobias against "beautiful words"; thus, he should be able to find favor with poetry lovers more interested in feeling than in pulling out meaning.

Émile Henriot. Le monde. July 2, 1958, pp. 8–9†

The easiest way to enter Yves Bonnefoy's universe would undoubtedly be to use the *wrong* method; I mean the method denounced in all of Bonnefoy's theoretical essays, the method every one of his poems seeks to divert us from—the simultaneously entrancing and harmful route of *concepts*. For although abstractions lead us astray, they can be very attractive: there is no doubt that, for Bonnefoy, ideas can be felicitous and numbers profoundly charming. . . . Would the peaceful harmony of abstractions and the charm of numbers and ideas—a charm that has obvious appeal to Bonnefoy himself—only serve to delude us? The essays collected in *The Improbable* tirelessly proclaim so. They constantly attack the same process, constantly drawing up the same indictment against ideas, or rather against concepts—for a concept is the caricature of an idea, a hollow idea. . . .

Bonnefoy's irrationalism, existentialist or romantic, leads to a nonphilosophy: to establish anything on concepts would be to build on emptiness; the only purpose of our thought should be to make us distrust thought. . . . In place of the sun of concepts, Bonnefoy would substitute the night of existence; for the overly neat and too smoothly articulated order of abstractions, he would substitute the disorder, the fleetingness, the wild but vivid penetrations of intuitions. [Feb., 1961]

Jean-Pierre Richard. Onze études sur la póesie
moderne (Paris, Éditions du Seuil, 1964), pp. 207–9†

[Bonnefoy's] poetry is serious, not to say somber, and evidences the obscurity and hermeticism of much of recent French literature. The study of Bonnefoy's poetry has been facilitated, however, by the publication of the two volumes of his essays, above all by the earlier, entitled *The Improbable*, which constitutes his *ars poetica*, and to a lesser extent by the later volume, *The Second Simplicity*. . . .

In revealing to us his theory of poetry Bonnefoy also reveals himself to be the most existentialist of poets, perhaps even the first true existentialist poet. . . .

One of Bonnefoy's most important symbols is the orangery which he uses to designate seventeenth century French classicism and more specifically Racine. . . . The hothouse with its windows which are so many thresholds, so many frontiers, remains a place of symbolic growth where death is conceived only as the invisible, as an absence. Bonnefoy's task, the "profound act," is to make of this "essential garden" of classicism an existential garden. . . . Bonnefoy's problem is to bring death into the orangery while maintaining the life of its fragile inhabitants. This he succeeds admirably in doing in his poetry.

F. C. St. Aubyn. *ChiR.* 17, 1, 1964,
pp. 118–19, 125–26

The three volumes of Bonnefoy's poetry are an attempt to build an edifice that will survive the dissolution of structural essentials experienced in the earliest of the texts, *On the Motion and Immobility of Douve*. . . . The total commitment to the building of this edifice makes of each succeeding volume not an independent structure, but a part of an evolving, cyclical concept. The entire cycle, prolonging the violence of *On the Motion and Immobility of Douve* in *Yesterday Reigning Desert* and seeming to find a tonal and substantive reconciliation in *Written Stone*, is both an extension and a denial of the initial experience of the ecstasy of death. The discovery, a sudden, excited, even joyous revelation, will be torturously disassembled, analyzed and refashioned, as a continuing sensory awareness, paradoxically ignoring the finality of death, will give meaning to the taut, apparently irreconcilable frame upon which the poetry is built. This triumphant perception also prepares us for the larger contradiction of the cycle: the search for a permanent place to contain an unstable poetic identity, expressed in a poetic structure that, responding to the disintegration and refusing to admit the formal measures of classical verse as a controlling medium, is of itself a constantly dissolving and shifting body. . . .

The disintegration of Bonnefoy's poetry is only an intermediate gesture which seeks to resolve itself in a light-bathed landscape. Here the elements of the body (a hand, a shoulder, a "mortal face"), annihilated as it were in death, rebuild not a dream landscape but a dwelling-place of stone and cold fire, more durable than the body it celebrates. The anguish and suffering are transitory displays and it is the joy and ecstasy of experience and discovery which illuminate this poetry. It is a poetry that honors the love of life, of death, of the body, of the minute, indissoluble things of this world. And like the poetry of the Renaissance which celebrated beauty in and beyond death, and the regeneration of beauty in line and verse, it is a feast of delight in the sensuous contours of the sparsely re-created body, present only in its most revelatory elements of line and genius.

Walter Albert. MLN. Dec., 1967, pp. 590–91, 601–2

Yves Bonnefoy represents the most "metaphysical" of contemporary meditations on art, on painting in particular, where the force of the gesture is necessarily inscribed within a limited framework. The complex interplay of that static outline with the momentum of the gesture has a parallel in the interwoven notions of presence and absence, speech and silence, perfection and imperfection, movement and the temptation to immobility which form the fabric of his poems, all of an apparent simplicity. Bonnefoy's quiet meditations have a transparency lent them by the space surrounding each gesture, each line. Or an illusion of transparency: the repeated motifs of ship, salamander, summer, stone, wind, and phoenix halt the linguistic movement by their recurring presence, while they confer on the texts a deep seriousness, a profundity attainable only by repetition and slow metamorphosis. For here the motion has come almost to a standstill. . . .

A major poet and a major critic, Bonnefoy . . . has the exceptional talent of raising a single word to the level of a poetic statement, of making a single object perceived—a withered leaf, a salamander—into an entire canvas of homage to time passing and to the present moment. His studies of the poetic gesture, whether painted or spoken, are no less solemn than his poetry itself; they translate to a different plane of meaning and of vision the contemplation of the work.

Mary Ann Caws. The Inner Theatre of Recent
French Poetry (Princeton, N.J., Princeton University
Press, 1972), pp. 8–9

BRETON, ANDRÉ (1896–1966)

André Breton's radicalism demands our sympathy. It is a good thing that a young man—and, in his wake, an entire generation—proclaims so insistently the absolute freedom of the mind. A fondness for the sublime, and the sometimes ridiculous ways in which the sublime manifests itself, coupled with a disgust and a vigorous hatred for the way people think on this planet, can occasionally lead us into regions close to those to which the mystics aspired, regions described in statements a Spaniard could be proud of, like: "It was the most beautiful of nights, the night of lightning." This fanaticism was necessary so that—even though surrealism pretends to place poetry within the grasp of every mind—poetry could regain its exclusivity and provocativeness, which rationalism was causing it to lose. And Breton points out the horrors of rationalism with the eloquence of a tribune.

It is in pursuance of this fine extremism that Breton begins his manifesto [*Manifesto of Surrealism*] with an attack on the novel. He is revolted by the concessions to current phraseology that the novelist's art seems to require; and right from the beginning Breton's dialectic alerts us to the simplicity to which he reduces the most complex problems. We can well imagine a novelist having a seizure of anxiety over facing the banal form in which he has to write his accounts, in which he must state the day, the hour, and the temperature. Nevertheless, Breton could also have conceived that a novelist can avoid this peril with as much grace as the poet avoids those perils presented to him by his own genre. . . .

Is this manifesto, advocating the right to dream and to fantasize, a call to arms for the unconscious mind following such fine examples as Freud's and Proust's? No. . . . Breton offers mathematical combinations, astral considerations, experiments in the desert. Instead of embracing the most complete and the most unexpected transformations, instead of rediscovering the formulas of the sensory alchemies whose secrets were guarded by the extraordinary Rimbaud, Breton's surrealism proposes nothing but a linear monotony—clever, willful, and inflexible.

Jean Cassou. *NRF*. Jan., 1925, pp. 30–32†

André Breton, by virtue of many admirable poems of a peculiarly bewildering quality, burning with implacable fires like the suns of another world, enriches poetry with a lucid and passionate vision, with an extraordinary clarity in the interrelations of his lacerating images, key images, images which fit together like the two pieces of a broken jar, the what-is and the what-will-be, as it were. Breton, whose theoretical texts are so definite, whose philosophical spirit is so clear-sighted, is accosted by poems as by people or events. He finds in them an immediate connection with life, and if he fails to see it straight away, it worries him and he seeks it. Always on the watch for chance encounters, he regards poetry as a reply to a question. He seeks the question in himself, and the reason for the answer in life. It is this which gives greatness to his poetry and to his life. Each poem is a fragment of the strange story of a voyage to the regions of "convulsive beauty." In *Nadja*, a true story, the story of something which happened, we have the equivalent in prose of Breton's poems.

Georges Hugnet. In Herbert Read, ed., *Surrealism*
(London, Faber and Faber, 1936), pp. 218–19

Mad Love . . . systematized a surrealist value that was not at all new: *objective chance*. Already in *Nadja* and *The Communicating Vessels* [Breton] had chosen to dwell on a number of external incidents: encounters, accidents, unexpected events, coincidences impossible to relate by a logical link but which resolved inner debates, materialized unconscious or avowed desires. Life and the dream, he had shown, were two communicating vessels, in which events were homologous, it being impossible for the individual to assert that the latter was more real than the former. This time he went further: he abolished any frontier between the objective and the subjective. There exists, according to Breton, between man and the world, a perpetual and continuous correspondence. There exists, above all, a continuity of events which can be antecedently perceived and whose correspondences remain invisible. Yet self-analysis permits their observation. . . . In the labyrinth of the events of his life, a man naturally chooses those which suit him, which suit his ultimate self, including misfortunes, diseases, individual catastrophes of all kinds.

This is to hold cheap, it will be said, the social conditions which more than any other determine the vicissitudes of our life, and for this reason some have censured Breton for not having completely closed the door to "mysticism." Breton posits a man sufficiently freed from social conditioning (but does such a man exist?) to obey only his own caprice and to receive orders only from his unconscious. That such a man exists is quite unlikely, but at least there are circumstances of life in which these exceptional conditions *can* be fulfilled, in which we adopt a "lyric behavior," in which we escape to a degree the constraining social necessities, in which reason, logic, the proprieties retreat before the unexpected, the marvelous, the sudden flash: these conditions are fulfilled in love. Passion and "mad love"—two expressions of a single state, a state of grace which unites the possible and the impossible, "natural necessity and human or logical necessity." [1945]

Maurice Nadeau. *The History of Surrealism*
(New York, Macmillan, 1965), pp. 205–6

When André Breton advocates a "hieroglyphic" interpretation of the world, in other words, an interpretation that is necessarily *esoteric*, he is obviously playing into the hands of those who base the legitimacy of a certain elite on a scorn for the "masses." Whether the race of overlords is one of priests, magi, warriors, or technocrats, it always brings concentration camps along with it.

When Breton declares his hope that a magic "key" will bring about the friendship of nature and the abolition "by enchantment" of "punishment," he is playing into the hands of those who want at any cost to turn our attention and our strength away from the merciless battle being waged today.

When Breton preserves nothing of traditional rationalism but a certain Kantian morality (the end and the means) whose aim is none other, in fact, than the reintroduction of the *sacred* into critical philosophy by an indirect route, he is playing into the hands of those who have always profited from the *sacred*. And it is not a coincidence if Breton uses the same terms as [Arthur] Koestler.

He plays into their hands once again when he strives to unite poetry with its *sacred* origins. It matters little what is *sacred*, in what way and to what extent. Those who genuinely love liberty have always attacked the very principle of dividing the world into two domains, one sacred and the other profane. Man will not be free—in other words, master of the world and of his destiny—until the very notion of the sacred has been erased from his mind.

Roger Vailland. *Le surréalisme contre la révolution*
(Paris, Éditions Sociales, 1948), pp. 59–60†

Breton, dedicated to disseminating new ways of thinking and feeling, does not abandon the effort to make himself *understood*—far from it. But what makes his work so particularly interesting is that he represents the farthest advance of purely poetic preoccupations in infiltrating the prose of our time. In Breton the carcass of classical prose—no matter how articulated, eloquent, and concentrated it appears to be (he has sometimes been compared with Rousseau and Bossuet, semi-seriously) —is no longer anything but an optical illusion, a thin crust entirely gnawed away from within by the unusual flow of poetry. Breton's originality lies in having resolved the modern problem of poetic prose, and having done so in the most paradoxical way, by carrying his solution over to the essay and to pure "literature of ideas."

From *The Lost Steps* and even the first *Manifesto of Surrealism* through *Arcanum 17*, Breton's work, considered from the point of view of form, shows a regular development in the direction of giving a sharper and sharper stress on the essence of its uniqueness, which lies in its treatment of syntax. . . . Breton's richest contribution to our language is probably his way of constructing a sentence: ample, long, sinuous, rich in examples, in sudden twists, and in interior echoes. Each sentence is constructed so as to hold the reader in suspense and uncertainty through its meanderings right until its final resolution, which almost never lacks an element of surprise.

Julien Gracq. André Breton (Paris, José Corti, 1948),
pp. 146–47†

Breton's prose writings occupy—by far—the most important place in his work. This poet, whose least significant page of prose shows evidence of inspiration sometimes completely lacked it when writing poetry. Perhaps his inspiration never failed him; perhaps he simply experienced more difficulty in expressing it through poems. Whatever the cause may be, the reasons for this paradox of a poet who was more successful in prose must undoubtedly be sought in the insufficiencies of his poetic art. That art was claimed from the beginning to be infallible and one that had to be followed blindly, but the very qualities of liberation in Breton's art (or the semblance of such qualities) are only so many shackles for a free genius. The fundamental surrealist rules proclaim the exclusive reign of dream and of a totally unbridled imagination, both considered capable of creating true poetry and true reality by themselves, without permitting any control by reason. I recognize the relative richness of the postulate—no control by reason—without thereby accepting the belief that this postulate by itself can nourish true poetry and true reality. Both poetry and reality were certainly rejuvenated by the surrealists on many occasions, but both were betrayed on many others. Significantly, Breton is usually much more convincing the less surrealist he is. In other words, he is never better able to convert us to his theses than when, to make his ideas accessible to us, he uses the language of everyone and makes references to common sense. . . .

Except for the occasional vivid flights and the more frequent dazzling showers of sparks that crackle as soon as one opens the book in which Breton's poems are collected [*Poems*], except for the few flashes that bring utopia itself suddenly, marvelously, within our grasp, Breton's poetry as an entity almost always seems to betray what he wanted to say through it, while his essays surpass in every way the medium that contains their message, while still releasing the medium and the message.

Claude Mauriac. *André Breton* (Paris,
Éditions de Flore, 1949), pp. 353–54†

The surrealists wanted to reconcile Marx's "let us transform the world" with Rimbaud's "let us change life." But the first leads to the conquest of the totality of the world and the second to the conquest of the unity of life. Paradoxically, every form of totality is restrictive. In the end, the two formulas succeeded in splitting the surrealist group. By choosing Rimbaud, Breton demonstrated that surrealism was not concerned with action, but with asceticism and spiritual experience. He again gave first place to what composed the profound originality of his movement: the restoration of the sacred and the conquest of unity, which make surrealism so invaluable for a consideration of the problem of rebellion. The more he elaborated on this original concept, the more irreparably he separated himself from his political companions, and at the same time from some of his first manifestoes.

André Breton never, actually, wavered in his support of surrealism —the fusion of a dream and of reality, the sublimation of the old contradiction between the ideal and the real. . . .

Of course he did not succeed (nor has anybody in our time) in the attempt to found a new morality. But he never despaired of being able to do so. Confronted with the horror of a period in which man, whom he wanted to magnify, has been persistently degraded in the name of certain principles that surrealism adopted, Breton felt constrained to propose, provisionally, a return to traditional morality. That represents a hesitation perhaps. But it is the hesitation of nihilism and the real progress of rebellion. After all, when he could not give himself the morality and the values of whose necessity he was clearly aware, we know very well that Breton chose love. In the general meanness of his times—and this cannot be forgotten—he is the only person who wrote profoundly about love. Love is the entranced morality that served this exile as a native land. [1951]

Albert Camus. *The Rebel* (New York,
Alfred A. Knopf, 1961), pp. 97–99

As I met the several apostles of Dadaism one by one, I penetrated further into the arcana of their system of unbelief. André Breton, by the autumn of 1921, was outstanding among them; by virtue of his cold intelligence and crushing power in argument, he had gradually assumed command of the Dadaist cenacle in Paris, and was their tacitly acknowledged "pope," or "archimandrite." . . .

At twenty-five, Breton made an imposing leader of a movement. He had a huge head, like one of the old Jacobin leaders, a mass of wavy brown hair, pale blue eyes, regular—though heavy—features, and jaws of granite. Like the men of 1793, he had in him a combination of fanatical idealism and ruthlessness. Whereas his closest friends, Aragon and Philippe Soupault, were spontaneous in manner, he was deliberate, speaking in long periods like an old-style orator and in a voice of deep and musical timbre. . . .

André Breton divided the world into fools and angels. A person unknown to him might be received at first with the most exquisite courtesy; Breton would listen to him attentively, using terms of such elaborate politeness that to some observers his good manners seemed to serve mainly as an armor of defense and were, on occasion, disconcerting rather than pleasing. Then in an instant his blue eye might blaze with anger at some idea he disliked, his heavy brows turn scowling, and he would proceed with measured words to tear the man before him apart, as if he enjoyed eating him up bit by bit. Though his air of pride and solemnity sometimes made him appear absurd, this complex young man could be very seductive in his friendships, and often used a delightfully paternal manner with his younger disciples, who sat at his feet submissively, but were also the recipients of his generous aid.

Matthew Josephson. Life among the Surrealists
(New York, Holt, Rinehart and Winston, 1962),
pp. 116–17

Perhaps even more than an exploration of unknown psychic territories, [Breton's] lifelong quest represented the regaining of a lost kingdom: the original Word, man before men and civilizations. Surrealism was his order of chivalry and his entire life was a Quest of the Holy Grail. . . .

He was one of the centers of gravity of our time. He not only believed that we humans are governed by laws of attraction and repulsion; he himself was the personal incarnation of these forces. I confess that for a long time the thought that I would say or do something that might provoke his reprobation kept me awake nights. I believe that many of his friends felt much the same way. A few years ago, [Luis] Buñuel invited me to a private showing of one of his films. When it was over, he asked me: "Would Breton think it within the Surrealist tradition?" I mention Buñuel not only because he is a great artist, but also because he is a man possessed of great moral integrity and freedom of spirit. These feelings have nothing to do with fear or respect for a superior (although I believe that if there is such a thing as superior men, Breton was one of them). I never considered him a leader, much less a Pope, to repeat the ignoble epithet popularized by certain swine. Despite the fact that we were personal friends, my activities within the Surrealist group were quite tangential. Nonetheless, his affection and generosity always amazed me, from the beginning of our relationship till the very end of his life. I have never known why he was so kind to me. Was it perhaps because I was from Mexico, a country he loved all his life? Apart from these personal reasons, I must confess that many times I write as though I were having a silent conversation with Breton: objections, answers, agreement, disagreement, homage, all these things at once. I am experiencing that sensation at this very moment. [1966]

Octavio Paz. *Alternating Current* (New York, Viking, 1973), pp. 47, 52–53

I lived near Breton, with Breton, every day for several years (two, three, or four, I no longer know). It was an unforgettable experience. We talked about poetry, dreams, Freud, images, Rimbaud, Lautréamont, Apollinaire, and Pierre Reverdy. After some moment of "illumination" we decided to write for ourselves alone, in two weeks, a work that would sum up, if I dare express it thus, our experiments, our years of apprenticeship. We entitled that work *Magnetic Fields*, we dedicated it to Jacques Vaché, and we baptized it "surrealist" in honor of Apollinaire, who had chosen that adjective for a text that we admired, a text that had shown us the path we wanted to follow—*Onirocritique*.

Side by side, with the best intentions, we wrote those pages that would bring about what Breton proudly called the "surrealist revolution." We were surprised—more than that, stupefied—when we reread what we had written. Sometimes we even "broke up" with laughter. I cannot forget Breton's laugh, the laugh of a child or a rooster. But I also remember my admiration in witnessing the blossoming of the poetic gifts of this cruelly intransigent man. Breton, who had been able only to write admirable prose (as has been often repeated, and rightly so) reached with an astonishing ease the heights only attained by Rimbaud and Lautréamont before him. . . .

His books have exerted an influence, have directed minds, through their extraordinary persuasive power. Nevertheless, I can firmly state that, despite all the legends, he did not take himself that seriously. To emphasize my point, I need only recall the admiration he had for the poet who was his most faithful companion, Benjamin Péret, whose sense of humor overwhelmed Breton. Undoubtedly, this friendship and admiration gave Breton the courage to publish *Anthology of Black Humor*, which is one of the most "disquieting" books ("disquieting" is an adjective he loved) to appear in the past half-century.

Philippe Soupault. *Le vrai André Breton* (Liège, Éditions Dynamo, 1966), pp. 6–8†

For many people who are not that well-informed, the name of André Breton is synonymous with surrealism. They are correct. Without Breton, even if surrealism had existed, it would have been nothing but a literary school. With him, it was a way of life. Like life, it brought contradictions, clashes, tempers, and quarrels. People have sufficiently reproached Breton for the ways in which he acted, before anyone else. Perhaps some of his stunts were unnecessary. His greatness erases them: let us move on. What remains is the imagination, the capriciousness, the invention, the discovery, the intellectual adventure, the moral adventure —everything that enabled surrealism to leave mere methodology. No resemblance here to the laborious efforts of the men who head movements.

Surrealism is beginning to become generally familiar as a way of writing, a way of painting. This is not enough (but who will say so?), because what should become familiar is Breton's life. . . .

Anyone who checks Issue 11–12 in the new series of *Littérature* will find, under the title "Erutarettil," the list of the great writers extolled by Breton in 1923. They are writers whose works are now available in paperback: Sade, Hegel, Lautréamont; at that time they were unknown or in disgrace. Breton changed the scale of values—not according to a system or a doctrine, but as he chose, by Olympian decision, one might say by an intuition that rarely failed . . .

One of the last times I met him I spoke to him about a dissertation about Dadaism that was defended at the Sorbonne. "Not a week goes by," he told me, "without my receiving a dissertation about surrealism. Or even two." He laughed briefly and added: "That is what they call culture."

Raymond Queneau. *NRF*. April, 1967, pp. 604–5†

The gravity which has contributed to make Breton one of the most remarkable prose stylists France has known in this century ruled out, from the beginning, all possibility of levity in his verse. One misses the joyous destructiveness which gave the early verse of Aragon its brilliance, just as one misses the inner turbulence which left its mark on the poems of Antonin Artaud. Time has confirmed the conclusion which in the twenties might have seemed premature; Breton's poetic tone takes its place between the violence of Péret's and the artful simplicity of Éluard's.

As a poet, Breton spoke with authoritative tones. So much so, indeed, that a malicious observer might be inclined to attribute special importance to his respect for Victor Hugo. From the moment when Breton's poetry began to evidence self-assurance, it was characterized by a tone which has done much to lend support to accusations that he assumed the role of pontiff. Breton's unshakable conviction that his was a privileged voice underlies many of his statements which lend themselves to misinterpretation. It is displayed even better in an innate respect for language patterns and an intuitive command of their capabilities. These qualities would strike a discordant note of harmony in the calculated cacophony of early surrealist writing were it not that Breton possessed to an uncanny degree the power to persuade us that mediation is, in his case, not a self-imposed role but a natural gift.

J. H. Matthews. André Breton (New York,
Columbia University Press, 1967), pp. 36–37

In spite of the title [*Nadja*], the initial and indeed the principal subject of the book is not Nadja's search for self-identity but Breton's. Nadja, whose name is the beginning of the Russian word for hope (and only the beginning) does not enter the book until after the first third of the text, and she fades out of it in the last part. She is important only as a stage in Breton's autobiography, as an example of the possible genius of the mentally abnormal and of their inexcusable treatment in "asylums," and as a contrast with the more "adaptable" behavior of the author and his friends. She troubles his mind temporarily, but she can in no way affect his general comportment or his permanent sentiments. This is a pitifully one-sided love story, for Nadja, who loves Breton as "the sun," is finally found by him to be less interesting than the more "normal" woman to whom the end of the book is addressed.

Breton undertakes the book then, not as a testimonial to the extraordinary character whose title it bears, but as an inquiry into what is individual about himself. What part of his personality continues through all the events which he experiences, all the gestures he makes, in the unique tastes he recognizes himself as having, and how does this individuality separate him from others?

Mary Ann Caws. André Breton (New York,
Twayne, 1971), pp. 62–63

Breton's philosophy did not prove popular in his lifetime. For one thing, his constant emphasis on the role of the individual as the basis of any new humanism, and the degree of liberty he attributed to the individual was incompatible with the leveling tendencies of the various types of collectivism that constitute society today. The championship of the unexploitable qualities of the essential man as opposed to the exploitable ones of men reduced to norms was completely out of tune with the processes of regimentation of work, study, play, and war. His very optimism irritated his philosopher contemporaries; for instead of confronting man with burdens of responsibility toward other men or toward

God, Breton's *table rase* left everything wide open, and therefore man remained free not merely to *choose* his destiny but to create it. If you declare the world "absurd" and deprive it of any significance, you give man a nonpersonal excuse for stagnation. But as Victor Crastre says in his distinction between Dadaism and surrealism, "Breton and his friends ventured to give significance to the world—or to create a world which might at last have a significance." By this presumption Breton made himself vulnerable and his philosophy forbidding. For him even the meaning of the word "absurd" was quite different from its later use. Life is absurd not in the nauseating sense of the word but so far as "absurd" designates the forces that out-distance the narrow limits of logic and gravitate toward the wondrous. To lull oneself in lyrical transcendence with the illusion that man must find his dignity in the act of suffering is poor comfort, according to Breton.

Anna Balakian. André Breton (New York,
Oxford University Press, 1971), p. 248

BRIEUX, EUGÈNE (1858–1932)

I think that [*The Three Daughters of Mr. Dupont*] is the best play Brieux has offered us. Why? Because in this play he has not striven for something beyond his power, at least not quite so much as he did in his previous plays. Often in this play he has restricted himself to writing only the play he should really be writing. . . .

I do admit that I hold a small grudge—maybe even a large grudge —against Brieux for this new play. As understanding as I am toward all the concessions in which "professional playwrighting" indulges, I am nevertheless unable to tolerate, without a brief confession of anger, the fact that the playwright has ruined one of the most beautiful scenes possible, the one in which the three daughters of the imbecilic and infamous bourgeois—who has refused to let one get married, who has expelled another, and who has forced the third into an unhappy marriage—meet and confront one another. . . . To write that horrifying scene . . . would have required, would have really required—ah! how beautiful it could have been—would have required a soul forever unreconcilable with those minds which, tomorrow, will praise Brieux for not having pushed matters to their limits. . . .

Here we have a writer—not a young one, but almost a new one— who is certainly worthy (and I am glad of it!) of the first rank among the writers of the younger generation, among writers who, having definitively given up the idea of literature—how I congratulate them for it! that sort of thing leads nowhere!—will be able to triumph in a genre that might be called "light comedy with a thesis." [Oct., 1897]

Catulle Mendès. *L'art du théâtre* (Paris, Bibliothèque Charpentier, 1900), Vol. III, pp. 362, 367–68†

After the death of Ibsen, Brieux confronted Europe as the most important dramatist west of Russia. In that kind of comedy which is so true to life that we have to call it tragi-comedy, and which is not only an entertainment but a history and a criticism of contemporary morals, he is incomparably the greatest writer France has produced since Molière. . . . The reason why Shakespeare and Molière are always well spoken of and recommended to the young is that their quarrel is really a quarrel with God for not making men better. If they had quarrelled with a specified class of persons with incomes of four figures for not doing their work better, or for doing no work at all, they would be denounced as seditious, impious, and profligate corruptors of morality.

Brieux wastes neither ink nor indignation on Providence. The idle despair that shakes its fist impotently at the skies . . . does not amuse Brieux. His fisticuffs are not aimed heavenward: they fall on human noses for the good of human souls. When he sees human nature in conflict with a political abuse he does not blame human nature, knowing that such blame is the favorite trick of those who wish to perpetuate the abuse without being able to defend it. He does not even blame the abuse: he exposes it, and then leaves human nature to tackle it with its eyes open. And his method of exposure is the dramatic method. He is a born dramatist, differing from the ordinary dramatists only in that he has a large mind and a scientific habit of using it. As a dramatist he must take for his theme a conflict of some sort. As a dramatist of large mind he cannot be satisfied with the trumpery conflicts of the Divorce Court and the Criminal Court: of the husband with the seducer, of the policeman with the murderer. Having the scientific conscience in a higher degree than Zola (he has a better head), he cannot be interested in imaginary conflicts which he himself would have to invent like a child at play. The conflict which inspires his dramatic genius must be a big one and a real one. . . . Not until the Académie Française elected Brieux did it occur to the boulevardiers that the enormous difference between him and their pet authors was a difference in which the superiority lay with Brieux. [1909]

Bernard Shaw. Preface to *Three Plays by Brieux* (New York, Brentano's, 1911), pp. vii, xvii–xix

One Sunday afternoon some years ago I found my way to a little theatre on the eastern boulevards of Brussels. The audience was sparse but tearful; the "melting mood," rightly extolled by Mr. Shaw, taking the unattractive form of a frequent and universal use of the pocket-handkerchief. The play given was *Blanchette*, by M. Brieux, member of the French Academy. I did not know then that *Blanchette* was one of the first successes of M. Antoine's Théâtre Libre, nor that M. Brieux had already achieved a limited and eclectic fame in England as *the* representative French dramatist through Stage Society performances of his later social dramas. Still less did I suspect that Mr. Shaw, of all sane men, would one day attempt the miracle of turning water into wine by devoting an entire preface to praise of this author's translated work. Shaw as prologue to Brieux is indeed a sight for gods and men. The high priest of unsentimentality, prostrate before the altar of bathos. The harlequin enamoured of pomposity. . . . And all this in order to prove that M. Brieux is the most important event in the European Theatre since Ibsen. . . .

[Consider] the domestic comedy of *Blanchette*. The ethics apart, it is quite skilfully and admirably written, for M. Brieux is a good stage craftsman. But consider it as the work of the alleged leading dramatist of France, writing for a revolutionary theatre some years after the appearance of Ibsen, and the dilemma is obvious. If it was sincerely done, then M. Brieux had nothing in particular to say; if it was insincerely done, then he was foisting upon the Théâtre Libre a piece of rubbishy theatricality which could have found a home in any one of ten fashionable theatres in Paris. In the light of the later plays, it is impossible to resist the former conclusion. *Blanchette* pointed the way for M. Brieux, and at the same time defined his limitations. Conventional domestic comedy was always his trade, and his social and political views are only window-dressing. There need be no doubt of the sincerity of M. Brieux's opinions, but they are for the most part so trivially expressed that they carry no conviction. In becoming a reformer, he ceased to be an artist.

Ashley Dukes. Modern Dramatists (London,
Frank Palmer, 1911), pp. 224–25, 227–28

I think it very notable that in [Brieux's] whole drama there is not one person of title. . . . M. Brieux never brings them in, and it is an immense relief. One keeps one's own commonness without shame; one is as good as anybody. It would be a mistake though, to suppose that the exclusion of people of quality works anything like the idealization of the bourgeoisie or of the working-classes. M. Brieux is far too honest a man for that; he knows his ground too well to have the heart to show it a flowery space or a well-trimmed lawn. . . .

I have been asking myself which of this dramatist's plays I think the greatest, and I am going to say *The Machine, The Philanthropists, The Escape, The Red Robe, The Substitutes, Maternity,* and *Faith,* and yes, of course, *The Three Daughters of Mr. Dupont*, though I have merely seen that on the stage, where no play has really its best chance. I cannot say from my no-knowledge of French life that these studies of it are true to it, but from my knowledge of human nature as I find it in myself and in my other enemies I think they must be true. It is from this belief and from the temperament of his work everywhere that I feel his prime characteristic to be honesty. Above his natural desire for effect, for "the creation of the beautiful," he seems to feel his heart bound to the truth. He is honest, honest, honest. A man may of course be too honest, but it is a good fault, and this fault one may detect in M. Brieux. A man, especially a dramatic author, ought not to be too honest; he unfits himself to comfort the tired business man.

William Dean Howells. NorthAR. March, 1915,
pp. 409–10

In the whole of [Brieux'] work there is not one character that deserves the title of dramatic creation. There is not one play that is more than an exploitation of personal or social failure. He has treated of almost every form of social evil, and debased his art by his treatment. His technique is most faulty in the study of character. The men and women of his plays do not reveal themselves through their words. For that, their speech should be in perfect accord with the slow unfolding of their character, no word superfluous or without significance. The dialogue of M. Brieux' plays is rather the description, translated into the first person, that a novelist might have given of his characters, a novelist addicted to commonplace language and the vicious cliché. . . .

It is to M. Brieux' credit that he chooses, sometimes, great themes. It is his failure that he cannot handle them. He lacks the power of personality, the dramatic imagination, to lift his work above polemics to the height of a criticism for all time. He has treated of painful things, and left them merely painful.

Storm Jameson. Modern Drama in Europe
(London, W. Collins, 1920), pp. 147–49

Born into the lower class, Eugène Brieux has something of the mentality of the man of the people on all matters: endowed with a great deal of innate common sense, passionate, generous, and enthusiastic about everything good or beautiful, but given a superficial education, he sometimes is not able to achieve an overall critical synthesis of the problems he wants to tackle on the stage.

In characterization, too, he brings to his plays the mentality of the commoner: for him, the "bourgeois" is always full of prejudices, greedy, immoral, and incapable of kindness, whereas the common man is filled with every virtue. The attitudes of the Théâtre Libre, in which he served his apprenticeship, have greatly influenced him. . . .

For Brieux, as for Alexandre Dumas, dramatic art is not an end in itself: it is not a goal, but a means. For Brieux, the virile sociologist of *Damaged Goods*, as for Dumas in such plays as *The Demimonde*, the formula "art for art's sake" has absolutely no meaning.

The theater of Brieux—a theater of thought and ideas in which so many problems are treated, so many varied and worthwhile questions are raised—has a very special moral value. It has a great social and humanitarian importance because of the many ideas of individual and collective responsibility it has planted in the soul of the public, as if it were sowing seeds in a field.

Cesare Levi. *Autori drammatici francesi* (Florence,
Felice Le Monnier, 1923), pp. 204–5†

In [*The Red Robe*] the cards are stacked at the playwright's pleasure, and his victory over the minions of the law is no equal battle. His piece, none the less, is capital melodrama, and its characters, like those in *The Three Daughters of Mr. Dupont*, are fairly vital. What a contrast appears in the technique of *Maternity* and *Damaged Goods*! No longer are the characters self-directed. They are simply puppets set up and manipulated by Brieux. Plot is also reduced to the lowest terms that doctrine may stand to the fore. . . .

In *Damaged Goods*, which achieved notoriety when forbidden by various censors, Brieux reached the limit of what the drama of propaganda can do. With a boldness equaled only by his lack of taste, he proceeded to discuss on the stage venereal disease in relation to marriage. His attitude, as becomes a modern social reformer, is scientific, not ethical. He declines to associate sin with sickness. He assumes that by presenting a particular case of distress caused by the marriage of an innocent girl to a victim of syphilis he can frighten parents into demanding for their children proper prophylaxis before marriage. . . .

In theme this production owes a manifest debt to Ibsen's *Ghosts*, but characteristically Brieux is concerned only with hygiene, whereas Ibsen was intent upon questioning a social ideal outworn and displaying souls at a tragic crisis. For Brieux the spiritual implications of Ibsen mean nothing. His interest is focused on preventing the transmission of disease. Ibsen's is focused upon substituting a true for a false ideal of marriage.

Frank W. Chandler. *Modern Continental Playwrights*
(New York, Harper and Brothers, 1931), pp. 208–9

[Brieux's] generous soul was offended by abuses, and he undertook to deliver us from them. He was impatient to find a solution, seeking the practical and immediate result. This side of Brieux placed the emphasis not on the internal reform of man but on the improvement of laws; he studied not a heart but an issue; he did not begin with the human to conclude with the human but began with a theory that was simply to be illustrated by means of a plot. This plot, fortunately, led him to a study of manners or a depiction of characters that, almost always, saves the play.

Even in those of his plays in which everything seems sacrificed to the presentation of an issue—like *Damaged Goods*, in which each character is only an entity, to the point of not even having a first name or a last name—the dramatist's instinctive gift always manages to provide the characters with hearts. Even in the first act, in the doctor's office, the young patient gradually assumes an identity and comes to life; we forget that he is there for a demonstration. A miracle!—he lives through himself and escapes from the hands of his creator. We recognize his ingenuous egotism and his naïve ferocity. What does the thesis matter? A masterpiece is in the process of being born... Alas, I have neglected the overly eloquent character who is always present in plays like this, and who, through the will of Brieux, almost never leaves the stage. Most of the time this character takes the form of a doctor, to whom the traditional role of "raisonneur" no longer suffices; one must call him a "lecturer." What a revenge on Molière's doctors! Brieux's doctors do not have the slightest humorous phrase to utter, and when they are speaking about alcoholism or other diseases, the spectator does not doubt their expertise.

But it should be repeated that even in those plays that certain critics have called "lecture-plays," Brieux the social orator never succeeds in altogether suppressing Brieux the observer of the human heart —the Brieux who, at the moment he is involved with the play of emotions, no longer remembers the thesis he wished to prove.

François Mauriac. *Discours de réception à l'Académie Française* (Paris, Grasset and Plon, 1934), pp. 38–41†

Uninfluenced by Shaw's panegyrics, we are at last able to do justice to Brieux without either exalting or belittling him. No doubt the unfortunate circumstances of his birth and upbringing turned him from the outset into a rebel—unlike Shaw, emotionally far more than intellectually. He was not a genius but a man of considerable if untutored talent. Most of his plays tend to be crude, sometimes excessively so; often they end in blatant melodrama or clumsy anti-climax. Nevertheless, he possessed a generosity and boldness of approach that at first shocked, and subsequently appealed to, a prudish generation. . . . His energy and courage were exceptional—but what about his talent? He could be embarrassingly naïve, with a strong leaning towards blatant rhetoric. His plays have definitely failed to stand the test of time; only the lively and stimulating *The Three Daughters of Mr. Dupont* and the rather gruesome but beneficent *Damaged Goods* are still—if very rarely—revived. . . .

No doubt the quality in Brieux that most impressed Shaw was a grim, puritanical earnestness of purpose unrelieved, incidentally, by even a glimmer of wit. Perhaps the word "puritanical" provides the clue to Shaw's predilection for Brieux. For in the more commonplace but boldly outspoken French dramatist the author of *Three Plays for Puritans* certainly detected something in the nature of an affinity. Here, indeed, was a matter-of-fact realist who regarded sexual love as an appetite that had to be controlled and, above all, not romanticized.

On the other hand, what he entirely overlooked was a no less significant characteristic of Brieux's: his almost mystical nationalism verging on a jingoism that in any other man would have infuriated Shaw. In 1914 Brieux threw himself passionately into the conflict, surrendering whole-heartedly to what Shaw denounced as "brainless war hysteria." Shaw's own attitude was closely akin to that of Romain Rolland, who showed me letters and cards from Shaw enthusiastically praising his pacifist work as that of "a good European." The play he admired most of all was a symbolical drama entitled *Liluli*, in which Rolland lashed out at the canting profiteers battening on the sacrifices of the combatants. Brieux, on the other hand, ignored the profiteers; he could see only selfless patriots and heroic soldiers.

John W. Klein. Drama. Winter, 1962, pp. 33, 34

BUTOR, MICHEL (1926–   )

[*Passing Time*] is a novel in the act of being constructed, and it is absolutely necessary for this construction to be ultimately unsuccessful. . . . If, in fact, the efforts of the narrator were successful, the final success would reflect back on the initial gropings, and those gropings would consequently appear planned. An attempt can only truly be shown as such if it is fruitless; if it succeeds, there is a danger that it will be regarded as nothing but the deluding—because simply aesthetic—

preparation for a success that was assured from the beginning and only put in doubt as a gesture.

Therefore, no regained time follows lost time: Butor is the anti-Proust, and lost time is never regained! Moreover, Proust only seems to lose time; this is really why he regains it. He does not even doubt that he can regain time, and this confidence is what allows him to set forth in search of time: he possesses it before writing his first sentence. He tells us so himself at the end of his novel, which he planned as circular: the time regained is the time when he made the decision to write, assured finally that the past was there, offering itself to his exploration. Butor, on the contrary, decides to write because he senses that the past is escaping him and that, if he does not fasten it by writing, he will never regain it, because one can only find again what has been preserved.

Two conceptions of time are involved here. For Proust, what has happened is indestructible, and each event only increases the substance of a past that a chance incident or a deliberate will can always recall to life. Of course, time passes, but passing means entering into eternity. For Butor, by contrast, time is absolutely destructive. If one is not careful, there is a danger that in the future one will experience only a series of discontinuous moments. Undoubtedly, one can remember and fixate the past—but this is just what must be done: it does not happen by itself. Memories are not at our beck and call, and there is no way of conjuring them up, of making them appear; they must be reconstructed. And the past, if it cannot be reconstructed, exists no longer.

Jean Pouillon. TM. April, 1957, pp. 1592–93†

At the end of the twenty-one hours or so that his journey from the Gare de Lyon [in Paris] to the Stazione Termini [in Rome] has lasted, the protagonist [of *The Modification*] has certainly not lifted the last veil, but at least he has learned a number of things, if only about his own feelings toward the girl he wanted to surprise in Rome, and toward Rome itself. Neither a psychological novel nor an historical panorama, Michel Butor's book, which is the minute description of a physical itinerary that overlaps a spiritual itinerary, seems like the narrative of a pilgrimage of initiation. Roman mythology—introduced through the thinking process of the traveler—is not the only thing that appears suddenly in the framework of daily reality: the story as a whole is placed on the level of a myth, without ever falsifying what I might call its "verism," because the details are so down-to-earth. . . .

It therefore seems that this story of a trip from Paris to Rome, in which no prosaic detail is omitted (the names of stations, ticket verifications, frontier crossings), has among its great organizing principles the idea of a *spiritual quest* accomplished according to traditional standards.

The Stranger and *The Plague*. No doubt it is not intended to be a Christian novel, but it is clearly not positively and confidently non-Christian in the way the earlier novels were. . . .

There are, admittedly, straightforward Christian parallels in *The Fall*. There are references to the Eden in which Clamence [the judge-penitent narrator] lived before his own fall. His very name, Jean-Baptiste Clamence, suggests John the Baptist, the *vox clamentis in deserto*. He refers to himself as a prophet preaching in the desert of stone, mist and stagnant water which is Amsterdam. But this biblical symbolism does not embody Christian convictions. The Christian doctrine of redemption, which goes hand in hand with the Christian doctrine of the fall, is explicitly rejected. There is a sense in which Camus means by the fall human fallibility, but this fallibility is not original sin. It is, rather, human guilt experienced without reference to any law; human guilt rendered all the more acute because there is no available standard of innocence. Clamence says that the worst human torment is to be judged without reference to laws and that this is precisely our torment.

John Cruickshank. *Albert Camus and the Literature of Revolt* (New York, Oxford University Press, 1959), pp. 183, 187

In an era such as ours when the figure of the writer-guide, the writer who can teach us something, seems to have practically disappeared, Camus, precisely such a writer, quickly commanded the attention of the critics and the public. He became so important that two years ago, when he was barely forty-four, the Swedish Academy awarded him the Nobel Prize. . . .

The unusual aspect of [Camus's] philosophy—if we can use this word—is that his nihilism does not exclude hope, does not exempt man from the difficult task of living and dying with dignity. In *Letters to a German Friend*, published in 1945, the writer's philosophical position opens up to quite a few interesting variations. But not even in the essays in *The Rebel* or those in *Essays of Current Interest*, two works published around the same time, can it be said that Camus achieved a satisfactory speculative systematization of his thoughts. I must admit, however, that it would be really strange to ask for even a minimum of systematization from an author for whom the two myths of revolt and hope were felt to be essentially an acknowledgment of the power of the irrational. . . .

Politically Camus was anti-religious without the anxieties of a professional atheist, and a leftist without a party. For him, the task of the intellectuals was only to denounce "troublesome conditions." An Algerian by birth, a Frenchman by culture, he undoubtedly dreamed of a solution to the Algerian problem that still, in some way, could unite Algeria's destiny to that of France. This feeling, as well as his unflagging admiration for Malraux, probably explains the fact that Camus, as far as we know, never took a hostile stand against De Gaulle, as others did. For Camus, the Frenchman, our days could no longer be the days of the rebel. They were rather the days of hope and anguished expectation.

Eugenio Montale. *Corriere della sera.* Jan. 5, 1960,

p. 3†

Albert Camus appeared in my life in April, 1941, in Algiers, where I had come as a refugee from France. I met him soon after my arrival, for in Algeria he was famous: the leader of a group of young journalists, aspiring writers, students, friends of the Arabs, enemies of the local bourgeoisie and Pétain. . . . I try to recall details, as if through them I could relive those days and learn something more about the young writer with whom I actually spoke little, since he felt no more like talking than I. I remember being totally obsessed by a single thought: we had arrived at humanity's zero hour and history was senseless; the only thing that made sense was that part of man which remained outside of history, alien and impervious to the whirlwind of events. If, indeed, such a part existed. This thought I considered my exclusive privilege. I felt that no one else could be so possessed by it; yet I yearned for someone to share it with. But there was no one. It was not an idea compatible with normal life, let alone with literature—or so it seemed to me. . . .

I saw him again in New York in 1946 on the pier where I had gone to meet his ship. In my eyes he seemed to me like a man coming straight from the battlefield bearing its marks, pride and sorrow. . . . He had won his position on the stage of the world; he was famous; his books were brilliant. But to me he had conquered in a more important sense. He had faced the question which I considered crucial and which had so absorbed me during the days that I first met him. He had mastered it and carried it to extreme and lucid conclusions. He had succeeded in saying, in his fevered way and in an argument as taut as a bow, why, despite the fury and horror of history, man is an absolute; and he had indicated precisely where, according to him, this absolute lay: in the conscience, even if mute and stilled; in remaining true to one's self even when condemned by the gods to repeat over and over the same vain task. In this lay the value of *The Stranger* and *The Myth of Sisyphus* for me.

Nicola Chiaromonte. *Dissent.* Summer, 1960,

pp. 266–68

One of the best photographs of Camus shows him standing at the imposing stone in the printing plant of a newspaper. With a pencil in his right
hand and the ever-present cigarette in his left, he is correcting one of his
editorials while an attentive printer stands beside him ready to run off
another proof. Camus looks confident and happy, although working
under pressure. Did he not say in the last year of his life that there were
two places where he had been supremely happy? One was on stage
either acting or directing a company of actors and the other was a newspaper composing-room. In both places he belonged to a team working in harmonious effort towards the realization of a specific aim. And in
both situations he was likely to be the moving spirit.

Unfortunately, Camus the journalist and the polemicist is still in-
adequately known in America. And yet, throughout his too-short and
most active life, he never abandoned the journalism that had been his
introduction to writing. In Algiers in 1938, at the age of twenty-five, he
had joined the staff of *Alger-Républicain*, and the following year his
forthright reportage on the misery of the Kabyle tribes of Algeria had
caused a sensation and incurred the wrath of the government. He was
even then working on his play *Caligula* and already planning his first
novel, *The Stranger*. Unable to find work in Algiers because of the
official distrust of him, he had gone to Paris, early in the Occupation
years, to work for *Paris-Soir*, one of the biggest dailies. Now beyond
doubt a professional journalist, he may even then have dreamt of one
day having his own newspaper marked with his personal stamp. The
opportunity came after he joined the powerful resistance movement
known as "Combat" in 1942 and helped found the clandestine newspaper of the same name, of which he became editor-in-chief. Despite his
postwar position as an editor in the Gallimard publishing house, despite
his growing fame from the publication of *The Stranger* and *The Myth of
Sisyphus* and the staging of his plays, *The Misunderstanding* and *Caligula*, he continued to edit *Combat* until 1947. There it was that he could
exert his most direct influence.

Justin O'Brien. ColF. Winter, 1961, p. 14

We possess some qualities and acquire others. It can be said of Albert
Camus that he possessed violence and acquired moderation. . . . Camus
could easily have gone from extreme violence to its opposite—absolute
passivity. But there is no trace of passivity in his works, which are
always governed by a heightened tension.

This inner tension is what makes Camus's works (*The Plague*,
for example) seem to result from firmly held beliefs; this tension is what
gives these works the power to persuade people to act. It might seem
surprising that so many pages are needed in *The Plague* to provide

a detailed description of an epidemic and its ravages, before reaching the conclusion given in the form of advice, or rather suggestion, that it is preferable not to abandon one's fellow men to a deadly fate, that evil must be fought, and that at the very least each man must declare himself the brother of those who suffer. But the *preparation* is precisely what makes the advice so urgent and so persuasive. If from the first page a call to solidarity had been hurled like a bomb, if that call had been a command, if man's destiny had been vehemently denounced, the reader would perhaps admire the writer's style but would not necessarily be convinced that the writer was correct. And the reader's energy would be all used up in this admiration; there would be no energy left for the subject matter. All the reader's work would have been done for him, and nothing useful would have resulted.

This principle of art, although universal and eternal, is usually misunderstood.

> Jean Grenier. Preface to Albert Camus, *Théâtre,*
> *récits, nouvelles* (Paris, Éditions Gallimard, 1962),
> pp. xv–xvi†

Kipling, Hemingway, Camus: the colonial progress to contemporary alienation. Independence, restlessness, self-dramatization, rapid sophistication, a tremendous reliance on a personal style are basic to them. It was superficial to equate Hemingway with "the dumb ox." He and Camus have closer affinities with a more ingenious imaginary beast: Kipling's "bull that thought"—that brave, sharp, giddy, clever, gay, fastidious animal which had faced death and had learned thereby a lot of skills. They were outside the heavy traditions of the bourgeois bull. These writers, who come so close to the skin and nerves of the natural man, do so by feeling for his surprising mind. . . .

An author's notes are usually haphazard, hit-or-miss ejaculations. They are meant for himself and it's no criticism that Camus is intimate without being informative [in his *Notebooks*]. But the notes do show that he was first and last an artist and that what we call his evasiveness is really the sharpening of his continual consciousness of his art. His philosophical ideas were not original but he was original as a moralist trying to work his way from a treble sense of alienation—a colonial, a man emerged from the hungriest working class and a modern man who has lost his belief in immortality—into an austere, new humanism. He was not, he said, a philosopher, but a man who craved "the knowledge on which to act." As an *engagé* his only uncompromising engagement comes from his early personal appreciation of death (he was tubercular): his hatred of capital punishment.

> V. S. Pritchett. *NS.* April 5, 1963, p. 492

Camus once jokingly proposed that he and Sartre should jointly state in a paid advertisement that they had nothing in common and declined to be responsible for each other's debts. This was an understandable reaction on Camus's part to inevitably being taken for an existentialist, even after he had written *The Myth of Sisyphus*, one object of which was to refute the so-called existentialists. Yet the amount of positive truth contained in such a statement would not have been very great, for despite all their differences Sartre and Camus have much in common. They are children of the same century—Sartre was only four years older than Camus. They lived for many years in the same city, Paris. They were both close to the Communist Party. (Camus was even formally a member of it for a time.) They were both writers and philosophers. But besides all this they are linked by something more profound which makes them brothers—though dissimilar ones—in spirit: a certain radical sense of what existence is for twentieth-century man, an endeavor not to dwell on fractional aspects such as society, religion, political action, nature, regionalism, family, and what not, but to go after the essence of existence itself and seek a fundamental solution for the problems it poses.

However different the solutions they propose, their kinship is not to be underestimated, for if we were to apply a counter-proof and seek a writer more compatible with Sartre than Camus or a writer of comparable stature more akin to Camus than Sartre, we should have some difficulty finding one. . . .

Both writers successfully attempted four main genres: the philosophical treatise, the novel and short story, the drama, and the essay. Taken as a whole, their work is marked by persistent traits which give it the character of a journey. Yet these journeys take them in entirely different directions. . . . [Camus's work] is a journey in the human sense of the word, a journey on which we encounter both the one and the other, light and shade, death and life, sense and absurdity, in the kaleidoscopic shifts of what world and himself mean and can mean to man. This is not an abstract, formal journey but a *real* search which knows no formal philosophical either/or discipline but is always both *envers* (reverse) and *endroit* (obverse). [1967]

Leo Pollmann. Sartre and Camus: Literature of
Existence (New York, Frederick Ungar, 1970),
pp. 111–13

The universal and symbolic implications of [Camus's] plays are stressed at the expense of the historical and concrete. With their elevated and unified tone, purity of language, minimization of physical detail, and concentration upon theme to the exclusion of superfluous humour, anecdote, and scenic ingenuity, Camus's plays are thus much more authentically classical in form than those of his contemporaries. And yet there is always something lacking too. That vital spark of human warmth, of truly theatrical tension when a dramatist who is the complete master of his effects grips his audience exactly as he wishes through his characters, glows sporadically in *The Misunderstanding* and *The Just* and perhaps comes near to being sustained only in *Caligula*. . . .

Incommunicable metaphysics, disparity of form and theme, faulty theatrical judgement, philosophical complexity and abstraction, cloying didacticism and failure to develop a sufficiently personal and artistically appropriate language to bear the weight of the play: these are the principal criticisms of Camus's theatre. Yet it would be quite wrong to regard it as a total failure. Like other "difficult" theatre—that of Claudel, for example—Camus's theatre possesses an undoubted resilience and a tendency, *given the right production*, to succeed at moments which seem frankly unstageworthy on the printed page. . . .

The real merit of Camus's theatre lies in the sphere of theme rather than form, in so far as it is possible to separate the success of one from the failure of the other. Camus's theatre constitutes the most sincere attempt in its genre to create philosophical theatre mirroring the metaphysical anguish of our age. At the same time it combats the nihilism to which such speculation can lead, and in this respect the author follows clearly in the tradition of the great French moralists. Camus's theatre is unequalled for the probity and passion with which it defended human values during a decade in France when they had never been more fragile.

E. Freeman. *The Theatre of Albert Camus* (London,
Methuen, 1971), pp. 160–61

Tragic drama deals by definition with what is extreme and outrageous in human life. The action of *The Just*, based on an historical event, is not meant to be taken either as a positive or a negative model of political behavior. It is rather a probing, under extreme circumstances, of the moral limits of political action. It leaves us with an awareness of the dilemma of trying to reconcile the passion for justice with an ardent love of life—stripped as we are of the traditional saving myths and beliefs. Camus's question is crucial: "Can man alone create his own values?" More specifically, is the search for justice possible in a world devoid of absolute values, that is, without resorting to the fictitious claims of a philosophy of eternity or the uncertain and dangerous claims of a philosophy of history? The answer is a severely qualified Yes.

Camus sets before us a brief historical episode insisting on the tragic cost of even a momentary victory over injustice. He rejects out of hand the different forms of nihilism which offer solutions without regard for the worth of human life. On the other hand, Kaliayev's irrational and politically imprudent idealism reaffirms a not unfamiliar moral predicament: the necessity of sacrifice to create and authenticate a purely human value. But even that moment of triumph over nihilism is qualified by the preceding agony of guilt and the inhuman arithmetic that equates murder and suicide. It is the answer of a twentieth-century humanist, clear-sighted and skeptical, who shows us that, left to his own devices, modern man must act to create his own morality, but that in doing so he becomes inescapably a tragic figure.

Alfred Schwarz. CompD. Spring, 1972, pp. 38–39

It seemed that Camus was a man who corrected himself incessantly, who corrected his style, his emotions, who did not let himself go, and who had a method or a means not to let himself go—a special kind of irony. It was a surface irony, I believe, an irony more feigned than real. He liked irony, but he sought after it; it did not come naturally to him. It was irony, not humor. There was little humor in Camus. That is a criticism I could make against him. But is it possible to be truly ironic when one believes in happiness? And from our first meetings, I discovered [in Camus] a man who had a passion for happiness. . . . I think that for him happiness came from the Mediterranean life, in a certain satisfaction the south can bring. . . .

I thank his disciples, who are often fanatics and sometimes deform a certain part of his thoughts, for having published [*A Happy Death*, a novel Camus had suppressed during his lifetime]. In it one sees everything that is touching and everything that is weak in Camus's thoughts. What is touching is the search for happiness; what is weak is the deification of happiness, the constant consecration that causes happiness finally to flee. . . . By this very notion of happiness, I see Camus as having escaped the duty of a true revolutionary, who never pronounces the word "happiness," but pronounces the word "justice." Because "happiness" prizes each individual person, whereas "justice" prizes the community.

Max-Pol Fouchet. MagL. Sept., 1972, pp. 31–32†

[Camus's] first attempt at extended fiction offers an instructive lesson in the strategies of the imagination. Though shot through with brilliant rays, *A Happy Death* is a chunky, labored work, cumbersome for all its brevity, so cluttered with false starts and halting intentions that it occludes its own themes. In Camus's published *Notebooks*, it first appears as some chapter titles listed in January of 1936, when he was twenty-two; the last relevant notation occurs in March of 1939, when work on

The Stranger was well advanced. An entry of June of 1938—"Rewrite novel"—implies a finished draft of *A Happy Death* by that time, but a month earlier, in a sketch of a funeral in an old people's home, *The Stranger* had begun to germinate, and some months later the uncanny first sentences of the masterpiece were written out intact. During the interval when passages for both novels compete in the *Notebooks*, those relating to *A Happy Death* suffer by comparison, seeming febrile and flaccid amid the sharp glimpses of *The Stranger*.

Wisely, Camus let the first novel be consumed by the second, reusing a number of descriptions, recasting the main theme (a happy death), and transforming the hero's name by the addition of a "u"—Mersault, the man of sea and sun, darkening to Meursault, with its shadow of *meurtre*, of murder. Technically, the third-person method of *A Happy Death*, frequently an awkward vehicle for alter egos (see, see the sensitive young man light his cigarette; now let's eavesdrop on his thoughts), becomes the hypnotic, unabashed first-person of *The Stranger*. Substantively, Camus has located, outside of autobiography, the Archimedean point wherefrom he can acquire leverage upon his world. Often in art, less is more, and one must depart to arrive. In the first novel, the author fumbles, trying to pick himself up by too many handles, and growing more handles in the process; in the second, he takes a short but decisive sidestep, becomes less himself and therefore more, and with this achieved narrowness penetrates to the heart of his *raison d'écrire.* . . .

Since *A Happy Death* arrives now with an excellent critical afterword by Jean Sarocchi, and since Camus suppressed the work, why belabor its weaknesses? Only to marvel at how its materials and concerns reemerge in *The Stranger*, transformed by their new position within a unified action.

John Updike. *NY*. Oct. 21, 1972, pp. 157, 163

CAYROL, JEAN (1911–   )

Jean Cayrol's most recent book, *Poems of Night and Fog* . . . comes to us in part from the concentration camps; only the great hymns at the end were written after the camps were liberated, but they are written as a memorial and tribute to his fellow prisoners.

Thus, the book is divided into two distinct parts: "Poems of Night and Fog" and "Public Tears." The first part, consisting of short poems in various meters, tells the story of a spiritual journey, of the achievement of serenity in the midst of horrible suffering. "Public Tears" contains vast, funereal, glorious liturgies, holy services in honor of the martyrs. . . .

It is true that the ordeal of night is very long. Long, cruel, and palpable, because Cayrol endured it physically, in his flesh and the flesh of those near him. Every poem is the movement from one state to a higher state; every poem bears the true scar of a conquest. Thus, the first part of the collection is a veritable Garden of Gethsemene: it bathes in a sweat of blood, which is contrasted with the gradual rise of hope. . . .

The poetic richness of the book . . . sometimes leads to excesses. The image frequently takes precedence over the rhythmical movement, and the words encroach upon one another under the flow of enumerations. The cause, in general, is a syntax too limited to support the pressure of a surprising creative imagination. Cayrol is fond of litany, a form which is appropriate to the solemn character of his poems but which contributes to their principal fault, an overabundance of symbols that are badly linked. This poet of undeniable inspiration needs very firm discipline for his epic temperament, already revealed in his preceding collections of poetry, to find a structure as complex as his vision.

These defects in his style should not diminish the admiration Cayrol's work deserves: in the short poems in *Poems of Night and Fog* and in the first funeral chant, the words are sometimes sufficiently under control for us to be able to hope that Cayrol will soon write the homogeneous and harmonious frescoes his inspiration seems to be leading him to.

Pierre Emmanuel. Poésie 46. May, 1946,
pp. 132, 134, 136–37†

There is a whole category of novels that are the story not of a man or of an event, but of a duration. . . . If this definition is accurate, Cayrol's novels, although the action in them is effaced or mysterious, are nevertheless genuine novels, for they are totally filled with a duration, which is that of a multiple birth. For Cayrol, content does not consist of a plot, in the usual meaning of the word; content is a continuum of episodes, meetings, and descriptions in which events are reduced to a sort of zero state, whose slenderness is disconcerting. . . .

Through these three novels [*Someone Speaks to You, The First Days, The Fire that Breaks Out*] . . . a man, men, and objects move from the irresolution of a world before history to the identity of a historical world, and finally beyond that world. This multi-form birth is like a movement that gradually touches all the materials in the work: men are born from objects, the possession of love is born from vicarious love, a man with a name is born from an anonymous voice, the narrative is born from a sharing of secrets, and finally the novel itself is born as a

perfectly formed human gesture and as a precious act of tenderness. . . .
For Cayrol . . . there is no duration without birth.

Roland Barthes. *Critique*. March, 1952, pp. 482–84†

[*All in a Night*] seems to show the precise importance of a theme that
is probably essential in Cayrol's work. In his fiction and poetry, amidst a
concert of loud tragic voices, another voice, apparently more restrained,
obstinately tries to make itself heard. . . .

This little voice is none other than simple "happiness." Certainly,
there is something paradoxical about its presence, because *All in a Night*
is linked in spite of everything to what might be called—with no pejorative intention—the tradition of despair, and linked to that tradition in
many ways. Cayrol's great desire for lucid awareness must surely be the
opposite of the "healthy" and overly convenient blindness that usually
accompanies cheap satisfaction or any other sort of comfort. But sometimes we forget, out of fear of deluding ourselves, that a romanticizing
of unhappiness is also one of the worst enemies of wisdom and soon
leads to irrationality. Madness is no more of a solution than blindness;
often it is also just as frivolous, just as complacent. Abandoning oneself
to despair is scarcely less degrading than abandoning oneself to blind
happiness.

François, the hero of *All in a Night*, walks alone on a cold, damp
night. He is trying to reach his own house, where he wants to spend his
thirtieth birthday with his father. He intentionally got off the train one
station too soon, to discover the surrounding countryside with which he
is so unfamiliar, having been more-or-less confined throughout his entire
childhood. Naturally, he soon gets lost. But he does not abandon his
project; he continues to be calm and confident. He continues to walk,
asks directions, walks back over the same ground, tries different directions, keeps moving in spite of sudden rainstorms and his own fatigue,
and only stops for a short time when he is offered shelter. . . .

While François is wandering, his memory is expanding. He patiently reconstructs images of his childhood—terror, claustrophobia,
absurdity—a whole atmosphere of systematic remorse and of misfortune, skillfully sustained by his father after the (suspicious?) death of
François's mother. Little by little, the landscape of this lost night takes
on shape and meaning: the places, the people, the things he has
glimpsed—all turn out to be more-or-less directly linked to the cursed
past haunting him. . . .

It is difficult to speak of this vibrant and free book without appearing to reduce it to symbolic constructions, which are denied by the real
presence in it of beings and things—real even for the least of them. And

symbolism would be scoffed at by the small, tender voice that persists in the midst of the uproar.

Alain Robbe-Grillet. *NRF*. Aug., 1954, pp. 317–19†

Appearing as a novelist in the immediate postwar period, Cayrol was already firmly established before the new novel became a literary issue. However, critics of the new school have considered him a kindred spirit, which he is indeed by aspects of his technique, theme, and concept of the novel. His writing stands quite apart from the French sociological or psychological tradition, belonging rather to that of the *Entwicklungs-roman*, the "duration" novel which Sartre and the new novelists all advocate. His hero moves blindly along in the adventure of his life, neither knowing where he is going nor ever really arriving. He is seeking something, his salvation perhaps, but all we can be sure of is that he will discover the world. The world for a man like Armand of *I Shall Live the Love of Others* is the world of objects, that of banal mechanical miracles of city streets along which he wanders.

Setting and structure of Cayrol's novels meet the specifications of the new novel; and his "Lazarian" themes—man's loneliness, his plight in a universe that fills him with awe and apprehension, his gropings to distinguish the true from the false, the real from the unreal—belong to the order of Existentialist and Phenomenological preoccupations. Moreover, younger writers can find in Cayrol the approved fictional devices of monologue and the restricted point of view. Cayrol himself has never been dogmatic in novelistic theory, but has given his blessing to Robbe-Grillet and the new school, who quite rightly hail him as a master.

Laurent LeSage. *The French New Novel* (University Park, Pa., Pennsylvania State University Press, 1962), pp. 79–80

With his most recent novel, *Foreign Bodies*, Cayrol returns for the first time since *Someone Speaks to You* to the *récit* [short narrative] entirely in the first person. The man who is speaking here . . . is endlessly telling and re-telling the story of his life, casting out the "foreign bodies" which fill his memory with things that never happened, replacing them with other distortions or inventions which resist our efforts to disentangle the true from the false, to separate actual events from imaginary ones created by Gaspard—subconsciously, perhaps—to deny his sordid past. Finally we realize that Gaspard's memory, which refuses the passive role of mere recapitulation in order to *create* a past which corresponds to his nostalgia, has become the agent and the expression of hope. We leave Gaspard finally as, catching his breath, he begins once again the long, confused story which has neither beginning nor end. . . .

The "inhabitants" of Cayrol's fictional universe, from Armand in *I Shall Live the Love of Others* to Gaspard in *Foreign Bodies,* are in constant motion, walking endlessly, seemingly at random, in the real space of the world of phenomena, a world both familiar and strange, disturbing and reassuring. If this motion seems to *spatialize* man's loneliness, it also incarnates his vague aspirations toward reconciliation and renewal and keeps him free to follow paths where chance encounters—chance for Cayrol being very much like the "objective chance" of the surrealists—may lead to recognition and to love. Love, one should note, is not for Cayrol the exalted passion of the Romantics, but a humble, patient, human emotion which may, nevertheless, bring the modern Lazarus back to life.

Carlos Lynes. In John Cruickshank, ed., *The Novelist as Philosopher* (London, Oxford University Press, 1962), pp. 202–4

[The protagonist of a Cayrol novel] is a man without gifts, without a heritage; if he looks encumbered, it is because he has appropriated the heritage of others. This man is always deprived of any reason for social existence and is therefore indefinable from the outside, is unrecognizable at first glance; he is nothing as he is first presented. It can scarcely be claimed that he is a man; this would be too much to say. He is "someone." . . . We know neither the age nor the face of the character who is the subject of the verbs in *Someone Speaks to You,* Cayrol's first novel. . . . This man is dead. He no longer even knows himself, either as man-space or as man-time, but only as the skeletal support of an action that will not clothe him until after a long delay. In a word, he is *dislodged.* For a long time nobody will know where he comes from, for he himself has little memory ("I don't remember details"), only rooms to pass through before entering his own. . . .

Thus *dislodged* from his own identity, man in Cayrol's novels can enter a deportation office as he would a hotel room, well informed of his situation, as it were, and with the time, as if incidentally, to perfect his self-oblivion. Time will lead him to recognize, the way one might "recognize" the color of his hair or a certain fault in his character: "Yes, I am deported." Not "I was," but "I am." Deported—that is, placed beside oneself, outside oneself. For good measure, his room will also be taken away.

Daniel Oster. *Jean Cayrol et son œuvre* (Paris, Éditions du Seuil, 1967), pp. 32–33†

CÉLINE, LOUIS-FERDINAND (1894–1961)

This enormous novel [*Journey to the End of the Night*] is an important book, with a power and scope we are not accustomed to finding in the works of the dwarfs of bourgeois literature, with their hair so carefully curled. A thousand reservations come to mind, but they cannot prevent me from putting this novel in a different category from all those very proper, very idealistic novels that seem to be written by little trained dogs.

Journey to the End of the Night is a picaresque novel; it is not a revolutionary novel, but it is a novel about the "underdogs." . . .

Céline is not one of us [that is, not a communist]: it is impossible to accept his profound anarchy, his scorn, and his general feeling of repulsion, which do not exclude the proletariat. His pure rebellion can lead him anywhere: to join us, to fight against us, or to go nowhere at all. He lacks the spirit of revolution; he does not perceive the real explanation of the miseries he denounces, the cancers he reveals; he lacks the concrete hope that carries us forward. But we can acknowledge his sinister picture of the world: he strips away all masks, all camouflage; he strikes down the trappings of illusion; he increases our awareness of man's present decay.

Time will tell where this man, who is not fooled by anything, will go. Céline's literary language is a transposition of the speech of the people: but it becomes artificial toward the end. The reason is that this book is two hundred pages too long. Céline did not stop after having said everything.

Paul Nizan. *L'humanité.* Dec. 9, 1932, p. 4†

Céline did not win the Prix Goncourt [for *Journey to the End of the Night*]. So much the better for Céline. . . .

For us, the important thing is not to find out whether Céline's depictions in this book are horrible; the question to ask is whether they are true. They are. And what is even truer than the depictions is the incomparable language, the most natural and the most artificial of languages, a language that has been entirely invented but is all of a piece like the language used in tragedy. Céline's language is as far removed as possible from a slavish reproduction of the speech of the wretched; his language was created precisely to express what the speech by the wretched could never express—their puerile and gloomy souls, their gloomy childhoods. Yes, here is the cursed side, the shameful side, the rejected side of our people. Indeed, we must acknowledge that there are more reassuring images of modern society, like the military image, for example: on the right, the *good* poor, who earn a stripe and a promotion; on the left, the *bad* poor, who have to be thrown into the brig. . . .

A true Christianity can be reconstructed only if it is willing to take certain chances. And the modern world does not seem very determined to take those chances. Therefore, this journey to the end of the night is not about to end—but the end will certainly come into view. The end of the night is the sweet pity of God . . . the depths of Eternity. [Dec. 13, 1932]

Georges Bernanos. *Le crépuscule des vieux* (Paris, Gallimard, 1956), pp. 341, 345–46†

Louis-Ferdinand Céline walked into great literature as other men walk into their own homes. A mature man, with a colossal stock of observations as physician and artist, with a sovereign indifference toward academism, with an extraordinary instinct for intonation of life and language, Céline has written a book which will survive, independently of whether he writes other books, and whether they attain the level of his first. *Journey to the End of the Night* is a novel of pessimism, a book dedicated by terror in the face of life, and weariness of it, rather than indignation. Active indignation is linked up with hope. In Céline's book there is no hope. . . .

Céline does not at all set himself the goal of exposing social conditions in France. . . . The present social system is as rotten as every other, whether past or future. Céline, in general, is dissatisfied with men and their affairs.

The novel is conceived and executed as a panorama of life's meaninglessness, with its cruelties, conflicts, and lies, with no issue, and no light flickering. . . . From chapter to chapter, from one page to the next, the slivers of life compose themselves into a mud-caked, bloody nightmare of meaninglessness. Receptivity which is passive, with its nerves sliced open, without the will straining toward the future—that is the psychological base of despair, sincere in the convulsions of its cynicism.

Céline the moralist follows the footsteps of the artist, and step by step he rips away the halo from all those social values which have become highly acclaimed through custom, from patriotism and personal ties down to love. . . .

Céline's style is subordinated to his receptivity of the objective world. In his seemingly careless, ungrammatical, passionately condensed language there lives, beats, and vibrates the genuine wealth of French culture, the entire emotional and mental experience of a great nation, in its living content, in its keenest tints.

And, concurrently, Céline writes like a man who has stumbled across human language for the first time. The artist has newly threshed the dictionary of French literature. Pat expressions fly off like chaff. And, instead, words that have been excluded from circulation by academic aesthetic and morality become irreplaceable to give expression to life in its crudeness and abjectness. [May, 1933]

Leon Trotsky. *Leon Trotsky on Literature and Art*
(New York, Pathfinder, 1970), pp. 191–93

The 700 pages of James Joyce's *Ulysses* seem to have been written all in one breath. One gets the same impression from *Death on the Installment Plan*. What is extraordinary about the book is its richness, its abundance, its torrential flow. The author wanted to put everything into this book, just as everything is put into a cathedral: the earth, heaven, hell, purgatory, the virtues, the sins, the seasons, the flesh, and the spirit. Not only does a cathedral have pillars, vaulting, walls, buttresses, and every other architectural feature; there are also statues, thousands of statues, an extraordinary profusion of statues. And while some of these statues are edifying, others are thoroughly inappropriate. . . .

Death on the Installment Plan was inspired by the most truthful spirituality—the spirituality of the medieval men who built cathedrals and who were able to gaze into hell, drew up inventories of the infernal regions, and pushed the devils and the damned pell-mell onto the town square with great sweeps of the broom, laughing aloud at the baffled witches and their ignominious sabbath.

The same distinction can still be made today between what can be seen and what cannot. What can be seen in Céline's novel is a vicious child. His mother is somewhat sickly and kills herself through overwork. His father is garrulous and moralizing, something of a tramp whose bad luck has given him a catastrophic outlook on life. This bad luck also undermines young Ferdinand's best resolutions, and outraged by his father's morality lessons, shouts, and slaps, the boy finally throws himself on the old man and half strangles him.

What cannot be seen is the whole background of misery and rancor, the irony of an unequal, impossible, and derisive struggle between ineffectual free will and implacable destiny—the grandeur, in spite of everything, of the ridiculous and pitiful human fate, the calamitous human condition. And Céline shows us these invisible devils, and we thereby become reconciled with ourselves and with his characters, who are likable in spite of everything.

Charles Bernard. Quoted in Robert Denoël, *Apologie de "Mort à crédit"* (Paris, Éditions Denoël et Steele, 1936), pp. 18–19, 21–22†

[*Death on the Installment Plan*] is a long, dull book lacking the tragic quality that distinguished *Journey to the End of the Night*. Despite the title, which is an original way of saying the autobiography of an underdog, death no longer is one of the central characters, and the absence of the war cramps the author's style considerably. But the same unremitting violence, the same prolonged paroxysm, marks everything he writes. There is no relief for the reader, whom Céline attempts to crush just as the hero's father constantly attempts to crush his son by jumping up and down, foaming at the mouth, letting off steam through his distended nostrils, breaking up the furniture, and finally puking all over the chaos he has made. In fact there probably never was a book which contained, in the literal sense, so much vomit. . . .

Céline has been most frequently compared to Rabelais and James Joyce. To be sure, he has in common with them lengthiness, a love of scatology, and a dissatisfaction with the current vocabulary, but he lacks their learning and careful composition. When Rabelais and Joyce enrich the language, for instance, they make subtle graftings and invent onomatopoetic images, whereas Céline simply scrambles common words as a strong man bends iron. He dominates language as he does the rest of his material, crushing it with a heavy hand. His special sense of the comic manifests itself most often in elephantine exaggeration, not unlike Rabelais at his worst—when he is carried away with the gigantic aspect of his heroes. . . .

In reality Céline belongs to the strictly contemporary school of hard-boiled writers, of which we know more here than they do in France. In saying that his work will survive, Leon Trotsky revealed his short-sightedness as a literary critic. In a very short time *Death on the Installment Plan* and all the novels of that school will possess merely an archeological interest.

Justin O'Brien. *Nation.* Aug. 27, 1938, pp. 207–8

One may be shocked by *Bagatelles for a Massacre*; one may grow tired of it; one may declare the book unreadable or idiotic; but it is impossible for a Frenchman born a Frenchman not to read at least a few pages with a feeling of relief. . . .

I am well aware of what reasonable people will tell me: "Céline exaggerates. He would ruin the best causes. A reasonable anti-Semitism can be supported, but not an animal anti-Semitism, a violent anti-Semitism. In this book the Jews will seek and quickly find the best arguments against the people who attack them." And I am very well aware of all the exaggerations in this work. But after all, when you choose to visit a lion, you do not give him spinach to eat. And my goodness, while reading this book, I was not at all sorry to be visiting Céline.

Of course, he exaggerates. His picture of literary history is false, but quite unsurprising in a man of letters, who has been endowed with all the faults of his profession. Despite appearances, there has always been an affected writer in Céline: the title of this book is good proof of that, as well as the descriptions of symbolic ballets, which open and close the book. He is the Giraudoux of the sewers.

Moreover, his obsession with Jews makes him see Jews everywhere. The critics: All Jews or Jewish tools! Famous authors? All Jews! Cézanne? A Jew! Racine? Another Jew! (Celine's assertion here is meant to be taken quite literally, and he analyzes the Semitic spirit in Racine!) The Pope, the Church, the priests? Jews! The Kings of France? "Don't you think they have funny noses?" It is obvious that it would be rather difficult to debate the Jewish question seriously wth anyone with such opinions. And I am not denying that his exaggerations eventually damage the cause he claims to support, and damage it a little more seriously than the author believes. If I reasoned as he does, I could (with less verve than he has, I admit) assert that this book, in its excesses, was written by a certain Celinemann under the pseudonym of Céline, in order to discredit anti-Semites. . . .

You can have any opinion you like about the Jews and about Céline. I do not agree with him on all grounds. But I am telling you: this enormous book, this magnificent book, is the first sign of a "native uprising." You can find this uprising excessive and more instinctive than reasonable; but after all, we Frenchmen are the natives. [1938]

Robert Brasillach. *Les quatre jeudis* (Paris, Éditions Balzac, 1944), pp. 230–31, 234†

Oh yes/the rising american writers/the writers of 1940 to 50 will STILL have to read a FRENCH author/I mean ANOTHER french author: one not yet in the school books/one no AMY Lowell will bring home in a sachet case/

France stank/and the stink is recorded/It is recorded with a COPIA: whereof probably no frog since Rabelais has been capable but the copia/the supply of words is an accessory/it is the clear view that makes CÉLINE important/

Yaas, I am talking of CÉLINE/last book suppressed I hear in Ole Bro. Pétain's France/dont like the SUBJECT/

some folks don't like the SUBJECT/now WHY dont they like the subject/Céline was all out to save France/I reckon he is still out to pick up the pieces/40 million population in France in 1938/25 million frenchmen/soon to be a minority/Céline was tellin'em and they did NOT listen to Céline/ . . .

His best KNOWN works are/*Journey to the End of the Night/Death on the Installment Plan/Bagatelles for a Massacre/*

Bonjour Ferdinand/I dont hold it my duty any more to run a chronicle of French publications/but I still Know a real book when I see one/whatever the contents/Ferdinand has GOT down to reality/Ferdinand is a writer/Next one will be the last one/ [May 14, 1942]

Ezra Pound. *"If This Be Treason..."* (Siena,
Tip. Nuova, 1948), pp. 24–25

Even people who do not think Céline important as an artist must admit his importance as a historical phenomenon. His antisemitic pamphlets, like his cynically disillusioned and satirical confessions, caught the mood of their generation to perfection and sold in the millions. Céline's books are more than bundles of paper. They are not forgotten as soon as they are read. They echo in the mind long after, for they pretend (not altogether in vain) to some intellectual substance as well as to raw emotional power. His books are really acts. They are, to use Milton's figure of speech, like those fabulous dragon's teeth which, being sown up and down a land, spring up armed men. Céline's books sprang up instead as men who threw away their arms. The French debacle of 1940 was as well prepared for by *Journey to the End of the Night* and *Bagatelles for a Massacre* as it was by *Mein Kampf.* . . .

Céline, who was never a Nazi himself, is yet more representative of the spirit which made the Nazis successful than they themselves ever were. Most of the Nazis, as has been shown in the trials since the end of the war, were petty opportunists and careerists, profiteers of circumstance, poor provincial windbags. Céline speaks with the thunder of the united voices of his millions of readers between the wars and during the war. He speaks with the authority of a world which has been physically smashed and intellectually read out of existence but still refuses to pass away. He is like the nightmare so powerful and persistent that it disturbs the rest of our waking hours.

Milton Hindus. *The Crippled Giant* (New York,
Boar's Head, 1950), pp. 10, 12

The secret source of that powerful novel *Journey to the End of the Night* was an oceanic self-pity, and a sweeping capacity for detail, speed and event disguised the fact. In Céline's succeeding novels, the self-pity has become hysterical and stylistically exhausting. *Guignol's Band* is made up of short breathless sentences, ejaculations, dashes, exclamations and asterisks and, in this respect, is a notable feat of typewriting by someone who appears to have had a knock on the head. This is, of course, also the condition of his characters. They are the foul-mouthed, feeble-minded of the London underworld: prostitutes, pimps, crooks and cranks, and the knock is the 1914 war. They keep themselves going by drink, by brawling, by commercial or perverted sex, and Céline's intention is to present them through the haze of their hallucinations. The result is a collection of personal nightmares. So far, so tedious. The redeeming side is that the book contains the corruption in long passages of gross and grotesque comedy, for part of each nightmare is knockabout farce and this is very well done.

There is no doubt that Céline is an artist in portraying people whose moral sense has been bitten off by rats. . . . He is susceptible to atmosphere and to the stupid, self-destructive and anarchic forces in human character, which, by an act of tough sentimentality, he detaches from the control of all moral sense. This ought to make his people mythical; they ought to be giants. They are in fact grotesques, but grotesques whose habits are petty and pathetic. Their obsessions are small and (if they were not almost pretentiously squalid) quaint. . . .

Macabre comedy, brutal hilarity are in Céline's vein. Behind the self-pity and the cynicism is an admiration of power and violence, a belief in frenzy and excitement and the sentimental exaltation of the irrational. In practice this may mean no more than falling down stairs dead drunk into a pile of crockery or beating an old woman with an umbrella. He does penetrate the sullen, private world of the conceited outcast; what offends is that he wallows in it very self-consciously, whereas the underdogs themselves do not know they are wallowing. He puts a lurid spotlight on them and then winds the handle of his literary barrel organ. Compared with *Journey to the End of the Night*, this is inferior stuff, but as a piece of caricature of the seamy kind, it has originality and anecdotal skill.

V. S. Pritchett. NSN. Oct. 2, 1954, pp. 412, 414

Céline valued friendship and always proved to be exceptionally loyal in his affections. During his entire medical career, which had such a great influence on his literary works, he demonstrated an admirable devotion and unselfishness, until the end of his life. In his last ten years, he even opened a medical office in his house at Meudon, less for financial reasons than to reestablish direct contact with medicine, through practice rather than books. A few poor patients came to see him; he could never bring himself to charge them, and he paid for their medicine. No, Céline was not a hard-hearted man; he was quite the opposite. The great affection he very naturally felt for children and animals should be sufficient evidence of that. . . .

I found only one weakness in him: the anger he let himself get carried away by. Nothing in this man, nothing in his conversation—which was full of well-being, gaiety and a verve as sparkling as the best passages in *Journey to the End of the Night*—no, really nothing could suggest any notion of nausea. Nature made him a fighter, by granting him extra strength, determination, and self-control, and his literary work is that of a fighter. Note that in Céline, the juncture of the poet and the doctor was of utmost importance and gave his work its orientation. If he had been an English teacher or an embassy attaché, he would probably still have undone the straitjacket of vocabulary and syntax. But he would not have written *Journey to the End of the Night*. The practice of medicine and the parade of the hundred thousand miseries in a suburban clinic sharpened, or at the very least firmly brought out, a feeling that was probably innate in Céline—a sense of sin, not against the divinity but against man.

Marcel Aymé. L'Herne. No. 3, 1962, pp. 213–15†

The appearance of *Journey to the End of the Night* in 1932 was a very important event for me. That was because of its radical upheaval of language—the eruption of a popular speech, with all its flexibility and poetic density, overturning sclerosed forms and a sclerosed language. The breaking of rhythm, the fracturing of the classical sentence, and the use of this new form constituted an aperture toward a visionary world. This novel was also important because it unmasked and dismantled appearances. There was a lot of tenderness and humanity in the *Journey to the End of the Night*. Céline, at that time, was anti-racist!

I felt great indignation and sadness when I later read his pamphlets. I attribute them to a veritable madness within him. It is impossible for me to protest against the political and moral reasons that, at least partially, motivated his ostracism. But I do believe that this ostracism also stemmed from the hostility provoked by genius. I never doubted that Céline's works would come back into prominence: revolutionary, like all great works, Céline's books today run parallel to the current concerns of novelists. Contemporary novelists are especially interested in form and language: these concerns explain why Céline today arouses interest.

Nathalie Sarraute. Arts. Dec. 22–28, 1965, p. 12†

During the Occupation, Céline associated with collaborationists and had connections in Vichy; but his contact with the Germans was minimal and his attitude concerning their future pessimistic. From the beginning he smelled defeat: "An army that can't draw revolution in its wake, in a war like this, is sunk. Washed up, the Fritzies." According to his ex-fascist friend Lucien Rebatet, he "was constantly pursued by the demon of persecution which inspired him to dream up fabulous systems in the hope of outwitting his numerous imaginary enemies." Nevertheless, he remained in Paris till 1944, writing the two parts of *Guignol's Band* and

Shooting Gallery, most of which was lost when his apartment was looted during the Liberation. He left for Denmark only after his nightmare visions had materialized and the B.B.C. had begun denouncing him as a traitor.

After eight months of wandering in Germany, he arrived in Copenhagen in March, 1945, where less than a year later he was imprisoned for his wartime activities and confined to a death cell for fourteen months, under threat of extradition to France. Paroled in 1947, he spent nearly five years in a primitive hut by the Baltic Sea. There he wrote *Fairyland for Another Time* and its sequel *Normance* while waiting for a French amnesty that came in 1951. He returned home to settle in Meudon (near Paris), where he continued to write until his death in 1961. Already by 1957, with the publication of the novel *Castle to Castle*, his reputation had begun to mend.

David Hayman. *Louis-Ferdinand Céline* (New York, Columbia University Press, 1965), p. 9

Céline has called men by all the vile names imaginable. He refers to them as *"les salauds"* [roughly, "skunks"] long before his famous fellow writer Jean-Paul Sartre, with the important difference that for Céline, hell is to be found not only in "the others," but in himself as well. Man then, is shown to be almost totally malevolent, stupid, absurd, grotesque, squalid, and *sale* (dirty) in the true sense of the word.

This brutal indictment does not change from *Journey to the End of the Night* to *North*, written almost thirty years later. If anything, it only deepens. For even the most cursory glance reveals that while the first diptych of *Journey to the End of the Night* and *Death on the Installment Plan* depicts the "vileness," absurdity, and futility of individuals, the second, comprising *Castle to Castle* and *North*, performs the same function for entire civilizations. While Bardamu, man and child, had wandered without aim or hope from Africa to Passy, from Detroit to Courbevoie, from Toulouse to Blême-le-Petit, in the early novels, entire peoples migrate in similar fashion and to the same end in the final works. The only difference is that the circles of their hell become more and more circumscribed as the catastrophe grows larger. They turn about in a continually tighter yet more gigantic trap. But the outcome is the same. The "No Exit" sign has not changed, only the lettering has become more grotesque. The vehicles which carry off the dead or dying, those who have succumbed within the trap, have also grown more nightmarish. The tugboat that draws away everything in its path so that silence may reign at the end of *Journey to the End of the Night* becomes "Charon's boat" with its hideous captain and mutilated passengers of *Castle to Castle*, or the cow-drawn chariot of *North* which carts off its load of drugged victims to a limbo even more shadowy than that of the tugboat of old.

Erika Ostrovsky. *Céline and His Vision* (New York, New York University Press, 1967), pp. 40–41

[Céline's] final trilogy is to be taken as an exact "chronicle" of his wanderings, beginning with his flight from France to Germany and ending with the momentary illusion that he had found safety in Denmark. That the work was written in three parts, consisting of *Castle to Castle, North,* and *Rigadoon,* is undoubtedly attributable, to some extent, to the chance success Céline enjoyed with the publication of *Castle to Castle* in 1957. . . .

Céline's chronicles are somewhat disconcerting if read in the order of their appearance. *Castle to Castle* tells various anecdotes about Céline's stay at Sigmaringen, the medieval village where Hitler interned the Vichy government in exile. *North,* published in 1960, begins with Céline's earlier flight from France in July, 1944, and ends with his leaving Zornhof, a fictional village near Berlin, to go north. *Rigadoon,* written in the last months of Céline's life and published posthumously in 1969, picks up Céline's flight as he leaves Zornhof and traces his travels to the north and then back to the south to Sigmaringen. In an entirely confusing manner, perhaps because Céline did not really finish the novel, *Rigadoon* skips over the Sigmaringen period (November, 1944, to March, 1945) and relates his later travels north to Denmark. In their general outline these three chronicles appear to be accurate in their presentation of Céline's journeys, though there is much confusion about specific incidents. Their principal interest, however, lies in Céline's vision of history as delirious farce. . . .

Castle to Castle is the only novel in the last trilogy in which Céline attains the mad rhetoric of his earlier works, for simulation of the characters' delirium demands the kind of verbal energy he displayed in *Death on the Installment Plan* and *Guignol's Band.* In *North* and *Rigadoon* a language in which violence is attenuated accompanies Céline's rejection of high comedy of character in favor of a vision of history as a bloody farce. The constant and mechanical recurrence of calamities, bombardments, assassinations, and close escapes produces a farcical series in which Céline, in spite of his persecution complex, plays a role comparable to Buster Keaton's in one of his chase sequences. . . .

[Céline's] visceral refusal has subsided—nausea has virtually disappeared from this trilogy—and in its place the reader encounters a powerful but absurdly egocentric view of the ravages of history. Céline's outcry against the incomprehensible unfolding of events that has led to his downfall is, ultimately, grounded in a paranoid clown's view of history as a personal apocalypse.

Allen Thiher. *Céline: The Novel as Delirium*
(New Brunswick, N.J., Rutgers University Press,
1972), pp. 169–70, 197–99

CENDRARS, BLAISE (1887–1961)

SWITZERLAND

On October 12, 1492, Christopher Columbus discovered America, a foundling child who has come a long way since then. For the last few years, even our artists have been feeling its influence. Our musicians use its ragtime, our painters use its landscapes of iron and stone, and our poets use its posters, its advertisements, and its movies.

Blaise Cendrars is, of all Frenchmen, the one who has been the most successful in achieving this new exoticism—a mixture of motors and Negro rituals. He does not follow fashion, he intersects it. The use of this material is legitimate in his work. He has traveled. He has seen. He testifies. He returns from the Americas and from the war like a prospector for gold, and he throws his huge nuggets on our table. He sticks his knife into the ground next to him. He has only one arm now, his left arm. The right one was torn off by a German shell. It seems as if the war removed his writing arm only to have his poems blossom in even more dazzling colors. [1919]

Jean Cocteau. *Carte blanche* (Paris,
Éditions de la Sirène, 1920), pp. 104–5†

Now's the time for the Homeric hymns of the railroads. Blaise Cendrars has written some of them already in salty French sonorous and direct as the rattle of the great express trains. . . . [In *The Prose of the Trans-Siberian and of Little Jehanne of France*] he goes on piling up memories of torn hurtling metal, of trains of sixty locomotives at full steam disappearing in the direction of Port Arthur, of hospitals and whores and jewelry merchants, memories of the first great exploit of the Twentieth Century seen through sooty panes, beaten into his brain by the uneven rumble of the broad-gauge Trans-Siberian. Crows in the sky, bodies of men in heaps along the tracks, burning hospitals, an embroidery unforeseen in that stately panorama unfolding rivers and lakes and mountains in the greenish dusk of the shed at the Exposition Universelle.

Then there's *Panama; or, The Adventures of My Seven Uncles,* seven runaway uncles, dedicated to the last Frenchman in Panama, the barkeep at Matachine, the deathplace of Chinamen, where the liveoaks have grown up among the abandoned locomotives, where every vestige of the de Lesseps attempt is rotten and rusted and overgrown with lianas except a huge anchor in the middle of the forest stamped with the arms of Louis XV. . . .

And Blaise Cendrars has since written the history of General Johann Sutter, *Gold,* a narrative that traces the swiftest leanest parabola of anything I've ever read, a narrative that cuts like a knife through the washy rubbish of most French writing of the present time, with its lemon-colored gloves and its rosewater and holy water and its *policier-gentleman* cosmopolitan affectation. It's probably because he really is, what the Quai d'Orsay school pretend to be, an international vagabond, that Cendrars has managed to capture the grandiose rhythms of America of seventy-five years ago, the myths of which our generation is just beginning to create. (As if anyone ever *really was* anything; he's a good writer, leave it at that.) In *Gold* he's packed the tragic and turbulent absurdity of '49 into a skyrocket. It's over so soon you have to read it again for fear you have missed something.

John Dos Passos. *Orient Express* (New York,
Harper & Brothers, 1927), pp. 158, 160, 162

His poems of eighteen years ago have the quality of motion pictures taken from a shaking express train, a quality which Cendrars tried for deliberately. Was he not cultivating the two hemispheres as his garden patch? His pages are peopled with allusions to, rather than pictures of, tropical seaports, Oriental deserts, locomotives, revolutions, skyscrapers, wars. Moreover, his poems date from a period in French literature when it was a fashionable affectation to use the names of outlandish places like Mississippi or Timbuktu, or foreign words like "cocktail" and "policeman." The effectiveness of such tricks sometimes disappears in translation; but the overwhelming effect of mobility, of breathless speed, is successfully captured.

"Forgive me for not knowing the antique game of verse," the poet says. *His* verse is to be free, discursive, profane. Or now it may be in the form of telegraphic jottings, or Whitmanesque catalogues of places and sights and people. But his poems seldom touch a great music which would hypnotize us into reading them over and over again. They compose rather the journal of a modern poet; they give us his nostalgias and his visions, often penetrating, violent, yet as bewildering and neutralizing in their total effect as prolonged sight-seeing from an observation car. Cendrar's deficiencies, I have always felt, result from his own poetic limitations. Apollinaire and Soupault, with much the same approach, have remained artists. The poems of Cendrars leave us but the notebook of a colorful and itinerant modern personality who has come to know all the trains by the sound of their wheels.

Matthew Josephson. *Nation*. Dec. 2, 1931,
pp. 616–17

Cendrars improvises with bold skill in plunging into the whirlwind of the period after World War I, and from this world he sometimes extracts the head of an eternal human being that has been mutilated by modern machinery, sometimes just a foolish novelty. Even when a keen need for the elementary casts him across forests and oceans, mountains and deserts, his sense of tragedy still forces him to depict a disturbing universe; the whole universe is put into the roller coaster of a carnival, a carnival that would be the last carnival, condemned to end in an immense fire. . . .

Cendrars, who wrote *Negro Anthology*, gives his halting prose as well as his free verse a superstitious and idolatrous appearance; he imparts a movement to his works that sometimes hurries with a riotous fury and sometimes has the slow drift of the last days of the earth. He will leave behind a curious stock of images. He alone can discover in the electric tramways moving along the avenue a resemblance to howling monkeys holding onto one another by the tail. But alas, he alone can also write: "When I let myself follow my destructive instincts, I find the triangle of a metaphysical solution." The fact is that when he encounters the airplane, the radio, the movies, and all the devices of destruction, he gets dizzy, and then he launches into strange intellectual bragging. In addition, he becomes very rushed, and does not pay attention to details. . . .

The rather dull litany of his poems gives rise to raw facts, one after the other, like trees seen from the window of a moving car, without any extension into his spirit. Those facts are unassimilated, and therefore inert and heavy. Cendrars's is an overly simplistic contact with reality, a tragic contact but one that wearies the reader, crushes him, and lulls him to sleep. This is all the more true since the verse he uses, a prose-verse, envelops each sensation as a separate entity, without fusions, links, or inflections. His verse gathers enough material to create living beings, but never gives them life. Poetry means creation. An art like Cendrars's does not create; it records.

Henri Clouard. *Histoire de la littérature française,*
du symbolisme à nos jours (Paris,
Éditions Albin Michel, 1949), Vol. I, pp. 575–76†

Many are the things which have been said against this writer . . . that his books are cinematic in style, that they are sensational, that he exaggerates and deforms to gross excess, that he is prolix and verbose, that he lacks all sense of form, that he is too much the realist or else that his narratives are too incredible, and so on ad infinitum. Taken together there is, to be sure, a grain of truth in these accusations, but let us remember—*only a grain*! They reflect the views of the paid critic, the academician, the frustrated novelist. But supposing, for a moment, we accepted them at face value. Will they hold water? Take his cinematic technique, for example. Well, are we not living in the age of the cinema? Is not this period of history more fantastic, more "incredible," than the simulacrum of it which we see unrolled on the silver screen? As for his sensationalism—have we forgotten Gilles de Rais, the Marquis de Sade, the *Memoirs* of Casanova? As for hyperbole, what of Pindar? As for prolixity and verbosity, what about Jules Romains or Marcel Proust? As for exaggeration and deformation, what of Rabelais, Swift, Céline, to mention an anomalous trinity?

As for lack of form, that perennial jackass which is always kicking up its heels in the pages of literary reviews. . . . *Oui*, Cendrars is full of excrescences. There are passages which swell up out of the body of his text like rank tumors. There are detours, parentheses, asides, which are the embryonic pith and substance of books yet to come. There is a grand efflorescence and exfoliation, and there is also a grand wastage of material in his books. Cendrars neither cribs and cabins, nor does he drain himself completely. When the moment comes to let go, he lets go. When it is expedient or efficacious to be brief, he is brief and to the point—like a dagger. To me his books reflect his lack of fixed habits, or better yet, his ability to break a habit. (A sign of real emancipation!) In those swollen paragraphs, which are like "a howling sea" and which some readers, apparently, are unable to cope with, Cendrars reveals his oceanic spirit.

Henry Miller. The Books in My Life (Norfolk,
Conn., New Directions, 1952), pp. 66–67

Up until a few years ago, Cendrars' adventurous life could be discerned through his novels (which perhaps may not survive him) or by reading his first verses (his most enduring work). But at the beginning of 1952, the story of his life was broadcast in ten of the thirteen radio interviews he had with Michel Manoll, and which later appeared in volume form under the title *Blaise Cendrars Speaks To You*. None of the prose books Blaise wrote equal this spoken portrait. It is not easy to summarize the extreme intricacy of the narration and even harder to give an idea of its inimitable verve.

A man who by himself is a whole epoch, perhaps the last great epoch of modern French art, Blaise was the quintessence of cosmopolitanism filtered through the sharpest Gallic wit. . . .

What is the value of Blaise Cendrars' poetry? It has never been doubted that it merits the place of honor in the tremendously vast production of the writer. With *Easter in New York* and the subsequent *The Prose of the Trans-Siberian and of Little Jehanne of France* Cendrars took his place in the group of poets who were called Cubists: Apollinaire, Max Jacob, Reverdy, Cocteau and even Fargue and Larbaud in certain of their poems. One would fall into a confusion of dates anything but clarified by critical studies if one accepted the contention that Apollinaire was influenced by *Easter in New York* when writing "Zone," the first short poem in the *Alcohols*. But perhaps the investigation would serve no purpose because "Zone" is not Apollinaire's greatest work and above all, because poetry expressed in irregular, more or less Whitman-like lines—a cosmopolitan poetry like a mosaic, and dazzling with its post-Rimbaudian illuminations—was in the air and would in any case have evolved, even without the influence of pictorial Cubism.

Of course, this was not Cendrars' view; he affirmed that Cubist painting was fifty years behind poetry.

Eugenio Montale. *Atlas*. March, 1961, pp. 86–87

After 1920 [Cendrars's] star dimmed considerably, almost undergoing a total eclipse for more than twenty years. Only a few American writers seemed to realize that a great poet of the French language was pursuing an extraordinary life and oeuvre, with incomparable strength and vitality. Did not John Dos Passos call Cendrars the "Homer of the Trans-Siberian"? Thus, the poet found a large audience outside of France before Frenchmen paid him much attention. The novel *Gold* was reportedly Stalin's favorite book. Then suddenly, along with the poetic explosion of the years 1945–50, Cendrars's star rose gradually in the literary firmament again. . . .

His exuberant excesses make it difficult to approach works that have intentionally been made arduous. If one adds to this his errors in language, the falterings in his style, his disorganized sentences that are belched rather than pronounced, and his choice of a popular vocabulary that sometimes borders on indecency or triviality, one can immediately see how far Cendrars is from what might be called perfection.

But there is a more serious reservation to be made. Cendrars's thought, although it is sincere and authentic, still remains narrow and incomplete. . . . His way of discussing fundamental problems of man and life with an often disdainful lack of interest leaves the disagreeable impression of superficiality. Man is a web of contradictions, we would agree, but is it not the task of great writers to resolve those contradicions and find a precise meaning in the human adventure? . . .

If the limitations of Cendrars's work can be clearly seen, his strengths are equally obvious—and what strengths! The poet seizes his reader's emotions so forcefully, and creates so much sympathy through imperceptible bonds, that one is first struck by the brilliance of his writings. It is a genuine pleasure to read Cendrars. His crackling style sets off sparks of genius, whose discovery alone is an ineffable source of poetic joy.

Jean-Claude Lovey. *Situation de Blaise Cendrars*
(Boudry, Switzerland, Éditions de la Baconnière,
1965), pp. 309–11†

Easter in New York, [Cendrars's] first generally known poem, draws on liturgical tradition and has the rather monotonous movement of litany. More interesting is *The Prose of the Trans-Siberian and of Little Jehanne of France* with which Cendrars reached his mature style. This long, uneven poem (the title-word "prose" is taken in the medieval Latin sense of a sequence of rhythmic lines) evokes a railway journey across Russia, which is at the same time a journey into the self. . . . The poet is accompanied by a prostitute ("She is quite naked, has no body— she is too poor") who, by her name, Jehanne [of Arc], suggests France. Actually she seems to represent the poet's stable moorings as she constantly asks, "Blaise, tell me, are we very far from Montmartre?" He consoles her by describing tropical paradises beneath and beyond Siberia: real geography assumes quite anagogical meanings in the poem. . . .

The Eiffel Tower (which also obsessed Cocteau and Apollinaire) serves as an end point to the horizontal journey across Russia, and the reader senses more acutely the metaphorical dimensions of Red Square and crossing Siberia. Paris is the figurative center of the world, and journeys from its nostalgia-filled reality become harrowing quests into a land of fire and spinning motion, of demonic violence. No illumination comes of the quest, however, and the poet finds himself back in the city, brooding on Jehanne, dead apparently like his youth in Russia, and contemplating the sinister image of the Tower, at once a point of stability and a reminiscence of the tortuous journey. The various parts of [this poem] are ingeniously linked in a way which isolated quotations can but meagerly suggest.

John Porter Houston. *SoR*. Spring, 1970, pp. 563–64

CÉSAIRE, AIMÉ (1913–   )

MARTINIQUE

[In 1942] Aimé Césaire gave me a copy of his *Notebook on a Return to My Native Land* which had been published in a limited edition by a Paris magazine in 1939. The poem, which must have gone unnoticed then, is nothing less than the greatest lyrical monument of our time. It brought me the richest certainty, the kind that one can never arrive at on one's own. Its author had gambled on everything I had ever believed was right, and he had incontestably won. What was at stake, with all due credit to Césaire's own genius, was our common conception of life.

Now that a bilingual edition in the United States has given this work wider circulation, people will see in it first its exceptionally rich movement, its exuberant flow, and a faculty of ceaselessly scanning the emotional world from top to bottom, to the point of turning it upside down. All these characteristics distinguish authentic poetry from the false, simulated poetry, of a venomous sort, that constantly proliferates around authentic poetry. "To sing or not to sing": that is the question, and there could be no salvation in poetry for anyone who does not "sing," although the poet must be asked to do *more* than sing. And I do not need to say that for those who do not sing, any recourse to rhyme, fixed meter, and other shoddy baggage could never deceive anyone's ears but those of Midas. Césaire is, before anything else, one who sings. . . .

Césaire's poetry, like all great poetry and all great art, has as its highest merit its power to transform what it uses; he begins with the most unlovely material, among which we have to include ugliness and servitude, and ends up producing the philosopher's stone, which we well know is no longer gold but freedom.

It would be useless to try to reduce Césaire's gift of song, his ability to reject what he does not need, and his power of magical transmutation . . . to a specific number of technical secrets. All one can validly say about these qualities is that all three contain a greater common denominator, which is an exceptional intensity of emotion in the face of the spectacle of life (leading to an impulse to act on life so as to change it) and, as such, this intensity will retain its full force until some new order comes into being.

André Breton. *Hémisphères*. Fall–Winter, 1943–44,
pp. 8–9†

A poem of Césaire . . . bursts and turns on itself as a fuse, as bursting suns which turn and explode in new suns, in a perpetual surpassing. It is not a question of meeting in a calm unity of opposites but rather a forced coupling, into a single sex, of black in its opposition to white. This dense mass of words, hurled into the air like rocks by a volcano is the negritude which arrays itself against Europe and colonization. That which Césaire destroys is not all culture, it is the white culture; that which he conjures forth is not the desire of all, it is the revolutionary aspirations of the oppressed Negro; that which he touches in the depths of his being is not the soul, it is a certain form of humanity concrete and well determined. One can speak here of an automatic writing which is at the same time engaged and even directed; not that there is the intervention of reflection, but because the words and the images continually express the same torrid obsession. At the bottom of his soul, the white surrealist finds release; at the bottom of his soul, Césaire finds the fixed inflexibility of vindication and of resentment. . . .

In Césaire the great surrealist tradition is achieved, takes its definite sense, and destroys itself. Surrealism, European poetic movement, is stolen from the Europeans by a black who turns it against them and assigns it a rigorously prescribed function. . . . In Europe, surrealism, rejected by those who could have transfused it into their blood, languishes and expires. But at the moment it loses contact with the Revolution, here in the West Indies, it is grafted to another branch of the universal Revolution; here it unfolds itself into an enormous and sombre flower. The originality of Césaire is to have cast his direct and powerful concern for the Negro, for the oppressed and for the militant into the world of the most destructive, the freest and the most metaphysical poetry at a time when Éluard and Aragon were failing to give political content to their verse. And finally, that which tears itself from Césaire as a cry of grief, of love and of hate, is the *negritude-object*. Here further, he follows the surrealist tradition which desires that the poem *objectivize*. The words of Césaire do not describe negritude, they do not designate it, they do not copy it from outside as a painter does of a model; they *make* it; they compose it under our eyes. [1948]

Jean-Paul Sartre. *Black Orpheus* (Paris,
Présence Africaine, 1963), pp. 36–39

The voice of Aimé Césaire, the black poet, which reached us right after the Liberation, was like a fresh breath; we heard tones that had never been sounded in French poetry. His first work, *Notebook on a Return to My Native Land,* a book woven of a single poem, seemed to obey no rule other than haste, as if it were appropriate to say everything at once, not omitting anything, as if it were necessary, here and now, to echo the most extreme urgency. This poem rose to the heights of French poetry like a meteor. What! A black voice finally refused to conform to our rhythms, to the rituals of our style, to the form we had imposed on the world—a form based on our landscape, our bearing, and our customs.

It seemed to me that this poem had been too quickly labeled as orthodoxy, surrealist orthodoxy, a literary preciosity of the same order as [André Breton's] *The White-Haired Revolver*. Césaire's poetry was quite a different matter: his revolt had a real basis; it was not related to any sort of ill humor or directed against a denigrated tradition. His revolt had its own sources . . . and its own mission [political freedom]. . . . It was marked by more haste, more determination, and more seriousness than the exercises of surrealism. Although we could become comfortable with surrealism—and we all got used to the *manifestos* of that school—we could not become comfortable with these cries, this long cry that was beginning to form its principles, to establish itself, and finally to bring in its wake things that were clearly going to threaten us.

Hubert Juin. *Aimé Césaire, poète noir* (Paris, Présence Africaine, 1956), pp. 19–20†

In Paris, at the Lycée Louis-le-Grand, Césaire met Léopold Sédar Senghor. This meeting led to a great friendship almost at once and to Césaire's discovery of Africa, the land of his heart, which he adopted immediately: "When I got to know Senghor [wrote Césaire], I called myself an African." . . .

In 1932 a little magazine called *Légitime défense* appeared; in it, communist and surrealist Caribbean students a few years older than Césaire violently denounced the corrupt society of Martinique, the misery of its people, and the ridiculous literary parrotry of its native writers. These were just the words that Césaire needed! For Césaire, Senghor, and Damas, that magazine was a true catalyst. The elders had their problems; they had to keep silent. That was not very important; a breach had been opened, and the three friends would make the roaring river of negritude rush into that breach. . . .

Césaire, Senghor, and Damas began by founding a little newspaper, *L'étudiant noir*, which brought together the black students in Paris on the basis of color rather than country of origin. This new grouping meant a recognition of two obvious and essential facts: that a black man is not a white man, and that all blacks have certain problems in common. This was a healthy reaction against the attitude of those Caribbean students who had rejected their origins, had tried to act like whites and like Frenchmen, even more so in Paris than at home, and had tried to forget their color! This first stage of negritude, this recognition of oneself, was followed, for Césaire and his companions, by an assumption of responsibility for their destiny as Negroes, for their history, and for their own culture. . . .

Instead of the classical French writers, *L'étudiant noir* set forth as models the spontaneity of black American writers, like Claude McKay and Langston Hughes, as well as the style of African sculpture, and the naturalness and humor of local tales, all of which were examples of a freedom of expression accordant with the original Negro temperament. . . .

For the first time, blacks spoke out to tell their fellow blacks "that instead of doing everything like a white man," they should, on the contrary, stay completely black, that their truth lay in their blackness and that it was beautiful. . . . Negritude was an enterprise undertaken to end the alienation of a whole race, and this movement laid the foundation on which the ideology of the decolonization of Africa would be built.

Lilyan Kesteloot. *Aimé Césaire* (Paris,
Pierre Seghers, 1962), pp. 20–23†

The Tragedy of King Christophe was published in 1963, two years after the death of Patrice Lumumba. Therefore, Césaire was aware of the circumstances of Lumumba's death when he wrote that play. But it was not until 1966, five years after Lumumba's murder, that Césaire finally decided, it seems, to deal directly with the African leader who was murdered in such a cowardly way.

Once again Césaire created a play about an African chief offered by destiny as a sacrifice to the Negro cause. *A Season in the Congo*, however, shows a development in Césaire's thesis about the Black Leader. In Christophe the portrait of the Leader was generally but not entirely clear. In Lumumba, who is closer to us, the portrait of the Black hero is made more precise. Césaire is able to repeat himself while renewing himself at the same time. *A Season in the Congo* presents the same theme as *And the Dogs Were Silent* and *The Tragedy of King Christophe*, yet the play is not the same. Even if the theme is the same, its presentation has evolved toward realism and precision. *A Season in the Congo* is also closer to historical truth than *The Tragedy of King Christophe* or *And the Dogs Were Silent*, whose stories are essentially invented.

The scenes of *A Season in the Congo* are short, quick, and, so to speak, choppy. The play is a kaleidoscope in which all of Patrice Lumumba's political life passes by. . . . Except for Lumumba and a very few others, the characters in *A Season in the Congo* are fragmented.

This is as it should be, for, whether he is present or not, all the scenes center and converge on Lumumba.

Hénock Trouillot. *L'itinéraire d'Aimé Césaire*
(Port-au-Prince, Imprimerie des Antilles, 1968),
pp. 156, 158†

In 1942 André Breton, the leader of the French surrealist movement, in flight from the Nazis came to Martinique and there met Aimé Césaire. These two poets developed a strong friendship. It was an important event in Césaire's life. André Breton brought Césaire to the notice of important literary circles in France. By 1944 Aimé Césaire was back in Paris and received with great fanfare. In 1956, *Présence africaine*, a literary magazine founded in 1947 by Alioune Diop, reissued the *Notebook on a Return to My Native Land*. *Présence africaine* served as a forum for some of the most outstanding African and West Indian writers and intellectuals like Alioune Diop, Léopold Senghor, Césaire, Damas and many others who later played an important role in the African Independence movement.

In 1946 Césaire fought and won the election as Deputy to the French National Assembly for Martinique. He also became Mayor of Fort-de-France, a position he has occupied to this day. Martinique is a constituency of the French National Assembly and is represented by three deputies. Most of the deputies have always advocated association with France as the cornerstone of their politics. Césaire's election meant that for the first time a man who identified with the economic and political realities of Martinique was to become a voice in the French National Assembly. For Césaire, the scope for expressing his intense hostility against French domination and assimilation was widened. He was now not only the ideologist of the oppressed but their representative. Indeed he could rightly claim that he understood their needs and their demands because he was one of them. In spite of his educational achievements, he had refused to be assimilated. His position as Deputy demonstrated the extent to which Césaire had embraced his beliefs in active participation. He had realized that only by the exercise of power could what he considered better political and cultural values be implemented. He saw the position he occupied as Deputy as a power base from which he could effect the desired change.

Mazisi Kunene. Introduction to Aimé Césaire, *Return to
My Native Land* (Baltimore, Penguin Books, 1969),
pp. 25–26

The memory of having been torn from the maternal breast, from a culture and spirituality of the soil that were deeply rooted in the Negro soul, is present throughout Aimé Césaire's works. He cannot forget the extent of the looting of Africa, and the poet grieves for this violated Africa as much as he grieves for his native Martinique. . . .

The first European plunderers and exploiters were sure of their superiority over the inhabitants of the countries "liberated" from the darkness of ignorance. [In his *Discourse on Colonialism*] Césaire is persuaded that the "main responsibility in this area lies with Christian pedantry for having set forth dishonest equations: Christianity = civilization; paganism = savagery. These equations could lead only to abominable colonialist and racist consequences, whose victims were to be the Indians, the yellow-skinned peoples, and the Negroes." . . .

Basilio [the Belgian King in *A Season in the Congo*] recognizes that once Belgian domination will have ended in the Congo, the spirit of the Negroes, their own personality, will be reborn. What he calls the "barbarous root" is the vital essence of the Congolese. It is the negation of colonialist omnipotence and is the most dangerous threat to the Church, guardian of the established order. . . .

Africa hungers for itself because it has gone through the traumatic experience of having its own negation forced on it. For Césaire, this experience extends all the way to Martinique, for the experience is not rooted in the obscure mysticism of a place or continent, which has been humiliated, but in the spiritual condition of a whole people. The African and the Martinican share the same fate. The torture they suffer makes time and place relatively unimportant. Only details differentiate the Rebel [in *And the Dogs Were Silent*] and Lumumba [in *A Season in the Congo*], King Christophe [in *The Tragedy of King Christophe*] and Césaire. . . .

The Negro hero, aware of the role assigned to him by Western society, mocks the vain attempts to enslave him by force and to make him deny his brothers.

Frederick Ivor Case. *ECr*. Fall, 1970, pp. 242–44†

Against the backdrop of the magical, enchanting world of Shakespeare's *The Tempest*, Aimé Césaire [in his play *A Tempest*] re-creates his vision of the black man's struggle against white tyranny. Original levels of metaphoric and thematic complexity recede to focus on the stark drama between oppressor and oppressed, between the desire for domination and the will to freedom. The setting is no longer a realm suspended in time and space where art and magic resolve the disorders and inequities of the temporal, political world. No longer can the play be considered in terms of spiritual and moral rebirth, as the movement from sin or crime through ordeal to contrition and forgiveness symbolized by the progression from tempest to the harmony of music. From the conflict between "civilization" and "primitive society," between colonizer and colonized, from the view of Caliban as "natural man"— all aspects of the play traditionally pointed out by critics—Césaire fashions a spectacle of racial conflict whose roots plunge deep into his own experience in colonial Martinique and whose chant echoes his early *Notebook on a Return to My Native Land*.

Césaire compresses the action into three acts and resolves the conflicts of Shakespeare's *Tempest* by the end of the second act: Ariel announces Prospero's forgiveness and the marriage of Ferdinand and Miranda. . . . The tension which has been building between Prospero and Caliban then intensifies freely. From Shakespeare to Césaire, Prospero evolves from the Renaissance symbol of Reason and what is best in man to the white colonizer whose very existence derives from power. Deposed not for his interest in the liberal arts but in a coup over his discovery of valuable new lands, Prospero rules over Caliban and Ariel as the colonial governor over native slaves. Usurping legitimate authority, as his brother did before him, he attempts to "teach" his values to the ignorant and resistant black indigene. But Caliban refuses the white culture as he rejects the white world's image of him as incorrigibly dirty and sexually obsessed. He will not deny his past and as a constant reminder of his disinheritance he will take the name X—as the Black Muslims do—to be "the man whose name has been stolen." Unlike Ariel, the non-violent mulatto integrationist who submits and seeks to stir Prospero's conscience, Caliban has become the black militant revolutionary whose cry, in English, "freedom now," links him to the universal struggle of his oppressed brothers. He prefers death with dignity: "death is better than humiliation and injustice."

Richard Regosin. *FR*. April, 1971, pp. 952–53

It has been noted that there is a fundamental unity among Césaire's heroes and that this unity arises from the author's presence in each of them. His presence is very apparent in the Rebel in *And the Dogs Were Silent*, who expresses Césaire's state of mind. He is doubly present in *The Tragedy of King Christophe*, speaking directly through the character of Metellus and showing his sympathy for one aspect of Christophe —his dream of grandeur for his people. In *A Season in the Congo* Patrice Lumumba's personality is too well known and his story is too recent for Césaire to transform them. The writer's voice, nevertheless, is often heard in the poetic and visionary remarks of his protagonist.

In his theater political questions have a central place, focusing on his greatest concern—the position of the black man in our era. But his theater is also "intentionally poetic." . . . Césaire's theater gives the spoken word, the dialogue, a special importance that stems from the lofty idea the author himself has about the power of language.

Rodney E. Harris. *L'humanisme dans le théâtre d'Aimé Césaire* (Sherbrooke, Quebec, Éditions Naaman, 1973), p. 161†

CHAR, RENÉ (1907–)

The world from which René Char's poetry draws nourishment is rural and Mediterranean. It is an astonishingly *unified* world, and this unity should be seen as one of the strongest guarantees of the authenticity of his poetry. A writer guided by images to this extent is a true poet, a man who would have been a poet even if he had never read Baudelaire, Rimbaud, Lautréamont, and Claudel. The remarkable way in which all of Char's words converge to construct a world, without clashing among themselves, would be sufficient proof that, for Char, metaphor is not a cold intellectual operation, an accessory, an appendage; on the contrary, metaphor is a donnée of Char's own sensitivity: it precedes all expression. Even more so because the results are independent of any intention, of any system. It goes without saying that Char is miles away from anything picturesque, and even farther from Provençal regionalism in language and subject. Yet the super-poem formed by all Char's individual poems is perhaps primarily a great landscape: undesigned, Mediterranean, and true, Greece and Provence combined into one. . . .

Space and light are the principal sources of the pure Mediterranean zest of Char's world. Space is ordinarily a sensation experienced only by the eye. . . . In Char's poetry, however, space perception is often linked not to the eye but to the entire body. The space perception is almost tactile, which explains its strange power. In Char's poetry there is a series of descriptions of space—three-dimensional, almost sculptural, and therefore very Greek once again. These descriptions can be traced to the poet's own physique: a giant, with broad shoulders, with movements as slow as those of the characters in the dreams in *Artine*. . . . Char, unlike all the rest of us, seems to feel space never above him but around him, and he communicates that wondrous sensation to us.

Georges Mounin. *Avez-vous lu Char?* (Paris, Gallimard, 1946), pp. 19, 23–24†

It is time to speak of Char. He has been writing since 1927, and since the Liberation has aroused a fervent interest within France. His novitiate served in the seminaries of Surrealism, and having published jointly with Breton and Éluard, from that dogmatic chaos he emerged gradually (and without apostasy) to affirm his own poetic truth. . . .

He does not regard himself as a source of universal and total salvation. What can one man do for another? At most, with a word or gesture, unveil momentarily a possible path, or as briefly retain, between thumb and forefinger, a wriggling, a slippery, a vanished reality: he cannot give eyes or hands. This "most" Char offers. Yet, and thereby he assumes the trappings of omnipotent deity, the means by which he realises his intentions are hard to discover: for while he inhabits a coherent poetic landscape, the barren or intermittently fertile regions of the *Midi* (the Vaucluse is his birthplace), the pressings of grape and olive have filtered into various receptacles.

Dominant in his recent work is the aspect of prose. . . . A poem, with Char, consists on occasion of a short phrase that, like much considerable poetry, will by many be judged "not poetry at all." He aims at the maximum density, not of imagery alone, but of meaning. A sequence of these self-contained blocks can form nevertheless a larger unit, as discrete rumbles of thunder build a storm. Thunder, maintained Heraclitus, governs all things. Or, when a poem has a greater apparent unity, something other subtends than a logical or narrative sequence, to ensure validity. . . .

It goes with Char as with Heraclitus, whom so greatly he admires: first comes the shock of recognition, cognition lags behind. There is no cult of obscurity, nor technical incompetence—the horseshoe of authentic poetry must of necessity be hammered out of glowing metal. Authentic, essential. If assurance of immediate surface comprehension were the Medean law, only the superficial, discursive, peripheral would have unfailing right of entry.

Kenneth Douglas. YFS. Fall–Winter, 1948, pp. 79–80

I would have less admiration for the originality of this poetry if its inspiration were not, at the same time, so ancient. Char rightly lays claim to the tragic optimism of pre-Socratic Greece. From Empedocles to Nietzsche a secret has been passed from summit to summit, and after a long eclipse, Char once more takes up this hard and rare tradition. The fires of Etna smoulder beneath some of his unendurable phrases, the royal wind of Sils Maria irrigates his poems and makes him echo with the sound of clear and tumultuous waters. What Char calls "wisdom with tear-filled eyes" is revived here, at the very height of our disasters.

His poetry, at once both old and new, combines refinement with simplicity. It carries day and night in the same impulse. In the intense light beneath which Char was born we know the sun sometimes grows dark. At two in the afternoon, when the countryside is replete with warmth, a dark wind blows over it. In the same way, whenever Char's poetry seems obscure, it is because of his furious concentration of images, a thickening of the light that sets it apart from the abstract transparence we usually look for only because it makes no demands on us. But at the same time, just as on the sun-filled plains, this black point solidifies vast beaches of light around itself, light in which faces are stripped bare. At the center of *The Pulverized Poem*, for example, there is a mysterious hearth around which torrents of warm images inexhaustibly whirl.

This is also why Char's poetry is so completely satisfying. At the heart of the obscurity through which we advance, the fixed, round light of Paul Valéry's skies would be of no use. It would bring nostalgia, not relief. In the strange and rigorous poetry René Char offers us, on the other hand, our very night shines forth in clarity and we learn to walk once more. This poet for all times speaks accurately for our own. He is at the heart of the battle, he formulates our misfortunes as well as our renaissance: "If we live in a lightning flash, it is the heart of the eternal." [1953]

Albert Camus. Lyrical and Critical Essays
(New York, Alfred A. Knopf, 1969), pp. 322–23

The impression I get from the poems and fragments of poems of René Char is that they are parts of something larger, from the same block. There is always a disturbing element about them, a sense of awe which comes over from whatever he writes. A Frenchman and an artist, he writes with all the respect of his kind of accuracy of detail. At the same time, were he a painter he would not paint like Picasso but Braque. He has all the attachment to nature, its birds and rivers and in short the whole topography of his native land which he knows and loves passionately. . . .

We are, the public is, on the whole dull witted. René Char is, a man schooled in a long life of multiple experiences, a man of extraordinary patience and courage both moral and physical; he cannot pause in what he has to do because we are too slow to follow him. The artist is inevitably an innovator, not because he wants to be, but because he must. . . .

René Char's poems are difficult for an American reader—not because of the French but because the sense of the words themselves is difficult to recognize in any specific poem. . . . Sometimes he catches no more than the tail of an idea as it were in passing . . . once he gets the theme he follows it in example and example with telling effect until gradually it becomes clear by the sheer persistence of what he has to say. It is a perfectly legitimate device of the artist and increases the pleasure of the reader by piling up the emphasis with variations of detail until the total effect is overwhelming.

William Carlos Williams. *NR*. Sept. 17, 1956, p. 18

The difficult way—the way of pain and the discomfort of having one's consciousness driven forward to a wider inclusiveness—is the only way to read any great poet. . . .

Char is difficult. He is not difficult to read sentence by sentence, for the most part, because he has saved his critical abilities for the composition of his poems, instead of writing bad books about other people. What makes him difficult is the fact that his themes are the great ones; they are the themes that are easy to see but hard to grasp, as God was for Hölderlin. I think one might find the experience of love a good analogy for the experience of reading Char's poems. Friendship is another good analogy. . . . Both experiences are pretty easy to fall into. It is so easy to be flattered by a superficial friend or delighted momentarily by a beautiful girl. However, it is not very easy to endure the sometimes shocking truths which good friends can point out to us, especially when those truths are concerned with our own selves. And it is not very easy to tolerate the pain that the beloved person can give us. Without either of those experiences, however, human life is nothing. The pain they offer is instructive. One cannot really realize that his heart beats unless he learns that the hearts of other human beings beat also. And one cannot really understand Char's poems without, in some sense, becoming a better person.

James Wright. In *René Char's Poetry* (Rome, Editions De Luca, 1956), pp. 116, 123

Once I was talking about *Leaves of Hypnos* to someone who asked: "That was Char's first book, wasn't it?" The error is more revealing than it might appear to be. Certainly, people neither neglected nor misunderstood his previous books, such as *The Hammer with No Master*. . . . [But] the poet's second period can be dated precisely from *Leaves of Hypnos*. His work had developed without any fanfare, slowly forming an edifice that became more impressive with each new volume of poetry, like a tower rising stone by stone in the light of day. When a tower or a poetic achievement reaches a certain height, the public *will* recognize it. The moment that Char's poetry reached this height seems to correspond to the publication of *Leaves of Hypnos*, an essential book whose importance has still not been fully measured. For the book is the drama of action and contemplation, of anguish and facing up to anguish.

World War I also produced one key book—*Calligrams*. But for Apollinaire, the war itself was a subject for poetry, a subject that on the whole he found congenial. Char, on the contrary, during World War II decided to put his faith in man, on man's *value*, while fighting as a maquis, with a full awareness of the immediate dangers as well as the perilous future that faced humanity.

The Resistance, then, gave Char's poetry a new direction. *Leaves of Hypnos* signaled that Char was confronting a stronger reality, was approaching the totality of human reality, at a time when the whole human condition seemed to be questioned and threatened with extinction. . . . It is certain that the new dimension in Char's work, in *Leaves of Hypnos*, arose from the contact between rebellion and reflective thought, between poetry and action.

Pierre Guerre. René Char (Paris, Seghers, 1961),
pp. 14–16†

Though he has the skill of an accomplished craftsman, Char stands outside the institutional and professional areas of the literary life; no one would ever mistake him for a grand man of letters. His poetry itself . . . makes its appearance at the edge of any living situation, on the very fringe of human actions as they occur. Char might say that poetry is the whole manner of being, physical, moral, and imaginative, of a person immersed in a multifarious existence: poems are hieroglyphics or notations expressive of that life. . . .

Char's true line of descent comes directly from Rimbaud, though he never enters that completely *other* spiritual dimension which was the adolescent poet's habitation. His poems do not fashion a whole universe suggesting the "true life" which in our ordinary lives is "absent." Instead, Char's poems are fragments, snatches of the difficult complex of existence at any moment, words in which such bursts of thought, feeling, and instinct receive a transfiguring power; they are—to use a French word appropriate to them—*témoignages*, testimonials to the perseverance and beauty and potentiality of the human estate. Char does not differ much from the Camus who so admired him: each supports the worth of life before the threat of death as absolute, yet each is also endowed with the same religious impulse, which has to seek its outlet within the limitations of the physical world and the meagre span of an individual existence.

Ralph J. Mills, Jr. ChiR. Autumn, 1961, pp. 47, 49

At the age of sixty, with twenty volumes of poetry published, René Char is considered by more and more critics in France as the greatest living French poet. . . .

In brief, it can be said that the chief theme of Char is a complete monography of the Poem, its genesis, form, function, and aims. A passage written by Maurice Blanchot in *The Fire's Share*, and often quoted since it was first published in 1946, sums up the poet's originality and work: "One reason for Char's greatness, the reason that he has no equal at this time, is that his poetry is a revelation of poetry, the poetry of poetry, and as Heidegger comes close to saying of Hölderlin, a poem about the essence of the poem."

The second essential theme in Char's poetry is that of rebirth, a theme which has been somewhat neglected by criticism, but will demand more and more attention since it has gained more importance in the poet's latest works. . . . Both closely related major themes of regeneration and the essence of the poem are essential in forming the meaning of one of the greatest poems by Char: "The Library Is Burning" in *Selected Poems and Prose*. . . .

In the past twenty years, Char's poetry has challenged the foremost critics to write an ever increasing number of penetrating analyses. But, for all the excellent decoding they have done, Charrian studies are only beginning. For instance, no stylistic study has yet been made on the famous aphorism, allegedly inherited from Heraclitus, but which also bears resemblances to those of several French moralists. In numerous homage poems . . . the poet has acknowledged his debt to Heraclitus, Rimbaud, Mallarmé, Nietzsche, among others, and also to his great friends of the postwar period: Albert Camus and Georges Braque. But criticism so far has merely repeated these opinions. It has insisted on Heraclitean as well as on surrealist influence, but hardly touched the Nietzschean. That influence, however, will undoubtedly be found far greater and more durable than the others.

Paulène Aspel. *BA*. Spring, 1968, pp. 199–202

From the moment he chose as the title of verses written between 1927 and 1929 the one word *Arsenal*, Char treated poems as weapons. . . . Although the theme of revolution is fundamental to his prewar poetry, Char did not resort to the verbal aggressiveness typical of the surrealist poems of Aragon. While Char proposed radical revolt, the idea of revolt remained subterranean in his writing. His imagery shows none of the joyous abandon that is the hallmark of Péret's verse. It is without the destructive playfulness of [Hans] Arp's. Indeed, the tone of Char the surrealist is nearer to the gravity of Breton, to whom *The Action of Justice Is Extinguished* is dedicated. This does not signify, though, that Char was without firm conviction when proposing integral revolt. Beyond question, he was deeply opposed to acceptance, which he saw as foreshadowing total inertia. . . . The *word* appears as the key to the prison in which society's unjust laws and his own unprotesting acceptance confine man. At the same time, it is the weapon with which man may arm himself, in his revolution against an unjust destiny. . . .

Despite the bitterness accompanying his expressions of protest, Char's verse during his years as a surrealist was distinctly optimistic in mood. He sought to penetrate the hard surface of misunderstanding, to undermine the firm structure of injustice. But if, in doing so, he had had no purpose beyond destruction or anarchy, his verse would have only limited value for surrealism. . . . Char is a miner searching for a gold-bearing poetic vein he feels certain he will find. He hunts a meaning he is sure will not evade him.

J. H. Matthews. *Surrealist Poetry in France*
(Syracuse, N.Y., Syracuse University Press, 1969),
pp. 117, 122–23

In 1936 René Char came close to dying of a grave illness, and the experience served to sharpen his sensitivity and increase his expressive power (see texts LXIX and LXX of *First Mill*). The poet's state of mind after World War II was quite different. What weighed most heavily on him was not that he had himself risked death during the four crucial years he spent as a maquis: he also had to witness innumerable deaths, and, above all, he had to kill. Char was never able to recover fully from this transgression. . . .

Char's work from 1950 to the present can be summarized . . . as a statement about the belligerence of death. . . . The death that is the subject of these poems is a voracious principle, something other than physical death; this death would take away your breath and thus expropriate your life while still leaving you alive, the result being that you would reach death already dead. . . . The fact that art, although tenuous, is the only resource against death does not mean that art makes it possible to achieve an immortality that would triumph over oblivion for eternity. . . . Instead, art is, at the same time, the poet exposing himself to death while still alive and the poet dying of poetry, only to give life to a poem.

Dominique Fourcade. *L'Herne*. No. 15, 1971, p. 29†

Char has confined his poetry to experience, and has entrusted this experience to the fullness and perfection of form; and he accepts language itself. Whereas surrealism tended toward liberation, toward a dislocation of the linguistic mechanism, Char has condensed the richest experience into the hardest and most explosive language. He has often ended up with maxims like those of Heraclitus, subsuming contradictions in the unity of a single tension. Imagery and metaphor (which have not always avoided preciosity; a meadow, for instance, is "day's watchcase") have been important elements in his poetry. But he uses them to create a passing glow, a flash of light rather than an object intended to be looked at. Like Char's aphorisms, his imagery and metaphors constitute a kind of gesture, a form of energy.

By condensing language, reducing it to the fundamental nuclei of its energy, Char isolates upon a page a number of atoms, so to speak, whose explosion will set off a chain reaction. His poetry sparks off and instigates much more than it actually relates; its unity is not that of a unifying consciousness but of a gesture that initiates. The tension maintaining the elements of language in violent equilibrium is that of a force coursing through life and opening up the future. The world's images glitter and glimmer like flint kindling the tinder of space. But this is a fire lit, rather than contained, by the poem. It gives one the taste and strength for life. The taste for life subsumes both the return toward primal innocence and a virile acceptance of life as it is. All times, like all contradictions, are fused: "Speech, storm, ice, and fire shall end by forming a common frost." Is this a prophecy or the reminiscence of a golden age? Neither. For past and future vanish in poetry's eternal present, in the golden moment of the poet's gaze riveted upon the world.

Gaëtan Picon. Contemporary French Literature
(New York, Frederick Ungar, 1974), pp. 141–42

Both Char and Rimbaud find that all forms of expression and all sources of creativity are valid. Moreover, they endeavor to capture the moment of harmony spontaneously albeit Rimbaud is literally spontaneous while Char concentrates only on the effect of spontaneity. Rimbaud relies on the dictates of his inspiration and intuition, while Char evinces a logical, almost mathematical, intellect at work; his reason is always in control of his feeling. Where Rimbaud is uninhibited, Char is disciplined; this is especially notable in Char's deliberate efforts to delete personal details and references, whereas Rimbaud's personal reactions prevail. Further evidence is found in Char's procedural progression from the particular to the general, while Rimbaud rarely goes beyond the particular. . . .

Rimbaud proposes verbal essence and accord only to find greater dispersion, incompatibility, multiplicity, and disillusionment in his own ability to express his vision. Char demonstrates a lived poetics and discovers reconciliation, harmony, and unity. He overcomes his early fears of illusion and death, but Rimbaud remains tormented by them. Char completes and realizes Rimbaud's vision: he brings the necessary corrective, human expression, to Rimbaud's immature faith in the non-human. It is impossible to predict the kind of poetry that a mature Rimbaud would have composed, but it is possible to suggest that his work would be similar to the poetry of René Char. Char is very much the student who profited from the successes and failures of his predecessor, and in fulfilling the vision he has remained loyal to it.

Virginia A. La Charité. PMLA. Jan., 1974, p. 62

CLAUDEL, PAUL (1868–1955)

The inexhaustible outpouring of metaphors gives Claudel's poetry a naïve, fresh sensuousness, which is perpetually effusive and dazzling and which summons the essences of things in all their reality and immediacy. Claudel, moreover, thinks in images and thinks with his senses. His very thoughts, like all primitive and truly profound thoughts, are sensuous. His thoughts are not an extract of feelings, some kind of subtle but fleeting fragrance obtained by distilling thousands of flowers. His thoughts are weighty and real and still attached to things.

Claudel's work is not a mechanical combination of abstract terms, but rather something analogous to the process of germination: painful, mysterious, slow, and groping. He also reaches a flowering, which, like the blooming of flowers, is completely imbued with colors, all exuding illumination and beauty. Thus, Claudel's language does not proceed through the *application* of images to thoughts; instead, thought itself is developed through words, a chain of primary images arising just as they do in an uncorrupted mind. These images are not only visual; we perceive them through all our senses simultaneously. They rise, grow, envelop us, communicate their vibrations to us, and, while bathing our whole bodies with a sensuous tide, they leave their secret meaning in our souls. One has only to welcome them to understand them, for they enter us from all directions at the same time, uttering the same truth simultaneously in several ways. All of Claudel's words, as well as having an appearance and a sound, have a texture, a smell and a taste. . . .

But to come under the influence of Claudel's sensuousness, to feel his power, one has to have retained one's primitive spontaneity and simplicity, or to be able to recapture them. One must still possess the wonderful childlike gift of understanding through images, of grasping ideas through illustrations, of not separating an idea from its tangible forms.

Jacques Rivière. L'Occident. Oct., 1907, pp. 162–63†

Let us note again the abundance of beauties of a truly lyrical nature in the early works of Claudel and the abundance of beauties of a dramatic nature in his mature works. In *Tête d'Or*, in *The Seventh Day's Rest*, and in *The City*, one often has the impression of a struggle between the characters taking place at a distance. The dramatic conflict makes them grapple with one another, but the lyricism often isolates them. They speak for themselves, not too concerned about the replies they receive; they express their feelings at length, and much more through words than actions. In some scenes, they seem alienated from one another, although they are caught up in the same conflict and set loose in the same circus.

But with *The Exchange* and all the plays that have followed it, one can see the blossoming of the poet's more genuinely dramatic gifts. The dialogue is more tightly knit; the characters look at each other and attack one another face to face. The lyricism, arising from a source just as powerful as in Claudel's earliest works, has become more closely related to the plot: it serves the action better, it heightens the seriousness of the drama more often, and it more naturally draws its power from the dramatic movement.

Georges Duhamel. Paul Claudel (Paris,
Mercure de France, 1913), pp. 106–7†

One of [Claudel's] seven plays is a translation of the *Agamemnon*; and his vocabulary shows signs of royal borrowing from the Bible. Critics speak, also, of the influence of Shakespeare, but the evidences are visible only to the eye of naked intuition, unclothed and uncorrupted by a knowledge of Shakespeare. But, Shakespeare apart, Aeschylus and the Bible are not the general food of modern French literature, which prefers its connexion with the Greek and Hebrew classics more delicately mediated; and Claudel's poetic language has, in comparison with the normal transparence of French style, an almost apocalyptic obscurity. Whether, therefore, he is the greatest of modern French poets or not, he is unquestionably in outward appearance the least French of them all. Not only is his language tumultuous and rhetorical, but his words leap from commonplace to recondite, while his lines are strangely shaped according to a plan which is by no means self-evident. The characters of his plays, moreover, do not speak; they chant; and not only one, like Cassandra, but all.

Yet, in spite of the initial strangeness, even upon those who approach Claudel's works in the order of their composition, the predominant effect is one of deliberate calculation. The lyrical frenzy with which the persons of his earlier dramas deliver themselves resolves into an argument built upon a firm structure of original thought. Even the impressive wealth of his imagery, the opulence of which has conciliated many hostile critics, is revealed as deliberate rather than spontaneous. His metaphors are links in a well-woven dialectic rather than the tumultuous visions of the seer. The novelty of his language is due rather to the logical precision with which he establishes the exact sense of his terms than to an instinctive love of words in themselves arresting. In brief, Claudel's work is not merely philosophic poetry; it is essentially philosophy in poetry.

John Middleton Murry. QR. Jan., 1917, pp. 79–80

Claudel is a conscious and deliberate artist rather than the drunken, uncontrolled genius depicted by current critical opinion; he is also an abstract philosopher, a rigorous dialectician trained to handle ideas, as well as a poet in love with images and the concrete. . . . One has only to open *The East I Know*, the masterpiece of Claudel's Mallarmé style. On every page one observes Claudel questioning the mysterious Orient, eager to learn and to explain, rather than to describe and to charm. . . . Claudel is at the opposite pole from Chateaubriand and Loti. He does not depict the color and shape of the objects; he interrogates them. The question he asks is Mallarmé's: "What does that mean?" And he answers with greater clarity than Mallarmé. As a physiologist, he explains what the brain is for him . . . as a botanist-philosopher, he discovers and reveals the secret of the coconut palm or the pine tree; as a teacher and a Cartesian eager for "clear and distinct notions," he makes us understand the difference between European and Eastern art. . . .

The talents of Claudel's I have pointed out—the penetration and depth of his intellect, the robust strength of his mind, his concern for clarity, and his liking for didactic explanations—have also made him a remarkable lecturer and, when he chooses to be, one of our most eminent critics.

Henri Peyre. NRF. Sept., 1932, pp. 432, 434†

[Claudel's] work is a beginning, a renewal which nothing before him could have made us foresee. Our first astonishment as we read him is to find ourselves present at the birth of a new, free, living, spontaneous French, more so than it has ever been since the sixteenth century. Each word with him seems as if created afresh, exempt from all wear-and-tear, a direct link having been re-established between the meaning and the sound, between the form of the sentence and the hidden movement of emotion and thought. Here poetic language escapes rationalistic withering, purist distillation, oratorical swelling, and does so, one would say, by a simple, effortless springing-forth, by the pure act of creation. And in the same breath the versification is transformed, beyond all the prosodic innovations attempted for a century and all the experiments with free verse, in a more vigorous and at the same time a more natural manner.

No other poet in our time has managed to fashion for himself a poetic instrument at once so new and so suited to the genius of his language, whose sources are, as the poet himself admits, along with the Bible, the prose of Rimbaud, of Maurice de Guérin and of Chateaubriand. The rhymed variations of this verse, with its strong final accent and its heavily emphasised caesura, resembles a greatly extended and more flexible alexandrine, but one which has kept its essential structure. And so Claudel's versification, like his poetic diction, though it keeps at a deliberate distance from traditional forms, never departs—and this is where it dissociates itself from the free-verse poets—from what in this tradition belongs to the very essence of French. [1936]

Wladimir Weidlé. The Dilemma of the Arts (London,
SCM Press, 1948), p. 114

The first version of [*The Tidings Brought to Mary*], written when Claudel was in China, in 1892, and rewritten in 1899 and 1900, was published in 1901 under the title *The Maiden Violaine*. It received its third and final form and present title in 1912. The changes it went through represent an increasing effort by the dramatist to make clearer and surer his dramatic conception, the sum and substance of which is the transition and ascension of life from the human level to the divine. The theme of the drama is the salvation of the soul in the world to come and in this. The characters in it are earthly, but their gestures and words bespeak the omnipresence and omnipotence of the invisible God among them.

The play has symbolic and liturgical connotations. The scene is laid in a medieval setting; the period is the beginning of the fifteenth century, one of the most troubled in the Middle Ages. Violaine, the heroine, symbolizes the Christian virtues of faith, hope, and charity. The charitable kiss she gives the unhappy leper . . . robs her of earthly love, marriage, and happiness. It becomes her cross. . . .

The action develops on two planes, the earthly and the divine. The scene is realistic, and yet dominated by the rising towers of Monsanvierge—symbols of purity, prayer, self-denial—whose bells chime the angelus morning, noon, and evening, as an accompaniment to the drama. . . .

The Tidings Brought to Mary is a *mystère*, a miracle play, which illustrates most poetically the Christian faith in the "Communion of the Saints," the belief in the sacrifice of self in the spirit and imitation of Christ. It is more than a stage play. It is a declaration of faith, a hymn of adoration, an action of grace.

S. A. Rhodes. The Contemporary French Theater
(New York, F. S. Crofts, 1942), pp. 136–37

Paul Claudel appears as the most demanding of contemporary poets. To be understood and followed, he requires from his reader a total spiritual submission and attention. It is not only the ornate and complex part of his work which tyrannizes the reader's intelligence, it is above all the harassing and well-nigh unbearable unity of his books. This unity provides his reader with no rest, no dream, no immobility. Claudel hammers in his truth without breathing between blows. Rightfully considered the most feared poet, he may also seem the most cruel. And yet, upon careful examination of his writings, it is impossible to discover precise examples of his cruelty. They give this general impression because they are unified in their criticism of the century's spirit. Paradoxically, Claudel is *par excellence* the poet of the world, the poet who has named the greatest number of objects in the world, the realist poet in his love for the humblest and most familiar objects; but he is also the most implacably hostile poet to the superficial world of our century. . . .

Paul Claudel closes, recapitulates, and subsumes the modern movement in poetry. It has often been said that Claudel's poetic power equals Victor Hugo's. This kind of remark reveals a basic misunderstanding of the two poets. Hugo's power is exclusively verbal. It bears no trace of the metaphysical struggle which is the glory and the distinction of modern poetry. And this is why Hugo's power is useless and impotent for men and poets today. . . .

After Baudelaire, who first stated the basic problem of modern poets; after Mallarmé, who was [the] master and theorist [of modern poetry] and whose brief work is a mine of secrets; after Rimbaud, who was its adolescent, that is, the one who underwent the experience in so personal and violent a way that we shall never be able to measure its profundity, comes Paul Claudel, whom we make bold to call the "poet." He is a poet in a more vital and more complete sense than these other artists. He is the poet of day who comes after a long line of poets obsessed with night.

Wallace Fowlie. Clowns and Angels (New York,
Sheed and Ward, 1943), pp. 112, 114–15

Although the delectation of Grace triumphs in *The Satin Slipper* on the one hand, and adultery is consummated and a crime is pursued to its conclusion in *Break of Noon* on the other hand, these two great works both teach the same lesson, a lesson that we have never received with such clarity and persuasiveness since the "*etiam peccata*" of Saint Augustine: sins, too, sins perhaps above all, serve the purposes of Grace. . . .

In both dramas the two women, Ysé [in *Break of Noon*] and Prouhèze [in *The Satin Slipper*], remain closely linked to the spiritual destinies of their lovers. This is the other lesson that can be drawn from *Break of Noon* and even more from *The Satin Slipper*. On the level of Grace, any encounter, even a criminal encounter, has a significance; it creates bonds that we cannot break. You [Claudel] teach us that we shall not save ourselves alone, that the thread of our destinies is woven on a loom on which many other threads intertwine with ours to form a final pattern that will not be revealed to us until after death. . . .

Those whom God has chosen cannot separate themselves from Him—this, too, is the meaning of these two dramas, which I prefer to all the others you have enchanted us with.

François Mauriac. Réponse à Paul Claudel (Paris,
Table Ronde, 1947), pp. 43, 45–46†

The roles of man and woman are not exactly symmetrical [in Claudel's works]. On the social level man's primacy is evident. Claudel believes in hierarchies and, among others, in that of the family: it is the husband who is the head. . . . The mere fact of being a male confers an advantage. "Who am I, poor girl, to compare myself with the male of my race?" asks Sygne [in *The Hostage*]. It is man who plows the fields, who builds the cathedrals, who fights with the sword, explores the world, conquers territory—who acts, who undertakes. Through him are accomplished the plans of God upon this earth. Woman appears to be only an auxiliary. She is the one who stays in place, who waits, and who keeps things up. . . .

In marriage the wife gives herself to the husband, who becomes responsible for her: [in *The City*] Lâla lies on the ground before Cœuvre and he sets his foot upon her. The relation of wife to husband, of daughter to father, of sister to brother, is a relation of vassalage. Sygne in Georges' hands takes an oath like a knight's to his sovereign, or a nun's when she makes profession of faith.

Fidelity and loyalty are the greatest human virtues of the female vassal. Mild, humble, resigned as woman, she is proud and indomitable in the name of her race, her lineage; such are the proud Sygne de Coûfontaine and Tête d'Or's princess [in *Tête d'Or*] who carries away the body of her slain father on her shoulders, who bears the misery of a rude and solitary life, the agonies of a crucifixion, and who attends Tête d'Or in his anguish before dying at his side. Conciliating, mediating, thus woman often appears to us. . . .

But if [Claudel's] women are thus remarkably devoted to the heroism of sanctity, it is above all because Claudel still views them in a masculine perspective. . . . In a sense we have here a new principle of subordination. Through the communion of saints each individual is an instrument for all the others; but woman is more particularly an instrument of salvation for man, and not vice versa. [1949]

Simone de Beauvoir. *The Second Sex* (New York,
Alfred A. Knopf, 1952), pp. 227–30

I was excited the other night upon leaving the Théâtre de l'Atelier after a performance of *The Hard Bread*. This was not just excitement one may feel after hearing a great work admirably performed but also the excitement of receiving the shock of a revelation—a double revelation.

The first revelation is that Claudel is decidedly not only a poet of genius but a very great dramatist, something I had not been completely convinced of even after the dazzling production of *Break of Noon*. The second revelation is distressing, and I state it with great concern about even uttering it: the crushing impression of reality that comes from the play—an impression that perhaps no other theatrical work by Claudel imparts to the same degree—can be explained by the fact that in this play the viewer feels he is directly in the presence of a personality that has been violently stripped bare; can one even wonder whether this personality is not that of the author? A single word can characterize that personality—and the word is ferocity.

The Hard Bread offers us the terrifying sight of a Claudel who has shed before our eyes all his religious and mystical superstructures. We see what his inner world and life probably would have been without the miraculous event he celebrated in "Magnificat." Now that I think about it, even in *The Tidings Brought to Mary*, I had been struck by the force with which a segment of humanity was presented, a segment, which seems to come out of the earth and which seems destined to return completely to the earth. I have always thought that the character of Mara merited a great deal of speculation and analysis. Still, Mara is only a dark spot in a mystery of light. If there is a mystery in *The Hard Bread*, it is a mystery of darkness. One would hardly be exaggerating in saying that it is the drama of the liquidation of Christianity, of France as a Christian country, and perhaps of France itself.

Gabriel Marcel. *NL*. March 24, 1949, p. 8†

There is no real separation in outlook, interest, even expression, between [Claudel's] poetic prose, his poems, and his drama. The drama is wider, vaster, more varied; but we find the lyric quality there too, pouring itself out in passages that range from almost disruptive humour to exquisite beauty. However the poems in lyric form do give us more immediate access to the poet himself, and suggest a personal development, even and perhaps exactly because the personal revelation is restrained. We gain by reading them in chronological order, by following the poet in his experiences and his moods, his ideas, his recurring themes, his adaptation of form to subject. . . .

Five Great Odes may be described in a line borrowed from one of them as *la déflagration de l'ode soudaine*, the sudden flash and explosion of the Ode. The Odes are pure and authentic Claudel, tumultuous poetry, originality in form and subject bursting fixed bounds, the outflow of a tremendous personality developed through experience and the storm and stress of suffering. They are the full contemporary exemplification of the theory of [his] *Poetic Art*, and by spirits attuned they were felt to be a revelation. . . .

Written from 1900 to 1908, published in 1910, they cover the period of various posts in China and journeys in the East. They were written before and after the experience of passionate love underlying *Break of Noon* and often alluded to in these and other of Claudel's poems; and they revolve in part round his marriage, which took place in 1906, and his family life.

The form is absolutely free. "O my son," said Cœuvre in [Claudel's] *The City*, "when I was a poet amongst men I invented verse that has neither rhyme nor metre." In the Odes we have neither. Long verses sometimes of a breathless quality are interspersed with others quite short and most striking. The vigorous, varying, impulsive rhythm, the movement expressive of intense feeling, crowding memories, lofty thought, produce what are really musical phrases.

Mary Ryan. *Introduction to Paul Claudel* (Cork, Cork University Press, 1951), pp. 35, 37

The central scene in *The Humiliated Father*, Scene II, Act III, where Pensée and Orian aim at a Corneillian grandeur, is merely unconvincing rhetoric. Deprived of that atmosphere of ineluctability which Claudel sought to infuse into the play, what seems like the sheer obstinacy of the heroes to act as symbols of historical movements or as instruments appointed by Providence for a definite task, destroys their individuality and makes their language sound as hollow as if it came from a mask. . . .

When the *dramatis personae*, besides belonging to the Christian world, belong not to the fabulous or legendary world but to history, the only forces which may drive them on are those of the human heart. That implies a power to scrutinize the psyche which Racine possessed to a supreme degree, and which in our time T. S. Eliot possesses to no mean degree, but which Claudel certainly does not possess; for whatever qualities he has, he is not a psychologist.

This trilogy, or this *Orestia*, as some critics like to call it, is not to my mind a great achievement; the poetry is poor, and in the case of *The*

Humiliated Father the dramatic element is so weak as to make the play not stage-worthy. While *The Hostage* is perhaps more dramatic . . . the poetry is poorer than in *The Hard Bread*, which is perhaps the best poetic drama of the trilogy.

Joseph Chiari. *The Poetic Drama of Paul Claudel*
(New York, Kenedy, 1954), pp. 126–28

The world of Claudel's dramas is the least conventional, the least reasonable, the least "theological" there is. This ambassador never staged monarchs or great personages who were not imperceptibly derisory: the King of Spain and his court in *The Satin Slipper*, interrupted at each instant in their maneuvers by the movements of the floating landing they had elected domicile upon; Pope Pius [in *The Hostage*], who goes to sleep in front of Coûfontaine (and it is this old man's somnolence which has the onus of representing on earth and the stage of the Théâtre-Français the Church's resistance to violence); the amputated Rodrigue [the hero of *The Satin Slipper*] who lets himself be taken in by the talk of a provocative actress sent by the King of Spain, and brings upon himself the ridicule of claiming unwonted powers before the court (and in what a tone of voice!), only to be given finally to two soldiers who do not even succeed in selling him.

The only characters Claudel takes completely seriously are those who are nothing but a simple passion, a sorrow, or an earthly possession. Mara [Violaine's evil sister in *The Tidings Brought to Mary*] is right in being jealous because she is ugly and awkward. Sygne [the heroine of *The Hostage*] is right in refusing at the last moment to make the sacrifice she nevertheless made, because "everything is exhausted" and no one can ask a human being to go any further. Turelure [in *The Hostage* and *The Hard Bread*] in his way was not wrong in pushing the monks of the abbey into paradise that summer of the Year I when the greengages were so good. . . .

What makes [Claudel] move so many men who are nevertheless alien to his beliefs is that he is one of the rare French writers who have made the din and prodigality of the world tangible. The new logic [his] *Poetic Art* spoke of has nothing to do with that of classical theodicies. Claudel does not take it upon himself to prove that this world is the best of all possible worlds, nor to deduce Creation. Taking it as it is, with its wounds, its bruises, and its staggering gait, he simply affirms that from time to time we find encounters in it that we had not hoped for, that the worst is not always certain. It is by this modesty, frankness, and humor that he acts beyond Catholicism. [March, 1955]

Maurice Merleau-Ponty. *Signs* (Evanston, Ill.,
Northwestern University Press, 1964), pp. 316–17

The poetic word, in Claudel's writings, does not covet any superhuman privilege. It does not claim to have any sacred property, which would place it in competition with religion. Its only goal is to give names to an *already* existent reality, which is the work of God. To believe that this reality . . . can be entirely the work of the poet would be blasphemy. Thus, before the poet has spoken, the things that he will name are already holy and sacred. The poet is content to recognize them in his turn and to add his modest praise to the symphony of created things. While Valéry worshiped "holy language," Claudel, fiercely hostile toward any philosophical idealism, intended to pay homage to "holy reality." . . .

Claudel's *Poetic Art* is concerned not so much with the creation of a work or the function of language as with the very structure of the world that is offered for our contemplation. Since the world exists, the Poem is a success from the outset. Indeed, this Poem never ceases to develop, and the poet's human song is perhaps capable of rediscovering ancient stanzas or anticipating those that will be created. The purpose of the human poet is to reassert a *simultaneity* that too many men are no longer able to perceive. But the poet does not create this simultanity; he observes it and deciphers it. From this understanding, there arises a feeling of *relaxation*, which is especially prominent in Claudel's work from *Five Great Odes* on, and which shows the poet's confidence and assurance in contemplating the work of God.

In Claudel's works, there may occasionally be casual remarks, jokes, simplicities, and here and there a few smudges (of a sumptuous color), which prove that the craftsman has not been infected by the sin of *angelism*. These elements do not in any way compromise a success that has been completely achieved through the real object which the poem is dedicated to and which inspired it.

Jean Starobinski. *NRF*. Sept., 1955, pp. 529–30†

Paul Claudel was the last peasant: he drew his great strength from the earth. His earth was mystical. Claudel was a giant, a God of this earth. What can be called his comic side and his humor are the expression of the enormous spirit of mockery of the peasant. Through this mockery the characters seem more insignificant than ridiculous. Even when Claudel seems to shower his heroes with the most violent sarcasm, seems to hold them in the deepest contempt, there enters into this sarcasm and this contempt a kind of serenity, the feeling of an all-powerfulness on the author's part and of such an insignificance on the part of the characters he abuses that this very insignificance saves the characters from the worst. They are not (or not even) hateful; they become picturesque. In the end, evil does not seem to be dangerous, because it is clear that it

only exists through God's will. Claudel may perhaps be the least charitable Christian poet, because the comic characters he puts on the stage
are too insignificant for anyone to take pity on.

In Claudel's works evil becomes almost funny; it is allowable—that
is, Claudel is more than willing to present it—in order to emphasize the
greatness, the sublimity, of the heroes: without evil, good would not
have any meaning. The Devil is comic. Only saintliness is tragic. The
ludicrous characters in Claudel's works are the figures of the Devil, and
that is why they are farcical. Evil is a farce; through evil God seems to
tease men and their souls; as cruel as it may be, a farce is only a farce.
The evil figures do not have souls; they are made up of appearances and
illusions. Evil essentially *does not exist*. One does not have any attachment, any pity, any real hatred either, for something that does not exist.
Claudel's serenity derives from his certainty that evil in itself is impotent, and that evil is useful as a temporary, uncritical test, willed by
God—and by Paul Claudel, who feels he is God's spokesman.

Eugène Ionesco. In *Cahiers Paul Claudel* (Paris,
Gallimard, 1960), Vol. II, pp. 26–27†

[During Claudel's adolescence his sister] Camille had waved a copy of
[Ernest] Renan's *The Life of Jesus* in front of her family and cried
out, "As far as religion is concerned, everything we have been taught is
nonsense; here is the proof." The tyrannical authority she enjoyed was
such that her outburst made a deep impression. The few beliefs which
may have remained deep within Paul's soul were destroyed by the teach-
ings he received at Louis-le-Grand. In a Paris lycée at that time it was
impossible for a student to acknowledge even the slightest degree of
faith. Everything was uniformly and completely black. . . .

[Years later Claudel] could not forgive Renan for never mentioning Jesus' clear and repeated assertion that He was the Son of God.
Claudel sees in this deliberate oversight a major imposture, a monumental deception compounding the responsibility of a master who drew
thousands of human beings into darkness, and very nearly made him
sink into the night. . . .

Driven to desperation by the entirely materialistic ideas dispensed
at that time in schools and universities and by the depressing moral
atmosphere of the period, he finally came to the point of considering
suicide. One day he actually put a gun to his head. But his vital instinct
prevailed. Divine Grace, in which the young man no longer believed,
kept watch over his exceptional destiny.

Louis Chaigne. *Paul Claudel: The Man and the
Mystic* (New York, Appleton-Century-Crofts, 1961),
pp. 38, 41–43

In 1886, Paul Claudel was seventeen years old. In that crowded and fateful year he discovered and was transfixed by the poetry of Rimbaud; he began writing his first play, a short pastoral farce on the theme of the Sleeping Beauty; he experienced a religious "illumination" on Christmas day, during a visit to Notre-Dame, which led to his formal return to Catholicism four years later and eventually to an obsessive need to enter monastic life; finally, the artist in him had a sudden intuition of what his work must strive to express.

During the next twenty years, until his marriage in 1906 (which brings to a close the period of his early works) Claudel was torn by a dramatic conflict between his artistic and his religious vocations. This conflict fed on the contradictions of his character, on the clash in him of neopagan and mystical tendencies. It reached a critical turning point in the year 1900 with his unsuccessful attempt to renounce his art in favor of the priesthood.

All the plays and poetry composed during this period (from *The Sleeping Girl* in 1886 to *Break of Noon* in 1905) acquire their fullest meaning when studied chronologically in the light of the conflict of vocations. These works are the fruit of this conflict. As Claudel struggled to turn his back on his poetic gift, he evolved, in spite of himself, a poetic program which served as counterweight to what might be called his yearning for sainthood. In this poetic program—a compromise born of the instinct of self-preservation—the poet-diplomat cast himself in the role of poet-priest to resolve the conflict of vocations; in effect, he appointed himself . . . "Ambassador of God."

Richard Berchan. *The Inner Stage: The Conflict of Vocations in the Early Works of Paul Claudel* (East Lansing, Michigan State University Press, 1966), pp. 1–2

Written in Japan between 1919 and 1924, [*The Satin Slipper*] first went onto the stage in 1943, at the Comédie Française under the direction of Jean-Louis Barrault, with music by Arthur Honegger. Written to be presented in two nights, it was cut down to a five-hour production in thirty-five scenes. Many Frenchmen were irritated with Claudel because of his Pétain poem, "Words for the Marshal," but on the opening night of *The Satin Slipper*, the élite of Parisian society came to the theater as well as many prominent officers of the occupying force. Paul Valéry sat in the front row, with Claudel directly behind him. At the beginning of the play, Honegger's overture was scheduled to be interrupted by the theater's loudspeaker, which in those days was also used to give directions in case of an air raid. On that opening night, just at the point where the loudspeaker was supposed to cut in on the overture, sirens sounded outside and actual warning instructions came through the sound system. The audience started to leave. The seventy-six-year-old Claudel, who had not heard the sirens, thought there was a misunderstanding and stood up to say, "Sit down, sit down, this is part of the play—don't worry."

Valéry finally made Claudel understand that it was a genuine air raid. Nevertheless, after a time the audience came back and the drama about Renaissance Spain went brilliantly. Indeed, it was so successful that, as the weeks passed and the play continued to draw crowds, the German censors grew uneasy (the last sentence of the play is, "Freedom for the captive souls"), and after the fiftieth performance they suggested to the management that it might be wise to play *The Satin Slipper* less frequently. After the sixtieth performance the Comédie Française dropped it from the repertoire. Barrault revived it in Belgium immediately after the liberation, at the Théâtre de la Monnaie in Brussels, where this work by the former ambassador from France was hailed "madly" after its final curtain, with the audience singing the French and Belgian national anthems and breaking seats and windows.

Harry T. Moore. *Twentieth-Century French
Literature to World War II* (Carbondale, Southern
Illinois University Press, 1966), pp. 200–201

We must remember that *The Satin Slipper* is much concerned with *creation*, in both senses of the word: with the divine or poetic act and with the created world, the work of the six days. . . . We must remember what the term *to create* means, in Claudel's definition . . . "to make something from nothing." And we must remember that for Claudel the created world was a *work of art* . . .

The puzzle begins to clear. The King [in *The Satin Slipper*] is an artist. He has created a *work* in exactly the sense defined above, and created it from nothing. His curious comedy echoes the improbable, playful artistry of the labours of God. More than that. Since the King is not only playful but cruel, he is a *parody* picture of God and of the artist. He is the artist as the eyes of science and administration see him. He is the divine Artist as He appears to the mind of rational man.

This view of the King is reinforced by the repeated suggestion that to turn one's back on His Very Catholic Majesty is to turn away from God. This is the double treason of Don Camille, and the arrogance of Rodrigue. . . .

The King and his scenario, then, are an image of God and His inscrutable purposes. They are thus an expression in brief and in caricature of what *The Satin Slipper* is at length and with less distortion: a picture of God at work. The play is experimental philosophy. . . . Its

enchanted me, you were formulating for poetry (concealed beneath the music) the great laws of self-purification and self-denudement that rule over any spirituality, the law of the work to be done as well as that of the eternal life to be attained, and whose supreme analogous pattern (though transcendent and supernatural) is to be found in ascetic progress and contemplation. You wanted of poetry only poetry in the pure state, the pure demon of agile grace, the pure agility of the spirit. And you were faithful to your vow; you left what you had, you risked everything at every moment, constantly unbinding yourself from yourself, reducing the matter and weight of body to such a point that people reproached you with having no more substance.

Not for a joke did the Greco-Roman charms of the rather plump Muse give place for you to the hardness of a Spirit come from the Orient of the sky. At that level you found yourself lifted, as if by trickery, to a struggle waged far above that of art and poetry, there where without the helmet and armor of Christ one is lost before beginning, you grappled with forces immune from matter, death closed in on you from all sides, it silently immobilized the reckless ones who loved you. There was no need to be a great wizard to have guessed the existence of that struggle against death that now you admit, now that death has lost. I was aware of the tragic in your practices and in your life; trapeze-swinging, acrobatic stunts, false bombs, false scandals—back of the circus gleamed the fangs of real beasts; you juggled so high and so squarely with your knives that an accident was not avoidable: one would see you with your heart opened by despair, or by the grace of God. [1926]

Jacques Maritain. *Art and Faith* (New York,
Philosophical Library, 1948), pp. 76–77

This morning, when I got back from Orléans, I found your [Cocteau's] book, and I read it, reread it, with amazement. What other era had a description, a determinant, a fixative, an engraving, a geographical map, a defender equal to *A Call to Order*? I wonder which exists more vividly —the era or your portrait of it? Great men are the only ones who can understand their own era: you were able to understand your era while you were creating it. You know just what I mean by that. I say "your era" because (God knows) I am not talking about [Victor Hugo's] Preface to *Cromwell* but rather, I daresay, about the color of the Eiffel Tower's dress after the fog. . . . What I have not yet said is how wonderful your definitions are. But you know that and today everyone knows it or will know it very soon. One is a better person after reading this book! I am very happy to say that, because it is unbelievable. This book is a moral book! I also love the passages in which you talk about me in that appropriate tone and spirit of justice which are all your own:

you always clarify things, and in such a way that nobody can pretend to be embarrassed by your praise. . . .

A Call to Order enabled me to measure your importance in the era and to measure everything that you have done so unpretentiously in the theater, music, and the other arts, your astonishing individuality in poetry (its extraordinary and perfectly original charms) and in the prose that only you can write. I would like someone to show me another book that has an idea in every line and an idea that is new, clear, devoid of pedantry. I would really like someone to show me another book so rich and new and so important. Have no fear: nobody will be able to write the history of the war years and the postwar years without mentioning your name. It would be impossible to omit it, and equally impossible, of course, in a history of poetry or prose. But I am saying things which you know better than I do and which you have heard and read a thousand times. [March, 1926]

Max Jacob. *Choix de lettres de Max Jacob à Jean Cocteau* (Paris, Paul Morihien, 1949), pp. 37–38, 41–42†

Always it is as the poet we must think of Cocteau—the person who says, "a thing can rarely at the same time be and seem true," who says he is "incapable of writing a play for or against anything"; and warns one that "it is not the poet's role to produce cumbersome proofs." M. Cocteau is haughty and dictatorial; he does not spread his cloak on the mud, he does not make promises, and his temperament permeates all his concepts; but he is fervent. His ardor of imagination, voracity of presentiment, inexhaustible fund of metaphor, and crisp fastidiousness comprise an apperceptiveness rivaled only by that of the animals. . . .

[In *The Infernal Machine*] Oedipus, successfully vivid, pants and arrests the eye, Jocasta half infatuates, the Sphinx—symbolizing the machinery of the gods' injustice—inspires fear, though her literal femininity and emphasized claws point to a crochet on M. Cocteau's part. He appears to have an unfeminist yet not wholly detached attitude to woman; Jocasta being, like the Sphinx, "of the sex disturbing to heroes." Burdensome yet seductive, she asks, "Am I so old then?" and adds, "Women say things to be contradicted. They always hope it isn't true." But also as part of the author's mental tendency, she is "poetic" and has the aspect of sculpture—dead, white, beautiful, with closed eyes.

At the end of the play, instead of a somber dimming of personality, as in the Greek play, there is an allusion to "glory," as completing the destiny of Oedipus, and horror is relieved. Ought it to be?

Marianne Moore. *Nation*. Feb. 6, 1937, pp. 158–59

Leaving Maurice Rostand, his childhood friend, to struggle with his smoky glories, an Aladdin's lamp in his hand, [Cocteau] set out for Montmartre where the poor Bohemians received him coolly. There was no love for either the rich or the elegant here. The artists were austere as men preparing revolutions generally are. Neither Apollinaire nor Max Jacob nor Picasso were pleased at the arrival of this young salon poet, but the interests that at first seemed opposed were actually not so. Cocteau wanted a new world to discover, the men in Montmartre wanted a clever advertising man. There was no need to be explicit. A surface friendship that actually concealed profound rivalries and terrible contempt served as a medium of exchange in all transactions. They offered Cocteau the key to a new vocabulary, a rediscovered imagery; he was introduced into the secrets of these tough, miserable men, greater and truer poets than he, and permitted to use the common coin, provided he vulgarized the knowledge of it and circulated among the public to whom he could speak so well this still unknown treasure which someone had to mint if the community was to survive.

I was not in Montmartre in those days, but what I am saying here I learned from the concentrated hatred of the writers and painters whom Cocteau has always called his friends, whose praises he has written a thousand times though he knows better than I how much they hate him as a man who had invented nothing, who has profited by everything, and who has appropriated by sleight of hand the poetic props of a theater he did not create.

An extraordinary potpourri of petals torn from the most diverse flowers, all of which have dried in his hands, Cocteau's work has neither a definite odor nor flavor. It is pale, almost uniform through its successive false transformations; it gives off only a melancholy perfume, like those roses we no longer can remember as beautiful, for they are nothing but a few ashes at the bottom of a bowl.

But it took me many years to be convinced of this truth which brighter men had realized long since; I became aware of it only when Cocteau's work, having ceased to interest remarkable minds, slipped down that natural slope that was to lead him, with halts for misunderstandings, toward the great bourgeois public which is his true public. The success of *The Parents Terribles* restored to the ageing writer the enthusiasm of the admirers of eighteen-year-old glory . . . his straight course as a prewar boulevard writer thus effacing by a bourgeois success the intermediary revolutions which, moreover, were not revolutions at all but merely the skillful, vulgarizing journalism of other men's revolutions. [1939]

Maurice Sachs. *Witches' Sabbath* (New York, Stein and Day, 1964), pp. 83–85

Jean Cocteau does not accommodate himself to established rules. He lacks that courage and humility which lead true artists to find satisfaction in conforming to the strict commandments of tradition. A poet like Paul Valéry knows the enrichment born of constraint. He cannot help being intrigued by the obstinacy with which poets of every age have sought to weigh themselves down with voluntary chains, but he submits to common practice. . . . Cocteau, however, invents, or believes he invents, the requirements to which he will subject his prosody, because verse is nothing but the "same old costume that each of us shapes to his own body." Agreed. The artist can set up rules of his own choosing. But it is still not permissible for him to cheat. The laws advocated by Cocteau are so subtle that any serious application of them is impossible. For Cocteau, these laws are not enriching shackles but excuses for facile games. . . .

Most of his poems present sequences of brilliant enigmas. More subtle than profound, his thoughts amuse us. They never move us. Everything is too carefully planned to be alive. Life, in all its complexity, is simpler, and Jean Cocteau's complexity is *too* simple. These high-wire exercises are no keys to the secrets of the world. The cry they elicit from us does not come from the deepest part of ourselves. It is a cry of superficial and delighted astonishment. It is the "Oh! The beautiful blue!" of a crowd entertained by a display of fireworks. . . .

Plain-Song shows us the heights Cocteau can ascend when he can be simple. But he scorns *Plain-Song*; he senses that his revitalization of sixteenth-century verse in this book brought nothing essentially new to poetry. And he is not wrong about that. It is not enough for him to be the second greatest man in Rome! He would rather reign in solitude: a poor kingdom of the artificial; the realm of the inane and the conventional. [1940]

Claude Mauriac. *Jean Cocteau; ou, La vérité du mensonge* (Paris, Odette Lieutier, 1945), pp. 62–63, 65–66, 76–77†

"In leaving reality behind," Gide had announced in 1904, "the theater is today weighing anchor." Jean Cocteau was the outstanding playwright of the new spirit, at least after his dramatic talent first fully revealed itself in *Orpheus*, a retelling of the Orpheus story in fantastic, whimsical, hilarious, grotesque, and somehow moving terms. His theory of the drama solves many problems that had proved too much for the fancy-dress tragedians and the poetic dramatists. First, he clarifies . . . the nature of theatrical as opposed to lyric poetry. His watchword is not poetry *in* the theater but the proper poetry *of* the theater. Second, he calls for a "cooling off" of the drama, which had indeed reached tropical temperatures in the nineteenth century—not excluding the New Theater movement of the eighties and nineties. This cooling is most triumphantly manifested in *The Infernal Machine*, where Cocteau minimizes suspense by having a chorus tell the whole story beforehand. He amply makes up for sweaty excitement and cheap thrills by richness of texture. Thirdly, Cocteau follows Apollinaire (instead of the symbolists and neo-romanticists) in requiring gaiety, fancy, and extravagance in the theater.

The crowning dramatic achievement of Cocteau (if we except the movie *The Blood of a Poet*) is his version of the Oedipus story *The Infernal Machine*. The deliberate, quasi-naïve, adroit series of pictures "flooded in the livid mythical light of quicksilver" is one of the legitimate triumphs of the anti-realistic theater. It does not, however, dispel all doubts about Cocteau's view of drama or about the future of his dramatic practice.

Eric Bentley. *The Playwright as Thinker* (New York, Reynal & Hitchcock, 1946), pp. 229–30

Most artists devote themselves to one medium; whether their complete *œuvre* is a single masterpiece, as in the case of Proust, or a succession of works, as in the case of Dickens, it is comparatively easy to grasp as a whole. There, in a uniform edition, is a row of books, The Collected Works. There is nothing left out. Both the general reader and the critic have a manageable task.

Now and then, however, an artist appears—Jean Cocteau is, in our time, the most striking example—who works in a number of media and whose productions in any one of them are so varied that it is very difficult to perceive any unity of pattern or development. To enclose the collected works of Cocteau one would need not a bookshelf, but a warehouse, and how then could one catalogue such a bewildering assortment of poems, plays in verse, plays in prose, mythologies, natural histories, travels, drawings, tins of film, phonograph records, etc.?

Both the public and the critics feel aggrieved. If they know about the drawing they resent the existence of the drama on which they are not experts, and vice versa, and are tempted to say "a dilettante" and pass on to someone from whom they know better what to expect. His fellow artists who know how difficult it is to succeed in one medium are equally suspicious and jealous of a man who works in several. I must confess that I found myself opening Cocteau's last volume of poems half hoping that they would be bad. They were not.

In addition to all this, Cocteau labors under the disadvantage of having become a public legend at a very early age and of having remained so ever since. One is usually right to distrust an artist who is notorious, for notorious people nearly always begin soon to act their own role and become fakes. In Cocteau's case, however, I believe one is wrong; he is the exception, thanks to his extraordinary lack of artistic vanity and self-regard. He has always been a poet in the Greek sense: a maker who forgets himself in a complete absorption with the task at hand.

W. H. Auden. *Flair*. Feb., 1950, p. 101

Poems, essays, novels, plays—all Cocteau's work has cracks, and through the cracks an anguish can be perceived. An extremely complex and suffering heart wants both to remain hidden and to open up. Does a profound understanding therefore make these works infinitely sad? They tremble. We know that our images convey information badly, but when expressions like "heavy sorrow," "deep despair," and "wounded heart" are uttered, what remains to be said? As soon as we perceive a man's suffering face—strictly controlling his pain and succeeding in harmoniously transforming it—how can we speak with precision without an offensive pedantry? Jean Cocteau? He is a very great poet, linked to other poets by the mark on his forehead that separates poets from other men, linked to all men by his heart. I must continue to insist on that link, because it seems that a deplorable misunderstanding has arisen regarding Cocteau. His graceful style was to become the prey of the vilest thing in the world—the elite.

The elite wanted to seize hold of this elegant form and take possession of it while overlooking the sensitive and bitter kernel it contains. It is time to reject this compromise violently and to assert our rights to a poet who is not light but serious. We refuse to give Cocteau the stupid title of enchanter; to us he is "enchanted." He does not charm; he is "charmed." He is not a wizard; he is "bewitched." These words are insufficient to counter the base frivolity of a certain crowd; I believe, however, that they give a good idea of the poet's true drama. . . .

Cocteau never gives us immodest lessons in morality—if he had to lecture to us, perhaps it would be with a malicious smile, the contrary of morality—but his writing is constructed with so much respect for the verbal matter it contains that his ethic, which is spiritual presence, is there at all times. What I invite you to discover in his style is therefore the severity, rarely relenting, of a way of life. Lightness, grace, and elegance are qualities that preclude laziness and flabbiness, but what other merit would they have if they were not applied to the hardest of materials? But while a dedicated artisan may choose to work with marble, the poet, through his choice of method and words, creates marble.

Jean Genet. *Empreintes*. May–July, 1950, pp. 24–25†

Bacchus is written in Cocteau's latest style, a concise realism that was well adapted to *The Parents Terribles* but has less relevance here. It is a hodge-podge of all Cocteau's theories, an anthology of remarks by Radiguet, Picasso and Genet. Too often, it is Cocteau imitating himself. . . . Cocteau may very well tell us that he is dramatizing a Byzantine legend which is five thousand years old, but he has not brought the myth into modern perspective as he did in *Orpheus*. Hans is less of a hanged or drowned god than he is a young man who is not quite sure which way to turn. . . .

Whatever its ultimate psychic origin, it seems clear that Cocteau envisages his own situation (and it is himself he is symbolizing in the youthful heroes and heroines of his plays) as one of passive suffering. The defeat and failure of his heroes do not have the cosmic overtones of the fall of Sophocles' Oedipus or Shakespeare's Macbeth. They are rather like children who choose to be disobedient in order that they may be punished, inflicting thereby a certain remorse on their parents. These characters desire and seek out punishment as a means of allaying their guilt at being different. This represents a transcendence, an involvement with others. They engage the world as victims to be punished, thereby transferring a part of their own guilt to those who punish them. To borrow an image from Cocteau's *Bacchus*, these characters force the rest of us to come and dance around the bonfire on which they are being sacrificed. The element of exaggeration here is obvious. Cocteau has not been burned at the stake; in fact, he has recently become a member of the Académie Française. But he kills off his characters just the same. They are expiatory victims in a universe to which, deep down, Cocteau has never become reconciled.

Cocteau never dramatizes the suppressed theme of homosexuality. Instead, he extends the metaphor of persecution to cosmic dimensions. In *The Infernal Machine* the gods themselves become the persecutors. Cocteau invariably refuses to find the truth of his characters' tragedy within themselves, where it belongs. Instead, he blames it on obscure forces beyond men, on their destiny. Through *Bacchus* we are brought to another mystery: What is the nature of this destiny which drives such lighthearted heroes to their doom?

Neal Oxenhandler. *Scandal and Parade: The Theater of Jean Cocteau* (New Brunswick, N.J., Rutgers University Press, 1957), pp. 115, 122, 124–25

[One evening years ago] I bought a secondhand copy of the issue of *Œuvres libres* containing *The Wedding on the Eiffel Tower*. I knew who Cocteau was only through the newspapers. . . . Idly and inattentive, I opened the issue, passed over the novels (a potential man of the theater, I already scorned that idle chatter) and reached the play whose strange title attracted me. . . .

At the first lines I read, something melted within me—a block of ice, transparent and impossible to traverse, that stood in my way. Everything fell into place, and at the same time—it was six o'clock—my neighbor the great bell, which no longer wakened me even in the early morning, began to ring to the evening Angelus.

Accompanied by its gruff, familiar droning (I did not hear it that night, but I hear it now), I finished my triumphal reading. It even seems to me that at that moment the sun emerged from behind a cloud. (Perhaps that is not completely true, but it serves to show the touching and somewhat color-photograph side of the scene.)

Cocteau had just given me a sumptuous and frivolous gift: he had just given me the poetry of the theater. [1960]

Jean Anouilh. *PCP*. Oct., 1961, p. 23†

Cocteau was one of my first French friends, and in my first years in Paris we were often together. His conversation was always a highly diverting performance, though at times it was rather like that of a feuilletonist out to make a "career." I soon learned to appreciate Cocteau's many sterling qualities, however, and we have remained dear and lifelong friends—indeed, he is the only close friend I have of the *Firebird* period. . . .

Cocteau is a master designer whose quick eye and economical line can fix the character of any quarry in a few loops. His best caricatures are as good as any but Picasso's, I think, and much modified by erasure, Cocteau scrawled his with photographic speed. When Cocteau first discussed his costumes and masks for the 1952 *Oedipus Rex* with me, he ended each description by scribbling the design on a piece of paper. Though this took him only a few seconds the drawings—I have them still—are each a talented print of his personality.

And his personality is generous and disarmingly simple. Artistically, he is a first-rate critic and a theatrical and cinematographic innovator of a high order.

Igor Stravinsky. In Igor Stravinsky and Robert Craft,
Dialogues and a Diary (Garden City, N.Y.,
Doubleday, 1963), pp. 44–45

Jean Cocteau seemed to me the pattern of those who refused to be labeled old men. . . . He was aware that being well known was as important to him as the air he breathed; and even more important than the notoriety was the effort he had to make to keep it up. . . .

This dread of slipping off the platform, even if it should only be for a moment, became an obsession during the last years of his life. There was not an article, not a preface, not a press release that he would refuse to write. Indeed, he burned himself out of his exhausting struggle for the limelight. His last coronary struck him when he had only just finished his own souvenir portrait for television. An admirable piece, his own through and through, and one in which he sought both to make his picture clear and to confuse it, as though he were looking into a reflecting pool that was sometimes motionless and sometimes ruffled by the breeze. It cost him a great deal in labor and anxiety. I went to see him at Milly a couple of days before the misfortune whose consequences carried him off, and he told me about his uneasiness. "I am not sure of having hit the right tone," he said. "I am quite sure you have," I replied with complete sincerity, for I felt that there was nothing more perfectly in Jean's line than that self-portrait.

He did not experience the peace of evening, but it was not made for him. I loved him; there were many of us who wept over his death; and by it the public has lost many a sparkling page, many an audacious drawing. It should not be forgotten that Cocteau had chanced upon his title, *Memory-Portraits*, for one of his most brilliant books: it is no doubt one of the most forgotten of his works, but it is the one posterity will choose when it calls upon this witness of his own age to provide his testimony. [1965]

Maurice Goudeket. *The Delights of Growing Old*
(New York, Farrar, Straus and Giroux, 1966),
pp. 197, 199, 202–3

Jean Cocteau wrote and directed his first full-length movie [*Beauty and the Beast*] in 1946; he created a fairy-tale atmosphere of sensuous elegance. As a child escapes from the everyday family life to the magic of a storybook, so, in the film, Beauty's farm with its Vermeer simplicity fades in intensity as we are caught up in the Gustave Doré extravagance of the Beast's enchanted landscape. In Christian Bérard's makeup, Jean Marais is a beautiful Beast; Beauty's self-sacrifice to him holds no more horror than a satisfying romantic fantasy should have. The transformation of the Beast into Prince Charming is ambiguous—what we have gained cannot take the place of what we have lost. (When shown the film, Greta Garbo is reported to have said at the end, "Give me back my beast.") . . .

Orpheus is the masterpiece of magical film-making. Though a narrative treatment of the legend of Orpheus in a modern Parisian setting, it is as inventive and enigmatic as a dream. Orpheus wants to get beyond the limits of human experience, he wants to reach the unknowable—the mystery beyond mortality. Jean Marais is ideally cast as the successful popular poet who is envied and despised by the younger poets; his conflicts, his desire to renew himself, his feverish listening for signals from the source of mystery, are the substance of the film. Dark, troubled, passionate Maria Casarès is his Death: attended by her roaring motorcyclists—the hooded messengers of death—she is mystery incarnate. . . .

The motorcyclists are part of a new mythology, they suggest images of our time: secret police... black heroes... the anonymous and impersonal... agents of some unknown authority... executioners... visitors from outer space... the irrational. They are the men you can't reach and you can't deal with; they stand for sudden, shockingly accidental death. The trial of Death is like a nightmare of a wartime resistance movement "underground" trial. Cocteau uses emblems and images of the then recent Nazi period and merges them with other, more primitive images of fear—as, indeed, they are merged in the modern consciousness. This gives the violence and mystery of the Orpheus story a kind of contemporaneity that, in other hands, might seem merely chic; but Cocteau's special gift was to raise chic to art.

Pauline Kael. Kiss Kiss Bang Bang (Boston,
Little, Brown, 1968), pp. 236, 326

Cocteau—taking as his model, as he told his mother, [Stendhal's] *The Charterhouse of Parma* (for its love intrigue and the scenes of Fabrice on the field of Waterloo)—puts his hero [in *Thomas the Impostor*] into the two sectors of [World War I] that he himself had known best, Champagne and Flanders, and he portrays imposture as a kind of poetry, requiring noteworthy feats of imagination. Even when Thomas is shot by an enemy patrol in no-man's-land, he pretends. " 'A bullet!' he told himself. 'I'm done for if I don't pretend to be dead.' But in him, fiction and reality were one. Guillaume Thomas *was* dead." Cocteau was particularly attached to *Thomas the Impostor* as an admirable illustration of the theme of the poet and his "lies." Gallant, outside society, dying in pursuit of his dream, his hero seemed to him the very essence of a poet. . . .

The Enfants Terribles is a novel of genius, weirdly prophetic in its forecasting of today's era of alienated youth. Its brother-and-sister pair of leading characters, Paul and Elisabeth, inspired by Jean and Jeanne Bourgoint, are among Cocteau's most striking literary inventions. No characters like them had appeared in fiction before, and Cocteau embodied in them qualities which, while always present in young people, were at the time this influential novel was written just beginning to grow into a wave that has since become tidal. . . .

On its publication in 1930, *The Enfants Terribles* became one of those books that are adopted as a kind of *vade mecum* by the young. Today Frenchmen and non-Frenchmen of middle age and over still speak of its extraordinary effect of revealing to them hitherto unsuspected depths of their adolescent selves, inspiring them with feelings of proud youthful exclusivity.

Francis Steegmuller. Cocteau (Boston, Little, Brown,
1970), pp. 287, 397–98

Jean Cocteau certainly overestimated the influence Radiguet exercised on him, particularly on Cocteau's evolution as a writer. There is less discontinuity than Cocteau claimed between those of his works that preceded their meeting and those that followed. Radiguet unquestionably brought Cocteau firmly back to classicism, and Radiguet undoubtedly freed Cocteau from what could have become bad literary mannerisms, but the ideas set forth in *Professional Secrets* are certainly Cocteau's, and his alone. And this is equally true of *Plain-Song* and *Opera*. Rather than the cause for change, Radiguet was the occasion for it, perhaps only the pretext. Radiguet's contribution consisted more than anything else in turning Cocteau away from the Parisian society from which Cocteau could not extricate himself and in which he was expending his energy. Radiguet forced Cocteau to devote this energy to creation.

Inversely, Cocteau minimized his own role in relation to Radiguet. It is known, for example, that Cocteau read and corrected the manuscript of [Radiguet's] *The Devil in the Flesh* and played a large part in the creation of *Count d'Orgel's Ball*. On a different level, Cocteau organized and orchestrated the great success that *The Devil in the Flesh* had, something he never deigned to do for himself, and Cocteau missed no opportunity to exalt Radiguet's genius everywhere, even at the Collège de France. In lowering himself, he raised Radiguet. Why? Because in Radiguet Cocteau had discovered the Angel. Undoubtedly the Angel had already had several other incarnations and would later have many others, but Radiguet was the Angel himself. . . .

When Cocteau wrote the play *Orpheus*, he had just turned thirty-six. A year and a half had passed since Radiguet's death, and Cocteau still had not completely recovered from that loss, from the sense of mutilation he felt. But now that he had some perspective on his suffering, he was angry with himself for having sought consolation in Maritain [and Catholicism], for having thus moved farther from Radiguet, for having almost betrayed poetry. While religion had separated them, drugs had brought them close together, and had given Cocteau the sense of abolishing the boundaries between waking and sleeping, between life and death, had given him the power to move freely from one to the other. Why should Eurydice not return from Hell? Why should Orpheus not go there to rejoin her? Why, in an identical yet different place, beyond space and time, should they not begin to live again, reconciled forever?

Jacques Brosse. *Cocteau* (Paris, Gallimard, 1970),
pp. 49–50, 111–12†

COLETTE, SIDONIE GABRIELLE (1873–1954)

Mme Colette Willy is a lively woman, a *real* woman, who dares to be natural and who resembles a little village bride more than she does a depraved woman of letters.

Read [*Seven Animal Dialogues*], and you will see how much truth there is in what I am saying. Mme Colette has chosen to take all the fragrance of gardens, all the coolness of meadows, all the warmth of the local roads, and all the emotions of man and to place them in two charming little animals. All the emotions: I avow that through the schoolgirl's laughter resounding in the forest I can hear the sobbing of a spring. You cannot bend toward a poodle or a tomcat without a muted anguish filling your heart. When comparing yourself to animals, you feel everything that separates you from them and everything that brings you close to them. . . .

Toby-Chien and Kiki-la-Doucette know very well that their mistress is a lady who would not harm a piece of sugar or a mouse; a lady who, to our delight, walks on the tightrope she has woven with words whose bloom she never ruffles, whose fragrance perfumes our air; a lady who, with the voice of a pure French stream, sings of the sad tenderness that makes animals' hearts beat so quickly. [1905]

Francis Jammes. Preface to Colette, *Sept dialogues de bêtes*
(Paris, Mercure de France, 1927), pp. 11–14†

The Vagabond . . . confirms the originality of [Colette]. The novel consists of memoirs arranged with a great deal of skill and undoubtedly a great deal of imagination, related in a confidential tone that gives them a great deal of charm. This novel transports us to a higher region: there are passages of truly Nietzschean detachment, concerning the pulling away from happiness because of a love for freedom. These passages contain the highest, most feminine, and truest philosophy. What a peculiar book, with its mixture of acrobatics, sensuality (perhaps something more than sensuality), painful melancholy, and haughty bitterness! There is no modesty—but all of woman's sensitivity. No hypocrisy—but all the mysteries of an enigmatic soul in which pleasure can be stifled by will.

The Vagabond may not be a work of art, but it is surely a treatise on feminine psychology. It is woman stripped bare, shown in her eternal situation of wanting what she does not want, of no longer wanting what is offered to her and what she desires, of pulling herself away from life out of a pride in living. . . .

Although one is entitled not to enjoy this book, one should not reject an entire work in which there are such beautiful and moving things.

Rémy de Gourmont. *Promenades littéraires* (Paris,
Mercure de France, 1912), Vol. IV, pp. 96–97†

Colette came late to the true novel—that is to say, the objective novel. . . . Her wish to focus on herself and her tendency always to write confessions seemed to justify the severe critics who claimed that women writers know only how to reveal themselves. But after *Mitsou* in 1919, Colette published a series of objective novels: *Chéri*, in 1920, *The Ripening Seed*, in 1923, and *The Last of Chéri* in 1926. She thus won the place she had been denied among creative novelists; and, just as [her earlier character] Claudine had become a social type, often cited in any classification of women, so Chéri immediately assumed an equivalent importance as the embodiment of the romantic gigolo. . . .

Chéri is no banal story of a liaison of an aging woman and a young boy. It is something infinitely more complex, something that should not repel any reader. . . . Freud's books try to teach us that the attraction of the adolescent male to the maternal woman is the most natural thing in the world. . . . Colette has given a definitive fictional treatment to this subject. Through restrained emotion and tender understanding, she is able to make us feel almost a sympathy for these somewhat ambiguous characters.

All the critics hailed this novel as an event, although they were divided into two camps: the admirers, and the indignant ones. But very few failed to perceive the vital force of a work about which Henry Bataille could say, in a striking phrase, "The last twenty pages of *Chéri* are Dantesque."

Jean Larnac. *Colette et son œuvre* (Paris, Simon Kra,
1927), pp. 148–49, 162–63†

"Death does not interest me [wrote Colette] not even my own." What interests Colette is accepting life, the successive ages of life as they come, and discovering the beauty of each age, a beauty that changes every moment. She establishes a peaceful kingdom around her, in which her sovereignty extends over gardens and over a population of animals. Everything is always alive around her, and her whole effort is to prolong and extend life. To plant, because planting is to prolong oneself; to survive; to look toward the future; to take care of the sick animal; to spare the toad at the edge of the pond. The only immortality that means something to Colette is a temporary immortality, incarnated in everyday gestures, the immortality of the peasant who identifies with his ancestors and works not for himself but for the family, which will not die and of which he is only one moment in time.

In her earthly wisdom, Colette is guided by someone else's example. It is not necessary to recount the extent to which Colette at last identifies with her mother, with the woman whom Captain Colette called Sido. *Claudine's House, Break of Day*, and *Sido* tell us about Colette's mother. One of mankind's deepest, most beautiful, and most consoling mysteries is the survival or rather the *rising to the surface* of one person in another, who is close to that person, at a certain time in life. For a long time Colette seemed to believe that she was nothing like Sido. But she gradually rediscovered her mother's traits. . . . They had been reshaped and changed in Colette, but all of them belonged to Sido. [1931]

Robert Brasillach. *Portraits* (Paris, Librairie Plon, 1935), pp. 22–23†

Colette is "authentic." She has the kind of style one would prefer not to call "style," because so many untalented writers . . . have gotten us into the habit of thinking of style as a self-conscious, artificial means of expression, one that even smells of the midnight oil. Colette writes the same way she thinks, feels, and speaks. Between what we read and what she has thought, felt, or spoken, *there is no distance*. Hers is a natural style. I am not saying that the only great writers are those with natural styles: exceptions can be found. But let me say, let me proclaim, and let me repeat that a writer with a natural style is the only miracle in literature. . . .

The literary clique that claims to set the fashion in France . . . expresses its scorn for Colette by its silence. They do not tear Colette apart; no, they ignore her. Or else they praise her only to indicate her limitations: "She is the queen of the kingdom of the senses." Which means, of course, that matters of the intellect are closed to her. But thirty volumes in which all her notations are true and human, thirty volumes without a trace of the literary or the artificial, so much overflowing poetry of simplicity and well-being, so much imperceptible finesse, nothing excessive and nothing insufficient, never anything "foolish," such a perfect lack of pretentiousness—does not all this constitute intelligence, *genuine* intelligence, active intelligence, the kind that does not have to isolate itself to contemplate and admire itself, the only kind of intelligence needed for living? . . .

There is perhaps a more valid reason for the half-silence of the intellectuals about Colette. . . . Critics do not know how to approach her works, because there is nothing to explain, nothing to criticize; her works need only be admired. [1934]

Henry de Montherlant. Carnets 1930–1944 (Paris,
Gallimard, 1957), pp. 165–66†

With the exception of Chéri, one of the most vivid of all her characters, [Colette's] masculine figures are easily effaced, leaving only a vague and slightly disagreeable memory. Always faintly sarcastic and contemptuous when she speaks of men, Colette never fails to endow them with beautiful bodies. She excels in sensuous descriptions of nude or scantily covered men, especially when these are young and sunburnt. Her scorn is reserved for their moral defects.

It is over her heroines that her heart expands. Her natural enthusiasm is for woman, to whom she invariably attributes the better judgment, the warmer imagination, the keener perception, the more intense feeling, and the greater self-control. Let a man deceive a woman in a Colette book, he is sure to be a monster of cruelty and ingratitude, she a dignified and suffering martyr. When the woman is the transgressor, this sympathy for the victim is replaced by prompt derision. While her heroines never neglect a chance to protest their undying love for some one man, under these lyric protestations there is a cool appraisal or some witty barb at their expense. . . . Colette's heroines are never lacking in physical desire; indeed, this is what makes them slaves to man. . . . Nevertheless Colette's heroines despise these instruments of their pleasure, for her psychology attributes to women what is usually considered a purely masculine trait.

But man, the necessity, is at the same time the woman's enemy, who "kills the thing he loves." Her heroines give their bodies, but withhold their souls, for they find all fusion with the masculine mind impossible. . . . Colette is too much of a feminist not to resent woman's subordinate position, and most of her heroines are invested with her own hostility towards man.

Milton H. Stansbury. French Novelists of Today
(Philadelphia, University of Pennsylvania Press,
1935), pp. 112–14

In Colette's sensitivity I can detect that of all French women, my female companions. This sensitivity consists of a desire for clarity, a constant struggle for physical pleasure, and a way of saying things very quickly, with a minimum of means and a maximum of music. Her traits, which one can discern from among a thousand writers—her style, with its spontaneous and ambiguous tendernesses; her love, so just and moderate even in its passions; her fondness for images, for verbs, and for a well-placed inflection in a sentence—all these elements are feminine and French. It is easy to understand why, in small-town libraries, at the home of a doctor, a wine merchant, or a horticulturist, it is Colette's books that look the most read, and the most carefully read. Indeed, whole passages from her books have been engraved in the memory of many an ordinary housewife, who is dazzled by Colette's ability to say things she herself might have said if it were not for the few meters, the little something, the invisible abyss that separates the housewife from the genius.

And Colette's genius, which French women feel is so close to their minds, of the same nature and essence, lies precisely in her answering all the questions about the inner life in the strictest way, like a generous oracle. She is infallible. . . .

A few critics thought they had raised an insurmountable objection by writing that Colette, although an incomparable artist, is not a great poet because she does not give answers, even tentative answers, to the harsh, tragic problems of the human condition; these critics claimed that she never participates in any contemporary quarrels or conflicts. But this is why French women praise her. For there are no problems! All problems have already been raised, all have been settled. Only the circumstances change, and Colette knows that well, better than anyone else.

Léon-Paul Fargue. *Portraits de famille* (Paris,
J. B. Janin, 1947), pp. 21–24†

In the first half of the twentieth century, Colette became an institution for many literary connoisseurs. That she was the finest French prose writer alive was an unchallenged opinion. Expert as she is as a stylist, exquisite as her chiseling of words and images can be at times, we believe that her prose is too ornate and too remote from the naturalness and simplicity of the very great works of art for her to rank with the truly eminent masters of French prose. Her mannerisms soon pall on the fastidious reader. Her characters are too monotonous and they wander complacently in an atmosphere of venal loves, carnal concerns, and gigolos, without rising to the stature of Proustian lovers or Toulouse-Lautrec's mournful seekers of joy. The men whom she depicts, including weak-willed Chéri and a number of vain Don Juans more often jilted than jilting, seldom come to life. They certainly never attempt to reach toward their partner's or their own inner life or to attain heroism.

Love, with Colette as in the earlier work of Paul Bourget and in Anatole France's faded *The Red Lily*, inevitably means lies. "There is a pleasure in being devoted to those who deceive us, who wear their lie like a finely adorned gown and open it only through the voluptuous pleasure of showing themselves nude." Thus wrote Colette in *Retreat from Love*. This woman, who went deep into the bitter abyss of sensation and whose many volumes endlessly illustrate Paul Valéry's celebrated epigram ("The deepest part of man is his skin"), failed to create solid works of fiction or characters likely to live in the memories of generations of readers. Her prestige discouraged French women writers for several decades. Today, however, she appears almost prehistoric, with her 1900 atmosphere and calculating demi-mondaines. A revolution has thrown her back into the era of an old regime.

Henri Peyre. The Contemporary French Novel (New
York, Oxford University Press, 1955), pp. 282–83

What a strange book [*Break of Day*] is! It was begun in 1927, at Saint-Tropez in the places that it describes, a thing which in Colette's books is exceptional for she always saw even landscapes better when she was some way away. If ever a novel appears to be autobiographical, that one does. Everything is in it, "La Treille Muscate" [Colette's and Goudeket's property near Saint-Tropez], the garden, the vineyard, the terrace, the sea, the animals. Our friends are called by their real names. Colette puts herself into it, describing herself in minute detail. Never has she pushed self-analysis so far. The transparent allusions to her past are authentic. The letters of Sido reproduce those which Sido wrote. The odours are those which still delight my nostrils, I have known those blue nights, I hear the chirping of the cicadas, I feel the buffeting of the wind, my hand lingers on the warm wall. Everything is there, except that *Break of Day* evokes the peace of the senses and a renunciation of love, at the moment when Colette and I were living passionate hours together, elated by the heat, the light and the perfume of Provençal summers. . . .

Colette was endowed with a solid appetite for the good things of this world . . . and derived a frank pleasure from their possession. But at the same time there was in her a secret austerity and later on it was she who, before me, decided that the time had come for the two of us to turn love into friendship.

Of all Colette's books this is the one I prefer. It comes midway in her work and I see in it the flower of her full maturity. [1956]

Maurice Goudeket. Close to Colette (New York,
Farrar, Straus and Cahady, 1957), pp. 44–46

The animals that people admire are often symbols of their own subconscious mind. Ernest Hemingway admires big, strong, combative animals. Jack London liked fierce dogs. Some people love birds—not caged birds, nor half-tame poultry like pigeons, but wild birds, flying freely and living harmlessly and making their own music. Colette admired the only animal which will live with human beings and remain almost wholly self-centered; the pet animal which refuses to be disciplined like the horse or to demonstrate loyalty like the dog; the animal which smiles, but never laughs, which can be graceful even in impossibly embarrassing situations, which is habitually polite—except in sudden crises of passion; the animal which, by its very walk, seems to convert a garden into a clearing in the jungle, and a dark room into a cavern full of ghosts; the animal which, although fed by human beings, remains its own master and sometimes dominates the other inmates of the house: the most cunning, the most cruel, and the most beautiful of all domestic beasts: the cat.

Horses can be mean; both dogs and men can be evil; but even when a cat is being fiendishly cruel or spectacularly sensual it cannot be called wicked. If you can imagine a series of novels written by an unusually intelligent cat, in a style varying from a silken purr to a melodious but occasionally threatening *meow*, and on subjects almost as remote from ordinary morality as feline ethics are from human ethics, you will have a very good notion of the books of that fluffy old thing with nine lives, Madame Colette.

Gilbert Highet. Talents and Geniuses (New York, Oxford University Press, 1957), pp. 82–83

During her lifetime Colette had received and accepted as much official recognition as any other French writer of the first half of the twentieth century. She was a member of the Académie Royale Belge, a member and president of the Académie Goncourt, and in 1953 she was made *Grand Officier* of the Légion d'Honneur. . . .

It is difficult to believe that if Willy had not suggested that Colette write recollections of her school days, she would probably never have written at all. The fact is that a year or so after their marriage, Monsieur Willy, always in need of money, did make the suggestion, and so Colette, having bought notebooks which resembled those she had used in school, began to set down her girlhood memories. Willy read the finished product, decided that it wasn't what he wanted and put it away in a desk drawer. Two years later, while arranging his papers, he rediscovered the manuscript, reread it and concluded that with a little spice added to it the novel would sell. In 1900, *Claudine at School* was published and signed "Willy." Its immediate success was such that Monsieur Willy ordered another novel and another, locking his young wife in a room for four hours every day to make sure that she would work. Coerced into writing, Colette slowly discovered that it could be a means of earning money (the 300 francs a month which Willy gave her as pocket money), and also that it was habit forming; soon she deliberately chose to spend certain hours of each day with pen and notebook. Thus one of France's most prominent writers began as a slave to literature and ended as an addict. French literature owes an unpayable debt to Monsieur Willy.

Elaine Marks. Colette (New Brunswick, New Jersey, Rutgers University Press, 1960), pp. 4, 36–37

As a writer, Colette is against the French grain. She, rather, *has* a grain: whereas the *génie français* has, since Racine, flowed classically without one. Where the whole tendency of French literature is, magnificently or banally, to substitute an abstract for a concrete and an intellectual antithesis for a tangible gesture, Colette's prose is forever bringing you up against whorls and knots—not merely substantives, but particular, even peculiar, substantives. . . . I could believe she never set foot in the country side, that she hired someone to coach her in her Burgundian accent, got her botany out of books, could not tell tulip from turnip, dog from cat or man from woman, and ate the revolting water-caltrop solely to provoke her friends' incredulity. . . . What is authentic is the literary power. . . .

Colette's perseverance in the truly Proustian creation she carried out in life as well as on blue paper measures her narcissism. Almost auto-erotically she played with her own name (she even got as far as "Willette Collie"); and by the same symptom she revealed that her sexual ambiguity went back to an indecision about whether to identify herself with her mother or her father. She inclined first towards the father. To call herself simply by her (and his) surname, Colette, shorn of female first names, was as blatant a claim to masculinity as the shorn hair which she adopted soon after. . . . Maturity and fame made Colette into "Madame Colette"—which was, of course, what her mother was. Colette's reconciliation and identification with her mother shewed itself not only in the open mother-worship she put (safely after her mother's death) into *Sido* but also in her ability to incarnate herself in the disreputable mother-figures of the novels: Chéri's mistress old enough to be his mother; the grandmother who, with an acute eye to an erotic detail, grooms Gigi's body for prostitution [in *Gigi*]. And the object who is cherished, groomed? Colette again. (She confesses in *The Blue Lantern* that the only flower she did not like was the narcissus. It must have come too near the bone.)

Brigid Brophy. NS. Aug. 9, 1963, p. 169

[*The Blue Lantern*] is a brave and gay performance by an old woman in pain, a kind of unaffected tribute to herself. . . . She writes about the progressive fading of the senses, accepts it, and values what remains behind: sights, sounds, smells, animals, and old friends. She speaks with love of Jean Marais, of Cocteau and [Marguerite] Moreno and the dying Fargue; she is charitable to the most egocentric of the young, remembering her own youthful "shudder of repugnance at the touch of old people." She watches children at play in the garden beneath her window, and writes of them with the unillusioned toughness she showed in the music-hall stories of long before. She writes of animals with an unsentimental anthropomorphism we Anglo-Saxons may have trouble understanding, because our culture precludes the unsentimentally anthropomorphic. . . .

On the whole, then, one sees *The Blue Lantern* as an agreeable act of self-indulgence, a cultist tribute to a writer whose notoriety has merged into her fame, whose grossness time and the worshippers have sublimated into a unique delicacy. . . . The major Colette is tragic, and *The Blue Lantern* is strictly not so; it is brave, amused, charming. Yet the aged hedonist, almost happy in her pain, experiences the last stirrings of that spirit of rebirth which is the other side of tragedy.

Frank Kermode. *NYR*. Dec. 12, 1963, pp. 3–4

A comparison between Colette and George Sand is inevitable at a superficial level at least because no other French women writers have known such fame and been so closely identified with their own work. . . .

In France, until 1900, and to some extent afterwards, all women writers were members of the aristocracy or like George Sand brought up by survivors from the *ancien régime*. Women have always been valued in France but only in relation to men, not in their own right. . . .

Colette seems to have been the first French woman writer who belonged uncompromisingly to the middle class, and the provincial middle class at that. It is here that the comparison with George Sand breaks down, for Colette never had the dash and authoritative attitude of her predecessor, *la dame de Nohant*. Colette was taught how to write, and it was a long time before she dared speak with her own voice. George Sand had less training, if more education, and her "collaboration" with Jules Sandeau was brief. Both writers affected men's clothes or manners for a time, one from romantic eccentricity combined with a wish to compete with men, the other from resignation and a temporary renouncement of men. . . .

[For Colette] happiness was hard to find and hard to keep. Colette seemed not to trust it and she lacked confidence because her personality and work, for all the naturalness they showed on the surface, were not natural at all, they had been organized by methods of various kinds, some haphazard, some controlled, but in any case somehow artificial. This is perhaps partly the explanation of her "amorality," her refusal or inability to see any distinction between what is usually called "good" and "bad." . . .

The role of a classic is surely not to teach readers what to do or think, but to show them a personal vision of the world and generally to enrich their lives. By an extraordinary chain of events and sheer hard work this is what Colette achieved. The schoolgirl with the long plait, the actress in front of her mirror, the journalist, the professional novelist, the beautician, the old lady who still made up her face carefully and tried to conceal her high forehead beneath her grey, blue- or mauve-tinted curls: a succession of women who were one, each fascinating the other to such an extent that they—she—could live not in search of time lost, but outside it.

Margaret Crosland. *Colette: The Difficulty of Loving*
(Indianapolis, Ind., Bobbs-Merrill, 1973),
pp. 244–46, 250, 261

One of the characters in *Gigi* says of her aging sister: "She prefers living in a splendid past rather than in an ugly present." This remark suggests the circumstances in which Colette wrote the story as well as the atmosphere of the story itself. It was written in 1942, a few months after Maurice Goudeket, Colette's third husband and constant companion, had been arrested by the Nazis and sent to a concentration camp. Moreover, Colette was by now completely bedridden with arthritis and often in great pain. But she continued to write newspaper articles in which she exhorted the women of France to avoid despair and cultivate hope, even happiness. *Gigi* should be seen in this light. It is a fairy tale of romance and happiness.

In *Gigi* Colette returns to the world in which her fiction first took shape—the world of the demi-monde in 1900. The milieu is one of elegant corruption, inhabited by women whose good taste and dignity are the result of strict adherence to the "honorable habits of women without honor." Sixteen-year-old Gigi, Colette's final idealization of youthful exuberance and innocence, is being brought up by her grandmother and aunt, two aging courtesans. Bursting with life, the coltish Gigi is a restatement of the same ideal of youthfulness that Colette, some forty years before, had embodied in the figure of Claudine. . . .

The characters in *Gigi* are shallow. Like other imaginative writers who are preoccupied with their own past, Colette attached a perhaps excessive importance to a form of life already vanished. Although the novel is beautifully executed, the material from which it is fashioned is thin. Still, the conversations are witty and full of sparkling humor. In fact, instead of being a portrayal of love, Colette's last fictional work is essentially a comedy of manners performed by a cast of stereotyped characters. As is true of any good comedy of manners, *Gigi* is a triumph of style.

Robert D. Cottrell. *Colette* (New York,
Frederick Ungar, 1974), pp. 113–14

COURTELINE, GEORGES (1858–1929)

Humanity's habits are not immutable. Even the gods change sometimes. We have already changed our way of laughing; it is indeed possible to imagine an age in which people will no longer laugh at all. In the future those who will wish to mold their faces in the shape of laughter will, when they read the books of Georges Courteline, receive a very clear idea of what this vanished habit was. Those who want to laugh now should make haste to rejoice. We are not yet at the point when we have to search for the bust of the god Laughter amidst the ruins. The god Laughter lives among us. When our statues will have fallen, when our customs will be abolished, when men will compute the years in a new era, they will say these simple words about the man who was able to make us so happy:

"He was a charming minor divinity, discriminating and good, who lived in Montmartre. He had so much grace that vulgar language, seeking an indestructible sanctuary, found it in his work."

Marcel Schwob. *Spicilège* (Paris, Mercure de France,
1896), p. 159†

If [Courteline] resembled his books, he would be jovial, badly dressed, and pot-bellied. He would look like a good fellow who was also something of a scoundrel, and nobody would be surprised to see him take a drink and then sprawl on his seat at a café, his vest unbuttoned, his paunch sticking out, tossing off mugs of beer and puns by the dozen. He would be a combination of a soldier on leave, an art student on a spree, and a joke-telling traveling salesman.

And now, here is Georges Courteline as he really appears: short, thin, sickly, his body buried in clothing that is too large for him, his hair unkempt and sparse, his complexion bilious, his chilled body under a woollen scarf: This man is sad; he seems to have just returned from a funeral. . . . But be careful. Courteline opens his mouth. And suddenly he is transformed. His eyes become animated, and they sparkle. His voice, alternately hollow and ringing out clearly, gives rise to funny sto-

ries. It is a running fire of wit, anecdotes, and sharp observations, underlined by jerky gestures. An enormous and excessive gaiety springs forth
from his speech. . . .

Excess is the characteristic mark of the age we are living in. In
every area, people forget about moderation and favor brutalities; everyone wants to make a loud noise, in order to be heard by the crowd.
Courteline is not exempt from these faults. Sometimes he goes beyond
the limits of taste and decency. He is unbothered by obscenity. But he
compensates for these excesses by his surprising qualities. One can say
of him what was said of his master Rabelais: When he is bad, he
outdoes the worst; when he is good, nobody else can be compared to
him.

Adolphe Brisson. *Pointes sèches* (Paris,
Armand Colin, 1898), pp. 99–100, 107–8†

While the bold, free comedy of Molière, which reflected the broad-
mindedness of Molière, who reflected the broad-mindedness of his century, was subdued and refined in [Jean] Regnard; while the comedy of
[Alain] Lesage rose from the buffoonery of the outdoor theaters to the
sharp satire of *Turcaret*; and while in Labiche comedy tended, through
the caricature of the grotesque and truculent bourgeois, only to provoke
laughter, in the bizarre fantasy of more than a hundred *vaudevilles;* the
comedy of Courteline, more profoundly drawn from life, more acutely
observed in the individual, has something bitter and sad—and it is
therefore more directly linked to the comedy of Molière.

Although the theatrical works of this subtle humorist are not numerous, although his comedies are almost all in one act, and although
they are miniatures of observation rather than large paintings, the manner of studying the individual, of analyzing him, and of reproducing him
with some particular characteristics, so as to individualize him among a
thousand others, is the same in Molière and in Courteline. One finds the
same originality, the same unexpected discoveries in the comedic, and
the same enormous buffoonery, which deforms the truth but which hides
a deep philosophical meaning. It is not too rash to say that, in two and
a half centuries, no comic writer appeared in the French theater with a
greater affinity of temperament to Molière than Courteline has. And it is
not too bold to say that the author of *Boubouroche* is a descendant of
the author of *Georges Dandin*. . . .

The boundlessness of Boubouroche's candor finds an equivalent
only in the boundlessness of Adèle's impudence. In this play we have
not merely two lovers named Boubouroche and Adèle facing each other
—one in love and gullible, who asks only to be convinced; the other
shrewd and cynical, who puts all her refined feminine art into maintain-

ing her position—but a weak man and a strong woman, who in their relations as lovers, counterbalance each other at all times. Here we have not only the confrontations between Georges Dandin and Angélique but also those between Alceste and Célimène [in *The Misanthrope*].

Cesare Levi. Rivista d'Italia. Dec. 15, 1920,
pp. 485–86, 492†

Courteline never wrote a comedy, any more than he wrote a novel, even in *The 8:47 Train*. Only one of his plays has more than one act: *Boubouroche*, which has two. *Boubouroche* and a few one-act plays were enough to entitle him to occupy the theater as a master, a master of laughter greater than Labiche, by reason of his dialogue, his style, and his movement. Like Labiche's, his comedy is bound to existence, to the way of life of the middle class, of its average member, but not, as in Labiche, the average citizen as seen from his own home. Courteline saw him, observed him, expressed him from the point of view of the place where he met him, which was the café.

Like Rabelais, Courteline is a great French writer without women. There is only one in his theater: Adèle in *Boubouroche*, just as the cashier in the neighborhood café where Courteline and his court elected to domicile their evenings was sufficient to represent her sex. To "the women's friend" Courteline opposed "the law's friend," La Brige, the anti-clerical bachelor, as big as life. The two other best-known preferred arenas of Courteline's comedy were again settings without women: the barracks and the office—the barracks before [World War I] and the office before the advent of the stenographer. If the war, the stenographer, and the decline of the neighborhood café did not unseat Courteline's comedy, it was because Courteline, like Rabelais and Molière, had built it on the rock. He has enemies, but they are enemies of laughter, young men who, like the old Fontenelle, have never admitted that it is possible to utter *ha ha*! [1938]

Albert Thibaudet. French Literature from 1795 to
Our Era (New York, Funk & Wagnalls, 1967),
p. 449

R.M.: There are three turn-of-the-century writers I would like you to say something about for us: [Octave] Mirbeau, Labiche, and Courteline.

P.L.: All I will say about Mirbeau is that *Business Is Business* seemed to me to be a very strong play, a very interesting play. It satirizes an entire class. As for Labiche, I am not very familiar with him. And Courteline doesn't interest me.

R.M.: How is it possible that Courteline doesn't interest you, since he is truly in the line of writers who are descendants of Molière?

P.L.: I don't agree at all. Courteline? An invention of Catulle Mendès, who called him a "son of Molière." [Marcel] Schwob went one better: "A charming divinity of laughter." I saw *Boubouroche* on stage. It is really overrated.

R.M.: You find comedy in it but no depth?

P.L.: It is overdone. Listen, the lover who lets himself be locked in a closet—you have to admit that the play is a bit much. There is more invention in it than truth.

R.M.: That situation of the lover is not impossible. Things like that have happened.

P.L.: No, no! It's a caricature.

R.M.: The truest situations can be caricatural.

P.L.: Now listen, you're not going to make me say that I enjoy that! You have your tastes, and I have mine.

Paul Léautaud. *Entretiens avec Robert Mallet*

(Paris, Gallimard, 1951), p. 230†

Pierre Loti and Claude Farrère were sailing one night on one of those improbable seas that are only navigated by naval officers in wartime, with the Southern Cross above their heads and a good ten days ahead of them before the next port, when Claude Farrère suddenly asked Loti the following question: "Who is, in your opinion, the most perfect writer of prose?"

And Loti the exquisite, Loti the précieux, Loti who had ten days ahead of him in which to consider his answer, immediately replied: "Georges Courteline."

The charming poet Hugues Delorme, who tells this story, adds that Claude Farrère had exactly the same opinion.

Colette, our great Colette, wrote: "I learned the language of animals with Sido; I am proud that I learned French with Georges Courteline."

Henri Bergson left this testimonial: "When you have read Courteline, you understand just how much depth there can be in comedy and how much philosophy in laughter."

I have taken the precaution of quoting these remarks to prove that one can be a comic playwright and a very great writer as well. There is a sharp prejudice against comic writers. When you say to a serious writer, "Well, you are forced to admit that the public likes that!", he answers, in the manner of [the composer Emmanuel] Chabrier, "That's true, but nobody else does."

When Courteline was alive, if anyone dared (like Catulle Mendès) assert that Courteline was a thousand times more important a writer than Paul Hervieu, Henri Lavedan, or Jean Richepin, people would laugh in his face.

And yet, I believe that the matter has been proven now. And in an irrefutable fashion.

Marcel Achard. *Rions avec eux* (Paris, Librairie
Arthème Fayard, 1957), pp. 157–58†

Courteline wrote nothing with more joy than *The Conversion of Alceste*. Perhaps the reason is because this play was written in verse, and so for the only time in his life he was able to reconcile the poet and the comic writer in himself. There is also nothing he wrote that better expresses his authentic misanthropy. We can still debate whether Molière [in *The Misanthrope*] was for or against Alceste. But there is no doubt whatsoever about Courteline's viewpoint. It was on the occasion of *The Conversion of Alceste* that Courteline confided to an interviewer: "One act, only one act: that is as much as I can do in the theater. I can't help it, I have no imagination. The subjects I think of do not admit of any development. My plots stop short after one act." . . .

The quality of imagination that he so cruelly lacked (constructing a plot or complicating one) happened to be precisely what the theater of his time needed least. Dramatic art could easily do without "carpenters," of whom it then had a plethora. What Courteline brought to it came just at the right time to rejuvenate a comic tradition that was worn out by plot complications and the most hollow improbabilities. Courteline brought an intensity of comic detail, a characterization of types that was both farcical and accurate, and the exemplary value of a comic situation carried to its paroxysm. A sketch by Courteline brought to perfection one kind of farce that, in a more diluted form, would lose its virulence and its hilariousness. The lessons Courteline had learned, in spite of himself, from journalistic constraint were applied willingly, throughout his easygoing theatrical career, in the form of the strict limits he was able to impose on his capricious creation.

Francis Pruner. Introduction to Georges Courteline,
Théâtre (Paris, Garnier-Flammarion, 1965),
pp. 19–20†

Courteline exerts practically no influence any more, even if his name is still known to the generation of writers and journalists who preceded today's "youth," which, in general, knows nothing about him.

It must indeed be admitted that part of his "little world" is dead: the barracks of 1968 are no longer those of 1880; the rations eaten on a straw mattress in a glacial and uncomfortable barracks-room have been replaced by the stylish dining-hall and the pleasant and well-heated rooms. Both noncommissioned and commissioned officers have become humanized; the army itself has become mechanized and automated.

The bureaucrats of today have to pass examinations and competitions to enter a ministry, where their presence and their activities are checked daily. . . . It is no longer possible to dream of offering half your salary to a colleague so that he will do your job.

Lawyers and judges are now rigorously educated and hired; their success or their advancement depends on their seriousness and their zeal.

Courteline has therefore aged insofar as he put on stage a world that has disappeared forever and insofar as he wrote his plays in a style that is too oratorical, too lofty, too literary. This style is irritating now; the proof is that his plays are almost never performed any more. . . .

The critic Jacques Guicharnaud remarked: " . . . The satire of bureaucrats, of military customs, and of the courts does not go beyond a few mannerisms or superficial absurdities. Realistic observation has its merits, but it imprisons the imagination (excluding the conclusion of *The Boulingrins*), and accuracy, even colored with a little bitterness, precludes any theatricality. The accumulation of so-called 'true' details quickly becomes out-of-date. . . ."

But Courteline will not die, because he remains the successor to Molière; he possesses the magic mirror in which men can recognize themselves.

Pierre Bornecque. *Le théâtre de Georges Courteline*
(Paris, A. G. Nizet, 1969), pp. 659–61†

The Commisssioner Has a Big Heart is a good introduction to Courteline. One of his favorite themes was the conflict between abstract or ideal justice on the one hand and, on the other hand, man-made law, as manipulated by lawyers and functionaries. In this play, the law, personified by the Commissioner, is trodden down and humiliated by a madman. This is, of course, a wishful, wistful idea: something Courteline would have *liked* to see. . . . The character of the Commissioner may well be filtered down from the first tyrant Courteline ever met, a schoolmaster under whom he suffered for several years at Meaux. . . .

Almost all his plays are based directly on his own experiences: his knocks at the civil service come from his thirteen years as an official in the Ministry of Culture; his army plays from his two years in Hussars; his leg-pulling of the law courts from some personal, drawn-out tangles with the French legal system and also from his father's work as a recorder at the tribunal in Tours; and his plays about the inscrutability of women were provoked by a couple of "let-downs" during his bachelor days in Montmartre. . . .

As a realist, Courteline had anything but an indulgent view of his fellow men. But he was not a pessimist. He was aware of their weaknesses, and bore down on them—hard. "Man is not wicked," he wrote in his last book, *The Philosophy of Georges Courteline*. "He is foolish, spiteful, boastful, unkind, stupidly skeptical and at the same time credulous. . . . But he is not, I repeat, wicked, in the exact sense of the term. . . ."

Out of this indignation came pure comedy. The writer Maurice Barrès told him: "When I read your writings I laugh like a monkey."

Albert Bermel. In Albert Bermel, ed., Three Popular
French Comedies (New York, Frederick Ungar,
1975), pp. 150–51

CROMMELYNCK, FERNAND (1888–1970)

BELGIUM

The Magnificent Cuckold and *The Childish Lovers*—these are the chosen titles of an author who takes the comedy of sex at its face value and yet laughs heartily at the imposture. He is no realist. By placing the scene of his action "in our time in Flanders" he achieves a singular detachment. We can believe anything of these Flemings, whose babes are surely as rosy as Rubens cherubs and whose skies luminous as the backgrounds of "Velvet" Brueghel. The inexhaustible generative force of Nature is in this people. They inhale exuberance from their flax-fields and cruelty from their cattle. . . .

Imagine these personages transferred to the drawing-room, and you have one of the hundred polite and weary comedies of sex—such a comedy as [Alfred] Capus or [Charles] Donnay or François de Curel might have written. M. Crommelynck, who abandons the plane of realism and seeks for the ludicrous essentials of his situation, escapes at the same time from the urbanity and the lassitude of these contemporaries. His *reductio ad absurdum* of the sexual motive imparts a new vigour to the theme. His comedy is cruel and grandiloquent, but it is elemental. The sap of nature runs in this tree that leans against the Wind of Flanders and casts a fantastic shadow on the plain.

Ashley Dukes. The Youngest Drama (Chicago,
Charles H. Sergel, 1924), pp. 87, 89–90

Can you imagine a Molière in a state of inebriation, a Molière who would also like to be as outrageous as Rabelais? That is Crommelynck.

[In *Golden Guts*] he shows us a poor devil maddened by a sudden inheritance, whose gold possesses him and finally chokes him. He is not like [Molière's] bourgeois Harpagon [in *The Miser*], pampering his vice for a number of years and coming to terms with it so as to derive as much pleasure as possible from it. This is a poor fellow born to earn his bread by the sweat of his brow, who is eaten alive by gold.

When we were in school, we congratulated Molière in our compositions for French class because he made his Miser a man in love. Crommelynck's hero also worships a girl—before he is possessed by his gold. But the gold separates him from his love to the point that, although we hear her sigh behind the door, the curtain falls before she has appeared on stage even once. No progression at all, and this is the weakness in this strong comedy: as soon as the play begins, the hero falls into an epileptic fit on learning of his inheritance. If Molière had shown us Harpagon falling into a delirium and howling in his search for his strongbox at the very beginning, he could not have sustained such a tone until the end. Crommelynck condemns his audience to a monotonous paroxysm, without rest or respite—treading the soil of madness.

François Mauriac. *NRF.* June, 1925, pp. 1051–52†

"Lord, preserve me from my gifts; as for my faults, I will take care of them myself." That is the daily prayer I propose to Crommelynck. But he will not pay heed to it. Because he prizes his inexhaustible invention, always to his own delight and often to ours; he prizes his wit, which extends in every direction like the beautiful branches of a tree; he prizes his vocabulary, which flows in abundance, and his imagination, capable of going astray but so real! Asking Crommelynck to exercise tighter control over so many riches is asking him to darken his life, to turn aside a gaze that can see gods, to lose his goat-footed cheerfulness—in short, to renounce his happiness.

Happiness illuminates this lively poet to such an extent that at times I am ready to prefer his joy to mine and to take his side, until, after the first act of *Hot and Cold*, he reduces an excellent dramatic situation to a brilliant shimmering of surfaces. . . .

Crommelynck's language is not easy: a rich language, charged with images, which sometimes makes us think we are listening to the very literary translation of a foreign play. It is not surprising that when we listen to Crommelynck we feel a tension analogous to that created by Claudel. We may be astonished, however, if we compare Crommelynck to Claudel, to find that Claudel sustains his plays better than does Crommelynck—through his faith first of all, through some great traditional conflict, and through a somber unity of the action, heavy but homogeneous. Crommelynck amuses himself and opens out where Claudel holds back; gets drunk where Claudel fasts. Dear Crommelynck, after you have had your fun, you should think a little about us, your audience. . . . [Nov. 25, 1934]

Colette. La jumelle noire (Paris, Ferenczi, 1935),
Vol. II, pp. 79–81 †

Giacomo Antonini . . . has seen in Carine the inability of human love to succeed, doomed as it is by the libido of man: the Italian critic could have found substantially the same thesis in . . . The Childish Lovers that anticipated Carine by nearly a decade. This was the undoing of Elizabeth de Groulingen grown old under her make-up and the veil of twilight in which she hides. A "stranger" loves the ideal mask of her, the flesh which he imagines. . . . But Elizabeth is old. The baron Cazou who is senile and broken was her lover in the days beyond time and its punishing. All the while, two children, Marie-Henriette and Walter, act out in counterpoint a similarly hopeless love story suggesting that the basic incommunicability of souls may be due to causes deeper than the barriers of the flesh.

The statement of this incommunicability is presumably more important than that of the flesh which is a mere vehicle. The flesh, although a latent presence in every play, will simply be used to describe different aspects of the failure of love, a frail agency, weaker than jealousy (The Magnificent Cuckold), weaker than avarice (Golden Guts), conceivably even weaker than fraud (Hot and Cold). However, the vehicle has frequently obscured the statement. André Rouveyre . . . who could not find very much to salvage in Crommelynck ("Let him be exported as quickly as possible; that will be best"), saw the Belgian playwright's drama as "Solely an object of venereal functions . . . that gives its characters the shabby aspect of maniacal patrons in a bawdy house." André Rouveyre was not allowing, in such condemnation, for one of the primary attributes of Farce that dates back to days when coarseness was accounted for by the greater intimacy then existing between art and life. . . .

In [Crommelynck's] hallucinatory world, love is not one of the primordial forces as in Maeterlinck. The great forces are the primal passions that have endured since a much earlier drama and that are not subject to social or superficial psychological contingencies. The only ambient atmosphere strong enough to contain them is that of the flesh, the essential world that antedates morality.

David I. Grossvogel. The Self-Conscious Stage in
Modern French Drama (New York, Columbia
University Press, 1958), pp. 234–35, 250

In spite of his limited output, the Belgian writer Fernand Crommelynck was one of the best dramatists writing in French during the inter-war years. Unlike so many of the plays of that time which are now only museum pieces, Crommelynck's plays have continued to be staged in Paris and to provoke reactions as keen as at their first performance. . . .

The Magnificent Cuckold is Crommelynck's best work and has been repeatedly revived. The most important of these revivals took place on December 31st, 1945, at the Théâtre Hébertot, when Georges Marchal offered a new interpretation of the part of the cuckold. Crommelynck intended *The Magnificent Cuckold* as a play on jealousy in the classical manner, and did not consider Shakespeare's *Othello* to be such a play because the hero's jealousy was the work of another, the villain Iago. One might, of course, argue that Iago merely awakened jealousy that was latent, but Crommelynck maintains that Othello was trusting, his jealousy was not innate, whereas his own hero, Bruno, was jealous by nature, just as Molière's Harpagon [in *The Miser*] was a miser born. . . .

He is such a complex character that the play admits of a number of different interpretations. It could be a farce; it could be a study of madness or a dispassionate analysis of jealousy.

Dorothy Knowles. *French Drama of the Inter-War Years* (London, George G. Harrap, 1967), pp. 65–66

The moving force in Crommelynck's drama is not an idea, a moral or doctrinal proof, but the literalness of life itself: a woman who loves love so much that she can no longer love herself, another woman who flees pleasure, a man who juggles with his desires. Crommelynck was born in an era that gave a *name* to hysteria in order to ward it off; his merit as a dramatist was probably to set aside the word and to keep the substance.

Certainly nothing could be more modern. Which does not mean fashionable. In fact, except for the years immediately after World War I, Crommelynck has never been fashionable. . . .

The very construction of his plays is free from the usual characteristics of the "play," because they drift into reverie, into garrulity, into idle chatter, and into childish stammering, without ever constituting an argument. How far we are from the beautiful constructions of an academic theater, in which cruelty proceeds along the innocent paths of rhetoric! Crommelynck himself yields to the delirium of lovers losing control of syntax or children playing with words. Sometimes, it must be said, these liberties alienate us from Crommelynck for a moment: sometimes his true language rings false. This is the only reservation I have about his plays.

Jean Duvignaud. *NRF*. May, 1970, pp. 777–78†

CUREL, FRANÇOIS DE (1854–1928)

No recent dramatist deserves higher esteem than that accorded to François de Curel, and every time the author of *The Fossils* and *The Guest* has a drama or comedy performed, we have the right to expect, if not a masterpiece, at least an honest, strong, and lofty work. This evening our expectations were once again not disappointed. What will the public think when it sees this play [*The Lion's Meal*] in which the dramatic interest is almost always buried under eloquent speeches that are sometimes admirable but often bombastic and sometimes trite, beneath rhetoric that is alternately revolutionary and Christian? I will not be so bold as to make a prediction. But whatever happens, Curel remains, in my opinion, a serious thinker whose ideas are perhaps not very personal but are very lofty; he will remain an honest craftsman whose art is spontaneous and austere. . . .

I was astonished . . . by [the] obvious indecision [of the conclusion] and, to tell the truth, by so much incoherence in the work of a thinker as serious as Curel. But if the ideas in this play lack coherence, they never lack depth, breadth, and general significance. And it is the task of a noble spirit to set into motion the most terrible and elusive problems of modern society—even if he does it rather in the manner of a cook who shakes the lettuce in a wire basket. [Nov. 27, 1897]

Catulle Mendès. *L'art au théâtre* (Paris,
Bibliothèque-Charpentier, 1900), Vol. III, pp. 448, 451†

More than anything else, Curel lacks genius. His plays are, suitably enough, very strong in thought and very timid in dramatic presentation. . . . Dramatic effects in his plays therefore remain almost completely subordinated to the exposition of ideas—an exposition that must be called excellent. The error for the dramatist is that the idea becomes more important than the character who expresses it. The *ideas* should be expressed only by the *action*—or, to say it another way, an *idea* in the theater has to be a character or a situation. The pseudo-ideas put in the mouths of characters can never be anything but opinions and must be subordinated to the characters. Ideas cannot be expressed *primarily* through the speeches of the characters. Ideas should be only the conscious content of the characters' actions. The unconscious support, which is more interesting, more important, and more forceful, is the character himself.

One can say, it is true, that Curel's characters are very well observed; one feels in particular that he took note of them very carefully and that his plays are carefully worked on. I admit very quietly that I prefer [Jarry's] *King Ubu*, but I have applauded with all my strength at performances of *The Lion's Meal* and *The New Idol*, and I have returned to see them several times. I have brought others to see them, too, because these plays, whatever their faults, are still far above the stupidities to which the theaters have accustomed us. And I have applauded so as not to provide a victory for the imbeciles, because certainly the role of intelligent people is to applaud, although they have the right to say whatever they like *later* in terms of reservations.

I do not think that plays like these can last, however; there is no *beauty* in them. . . . They make refined people exclaim, "How well-written that is!", just when the style ceases completely to be theatrically viable, without however providing any truly beautiful lines. . . . In spite of all these reservations, I admire Curel's very great—indeed, perfect—artistic honesty and his good faith, which has often moved me more than his plays. [1898]

André Gide. *Prétextes* (Paris, Mercure de France, 1913), pp. 84–86†

[For] Viscount François de Curel . . . playwriting is an avocation. His large fortune, extensive business and, above all, his keen interest in hunting, occupy the greater portion of his time. His ten plays cover a period of more than twenty years; the first eight were produced between 1892 and 1900, the ninth in 1906, the latest in 1914. Curel writes then to please himself, and if his efforts be judged according to the criterion of popular approval, he has not often pleased the public. As he himself once said, he was ideally situated to wait for ideas and the necessary impetus and inspiration to develop them. He has never been a "man of the theater," he was never forced to write down to his public. Following his own inclinations, and writing only when writing came naturally and easily, his work bears the imprint of great care both as to style and content. Abnormal cases in the psychology of crime, heredity, sex pathology, character analysis of the subtlest and most evasive sort, are what fill his strange plays. There is never any conscious effort to please or popularize, so that it is not difficult to see the reason of the failure of nearly every work. The love element, pure and simple, so cherished by all audiences, especially the French, is never introduced per se: he may at times tell a love story, but it is stripped of its romance, perhaps even of its legitimate appeal. This continual insistence upon the abnormal in human nature doubtless tells against Curel as a commentator on human nature in general, but we may always be sure to find in his works a sincere, masterly, and complete treatment of whatever strange corner or unfrequented byway of science the dramatist chooses to consider.

Barrett H. Clark. *Contemporary French Dramatists*
(Cincinnati, Stewart & Kidd, 1915), pp. 1–2

The master of the drama of ideas was François de Curel, one of those for whom the Théâtre Libre was created. He began there. Obviously, Curel's plays are not message plays, since as a rule he posed questions for argument without drawing conclusions. But his protestations must not be taken too literally when he defends himself against having put "ideas" into his plays and asks that they be taken simply as dramas of life—an adjunct to a hunting gentleman's fresh air. Ibsen raised the same objections against critics with respect to his own plays, and we know what talk means. In one of his forests Curel had a little hunting lodge whose shelves included the complete collection of *La revue philosophique*. It can be considered, symbolically, the laboratory of his plays.

It is not quite clear what qualities of a man of the theater were lacking in Curel. His plays are solid, occasionally powerful; *The Fossils* and *Inhuman Land*, the one at the beginning and the other at the end of his career, can be called masterpieces of workmanship. He wrote a good theatrical style, open, ventilated, solid. In *The Reverse of a Saint* and *The Soul Gone Mad* he created quite individual feminine characters, as living as those of any playwright of his time. He won his successes progressively against the resistance of the public, without making too great concessions to it, raising it to his own level almost by sheer physical force. And yet he soon became dated; inclusion in the repertory did not save him from that. He retained much more standing among people who read plays, and abroad, than among those who knew the theater. . . .

This fate derives from the dangerous game that he played: the game of the theater of ideas. Ideas automatically succeed one another, whereas emotions are eternal. Ideas have their specialists, the men who live with them. They have hardly more to do with men of the theater than the mistresses of an evening. And *The Lion's Meal, The New Idol, The Comedy of Genius* truly make the stage resemble a night school. Anyone who said of Curel, "He is a schoolteacher!" would be doing him an injustice, but he would be understood, at any rate, and he would establish a basis for discussion that would have to do with Curel and with the theater of ideas. [1938]

Albert Thibaudet. *French Literature from 1795 to
Our Era* (New York, Funk & Wagnalls, 1967),
p. 442

The drama of Curel represents a fusion of the thesis play, the prose tragedy, and the symbolic comedy. The conflict in it arises from a situation which suggests the possibility of action but which is complicated by psychological, intellectual, or spiritual involvements. In his first three or four plays the characters are caught in a labyrinth of contending passions; in those, like *The Lion's Meal*, in which he reaches the apex of his art, they are involved in a maze of human conflicts from which they can find a way out only by following the thread of clear reason. In the last group of plays, like *The Soul Gone Mad*, the maze becomes even more entangling, but here the author, merciful *deux ex machina*, intervenes, and smilingly guides his groping victims out of the dark. In all cases the dramatic interest lies in the fate of the *dramatis personae* rather than in the ideology they incarnate. . . .

Nearly all his men are self-portraits. Sometimes they show one aspect of his nature, and at other times other aspects. He reveals himself young and full of dreams at one time, grown old and disillusioned at another; idealistic in one case, realistic in another, and genially philosophical in others. He has identified himself with the creatures he has introduced into his theater from real life, and with those he has created out of pure cloth. Therein lies their strength, and also their weakness. Fortunately, they are saved from becoming abstract and arbitrary by the life-giving poetry which his spirit infuses into them. His is a virile, lucid, and eloquent poetry, full of moving parables, stirring tirades, lyrical outbursts, and symbolic connotations. Always, and everywhere, he is seen to be absorbed in the contemplation of the soul, one like unto his own, the soul of a man with a design for living whose social and spiritual concepts have become fused on the level of a common aristocratic ideal of human dignity and life.

S. A. Rhodes. *The Contemporary French Theater*
(New York, F. S. Crofts, 1942), pp. 86–87

The Fossils marked François de Curel's transition toward the world of ideas in which he was to crystallize his personality. Here he expressed himself in a lyrical naturalism consistent with his new preoccupations. Abandoning the scientific dissection of characters that was the heart of his method in his earlier plays, he began to have an ideal and a dream. . . . [In *The Lion's Meal*] he was still dependent on his own observations, but he could no longer deal with new experiences objectively and impartially. . . . Facts transformed themselves into ideas. These ideas became the framework into which he would fit reality in the future. These ideas haunted and obsessed him. He found them everywhere, without having sought them. At that moment, he asked nothing more of life and art than the confirmation of his ideas; he asked only for a means of expressing them. . . .

Since everything is relative, one might conclude that there are as many truths as ideas. This is why the thoughts of Curel strike us as transitory. They are not the systematic and logical construction of a mind seeking to prove a thesis. They are rather the sign of a mind divided into contradictory ideas. "Theater of Ideas" is therefore the best label to apply to his work.

Edith Braunstein. *François de Curel et le théâtre d'idées* (Geneva, Librairie E. Droz, 1962), pp. 103, 107†

DADIÉ, BERNARD BINLIN (1916–   )

IVORY COAST

In *The Circle of Days* the lyrical movement is different [from that of David Diop's poetry]. Humor, tenderness, and harmony with life have a different density. *The Circle of Days* is more like a Negro spiritual than a message bearing vindictive fire. It expresses a more secretive consciousness and inner life. But Africa is equally present, and as sometimes in the works of Langston Hughes, it is colored with an evangelical humor: "I thank you, God, for having created me Black,/for having made me/the sum of all sorrows. . . ."

Dadié's lyricism remains intimate and casual even when he makes accusations; he never appeals to the powers of hatred. . . .

Besides a tender humor, a joy in living seems to me to best define Dadié's originality. It is a joy that defies death: "Never a sad goodbye . . . Carry me/as if we were going to a celebration/hand in hand. . . ."

It is natural for the poet from the Ivory Coast to be sensitive to the magic of love. On this plane, Dadié attains the Dionysian fervor of David Diop. For Dadié, too, love is a participation in the elementary pulsations of life. . . .

The African charm that characterizes Dadié's stories also pervades his poetry, and leaves within us, as on his native sand, imprints of bare, agile feet!

René Depestre. PA. Dec., 1956, pp. 112–13†

Dadié belongs to the early post-First World War generation and for this reason his work reflects rather well the period of the true beginnings of the African evolution. Thus, he is a part of that group of intellectuals composed of doctors and teachers trained in Dakar who are commonly known as the "educated persons" of Negro Africa and who, to a large extent, make up our present-day governments. Consequently, he was caught up in the mesh of the movement, especially in politics, which shows us the constructive character of his book called *A Negro in Paris*. He thus follows the development of present-day Africa. . . .

His work is diverse and contrary and consists of legends, poems and novels, including [*A Negro in Paris*]. This book is splendid for its diversity of form: in some passages we find real poetic inspiration; in others, we have the impression that we are reading Voltaire or Montesquieu. It is well constructed and coherent, though in certain places the spirit of the work is somewhat lost.

I do not think this book seeks to transplant Western development —a part of whose culture we have acquired—into Africa. The issue is one involving her individual evolution confronted with Western culture, because it must be said that she can only evolve in terms of what she has received. This does not mean a mere copying but a synthesizing of her own in order to acquire her own individuality.

Joseph Miezan Bognini. *PA* (English ed.). 8, 1, 1961,
p. 156

As a counterpart of *Tales of Renart the Fox*, which belongs to the French Middle Ages, and the Cycle of Leuk the Hare, which belongs to the Senegalese soil, the Ivory Coast (together with [southern Togo and southern Dahomey]) offers us the Tales of the Spider.

Kacou Ananzè [in Dadié's *The Black Skirt*] personifies trickery, cleverness, and above all dishonesty and treachery, without the likeable and joyous traits that make Leuk and Renart so intensely vibrant. Kacou Ananzè incarnates the malicious spirit lying in wait for animals and men. Although surrounded by numerous other creatures, this character . . . creates the unifying element in this Book of Animals. Of the sixteen stories collected in *The Black Skirt*, ten are devoted to the spider. . . .

If Renart, Leuk, and their feathered and furry friends correspond approximately to their equivalents in nature, Kacou Ananzè, on the contrary, in no way shows the zoological features of the spider; he can reach the size of a man, bow down, stand up straight, and walk on two legs. His behavior is in every way reminiscent of that of the Ivory Coast peasant: he lives in a hut, cultivates his land, goes fishing, and does his shopping. Kacou Ananzè's anthropomorphism therefore precludes our classifying him as a zoological or mythical beast.

Roger Mercier and M. and S. Battestini. *Bernard*
Dadié (Paris, Fernand Nathan, 1964), p. 7†

[In *Boss of New York*] Dadié looks in an unusual way at "surprising America," and this "old west" about which "I thought everything had been said but which yielded things never revealed to anyone else." Dadié turns his gaze upon this land in which beauty and ugliness mingle without colliding. With a subtle knowledge of human psychology, he depicts this nation torn from a peaceful life by an infernal quest for supremacy. He explicitly describes this nation's shifting profile, letting America's whole ridiculous pretension be reflected through his naïveté.

Paris and New York do not make Dadié feel disillusioned, strangely uprooted, or sadly nostalgic. On the contrary, his trips allow him to observe minutely the "immense absurdity" surrounding him. From his deliberations there arises a grain of humor sufficient to set up that liberating distance which makes the "Negro," formerly condemned to being observed and kept at a distance, into a human being who observes and judges in turn. Dadié is a remarkable manifestation in literature of the movement toward awareness as a prelude to liberation.

Boss of New York, for some readers a simple "chronicle" of a trip, is actually an amusing satire revealing the unknown, fragile underbelly of Yankee power.

C. Quillateau. Bernard Binlin Dadié: L'homme et
l'œuvre (Paris, Présence Africaine, 1967), pp. 25–26†

[*A Negro in Paris*] is cast in the form of a traveler's book in which a foreign visitor writes a detailed and presumably "objective" description of the interesting customs and manners of his hosts. *A Negro in Paris* is extended irony, Dadié placing his main character, a West African, in the reverse role of many a rather smug European traveler to West Africa. Whereas the European would describe the quaint behavior of Africans for home consumption so that others might "understand" them, the narrator of this work describes Parisian mores with the same critical eye for relationships among minute, often ridiculous details. . . .

Dadié's basic theme seems to be that the Parisian is really a human being after all, and worthy of study, having a history and traditions which he reveres, gods whom he worships. And by drawing comparisons between the West African and the Parisian, the author suggests that Africans are as good as Europeans, or that Europeans are as bad as Africans, however the case might appear. The core problem is the understanding of persons of one culture by those of another.

Austin J. Shelton. ECr. Fall, 1970, pp. 217, 219

Like so many other French-speaking Africans, Dadié is continuously asserting the beauty of African life as a constant reminder that colonialism cheated the black man out of his heritage. . . . *Climbié*, like the other prose works of its family, portrays the quality of African childhood experiences. The general outlines of the pattern are common: tough elementary education, dogged by poverty, sadistic schoolmastership, and so on; life among the many relatives in the African extended family; childhood ambitions; secondary education which is perpetually haunted by the fear of failure; the day one sets out in pursuit of one's vision; new experiences in the encounter with white authority that invariably suspects and fears the "educated native."

Nothing spectacular happens to Climbié until he has finished secondary school and is working—towards the end of the book.

His development is like the muted process of plant growth in which the seed germinates, pushes through, always in an upward thrust, until it blossoms and lays bare its foliage, now exposed to wind, sun, rain, insects that lie in wait for its juices, in a way it never happened before. As with the plant, things happen to Climbié; he never "happens" to them, until he reacts to white domination once he is back home from Senegal. His development is fully rendered by the marvellously subtle shift in Dadié's style, especially in Part II; the style "grows up" with Climbié. And yet, again, like a plant, he is part of the landscape which we view through him. Dadié has portrayed for us, often in a volatile idiom that reflects his mercurial personality, a human and physical landscape that is alive, at once friendly and hostile, and indifferent.

Ezekiel Mphahlele. Introduction to Bernard Dadié, Climbié (London,
Heinemann Educational Books, 1971), pp. viii–ix

DAMAS, LÉON-GONTRAN (1912–　　)

FRENCH GUIANA

For a long time I have hesitated to write about *Pigments*—not because its merits as poetry are negligible, but because it is primarily a testimony: a Negro poet tells us his reactions to White Society. . . . This point of view explains the tenseness of Damas's tone, the violence of an inspiration that makes the poet defend himself against others' curiosity and suffer the scars of his condition. These scars are also the reasons for his pride, since he feels he is a Negro and asserts himself as a Negro. Because of this self-assertion, Damas's lyricism coincides with his analysis of what it means to be a poet, a central theme in contemporary poetry. Damas—who has, so to speak, more enemies than anyone else because of his race—also nourishes a more forceful hatred of all forms of oppression. . . .

The Negro has been exploited and is no longer sure of having his own consciousness. What black intellectual has not been corrupted by a certain desire for "assimilation," an attitude that disgusts Damas and makes him reject his childhood. . . . But the poet's very tragedy leads him to make protests that often go beyond his intentions: "I always feel ready to foam with rage/against everything that surrounds me/against everything that prevents me from ever being/a man." Certainly I understand this language only too clearly. But listen, Damas, what prevents you from being a man is also what prevents me from being one, and the color of my skin or of yours is not really important! Your poems are ours, as is your sense of lost grandeur, a feeling that can be experienced by anyone, man or nation, who is sensitive enough. Is not the knowledge that we share the same enemies the most beautiful reason for us to like one another?

Léon Gabriel Gros. CS. Sept., 1937, pp. 511–12†

For the most part, the French Negro poetry with which we are most familiar now (e.g., the recent work of Léopold Sédar Senghor and Aimé Césaire) is *engagée* [committed] in a European sense, supporting the Negro cause everywhere while often criticizing "white" civilization, and it owes a great debt to French culture and language; but it has its own idiom and standard of excellence that have developed from a new sense of Negritude bursting free. This poetry looks, at last, to Africa and speaks from an African heritage over the corpse, the still warm corpse, of colonialism.

However, *Pigments* is largely another thing, a little classic from another time. It is the poetry of a bitter Negro citizen of pre-war France —Damas, by the way, was among the first of the militant French Negro poets: Aimé Césaire, for instance, did not begin writing until the Forties. The result is often that kind of passionate social protest characteristic of the Thirties. . . . One is reminded more of Langston Hughes than of Senghor. But that is not necessarily bad, and besides, not all of the poems in [the present edition of *Pigments*] are products of the Thirties or a Thirties mind-set. Moreover, less subject to dating is the poet's art; it, like the whole idea of French Negro poetry or American jazz, is a product of a cultural blend; and the best analogy for Damas's art (and one that he insists on) is to jazz. That is, Damas's technique, whether his goal is direct social utterance or, just as characteristic, disinterested poetic utterance, or is a combination of the two, is best described as a jazz technique—endless theme and variation, incremental repetition, improvisation, and a kind of verbal counterpoint that adds up to a most impressive expression of a trapped man's Negritude.

C. E. Nelson. BA. Autumn, 1963, p. 476

Co-founder with Senghor and Césaire of the Negritude school, Léon-Gontran Damas was born in Cayenne, Guyane (French Guiana), South America. After completing his secondary studies at the Lycée Schoelcher in Fort-de-France, Martinique, he went on to Paris, where he studied law and met Césaire and Senghor. In Paris, Damas was an habitué of all the places frequented by blacks from many countries of the world who had been attracted to this intellectual "Mecca" and bastion of individual freedom. . . . Being a poor student, M. Damas lived intensely the intellectual and moral tragedy of his race, undergoing the identity crisis common to all his fellow blacks. His poetic sensitivity made him all the more vulnerable to that tragedy.

Damas's poetic works include *Pigments, Graffiti*, and *Black Label*. His poetry, in contrast to that of Césaire and Senghor, is unsophisticated. It finds expression through everyday words, common or noble, most often those words and expressions of the common people, colored at times by an outmoded gracefulness and the use of certain Creole terms, and all of it subjected to the rhythm of the *tam tam*, for with Damas, rhythm takes precedence over melody. Being unsophisticated, Damas's poetry is direct, brutish, and at times brutal; and not infrequently it is charged with an emotion disguised as humor, a characteristically Negro humor that has been the black man's saving grace in a harsh and cruel world in which he has had, for years, no other defense or technique of survival.

Edward A. Jones. In Edward A. Jones, ed., *Voices of Négritude* (Valley Forge, Pa., Judson, 1971), pp. 63–64

When *Pigments* appeared in 1937, it caused a sensation. Claude McKay's lines, "Am I not Africa's son, Black of that black land where black deeds are done," which Damas used as an epigraph, and the title's unmistakable allusion to color, were underlined in Robert Desnos' introduction. . . . "With Damas, there is no question of his subject matter nor how he treats it, of the sharpness of his blade nor the status of his soul. Damas is Negro and insists on his Negro-ness and on his condition as a Negro. . . . These poems are . . . also a song of friendship offered in the name of his whole race by my friend, Damas the Negro, to all his white brothers." . . .

As for Desnos' characterizing *Pigments* as Damas' "song of friendship . . . to his white brothers," this is true only by the most generous extrapolation. Why sweeten the pill? The short poems of *Pigments* are a bitter testimony, variations on themes of *pain*. They do reveal compassion for fellow-sufferers other than the Black man (the Jews under Hitler, for example). But nowhere in these pages does this reader find, nor does she ask for, "a song of friendship." If anger, tenacity and a certain despair are the impact of this first book of poems, this first major work of the Negritude group, they are valid, sufficient and important in and by themselves. . . .

"Et Cetera," which ends the book *Pigments* . . . reflects its historical moment. Senegalese soldiers were long known as among the best in
the French Army. Here the poet exhorts them to fight for their *own*
independence, "to invade Senegal," rather than defend their colonial
masters against the Germans. Doubtless this was among the Damas
poems recited in Baoulé translation by rioting African draft resisters in
the Ivory Coast in 1939. As a result, *Pigments* was quickly banned
throughout French West Africa, an early indication of the revolutionary
proclivities that the later poetry of Negritude, particularly Césaire's and
David Diop's, would demonstrate even more.

Ellen Conroy Kennedy. Black World. Jan., 1972,
pp. 8–11

DESNOS, ROBERT (1900–1945)

Verbal delirium reaches its probable climax in some of the poems of
Robert Desnos. During the years following the dadaist crisis, Desnos
applied himself chiefly to forming linguistic aggregates by simple mechanical procedures, aggregates for which he did not intend to be responsible, which were meant to be the outcome of an anonymous activity,
and whose poetic properties were to be discerned only subsequently.
It was a determined attempt to let words think for themselves; the
results could be studied later. It was a fishing for miracles; but miracles
are rare, and the method proved disappointing, at least for the reader.

Later, dreams supplied Desnos with the equivalent of an object, of
a subject matter, however evanescent, whose existence was to be subjected by words. In the sequence entitled "The Shadows" (in *Body and
Belongings*) beautiful streaks of remarkably coherent dream poetry
evoke the obsessive presence of those fabulous beings which in dreams
take the place of material things and wander through the whole field of
thought. But in Robert Desnos, the impact of the automatisms and the
inertia of words "at liberty" produced the ultimate consequences of the
"immense facility" inherent in surrealism; under the seeming discipline
of the alexandrine or even of the rhymed or assonanced quatrain, a
voice whispers or shouts a mad monologue, in which images drawn from
the common store of romanticism, from Musset and Hugo to Apollinaire, emerge like strange islets. It is the final deception—the known
and the unknown are mingled in a grimacing chaos, seemingly compounded of the fantasies of an overflowing collective unconscious. An
engine is running in a vacuum, the mind having broken with words,

having left them to all sorts of irregular loves which seem to produce a factitious and soulless lyrical exaltation. The experiment is interesting and was worth attempting, but once is enough. [1933]

Marcel Raymond. *From Baudelaire to Surrealism* (London, Methuen, 1970), pp. 277–78

There is a kind of solid if unspoken link among all those who met and admired Robert Desnos; they share a common pride. They can never mention their friend's name without feeling more generous, more rebellious, more energized by his qualities: a fraternal solitude that had something rough about it, and an innate attitude that invincibly drew him as if by a magnet toward the dangerous pole of things.

He could breathe only in a universe of legend, and of all who participated in surrealism during its great years he was one of the first to restore a legendary brilliance to every action and every object in our daily lives. Incapable of compartmentalizing his universe, incapable of setting up a frontier between life and dreams, when he would stroll his eyes were wide open to both domains at once, both mingled and enriched with a mind capable of great metamorphoses.

The same lost paradise that Nerval pursued until his death, the same ghost of a woman who is never named, can be sensed in Desnos's attitude and in some of his poetry, but transposed into a more violent and despairing register, which makes him less universal and also more vulnerable.

It would undoubtedly be absurd to attempt to predict the future reception of Desnos's work, because today we are still totally blinded by the first flames of surrealism. But it is impossible to believe that the powerful human electricity with which some of his poems are charged could be lost without having been fully transmitted.

Georges Neveux. *Confluences.* Sept., 1945, p. 679†

For two years Desnos played a role in the Resistance. How could it have been otherwise? . . . Every one of humanity's crucial hours has given rise to a poet's cry. Desnos cried in our night that liberty would return. And perhaps with a premonition that he would not be there to welcome the liberators awaited by an entire nation, he shouted in advance across the Atlantic Ocean, the English Channel, and the Mediterranean Sea: "Hello, hello, with all my heart hello." . . .

On February 22, 1944, a telephone call from a well-informed friend warned Desnos that the Gestapo would arrive in a few minutes. He refused to flee, for fear that his wife Youki would be taken in his place. When the Gestapo arrived, he was ready, ready for anything, with a smile. . . .

Youki protested so unremittingly to the various branches of the German police that she succeeded in having Robert's name crossed off the list of deportees. A few days later a high-ranking officer in the Gestapo was dining in a Paris restaurant with a few writers and journalists who worked for the Vichy press. He was being questioned about his responsibilities, about concentration camps and the famous people who could be found in them. He said that at Compiègne there were intellectuals, professors, doctors—even, he added, a poet. "His name is Robert Desnos. I do not think he will be deported." At that moment, one of the men at the table stood up. "Not deported!" he shouted. "You should shoot him. He is a dangerous man, a terrorist, a communist." The speaker was Alain Laubreaux. . . .

On April 27 Desnos was among the prisoners sent to Buchenwald. Ten days later the gates of Paris were thrown open to the Allied armies. Alain Laubreaux now lives in Franco's Spain. But if he ever sets foot in France again...

Pierre Berger. Robert Desnos (Paris, Pierre Seghers, 1949), pp. 86–89†

It is Robert Desnos who left a lasting mark on the practice [of sleep induced by hypnosis]. He was passionately devoted to that activity. . . . Nobody but Desnos charged headlong down every pathway leading to the marvelous. . . .

All those who witnessed these daily plunges made by Desnos into what was truly *unknown* were themselves carried away by a sort of vertigo. Everyone hung on what Desnos might say, on what he might trace feverishly on the paper. I think particularly of his puns, whose lyrical nature was totally original, and which he could produce one after another for a long time, at a prodigious pace. These puns, which were supposedly the result of a telepathic communication with Marcel Duchamp, who was then in New York, were collected by Desnos in *Body and Belongings* under the title "Rrose Sélavy."

I spoke of a prodigious pace. What was even more prodigious was Desnos's ability to transport himself at will, instantly, from the mediocrity of daily life right into the midst of a region filled with illumination and poetic effusion. Undoubtedly, a book is not the most favorable repository for poems of this kind. On the printed page, the facile, even trivial, puns seem to mar the effects: these poems are so spontaneous—they are 100 percent inspired, irrepressible, and inexhaustible—that critics do not know how to approach them. It goes without saying that "literature" and its criteria have nothing to do with such poetry.

André Breton. Entretiens [avec André Parinaud] (Paris, Gallimard, 1952), pp. 84–85†

The behavior of the surrealists disgusts me. . . . I would make only one exception—Robert Desnos. Robert was a very decent fellow; I had a lot of good laughs with him, and we met for drinks in a bar I had baptized "The Eye of Paris," because it was on Rue de Rivoli, under the arcades, two steps from the Place de la Concorde, and you could see everyone in Paris walk by without leaving your stool. . . .

Robert was a jovial companion. We did not talk about automatic writing, and the two or three times I tried to ask him about that disastrous gift the surrealists tried to load him down with, he just winked at me and gave me a funny smile, like someone who could tell the whole story if he wanted to! That is why I never took Desnos seriously as a medium, no more than I took Max Jacob seriously as a mystic. Desnos was a great poet. A genuine poet. Reread "Saint-Merri Quarter" [in *Fortunes*]. It is in the same vein as François Villon. One was from the Saint-Jacques district, the other from the Saint-Martin district. Left bank, right bank: the same thing.

Blaise Cendrars. *Blaise Cendrars vous parle* (Paris,
Denoël, 1952), pp. 49, 51–52†

André Breton's predilection for esoteric doctrines led to a new orientation for surrealism, and Desnos consequently broke with the movement. That break, combined with changes that had taken place in his personal life, led Desnos toward a more objective, more fraternal, and more popular kind of poetry, which was accompanied by a deeper philosophical understanding and which, in turn, led him toward a rationalist and Cartesian materialism and a dialectical conception of nature and life.

The intense delight in living that Desnos felt at that time was expressed in poems that were simple and clear, written in a precise and musical rhythm, perfectly easy to approach.

World War II, which made Desnos's poetry more active, also brought a soberness to his work. One of the most extraordinary phenomena of French poetry written during those four arduous years was the return to classical form. This return deeply affected Desnos's poetry, which became slightly hermetic without thereby breaking the link that united it to men.

Death was to interrupt brutally a creative evolution that was ceaselessly hurling Desnos's poetry, in both content and form, toward unpredictable adventures, but adventures whose human meaning cannot be doubted. Desnos's entire work, after all, confirms his message of confidence, hope, and love of life, a message that remains his clearest and most moving affirmation.

Rosa Buchole. *L'évolution poétique de Robert Desnos*
(Brussels, Académie Royale de Langue et de
Littérature Françaises, 1956), pp. 220–21†

The poetry of Robert Desnos in an Exorcism. This is partly to say that although he was one of the several co-inspirers of and early participants in the Surrealist movement, and one of the most admired experimenters with the techniques of Automatic Writing and trance-writing in its early "laboratory" period, Desnos has a somewhat curious relationship to it. From the outset, Desnos opposed several tendencies we may associate with the less attractive aspects of Surrealism.

In 1926, three years before Desnos dropped out of the Surrealist circle at the provocation of André Breton, Louis Aragon had written: "The vice called Surrealism is identical to the ardent and unruly use of the omnipotent poetic image." In even his earlier poems . . . Desnos appears dissatisfied with the Surrealist exploration of imagery. In one of the best-known of his early poems, "The Spaces inside Sleep," Desnos speaks of his desire to experience his passions with a non-literary purity. . . . Already, Desnos seems to be accusing Surrealism of having habits; of involving not only a certain imagistic process, but also a predictable kind or *class* of imagery. . . .

Desnos's diction follows suit. It is unique in its combinations of the lyrical and the low, dignified and ecstatic, hilarious and serious, romantic and colloquial. . . . In the later poems these exorcisms extend beyond a boredom with "poetical" approaches to technique, to the more dangerous realm of officially approved poetic "feeling." This is especially risky in view of the fact that a good part of his work is love poetry, many of his love poems being among the most admired of the *genre* in France. Even in this haven of human illusion, one senses Desnos rigorously ridding himself of traces of empty poetry. One result is that, in the face of thousands upon thousands of relatively conventional love poems (and at least a million awful songs) Desnos asserts that the health and strength of passion *depends* on absence as well as presence.

Michael Benedikt. Introduction to Robert Desnos,
22 Poems (Santa Cruz, Cal., Kayak, 1971), pp. 5–6

[In his early poems] Desnos's voice vibrates even when playing games whose rules were apparently arbitrarily drawn up. His voice collides with the limitations of language; this voice refuses to lose a single particle of life. Therefore, I do not share Pierre Berger's opinion: "From 1922 to 1923 Desnos devoted himself solely to experiments and poetic research. Needless to say, he knew that the road he was taking led to a dead end, but was not that dead end necessary?" . . . To claim, as Berger does, that an artist consciously chooses a dead end seems to me an insult hurled at the artist, even if the critic's purpose is to provide, a posteriori, some sort of excuse for the artist's "failures." . . . Desnos practiced his craft every day. He wrote poems. Every poem renewed his poetic life, even if the poem were a series of puns. Life is too short to set up dead ends for oneself. Creation is too difficult to engage in it with no goal in mind.

Therefore, it is exciting to follow all the experiments made by Desnos, trying to break down the resistance of a material more ephemeral than any other—language. The multiplicity of his creations, the multiplicity of the rockets set off by his mind, the elegance of his pranks, and the metaphorical resonances of his puns formed the basis of his poetic universe. It is true that he yielded to the fashions of the period, but fashions can be liberating for people of talent. It is true that he sometimes abused his fluency by playing with numbers and musical notes. It is true that he sometimes leaned toward a system, although he himself was unsystematic. Nevertheless, his poetic temperament could easily adapt itself to these escapades.

René Plantier. *Europe*. May–June, 1972, pp. 67–68†

DIB, MOHAMMED (1920–   )

ALGERIA

The Big House is a work of high literary merit. The descriptions, never gratuitous, are handled with disconcerting skill. Words vibrate as well as depict; invocations to hunger are hallucinatory chants. . . . The curses of Aïni, the mother, are heartrending in their sadness. . . .

To live this book and understand it, we must not stay at the door of *The Big House*. By resisting a background that is unfamiliar, by looking for a plot to find out "where the writer is leading us," we run the risk of simultaneously missing the poetry and the fictional elements. We must be willing to cross the Mediterranean, to leave the Algeria of the tourists, the European quarters, the homes of the rich Arabs, and to restrict ourselves to Dar Sbitar.

Jacques Richet. *Esprit*. April, 1953, pp. 646†

In his trilogy [*Algeria*], strongly reminiscent of John Dos Passos' *U.S. A.*, Dib attempted to paint a huge fresco of Algeria on the eve of World War II. Through the eyes of the young Omar, whose adventures give pattern and unity to the trilogy, the reader understands the material and moral distress of the Moslem population and the underlying unrest which was soon to set Algeria on fire. In fact, the real hero of the trilogy is Algeria herself, just as America was the hero of Dos Passos' masterpiece, and the slow moral, intellectual and emotional awakening of Omar symbolizes the birth of an Algerian conscience, eager to be recognized, intent upon gaining such recognition by whatever means are necessary. . . .

In the first volume, *The Big House*, Dib gives us a vivid description of the squalid conditions of the working classes, trapped in urban tenements, unable to live a morally or materially decent life. . . .

In the second volume, *The Fire*, Dib has moved his young hero to the country where he becomes a witness to the moral and material poverty of the native peasants, the *fellahs*. Again, he discovers that his countrymen are not happy and, as the volume comes to an end, he silently watches the start of the fire which will soon spread throughout the whole country; "a fire has been started which will never extinguish. It will keep on burning, slowly, blindly, until its bloody flames embrace the whole country with their sinister glow."

With the last volume, *The Loom*, we return to the city. Omar, now a young adolescent, begins his apprenticeship as a carpet weaver, as Dib himself once was. The fire which began in the country is now spreading to the urban centers as well, as the *fellahs*, hungry and bare, invade the city to join miseries with their urban countrymen. As the trilogy comes to an end, Omar, now of age, stands out clearly as the symbol of increasing Algerian unrest. He has seen the birth and development of the rebellious spirit of the native population while he has gained, at the same time, a personal awareness of the wretched conditions of Moslem life. In the course of his mental, spiritual, emotional and physical growth, Dib's young protagonist has learned the real meaning of human dignity. He will not rest until he has achieved, for himself and his fellowmen, this new self-awareness, self-respect, and individuality.

Georges J. Joyaux. *YFS*. Summer, 1959, pp. 34–35

Perhaps from [my experiences during World War II] I can understand the poet of *Guardian Shadow*, and from my own barracks of Croucy-sur-Ourcq I can follow Dib into the Algerian war through the Aurès he creates with words, through the hills of dried grass and fire. . . . In 1960 when the Algerian poet says "Aurès," no one can prevent him from envisioning images of that region of Algeria. Whatever the weight laws may carry, there are no laws that can repress the sadness, the invincible sadness. . . .

Guardian Shadow is a book with two windows, one of which opens onto Algeria and the other onto Europe—Antwerp, Bordeaux, Paris. Perhaps one has to have crossed these European streets, these river banks in our climate in order to appreciate his poems about Algeria in which "The new mint has blossomed,/the fig tree has borne its fruits"; in order to understand these poems with all the nostalgia of a man for whom "Paris in the dark is a kind of hell"; in order to recapture these poems with Dib, this companion we have encountered in European cities. And suddenly I feel that he is no longer a stranger to me, not because of the language that we share, but because of the vision, the *illuminations*, in Rimbaud's sense of the word, by means of which he welcomes me to his domain and offers me the hospitality of his village; I feel that I am no longer a stranger to him when he describes to me what is natural to him. . . .

I am not sure that I really understand him, that I have a right to understand him; I am surprised by his hospitality in letting me enter [through his poems] the intimacy of a house in which I feel that I am some sort of desecrator.

Oh Mohammed, why is there this confidence between you and me? What do we have that does not separate us? And he smiles for the first time and answers, "The future."

Aragon. LetF. Jan. 26–Feb. 1, 1961, p. 10†

Spurred by his desire to see things clearly, Dib has tried to present the evolution of Algerian society by revealing that the people are not prisoners of daily life: they transcend it through their great desire for freedom. Dib dreamed of being the Balzac of Algerian literature, but a Balzac transformed by Marxism. To be sure, those who read [*The Big House*] today are disturbed by the belabored style, the homilies, and the certainty of a man who knows he is right. But after all, Dib has developed since then; he did not lock himself into the simplistic realism of his first novel. . . .

The trilogy *Algeria* is in its own way a history of Algerian daily life, made of thinking, and growing self-awareness. At the very time when people were debating whether there were such an entity as the Algerian nation, Dib demonstrated its existence. Historians will perhaps find much of interest in this social panorama. . . .

Like the nineteenth-century novel, the Algerian realistic novel has a chronological, linear narrative, vivid characters, and a functional organization of time and space in which objects have a well-defined place. But those objects do not exist for themselves; their role is to express human concerns, to reflect the social milieu.

Abdelkabir Khatibi. Le roman maghrébin (Paris,
François Maspéro, 1968), pp. 56–57†

Dib opens *God in Barbary* with a dialogue of ideas. Since ideas are necessarily less personal than characters, the result is that, instead of helping the reader to separate the characters, the first chapter only merges them in the reader's mind. . . .

In this poetic novel, also in some ways a detective novel, the opening chapter is not the only one in which there is a dialogue of ideas; the most shopworn ideas clash with the most utopian, and Marxism clashes with a Tolstoyism that dreams of salvation through the most deprived *fellah*, just as the writer of *Resurrection* dreamed of salvation through the Russian peasant. Dib does not need to take sides for us to perceive considerable confusion in the minds of some of the Algerians obsessed by the problems of their country and its future. . . . Those Algerians misunderstand what is essential. . . .

Dib strongly feels that "To be or not to be" . . . must be interpreted for the time being in his country as "To eat or not to eat." . . . "In Algeria, hunger kills thought before it can be born." . . . The injustice of a divided society is that the Pasteurs, the Prousts, and the Debussys fail to develop properly because nothing can compensate for the intellectual inadequacy of their original environment and the inadequacy of their education. And in the poorest nations, the Pasteurs will never even learn the multiplication tables, the Debussys will never even learn the scale, and the Prousts will never even learn the alphabet. Are the victims themselves completely innocent? Of course not: "By living so long in the darkness, we have ended up by signing a pact with the monsters and worms that take refuge in the darkness. This pact must now be broken, and we must dare to look at the daylight, to stare directly at our sun in Barbary."

André Wurmser. *LetF*. Sept. 23–24, 1970, p. 8†

[*He Who Remembers the Sea*] paints a mural of horror which is purposely free of realistic blood and gristle. In a "Postface" to *He Who Remembers the Sea*, Dib admits that he has tried to create a legendary, timeless commentary on the Algerian war in the style of Picasso's *Guernica*—but in words. Even had he not told us of his indebtedness to Picasso, the frequent references to the Minotaurs in the streets (French troops? Forces of evil? The universal war machine? Or, perhaps, even Minotaurs?) and to the strange proliferating city would suggest the kinship.

The novel—if, indeed, it is a novel and not a prose poem—hovers tantalizingly between the logically and historically explicable and the hallucinatory world of the illogical and the unknown. The legendary, millennial quality of the poem-novel is communicated by the author's abrupt transitions to the image of the sea which is a mother image and a life-death image throughout. . . . The ageless backdrop to the prose-poem is the sea whence man came . . . and the theme of the four elements is the common denominator of most of the scenes or "states of soul" of the novel which deal repeatedly with water, space, earth, stone, stars, and flames. . . .

Dib invents a fantastic environment of daily miracles. The place he invents in his poetic prose, and the poems which are basically marginalia to that prose, is new to us, but he makes it our natural habitat. . . . He deliberately places us in a series of images and a syntax which are disruptive and disquieting; yet, at the same time, he reassures us of the fundamental integrity of his poetic world by steeping it in the eternal elements and the familiar primordial objects of the universe.

Eric Sellin. *JNALA*. Sept., 1971, pp. 52–54

DIOP, BIRAGO (1906–   )

SENEGAL

Birago Diop is indeed an enchanter, because he is a storyteller, a real one, a member of the race that is on the road to extinction in European countries, one of those people who grab hold of you, whether you like it or not, to make you see miracles through their eyes and listen to secrets through their ears. . . .

On some evenings—"for in the black country, tales are not to be told until nightfall"—the old storyteller Amadou Koumba told Diop tales he had already heard as a child; but Amadou also taught him others and embellished them with maxims and proverbs. Diop absorbed them, around the fire, while the tom-tom rolled, and the crowd beat on inverted calabashes in time to the chants. And the stories and legends bore fruit [in *Tales of Amadou Koumba*].

That is how we—the deaf, blind, busy, and gloomy—get to know Fari the She-Ass, Golo the Monkey, Kakatar the Chameleon, Koupou-Kala the Crab, Bouki the Hyena, Leuk the Hare. . . .

There is a whole universe in which human beings play an almost exclusively subordinate role. It is a whole world—a world that is very young and very old. It is old because it has wisdom and humor, but young because of its new ways of looking at things, and that extra-keen, dazzling faculty of perception which you only have at the dawn of life but which you retain if you are a poet.

Magdeleine Paz. *PA*. No. 5, 1948, pp. 890–91†

The first virtue of the Negro-African storyteller, as of any true artist, is to cling to reality, to *make things live*. . . . Birago Diop, following the model of Amadou Koumba, depicts the men and animals of Africa such as we perceive them. Not only men and animals, but also the "bush" with its poor villages and immense sandy spaces. . . . But, beyond the silhouettes of the living, the storyteller reveals their *essences*, those inner realities that are their miseries and their dreams, their work and their worries, their passions. He shows us the role played by food in these villages that are periodically threatened by drought and famine.

Because nothing that *exists* is foreign to him, the Negro-African storyteller integrates into the traditional subjects those of today, especially those of "colonial" life: the Commandant de Cercle, the School, the Hospital, the Machine, the Marabout and the Missionary, trading and money. . . .

As a faithful disciple of Amadou Koumba, Diop renews his links with tradition and revives ancient fables and stories—in the original spirit and the original style. He renews them, however, by translating them into French, with an art that, while respectful of the genius of the French language—this "language of graciousness and courtesy"—at the same time preserves all the qualities of the Negro-African languages.

Léopold Sédar Senghor. Preface to Birago Diop, Les nouveaux contes d'Amadou Koumba (Paris, Présence Africane, 1958), pp. 14–15, 22†

There is as much cunning and malice in [Diop's stories] as there is in Aesop and La Fontaine. One must hardly ever allow oneself to deviate from Nature and realism in order to please Man, even when confronting him with hard truths. With Diop's latest book [*New Tales of Amadou Koumba*] we have to deal with a three-fold moral criticism.

This is proved by his story called "The Bone." The central character is Mor Lame; his gluttony is not explained but is *dissected and exposed* with a skill which the reader should be allowed to unravel for himself. But will one say that the author does not mean to do the same for Moussa? Moussa is "the more-than-brother," the "Bok-m' bar" and incarnates parasitism which is the cancer of African families. . . .

The third complex criticism concerns the authority of Serigne-le-Marabout (a witch-doctor), against which nobody seems to have the right to rebel. This authority incarnates a shocking tradition which, alas, still exists. . . . Serigne is a cad, an evil-doer whose many negligences are castigated in the story "The Excuse." . . .

Must it be repeated for the benefit of those who have not yet understood, that the significance of Negro-African literature lies in the disinterment of abolished Negro cultural values? Birago Diop, certainly as wise as his master, Amadou Koumba, sets into his stories more than one jewel of Negro-African speech. . . . The author is equally a poet, and he proves that in his latest work he has mastered the secret of writing, which is perhaps the most difficult of all diagnoses.

Olympe Bhêly-Quénum. PA (English ed.). 8, 1, 1961, pp. 160–61

The *griot*'s [storyteller's] function in the community was as much to instruct as to entertain, and many of [the *Tales of Amadou Koumba*] are fables, pointing a clear moral, particularly those in which the characters are humans. This moral is often as direct as in traditional folktales. . . . In "The Inheritance," we have the most elaborate allegory of all the tales—a sort of multiple fable, with several layers of meaning. All man's existence and its many possible vicissitudes are illustrated symbolically by the fantastic adventures of the three sons in their pilgrimage. At the same time their father's mysterious bequests contain a message about community living, just sharing and a wise assessment of the value of worldly goods.

Sometimes Birago Diop's tales seem to have a more doubtful moral. Are we to believe that loyalty and diligence in a lifetime of service are always repaid by neglect and cruelty in old age? Is a good turn always repaid by evil? Is it so that we should rely on Falsehood if we are to get on in this life, as obviously Truth is a bad guide? And what of the more tragic element of "Little-Husband," where we see a love that dare not declare itself hound its object to death? In these tales, and particularly in those where conventional ethics are cynically reversed, Birago Diop adds the more sophisticated element of irony to the straightforward morality of the traditional fable, and proves himself more than the mere mouth-piece of his household *griot*. Just as he showed up many of the foibles of human nature in his portraits of man and animals, so here too there is satire, sometimes more subtle and deep-seated, of human and social weaknesses.

Dorothy S. Blair. Foreword to Birago Diop, *Tales of Amadou Koumba* (London, Oxford University Press, 1966), pp. xiii–xiv

Birago Diop, Master Griot, was born in 1906 at Ouakam, a suburb of Dakar. After completing his education at Toulouse and writing most of the poetry published later as *Lures and Lights*, he was a qualified veterinary doctor and, returning to Africa, he met Amadou Koumba N'Gom, the old griot, whose stories became the inspiration for almost all Diop's future work. . . .

His work as a veterinary officer, requiring an objective approach to men and animals, tempers the passion which he might feel through his involvement in the movement for African freedom. It also gives him the sense of dispassionate commitment to the problems, needs and weaknesses of men and animals which is expressed in his stories. In return, his involvement and feeling for animals and men must surely temper the clinical attitude of the practician. This, too, is seen in his stories; everything, good or evil, is approached with the same equable humility and humour.

Like La Fontaine, Diop has spent his life in close contact with men and animals, and in observing them. The "tales," so he tells us in the introduction to *Tales of Amadou Koumba*, were written to fulfil his own need to re-establish contact with his own country while he was in exile in France and then, later, when he was traveling through the Sudan, Upper Volta and Mauretania as veterinary officer and in Tunis as ambassador. Apart from the similarity of the vagabond life, there are many other comparisons to be made between the seventeenth century fabulist and Diop. In the first place, they share the same interest in popular, traditional tales. They have, too, the same capacity for objective but charitable assessment of human behaviour. Finally, and the point at which they meet as artists, both have a profound understanding and feeling for the rhythm and vocabulary of the French language; Diop, too, introduces African dialects and onomatopoeia into the stories to give greater effect, using them to establish links with the popular, oral tradition which is the source of his inspiration.

A. C. Brench. *The Novelists' Inheritance in French Africa* (London, Oxford University Press, 1967), pp. 14–15

[In *Tales of Amadou Koumba*] the woman is placed under guardianship, first that of her father, then that of her husband. Many tales illustrate the unlimited powers of the father. The father disposes of his daughter as he pleases; he can marry her off to anyone he likes. He does not have to answer to anyone. He does not take the trouble, in any of the tales in the book, to consult his daughter on the choice of her future husband. Tradition makes it the daughter's duty to bow to her father's will, as she later will have to submit to her husband's wishes when he gets the notion to take other wives. In "An Errand" Mor, Penda's father, decides to find an intelligent husband for his daughter; yet he does not choose the best way to reach this goal. Nowhere is Penda's consent to this marriage ever brought up. She seems rather like a kind of trophy, since she will belong to the man who will send Mor dried beef in return, by means of Bouki the Hyena, the intermediary. . . .

The marriage guardianship is maintained with equal strictness; but the clever wife can turn things to her advantage. Generally, she is not recognized as having any particular rights in marriage. She has only duties; at least, she can only assert her rights insofar as she carries out her duties perfectly, duties that exceed her rights to the point of practically canceling them out. This situation comes from a combination of traditional African and Islamic attitudes toward women. . . .

In Birago Diop's tales, humor and satire triumph; he leaves no room for sentimentality. . . . Since he does not have any intention of producing an ethnological document, Diop does not make the effort to define precisely woman's place in society. His indictment of women should not be taken literally. . . . These delightfully sketched portraits of women are too suffused with the author's humor to have originated from any motive other than the desire for healthy amusement.

Mohamadou Kane. *Les contes d'Amadou Coumba* (Dakar, Université de Dakar, 1968), pp. 75–76, 78–79†

DIOP, DAVID (1927–1960)

SENEGAL

The works of this twenty-nine-year-old Senegalese writer display a lyricism directed toward practical goals. The poems he writes are militant, but . . . he bears essentially poetic arms. David Diop celebrates our African riches with humor and sensuality. His voice is always sober and concise. Yet his concern for exactness never stifles the final object of the poem. A spirit of healthy rebellion—sometimes underlying the poem, sometimes right on the surface—dominates his lyricism. His poems are a "hymn to the taut muscles," in which the lyrical vitality is never locked in a "coffin of words." . . .

In *Hammer Blows* "the heart and the brain are joined in the straight line of battle," and their union is a lesson in morality that we should remember as we see around us so many intellects who discredit the power of the heart in the name of a colorless and frozen intelligence. Through the culture of his people the poet finds the universal meaning of humanity. It is therefore not surprising that he brings us hope. . . .

Diop also knows how to write about the dizziness of physical love. To his eyes, the act of love is not a biological or recreational act but one of the most dazzling forms of participation in the world, in life. Love is a glorious dance in the sun by the senses, a dance during which the partners, who become equals through the incandescent virtues of blood, discover the riches they have in common.

René Depestre. *PA*. Dec., 1956, pp. 110–11†

Hammer Blows is a thin booklet, but there is more in this short work which is disturbing in its compactness than in many modern *complete works*. Before qualifying this poetry—which is always a means of curtailing it or justifying what is foreign to it—let us recognise its funda-

mental merit, which is of being *poetry* above everything else. The closer
a work comes to the *intrinsic poetic phenomenon,* the more it defies
analysis. . . . This is true of David Diop's poetry. It is difficult to analyse
by reason of its singular poetic compactness and its high content of
poetry. The work is complete in itself and perfectly impervious. It is like
those works of art whose beauty is beyond question but defies explanation.

On reflection, it may perhaps be suggested that this verbal achievement cannot be accounted for solely by talent and that unexplainable
spontaneity causes a poet to write poems in the same manner as apple-
trees yield apples. Indeed, on closer examination, one finds that the
great impulse that underlies, illuminates and sanctifies David Diop's
lyricism is beautiful as the daylight and life itself—Love. Love with a
capital "L," in all its forms with all its subtleties and climes. Filial love
. . . passionate love with that irresistible breath which comes from deeper
than the heart . . . the love of the fighter who exorcises the subtle devils
and unmystifies . . . the man who claims the penalty and assumes the
crimes of others . . . and lastly outright love: love of life, rhythm, and
grace. . . .

Hammer Blows is a work of profound faith in Man. The poet's
African temperament breathes through these verses which are written in
a generous, fiery vein.

PA (English ed.). June–Sept., 1960, pp. 244–45

In September 1960 the young poet David Diop died in a plane crash off
Dakar. With him went his wife and all his manuscripts. At the age of
thirty-three the most promising of West Africa's younger French poets
was thus snatched from the scene, leaving only a single pamphlet of
seventeen short poems behind him. That little pamphlet, *Hammer
Blows*, was enough to establish David Diop as the most interesting and
talented African poet of the fifties. Its appearance in 1956 aroused
hopes of a career which never happened, but the unifying passion and
fire of these few poems earn Diop a place here as the spokesman of a
new age, the age for whom Senghor must appear a figure too deeply
committed to the idea of a French Community uniting many peoples
under the umbrella of a single civilization; the age, in short, of the
Guinean Revolution.

David Diop was born in Bordeaux in 1927, the son of a Senegalese
father and a Camerounian mother. His youth was spent partly in
France, partly in West Africa. This background might superficially suggest the "cultural mulatto" far more strongly than Senghor's. In fact, we
are now in a new political atmosphere. Diop uses his French culture, not
to seek a reconciliation, a synthesis, or even a polarity of tensions, but

to unleash an unrelenting hatred of Europe and all that it stands for. Across centuries of bitterness and hate, he proclaims the dawn. It is a dawn to which Europe has contributed nothing but the prelude of darkness. But if the extremity of his position may repel in cold prose, the urgency and fervour of his verse give it the quality of a "Marseillaise."

Gerald Moore. *Seven African Writers* (London, Oxford University Press, 1962), p. 18

David Diop's literary career began while he was still a student at the Lycée Marcelin Berthelot near Paris, in the late 1940's. His teacher, Léopold Sédar Senghor, was impressed with the youngster's "original inner life" and selected several early poems for inclusion in the history-making *Anthology of New Negro and Malagasy Poetry* (1948), which Jean-Paul Sartre prefaced with the famous essay "Black Orpheus." Later, David Diop contributed to *Présence africaine*, the cultural review of the Negro world edited in Paris, and participated in the Negro Writers and Artists Conference in Paris (1956) and Rome (1960). . . .

Until his untimely death, David Diop was emerging as a leader of the younger generation of "negritude" writers, those who reached their twenties in the postwar years. Many of his poems take up images, themes and accents already introduced by such older French-speaking West Indians in the negritude school as Jacques Roumain and Léon Damas. The influence of Aimé Césaire on David Diop's work is especially strong. While the younger poet's gifts cannot be compared with Césaire's, his work has a distinct personal stamp that stems from its directness, simplicity, and raw emotional power. The impact of every line, every word, is intentional. The angry young man meant his poems to "burst the eardrums of those who do not wish to hear them." . . .

The incident that inspired the poem ["To a Black Child"] is the 1955 lynching in Mississippi of a Chicago youngster named Emmet Till. David Diop had not been to America, but like nearly all Africans and West Indians in the negritude movement, he identified closely with the American Negro. He was deeply shocked by the Till affair, and by the fact that the murderers, though known, were acquitted in a trial that made a mockery of justice. . . .

Léopold Sédar Senghor had hoped to see his young countryman's talent mature, his bitterness and anger soften with understanding and compassion. It was President Senghor who pronounced the funeral oration in Dakar, recalling David's courage during the "long calvary" of his youth, the months and years of sickness [in sanatoriums with a recurrent illness that plagued him from childhood]. These, and the more purely psychic anguishes, David Diop has recorded in a series of lucid images: "ragged days with a narcotic taste," "anxious hangings on the edge of cliffs," and "sleep inhabited by alcohol," together with a love that brought "necklaces of laughter," his second marriage. "Through your long hospital nights," said President Senghor, "you identified with your crucified people. Your sufferings became their sufferings; your anguish, their anguish; your hope, their hope." Senghor's words were a generous tribute to a voice he found "hard and black as basalt," a voice destined never to reach maturity, but which sang ardently and unforgettably of "Africa my Africa."

Paulette J. Trout and Ellen Conroy Kennedy.
JNALA. Spring–Fall, 1968, pp. 76–78

According to Gerald Moore, David Diop "uses his French culture . . . to unleash an unrelenting hatred of Europe and all that it stands for." Considering the poet from another viewpoint, the editors of *Présence africaine* interpret Diop's "fundamental drive" as "Love." A more comprehensive description of Diop's inspiration might define him as a poet of passion. *Passion*, derived from the Latin *patior, pati, passus sum*, which means *suffer*, is not limited to erotic experience. Rather, it is violent and intense emotion which may run the gamut of feelings from hatred to love, and from the limits of pain to those of pleasure. . . .

"Negro Tramp" reveals several of the fundamental elements of Diop's passion: abomination of the whites ("their big mouths full of principles"); compassion for others who suffer; a belief in the fertility of revolt ("I excite the hurricane for future fields"); and an almost paradisiacal dream of what will come. In this way, Diop's fury against the oppressor provides the ferment for his dreams of revolution. . . .

But Diop's poetry goes beyond his hate. Often his poems fall into two-part structures. After his tirade against what oppresses him, he soars upward to hope. . . . Mediating between his hatred and his vision are the poet's compassion and faith in creative revolt. . . . As Diop treats it, rebellion is not an act of hatred; rather, it is a process of creative violence which includes notions of fertility, hope and even love. Through revolt he seeks to overcome his suffering and his subjection. Storms, symbolic of the forces of destruction, are for him images of reconstruction. He calls them "virile tempests." Often erotic imagery describes the passion of his re-creation since he regards revolt as fertile when nourished by love. In "The Vultures," for example, his hands, "profound like revolt," will "impregnate the belly of the earth." Hope, in the figure of spring, will be born in the flesh beneath his steps imbued with light. . . . Revolt merges with the erotic impulse in the passion of Diop's re-creation.

Enid H. Rhodes [Peschel]. ECr. Fall, 1970,
pp. 234–35, 237

DRIEU LA ROCHELLE, PIERRE (1893-1945)

With his first book, *Interrogation*, published in 1917, which Barrès called "the most beautiful book about the war," Drieu la Rochelle, in fiery and explosive phrases, found the essence of the soul and formulated the heroic desire of his generation, the generation born between 1890 and 1900, young men who were thrown into the trenches straight out of school or their apprenticeships, without having had a chance to live. An idealistic and vigorous elite leading the eager masses, who had been cured of alcoholism and petty politics by physical exertion, toward a life of struggle and economic and spiritual conquest—this is the picture painted by Drieu la Rochelle of the aftermath of the war's butchery. . . .

Measure of France . . . is the result of a long and merciless meditation. Descartes, shut away in his cozy Holland, meditated not on the consequences of the Thirty Years War but on the foundations of knowledge. Drieu la Rochelle, however, did not take refuge in any ivory tower to find the liberty of his intellect and imagination. He felt compelled to set forth, for himself and for us, all his reasons for optimism and pessimism, to define with anguish and sincerity his vision of France and the world after the war.

It is a hasty vision, and undoubtedly in many ways false, but it is striking in its harshness and its occasional cynicism. . . . One can appreciate the value of this little book, which Péguy would have liked; its gaps are also evident. But an analysis of the book cannot indicate the enthusiasm of the demonstration, the brilliance and at times the density of the expression, and the passion that burns within these pages. The chapter devoted to Raymond Lefebvre's death is one of the most beautiful works of testimony we have about the generation that reached maturity in 1914. As Barrès and as Péguy did for their generations, Drieu la Rochelle has assumed the role of major witness on behalf of his.

Benjamin Crémieux. *NL*. Nov. 25, 1922, p. 2†

The Comedy of Charleroi is a book of memoirs: in it [Drieu la Rochelle] expresses himself directly, without characters, and he relates facts that have long since been assimilated, transformed, and made ready for life within a book. Uneasy with fiction, because lacking a sustained interest in people other than himself, Drieu la Rochelle is an excellent writer when he speaks about himself. He describes, in his own voice, his tall body, his gestures, his mannerisms, his crude language, his outbursts of lyricism, his hours of fatigue or disgust, his constant need to see clearly and to find himself. In this book the joy in the narrative and the happiness of the tone are both delightful. The language is oratorical, but not inflated, sometimes awkward and complicated, but more often strong, steady, clear in its violence, full of felicitous discoveries, bold strokes, and surprising foreshortenings; an elevated language. . . .

Drieu la Rochelle is likable when he is moved, angry, or indignant. I do not like him when he becomes bored; and boredom fills half his books. But in this book he has found his subject; he has become involved. *The Comedy of Charleroi* is not a depiction of the war; it is the story of the relationship between one man and the war. . . .

Yet, as sincere as the book is—perhaps one should say because the book is sincere—the reader feels he can perceive an indefinable undercurrent that is almost inhuman. Undoubtedly, this undercurrent is part of the meaning of the work, as is Drieu la Rochelle's personality. But it is hard not to be struck by the indifference this strange man, this ardent dilettante, shows toward other men. When he approaches others, it seems to be less out of true friendship than out of curiosity or out of a fondness for his own reflection. His self-satisfaction contains an unconscious cruelty. And at times it would seem as if the entire war were only important insofar as it revealed Drieu la Rochelle's own personality to him. [1934]

Marcel Arland. *Essais et nouveaux essais critiques*
(Paris, Gallimard, 1952), pp. 266–68†

If, according to the contention of some psychologists, it is only the unhappy, thwarted nature who seeks refuge in creative art, Drieu la Rochelle is another soul in pain who found relief in literary expression. Unfortunately the degree of pain is not the gauge of inspiration, and Drieu la Rochelle's is not a brilliant talent. He himself admits that he has no natural gifts, and in his autobiographical novel, *The Young European*, he confesses it was because he gradually found himself without money, friends, children, and a vocation that he first turned to writing. Begging his public's indulgence for having embraced a literary career, he asks: "What was left but to become a writer if only to bid farewell to the human forms which one by one were disappearing over my horizon?" However, it was more than through cowardice and to earn his daily bread that Drieu la Rochelle became a man of letters. Idealistic and patriotic, he is fundamentally a moralist and a disciplinarian, whose instinct is to preach and reprimand. Drieu la Rochelle's characteristic note is acerbity and ill humor, which, without the saving grace of genius, makes him a dreary and forbidding writer. . . .

Drieu la Rochelle's specialty is to write novels on love in which nobody loves, and, whether intentionally or not, the conversation never

rises above a certain smartness. Perpetually philosophizing and gener-
alizing, Gille [in *A Strange Kind of Journey*], caustic but less penetrating perhaps than Drieu la Rochelle imagines him, concludes: "Women
love nothing. Least of all do they love love. That is reserved for men.
Women do nothing, are nothing. Even in the choice of their jewels and
clothing they depend on men." . . . When not only the hero, but each
member of this rich and futile milieu joins in such reflections as:
"Madame, you must resign yourself to seeing your daughter marry an
attractive man who will be unfaithful to her, or an unattractive one to
whom she will be unfaithful," the reader is apt to lose sight of the satiric
import of the novel, to flounder aimlessly in its mire of tarnished epigram and cheap cynicism.

Milton H. Stansbury. *French Novelists of Today*
(Philadelphia, University of Pennsylvania Press,
1935), pp. 176, 184–85

Dreamy Bourgeoisie, which Drieu la Rochelle intends to be a severe
attack, is ultimately marked by an extreme complacency toward the
bourgeoisie, and every page shows signs of a hidden complicity.

I am well aware that a bourgeois writer, for whom the requirements for creativity are inseparable from the maintenance of a certain
living standard (Drieu la Rochelle once wrote that he needs 60,000
francs a year to live on), can nevertheless sense the extreme poverty of
the bourgeois world he feels attached to. Like some other intellectuals,
Drieu la Rochelle is drawn to the proletariat, even more strongly than
some workers are drawn to the bourgeoisie. But to follow this impulse
to its conclusion, an intellectual would have to go so far as to take a
stand on behalf of the proletariat, and to take such a stand would
immediately cause considerable difficulties for a bourgeois intellectual,
concerned with maintaining both the living standard offered him by his
class and the high opinion that class has of him.

An intellectual like Drieu la Rochelle believes that he can resolve
this contradiction by becoming a fascist. Fascism gives him both op-
tions: he is still socially a member of the bourgeoisie, but he appears to
belong to the proletariat, according to fascist demagogy. But since this
proletarian appearance is just a lie, designed only to mislead and then
crush the people, what the intellectual gains in self-satisfaction, he loses
in talent. He becomes a fool. . . .

Dreaming of belonging to the people, but not daring to do so,
Drieu la Rochelle is satisfied with the bourgeois caricature of the proletariat fabricated by fascism. A liar in his politics, he is consequently a
liar in his writing, confusing baseness with strength and vulgarity with
simplicity.

Paul Nizan. *L'humanité*. Aug. 7, 1937, p. 8†

Drieu la Rochelle has a very keen sense of the contemporary world and the tragedies to which it gives rise. He has never ceased describing and writing about war, the decadence of the ruling class, and women; he has never ceased meditating about the problems of leadership. He has done so with greater or lesser success according to how close he remains to concrete details, but every time he can "come to grips with the object," as the hero of *The Will-o'-the-Wisp* wished to do at the moment of his suicide, Drieu la Rochelle carries us away with a dark and piercing song. If anyone is capable of some day writing the novel of twentieth-century civil war, it is not André Malraux, who sees only one side of things; it is Drieu la Rochelle.

Boldly, unequivocally, on several occasions he has taken firm and dangerous political positions. But the future will say that he was never a conformist. He says what he thinks to his friends and his allies, and during the most difficult times he has been the very voice of our disappointments and disillusions. He is an honest man capable of speaking out and enumerating the errors committed on every side. He has done so in a simple if grumbling manner, never abandoning his task; in this intellectual aristocrat it is heartening to find a temperament akin to that of the common people, the decent folk who suddenly shrug their shoulders, stop a moment, and take up their work again, muttering, "What a pity!" And Drieu la Rochelle's own task, despite all opposition, is to be sincere with himself, to depict the agony of the bourgeoisie . . . and to point the way toward the future. [1943]

Robert Brasillach. Les quatre jeudis (Paris,
Éditions Balzac, 1944), pp. 281–82†

In 1939 [Drieu la Rochelle] published his most important novel, *Gilles*, which will be studied for many years as the most complete portrait in fiction of the moral and intellectual development of a French fascist. . . . This strange novel, baffling, uneven, full of a tormented symbolism, was recognized by the critics as the odyssey of the inter-war generation in search of a cause for whose bright flame they might fight, finding only the cold ashes of one disillusionment after another. That Drieu la Rochelle, like Gilles, was eager to destroy his own world is unmistakable, though his reasons are not always plain. . . . Whatever its cause, this malady of the spirit was an admirable preparation for his adherence to fascism. Like many another man of his age, he felt the need of a religion, and satisfied it by deifying a political theory. And regular attendance at the Nuremberg congresses only served to confirm him in his faith.

When the Germans entered Paris he remained constant to his openly declared convictions, and became a loyal supporter of the Vichy government and its foreign masters. . . . Drieu la Rochelle assumed the editorship of *La nouvelle revue française*, many of whose contributors had, like himself, welcomed the New Order, though some, following the example of André Gide, had promptly resigned. . . . The director of the *NRF* (whose enemies said there was nothing left French about it but the name) was expected to spread fascist propaganda among the intellectuals, and this Drieu la Rochelle did faithfully, both in articles and in well-advertised speeches. He expressed amazement that the French people refused to accept their defeat as part of the inevitable course of history, as he did himself. He urged them to enter gladly into that death which was necessary before they could enjoy their resurrection, to forget what they had been for so long, to discover within themselves the hidden source of life and of miracles which would transform them into a young, vigorous, brutal nation. But, again like Gilles, he found his pleas in vain, and the New Order on which he had staked his fortunes proved to be only the last and greatest of his illusions.

Beatrice Corrigan. UTQ. Jan., 1945, pp. 203–5

I am not undertaking a defense, an indictment, or a rehabilitation. We do not have to give Drieu la Rochelle back his place: he still occupies it. At first sight, his position is certainly not very important. I have reread his essays: they are often hasty, facile, and confused, consisting of ideas that occurred to him after evenings of tobacco and whisky, ideas that he went over and over again in an interminable dialogue with a friend or with himself, on bar stools or in the streets of Paris at night. Perhaps his position is not very important—but it is his: that of a man, a novelist, and a political writer who was always spoken of as a failure, who himself willingly used the word "failure" about each of his books. Nevertheless, literary history is full of those immortal failures whose frail ghosts—but ghosts that become more solid from year to year—trample upon the dust and ashes of those who were once thought successful.

A frail and tragic ghost. We are tired of asking our brothers to justify themselves, especially our brothers who have been killed, especially this brother who killed himself. Not that I approve of the path he took: I still believe that he was horribly mistaken. But it was first of all the wrong path for himself. What a path! His suicide [in 1945] shows his absolute despair. The survivors on all sides should think about his death: they managed their affairs well, those who succeeded in not drowning in that ocean of whirlwinds and abysses. . . . This man ended in despair only because he had begun in despair.

François Mauriac. TR. June, 1949, pp. 912–13†

[Drieu la Rochelle] blamed the times for the somberness of the picture in [*The Will-o'-the-Wisp*]; he had only reported faithfully on what was happening to a part of French youth.

The title was equally symbolic, with an even more definite reference to decomposition and decadence. Alain shares with the will-o'-the-wisp a certain lack of substance, a lightness and a fleetingness not without charm. He is the emanation of a rotting society. He seems sometimes to be one of those "flowers of evil" imagined by Baudelaire, who had placed drugs, suicide, and alcohol among the forbidden means offered to man to break the walls of his prison. . . .

The author adopts the omniscient point of view and we follow Alain's intimate thoughts and reactions. It is a picture from the inside. The author has imagined with a horrified fascination the situation of a man who has decided to end his life and who sees everything and everybody in the special light of impending death. There is such an appeal for Drieu la Rochelle in this particular situation that his imagination goes back to it again and again. In one form or another it finds a literary transposition in all his novels. . . .

The plot is not very important. What matters is Alain's quest for a reason to live and his failure to find any reason. In that respect *The Will-o'-the-Wisp* opens the series of Drieu la Rochelle's great books of the 'thirties sounding the depths of the more somber side of man's fate. Alain, being a kind of outlaw who refuses to follow the rules of the social game, sees through the lack of sincerity of people around him. Everybody is vaguely frightened by Alain's possible outburst of truthfulness—a truthfulness which does not admit any compromise since it measures everything with the authentic detachment of someone who has chosen death as the alternative to an unsatisfactory world. . . .

The characters in later novels will have wider scope and meaning for the average reader. Gilles, in his many incarnations, will reveal more facets of contemporary society and therefore more facets of the decadence, corruption, and hypocrisy which Drieu la Rochelle hated. But none of the later characters or novels will have a more chilling impact.

Frédéric J. Grover. *Drieu la Rochelle and the Fiction
of Testimony* (Berkeley, University of California
Press, 1958), pp. 89, 94–95

Whatever the cause, his political involvement and his thought suggest more than anything else a nihilist's desire to destroy a world that [Drieu la Rochelle] disliked. Thus his mania for predicting disasters to come.

His real talent was the use of devastating satire in his novels to depict the social and political life of what appeared to be a narrow, cramped society living on borrowed time. Even his vision of purity, insofar as it took on any tangible outline, was directed toward the opposite pole from the bourgeois France that he could not accept. Every authentically conservative sentiment of the day was made a target by the themes of his work, from his advocacy of socialism to his appeals to revolutionary violence and the abandonment of bourgeois goals. But, especially, a society dedicated in those years to inaction was urged to break with its main characteristic.

That there was an air of unreality in his thought is undeniable; but paradoxes and contradictions can abound when the object is to shock the bourgeoisie. Drieu la Rochelle's work shows the spirit of adolescent rebellion against the comfortable mediocrity of the materialistic view of life, the politicians who articulate its values, and the myths associated with it. His views went beyond the spirit of *incivisme* [lack of civic-mindedness], which permeates all classes in France. Indeed, it appears that his flight was not so much toward totalitarian political systems as it was away from any conceivable regime in France. To remain at least a nominal collaborationist to the end was to give proof of one's nonconformity and spirit of total opposition to the majority, even if that majority consisted of one's own countrymen undergoing the rigors of the Occupation.

William R. Tucker. *The Journal of Politics*.
Feb., 1965, p. 175

The author of *The Will-o'-the-Wisp* is Pierre Drieu la Rochelle, a Frenchman who wrote between the wars and is largely unknown to Americans. Unknown for good and sufficient reasons, if this short novel is anything to go by. For this is the kind of bad novel that could only happen in France (every literature has its troubles): a witch's brew of bad classical technique, undeviating *angst* and second-drawer café-philosophy. . . .

The novel's only real claim to interest—outside of the fact that it has been made into a passably good movie—lies in the fact that it ends with a suicide, and the author's own life ended with a suicide: a grim proof of his credentials. Ironically enough, even the suicide is largely "literary"—set up from page one and pushed remorselessly throughout.

Wilfrid Sheed. *NYT*. March 21, 1965, p. 4

Pierre Drieu la Rochelle . . . was able to speak only with despair of the future of mankind and in particular of the French nation. In an epilogue to *Gilles*, he called decadence the directive theme of his work and characterized the inner form of his narrative prose by calling it an accounting. He thought of himself as occupying a position somewhere between Céline, Montherlant, and Malraux. Drieu la Rochelle formulated his political commitment in essays which aroused great interest and much controversy. His place in French narrative prose appeared clearly defined—after *The Man Covered with Women* and *The Will-o'-the-*

Wisp—with the publication of *Gilles*. This extensive work, which [Gaëtan] Picon lists among the great novels of the century, was written after 1934. When it appeared, none of the critics had the courage to praise it without qualification. The subject was too ticklish late in 1939. . . .

[Gilles] feels persecuted by the trauma of ubiquitous sterility spread by the egalitarian principle. Sterile is the politics of socialism; sterile the formalism of Marxism; sterile and flabby appears, to Gilles, the literary revolt of surrealism (here the work is clearly a *roman à clef*); sterile finally is his young wife Pauline. Boldness, that is, the will to power and to self-realization, the hero finds only among the Fascists. In the falangists of the Spanish Civil War he celebrates positive symbolic figures, for they are able to face death without material backing. We know that Drieu la Rochelle originally intended to give his novel the title of *Death and Money*, in order to name and label the ultimate horror. The dreadful confusion of the hearts, caused by the monied bourgeoisie and by bolshevism, implies ultimately also a pervasion of the relationships of love which become interchangeable. In his description of the ephemerality of things erotic, the author comes close to equaling the mastery of Aragon.

Winfried Engler. *The French Novel from Eighteen Hundred to the Present* (New York, Frederick Ungar, 1969), pp. 121–22

DUHAMEL, GEORGES (1884–1966)

People had told me [that *The Light*] was a pleasant play. Two ladies, who had seen it before I did, summarized their impression thus: "I wept!" How can I collect my thoughts? *The Light* is indeed the most boring evening in the theater I can remember. Duhamel has put on stage a young man who has been blind from birth and a sighted young woman. The blind man celebrates the pleasures of the sense of touch, which is well developed in him as it is in all blind people, while the girl celebrates the pleasures of sight. This goes on for four acts, all in an ultra-literary style. Ultimately, the girl becomes blind, too, because she has looked at the sun too much. Then the two young people realize that they are in love, and love finally makes them see clearly. It is so childish!

I am not saying that the play does not have nice touches. It would perhaps be very beautiful to read, although I personally do not particularly care for this kind of literature—all that lyricism, all that affectation. I would put down the book at the first page. But on stage, it is frankly unbearable. I do not go to the theater to hear pages of a book, poetic verses, well-spun metaphors—nothing but literature, in short. On stage there has to be action, life, reality, especially when we are presented with contemporary characters. In *The Light* there are only phrases. As for the subject of the play, I know a novel by [Lucien] Descaves, *The Walled-In People*, in which the events are far more varied and far truer to life than these four acts by Duhamel. . . . I had such a need to refresh my mind after *The Light* that I reread [Molière's] *The Misanthrope*.

> Maurice Boissard. *MdF*. May 1, 1911, pp. 193–94†

As a result of the justified success of his books on the war, *Life of the Martyrs* and *Civilization*, Duhamel has acquired real prestige. Since he is interesting, people listen to him. Since he has strong convictions, he takes advantage of his success to make the public share them. *The Possession of the World* and *Conversations in the Turmoil* are doctrinaire and popularizing works. . . . Duhamel is a good man, and therefore worthy of all our sympathy. He is not one to forget the war; he avows that he cannot and does not want to stop thinking about it. He came out of the war disillusioned, like everyone else, but more so because of the extent of his illusions. . . .

[His doctrine] consists of teaching men to look both inside and outside themselves, and to love what they see, of educating each man's senses and heart (if not his mind), of inculcating a taste for nature, art, reading, friendship, and reverie, and in this way of promoting a pastoral state of mind, a guarantee of eternal peace. Maeterlinck, when he wrote *The Treasure of the Humble*, recommended similar gymnastics to us.

It remains to be seen how men will adapt themselves to this doctrine. I am not speaking about a certain number of men to whom this advice can indeed be useful. I am speaking of men in general. How will you persuade them to give up material goods, which they know and appreciate, for a moral good they are unaware of? How do you account for their passions in your system? "I am appealing to their hearts in the name of love," Duhamel answers us. The goodness of his heart intoxicates him, and this intoxication clouds his thinking. He sees the clash of self-interest, jealousy, and discord everywhere; from this clash he concludes that people must disarm and love. This is a strange logic. First of all, who will decree the commandments of love? A man? It will really have to be a man; we have here a religion without God.

The most serious point of his doctrine, however, is not so much this noble confidence in the goodness of our hearts, as the anathema on reason, as creating an obstacle to love and harmony. Faced with the ruins of the present time, Duhamel proclaims that reason has failed; that is why his ultimate recourse is to the emotions.

Henri Ghéon. *RevU*. April 1, 1920, pp. 98, 100†

[Duhamel's] works, because of their truthful sadness and boldness, have often been compared to those of the naturalists. How can we protest enough against this comparison? Historically, naturalism (according to the theories to which it gave rise) arose as a school of journalistic reporting. One of Huysmans's heroes, I believe, says: "I have to go to the slaughterhouse of La Villette at six o'clock to note the effects of a sunrise." This subjection to realism, this codified myopia, horrifies almost all of today's writers; and Duhamel, even if he is a great observer, is not at all attracted to this method.

Nobody is less obsessed by external reality than he: he seeks souls under people's gestures and words. Facts and objects in themselves are not interesting to him. He wants to know man *through* facts and objects. That is undoubtedly why he wrote several short stories on trivial, almost negligible subjects. From his point of view, nothing is insignificant in itself; it is up to the artist to make everything significant. This ability is not within the reach of everyone. For this task talent can never be replaced by the most serious industriousness. And now that literature has completed its apprenticeship in realism, now that it is quite natural for an open mind to see the external world clearly, it is necessary to rediscover the inner world beneath those external elements.

André Thérive. *Georges Duhamel; ou, L'intelligence du cœur* (Paris, Vald. Rasmussen, 1925), pp. 25–26†

Duhamel's Louis Salavin [in *Life and Adventures of Salavin*] is described by the publishers as "lovable," but all the same I should not care to meet him. In life he would not be readily comprehensible and might even prove exasperating. In a novel he is perfect—not because he is a "character" but because he is the type of person whom the omniscience of fiction, exploring every cranny of a man's mind, every shadowed part of his personality, can illuminate. We come to know him with a completeness that does indeed make us love him; but he is not, as we speak of people generally, "lovable." He is a misfit, but not one of those romantic or sentimental misfits who are hopeless dreamers, vagabonds, knights born into the wrong age. He is a terribly self-conscious, self-probing neurotic, an intellectual *manqué*. He has a positively calamitous knowledge of his own shortcomings, and his instinct for self-preservation lies entirely in some dangling incoherent desire to convert his shortcomings into virtues. At bottom he seeks what all intelligent people who are not naturally well-adjusted seek: a successful formula for living.

Salavin makes a drastic choice. Aware that he cannot find salvation through worldly achievement, through anything he can do, he seeks it through personal purification, through what he can be. He decides to become a saint. . . .

Though the book drives off at furious tangents, it yet keeps its feet on the ground because no matter how much Salavin insists on playing the moralist, Duhamel just as constantly insists on remaining the psychologist. Against Salavin's idealistic and aberrant values, Duhamel places saner, almost maliciously saner, values of his own. He has saturated himself in his character, been warmed by Salavin's erratic heat, even indulged him; but he has never succumbed to him. The irony of Salavin's position cuts, as it should cut, both ways. Like all men with the earmarks of fanaticism, and again like all men who, however noble their ideals, are hopelessly wrapped up in themselves, Salavin is at once a comic and a tragic figure.

Louis Kronenberger. *NYT*. Nov. 8, 1936, p. 5

In some men love for music and poetry is a defense against life. Because they are born without a protective shell, they try to move through life surrounded by a cloud of harmony, much as certain fish stir up the water around them to escape being devoured by their fellows. In this sense, Bach and Mozart protect Duhamel. . . .

Duhamel was human—all too human; he would never have been able to endure the agony of others' pain [during World War I] without some appropriate defense—in his case, his memory of music. Even today, when no man's pitiful life blood is spilling over his hands, it protects him, for everyday life is quite enough to bathe one in others' blood.

Duhamel has always found the melody he himself needed for shelter. And if a friend could not remember a particular air that was dear to him, Duhamel reached down within himself and, little by little, drew it up from that mysterious lair where all the music of the world seemed to lie enchained.

He did not always fetch it up on the instant. For hours and hours, Orpheus may have wandered in the limbo of sleeping sound—Duhamel went on laughing and talking. Nothing suggested that a part of him was working secretly to discover the charm that will awaken the elusive phrase. I remember one summer at Estoril when I heard his friendly voice at the other end of the wire: "I found your rondo!" It was a Mozart rondo I had been talking about to him the evening before; we had tried to remember it, but neither of us could. As I was hurrying down to rejoin the friend who had rescued my melody from silence, suddenly the tune came back to me too, like a child delivered. [1937]

François Mauriac. *Second Thoughts* (Cleveland, World, 1961), pp. 109–10

Duhamel incarnates a humanism that avoids aesthetic and moral dryness as well as metaphysical blindness—a humanism saved by a secret fever to go beyond itself. In the same way, and for the same reasons, it could be said that he represents a certain perfection of the bourgeois, especially of the French bourgeois, who in Duhamel's works achieves his goals and surpasses himself at the same time. Just as [François] Mauriac incarnates well the devout bourgeois, with the slightly tense, bitter, and grating qualities that devotion can assume when it is used in the struggle against worldly temptations, Duhamel, with more ease and more peace, is the decent bourgeois, the literate, sociable family man. . . .

The cult of science, the taste for art in general and poetry and music in particular—everything that naturally elevates man's heart shines in Duhamel as it does in his heroes. His moral style as well as his writing style has an unusually rich harmony. Just as Duhamel the prose stylist was able to rediscover the clarity of the classical sentence while enlivening it with subtle vibrations that both prolong and purify romantic and symbolist art, Duhamel the moralist corrected the dryness of a merely reasoned morality by adding a few drops of discreetly filtered humanitarian lyricism. The prudent Frenchman, the friend of moderation, who prefers the decent butcher shop of his village to the gigantic canned-goods factories of Chicago, is the same one who condemns industrial civilization because it takes away the average man's taste for meditation and the feeling for great art. What is more, he is the same man who, in *The Possession of the World*, places the highest wisdom in love.

Pierre-Henri Simon. *Georges Duhamel; ou, Le bourgeois sauvé* (Paris, Éditions du Temps Présent, 1946), pp. 192–93†

Duhamel's father was a doctor who started practicing medicine late, never became very successful for lack of order and efficiency in his life, and bequeathed little else to his family but the memory of an entertaining visionary buffeted by life but always obstinately smiling. He appears several times in the novels of his son. Duhamel was also a doctor, one of many in Europe who turned to literature; Céline and Luc Durtain were also medical men who won fame as novelists . . .

He owed much to the practice of medicine, the most fertile training ground for one who would be a novelist. He probed the secrets of men and women and diagnosed the psychological causes of some of their diseases. He observed the concrete instead of theorizing from books and systems. He visited people when they were off their guard, in a disorderly bedroom, with their hair, faces, and clothes unprepared for the social comedy that one plays in healthy life. He heard confessions from wives hating their husbands, from heartless husbands, and from human beings suddenly become abject in their fear of disease and of death. But that experience did not make Duhamel bitter or cynical. It did not even make him gruff and imperious, like many doctors who think they will be obeyed and respected more by their patients if they utter laconic oracles and scold with sharp finality.

Pity is the controlling sentiment that Duhamel tried to reintroduce into literature, after the naturalists and certain intellectual cynics had disaccustomed readers to such an outmoded feeling.

Henri Peyre. *The Contemporary French Novel*
(New York, Oxford University Press, 1955),
pp. 46–47

[Duhamel's] two main fictional works are cycles that reflect the changing temper of those two strongly differentiated decades, the twenties and the thirties. In the twenties, the decade of individual "anxieties" and maladjustments, Duhamel published the five-volume *Life and Adventures of Salavin*. In the thirties, a decade of social restlessness, appeared *The Chronicle of the Pasquiers*. . . . Though certain volumes of the Salavin cycle still have considerable appeal, neither the Salavin nor the Pasquier cycle is entirely readable today, and large sections of the latter seem incredibly tedious. It is fortunate that Duhamel prudently conceived each volume in the two series as an entity that might be read separately. . . .

[In writing *The Chronicle of the Pasquiers*] Duhamel may have had in mind Zola's great cycle *The Rougon Macquarts*, but he seems closer to Galsworthy. His account of the rise and development of a lower middle-class family from the 1880's through World War I has a certain documentary interest but is otherwise fairly arid. This, perhaps, is because the Pasquier family is too close to the Duhamel family to allow for the play of imagination, compassion and humor that mark the best pages of Salavin. In the first volume Duhamel presents the family, evoking the figure of M. Pasquier, who is drawn from memories of his own fantastic father. We then follow the Pasquier children as each one moves rather conveniently into a niche in one of the different professions open to the middle class: clerk, businessman, musician, actress, scientist; for the Pasquier children are singularly gifted. They too, like

Salavin, have a special novelistic function. They realize the intellectual and artistic aspirations latent in a certain class of society. The scientist, Laurent, tells the story and points the moral. As Laurent grows older, we begin to find him something of a prig and feel only a perfunctory interest in the family trials. The climax of the book, the war of 1914, is also one of its weakest points. There Laurent, and Duhamel with him, deep though their concern may be, deal largely in platitudes. . . .

[Duhamel's] books, after the Salavin cycle, lack that generous and total involvement in life that characterizes the living novel. In a sense Duhamel is the Anatole France of his generation, but a France in whom earnestness has displaced whimsicality. The violence of the times proved too powerful for Duhamel to cope with.

Germaine Brée and Margaret Guiton. *An Age of Fiction: The French Novel from Gide to Camus* (New Brunswick, N.J., Rutgers University Press, 1957), pp. 63, 65–67

Georges Duhamel started out, like the heroes of his novels, as an optimistic and open-hearted dreamer. With a few friends, he attempted, at the beginning of the century, to create a sort of collective community. This communal life was a failure, and the experience confirmed the pessimism about human groups that had already been instilled in Duhamel by a family circle rather similar to his fictional Pasquiers. A doctor and an assistant medical officer during World War I, he lived with the wounded for four years. He saw mutilated and bleeding Frenchmen of all classes—workers, peasants, and bourgeois—and he learned to respect and love these martyrs. From the war experiences he began to formulate three basic ideas around which he was to build his work: a hatred for any civilization that was mechanical and murderous; a love for a spiritual and humane civilization; finally, the notion that in France, and in a few small countries in Europe, Western civilization found its highest expression.

Duhamel was a Frenchman in love with his country. He loved everything about France: its countrysides and its cities; its monuments; its paintings and its books; its language, whose words, when used with taste and precision, gave him a physical joy; its cuisine, about which he spoke as a passionate devotee; its wines and cheeses, whose fine perfection was equal in his eyes to a beautiful style. He respected this French sensuality because it stayed delicate and moderate. . . .

His love for a traditional, sensuous, tender, and unselfish way of life made him aggressive and severe toward ways of life that were industrial, efficient, and gregarious. He went to the Soviet Union and was not happy there. . . . He went to the United States and wrote a book

about it, *Scenes of the Future Life*, in which Duhamel the apostle transformed himself into a pamphleteer. Unable to speak English, he was
exasperated by the treatment he received from the immigration authorities, by some aspects of technological overdevelopment, and by an excess of comfort. . . . Above all, he blamed this civilization for killing the
culture of the individual, which he thought was the only culture. A
musician, accustomed to playing in chamber-music groups, he was irritated by America's "false music, that canned music, that musical
hash."

André Maurois. In *Georges Duhamel (1884–1966)*
(Paris, Mercure de France, 1967), pp. 15–17†

Duhamel's death put an end to several years of moral suffering. Not
only had he witnessed—and helplessly—the splitting, crumbling and
disintegration of a world he had known so well, but he also foresaw a
third and deadly world holocaust. His sadness was profound.

Duhamel was also pained to learn that he now belonged to a past
generation, that he was no longer in tune with the young for whom he
had always felt such warmth and such rapport. His books, though still
read, were no longer devoured with the same fervor and ardor they had
once been. In the 1920's, his works had been best sellers, conversation
pieces. In the 1960's, they were looked upon as fine literature, not as
indispensable or controversial volumes. His message of good will, of
study, of classical education, and of a return to nature fell on deaf ears.
He felt most strongly the sting of hurt, the bitterness of misunderstanding, and fear for the future.

Duhamel finally and regretfully accepted the fact that man cannot
learn from past mistakes, that each of us has to experience bitterness
and sweetness for himself. A man's personality, he concluded, is so filled
with turmoil that he is unable to assimilate his swelling feelings of anger
and hatred. These, therefore, have to be expelled, leveled at others in
some aggressive manner. Then only through violence, man thinks—and
erroneously—can equilibrium be achieved. . . .

Duhamel's major works fit into our contemporary fad-mad, psy-
chedelic world mainly as counterweights. He is a representative of the
heart, of feeling, understanding, balance, harmony, and stability. These
character traits are so submerged in today's violent, ebullient, ruthless
society as to be virtually nonexistent. One gazes at Duhamel's works,
therefore, with a twinge of nostalgia, longing, and melancholy. . . .

Bettina L. Knapp. *Georges Duhamel* (New York,
Twayne, 1972), pp. 174–76

DURAS, MARGUERITE (1914–   )

In *A Dam against the Pacific* Marguerite Duras revealed an original and bold talent. I admired that novel a great deal. I find the same gifts in her new book, *The Sailor from Gibraltar*, but not her own authentic personality. . . .

[Anna] has loved only one man, a sailor from Gibraltar. . . . She loved him; he left her; she pursued him, waited for him; two or three times they met again and "rekindled the flame." Then he fled again, or rather he vanished one evening, and she has never stopped waiting for him. She pursues him by boat, from port to port, from country to country. . . . Anna will never again reach the mysterious place in which the Sailor from Gibraltar has undoubtedly found refuge from love and from the police. And her strange lover of the moment, Anna's confidant, shares the delights of this pursuit with as much unsatiated ardor as Anna. The Sailor from Gibraltar looks very much to me like the symbol of happiness.

The reader, somewhat worn out by so many voyages, by disillusions, and intoxications of every variety, closes the book with a sort of relief. But he will not forget it. . . .

Gérard d'Houville. RDM. Dec. 15, 1952,
pp. 728–30†

Nothing could be more misleading than the title *Moderato Cantabile*. The novel sings, yes, but in Marguerite Duras's works the emotions are never moderate. Often at the beginning of her books her central characters are established in a misleading equilibrium, as if in a lethargy. Then a break—an awakening—takes place, and the awakening is always spectacular. This is what happens in the extraordinary love scene in the automobile in *A Dam against the Pacific*, in the drunkenness of the minor bureaucrat who is about to change his ways in *The Sailor from Gibraltar*, in the mother's sudden entrance into the night club in *Whole Days in the Trees*. In *Moderato Cantabile*, the occurrence of a crime sets everything in motion. . . .

The whole story is not narrated, or even suggested. Instead the woman in the story makes a discovery, and the reader, if he is up to doing so, is invited to make the same discovery. Undoubtedly, the details of interpretation matter little, and errors are permissible. The main thing is to feel the power of the dialogue, to feel the electric charge that magnetizes every phrase, every word. That charge is so great that the actions and words can be reduced to a minimum. One hand placed on another hand becomes more erotic than a ten-page bedroom scene in a book by another writer. The simple description of the long boulevard by the sea along which the woman must walk at night, dragging her tired child behind her, when she has had too much to drink and is running out of time, conveys with every repetition the weight of her burden and the courage necessary for escape.

I would be tempted to call *Moderato Cantabile* an extremely interesting experiment if I did not know that for Duras there are never any experiments. She throws herself wholeheartedly into every new book as if into a battle, with an intrepid courage. This time she has clearly won a victory.

Roger Grenier. TR. July, 1958, pp. 122–23†

The Square is a very short novel, mostly in dialogue, with hardly any description or supports like "he said" and "she said." It is a conversation between a couple sitting in the late afternoon on a bench in a Paris square. He is a hawker, she is an overworked servant girl. They each have a philosophy of life, which is what the novel is about. . . .

This novel was, I believe, praised by Beckett, whose own characters the two nameless and, largely, faceless people on the bench resemble. By its very simplicity the idea of the book is highly ambitious. Ingredients: a man and a girl in a public square, never moving, only talking—what ingenious possibilities for a novel! But I do not think *The Square* has succeeded; it seems to me an interesting and sophisticated exercise-piece.

I am the last person to object to any movement which aims at the elimination of clutter from the novel, or to anybody's larking about with the novel form. But in order to practise economy you have to have some substance to practise it upon. The only excuse for presenting a novel in an abbreviated form is that it should convey a lot more than it says; the effect should be compressed, dynamic. My objections to *The Square* are therefore not directed against its intentions but against the book itself. These objections are as follows:

1. It reeks of art.

2. Short as it is, it is too long. That is to say, its action and development would justify a short story of not more than 2,000 words. Its present length of, say, 30,000 words is monotonously drawn out with repetitious talk.

3. The dialogue is insufficiently differentiated. (This may be partly the translators' business.) Consequently it is sometimes difficult to see who is speaking.

4. The experiment of an almost total dialogue-novel has almost

succeeded in changing the genre, so that it looks and sounds like a radio script.

Muriel Spark. Obs. July 19, 1959, p. 11

In my opinion, Marguerite Duras's work should be linked to that collection of widely varying attempts that is called the "new novel." The primary reason is the importance given to tempo in her work, the role that duration constantly plays in her writing. While all her works deal with passion (its development, its dangers, and its inevitability), passion is almost always . . . seen in terms of time, in terms of its essential relationship with the contradictory and complementary effects of duration. Time and passion: to be sure, this is not a new coupling. What *is* new, however, is the shift of emphasis, the importance given to a particular aspect of duration (which is stressed to the point of making it the protagonist of the story) and the constant concern with communicating the ambiguity of perceived duration to the reader.

The almost obsessive preoccupation with time, and the discovery of the novelistic possibilities of subjects that have their own time (or a dislocated time, like the world of memory)—these are undoubtedly among the most prominent features in the "new novelists," all of whom have read Proust, Joyce, and Faulkner. It is worth noting, however, that the "new novel" is often the story of a man, more precisely, of a narrator, who tries to come to terms with time, a story of how difficult it is to account for past time (Butor, Simon), a story that sometimes gives up or deliberately rejects any temporal perspective (Robbe-Grillet). But for Duras, duration and its effects are not technical problems . . . but a theme. And her very personal interpretation of this theme is what gives this novelist her special place in the French novel of today. What best characterizes her contribution (and is also the sign of her success) is undoubtedly the durable memory she leaves her readers of having been, for the space of a reading, subjected to a unique tempo. . . .

Jean-Luc Seylaz. Les romans de Marguerite Duras
(Paris, Archives des Lettres Modernes, 1963),
pp. 40–41†

We know that one of Marguerite Duras' favorite themes is absence and some of her characters hardly even seem to exist.

It may all be very clever, very profound and very moving, but it is also very convenient. Nothing is easier than to create a lifeless character who is barely explained by the author and who is the subject of fitful and vague discussions among the other characters, who are themselves without substance.

Such is the case of *The Vice-Consul.* Marguerite Duras calls her character Jean-Marc de H. He had been the French vice-consul at Lahore. He had been suspended from his duties for firing shots in the gardens of Shalimar, which were full of lepers and dogs. Some of them were killed. Now the vice-consul is waiting in Calcutta while his case is being decided. . . .

Why did he fire shots in the gardens of Shalimar? The author is careful not to tell us. It wouldn't be modern. And besides it would need imagination, some sequence of ideas, some knowledge of life and people, all those things which have been banished and declared obsolete, no doubt because they are very difficult to acquire.

In the same way, if the tools of the classic novelist have been abandoned is it because they are really out of date? Or isn't it rather because the "new novelists" are incapable of handling them? There is, to say the least, considerable doubt on this point.

Similar comments are inspired by the writing. There are one or two sentences in *The Vice-Consul* which are pleasant to read. The rest of the book alternates between banality and confusion.

Kléber Haedens. *Atlas*. April, 1966, pp. 254–55

The Afternoon of Mr. Andesmas hardly contains a story. Practically nothing happens in the afternoon described. An obese old man simply sits on the balcony of his mountain cottage and, from time to time, casts a glance on the village below. His solitude is absolute, painful, and poignant, and the gay musical fragments which sporadically reach his ears from down below emphasize his spiritual and physical loneliness. . . . Life is thus construed to be neither absurd, nor unjust, but simply terribly mediocre. Sometimes one falls in love, one marries, one has children or a clandestine affair. Impossible passions and calamitous dramas occur, incarnation and superiority seem within reach, only to fade quickly and plunge the victims into the antechamber of hell where neither hope can animate nor desire can stop the onrush of permanent acquiescence.

The lesson of *The Afternoon of Mr. Andesmas* crystallizes Mme. Duras' previously exposed views on the mediocrity of life. In her twenty-year-old career as playwright, film writer, and above all novelist, she has succeeded in synthesizing the qualities of what is generally called the "American Novel" with the engaging aspects of the New Novel now raging throughout Europe. She has managed to become neither so famous as Hemingway, for example, nor so notorious as Alain Robbe-Grillet. But her ability to combine the forces of the old with the lucidity of the new seems to assure her place in modern French literature. Her middle-of-the-road position represents, perhaps, the writer's own tacit assent to the inferiority of existence. Marguerite Duras, then, already widely known and appreciated by war-torn European readers who, more than others, have cause to question our "best of possible worlds," deserves a greater reception among the American intelligentsia, indeed among all *aficionados* of better writing.

Alfred Cismaru. DR. Summer, 1967, pp. 210–11

Duras' plays are all based on the aim at an absolute break or its realization. They are probing examinations of the leap into something other, a leap by which the characters invent or rediscover their authentic destinies. . . .

"The love that flows between them, stifling," at the end of *Suzanna Andler*, is beyond expression; it is a dazzling and radically new fact. . . . The "flow" of love at the end of *Suzanna Andler* has some resemblance to the denouement of *La Musica*. A marriage has fallen apart and ended in divorce. The husband and wife have both taken lovers, and they can thus remake their lives according to a bourgeois pattern. Instead of such a mediocre solution, Duras has husband and wife meet again for a few hours and discover a new form of love for each other—a new beginning, absolute but sublimated, for they will separate again, forever. Although they go on to their respective lovers, they have made the leap into a legendary situation—that of impossible love. The passion between them will grow, but it is beyond realization and beyond language, for it both unites and separates them.

At the end of these two plays something radically new has been initiated. The bourgeois stagnation of people who are bound socially, but isolated psychically, explodes. The beginnings of true communication are effected, which, for want of anything better, is called love. A clearer and more comprehensive explanation of things would no doubt destroy the absolute novelty of the event or, more precisely, the advent. A kind of private apocalypse is anticipated, which is both desired—for through it the characters come out of themselves to make contact with others—and dreaded, for, like all apocalypses, it can take place only if everything that exists is destroyed.

In Duras' works increasing emphasis has been placed on the necessary phase of destruction, an explosion of the present state of things, ranging from a rejection of bourgeois conventions to actual murder.

Jacques Guicharnaud. YFS. No. 46, 1971,
pp. 114–16

Duras has been writing since childhood, but it was not until 1944, when she was thirty, that she published her first novel. Since then her work has branched out in many directions: fifteen short novellas—or we might best call them prose narratives—the last entitled *Love*. Her work has become increasingly strange and hard to read, but it obsesses and fascinates those readers who have once entered Duras' world. She has written a book of short stories, two volumes of plays, and film scenarios, of which the best-known is *Hiroshima, My Love*, the film for which she wrote her first script. Lately, fascinated by the medium, Duras has started to produce her own films.

There is a kind of fluidity or plasticity in her writing that allows a narrative to become a play or scenario; indeed, her works sometimes go through the three media—narrative, play, script. Technically, Duras' narratives have tended toward musical forms, modulating basic themes that occur hauntingly throughout her work: madness, suffering, solitude, but also love. Her prose narratives set up highly stylized, simple scenarios in which characters, identified only by name, embody the buried unconscious needs and frustrations that, in Duras' view, haunt modern lives, blocked by the orderly mechanical patterns of bourgeois existence. Because they embody these emotional needs and deprivations, they enter into strange dialogues, encounters, and relationships. But whatever the characters and scenario, underlying them all is the theme of love— love as a mode of perception and total dispossession of the self, a love that includes the sexual as *one* of its modalities, but which does not exclude different modalities breaking with bourgeois patterns of exclusivity.

Germaine Brée. *Women Writers in France* (New Brunswick, N.J., Rutgers University Press, 1973), pp. 66–67

ÉLUARD, PAUL (1895–1952)

Paul Éluard belongs to a generation that has made serious experiments. This generation, influenced by some of Mallarmé's investigations—undoubtedly even more influenced by Rimbaud—has tried not to subject its inspirations or its writings to any preestablished rules; this generation has tried to abolish by its own example the constraint of faultless models and the prudent, calculated impulse that stems from knowledge. The young poet of today wishes to write down an intimate incantation using words born spontaneously in his mind—a series of words or syllables apparently improvised by the subconscious—disdaining any logical, ritual, rational, or even explicable connection between the words. "What does it matter?"

There is no doubt that some of these young writers, and Éluard above all, have at times created—no, I cannot use that word, since it implies design—have at times *gathered* strange effects of involuntary rhythm this way, have found images, created or evoked, that are simple, lively, and unexpected, images that a more deliberate artist could never have produced. In *Capital of Pain* there are curious successes of this sort; there are also a great number of passages that the reader could easily live without. Often, after a strange leap into the dreamlike or the beautiful, the impulse seems to give way, exhausted, or is broken up by some triviality whose coarse appearance spoils the freshness and simplicity that first made us so enthusiastic.

Perhaps I am mistaken. Éluard, it seems to me, senses the dangers of maintaining a role that forbids him even to serve as a filter for his own feelings. Choice intervenes, as does unified organization, especially in the series "New Poems" [in *Capital of Pain*], which consists mainly of prose poems. I would consider it unfortunate, given Éluard's innate gifts, if he did not someday reach the point of understanding the necessity for an equilibrium—even one that gave predominance to instinct—between the mysterious suggestions of long, undefined reveries and the fruits of deliberate thought. A man of Éluard's intelligence and education cannot escape deliberate thought even if he wants to—and frequently he proves as much.

André Fontanas. *MdF*. Jan. 15, 1927, pp. 405–6†

Since about 1924 Éluard's thought has gravitated around the reality of love, or the reality of solitude, which is only the absence of love. It grasps ever more tightly and deeply that elusive point where the flesh and the spirit, realism and idealism—to use André Breton's terms—"are no longer perceived as contradictions."

It is metaphysical poetry in that it makes love a cosmic drama, in the resolution of which the whole universe is interested; it takes place in "the abysmal darkness which tends fully to a dazzling confusion" (*Immediate Life*) and only the presence of which can be felt, since the darkness itself remains inaccessible to the methods or formulas of psychology.

The climate of this poetry is purity. . . . There dwells in Éluard an ardent inexorable aspiration toward purity, toward the absolute of love. He does not know what he is, toward what end he is moving, what revelation awaits him—and always fails to materialize. In "New Poems" [in *Capital of Pain*], he sometimes abandons himself to sweetness, his joy breaks out and is prolonged in a tranquil luminous ecstasy. . . . This peace is precarious. One cannot establish oneself in love, where desire alternates with despair, presence with absence. Solitude soon prevails in a mental universe where the mind spins amid deathly silence. "The new star of love" will not rise.

And yet, She comes closer, She moves away, always alive; nothing exists except in Her look, in a long dream in which night is mingled with day, in which all things are incessantly shattered, to be vainly reborn in a radiation of innocence duplicated by darkness, in an anguish sometimes interrupted by a humble and tender jubilation of the soul. A process quite different and far more serious than that of chivalrous love, however lofty, than idolatrous submission to a *domina*. Here we have to do with a spell, a "possession" that makes self-possession impossible, that makes solitude an ever-yawning abyss, and love a temptation stronger than life. And in the universal solitude nothing answers, no echo, no reassuring voice dropping from a transcendent beyond. [1933]

Marcel Raymond. *From Baudelaire to Surrealism*
(London, Methuen, 1970), pp. 281–82

Paul Éluard, one of the original members of the Dada "school," moved into Surrealism, under the leadership of André Breton, when "the Dada anarchy" was outlawed. He has held closely to the tenets of Surrealism through all their hardening and stiffening, in spite of the fact that his gifts seem perfectly opposed to all that Surrealism once stood for, and all it stands for now. The reasons for his alliance with Dada would be somewhat difficult to determine.

It was natural, certainly, that a talent like Éluard's—simple and sensitive, quite unclouded by the fumes of the macabre, and undisturbed by the sardonic horse-play and involved cynicism of his sturdier contemporaries—should be forced, during the post-War years, to take on some kind of protective coloring, make some defensive alliance, in order to exist. Such a talent was one of the exact kind to move his contemporaries to parody. Éluard's complete complaisance to Surrealist doctrine, before and after Surrealism's alliance with "the revolution," permitted him to go on writing; but his passivity has lapsed, at times, into a kind of masochism, vitiating his work and making his "thinking" ridiculous. He has never rebelled against Breton's manifestos and excommunications; he is, in fact, the complete complement of Breton, who has been called the Saint-Just of Surrealism. He obediently became a Communist when Surrealism, the party wedded to complete nonutilitarianism and to the exploration of the wayward subconscious, automatism and the dream, developed a dogma equally unyielding, and in many ways paralleling Communist dogma. Éluard has obeyed, it is true, without once changing his fundamental poetic nature. He stands today in the peculiar position of a poet who has remained a depository of one kind of poetic expression . . . while paying more than lip-service to doctrines in every way inimical to the development of that expression. . . .

That Éluard's gifts should have been forced, by the fashion or neurosis of his period, to disguise themselves as "unconscious" (so that their true imaginative flights will not lie open to scorn), and be reduced to the level of a word game, is peculiar enough. That they should have been twisted into the use of propaganda, and made to function under manifestoes, literary and otherwise, will certainly amuse future critics and diagnosticians of his era. [1939]

Louise Bogan. A Poet's Alphabet (New York,
McGraw-Hill, 1970), pp. 112–13, 122

There are few French poets in whose work the symbols are as direct and as visible as in Éluard's. The most important of these symbols, the one that determines all the others and constantly draws the others to itself, is the first person singular, the "I." This "I" . . . flows out in every direction from the poet's pure, lyrical personality. Éluard's "I," which constantly recurs in his poetry as a criterion of absolute evidence, is a perfect example of the *universal* "I." Although this "I" is inseparable from the poet's temperament, his own way of grasping the world, this "I" is also the principle of internal cohesion of a larger world rehabilitated by language, a world from which any merely personal drama is excluded—although the tragic destiny of each man does not thereby disappear. . . .

Éluard's poetry never contains the name of God; his poetry ignores the religious drama, the incommensurable solitude of man before the Lord of all creation. . . . The frequency of a mystical language in Éluard's poetry stems from womankind. What the poet adores in woman —in *the* special woman—is the permanence and the unique light, "which lighteth every man that cometh into the world" (the definition of "the Word" given in the first chapter of the Gospel according to Saint John). But in Éluard's poetry it is as if the mystical connection has been reversed, with the deity adoring his own image: the symbol of the *mirror*, or the gaze whose function is to reflect, is constantly joined to the symbol of woman. And, as I have said, all these symbols proceed from a more primitive symbol, that of the universal "I," which asserts itself at every moment in the unity of its metamorphoses.

Pierre Emmanuel. Le je universel chez Paul Éluard
(Paris, GLM, 1948), pp. 14–15, 29–30†

All who gave to the Resistance in the fullest measure of their means cannot forget the large part played by Paul Éluard in its organization. This poet, whom nothing seemingly designated to lead difficult and dangerous action, gave himself to it completely; at the same time that he was writing poems whose publication contributed immeasurably to the spiritual resurrection of France, he helped in rallying a great number of young writers. . . .

He sings the misery of a country which will not despair and which finds in its suffering the very reason for its revolt. He evokes Paris, Paris which sings no longer in the streets, her unresigned people, the faces of the innocent being led to death, the struggle carried on by so many heroes who had nothing left but the desire to wipe out the despicable invader. All who have met Paul Éluard in the streets of this city where he has always lived have understood the esteem in which he holds this people who "tolerate no injustice." He went from one neighborhood to the other, carrying a brief-case loaded with forbidden papers and clandestine editions, each day risking recognition and arrest. After the publication of *Poetry and Truth 1942*, which the German Institute denounced as a dangerous tract, he changed residence each month, taking with him only crumpled bits of paper on which he wrote the first drafts of his poems. For a long while his existence was one which so many intellectuals have known; but few of them have expressed, as he has, all its misery and grandeur.

Louis Parrot. In Paul Éluard, *Selected Writings*
(Norfolk, Conn., New Directions, 1951),
pp. xxii–xxiii

Éluard Dada, Éluard surrealist, Éluard of the Resistance, Éluard of the Communist Party, and—if you want to be complete—Éluard the unanimist in his first writings: these are the different figures literary historians will probably enjoy differentiating in Paul Éluard, as they sift through his life and divide it up into periods, as if it were possible to slice up coldly so unified a destiny without running the risk, through fragmentation, of missing precisely what constituted the unity of that destiny, and what must therefore correspond to the permanent and essential traits of a life such as Éluard's.

From the strictly formal point of view, of course, it is undeniable that such divisions can be seen in Éluard's work, as in the work of many artists and poets. But once we pursue an examination beneath the surface, our interest becomes the profound sources and not merely the efflorescences of these sources—and continuity becomes obvious. Soon we can perceive an image of the fundamental Paul Éluard, whose development consisted of moving—not without detours, conflicts, setbacks, and tribulations—"from the horizon of one man to the horizon of all." . . .

The same movement toward others that had gradually led Éluard to emphasize explicitly emotional poetry over poetry dominated (at least in appearance) by free invention, led him to make his poetry militant in the highest and most complete sense of "militant poetry": a weapon in the hands of a man who not only was involved in political struggle but struggled for man and for poetry itself, insofar as poetry was a sign of and a means of attaining complete humanity.

Michel Leiris. *Europe.* July–Aug., 1953,
pp. 50–51, 56†

I was traveling in Belgium when I learned of Paul Éluard's death. The wife of the mayor with whom I was staying announced the death to me in a quiet and solemn voice, as if it were the death of a close friend. In the course of my travels I discovered that the whole nation was in mourning. This was the greatness of Éluard: during his own lifetime he became a classic for men and women who did not otherwise pride themselves on their interest in literature. Somewhere André Gide defined classicism as "controlled romanticism"; this definition precisely describes Éluard's work.

His whole work does nothing but express, day after day, a life that was lived passionately. It was standard to call Éluard the poet of love. And it was true. What was so admirable and unusual was that this love was "unique" in all its metamorphoses. Éluard only loved and only sang about one woman throughout his career, always the same woman, who disappeared "in order to reappear." In this sense, "love chooses love without changing its face."

Through this woman, through his unique love, the poet-soothsayer discovers and re-creates the world. . . . He abandons himself to the woman's *attraction*, to the rhythm of her eyes, the way a dove abandons itself to a serpent. . . . But the *abandon* of the lover-beloved is an active abandon. The cultivation of passion enables the lover to forge the language of a seer. The poet develops this language patiently and precisely, by methodically putting the laws of grammar into disorder. He does more, because he has to transcribe an intangible world; he creates for himself a "tangible language" by establishing new relationships among words and by making "customary use of the most uncustomary images." Once he does this, he only has to call "things by their names" for them to blossom and flower, creating and transcribing a new world.

Léopold Sédar Senghor. Europe. July–Aug., 1953,
pp. 167–68†

Critics who sought to establish degrees of so-called "accessibility" used to say in the twenties and thirties that Éluard was a poet for a hundred amateurs of Éluard. This was true in so far as Éluard's poetry was at that time unknown to a wide public. Then the Second World War broke out. Millions of Frenchmen copied out poems by a man they had not heard of before; with those poems, hostages faced execution and partisans went into battle. The "poet for a hundred amateurs" turned out to be understandable to everyone and understood by all.

Perhaps the reason was that Éluard's poetry had changed? Was he writing differently? When one speaks about poets who become Communists it is usual to establish a turning-point in their work: until the year so-and-so he wrote about love and wrote incomprehensibly; in the year so-and-so he saw the light and began writing about public issues in a manner accessible to all. This kind of classification seems to me somewhat oversimplified. In the case of Éluard, it is altogether inapplicable: it is difficult to find a turning-point in his work; there exists a direct link between his early poems and those he wrote shortly before his death. Naturally, new thoughts, new subjects, fresh hope appeared: they were brought in by life itself. But Éluard was outraged in his youth by war, injustice, and the violation of human dignity; and in his last years he did not abandon the theme of love. . . .

If we compare Éluard's poems on political subjects with his lyrical poems, we see no split between them. When he was writing about the *maquis*, about the grief of Mount Grammos, about the fighters for peace, the thoughts and feelings that inspired him were the same as those which had dictated his poems about personal sorrow, love, and death. What predetermined Éluard's political life? Above all, his inexhaustible desire for justice. . . . He truly suffered from injustice, not only as a citizen but as a poet. He loved freedom no less than justice and never opposed one love to the other. He responded to freedom with his whole being. Better than to any other contemporary, Pushkin's words apply to Éluard: "In my cruel age I have glorified freedom." [1958]

Ilya Ehrenburg. *Chekhov, Stendhal, and Other Essays*
(New York, Alfred A. Knopf, 1963),
pp. 238–39, 242

The dominant characteristic of Éluard in his earliest surrealist poetry was the love theme. In his later period, love remained for him, as well as for Aragon and Breton, an expression of the innermost recesses of human personality. A spontaneous physical and spiritual relationship with the loved one makes her the intermediary between the creative sensibility of the poet and the sensations to be conjured from the earth. In her are reflected the beauties of the material world and the impressions of the poet. Love makes the senses keener and the imagination more acute, delivers the poet better than anything else from the notions of time and space; love is at the same time the center and the circumference of his universe: "world where without you I have nothing." From personal love to communion with all of humanity is a natural step and one which inspired him to say, despite all the hatred about him: "I love for the sake of loving and I shall die of love."

It is in *Uninterrupted Poetry*, written immediately after the termination of hostilities, that Éluard gave his most complete expression of his parallel loves for his wife and for humanity, and the ultimate relationship of these feelings with the universe. With the surrealist's belief that this world is all, and that there is enough here if only we develop sufficient elasticity of insight, he proceeded from the narrow perception of the blind of eye and of heart to the apocalypse of the visionary. He draws upon multiple perspectives as he and his loved one rise step by step, widening the scope of their senses and exploring their powers of divination. . . .

But the mirror was to break. Éluard suffered soon after the war the excruciating tragedy of losing his beloved wife, Nusch, in an accident. He and his friends did not think that he could survive the devastating blow or bear the resulting solitude. Yet, his next volume, *A Lesson in*

Morality, is a reiteration and a reinforcement of faith in the ability of a poet to transform the world and attain its inner unity. [1959]

Anna Balakian. Surrealism: The Road to the Absolute
(New York, Dutton, 1970), pp. 220–21, 223

The hand of a man who picks a rose feels the prick of the thorn before the action of picking the rose has been completed, and his whole being is immediately affected by a physical sensation that sets the complex life of the individual in motion, his body as well as his mind. Thus, if I can borrow an expression from Hegel, Éluard is struck not by the abstract essence of objects but by their concrete reality. The power of physical sensations creates his poetry. . . .

The words Éluard uses . . . are most frequently chosen from among those signifying an object, or an immediately perceptible aspect of an object. There are no chiseled jewels and no abstruse terms in his poetry; rather, there are clear words, words used every day—the most easily recognizable words. His is a poetry created for everyone, created from everyone's thoughts, a poetry offering us the rewards of what we could see ourselves if our eyes were open wide enough. Rimbaud exploded, Verlaine sang, Mallarmé measured, and Apollinaire modulated; Éluard owes scarcely anything to these earlier poetic experiments, which he nonetheless respected almost with affection and whose value he recognized. . . .

His language does not strive for alchemy; it has no aim other than economy of means in saying what is essential. For Éluard, vocabulary definitely does not mean an agreeable freedom offered to the writer; rather, it means a possibility of coming to a better understanding. The term he chooses is *sign*: the word is the sign of an idea, and the idea serves to deepen thought. The primary function of language, according to Éluard, is to enable people to communicate with one another. Language serves knowledge by fixing an idea; therefore, one must always seek the most accurate word, the one best able to halt the march of reality, which is constantly in the act of changing.

Louis Perche. Paul Éluard (Paris, Éditions
Universitaires, 1963), pp. 47, 76–77, 80†

Ever since Éluard's 1926 poem "Pablo Picasso" the ties of affection between the two men [became] constantly stronger and closer, aided, in the early days, by the association of the surrealists with Picasso, who illustrated several collections of Éluard's work. In 1936 the poet delivered a lecture on Picasso in Barcelona, to accompany a retrospective exposition of his painting. But poet and painter became active partners only after the outbreak of the Spanish Civil War, which stirred up their consciences and brought about a mutation of their art. Together they took up an unshakable position in the face of those climactic events. The great stanzas written by Éluard at the time form an echo to Picasso's *Guernica*. Their taste for life, their intrinsic force, their will to transform pain and hardship into the joy of creation are the common denominators of their friendship. To the most realist of painters and the most visual of poets—neither of whom can imagine life without love— art is the act of living and seeing and not of imagining and dreaming. Based on the physical, it demands the support of the real, and flees from anything gratuitous. . . .

[In 1945 Éluard] showed me some of his own manuscripts, and I was surprised by the number of changes and corrections he had made. His poems are so simple, so clear, in the reading, that one would think they had been written in a single burst of inspiration. Éluard shatters this illusion. Not one of them has been born of the tip of the pen. He writes them laboriously, sometimes struggling with them for a long time. "There is just as much of the conscious will as of spontaneity in a poem," he tells me. "Few fortuitous images can take their place in a poem, just as they occur. They must be clarified, mastered, according to the feeling that dominates the poem. Intoxication demands to be carefully written out, verbal frenzy to be controlled by the sensitivity of the poet." [1964]

Brassaï. *Picasso & Co.* (Garden City, N.Y.,
Doubleday, 1966), pp. 151, 155

In Éluard's idiom nature is not a symbol or image of the beloved, the beloved is not a symbol or image of nature. The union has gone far beyond such a level. And through it a vital relation of man and nature has been re-established, recognising alienation but overcoming it in the ceaseless adventure of experience. More, this relation, based as it is in the union of man and woman, is one of love. Man is not only reunited with nature; he is also merged with it in terms of a love that takes him right into the heart of the meaning of process. There is no abstraction of purpose, but everything has purpose within the unitary process that embraces both man and nature. The demarcation of human and natural is affirmed only to be broken down, broken down to be affirmed.

Woman is the intermediary; and because of her greater power of participation in process, both passively and actively, because of her "generosity of blood," she heals the wound of alienation. Through her existence in all things, she ends the emotion of *absence*, on which the paradoxes of poetry from the Trobadors or Hafiz to Mallarmé had been based. The element of estrangement and violence in the Rimbaudian derangement of the senses is eliminated by this comprehension of the transformative process of life and art. The senses are separate and are one, and are part of the flow and change, the formative movement, of nature. Focused in touch, in Éluard's trembling fingers, they achieved this new unity of man in woman and woman in man, in the perpetual flow of love.

This love, dynamically centred on the love of man and woman, is also love of all men—a universal love saved from all abstraction or emptiness by its origin and endless renewal in the senses. Éluard incarnated this love, as no one I have known or can imagine. He was a man indeed of such transparent honesty, kindliness, gentleness, that he inspired affection in all who knew him. Even his anger was always an aspect of his love. . . . Once I mentioned an English writer who had said he'd rather see the atomic bomb used than meet a Communist world-triumph. Éluard was so affected that he rose and could not keep still, he moved anxiously about the room with the horror chilling him, his hand touching familiar things. "Why, rather than have the bomb used I'd prefer to see class-society last for ever." Yet the thought of class-society thus lasting would have meant the end of every dream and hope he had for men. [1968]

Jack Lindsay. *Meetings with Poets* (New York,
Frederick Ungar, 1969), pp. 204–5

Éluard's surrealist verse, passion oriented, is neither the love-sick sigh of adolescence nor the professional smile of the Don Juan. It ignores politics as well as philosophy. If some of the surrealists can be called literary dilettantes—those who take themselves more seriously than they do their work—Éluard belongs to another, smaller group of those accepted (sometimes only temporarily!) for personal reasons, despite Breton's comment that Éluard wrote automatically. . . .

Although Éluard broke with Breton in 1938 on the question of how best to oppose the Nazi menace, there is no radical change in the thematic content of his poetry. The influence of the rupture appears, but in veiled terms only, as is almost invariably so when Éluard is dealing with persons and situations close to him. Whether this reflects an artistic attempt to universalize the particular or some deeper reticence at placing his sorrows and pleasures before a scandal-hungry public, or both, is not of major importance in this context. There can be no doubt that Éluard consciously refrained from revealing all, or that he modified his themes in the direction of comprehension (the subjective element is always under control), and that, as a matter of course, he rejected the fanciful structure of his more doctrinaire colleagues. While this in no way denies that the point of departure was some inspirational gift of the gods, the end result so clearly reveals an *intellectus agens*, a poetic vision deficient

What I wish to remember above all is that during the sad hours of the Occupation, Emmanuel's poetry was—along with that of Aragon, Jouve, Éluard, and a few others—the lyrical expression of the French Resistance.

In 1942 *Fight with Your Defenders*, that vibrant call to Resistance, appeared in Switzerland; later, when France had not yet been liberated, *Day of Anger* and *XX Cantos* were published in Algeria. *XX Cantos* are to Emmanuel's vehement work what Hugo's *Songs of the Streets and Woods* are to his *Punishments*. For Emmanuel has more than one lyrical vein, and if some of his songs have an epic quality, others move us by their bareness and simplicity. Emmanuel is indeed one of those rare thinkers, like Baudelaire and Valéry, who are able to apply an intellectual system to creative activity.

Georges Cattauï. RdP. July, 1968, pp. 143–45†

[In Emmanuel's work] after a long, sometimes hesitant, approach man prepares himself for mystical union with God. For a brief moment that union seems to be attained; for a moment man seems to be lost in infinite totality, in contact with a divine Being who seems to fill man with His inexpressible abundance. After this eternal instant—so brief that man cannot even say whether he has really experienced it or not—he finds himself alone once again, thrown back on the shore of his own self. At the very least, mystical union was a partial failure. . . . The cause of this semi-failure lies in the more-or-less conscious refusal, mingled with desire, that man opposes to his own impulse toward elevation, preventing himself from reaching the goal toward which he has been aiming. It is as if a love-hate is alternately or simultaneously propelling him and then pulling him back.

The consequence of this semi-failure is that it modifies, if not deepens, the understanding of the fundamental relationship between man and God, which will be henceforth marked by a *dialectical reciprocity* in which refusal and quest are paradoxically combined. . . .

The impulse behind Emmanuel's poetry is essentially an aspiration toward unity with God, the search for a unitary relationship with the Absolute. Nevertheless, his poetry can be called neither strictly mystical nor strictly Christian—Pierre Emmanuel is correct in saying so. His poetry is *the expression of a mystical intention with a Christian inflection*.

Sven E. Siegrist. Pour et contre Dieu: Pierre
Emmanuel; ou, La poésie de l'approche (Boudry,
Switzerland, Éditions de la Baconnière, 1971),
pp. 331, 333†

FARGUE, LÉON-PAUL (1876-1947)

Fargue's *Poems* places a large obstacle before the average reader: this book does not have Vanity as its principal author. *Poems* does not deal in the usual currency passed between men who have no inner life—self-indulgence. We are no longer accustomed to such books: anyone who reads nothing but contemporary writing is almost completely unaware that such books ever existed. . . .

There is another obstacle that the reader must surmount before being fully able to appreciate Fargue's poetry. This poetry does not smile at the public, flatter the readers, or treat them with exaggerated politeness. So many modern writers are reminiscent of those young flower girls who stand along the roadside near famous sites, run up to cars, and force strangers to buy their flowers by throwing them into the car. Fargue's poetry could be compared instead to a beautiful statue in the center of an open space in a park: one should approach the statue and see it from every side. But this analogy pertains only to Fargue's attitude toward the public. His poetry does not have the immobility of statues: it is living and breathing flesh, with no trace of Parnassian impassiveness. Fargue's poetry has, quite simply, the high dignity of art, which the Greeks expressed by making the Muses virgins.

The last obstacle in approaching Fargue's poetry, and not the least, is that his poetry is so well constructed, so carefully stripped of ornaments and emphatic punctuation, its form so sober, clear, and spare, that the reader must be very attentive to grasp all of its merit on a first reading. [1912]

Valery Larbaud. *MdF*. June, 1963, pp. 255-57†

I have just reread Fargue's poems. . . . I had to abandon my facile preconceived notion about Fargue's similarity to Arthur Rimbaud. This notion, arbitrary yet almost reassuring, had nonetheless been appealing. Why? Undoubtedly because Fargue, whenever he is asked, reads aloud [Rimbaud's] "The Drunken Boat" in a voice overwhelmed by love.

Rimbaud's masterpiece generated a whole vogue for exotic poetry, adventure poetry. . . .

Fargue's poetry does not have the excesses of [that of Rimbaud's followers]. Fargue's discreet yet tumultuous sensitivity releases a strangely private sob that has its source in Fargue alone. But if I were to look for influences, I would go to the vivid imagination and enchanting labyrinthine structures of Jules Laforgue, the impeccable style of Colette, and the heartrending and truthful *andante* rhythm Oscar Wilde discovered through his suffering. . . .

I have recently been reading Issue 10 of the magazine *Commerce*. No matter how prepared one may be for Fargue's verbal sorcery, the spell cast by "The Shipwrecker's Second Tale" is nevertheless surprising. Fargue's humor has the casualness and the touchingly serious inventiveness of children's games. Fargue's skillful drollery has the cadence of a classical poem (for perfection in drollery necessitates as much mastery as perfection in an ode or a sonnet). One can justifiably claim that Fargue alone possesses the gift for robust nonchalance.

Comtesse de Noailles. *Les feuilles libres.*
June, 1927, pp. 22–23†

The Prix de la Renaissance has just been awarded to M. Léon-Paul Fargue, though without making it clear whether it is to honor the whole of this author's work or the latest volume, which according to the papers is called *After Paris*, but which is not yet on sale anywhere.

What more does M. Léon-Paul Fargue need to attain glory? He edits a revue entitled *Commerce*, a beautiful and luxurious publication which appears with charming irregularity. He has published a considerable number of little booklets which were united two or three years ago in two volumes, *Spaces* and *Under the Lamp*. He starts a revolution at the [Café des] Deux Magots each time he shaves off his beard or allows it to grow again. We are unable to give any information as to the present state of this face which has recently been adorned with laurels. To crown his success, his friends never speak of him but by his Christian name, and Léon-Paul bids fair to become as illustrious as Jean-Jacques.

In view of all this, it must be a little galling to be discovered, crowned, and rewarded with paper francs like any young author who has just brought out his first book. When you're already turned fifty! [1931]

Robert Brasillach. Quoted in André Beucler,
The Last of the Bohemians: Twenty Years with
Léon-Paul Fargue (New York, William Sloane
Associates, 1954), pp. 128–29

It has often been said, and rightly so, that for Fargue poetry was to an exceptional degree not an intentional choice but a calling, the satisfying of a passion. This quality is evident at every point in his work, as is the profusion of special gifts that hard work alone cannot achieve. But it would be wrong to assume that reflection, as well as all sorts of subtle calculations and expert deliberations, had no place in Fargue's private world. In fact, he meditated a great deal, about himself, about his predecessors, about his imitators. He certainly did not have any theories; or rather, he put on an affectation of avoiding formulas that would have seemed too general. But—at times practically in secret—he did elaborate very firm principles, and he stuck to them. He was not very concerned about changes in fashion, even when those changes seemed likely to favor his own preferences. He distrusted modishness.

Against anything that was central to the art of writing, against any of the main disputes or questions of our age, Fargue kept a very keen vigilance. He was always able to differentiate between shades which are apparently close which consequently are lost on writers of cruder or less discriminating vision. Therefore, Fargue came close to losing his temper when people praised him or honored him as a precursor [of surrealism] by comparing him with those who consider verbalism an autonomous spark, an independent source of creation, when Fargue knew very well that his intense verbal gift and the delight he took in applying this gift were of a quite different order, a different "shade." He even made fun of hermeticism in poetry, although his poems do seem to a large extent full of obscure allusions and enigmas. But Fargue was not being self-contradictory, nor was he merely defending himself against annoying flattery; he had a precise idea of his own approach to poetry.

Jules Romains. CS. 286, 1947, pp. 929–30†

In 1943 Fargue was struck with a hemiplegia that confined him for the rest of his life. . . . The stroke removed an essential quality from his work, but intensified his journey into the interior; immobility caused him to call upon the reserves of memory and dream, on a generous, active past that shimmered in the white light of remembrance, the days of the *belle époque*. Memories crowded into his solitude, crackling under his pillow, he says, like insects of glass.

But there was an irreparable change in the legend of Fargue the "old boy," trailing around Paris for hours on end in his own faithful taxi; a change from the noctambulant, irresponsible poet, the idler on the alert, the gourmand, always turning in the enchanted circle of Paris. . . .

A collection of short pieces, half essay and half prose-poem, published under the title *Total Solitude* in 1941, is perhaps the best expression of every attitude that had developed in Fargue. Heaven and Hell, the Deadly Sins, the virtues, the Music of the Spheres and the Dance of Death, the Feast of Fools and the Chain of Being are his skeletal beliefs: his preoccupations are chimera and mutability, his own sensibility and vulnerable heart, and the hazards of the brittle mould of flesh. His method was to write a "literature of enchantment": he expressed a horror of style "that does not whet the appetite," for style, he claimed, should be a Twelfth-tide cake with a hidden reward for the good reader. In practice, this brought certain difficulties in its wake; in fact, the reader suffers occasional indigestion from too rich a material and too liberal a love of such devices as telescoped metaphors, puns, conceits, Spoonerisms . . . inversions, and categories of things to all appearance unrelated but whose clandestine marriage he loved to make public— although it must be said that Fargue is masterly in the quick discernment of "occult resemblances," the *discordia concors* that is part of the substance of poetry.

TLS. July 22, 1955, p. 410

Fargue, a poet of quality, was admired by an elite and soon given recognition by those *he* admired. But never during his lifetime did he receive the widespread acclaim he deserved. No matter how modest and even unfulfilled his poetic work may have been—as in fact all poetic work is—Fargue's excellence should have been sufficient to bring him more fame. But the man himself, unconcerned, was too much a poet to gain fame by organizing a literary career. . . .

Fargue was the younger spiritual brother of Valéry and Claudel, and he contributed his share to the new song. He was closer to our century than Jammes, closer to the heart of French poetry than Apollinaire, and he was praised very early by Gide for a poem in *Tancrède*. During the heyday of modernism Fargue was able to capture a specific aspect of the French spirit as it then existed. Fargue sounded a note that rang true, a note he alone sounded in the symphony created by half a century of French poetry. . . .

He belonged to no school or movement; he belonged only to the French poetic community, where the living and ever-increasing sum of an evolving heritage is gathered. Fashions, tendencies, or literary doctrines could alter, the stream itself could change its bed, but Fargue followed his own path, according to his own requirements. The same tonality marks all of Fargue's poetry, from his first poem on. The same inflection, simple yet personal, seems to carry his work along from the first measure of the song to the last. Fargue was always, ceaselessly, himself, propelled by his inspiration and faithful to it, approaching every frontier without ever doing anything alien to his own nature.

Saint-John Perse. *NRF*. Aug., 1963, pp. 197, 199–200†

François Villon's Paris was closer to the Paris writers knew before World War II than our Paris is to theirs. Of all the writers who celebrated Paris before World War II, Fargue is the one who experienced the metamorphosis on a completely emotional level—in other words, he lived through a Baudelairean farewell to the self as the city rearranged itself in new proportions and overturned its own horizons. The Paris Fargue had celebrated in *The Parisian Pedestrian* was indeed the city as it was before World War *I*. . . .

To consider Fargue only the poet of Paris, because he proclaimed himself—not without pride—the city's exemplary pedestrian, would be to overlook important aspects of his poetic work. Moreover, it should not be forgotten that Fargue's total output falls into two genres (related, to be sure, but strangely and meaningfully separate): poetry, from which Fargue abruptly turned away, as if he had chosen Rimbaud's sudden silence in that area; and his essays written for newspapers, read on the radio, finally gathered in various volumes—essays that make Fargue's Paris unforgettable.

Hubert Juin. *MagL*. Oct., 1973, pp. 44–45†

FAYE, JEAN-PIERRE (1925–   )

The most recently baptized of literary categories, the "new novel," a phrase to which I would object primarily because it means nothing and because it makes honorable people say a lot of foolish things, also provokes so much exasperation and so much sarcasm in many critics that I shall be very careful not to affix that label on *Between the Streets*, the most unusual, the most baffling, and perhaps the most original novel published in a long time. . . .

From the very first words, in fact, with no intermediary, we find ourselves inside the narrator's own skin: we will henceforth feel only with his skin, his nervous system; we will see only with his eyes; we will understand only with his brain. In addition, in this vision, feeling, and understanding we will not be one second ahead of the narrator or one second behind him. Jean-Pierre Faye has removed optical distance and organization from his novel, the methods by which a writer makes it easier for the reader—and for himself—to approach a fictional character and understand his state of mind, his thoughts, and his mental processes, even when they are instantaneous. In other words, this text does not include a single one of the arrangements, or the light touches, by

which Faulkner, for example, organizes even the stream of consciousness of an idiot [in *The Sound and the Fury*].

Faye immerses his reader in the discontinuous brutality of immediate experience, in the maddening eruption of sensations that are never
analyzed but are immediately associated with one another or conceptual-
ized without any explanation. . . .

In *Between the Streets* we therefore participate in the obstinate,
hesitant moves of a man trying to orient himself within a country, a city,
a society, and an action that are foreign to him. What is his goal? . . .
Does he not ultimately seek to conquer the central fact of his condition
(of the entire human condition?): his situation as a foreigner? If he
finds *his* place in the vast urban and social landscape that is infinitely
dispersed, concealed between the streets, then he will find his identity, his own personal angle of intersection with reality.

Olivier de Magny. LetN. Nov., 1958, pp. 605–7†

It is certainly true that *Analogues* often makes one think of a book of
rough sketches like those used by painters. Not because the scenes that
comprise it are blurry, vague, or unfinished, but because they interrupt
each other, cut each other off, and break off (if necessary, with an
"etc."); they never conclude, and their only meaning and significance is
in the resulting counterpoint. The old technique of counterpoint is
strangely rejuvenated here: the scenes Faye places side by side are not
alternate views of the same reality but are primarily *pages*, fragments,
bursts of written material arranged like the facets of a prism or the
reflections in a prism of a multiple universe. This multiple universe is
that of Jean-Pierre Faye, or more precisely, of his preceding novels.
From *Between the Streets* to *The Break* and *Pulsation*, this novelist has
been following a difficult narrow route, along which he has sought to
exercise his penetrating, shifting, vigorous vision of things, a very personal vision. The idea of adding to these first three novels a fourth that
would be, as he says, their "multiplication table" was interesting insofar
as it allowed him to return to everything that was latent, implicit, invisible, and "possible" in the relationships that united the characters in his
earlier books, to "multiply" those relationships, and to develop them by
analogy. . . .

Faye's point of departure—the juxtaposition of flat, static, concrete
scenes—clarifies the conception of a book like this one as well as a
whole area of contemporary literature: the written words take on a
value totally independent of the collection of ideas or actions they express. The written words have the characteristics of concrete raw material, comparable to the material manipulated by composers in music

that is called, indeed, "concrete." Written words become part of a *composition* just like visual or aural material. . . .

I do not pretend that there are no risks in this kind of attempt. But a method that would not work for other writers can work for a writer whose vision can instinctively create rapid forms, sharp angles, and movements of light out of the tissue of reality. I think that Faye is such a writer. . . .

Raymond Jean. *Le monde.* Aug. 29, 1964, p. 7†

The central theme of Jean-Pierre Faye's *The Canal Lock*, which has just won the Prix Renaudot, is once again a divided world, torn apart by two opposing sides. . . . But the novel is hardly about racial or political rivalries; it touches on them only very tangentially. The problems are internalized. The disorder that is the subject of this book is none other than the disorder of the secret universe each one of us carries inside.

To illustrate such a drama, Faye has written a book whose quality and whose richness are unquestionable, but the book is so unrelentingly hermetic (albeit less so than Faye's previous books) and the writing is so unusual that more than one reader may well put down the book after a few pages. . . .

The richness and originality of this book undoubtedly result from a skillful, subtle counterpoint, by which the world of reflective thought and the world of purely physical sensation constantly confront one another: the world of imagination and desire is confronted by the world of imposed facts. Several themes are intermingled—not presented one after the other but perceived simultaneously. This novel uses to the fullest both the rigorous analysis of the "new novel" and the poetic juxtapositions of surrealism. But the audacious synthesis of two so different literary movements contributes to the book's obscurity, and this obscurity may well be an indication that Faye has not completely mastered his art, which can be seen most clearly in the incantatory power of his images and the skillful construction of some of the conversations.

Louis Barjon. *Études.* Jan., 1965, pp. 82, 85†

In *Analogues*, a book that is not for anyone who does not have twenty hours at his disposal, Faye concludes his tetralogy by building a solid form in space, a trihedral, out of his three previous "novels" (or triangles).

It is impossible to recount the story contained in these four "novels": the story is formed out of novelistic *equations*, and nobody would ask the physicist Heisenberg to recount what one of his equations means, as if it were a comical or amusing story; the equation fills a whole blackboard with symbols that are meaningless to the uninitiated.

Faye is a geometrician of the novel. And geometry cannot be summarized; it is studied. To read *Analogues* and the books that preceded it, one needs index cards, diagrams, and a blackboard.

Nevertheless, Faye does not lack a novelistic imagination. In 1964, the same year as *Analogues*, he also published *The Canal Lock*. . . . Berlin, a city of encounters, a city of intrigues, a city cut in two, is the "double" of Jerusalem, which is also cut in two. . . . The fine paradox and the fine boldness of the novel is that such a specific contemporary subject, which could inspire adventure novels or pseudo-journalistic novels, is treated in a wonder-struck, slow-moving, mysterious, poetic, and intentionally imprecise style. I know perfectly well that Faye, primarily an artist, primarily interested in the novel as "written material," did not wish to "deal with a subject," especially a subject that is specific, limited, historical, and novelistic. But he did take up the challenge; and he has shown that the "phenomenological" novel of cerebral aestheticism, which so many intellectuals are now championing, can have the same apparent "subject" as a novel by a good reporter or by a novelist who specializes in topical issues.

R.-M. Albérès. *Le roman d'aujourd'hui* (Paris,
Éditions Albin Michel, 1970), pp. 253–55†

Although [the narrator's] relationships with the three young women [in *The People of Troyes*] are never clear, a number of erotic suggestions and mysterious anecdotes constantly lead us to wonder how these ambiguous ties will be unraveled and what new liaisons will be formed. This is the suspense.

Since Faye's language is as complicated as possible, and fiendishly neomedieval, this suspense is maintained by the method of reading imposed on the reader. The reader must ceaselessly make inferences and deductions, as if the novel were a detective story, in which the whole interest consists of seeing through the tricks of a writer who constantly tries to confuse the reader. With one exception: here the clues are in the *words* and the style, not in the facts. . . .

For the inattentive reader, the text resembles a rebus, and each passage is cloaked in an obscurity difficult to penetrate. Can one find pleasure in the perpetual exercise of exegesis required to read a hexagram? Certainly, but one may also wonder why the writer took this roundabout way of telling a story. But one could just as well seek the reasons that prompt a mystery writer to surround a murder with enigmas. The problem is simply the choice of genre.

But then, why should devices borrowed from a minor genre be used in an intellectual novel with lofty ambitions? Undoubtedly because today films and television are supplanting fiction's traditional story-telling function. To prevent fiction, superseded by visual media, from falling into disuse, writers have to teach the public *to read differently*.

Marc Saporta. *QL*. April 16–30, 1970, p. 7†

Seemingly casual references to the town of Cicero, to Henry George, and others in *Between the Streets* are echoed in *The Break* by the mention of Guernica, Jules Guesde, La Bourse du Travail, La Libre Pensée. They should serve to establish within the reader's consciousness the network of a canvas upon which a meta-text can be woven—one that possesses a definite political orientation. For a number of readers, however, this did not happen. French reviewers of those two works made no mention of any political overtones. This seems hard to account for, even if one grants that the American setting of the first text might have made political references more obscure. One possible explanation is that those who read Faye in 1958 and 1961 were prejudiced by the label of poetry pasted on his previous publications and by the affinity they detected with other young writers whose absence of overt political statements in their fiction they had misinterpreted. Be that as it may, it became impossible to ignore the political context of *Pulsation*. . . .

As the plague in Maurice Blanchot's *The Almighty* was metaphorical, schizophrenia in Faye's fiction appears to correlate to the plight of the uncommitted. V. [in *Pulsation*] seems as much lacking in political or social awareness as he is incapable of true emotional involvement. He goes to Munich for purely selfish reasons. Once there, he makes some half-hearted attempts to locate his former mistress, Merie. But everything that happens to him is accidental. It simply turns out that the woman who occupies the room next to his and with whom he strikes up an acquaintance is connected with the F.L.N. (the National Liberation Front of Algeria). It is by sheer coincidence that he meets Merie again, who is also working for the F.L.N. and gives him a copy of a book directed against French colonialism—which he does not refuse. It is merely by accident that he later drops the book in the street, thus allowing it to be identified by members of *La Main Rouge*, the rightist group, who are following him because of his meetings with F.L.N. sympathizers. The rightists quite logically conclude that his encyclopedia business is merely a cover for his distributing F.L.N. propaganda, and, on the last page of the book, they kill him. There is, however, no overt statement in the text that specifically justifies any of the points I have just made, nor is it even stated that the action takes place in Munich. Rather, the work is so structured as to make such conclusions, in my opinion, inescapable. . . .

In the final analysis, as all elements in *Pulsation* converge, they point to V.'s illness being not so much schizophrenia as alienation. It is

a total alienation, beginning with the Marxist connotations of the word
... and broadening to include the self.

Leon S. Roudiez. *French Fiction Today* (New
Brunswick, N.J., Rutgers University Press, 1972),
pp. 323–24, 326–27

FERAOUN, MOULOUD (1913–1962)

ALGERIA

Neither *The Poor Man's Son* nor *Earth and Blood* can be said to have
propaganda as their immediate goal; but only an idiot could claim that
these novels are meant to serve those who cheat the poor and humiliate
the native population. From my first acquaintance with *The Poor Man's
Son*, when it appeared in 1950, I liked Feraoun from a distance, without
having met him. I knew nothing about him except that he was a poor
man from Kabylia [a region of northern Algeria], the son, grandson,
and great-grandson of poor people; that his hard work and intelligence
had enabled him to become a schoolteacher, a writer, the headmaster of
a high school, and one who could bear witness on behalf of a people
whose eyes are so often blue, whose complexion is so often fair, and
whose hunger is so often unappeased. I felt his modesty, kindness, and
straightforwardness on every page of *The Poor Man's Son*, a book that
is a little awkward, a little slow, and even a little monotonous, but
irresistible nonetheless; I could not put the book down until I had finished it. Olives, figs, the rough field, hunger, the customs of the çof [the
clan], troubled love affairs, and the suffering of the humble—these are
the elements, only these, and the setting is always the mountains. In this
novel there is no attempt to be picturesque. . . .

   This winter, I accompanied Emmanuel Roblès to meet Feraoun at
the large new school that he heads in Fort-National. . . . I came to know
a man who was just as I had imagined him from his first novel: how
could I fail to like him! Since then, I have read *Earth and Blood*, a true
novel in which I can detect the virtues of the teacher. . . .

[René] Étiemble. *NRF*. Sept., 1953, p. 518†

Mouloud Feraoun's first novel, *The Poor Man's Son*, very modestly tells
an almost entirely autobiographical story, that of a native schoolteacher.
An education and a standard of living that our affected Parisians would
call petit-bourgeois—or simply minimal—represented, for the Kabyles,
the realization of a scarcely reasonable ambition. Such humility immedi-

ately reminded me not only of the tales of some Turkish realist writers of recent years (writers who, like Sabahattin Ali, describe life in the villages of the interior of Anatolia in analogous terms) but also of the stories and novels of the Italian *veristi*, who depict the life of the common people in southern Italy. . . .

In his second novel, *Earth and Blood*, Feraoun introduces us to a young Kabyle villager who leaves his town before World War I to find work and to make his fortune—for everything, even fortune, is relative —in the mines of northern France. . . . Feraoun's plot, limited to a few incidents, could just as easily have been set in Corsica, Sardinia, or Sicily as in Kabylia; from Mérimée and [Giovanni] Verga to Giono and [Ignazio] Silone, French and Italian novels have been filled with stories of love and revenge set under the blue skies of the Mediterranean, in countrysides that have been stripped bare by a thousand years of erosion. But Feraoun introduces two new elements: an understanding of the amazement and anguish of the North African immigrant in his first confrontation with the urban and industrial civilization of France, and a detailed analysis of the social structures of a rural community of Kabylia. Many an ethnographer would be proud to have written Feraoun's explanation of the role played in this archaic society by the clan or the family, a role similar to that played by the *gens* in the ancient Roman Republic. Equally worthy of an ethnographer is Feraoun's explanation of the patriarchal village customs his hero rediscovers when he returns, already Europeanized, from France, after having saved enough money to retire in his native land. More objective than Mouloud Mammeri in his analysis of the facts he sets forth, Feraoun is also less lyrical; the dryness of his prose and his insistence on giving the reader information serve to remind us occasionally that he is a schoolteacher by profession.

Édouard Roditi. Preuves. Aug., 1954, pp. 87–88†

From the literary point of view, Feraoun's first novel, *The Poor Man's Son*, is his most successful. . . . Feraoun's two subsequent novels (*Earth and Blood* and *The Climbing Roads*) are uneven. They do well enough in relating actual experiences, but they lack creative power. In *Earth and Blood* the Parisian woman who lives secluded in Ighil-Nezman is strangely lifeless, reduced to a few conventional characteristics, whereas she should have been central to the structure of the novel; the episodes that take place in France are vague. Feraoun is unable to recreate anything that does not fall within his familiar sphere.

Therefore, in reading his books, one should look only for an exact depiction of a little world, like many others but with its own special qualities: the mountainous region in which he grew up, the village with its *djemaâ* (public square), its *karouba* (neighborhoods), its important citizens, its works and days. In this connection, I hope people will also read his [book of essays], *Days of Kabylia* . . . a series of rough sketches portraying the life of the village in several tableaux. All of his talent as a storyteller is revealed in these essays: his observations that are sly and tinged with humor, the sharp accuracy of his perception, his gift for description, his desire not to take anything too seriously, his feigned impassiveness. . . .

The Algerian war split him in two, casting his Kabyle and French loyalties into two opposing camps. He suffered deeply and concealed his pain under the appearance of blasé good naturedness; but his suffering could be induced from many of his reactions. . . .

It would be an error, because of his assassination, to make Feraoun a political martyr. He was a quiet man, a private man if there ever was one, the kind of man least eager for publicity. If he incarnated something, it could only have been the Algeria of silence, the Algeria about which no one ever spoke and about which it is so difficult to speak objectively even today.

Édouard Guitton. *TR*. Oct., 1963, pp. 67–68, 70†

Too much pity and kindness weigh down [*The Poor Man's Son*], which is the autobiography of a man of good will. . . . In Feraoun's two other novels the realism becomes less academic, humor begins to appear, a style takes shape, and the characters begin to stir, love or hate, in short to have a substantial life. . . .

Dramatic density is a secondary consideration in Feraoun's novels, which are essentially ethnographic portraits of Kabylia. . . . There are long descriptions of daily life—descriptions that are often handled didactically and thus come close to boring the reader. Feraoun uses allegories and symbols, particularly when he tries to show the perfect integration of the fellah and his land. . . .

In his last novel [*The Climbing Roads*] bitterness and disillusionment are present; the colonial system is directly criticized. Feraoun names the evil, but he goes no further. Out of prudence, out of realism. Other writers would express rebellion and give detailed analyses of the psychological mechanisms of colonial alienation. Algerian nationalists accused Feraoun of being an idealist because he did not pay enough attention to the contradictions of the colonial situation and the conflicts of acculturation. By remaining at a distance from political events, the Algerian writer runs the risk of being called an aesthete. On the other hand, if he wants to serve the national cause by using the novel as a means of propaganda, he risks compromising his art. Either way, the writer is condemned to having a guilty conscience.

Accused of being a "sentimentalist" during the Algerian war, Feraoun has been "rehabilitated" after independence, now that daily life has become more important than political issues.

Abdelkabir Khatibi. Le roman maghrébin (Paris,
François Maspéro, 1968), pp. 50–52†

Right until the tragic day of March 15, 1962, Feraoun's life was simple and straightforward, devoted entirely to his family, his friends, his professional obligations, and his literary creation. His life was in many ways reminiscent of Federico García Lorca's. Like García Lorca, Feraoun was entirely dedicated to his work, was inspired by the people of his land, and was riddled by killers' bullets. Like García Lorca, Feraoun was obsessed with death, especially violent death. . . . It seems that both poets, the man from Kabylia and the man from Andalusia, had the same foreknowledge of their destinies. . . .

With *Earth and Blood* and *The Climbing Roads*, Feraoun created' two novels so fine that they alone are enough to keep his memory alive. . . . For both books the writer revitalized the most important themes that have haunted the human mind since antiquity. It is indeed appropriate to refer to ancient tragedy when examining the destinies of Amer-ou-Kaci and Amer-n'Amer, trapped in the fatal conflict of love and revenge.

Finally, his *Diary* . . . which covers the years 1955–62, will remain the most extraordinary document on the Algerian revolution. In this work events are not seen by a far-off observer but are intimately experienced and suffered through by a man who hated violence yet whose keen sensitivity was put through a harsh ordeal every day. Feraoun kept this diary until the eve of his death, March 14, 1962. . . .

[The next day] a commando of the OAS murdered him and five of his companions.

Emmanuel Roblès. PFr. Autumn, 1970, pp. 147–49†

FEYDEAU, GEORGES (1862–1921)

It seems to me that because of the fertility of its comic devices, the perpetual flashes of unexpected mistaken identities, and the inexhaustible mirth of the dialogue, Feydeau's new play [*The Lady from Maxim's*] is superior to all the plays he has written until now.

What surprises me most is the sure hand with which the most extravagant antics are ordered, explained, and justified. The misunderstandings bounce back on one another, and there is not a single one that is not fully developed, not one that does not make you say to yourself, when it occurs, "Yes, that's true, that couldn't happen any other way." There is not a single useless detail, none that does not have its purpose in the action. There is not a word that, at a given moment, does not have its repercussion in the comedy, and these words—although I do not know how it happens (it is the gift of the playwright)—sink in your memory and reappear just when they are supposed to cast a vivid light upon an incident—an incident which we did not expect but which seems quite natural, which charms us both by its unexpectedness and by the impression that we should have foreseen it. . . .

Everything in [Feydeau] is ordered with the mathematical precision of clockwork, and everything moves with the speed of the most unbridled buffoonery. *The Lady from Maxim's* was played, as it should have been, at a frenzied pace. [Jan. 13, 1899]

> Francisque Sarcey. *Quarante ans de théâtre* (Paris,
> Bibliothèque des Annales Politiques et Littéraires,
> 1902), Vol. VIII, pp. 189, 195†

Georges Feydeau . . . best known out of France for *The Lady from Maxim's*, is the author of many another piece of rollicking fun, more or less Rabelesian in quality. Although his plots, like this, are far from normal, they are so evidently capers of the imagination removed from the actual that they bear no ethical import. In *The Lady from Maxim's*, for example, a physician, having imbibed too freely one evening, awakens next morning to find that he has brought home a fair dancer, who must be got out of the way of his wife. The credulous wife he sends to the obelisk in the Place de la Concorde at the command of the Angel Gabriel, to meet one at whose word there will be born to her a noble son. . . . Errors accumulate, and the laughter grows, the first act alone keeping the audience convulsed for an hour.

Sometimes Feydeau, as in *The Sucker*, spins a plot over-long and involved. As a rule, however, he is too volatile to weary, even though play after play exhibit the same old deceptions of husbands and wives, and chance meetings between those who seek to evade each other.

> Frank Wadleigh Chandler. *The Contemporary Drama*
> *of France* (Boston, Little, Brown, 1920), pp. 163–64

There are three periods in Georges Feydeau's work, and all three are ruled by the female character. When the heroine changes, the style, pace, and quality of the comedy change too.

The first period is dominated by middle-class ladies. They have not sinned—yet—but they dream about it all the time. They are charming, unstable, and a bit mad. They are despotic mistresses and rather un-commendable wives. . . . They are more emancipated than the heroines of Labiche, but not unlike them. . . . This is the period of *The Master Goes Hunting!, Your Deal Next, The Sucker, A Flea in Her Ear,* and *The Hotel of Free Trade.*

The second period deals with the *cocottes,* or *dégrafées* as they were called at the time—Amélie, Bichon, Crevette. These girls have character. They are amusing, aggressive, ridiculous. A whole cosmopoli-tan menagerie, a whole rich fauna of rakes, weaklings, refugees, and deadbeats follow in the wake of these ladies. . . . This is the era of sparkling successes—*The Lady from Maxim's, I Don't Cheat on My Husband,* and *Keep an Eye on Amélie.*

The last period is the reign of the untamed shrews: it is also the period of his masterpieces, his one-act plays. Feydeau has now given up cataclysmic encounters, disguises, pistol shots, conditional threats, brawls, booby-trapped rooms, apparitions, magnetism, spiritualism, anesthetizing ecstasy. He abandons all his accessories, concentrating on nothing but his excruciating buffoonery, which he will bring to bear upon a married couple—a weak and rather stupid man in the clutches of a terrible, fascinating, and pitiless shrew. [1948]

Marcel Achard. In Eric Bentley, ed., Let's Get a
Divorce!, and Other Plays (New York,
Hill and Wang, 1958), pp. 361–62

The relationship [between Feydeau and Achard] is clear despite all the differences of time and temperament. Their similarity, which has be-come more evident as Achard has matured, is not based on the simple fact that both the dramatist of the past and the current dramatist write in the comic vein, for there are comic writers of all sorts. Their simi-larity can be seen first in the same inspiration and in what I would almost call an identical philosophy, and the similarity also extends to the level of craftsmanship. Feydeau is more bitter and stricter, Achard more discreet and more easy-going. Yet both belong to the same genus of clear minds and spontaneous artists in whom laziness and hard work, technique and fantasy, irony and naïveté result in very delightful synthe-ses. . . .

Even if Feydeau's wit should elude us, we can still find in his plays the intellectual satisfaction we derive from good detective stories. Each of his works gives us the pleasure of a coherent architecture—which is logical, if need be, even to the point of absurdity—the security of a geometry that is finally revealed to contain no secrets, and the comfort-able thrill of an acrobatic virtuosity so masterly that we know as soon as the play begins that the acrobat is not risking breaking his back.

Feydeau's works would, however, be insignificant if he had completely enclosed them in this perfect but sterile circle, in this closed and restricted world. The special merit of Feydeau is precisely that at certain points something irrepressible breaks through the tidy structure in which he had stubbornly labored to confine it. . . . Behind this playwright author, there is a man: probably a desperate man, one who thinks, it is true, that he no longer believes in anything. But, in fact, he is a man endowed with a rare power of penetration, and he is sensitive to the point of ferocity. This man, in love with the absolute, used mockery to avenge himself for having been forced to judge life and the century unequal to his hopes. In short, he is a moralist and a poet who wholly belongs to the great tradition of French literature. [March, 1948]

Francis Ambrière. *La galerie dramatique* (Paris,
Éditions Corrêa, 1949), pp. 278, 280†

Vaudeville demands a more heightened tone than comedy. One might say it has more shadings. It is midway between comedy and operetta in form. It is brassy. We first approached the problems of staging *vaudeville* in 1947 when we performed Georges Feydeau's *Keep an Eye on Amélie*.

Feydeau is the undisputed master of this kind of play. He deserves to become a classic. After Molière's farces, Feydeau's are the ones that have been performed most successfully. Feydeau's profound humanity never loses any of its integrity even when he indulges in the wildest flights of imagination. Moreover, there is an intentional madness in Feydeau. His writing is extremely well-thought-out and tightly knit. If we try to change a word, Feydeau's sentence loses its force.

Through burlesque, he creates the atmosphere of dreams. At times we believe, we truly believe, that we are dreaming; we could almost believe that our dreams have been invaded by madness. . . .

One of Feydeau's characteristics is to put associated ideas into concrete form. As soon as a few ideas are connected, his subject immediately exists. Often in life people speak before thinking, which gives them a charming grin of stupidity. Often in Feydeau's plays words come out of characters' mouths before they think, and laughter spreads lightly and quickly.

Feydeau is never coarse because he is always self-aware. He constantly remains well-behaved. The ridiculous moments come from life, not from the characters, the majority of whom are sympathetic.

Jean-Louis Barrault. *Une troupe et ses auteurs*
(Paris, Compagnie Madeleine Renaud–Jean-Louis
Barrault et Éditions Jacques Vautrain, 1950),
pp. 51–52†

The characters [in *The Hotel of Free Trade*] are not individual or unique. They are universally recognizable types. They correspond to the classical humors of Ben Jonson or the inevitable and classic roles of the *commedia dell'arte*. The dominating wife dominates, the henpecked husband with a roving eye lets his eye rove. The worm turns: the pretty, impulsive woman gives way to an impulse which her prettiness provokes. The characters don't utter witticisms or felicitous phrases, but talk in the flat and exact tones of the middle class to which they belong; and what they say is funny because it is true to type. . . .

Feydeau's plays are written with an expert eye to the visual effect. When well acted, they are funny to watch, as well as funny to listen to. In fact, in many good productions of his plays the dialogue is completely lost in the laughter of the audience; but then what is happening always tells its own story, even if the words are not heard. His farces have much in common with the early silent films of Mack Sennett and the Keystone Kops, a fact which was noticed by the critics when *The Hotel of Free Trade* was produced in London. . . . I have considered the idea of producing *The Hotel of Free Trade* as a silent film, since so much of the humor comes from mime and action. Its situations are concerned with the complications and ludicrous calamities of everyday life, and are arranged in a pattern of such perfect precision and increasing momentum that we welcome each step toward pandemonium with the same delighted expectation with which we view the approach of a self-important character toward a banana peel.

The play does not attempt wit, nor is it profound. The laughter it provokes is from the belly rather than from the head. It appeals to the child in all of us. It is a riot which should never be allowed to degenerate into a romp. It requires great expertness from the actors. . . . However wildly pandemonium may reign in the plot, the actors need the control and the exactitude of tumblers and tightrope dancers. They have to be *in extremis* without going to extremes. They have to be stylish but with panache; over life-size without being untrue. While the whirlpool of comic incident increases in speed and violence, the orchestration of the playing must be disciplined to a musical beat.

Peter Glenville. TA. April, 1957, pp. 86–87

I had the opportunity to see [Feydeau's] last *vaudevilles* during their original runs. They still brought down the house. Then came the period of disfavor for Feydeau's plays, from which they have now emerged. [In the early part of the century] farces were performed at a much more frantic pace, with exaggeration and contortions. The lines were strongly underlined by traditional effects, always the same, which were borrowed from a repertory of gestures just as fixed—and as false, if you like—as the conventional language of pantomime. The characters were typed once and for all; they appeared from playwright to playwright, from play to play, and their conventional nature was even more accentuated by the fact that the same kind of role was always played by the same actor. . . .

It has already been noted that Feydeau is superior and has aged better as a satirist than as a farceur. Today it is the first two acts of *Keep an Eye on Amélie*—in which the exposition is unfolded and in which Feydeau the satirist is more at ease—that are particularly effective. The last two scenes of the play, however—in which the speed of the action puts Feydeau the farceur to the foreground—now sound hollow.

But Feydeau's satire, even if his best feature, is directed at mores that have undergone profound changes. The world of cocottes and merrymakers, in which *Keep an Eye on Amélie* is set, no longer exists at all; even in 1908 it had no connection with the society of the day, and consequently no chance of remaining alive and forever true. Moreover, these mores govern the comic situations in the play, so that these situations themselves may no longer be funny. . . . I do not wish to speak ill of the young girls of today, but when the godfather Van Putzeboum finds in the bachelor Marcel's bed the girl he considered his fiancée, it is no longer such a shocking revelation.

Philippe Hériat. CRB. Dec., 1960, pp. 23–25†

Quite recently, I read one of [Feydeau's] plays, *A Flea in Her Ear*, extremely carefully. I can hardly remember the plot at all. What was interesting was the mechanics of the plot. People have talked a lot about Feydeau's clockwork style, but I don't think anyone has really analysed it sufficiently. People have also claimed that his plays contain a critique, or at least a scathing portrait, of the society of his time. In fact, as far as content is concerned, his plays are entirely devoid of interest, they're stupid. But their mechanics *are* interesting: the mechanics of proliferation, of geometric progression, mechanics or patterns for their own sake. [1966]

Eugène Ionesco. In Claude Bonnefoy, Conversations
with Eugène Ionesco (New York, Holt, Rinehart
and Winston, 1971), p. 51

I suspect that, like Feydeau's contemporaries, the rank-and-file spectator of today sees in him an ingenious fabricator of what the French used to call "digestive comedy," a nonintellectual after-dinner theater whose characters might, likely as not, cavort about in their underpants to bring down the house; a theater admittedly superficial, unconcerned with the many deep, problematic, philosophical plays of the avant-garde. . . .

And, no doubt, Feydeau is very much a part of this popular tradition. Still, while the greater public accepts the comic madness of his plays as farcical clowning and slapstick . . . many, on the other hand, see in this madness the possibility of a more serious twentieth-century interpretation, and one not unrelated to that selfsame offbeat and obscure theater of today's avant-garde. For many, Feydeau represents a foretaste of that contemporary theatrical current which, for good or ill, has been dubbed "Theater of the Absurd." . . . It is in the very grotesqueness of the typical Feydeau situations that he seems to emerge as a forerunner of the "absurd." [Feydeau's plays share] another characteristic that pervades a good part of this avant-garde theater: that is, the projection, in theatrical terms, of the aimlessness and unpredictability of man's fate in a haphazard (or, at least, inexplicable) universe, in which things—mainly bad—will happen to him for no obvious or compelling reason. . . .

There are those unfortunates who, thanks to an innocent peccadillo, are made to suffer the torments of Feydeau's comic hell. Saint-Florimond [in *Champignol in spite of Himself*] may, indeed, be pursuing Madame Champignol with less than honorable intent; and Dr. Petypon [in *The Lady from Maxim's*] did bring home the notorious "Môme Crevette." But neither man has yet been guilty of any real breach of propriety. Nevertheless, they are enmeshed in the maze of circumstances, whose cause—their creator's wanton caprice—they cannot even begin to perceive. . . .

[Feydeau's] cruelty can have near-tragic overtones. With a shift of emphasis many a Feydeau hero would feel uncomfortably at home in Artaud's "Theater of Cruelty" and its present-day descendants.

Norman R. Shapiro. Introduction to *Four Farces by Georges Feydeau* (Chicago, University of Chicago Press, 1970), pp. xliii–xlvi, xlviii–xlix

During the thirty years following Feydeau's death, he was considered so bad that not only was he no longer performed, but when, by chance, a bad *vaudeville* was performed, the critics would write, "It's a Feydeau," which was meant to be the height of abuse. Since World War II, Feydeau has been performed again, has been performed all the time, has been performed everywhere, no matter how; and we keep finding him admirable. Feydeau has been deified. . . .

Why is there this renewed interest in Feydeau's plays today? Because his *vaudevilles* are mathematical wonders; because these mysterious messages, these ambiguous telegrams, these innumerable traps, these disguises and substitutions, these double meanings and double roles, these fake rooms, these turning beds, these revolver shots that do not kill anyone partake of the same mythology as James Bond. Because psychiatry and psychoanalysis have made us familiar with certain personality confusions. Moreover, in Feydeau's plays everything ends in an immense, gigantic burst of laughter, which is reassuring and liberating. . . . And *A Flea in Her Ear* is just that—with genius. Here is the real reason, the only reason, why no other writer of *vaudevilles* has ever cast a spell as strong or as lasting: Feydeau had genius; the others did not.

Jean-Jacques Gautier. *Théâtre d'aujourd'hui* (Paris, Julliard, 1972), pp. 76–77, 261–62†

Feydeau is the quintessence of French farce, as it developed traditions somewhat different from those of English farce in the nineteenth century. . . . The traditions of French farce, unattenuated by Victorianism, allowed Feydeau to deal with the same areas of real life that were dealt with in serious drama. . . .

In the tradition of farce, all must end well—but, after the dizzying adventures of his "toys of fortune," we are rarely prepared to conclude that all is for the best. Happy endings in Feydeau are only temporary solutions. They are temporary solutions because life lies at the center of Feydeau's plays. Rather than evasion into a misty world of wish-fulfilment, we are brought face to face with the absurdity of our predicament, incarnated in a mechanism of such perfection, speed, and violence that human struggle is useless. Here lies the fundamental seriousness of Feydeau. Expressed in the entire structure of his plays, his view of man's lot does not reaffirm our lazy pretenses, but serves, as all serious theater must, to raise doubts. It destroys our self-satisfaction and security, throws all into question, and by its very violence strikes deeper than more serious ideas expressed discursively might do.

Leonard C. Pronko. *Georges Feydeau* (New York, Frederick Ungar, 1975), pp. 194, 196

FRANCE, ANATOLE (1844–1924)

The true Muses, the Greek Muses, played their heavenly flute at Anatole France's cradle, and he has remembered their song all his life. His first poems were published under the title *Golden Poems*, undoubtedly with reference to the "Golden Verses" that Pythagoras brought back from Asia for the education of Greece. . . . France's *Golden Poems* sparkle with a brightness and honesty that can be called Pythagorean, since everything in them is worthy of that distinguished philosopher who, so many centuries before Christ, could establish a congregation of monks and wise men, a congregation possessing all the virtues. . . .

It seems to me that such poems remove France completely from the common lyric fold and grant him membership in a special chamber, one I would like to call the Pythagorean Institute of Poetry. It is a venerable place where one can find assembled wise men who have been poets as well as poets who have made use of philosophy. . . . Only purely intellectual poets are accepted, here, those whose emotions are not displayed openly but are only revealed through modest veils woven by passionate and penetrating meditation. Some abstract quality is mingled with their desire and is expressed alongside it. Their cries are nonetheless ideas.

I hardly need to inform you that such idealistic works have been rare in the nineteenth century. Since the death of André Chénier and Racine's fall into unpopularity, especially since 1830, despite the fact that our language (it was born a metaphysical language) lends itself naturally to this kind of poetry, the noble institution of which I have been speaking has scarcely opened its doors except to Alfred de Vigny and Maurice de Guérin, before receiving Anatole France.

Charles Maurras. RH. Nov., 1893, pp. 566–68†

I should like France more whole-heartedly if certain rash people did not try to make of him a writer of importance. That sets me wondering. I fear that perhaps I have not been fair. . . . I read this sentence [of France's] which I applaud: "One thing above all gives charm to men's thoughts, and this is unrest. A mind that is not uneasy irritates and bores me." I am reminded of Goethe's remark: "The tremor of awe (*das Schaudern*) is the best in man." Alas! this is just it; no matter how I try, I do not feel any tremor in France; I read France without a tremor.

He is fluent, subtle, elegant. He is the triumph of the euphemism. But there is not restlessness in him; one drains him at first draught. I am not inclined to believe in the survival of those upon whom everyone agrees right away. I doubt very much if our grandchildren, opening his books, will find more to read in them than we are finding. I know that, as far as I am concerned, I have never felt him to be ahead of my thought. At least he explains it. And this is what his readers like in him. France flatters them. Each one of them is free to think: "How well put that is! After all, I wasn't so stupid either; that's just what *I* was thinking *too*."

He is well-bred; that is, he is always aware of others. Perhaps he does not attach any great value to what he cannot reveal to them.

Besides, I suspect that he hardly exists at all behind and beyond what he reveals to us. Everything comes out in conversation, in relationships. Those who frequent him appreciate being taken right into the drawing-room and the study; these rooms are on one floor; the rest of the house doesn't matter. In my case, I am annoyed not to have any hint of the near-by room in which a crime is committed or of the room in which people make love. [April 9, 1906]

André Gide. *The Journals of André Gide* (New York, Alfred A. Knopf, 1947–51), Vol. I, p. 179

Anatole France is no longer young, but his celebrity is of comparatively recent date. On April 16, 1904, he completed his sixtieth year, but only for the last eleven years has he really been famous.

He began as quite a young man to write literary and historical essays and tasteful poems, but he was thirty-seven when he first attracted attention by his simple tale, *The Crime of Sylvestre Bonnard*, and it was not until 1892–93 that he gave proof of his originality. . . .

In [Anatole] France's literary life, after a preparatory stage which lasted fifteen years, there are two periods, which differ so much from each other that one might almost say: There are two Frances.

In the first of these periods he is the refined satirist, who, from a station high above the human crowd, observes its endeavours and struggles with a superior, compassionate smile. In the second he appears as the combatant. He not only attaches himself to a party, but affirms as he does so his belief in the very things at which he has jested and scoffed— the sound instinct of the people, the significance of the majority, the increasing reality of progress—in the doctrines which as a thinker he had declined to accept, those of democracy and socialism.

Georg Brandes. *Anatole France* (New York, McClure, 1908), pp. 9, 24–25

Voltaire read human nature into Joan of Arc, though it was only the brutal part of human nature. At least it was not specially Voltaire's nature. But M. France read M. France's nature into Joan of Arc—all the cold kindness, all the homeless sentimentalism of the modern literary man. There is one book that [France's *The Life of Joan of Arc*] recalled to me with startling vividness, though I have not seen the matter mentioned anywhere; [Ernest] Renan's *The Life of Jesus*. It has just the same general intention: that if you do not attack Christianity, you can at least patronise it. My own instinct, apart from my opinions, would be quite the other way. If I disbelieved in Christianity, I should be the loudest blasphemer in Hyde Park. Nothing ought to be too big for a brave man to attack; but there are some things too big for a man to patronise.

And I must say that the historical method seems to me excessively unreasonable. I have no knowledge of history, but I have as much knowledge of reason as Anatole France. And, if anything is irrational, it seems to me that the Renan-France way of dealing with miraculous stories is irrational. The Renan-France method is simply this: you explain supernatural stories that have some foundation simply by inventing natural stories that have no foundation. . . .

When you find a life entirely incredible and incomprehensible from the outside, you pretend that you understand the inside. As Renan, the rationalist, could not make any sense out of Christ's most public acts, he proceeded to make an ingenious system out of His private thoughts. As Anatole France, on his own intellectual principle, cannot believe in what Joan of Arc did, he professes to be her dearest friend and to know exactly what she meant. I cannot feel it to be a very rational manner of writing history; and sooner or later we shall have to find some more solid way of dealing with those spiritual phenomena with which all history is as closely spotted and spangled as the sky is with stars.

Joan of Arc is a wild and wonderful thing enough, but she is much saner than most of her critics and biographers. We shall not recover the common sense of Joan until we have recovered her mysticism.

G. K. Chesterton. All Things Considered (New York, John Lane, 1908), pp. 268–69, 271–72

Thaïs, in subject and style, might, to a superficial reader, seem to be the work of a devout son of the Church. . . . The theology of the tale is irreproachable, and the style too is of the strictest orthodoxy: there is hardly a phrase that is not borrowed from the biography of some saint. Just as the smell of books and parchment pervaded The Crime of Sylvestre Bonnard, the pages of Thaïs are fragrant with an "odour of sanctity," that strange perfume of which the physiologist Georges Dumas has given us the chemical formula.

On second thoughts, Thaïs appears as one of the most insidiously unchristian, or rather antichristian, books in modern literature. It is the last flower of the school of aesthetic Christianity which began with Chateaubriand. "Christianity is beautiful, therefore it is true": such was the central argument of Romantic apologetics. [Ernest] Renan, a Chateaubriand with a scientific training, said: "Legends are nought but legends: but, if they are beautiful, they are respectable, and have in them that element of truth which is inseparable from beauty." Anatole France goes further: "Legends are legends. To the modern mind, they are absurd and laughable; but we refuse to pay them the homage of combating them seriously. We are liberal enough to enjoy, at the same time, the charm of their beauty and the humour of their absurdity." Thus we have a story to the full enjoyment of which apparent belief in miraculous Christianity is indispensable: yet the undercurrent of unbelief, at times of hostility, is ever perceptible. This discord mars the impression of the book: we are puzzled, uneasy. The irony is too continuous to be thoroughly enjoyable; and its presence is sufficient to spoil the spiritual passages, which, whilst faultlessly beautiful, are obviously insincere.

Anatole France ought to have written *Thaïs* ten years before. In 1890 the eighteenth century had taken too strong a hold of him. The style suffers from the same duality of purpose as the thought. *Thaïs* is a work of art, the most carefully finished perhaps in the production of a master craftsman. But the art is too evident; the ironical notes make the pseudo-hagiographic passages unconvincing, and there is nothing so dismal as a prolonged and unconvincing pastiche.

Albert Léon Guérard. *Five Masters of French Romance* (London, T. Fisher Unwin, 1916), pp. 68–70

France never liked anything in the modern world except the remains of the past; an uneasy antique dealer, he was waiting for his shop to be looted and thought he did well by moving to the side of the wolves: the wolves judged that he howled badly. . . .

Was he a great artist? There are antique dealers today who pay a great deal for old wood they can use in reconstructing old pieces of furniture with a learned naïveté. These pieces of furniture are not fakes: they are made from the same material, using the same process— even the most clever experts get taken in by them. Thus, France faithfully re-created antiques; they are beautiful like antiques; they are just as beautiful as real antiques. Through his golden legends and memoirs, this old woodcutter gathered branches of trees where nymphs quivered; he brought back marbles that still retained the contours of a divine torso. . . .

This man of the political left needed to step back several centuries to observe people and morals; he could only breathe easily under kings. In short, he was a stranger to the modern world, an enemy of his time to the point of unscrupulously surrendering the modern world to the barbarians. . . .

"Our good master" is not a master: what kind of master has no disciples? And who among today's writers ever accepted his guidance? It is not his skepticism that separates us from him, for there are skeptics who nourish us: we cannot live without Montaigne. But in France's negation, there is something weak and poor; it is the opposite of any faith. It does not lead to anything; it is the end of everything.

François Mauriac. *RH*. Oct. 18, 1924, pp. 357–58†

When one thinks of the genius of Anatole France, it is impossible to forget about the spirit of his nation. Just as Dostoyevski and Tolstoy, each in his own way, expressed the soul of the Russian people with complete fullness, so, in my eyes, Anatole France is in every way in profound communion with the spirit of his country. . . . I am not comparing aesthetic values but rather the degree of perfection to which the spirit of a particular nation is expressed; from this point of view, Anatole France is, for me, absolutely equal to the greatest geniuses of every country. . . .

I find France especially astonishing in his courage and his mental health; in truth, he was the ideal "sound mind in a sound body." He lived during a trying period, shaken by all sorts of social catastrophes, and I do not recall his clear-sighted eye ever making a mistake in evaluating current events, although it is not easy for me to understand how his attitude during the war could be reconciled with his attitude toward communism. He possessed, to the highest degree, the caution of the intellectual aristocrat, and this noble caution never allowed him to increase the sadness of this world by complaining about his fellow-men or by relating his own sufferings; yet it is undeniable that this amazing man suffered a great deal.

Maxime Gorki. *RevE*. Dec., 1924, p. 3†

[Anatole France's] work exists and subsists. Its merits are as clear as itself. Everybody knows and appreciates the perfection of an art refined to the point of exquisite simplicity. But what are we to say to that singular circumstance, the wide favour it has obtained? and more than that, the almost popular fame it owes to the eminent seduction of the purity of its form? The thing is almost unbelievable. It is a phenomenon without parallel in modern literature, since we usually find that the great public reserves its welcome for those books whose substance devours their form and whose effects are independent of the delicacy of their means.

This phenomenon is doubtless to be explained by the virtues of our language, which this expert author mastered so thoroughly and wrote so nimbly. He demonstrated that it was still possible, in our language, to make patent the priceless value of a prolonged culture and to combine and sum up the heritage handed down by an uninterrupted series of admirable writers. . . .

My illustrious predecessor [in the Académie Française] was not ingenuous. He did not expect humanity to differ very much in the future from what it seems to have been in the past; nor did he expect hitherto unknown marvels to be born of the fervour of men and the search for the absolute. There was in him no invincible faith in the adventures of the spirit; but he had read so much and so well that his general and intimate knowledge of everything readable in the past (and even unreadable) had rendered him immune to the present, independent of the future. He was born in books, reared in books, and ever changed by books.

Paul Valéry. *The Dial.* Nov., 1927, pp. 367–69

I met France in 1920 at the home of an American friend, Edward Wasserman, who had come to Europe during the war, and for whom France felt a paternal affection.

France was no longer very active, and the features of his face at times took on an extraordinarily ungraceful immobility, but in conversation his appearance of rigidity was compensated for by bright, keen glances and by rather poetic hand movements. Sometimes there were also streaks of kindness in his face; then suddenly that sweetness of an old shepherd would give way to a hard, angry, scornful expression. I have rarely seen such abrupt changes on a face, an oasis of universal love transform itself thus into a hostile desert. . . .

I remember that on that day at Edward Wasserman's France found an appropriate anecdote for each of us. That whole conversation seemed lively and varied to me. On leaving, however, I had the impression of having spent an hour with a collector who had opened up his boxes and given each one of us a little engraving he himself did not value.

Jacques de Lacretelle. *NRF.* July, 1930, pp. 38–39†

It has become the fashion to disparage France as a writer; but that is partly because people expect to find in him things that he cannot supply, even though he may sometimes attempt to do so—and not for the things that are actually there. For Anatole France does not represent merely a dimming of the eighteenth-century Enlightenment as Taine and Renan do; he shows that tradition in full disintegration; and what he is telling, with all his art and wit, is the story of an intellectual world where principles are going to pieces. . . .

In his political role, France is a socialist; yet the whole purpose of two of his later books, *The Gods Are Athirst* and *The Revolt of the Angels*, is to show that revolutions must eventually result in tyrannies at least as oppressive as those they were designed to displace. And when he undertakes, in *Penguin Island*, to write a sort of outline of history, he has modern industrial civilization blasted off the face of the earth by embittered proletarian anarchists. But no freer and more reasonable order succeeds: the rebels are wiped out with their masters, and such men as are left on earth return to their original condition as tillers of the soil. We are back with the cycles of [Giovanni Battista] Vico again and might as well not have got rid of God. *Penguin Island* is presented as a satire, to be sure; but we know from France's other work that this kind of idea haunted his mind. "Slowly, but surely," he had written at the head of his political papers, "humanity realizes the dreams of the wise"; but he had moments when this assurance was destroyed by the nightmares of science, which was no longer for France . . . the school of discipline, the source of strength, that it had been for Taine or Renan or Zola.

Edmund Wilson. To the Finland Station (New York, Harcourt, Brace, 1940), pp. 61–62

Anatole France was born as Jacques-Anatole-François Thibault and lived to eighty. His great-grandmother was called Françoise, his great-uncle was called François, his father was called François Noël. They were from Anjou, where the peasants shorten François into France, even as the Germans say Franz. The great novelist had therefore a right to call himself France—an otherwise unforgivable impertinence—and he made good his title to the name. He was born in Paris of a mother who belonged to Chartres. Nothing could be more French in the most intimate sense than this descent: Anjou, Chartres, Paris. No purer flower was born from the French earth. . . .

Anatole France began as a charming individual and ended as a formidable figure, whose true greatness is hardly seen even now. He is thoroughly at one with the period, and yet in him is the full fruit of a much longer tradition. Just as Mallarmé flowers in Valéry, Voltaire flowers in Anatole France. *Candide* culminates in *The Revolt of the Angels*, in which, on a much grander stage, Voltaire at last bows to Leibnitz and agrees finally, through Satan's mouth, that all is for the best in the best of all possible worlds; the accent is still on *possible*. *The Simple Man* reappears as Evariste Gamelin in *The Gods Are Athirst*; the man who looks for justice with too undivided a mind becomes all too quickly a terrorist. . . .

Much has been said of France's style. He deserves his name, France; he writes French in perfection. It is true he does not achieve the sublime any more than Voltaire does. Neither Bossuet nor Paul Valéry are in his orbit. But the ordinary cultured man is fully at home in Anatole France's perfect French—throughout the world. The whole world will have to learn French to enjoy Anatole France—and neither Bossuet nor Valéry would make the world do that. The world has

GARY, ROMAIN (1914–   )

The attention of the general public was first focused on Romain Gary with the publication of *A European Education*, which received the Critic's Prize in 1945. The book was still a bit thin and raw, but it showed promise. One might have objected that the title was, as it were, wider than the subject: the novel relates the adventures of a small group of Polish partisans, hibernating in the forests of their country overrun by the Germans—nothing very spectacular, just a continuous fight for survival against the elements, the cold and snow of the winter, and a few attacks against enemy convoys or reprisals against traitors. There are about thirty short and sharp episodes centering around the main hero, Janek Twardowski: at first a child, whose father has been killed by the Germans, he rushes through a hurried adolescence to a precocious manhood. Love and death fly over most of the scenes, producing a curious mixture of tenderness and hardness, deftly underlined by the humoristic touches of the style and set against a general tonality of dry wonderment at the meaning of such harsh destinies. . . .

The setting and the tone of the whole book pose an interesting problem of aesthetics. There is no doubt that to French ears the novel *sounds Slavic*; how authentic that sound is, is another matter. Nevertheless, it is interesting to reflect on the means by which this effect is achieved. It is evidently at first sight a matter of the generous use of Polish and Ukrainian names coupled with a smattering of local color. But there is more to it than these obvious devices. I should like to call attention especially to a certain elemental quality of the dialogue, which is devoid of any literary overtones, and which is apt at times to treat primeval philosophical problems with a bottomless ignorance and a most serene innocence. . . . There is no doubt, however, but that this elemental approach gives a maximum of strength to the light structure of abstract thought and of philosophical feelings which run through the book: the abhorrence of hatred, the deep need for human fraternity, the desire to give a meaning to life, and a subdued rancor toward God, who does not appear to take pity on the hearts of his creatures.

Jean Boorsch. *YFS*. Fall, 1951, pp. 51–52

In Romain Gary's *The Roots of Heaven* we rediscover the density of mysteries, men, and animals, the taste for adventures, and the love for a sultry continent still entangled in its past—qualities that enlivened the first novels by Kipling, with Africa replacing Asia here. . . .

Morel [the protagonist] has no political ambitions. He thinks only of protecting the elephants—at least so he says, but in fact his actions have a wider meaning. He is a defender of nature, and of all sorts of other things, as the reader gradually discovers. Because of its implications, the book, which can be taken on the surface as an excellent adventure novel—full of action, surprises, and suspense—can gradually be seen to convey the concerns of many people today. . . .

This book has an important subject, a well-plotted intrigue that is rich in unexpected turns, and a vitality that makes the whole narrative astonishingly compelling. All these merits should guarantee the book's success and make it a strong contender for every literary prize at the end of this year. I do have a few reservations, however; there is some repetitiousness, the prose is too much like the spoken language, and the style is sometimes heavy and rough. Gary would have had to have been more continuously sensitive to the values of art and poetry to justify fully any comparison with the two great English writers [Kipling and Conrad] whose work often came to my mind while I was reading *The Roots of Heaven*. But there is no need to quibble and thus spoil our pleasure; this book is both exciting and beneficial.

Marcel Thiébaut. *RdP*. Dec., 1956, pp. 150–51, 153†

M. Gary's *Lady L.*, in spite of the eighty years it covers and the great number of events crammed into its 190 pages, is really, constructionally at any rate, a short story. Lady L., splendid old dowager and grandmother of various pillars of society, learns that her memento-stuffed garden pavilion is due for demolition. The news throws her into a panic, and she begins to think back over her past life. We see her, in a series of flashbacks, as a young prostitute in Paris, taken up by anarchists, groomed, and lobbed like a beautiful bomb into high society. The point we keep coming back to, of course, is What is in that pavilion? There are several interludes in which the recipient of these confidences is rather tiresomely incredulous about Lady L.'s revelations. . . . We are told that the proof of all she is telling him lies in the pavilion.

M. Gary traces Lady L.'s remarkable life with a fine economical style, but he has so much to be economical with that at times his novel reads like a synopsis for the film that will undoubtedly be made of it. In Lady L.'s final bout of reminiscence she is married to an aristocrat and in love with an anarchist. Who shall have her lover—herself, or The Cause? And so, at last, we come to the pavilion. I will not reveal what is in it, except to say that it isn't Guy de Maupassant.

Keith Waterhouse. NS. Sept. 19, 1959, p. 366

Nicholas Berdyaev, the philosopher, once remarked that atheism has often been a characteristically Russian reaction to the idea that God could be the creator of a world racked by misery, cruelty, and injustice. Romain Gary is not an atheist—if only because, like his irascible Franciscan Father Fargue in *The Roots of Heaven*, he could never quite renounce the hope of one day rejoining those Free French comrades-in-arms who perished during World War II. Yet his books ring with the echo of a profoundly Russian, if not Manichean, bafflement before the spectacle of a world bristling with new satanic inventions—atomic bombs, brain washing, concentration camps.

This deep sense of protest is as evident as ever in his latest book, *Promise at Dawn*, which opens with an imaginary evocation of the grinning gods of stupidity, dogmatic truth, mediocrity and servility. Its original title was to have been "La lutte pour l'honneur"—"the struggle for honor"—but no one needs to know it to realize that this romanticized autobiography is something more than a "life with mother" story. It is the story of a young boy's endeavor to achieve manhood in an age of crumbling values and revolutionary upheaval, and it explains, more explicitly and movingly than Gary has ever done before, why his books are so haunted by a sense of solitude, of bereavement, of a paradise irretrievably lost.

If human life is, in the nature of things, a long process of disenchantment, *Promise at Dawn* is a reminder that the initial enchantment of youth, far from being an exercise in self- or child-delusionment, is what ultimately permits man to raise and ennoble himself above his merely brutish condition.

Curtis Cate. NYT. Oct. 15, 1961, p. 1

What has driven Morel [in *The Roots of Heaven*] to seek intimate knowledge of as well as protection for the roots of heaven, specifically the elephants, is a suffering so extreme that only an unworn image could save him. In a Nazi concentration camp, where a systematic attempt to destroy the spirit was made, Morel knew an attack on the soul that no idealist like Ghandi or Schweitzer ever encountered. The way he survived was to keep in his mind the picture of wide-ranging elephants as an image of freedom. This ordeal was the beginning of his career as a new idealist. His real work from then on would be to bring himself and others into an emotional as well as a mental relationship with an image and at the same time to establish once again a vital contact with nature. To do this work he had to shed completely the materialistic philosophy of the West. Morel is western man, voluntarily dispossessed, beginning a new religious life on the frontier of the world; Schweitzer, on the other hand, is simply the old humanitarian who brings modern medicine to primitives. Morel though finds a way for himself and other dispossessed westerners to get into contact with the power and beauty of heaven. . . .

The break with western materialism is underlined by Gary in the contrast he draws between Morel's idealism and the political idealism of the revolutionary leader Waïtari. Revolutionary doctrine will only bring western totalitarianism to Africa; everything that Morel suffered in Germany will be repeated on the last great frontier of the world. Today the search for the political kingdom often leads to inhumanity; the spiritual kingdom is becoming man's chief hope. But the journey to the new kingdom is filled with great pain and only a few can begin to take it. Gary makes much of this as he also makes much of the necessity of beginning with one particular symbol. Elephants will seem to most people to be a strange, even absurd symbol, or root, of heaven; but the complexities of Morel's life suggest that in times of total spiritual collapse man must accept what he can receive. To put it another way, strange visions come in time of great suffering. But Gary makes it clear that his hero is making a beginning.

Ted R. Spivey. *Religious Themes in Two Modern
Novelists* (Atlanta, Georgia State College, School of
Arts and Sciences Research Papers, 1965), pp. 16–17

White Dog was a creature who sought refuge with Romain Gary and his then wife, Jean Seberg, during a California rainstorm. . . . What seems to begin as a tale of a sixty-year-old boy and his dog rapidly turns into a nightmare when it is discovered that the creature they are sheltering is a savage attack dog—trained to respond instantly to the sight of a black man (White Dog being the name Blacks give such dogs). Gary cannot ask his wife to put to sleep her most cherished principles and beliefs nor will he betray an animal whom he loves simply because it has been diabolically trained to dispute their views, tooth and claw.

Something within us wants to say "only a Frenchman"—with rueful admiration for that nation's devotion to symbols and irony—only such a man could have found himself in such a muddle or written such a book. Gary turns it into a decathlon event. Responding as intellectual, novelist, Frenchman, American, husband, veteran activist (semi-retired), devout humanist, and survivor par excellence, he develops a household crisis into a full-scale allegory. . . .

It's a good book reaching out in all directions—ghastly and funny and wise at once. I admire the author, finally, as a survivor and am somehow touched that he has lived to witness his own maturity. Moreover, his insight and his passion compensate for the fact that, on occasion, something less than first class in me responded to *White Dog*, for one does suspect him of fiddling the truth to compose a catchy thought, does imagine the author capable of using us, just a little perhaps, to help make himself a legend in his own time.

Julia Whedon. Harper's. Jan., 1971, p. 96

GASCAR, PIERRE (1916–   )

The six stories [in *Beasts*] are so closely related that we have little reason to think that we are in error as to the nature of these "beasts," which, although they do not function as protagonists (who are always human) still form a secondary layer of great importance. And, since the word "divinity" recurs several times in the course of these stories, there is one obvious comparison that should be made: the beasts here are like the invisible presence of God in a book whose subject is faith. . . . But Gascar does not give us some vague symbolism: the scenes here have too much force and presence. Despite their hieratic overtones, these animals are only too easily recognizable as the cat we tried to tease one day and the rat that suddenly ran between our legs. This part of ourselves is certainly a part of our flesh and is, at the same time, sacred, troubling, alarming, and most often cursed; it is something like an externalization of our damned and unhappy souls.

In each of these tales the form is identical: a man who had previously lived without worry, in the light of day—in other words, in ignorance—finds himself suddenly plunged into a "subterranean world" whose importance he had underestimated. . . .

In a parallel movement, the beasts, who always come into view as exterior existences, take their places very rapidly in the minds of man. They first erupt into man's daily preoccupations, for example, in his work, they move into his dreams, and finally they occupy his whole thoughts, his whole life. . . .

This nightmarish proliferation is opposed by established order, logic, and health—which take the form of public services and especially of military society. Gascar generally places soldiers in opposition to his ghosts. But do not the most secure of them make compromises? One example is a young officer who discovers the only way to fall asleep in the midst of the incessant barking of a pack of dogs: he chooses the howl of one particular dog and *mentally barks along with him*. But in this contaminated sleep, what difference is there between defeat and salvation?

                                    Alain Robbe-Grillet. *NRF*. July, 1953, pp. 142–44†

One readily observes an historical continuity between Kafka's art and that of Pierre Gascar, in his stories in *Beasts* and *The Season of the Dead*. I am thinking particularly of Kafka's beast fables. But something has happened between Kafka's time and that of M. Gascar, a vexing of the nightmare out of which William Butler Yeats, casting a cold eye upon the future, envisioned the pitiless horror of the Apocalypse. These later animal fables came out of concentration camps on the Eastern Front, and in view of this new historical donnée, one feels that, Kafka or not, if M. Gascar's stories had not been invented they would have had to exist anyway.

There was still, for Kafka, the stable pattern of the family, the triad of the tyrannical father, the compassionate mother, and the son who staves off anarchy by taking any necessary suffering upon himself; if he protests, it is as a reasoning creature who has no doubt that a rational explanation for suffering will be available. There were also analogical patterns in the other social institutions, the state, marriage, and religion. His private psychic life repeated these analogies, almost as if a rational consciousness guided his dreams. Thus the behavior and the language of the animals he saw in dreams seemed to offer useful knowledge in parables of the social theme.

But M. Gascar's world is that of the bestial floor itself. His material is only the suffering. The duties of conscience fail here: there is no part of the mind that can conceptualize this state of being. In these pieces, the beasts do not argue their ethic in parables of human behavior; they howl and bite.

                                    Dorothy Van Ghent. *YR*. Autumn, 1956, pp. 149–50

Pierre Gascar (whose real name is Pierre Fournier, but whose pen name may denote his Gascon origin) ranks among the most original talents of contemporary France and easily, along with Paul Morand and J.-P. Sartre, among the best authors of *récits* [novellas] and short stories since Maupassant. . . . Of all the storytellers in France today, he may be said to be the closest approximation to Hemingway, with no trace of any American influence on him.

He has very sparingly offered revelations about himself, his metaphysics and his technique, and has shunned all publicity. But his novels have allowed readers to catch a glimpse of a melancholy childhood, spent in hardship and brooding solitude: his mother had died before he was ten and there was little affection spent on him. He refused to become a priest. As a teen-ager, he earned a meager subsistence working at all kinds of hard trades. World War II kept him in the army for eight years. A prisoner of war in Germany, he was made to serve as the gravedigger for his camp; he became familiar with mental agony and death there, and he observed animals, horses especially, whose behavior and uncanny psychology he conjures up with a vividness unmatched since D. H. Lawrence. He has kept away from Existentialism and from the new, dehumanized or antihuman type of fiction. His few philosophical reflections, interspersed in his stories, are neither original nor pretentious. Yet he has a tormented soul and an exciting writer's conscience.

Henri Peyre. SR. July 10, 1965, p. 40

[*In Women* and *Suns*] M. Gascar writes about people who experience excruciating pain of soul. There is no mistaking his meaning: suffering does not merely occur in human life, but the essence of human life is suffering. This is legitimate enough a conception . . . but it is badly expressed. For example, M. Gascar is too insistent about wringing a certain horrible beauty out of the repulsive. . . .

M. Gascar also tries to cast sudden light into the dark corners of the mind. In Tolstoy, the effect of such sudden insights is overpowering; here, it is not. The principal obstacle is that, except for brief moments of forgetfulness, M. Gascar's people are not human. They are ambulatory symbols, so abstract that we cannot identify with them and therefore can never see that a truth about them is also a truth about ourselves. Worse, the alleged insights are far from original and are badly brought off. . . .

There are passages of striking beauty and genuine poetry; and, better, there is clear evidence in every story that M. Gascar knows where he wants to go and is doing his level best to get there. Certainly these virtues do not make up for what is wrong with [*Women* and *Suns*]; but they do constitute unmistakable evidence that M. Gascar is a craftsman of great promise who deserves our attention.

David Earl Chalfan. SSF. Winter, 1966, pp. 266–67

Two years ago, almost to the day, I stressed the merits of a book by Pierre Gascar called *The Chimeras.* That gave me the chance to enumerate the three fundamental qualities of his work: a highly developed and rigorous form, the somewhat lofty solitude out of which the author writes, and the force of the symbols that he likes to deploy and develop.

All these qualities can be found once again in *The Ark,* more homogeneous but more disconcerting than the three stories comprising *The Chimeras.* . . . The starting point for the author's reflections is the village of D., which is ancient, isolated, and classified as an historical monument to preserve the ruins of an abbey. D. also has what the guidebooks curiously call a "natural asset"—caves. These caves seem to be Gascar's real subject. . . . Little by little, the author opposes the inconsequence, the baseness, and the horror of the world above ground —our world—to the underground world of the caves. . . .

The tone of the book increasingly emerges from a strange yet appealing mixture of dreams and vulgarizations, of myth and realism. The fundamental symbolic meaning is . . . that the caves, used in the near future as a shelter from atomic weapons, will become the ark for a new preservation of the human race and of a few insects, mosses, and bats. But by the time this symbol is developed, the reader has been led in so many other directions that he no longer accords the highest importance to what should have been the heart of the allegory, since it gives the book its title.

François Nourissier. NL. March 11, 1971, p. 2†

GATTI, ARMAND (1924–   )

For France today, *The Toad-Buffalo* is extraordinarily daring. Its setting and action have nothing specifically to do with France. On the contrary, Gatti has pointed out that he has made free use of factual material picked up during extensive travels in Central America. The principal character is the dictator of a fictitious country whose words and acts are in part borrowed from Trujillo, Armas of Guatemala, Martínez of San Salvador and Somoza of Nicaragua. In addition, he makes "a gift of his person" to the state, using the words employed by Pétain at the time of the armistice with Germany. Gatti's Don Tiburcio, however, carries out his offer literally, depriving himself first of one leg, then of the other, then of his arms.

As the evening progresses, these members are strung up like banners around the stage, a grotesque commentary on the essential insanity of personal rule, while the actor playing the part is artfully reduced to a basket case. . . . Gatti has swept out of his theater everything that stands in the way of swift and immediate dramatic communication and is not bound even by the physical limitations of his actors. In the supremely macabre climax of *The Toad-Buffalo* he has the severed head of Don Tiburcio hopping about the stage in pursuit of his successor.

Gatti's vision goes beyond himself, beyond despair, which distinguishes him from his *avant-garde* elders and contemporaries, and he writes in a style that is both colloquial and poetically evocative. There is every reason to hope that as more of his plays are presented to the public he will restore universal human values to a theater that has become increasingly self-absorbed and hermetic.

Gordon Merrick. NR. Feb. 15, 1960, p. 20

Dürrenmatt claims to have no biography, thus demonstrating that he means to separate his life from his works. But Gatti has a biography that explains and could justify, if it were necessary, all of his works. His parents: a Russian mother and an Italian father. Gatti himself was born in Monaco, to which his parents had emigrated. His father was a street cleaner who died when Gatti was fifteen, virtually in the same way as does the street cleaner Auguste G. [in *The Imaginary Life of the Street Cleaner Auguste G.*]. When Gatti was nineteen, his short pants having scarcely touched the University benches, he fought in Corrèze with the Maquis. The Germans arrested him, condemned him to death, then granted him a reprieve and deported him to somewhere near Hamburg. . . .

The Imaginary Life of the Street Cleaner Auguste G. is a very angry return to the past, as well as an act of gratitude to a father who wanted his son to lead a life worthy of a man. . . . Gatti shows us his characters from within, with beautiful lyric flashes, and the play—based on a news item—widens in scope as it proceeds. At the end, when Auguste G. dies, it is not one man but thousands of men who die before us—for the Revolution, that sea serpent, that mirage.

Renée Saurel. TM. June, 1964, pp. 2283–84†

One of Gatti's favorite methods is to base a play not on a chronological flow of time but on a meeting point of the past, present, and future. A striker mortally wounded by the police sees during his agony the events of his past reenacted, as well as one possible future event (*The Imaginary Life of the Street Cleaner Auguste G.*) The meeting, in a fairground, of a former prisoner of a concentration camp and the widow of a man who had been shot provokes not only a confrontation of their respective pasts but a "murder" of those pasts and finally their unavoidable resurrection (*The Second Life of the Tattenberg Camp*). The story of Sacco and Vanzetti is simultaneously and currently performed in five theatres in different cities, and the fictitious spectators, each in his own way, relive the trial of the two anarchists, thus representing the trial's future (*Public Hymn before Two Electric Chairs*).

All three plays are extremely complex in form (even if some of the dialogue is very elementary), for the meetings, parallels, and contrasts between groups of men, eras, expressionistic symbols, and levels of reality are multiplied. In *The Imaginary Life of the Street Cleaner Auguste G.*, for example, one sees onstage, sometimes simultaneously, Auguste at nine years old, Auguste at twenty-one, Auguste at thirty, Auguste at forty-six (the year of his death), and "ageless" Auguste. In *Public Hymn before Two Electric Chairs* the spectators from Boston, Los Angeles, Hamburg, Turin, and Lyon alternate or join together, and in *The Second Life of the Tattenberg Camp* there is a mixture not only of the camp's dead and survivors but of giant puppets and imaginary characters out of a Viennese parade. Thus, as a whole, Gatti's plays may be described as clusters built around a central adventure and radiating in space and time. Compared to such complexity, Salacrou's innovations in *The Unknown Woman from Arras* now appear somewhat mild.

> Jacques Guicharnaud, with June Guicharnaud.
> *Modern French Theatre from Giraudoux to Genet*,
> rev. ed. (New Haven, Conn., Yale University Press,
> 1967), pp. 206–7

In Gatti, without a doubt, there lies a potential *poet* of the people's theater—the sort of theater that everyone is trying to invent. But the paradox—a double one—is that this "poet" does not seem to have found his language yet, and that this "people's" dramatist seems to write only for complicated people. Generous, inventive, and revolutionary, Gatti is a lyric dramatist. And I believe that lyric theater—with or without music—is one of the two directions, along with the theater of comic satire and clowning denunciation, that can be taken by a people's theater.

We are searching for a lyric poet of the theater who is neither a Claudel—God preserve him, and preserve us from him—nor a Genet, whose ethics and dramaturgy can unfortunately reach only an audience of intellectuals. Gatti could be that poet. Alas! This left-wing Claudel is a poet with no language, or at least a poet whose language, even today, still only stammers. Yet he is a poet of dramatic structure and of theatrical space; he has a poetic *idea* of the theater, an idea that is not so far removed from the great vision of the baroque period. His plays are based on complicated contrivances, but contrivances that are often uselessly complicated; on abundant and tangled ideas (about staging and meanings), but ideas that are often very confused.

Using methods taken from novels, plays, and films, he loves to turn time and space upside down, to superimpose the imaginary on the real—in short, to handle theatrical machinery as it needs to be handled. But the material he presents us with is as confused as it is rich, and it is presented in a language that never reaches inspiration. The breath of lyricism animates the visual concepts, but it rarely enters the verbal aspect of the plays, an aspect that often remains rather elementary.

Gilles Sandier. *Théâtre et combat* (Paris, Stock, 1970), p. 106†

In spite of Sartre's defiant claim: "Marxism is our culture," the fact remains that militant ideologists rarely possess those qualities of sensibility and introspection that go to make good poets. One of the exceptions is Armand Gatti. Brought up in the lower depths of poverty and insecurity, forced to struggle for survival in the heart of a flamboyant, almost fairy-tale city of shameless wealth and even more shameless waste, all the conditions were assembled that should have turned Gatti into a dogmatic insurrectionary. Instead, he became a dramatist, or more precisely, a poet of the theatre; and the fascination of his plays lies precisely in the manner in which their anger and their ideology is deepened through compassion and at the same time individualized through fantasy and dream. *The Second Life of the Tattenberg Camp* is unquestionably a political play: its theme is one of horror, mass murder, the gas chambers, the extermination of Jews; yet simultaneously it is a lament for human destiny and a carnival of the absurd. . . .

For Gatti our life may be absurd; but it is the only one we have, and even if it is absurd, this is no reason for it to be insane and cruel and murderous as well. To fight against tyranny is significant for the fighter and for those who believe and hope in him, even if it may prove meaningless in the context of eternity; and so heroism *is* possible, for all that death is as omnipresent as it is in Ionesco's *Killing Game*. Gatti, therefore, is more than willing to adopt the *techniques* of absurdist drama (and to invent a good many others of his own into the bargain); but his characters are meaningful and "in the world," and this world is one of violence, torture, and insane destruction.

Richard N. Coe. *YFS*. No. 46, 1971, pp. 60, 63

GENET, JEAN (1910–   )

Jean Genet has become the subject of many discussions. His great love of books having led him to acquire them without paying any money for them, the young poet was brought before a police court for the seventh time. The excellent weekly *Comœdia* . . . wrote about the incident as follows: "The press has created some stir about the trial of Jean Genet. The poet and vagabond, one might recall, was sentenced to three months in prison for stealing books. The sentence would have been even stiffer, and would have included deportation, if Jean Cocteau, in a letter to the police court, had not called Genet the greatest poet of the age. Cocteau's praise will be discounted as representing charity on the one hand, and defiance on the other. Yet we have read poems by this disciple of Rimbaud and Verlaine that have surprising strength in their rather shocking way. In fact, the book he stole was a collection of poems by Verlaine. And when the presiding judge asked Genet if he knew the book's price, he replied: 'I know its value, but not its price.' "

P. S. [Pierre Seghers]. *Poésie 43*. July–Sept., 1943, pp. 74–75†

The Maids created controversy not only among critics but also among the spectators, some of whom demonstrated against the play almost every evening. . . . What fault did they find with Genet's play? The fault was much more a lack of tact than a lack of talent. It is truly painful to witness a debate on stage over the relationships between masters and servants, at least in their present incarnations. The classical theater, however, is full of scenes about, allusions to, and discussions of these relationships; but such relationships were not the same in society of old as in contemporary bourgeois society. It would be impossible today to write a Marivaux play with the same cast of characters, or to present the same confidences between masters and servants. Genet, moreover, has not written a comedy of manners: he has painted a rather extraordinary picture of the hatred two sisters feel toward their mistress, and of their decision to poison her, which, however, they do not carry out. Only Strindberg, among earlier playwrights, could have conceived of such a subject and dramatized it successfully. Genet has depicted a cell in Hell in which an insane hatred is expressed and in which the smoke of poison and the musty odor of dubious sexuality fill the air. These two servants are damned women. . . .

The reactions of the critics and the public led to a counterattack by the "spoken press," in which Genet's friends labeled him a genius, a victim of the Pharisees and bourgeois hypocrisy. . . . Let us put *The Maids* in its true place. This play has revealed a dramatist to us, one rather too haunted by bad dreams, too verbose, and not yet able to pace a scene, but a dramatist who is certainly capable of someday writing a gripping work.

Gérard Bauër. *RdP*. Aug., 1947, pp. 148–49†

Jean Genet's *Deathwatch*. Jean-Jacques Gautier (may he forgive me for turning critic too) writes the expected article. "Enough of these ignoble plays, etc. . . ." The funny thing is that the only real criticism of this play would be to reproach Genet with putting into it nobility of sentiment and language which border on the inhuman. Genet is a moralist in the sense that he has moral standards from which he never deviates by a hair's breadth. As a result it sometimes sounds as if he were preaching. Besides, Genet is a writer of fables, who makes his animals talk. He invents, or rather expresses, the psychology of dumb creatures who have none, or who may possess such a subtle type of psychology that they can express it by silence or violence. His vocabulary is therefore enormously superior to that which his characters would use. They therefore become heroes, high-minded complicated beings who translate into words shades of meaning coming from a world besides which conventional "elegant society" would seem in comparison disgustingly clumsy. [1949]

Jean Cocteau. *Maalesh* (London, Peter Owen, 1956), p. 15

The general impression of [Genet], such as it is, seems to leave out the heart of the matter, which is that however repellent his preoccupations, and however childish the philosophical equipment that he shares with many of his betters in that line, he is with little question one of the most gifted French prose writers of this generation, and the only one to have created a world nearly comparable in compulsion if not in scope to that of Proust or Céline. He is successor to both of them, and their only one, though he has a closer ancestry among the poets of the nineteenth century.

Unfortunately, public prudery being what it is, it will probably be a long time before his reputation will be based on much more than hearsay in this country. It is hard to see how the books could be made generally available here except in mutilated form, or even how they could be mutilated, since Genet's sexual candor, to put it mildly, is not eruptive as in Sartre but entirely of the grain; to doctor his writing for commercial purposes would be to operate on every line. . . .

Although *Miracle of the Rose*, which I should judge was the first of his published books, is the only one that is actually set in prison and describes prison life at any length, really prison, both as poetic symbol and as the origin and standard of values, is his whole world, and all the material that he develops more skillfully later is present in the autobiographical *Miracle of the Rose*, which twists back and forth between an adult prison and an extraordinary lyrical evocation of childhood in a reformatory called Mettray. The main theme, always the same, stems from the constant, conscious opposition of this world to "yours," the world of habitual morality, which is to be rejected on the quaint grounds of excitement and the "attraction of the forbidden" but also in the higher interest of "moral solitude," freedom and purity.

Eleanor Clark. *PR*. April, 1949, pp. 443–45

When we yield to the artist's demands, it is *his* universe that we are approving. . . . I know: there is a defense. One can pull oneself together, can stop reading, can thrust the book aside with disgust. But, in the first place, Genet expects this disgust, he hopes for it: is it not the inverse of a Perpetual Adoration? He is delighted that, more or less everywhere in the world, his books are the impassive objects of impotent fury. And besides, what is disgust? Quite simply an incipient vomiting. And what you vomit must in some way have been inside you.

How Genet laughed at [François] Mauriac's painful efforts to vomit him out: he would have liked, I think, to speak to him somewhat as follows: "The disgust which you manifest when confronted with my books is a magical effort to reject that Other who is no other than yourself. But when, in desperation, you make such a fuss, it is already too late. One does not vomit up one's soul, and it is your soul that is rotten. Is there any way of my knowing, when confronted with your wild frenzy, what loathsome instincts have awakened in it? After all, you were considered a specialist in Evil before I appeared on the scene. We are confreres. You, however, had got into the habit of stopping in time, out of respect for your public, or else, after describing lost, ignoble souls, you wrote a preface to praise the divine creation and to recommend that we practice Christian charity. I, on the other hand, do not write a preface. I have led you further than you wanted to go. In unmasking myself, I unmask you. You are an evildoer, like me, but a shamefaced evildoer. Your fury sheds a very singular light on your own works. Wasn't Thérèse Desqueyroux a poisoner? How glad I am to write openly and how the wickedness that dares not speak its name must suffer." He would be greatly disappointed if it occurred to anyone to say to him that M. Mauriac's clownish indignation simply expressed a mediocre author's hatred of a great writer. [1952]

Jean-Paul Sartre. *Saint Genet: Actor and Martyr*
(New York, Braziller, 1963), pp. 497, 501–2

Sartre himself noted a curious difficulty at the basis of Genet's work. Genet, the writer, has neither the power to communicate with his readers nor the intention of doing so. His work almost denies the reader. Sartre saw, though he drew no conclusions, that in these conditions the work was incomplete. It was a replacement, half way from the *major* communication at which literature aims. Literature is communication. . . .

[But] in fact there is no communication between Genet and the reader—and yet Sartre assumes that his work is valid. He suggests that it is based on consecration, then on poetic creation. According to Sartre, Genet had himself "consecrated by the reader." "To tell the truth," he adds immediately, "the reader has no knowledge of this consecration."

This leads him to maintain that "the poet . . . demands to be recognized by an audience whom he does not recognize." But this is unacceptable. I can assert that the consecrational operation, or poetry, is communication or nothing. Genet's work, whatever a commentator may say about it, is neither sacred nor poetic because the author refuses to communicate. [1957]

Georges Bataille. *Literature and Evil* (London, Calder and Boyars, 1973), pp. 160–61

For some months we had been hearing about an unknown poet whom Cocteau had discovered in prison, and whom he maintained to be the greatest writer of his age. At any rate, this was how he had described him in July 1943, when composing a letter to the presiding magistrate of the police court in the nineteenth arrondissement, before whom the poet, one Jean Genet, was up for sentence, with nine previous convictions against him for theft already. [Marc] Barbezat intended to publish some of his poems and an extract from a prose work in [the journal] *L'arbalète*, and his wife Olga—brunette Olga, that is—occasionally went to see him in prison. It was from her that I had learned of his existence, and discovered one or two facts concerning his life. He had been placed with foster parents, a peasant family, soon after birth. The larger part of his childhood he had spent in reformatories. His career as burglar and pickpocket had taken him all around the world, and he was, on top of all this, a homosexual. He had taken up reading in prison; this had led to his writing poems and, subsequently, a book.

Olga Barbezat was ecstatic about his talent, but I was less impressed than I might have been in my youth. The gutter-Bohemian of genius seemed to me a somewhat stereotyped figure; and knowing Cocteau's taste for the offbeat, not to mention his passion for discovering people, I fancied he might be overboosting his protégé's claims. But when the first section of *Our Lady of the Flowers* appeared in *L'arbalète*, we were very much impressed. Genet had obviously been influenced by Proust and Cocteau and Jouhandeau, but he nevertheless possessed a voice of his own, a quite inimitable style of utterance. It was a most uncommon occurrence nowadays for us to read anything that renewed our faith in literature: these pages revealed the power of words to us as though for the first time. Cocteau had read the situation aright: a great writer *had* appeared. [1960]

Simone de Beauvoir. *The Prime of Life* (Cleveland, World, 1962), p. 458

While I would like to make it clear that *The Balcony* is an event of at least relative importance, I do not at all wish to hide the disgust and even moral outrage this play makes me feel. . . . I do not consider Jean

Genet to be any more of a genuine dramatic author today than I thought he was yesterday. But *The Balcony* still has an undeniable sort of existence. In it one should see a derisive condemnation of what our civilization risks becoming through the fault of people whose minds are being decomposed by a great toxic force. . . .

One thing is certain: all the snobs of Paris and elsewhere will come to cheer *The Balcony*. That is normal; it could not be any other way. It is more distressing to think of the nice people who will rush after the snobs so as not to miss the boat and who will come and perplexedly contemplate this long black mass, this ritual in reverse. . . . What must be said is that this play, which is blasphemous and—from start to finish—sacrilegious, is at the same time a dismal entertainment that eventually tires those it began by shocking.

Gabriel Marcel. NL. May 26, 1960, p. 10†

The subject of [*The Balcony*], perfectly clear and almost "didactic," is no less than the essential transformation of industrial society in the first half of the twentieth century. . . .

In modern Western society, as almost all contemporary sociologists tell us, the separation between economic power and political power tends progressively to disappear; both powers, although not yet identical, tend to blend into one another. Genet simply records this fact by showing Irma simultaneously become queen and proprietor of the house of illusions in the newly established order.

The other great transformation that constitutes the central subject of the play is the entrance of the chief of police into the popular consciousness and his rise to the same prestige other dignitaries have. In Genet's play this transformation takes place with the help of the defeated revolutionaries (embodied by Roger), for whom the hope of a technical organization of power has now become more important than the promise of authentic life represented by the revolution. Instead of the beautiful girl who sang of life, they now dream of becoming chiefs of police. . . .

Whether he intended to do so or not—and certainly with a completely different view of the world—Genet has written the first great Brechtian play in French literature.

Lucien Goldmann. TM. June, 1960,
pp. 1189, 1193, 1196†

[In *The Blacks*] one is asked to consider a theme which may be the central moment of the twentieth century: the passage of power from the White to those he oppressed. But this theme is presented in a web of formal contradictions and formal turns sufficiently complex to be a play in itself. Pirandello never made this mistake. His dance of mirrors was always built on pretexts which were flimsy. If one's obsession is with the contradictory nature of reality, the audience must be allowed to dispense with the superficial reality in order to explore its depths. The foreground in *The Blacks* is too oppressive. One cannot ignore it. White and Black in mortal confrontation are far more interesting than the play of shadows Genet brings to it. If he insists with avant-garde pride that he will not be bullied by the major topicalities of his theme, and instead will search out the murmurs, the shivers, the nuances, one does not necessarily have to applaud.

Certain themes, simple on their face, complex in their depths, insist on returning to the surface and remaining simple. The murder of Lumumba is thus simple. It is simple and it is overbearing. It is inescapable. One cannot treat it as a pantomime for ballet without making an aesthetic misjudgment of the first rank. It would be a strategic disaster of conception. So with Genet's choice to add the minuet to Africa. One is left not with admiration for his daring, but with a dull sense of evasion. How much real emotion and complexity we could have been given if literal White had looked across the stage at literal Black. His rhodomontades and escapades leave us finally with the suspicion that Genet has not escaped the deepest vice of the French mind: its determination, no matter how, to say something new, even if it is absurd. And it is this vice which characterizes the schism in Genet as an artist, for he is on the one hand major, moving with a bold long reach into those unexplored territories at the edge of our awareness, and with the other, he is minor, a Surrealist, destroying the possibility of awareness even as he creates it. [1961]

Norman Mailer. *The Presidential Papers* (New York, G. P. Putnam's Sons, 1963), pp. 208–9

Many people are shocked by Genet's plays. They are frightened when confronted with a world they know really exists—a complete world. Ionesco, for instance, never stayed to see the end of *The Blacks*. As a white man he felt uncomfortable; he felt he was being attacked; he sensed the great pleasure the Negro actors took each time they insulted the whites. If people are shocked by Genet's plays, they are completely disarmed by his other great quality—his ability to evoke laughter, and laughter relaxes the spectator. If a spectator is shocked by the obscenities he hears on stage, he is won over by the sheer beauty and poetry of Genet's language. Even those who feel they are being mocked and ridiculed are struck by the "truth" and burning sincerity of his poetry and are held by a sense of "fair-play." There are, of course, bigots like Gabriel Marcel who turn away. . . .

What I try to do when directing a play is to translate the author's ideas, his aesthetic that is, both visually and emotionally. I want the audience to feel the immense jubilation Genet felt when he wrote *The Blacks* and *The Screens*. It's the jubilation of a child who punishes others and at the same time punishes himself. Take *The Blacks*. It's anti-white, but don't think for a moment that it's a glorification of the blacks either. The play is purposely ambiguous—what with blacks acting out their ritual in front of a white audience which isn't white at all, but made up of blacks disguised as whites. Genet is not shedding tears over the fate of the blacks. He is showing humanity with all its passions, its hatreds, jealousies, and vices. He is trying to penetrate the inner core of man, to understand it. He is searching for man's motivations, really Genet's motivations. Each time Genet writes, he tries to get to the bottom of things. This is the only way he can find himself and so liberate himself. The pen is his only friend and confidant. My role as director is to make this clear to the spectator.

Roger Blin. *TDR*. Spring, 1963, pp. 113–14

The Blacks is a depth charge of evil which plunges through the placid surface of rational discourse and social benevolence to the dark sea floor of the unconscious, where myths of danger, sado-masochistic fantasies, and primitive sacrificial rites explode on us unaware. Taken as a programmatic essay on relations between the races, it is, of course, intolerable—but Genet's art never functions programmatically. It is, rather, imaginative and metaphorical, creating a world contiguous with our own but not identical with it. Appealing to whatever has remained unconditioned and uncivilized in the spectator's soul, Genet fashions his plays as cruel purgative myths—deeply subversive in their implications, profoundly liberating in their effect.

No art, however, is totally self-contained. And Genet, whose criminality and depravity not only attack but exemplify the degeneration of our culture, may well go down as the dramatic artist who presided over the disintegration of the West. Unlike Artaud, whose theories of cruelty were animated by a robust spirit and a healthy conscience, Genet is sick with evil, impregnated with it, consumed by it. His art, however, is his health, and he has managed to wring from his pathology myths which are beautiful, spontaneous, and profound. If he can cure himself, then he may help to cure us, and the dying civilization he chronicles may again revive.

Robert Brustein. *The Theatre of Revolt* (Boston,
Little, Brown, 1964), pp. 410–11

If we experience sympathy for Genet's outcasts and reprobates, feeling some measure of guilt and responsibility for their condition, we shall move on to thoughts of amelioration or social reform which he himself vigorously rejects (his total rejection of prison reform in *The Criminal Child* must make painful and depressing reading for our psychologists and sociologists of crime). On the other hand, if we largely ignore the matter of Genet's writings and respond primarily to his remarkable literary imagination, we remain insulated by art from the only world of experience which he cares to write about and which he thinks to be worth living. In some curiously complicated way, it seems that his very articulateness, his existence as a literary voice, works against him as a practising "anti-moralist." Genet himself, on the other hand, has the last word if he causes us to reject his ideas but to admire his artistic presentation of them. Once we do this, we are accepting literature as a phenomenon without a moral existence using the term "moral" here in its widest and most humane sense. Nihilism will then have reached its ultimate expression by encompassing both the content of art and the formulation of this content in words. If we allow ourselves to adopt such an attitude, Genet's ideological attack on our world will have manoeuvred us into a position in which defence has become impossible and willed crime emerges as the only form of integrity.

John Cruickshank. *CQ*. Autumn, 1964, p. 210

The Screens . . . is a sprawling mosaic of Algerian life under French colonial rule. Three characters run through it—a young man named Saïd, his mother, and his repellently ugly wife. Genet's text embraces squalor almost as if it were a benediction. Metaphors of filth and putrescence multiply, and violence takes on an aura of sensual exaltation. On the one hand, the occupying army is exhorted to think of itself as "the mighty phallus of France." On the other, Saïd's wife implores her husband to "choose evil and always evil," for "I want you to know only hatred and never love." Genet sees the two sides as equal partners in a game of mutual debasement. Ever since the play opened [in Paris], performances have been interrupted by catcalls, walkouts, vegetable missiles, and exploding firecrackers, although the Algerian war ended long ago.

[Jean-Louis] Barrault [who directed the production] contributes to the programme a dazzling facing-both-ways essay in which he declares that drama differs from the other arts because it takes place in public. This means that in the theatre "there is perhaps something more sacred than liberty; namely, respect for human beings." At the same time, he is careful to point out that a writer must be true to his vision, however outrageous it may be, and that *The Screens* is a case of "legitimate provocation." My own view of the play is that it resembles a swamp of self-indulgent images from which pinnacles of tough theatricality occasionally protrude—a Sargasso Sea dotted with the wreckage of a potential masterpiece. [Oct. 15, 1966]

Kenneth Tynan. *Tynan Right and Left* (New York, Atheneum, 1968), p. 191

Apart from a short appreciation of Giacometti, an essay about an acrobat, and a number of prefaces to his plays, Genet has not added to the prose works published in his *Complete Works*. This confirms his remark, in the *Playboy* interview, that Sartre's study made him almost unable to continue writing, and emphasises how curious the relationship between Sartre and Genet is. Had it not been for Sartre, far fewer people would have heard of Genet, and his work would certainly have been studied from a very different point of view. It is also rumoured that it was only because of Sartre's influence that Genet consented to the publication of his *Complete Works*, and that Gallimard agreed to undertake it.

The way Sartre uses Genet as a pretext for his own ideas on the wickedness of bourgeois society lends weight to Philip Toynbee's remark that their relationship is "rather that of the bearded lady in the tent to the voluble huckster outside," but there is, in this respect, one significant difference: no previous literary huckster so vaunted the fascination of the beard that the lady became unable to grow any further hair. This seems to be what happened to Genet, though it could also be argued that his sources of inspiration had virtually dried up, as far as his prose work was concerned, before Sartre ever showed him the manuscript of his analysis. Only *The Thief's Journal* was, in fact, published after 1947, and Sartre is quite right to see it as a "literary testament, or at least a conclusion." It breaks no new ground, and frequently seems contrived and over-intellectual when compared to *Our Lady of the Flowers* or *Miracle of the Rose*.

Philip Thody. *Jean Genet* (New York, Stein and Day, 1969), pp. 19–20

The lady at the desk of the [Café des] Deux-Magots handed me the copy of *Miracle of the Rose* Simone de Beauvoir had left there for me. It's heavy, I commented. . . . That evening: *Miracle of the Rose* weighing down my bed. The book is inside a chest, between two covers that fit together. I have brought a de luxe edition home with me: it's a first. I am not turning pages, I am lifting engravings. Each page has the serenity of a sheet of thick blotting paper. . . . I lean my elbow on the pillow, we tilt, the book and I together, towards the wall, and we begin to give ourselves to one another. I am falling into my reading of *Miracle of the Rose* as one falls in love. . . .

I sit and read *Miracle of the Rose* again. Fever, palpitations, shivers, just the way it was when I read it first, nineteen years ago. I was an adolescent of thirty-eight, I was discovering the happiness of adoration, the joy of admiration. Now I am an adolescent of fifty-seven, I am discovering the happiness of adoration, the joy of admiration. For whom had I caught that fever? For whom was I in a swoon? For Harcamone, the convict condemned to death. I reread Genet and my heart beat faster. . . . I can open Genet anywhere. The griefs and agonies in Genet are my litanies. I am raised up like Harcamone; see how I hover over his majestic misfortunes, his sumptuous experiences, his rituals, his carnivals, his metempsychoses, and Genet's ultimate alchemy when he transforms imprisoning chains to flowering bracelets. . . . Every book he writes is a commemoration of transfigured sufferings. At his high mass I hurry to be early, to get a seat in the front row. [1970]

Violette Leduc. Mad in Pursuit (New York,
Farrar, Straus & Giroux, 1971), pp. 71–74

Genet began his career politically in the nineteen-thirties on the moderate Left—radical, radical-socialist or social-democrat—and has since moved progressively further and further left, abandoning socialism in the end for a brand of anarchism so intransigent, so uncompromising and so totally negative that it can only express itself by paradox: where *all* organised political parties of whatever complexion are equally unacceptable, then it is possible for Genet, with complete sincerity, to glorify the efficiency of the police state in one play (*The Balcony*) and to exult in the destruction of the armies of that same state in another (*The Screens*); to show an oppressed race conquering its temptation to assume the values and the culture of its oppressors in *The Blacks*, and, in the final scenes of *The Screens*, to show another oppressed race gaining the victory over its oppressors precisely through the efficiency with which it imitates them. . . .

The combined influence of Sartre, Brecht and—more problematically—of Antonin Artaud has been so strong that, of the five plays he has published, *Deathwatch* alone can be said to be wholly free of commitment. War and colonialism, the oppression of minorities, race-hatreds, revolt and revolution: these seem hardly the ivory-tower topics of a mystic and an aesthete. And yet in fact—most brittle of all Jean Genet's many paradoxes—they are precisely this.

Richard N. Coe. In John Fletcher, ed., Forces in
Modern French Drama (New York,
Frederick Ungar, 1972), pp. 158–59

GHELDERODE, MICHEL DE (1898–1962)

BELGIUM

[Ghelderode's] art is not at all intended to please. One has only to think of the enormous flattery of public approval the Boulevard theater offers to measure how far the dramatic work of Michel de Ghelderode, particularly a play like *Hop Signor!*, is from the usual guideline of pleasing the audience. His work is far as well from the classical theater —I am speaking of French classicism—which was also founded on the art of pleasing the public. We have to acknowledge that most of the public does not have the sensitivity to grasp the fascinating magic, the invisible rays, that emanate from Ghelderode's universe. Indeed, a part of this universe—its most important and most secret radiations—will always escape the ears of the majority (except in such specifically popular works as *Barabbas*), just as ultra-frequency sounds escape us and as some rays escape our eye.

We might call Ghelderode's an ultra-violet theater, and moreover an ultra-violent one, in which the characters may have an epileptic fit or worse at the end of every scene. In the presence of these mesmerized characters moving around the stage, I cannot help dreading a sudden metamorphosis or sudden death for them. They exist in a region of great crises, in the critical zone in which phenomena are transformed, in which light becomes sound or a fatal penetrating ray, which makes the invisible visible. It is a zone in which sensual pleasure is transformed into suffering, even into paroxysm, in which chastity becomes a superior form of lewdness. . . .

[Ghelderode's] brand of Satanism is infinitely more sincere, less literary, than that of writers like Barbey d'Aurevilly and Baudelaire. Ghelderode's characters are genuinely possessed. They are possessed by the Cross or possessed by the Flesh, and barraged by the whole range of sparks discharged between these two poles.

Paul Werrie. *Théâtre de la fuite* (Brussels,
Les Écrits, 1943), pp. 158–59†

There is in Ghelderode's comedy the great force ordinarily found only in tragedy. In the first place he has the skill and forceful genius for creating "types"—without which the farce would find it difficult to exist. Even the names which he gives his characters are true to type, and when the curtain rises we already have an idea of what awaits us.

Ghelderode's nonconformist art is magical, and it does not seem to follow any rules, or rather rules with which we are not familiar. Consider the vast difference between our theatre and that of the Greeks, or the Elizabethans. Remembering the distance between contemporary man and the man of the Renaissance, one cannot ask theatre to follow the rules of a chess game in which one logic is admitted. Ghelderode's dramas are partly pathological in that they emanate from the subconscious to the conscious; the barriers which separated the spectator from his neighbor or from the actor are completely broken down and there is a sense that all present are accomplices.

Ghelderode certainly would have liked to create for the Elizabethan scene which made possible continuous action without interruption to change locale. We find this "movie" technique in *Christopher Columbus*. In this work Ghelderode violates the exact facts of history, but in so doing he contributes to psychology of the discoverer. Columbus is no longer the man looking for a new continent, but rather looking for an opportunity to escape his fellow man. He leaves to discover himself and to contemplate rather than to explore. And when the King locks him up, asking what he's going to do, Columbus replies, "Voyage." . . .

Perhaps the actuality of Ghelderode's work is to remind us that there are certain eternal things which one cannot classify, dissect and prove, and that humanity continues in its mystery and fear and ignorance. Where our contemporaries attempt to discover rational explanations, Ghelderode uncovers the demons found in the best places in the Middle Ages—and all still very much of our time.

Jean Francis and Roger Iglesis. *Chrysalis.* 3, 3–4,
1949, p. 9

[The character] Jean-Jacques, the author, has a curiously secondary role in [*Exit of the Actor*], essentially [the drama] of Renatus, the incarnation of the actor, with whose death and resurrection it is concerned. Whereas Jean-Jacques remains at all times a creature of flesh and blood, albeit one occasionally endowed with remarkable intuition, Renatus is able to loose his earthly bonds, releasing the symbolic spirit of the character. The role of the author is more confined within his terrestrial shell through the added contrast of Fagot, the prompter—*le souffleur*, insufflator of life wherever are found scenic machines, on the stage, in the church, or at an actor's funeral—hence, the spirit of the dramatic rite, of the Theater. . . .

This play is first of all about the stage. All its characters are actors, or at least performing spirits in the making of the theater. The author, who remains throughout a lay protagonist, is nevertheless on intimate terms with the demiurges. He is able to span the planes between his earthliness and their otherworldly realms by the deep and amicable understanding that he has of their individual personalities. He is Baudelaire's poet walking amidst familiar symbols. . . .

Jean-Jacques is primarily what Gide would have called a "disquieting" influence, though a strangely reluctant one. It is he who has contaminated Renatus with his plays and instilled in him the persistent theatrical illusion. . . .

For [Ghelderode], the real actor is one marked by the somber powers of the stage and scarcely distinguishable from all who bear its fateful impress. He is an intuitive creature, attuned to the same otherworldly waves actuating the author: both are impelled and inspired by forces apprehensible only to the few elect, the outcasts who toil within this sanctum.

Renatus is the prototype of such creatures, bearing with varying degrees of fortitude the aboriginal curse of his extraordinariness. The actor's agony, like that of the author, stems from his inability to escape, to be other than what he is and will be for all eternity, despite the torturing acuity of his vision. The only consolation that he may countenance is as bitter as the early Camus, whose neo-stoicism it recalls: his awareness of this somber fate gives him dignity.

David I. Grossvogel. *The Self-Conscious Stage in*
Modern French Drama (New York, Columbia
University Press, 1958), pp. 254, 256–57, 262–63

[Ghelderode] concluded his *The Ostend Interviews* with the following statement: "Men are not lovely, not often, and it's very well that they are not even more ugly; but I believe in *Man*, and I think that this can be felt in my work. I don't despair of him, and I find him interesting, capable of everything—and of its opposite." Herein lies the key to everything he ever wrote, and this is especially true of *Pantagleize*, probably his finest play.

Pantagleize is Ghelderode's drama of Everyman and it deals with the problem of commitment in life. When the play opens, Pantagleize has no real identity in the society in which he lives. . . . Pantagleize is vaguely uncomfortable that he does not have a sense of his own destiny, but he has accepted this fact and is really quite relieved that he is free of such a burden. . . . Pantagleize has no intention of getting involved with the revolution, or with anything else for that matter. But his innocent remark, "What a lovely day!" starts a chain of events which enmeshes him inextricably in the revolution and leads to his death. In the process, however, this Chaplinesque character begins to live: he falls in love, he enjoys the power and prestige of being a leader of men, he is exhilarated as he participates unwittingly in desperate adventures, and he is confused as he faces the final judgment and death.

Using the technique of a kind of modern baroque amplification to create a burlesque of man's condition, Ghelderode shows us that the contemporary Everyman does not choose his identity, rather it is thrust upon him. But strangely enough, when this occurs Pantagleize manifests a rich and warm humanity. . . . Just before he dies, Pantagleize decides that he will never again bother about his destiny, but in that one day he revealed the richness, the joy, the pain, the sadness, and the ludicrousness of each man's destiny, and in so doing he affirms the humanity of us all.

Robert W. Corrigan. Introduction to
Robert W. Corrigan, ed., *The New Theatre of Europe*
(New York, Delta, 1962), Vol. I, pp. 23–24

Ghelderode's world is medieval Flanders, and his view of the world can best be described as savagely grotesque. His plays are sadistic caricatures shot through with a ribald scatological humor which reminds one of the pictures of his countrymen Hieronymus Bosch and Pieter Breughel and of the anonymous woodcuts of the danse macabre. Indeed, Ghelderode has specifically set some of his plays in a fictitious "Breughellands" where the painter's grotesque and ribald creations come to life. . . .

[*The Blind Men*] is a short sketch inspired by Breughel's painting "The Parable of the Blind," now in the Museo Nazionale, Naples. Breughel's picture shows six blind men walking along one behind the other and about to tumble into the ditch into which their leader has already fallen. Breughel based his picture on the Biblical proverb, "they be blind leaders of the blind. And if the blind lead the blind both shall fall into the ditch." In Breughel's picture, as in Ghelderode's world, the blind men are the helpless victims of a system perverted by the Devil's ascendancy. If the Devil were not in control of the world, the men would not be blind, there would be no treacherously placed ditch for them to fall into, and they would not be instinctively led to disaster anyway, but rather to the church in the background of the picture.

The literal presence of the Devil and his cohorts was a real concept to Breughel, as it undoubtedly is to Ghelderode as well. But Ghelderode makes the plan of the picture somewhat harsher. In Ghelderode's world the Devil makes men perverse: they are the victims not of their alien surroundings but of their own twisted and willful natures. The characteristic of the damned in religion, after all, is that they heed the promptings of the Devil instead of the voice of God. Ghelderode's blind men (reduced to three, presumably for convenience of staging) are pilgrims on the way to Rome, where they believe they have now arrived, although they have actually been wandering around in circles for weeks and are still in Flanders. A one-eyed man warns them that they are in dangerous country and offers to lead them to a monastery where they will be safe. The blind men refuse to believe him and scornfully reject his help. They trudge off and are swallowed up in a bog. Breughel's blind men are merely comically ducked in a ditch, but Ghelderode's deliberately turn down an offer of salvation and die.

> George E. Wellwarth. *The Theater of Protest and Paradox* (New York, New York University Press, 1964), pp. 98, 100–101

Michel de Ghelderode was a solitary who lived for the greater part of his life in a room full of dress-shop dummies, macabre marionettes, old armor, and seashells. . . .

Born at Ixelles, in Brabant, Ghelderode was the son of the principal clerk of the Archives Générales, a man who believed that in the modern world of conformity the best occupation a man could have was that of civil servant. In boyhood, his nonconforming son Michel built for himself what he called a second life, a dark life which he kept hidden like a treasure. When he was sixteen, a serious illness took him away from his classical studies, and he began producing poems, which he later lost; he also kept a journal. But he didn't seriously take up writing until 1916–17. The puppet performances of the Belgian marketplaces had always fascinated him, and the elements of their plays are often reflected in his own work, along with his lifelong enthusiasm for such novels as *Don Quixote* and *Til Ulenspiegel.* . . .

Ghelderode . . . though he wrote in French, and in a wildly poetic French, was Flemish in spirit. His plays not only have their puppet-play elements, but also phases of the macabre, the supernatural, the carnal, the monstrous.

> Harry T. Moore. *Twentieth-Century French Literature since World War II* (Carbondale and Edwardsville, Southern Illinois University Press, 1966), pp. 31–32

Ghelderode's Flemishness has the stamp of the time of the Spanish occupation. He is someone who, quite literally, has never gotten over that occupation, has still not recovered from it. For Ghelderode, the Spaniard is the occupier in the fullest sense of the word, one who not only gives orders to the occupied man but who also haunts him, fascinates him, and takes possession of his soul. The occupier eventually forms a couple with the man he occupies; the two hate each other, but their cohabitation can never come to an end. Each one sucks the blood of the other, and ultimately it is impossible to say which of the two, the oppressor or the oppressed, is more powerful, which one dominates and contaminates the other.

Ghelderode's work is that of an occupied man. Undoubtedly this is one of the reasons for his sudden popularity in Parisian theaters shortly after another Occupation. Occupation is night. Ghelderode's work is nocturnal. Everything happens at night or in crypts, in buried rooms in which day never dawns. The monsters Ghelderode lets loose on stage . . . are hallucinations caused by terror, by the fever of an occupied man. These characters are the exaggerations of insomnia, the phantoms of nights that early curfews have made interminable. It is Breughel's village fair—but threatened, watched by patrols, spied upon by the dark men of the Inquisition, with the scaffold erected two steps from the cabaret.

Félicien Marceau. *Les années courtes* (Paris, Gallimard, 1968), pp. 291–92†

The Aristotelian aesthetic of a brief disturbance between two periods of calm does not suit a comic theater, which encompasses Destiny and Becoming, Creation and Chaos. In Ghelderode's theater, in which personalities crumble, myths disintegrate, and reason dissolves, the need, from the very beginning, was indeed for a new, non-Aristotelian aesthetic. Like Artaud, Ghelderode strives to discover a physical and concrete language for the stage, one that stresses movement, disharmony, and paroxysm. The main assumption of this theater is Revelry: plays will be set in the time when all is possible, the time of flouting all taboos through violence, danger, and scandal. Ghelderode's aesthetic will be the foundation for those impressions, correspondences, and analogies that, acting on the senses, cause physical shock on the viewer's nerves and mind.

The importance given to the setting attests to its symbolic value. At times, however, it expresses, through concrete dialectics, the disharmony between the character and his setting, the distance between the actor and the object. The optics of the dream always accentuates the "reflection" of the real and the imaginary. Burlesque humor, broad laughter, or clownery underscore the disintegration of the rational. Finally, language often reduced to stomach rumblings, or annulled by pantomime, sometimes still rises to the level of incantation and poetic magic, although even here language can be made inarticulate and deformed by the joining together of strange figures of speech, by odd syntax, or by the use of foreign languages (English, Flemish, and so forth), in which case it expresses the fundamental incoherence of man. Such is Ghelderode's conception of theater.

Jean Decock. *Le théâtre de Michel de Ghelderode:*
Une dramaturgie de l'anti-théâtre et de la cruauté
(Paris, Librairie A.-G. Nizet, 1969), p. 212†

GIDE, ANDRÉ (1869–1951)

Whether he writes a journal, or treatises, or poems, Gide remains himself, and among the apparently radical differences that can be noted
among the orientations of his books . . . a constant personality can be
found, composed of a few principal traits whose relative dominance is
the only thing that varies. In greater or lesser reliefs, there is not a single
work by Gide that does not contain all these traits. . . .

Gide is a sensitive person; his soul is afraid of the slightest touch,
for that would be enough to shake it completely. The external world
produces a violent impression on him, for better or for worse; but it
does affect him, and his sensitivity is so delicate that it seems mystical,
at times analogous to that of those heroes of Maeterlinck who are
troubled by a flower and gripped by silence. Music, the art of pure,
vague, and subtle expression, especially the music of the great romantics
like Schumann or Chopin, throws Gide's being into profound ecstasies.
He has his simple side and his complexities. Once he spoke of the
emotion he felt at seeing "his hand on the table"; at another time he
spoke of the joy of nearly touching the object of his desire, having
only to move his arm forward, and of passing it by. But just as he took
pleasure in chastity, so will he take pleasure in possession. He speaks in
one of his works of the inextricable complexity of his emotions, which
are such the slightest perception awakens complicated systems within
him, systems that form a sort of network of intimate sensations; this is
why his emotions are often contradictory. He trembles at formal beauty
as at moral or religious beauty. . . .

This sensitivity denotes an infinite tenderness and might make one
take Gide for a melancholy man. At times his writings have a gray,
subdued tint, as if they were covered with a haze of vague sadness. But
nothing is healthier than this soul, nothing more beautifully alive: for
the tender and sensitive man is also a passionate man. The very subtle
perceptions of his heart bring about an awakening of all the forces he
has held in check.

Henri Ghéon. MdF. May, 1897, pp. 244–45†

I have just received the third number of *La nouvelle revue française*, in
which I find the last part of *The Narrow Gate*. I am still suffering from
the emotional shock (and the great perplexity) which its perusal provoked in me. Having read it in serial form, I have carried your
[Gide's] book within me for a long time, but I shouldn't like to say

that I've understood it perfectly, despite the high quality of an admirable style which insinuates itself into one's being like some warm and intoxicating liquor. One seems to be enveloped on every side in that solemn end-of-summer atmosphere, that "gilded ecstasy" of which you speak in your concluding pages. The language is suave and mature—a suavity full of anguish. A Dantesque sweetness but beneath it is something terribly bitter—I don't like to say despairing. . . .

The coarse literature of the last hundred years has put us off the scent, where the study of our deepest feelings is concerned. NO, sexual satisfaction does not mean the satisfaction of love and passion; it is a diminution, and always a transformation. It is not a question of Platonic niceties. The sentiment of "refusal" lies deep in the heart of womankind and is even found among the animals! There is no richer or more complicated dramatic subject, and none more filled with pathos for a masculine reader—whence our interest in all those books ([Eugène Fromentin's] *Dominique* is the most moving of them) in which we watch passion at grips with duty. The strength of your book is that there is no question of external duty, but only of an inner voice. That is also what many readers will find exasperating.

Let us turn to the Christian problem, which leaves me very much in doubt—what was your intention? Is yours a Christian book? Have you simply represented God as an atrocious, unspeaking tormentor? Your noble Alissa, dying broken-hearted between your clean bare walls, distressed me deeply. [May 10, 1909]

Paul Claudel. In The Correspondence between Paul
Claudel and André Gide (New York, Pantheon,
1952), pp. 89–90

In the presence of a scene in which the most subtle external reactions are superimposed on the deepest layers of emotions, but in which their fusion is so complete that nothing can be left out, one may well repeat the words of Benjamin Constant: "There is truth only in nuances." Everything is in the nuances, and they omit nothing. An exquisite restraint presides over Gide's choice of external details [in *The Pastoral Symphony*]; only a few are employed, but none is unimportant. . . . *The Pastoral Symphony* makes one think of [Louis] Lenain's paintings in the Louvre—paintings in which the setting always has a domestic, private feeling, in which the drama is acted out entirely internally, behind the motionlessness yet impassioned stillness of the faces.

Art of this nature quite naturally excels in "preparation." . . . In *The Pastoral Symphony*—which, in this respect, is somewhat similar to the best works of Ibsen—the artist's role consists in gradually creating, in gradually preparing, the atmosphere, in making the setting of the action an inhabited place. . . .

Never has Gide developed this art of preparation further than in *The Pastoral Symphony*, with its two harmoniously united parts; but a moment arrives when Gide becomes the victim of this very art, and one has to admit that the ending of *The Pastoral Symphony* is abrupt. We had been witnessing, with nothing glossed over, the gradual development of emotions, each viewed separately and shown as operating only internally. But when all the emotions surface externally and explode, and when, through their convergence, the crisis comes to a head, no sooner are the events set in motion than the invisible presence through which the narrative had been sustained withdraws after the briefest comments and leaves us in the lurch. Here Gide resembles a man who had planted his field with the greatest care, and whose harvest promises to exceed all expectations: then, when the time comes to bind the sheaves together, Gide leaves everything as it is and takes off. [Jan., 1921]

Charles Du Bos. *Le dialogue avec André Gide*
(Paris, Au Sans Pareil, 1929), pp. 12–13†

Gide confides to me that he "absolutely must" publish *If the Grain Die...* and *Corydon* without further delay. I do my best, I do all I can think of, to dissuade him. . . .

He has always been haunted by the tragic destiny of Oscar Wilde. It's quite possible that he believes he has a supreme duty, a higher mission, to fulfill; and that what he is yielding to this moment is a nostalgic summons to martyrdom. [Jacques] Copeau thinks so; and so, perhaps, may others. I myself think that it results from his intoxication with Russia. For months he has been living in daily intimacy with Dostoevski, while preparing his lectures for the [Théâtre du] Vieux-Colombier. The idea of public confession is infectious; like the hero of a Russian novel, Gide is burning to affront Society and invite its punishment. Outrage, opprobrium, the pillory—those are the things to which he aspires. He has such a strange inspired smile when he disposes of my objections! Doubtless he feels enhanced and self-glorified when he thinks of how he will be misunderstood and shunned and despised—and of what a price he will be paying for his sublime sincerity. For I can sense, in this adventure, some half-formed longing for *expiation*; a new mark, in fact, of those moral reflexes which he has inherited from his puritan ancestors. It is an extension, I would say, of his latent sense of sin—not that he knows of its existence; he would certainly deny it—but I have often noticed the vestiges of it in his behavior: above all, for instance, in his perpetual wish to explain and defend himself, to *justify* himself, in fact. For it is to that that this great rebel, who believes

himself completely emancipated, has hitherto devoted, on his own ad-
mission, the best part of his intelligence and of his gifts.

It is a waste of my time to try to convince him. He will publish his
Corydon; he will publish *If the Grain Die...* In his present exalted state
of mind he is ready to sacrifice everything—his good name, his growing
reputation as a writer, his peace of mind. . . . He is inaccessible to
reason. He follows what he calls the natural incline of his career; the
more disproportionate the sacrifice, the more intoxicating his own mystical enjoyment. [March, 1922]

Roger Martin du Gard. *Recollections of André Gide*
(New York, Viking, 1953), pp. 34–38

[*The Immoralist* and *The Narrow Gate*] would need to be taken
together to form a tragic axis, whose presence we would expect because
of other Gide works. Either of these two narratives taken separately
does not contain this tragic axis. *The Immoralist* is a drama of married
life; *The Narrow Gate* is a drama of an engagement. Alissa [Jérôme's
fiancée in *The Narrow Gate*] has the time—all the time that Jérôme
grants her—to perceive and crystalize in her mind everything that would
have made their life together hopeless; Marceline [Michel's wife in *The
Immoralist*] has only enough time to sacrifice herself. The conflict, the
confrontation, of two people would have acquired supreme tension and
complete significance if Alissa had been the wife of Michel; and Marceline could have both saved and improved herself if she had been
Jérôme's fiancée.

But the two works are indeed separate; collision is avoided, they
correspond to two different swings of the pendulum. Their connections
show that Gide had difficulty in treating an overtly dramatic conflict. . . .
Jérôme's passivity is just as significant in this regard as Marceline's. His
passivity also shows that Gide does not separate his art from his life,
and that he will always have difficulty in bringing to his work the detachment that allows the artist not to feel involved in his creation. This
granted, one can nevertheless appreciate how our psychological understanding is heightened by Gide's isolating approach, how the successive
rather than simultaneous presentation of Michel and Alissa gives the
analysis of each the purity of a laboratory experiment.

Taken on their own terms, these two short narratives occupy a
place of distinction in Gide's oeuvre. . . . If any contemporary works
deserve to be called classics, these two do, because the clarity of what is
said and the mystery of what is suggested correspond to real lights and
shadows. Gide will perhaps push his investigation of man further; he
will most likely come to better terms with his own inclinations and

passions. But he will never write anything more touching than Alissa's Journal, nor anything more illuminating than Michel's awakening recognition of himself.

Ramon Fernandez. *André Gide* (Paris, R.-A. Corrêa, 1931), pp. 114–16†

What separates [*The Fruits of the Earth*] from [*The New Fruits*], much more than Communism does (half of *The New Fruits* antedates Gide's agreement with Communism) is [Gide's] *Journal*. . . .

There is the journal which precedes the essential works of its author—that of Stendhal; and the journal which follows them—that of Gide. The latter sort develops parallel to experience; and perhaps it is this *acquired* experience which gives to *The New Fruits* its special sound. [Subdivisions entitled] "Encounters" have replaced [subdivisions entitled] "Lays"; expression through facts has replaced expression through lyricism. The metaphorical system set up in *The Fruits of the Earth* by means of adjectives establishes itself this time more mysteriously through juxtapositions of facts. This is not the place to develop the idea, which means much to me, that all art rests on a system of ellipses. But at least their force and nature can be seen; the most urgent action of this book is in its silences, in the realm of suggestion where the meaning of the "Encounters" becomes one with the pages of affirmation.

The form is new, and will perhaps be imitated. The preference for external composition, moreover, seems to me to become weaker in Gide as the *Journal* grows: his evolution, from Racine to Stendhal, becomes more pronounced from year to year.

As for the significance of [*The New Fruits*], it is a double one. Taking the book by itself, it will be determined, like that of all Gide's significant works, by the justification it brings to a particular group of readers. Gide's strength—as artist and as moralist—lies in the fact that he is almost always a *justifier*. This is the case with all modern writers who exert a moral influence. The reader returns to the artist in the form of admiration what the latter gives him in the way of justification. This book will justify many of those who wish to *think* their generosity intelligently: I believe they are numerous.

The other significance, and the more important: the place of *The New Fruits* among the works of Gide. It opens a cycle or closes one, depending upon whether Gide will go on to limit himself to his *Journal* or not. But on this score, only life can tell. [Dec., 1935]

André Malraux. In Justin O'Brien, ed., *From the N.R.F.* (New York, Farrar, Straus and Cudahy, 1958), pp. 203–5

In *The Fruits of the Earth* under the awful Romantic style many of the ideas and sentiments were sound—by which I mean recognizable as human. In *The Vatican Cellars* the feelings are upside-down, but the style is becoming clearer and simpler. Perhaps the autobiographical fragment *If the Grain Die...* marks Gide's best period; there his style is openly declared and most effective.

Then a queer thing happened to Gide, and perhaps posterity will decide that there were two writers of the name of André Gide. Can he really have gone to the Congo and to Lake Tchad, and written those two most delightful travel books, *Journey to the Congo* and *Back from the Chad*? I think those are the books that are most likely to be read for generations; but the later the generation the less it will understand that Gide could write such books. The man who had preached the gospel of the "gratuitous act," homicide without cause or reason, is profoundly shocked because Negroes are not well treated. Behind the symbolist poet of André Walter [in Gide's *The Notebooks of André Walter*], a long-dead romantic humanitarian is now resurrected, a man who cannot bear cruelty to any living thing, and who feels that he is a brother to the crocodile and the hippopotamus; a man who reads Milton by moonlight on the Congo river—a delightful man, who writes like an angel. Why did he have to come back? He should have stayed on the Congo forever.

Denis Saurat. *Modern French Literature, 1870–1940*
(New York, G. P. Putnam's Sons, 1946), pp. 125–26

A product of the Symbolist school, [Gide] never renounced his faith in the idea of perfection, in the virtues of a finished form and a fine style. The major part of his existence as a writer is dominated by a desire to live in accordance with the ideal of a true and harmonious art. For Gide, to be faithful to the act of writing well does not imply that one must be unfaithful to or betray anything else; it means to follow the road that leads the farthest, that makes possible the most important, the boldest adventures. Why? An act of faith, based on a centuries-old cult and the example of the masters.

In his mature years, instructed by experience, Gide could still write: "It is very difficult for me to believe that the wisest, sanest, most sensible idea is not also the one that, projected into prose, yields the most harmonious and beautiful lines" (*Journal*, 1928). The elegance and harmony of a felicitous structure are not then mere aesthetic satisfactions that the author allows himself, as a kind of reward for yielding to his own talents. What is hoped for goes far beyond that: it is the assurance that, when all has been put in question, the shape and structure of his sentence will remain as the measure and safeguard of its value. . . . *Be perfectly sincere*, demands the Gide of 1892, and the other

Gides reply in full faith: All right, then; write in conformity to the innate harmonies of the language, and in such a way that once the phrase is traced, once the work is finished, all the resources of the language will not permit the least word to be changed. [1949]

Maurice Blanchot. In David Littlejohn, ed., <i>Gide:</i>
A Collection of Critical Essays (Englewood Cliffs,
N.J., Prentice-Hall, 1970), p. 53

First of all, *The Counterfeiters* is an impression of life; the counterpoint of contradictory ideas is less striking than the counterpoint of mood. Gide alternately plays all the instruments he had mastered in his shorter books: the comedy and fantasy of the *soties* [satires], the complacent unconscious irony of *The Pastoral Symphony*, the satire of *Marshlands*, the pathos of *The Narrow Gate*. He refused to confine himself to the immemorial subject matter of the novel: the loves and ambitions of men and women in their third and fourth decades. Nothing is lacking to his human comedy but an intelligent and middle-aged "good citizen" and a happily married couple. Otherwise, there is an almost too calculated counterpoint of sex and age—the story moving from the divine imaginativeness and diabolic cruelty of children to the anxiety of adolescent boys and the willfulness of adolescent girls; from the resignation of neglected wives and spinsters to the bewilderment and querulous jealousy of the very old.

    The Counterfeiters is also a love story, as most novels are. It was certainly one of Gide's intentions to prove, perhaps in answer to Proust, that homosexual love could be "normal" and happy. Édouard's love for Olivier has its hours of harsh desire and jealousy, but also its hours of idealism and self-sacrifice, of calm tenderness and intellectual companionship. The argument may seem weighted in Édouard's favor to the reader who is unbendingly hostile. But Gide is comprehensive enough to admit the attractiveness of Bernard's idealization of Laura and the urgency of his desire for Sarah. And honest enough to admit the existence of a Comte de Passavant, as unpleasant as any Proustian invert.

Albert J. Guerard. <i>André Gide</i> (Cambridge, Mass.,
Harvard University Press, 1951), p. 154

Well, yes, Gide was careful, he weighed his words, hesitated before signing his name, and if he was interested in a movement of ideas or opinions, he arranged it so that his adherence was only conditional, so that he could remain on the margin, always prepared to retreat. But the same man dared to publish the profession of faith of a *Corydon*, the indictment of the *Journey to the Congo*. He had the courage to ally himself with the Soviet Union when it was dangerous to do so, and greater still, he had the courage to recant publicly, when he felt, rightly or wrongly, that he had been mistaken. Perhaps it is this mixture of prudence and daring which makes him exemplary. Generosity is only estimable in those who know the cost of things, and similarly, nothing is more prone to move us than a deliberate temerity. Written by a heedless fool, *Corydon* would have been reduced to a matter of morals. But when its author is this sly Chinese who weighs everything, the book becomes a manifesto, a *testimony* whose import goes far beyond the scandal which it provoked. This wary audacity should be a "Guide rule for the mind": withhold judgment until the evidence is presented, and when conviction is acquired, consent to pay for it with your last penny.

Courage and prudence. This well-measured mixture explains the inner tension of his work. Gide's art aims to establish a compromise between risk and rule, in him are balanced Protestant law and the nonconformity of the homosexual, the arrogant individualism of the rich bourgeois and the puritan taste for social restraint, a certain dryness, a difficulty in communicating, and a humanism which is Christian in origin, a strong sensuality which would like to be innocent; observance of the rule is united in him with the quest for spontaneity. This play of counterbalances is at the roots of the inestimable service which Gide rendered contemporary literature. It is he who raised it from the worn groove of symbolism. The second generation of symbolists were convinced that the writer could only treat, without loss of dignity, a very small number of subjects, all very lofty, but that within these well-defined subjects, he could express himself any way he liked. Gide liberated us from this naïve *chosisme* [Sartre's own word designating the rule of the thing (*chose*) or the tyranny of subject-matter—Trans.]: he taught or retaught us that *everything* could be said—this is his audacity —but that it must be said according to specific rules of good expression —that is his prudence. [March, 1951]

Jean-Paul Sartre. *Situations* (New York, George Braziller, 1965), pp. 64–65

I read all Gide's works, responding in my turn to *The Fruits of the Earth* with the personal upheaval so often described by others. Mine came the second time around, perhaps because on the first reading I was a young, unenlightened barbarian, but also because for me there was nothing revolutionary in the senses. The shock was decisive in quite a different way. Long before Gide himself had confirmed this interpretation, I learned to read *The Fruits of the Earth* as the gospel of a self-deprivation I needed.

From that point on, Gide held sway over my youth, and it is impossible not to be always grateful to those we have at least once admired for having hoisted us to the highest point our soul can reach. In spite of all this, however, I never saw Gide as my master either as a writer or a thinker. I had given myself others. Rather, Gide seemed to me, because of what I have just said, the model of the artist, the guardian, the king's son, who kept watch over the gates of the garden where I wanted to live. There is almost nothing in what he has written about art, for example, that I don't entirely approve of, although our century has moved away from his conception.

The reproach made of Gide's work is that it neglects the anguish of our time. We choose to believe that a writer must be revolutionary to be great. If this is so, history proves that it is true only up *to* the revolution, and no further. Moreover, it is by no means certain that Gide did move away from his time. What is more certain is that this time wanted to move away from what he represented. The question is whether it will ever succeed, or will do so only by committing suicide. Gide also suffers from that other prejudice of our day, which insists that we parade our despair to be counted as intelligent. On this point, discussion is easier: the pretext is a poor one.

Yet I had to forget Gide's example, of necessity, and turn away very early from this world of innocent creation, leaving at the same time the land where I was born. History imposed itself on my generation. I had to take my place in the waiting line on the threshold of the black years. We fell into step, and have not yet reached our goal. How could I not have changed since then? At least I have not forgotten the plenitude and light in which my life began, and I have put nothing above them. I have not denied Gide. [Nov., 1951]

Albert Camus. *Lyrical and Critical Essays*
(New York, Alfred A. Knopf, 1968), pp. 250–51

Nowhere does the didactic intent of *The Fruits of the Earth* become so apparent as in the Foreward and the Envoi. To be sure, the poetic prose abounds with vocatives and imperatives; the poet constantly tells Nathanaël how to face and embrace life. His message is one of the necessity of finding and asserting oneself. . . .

The four cardinal points of the doctrine are restlessness, uprooting, readiness, and fervor. The most fundamental is the first, for without restlessness and dissatisfaction it is impossible to achieve anything in life or to attain the divine fervor that gives life its zest. Already the hero of *Marshlands* is ineffectually aware of this, but fails to get beyond the initial unrest; and throughout his career Gide will not cease to proclaim that his function is to disturb.

Uprooting, the second point, is a necessary corollary of unrest: to launch out into the unknown one must break with tradition, getting away from the restrictive influences of family, heredity, conventions, and the patterns of one's own thought. Man is ever attached to his comforting and convenient habits; as soon as he settles somewhere, he begins to secrete a shell that exactly resembles him. But here Gide teaches that one must resist that natural tendency and flee whatever has taken on one's resemblance. . . .

Through initial uprooting and permanently cultivated unrest, one should maintain oneself unattached, ready and receptive for whatever comes. . . . Nathanaël is taught not to prepare any of his joys, for *another* joy, in its place, will surprise him. Taking nothing for granted and maintaining a constantly fresh vision, the wise man finds everything a source of wonder and amazement.

Fervor, the fourth point of the doctrine, means nothing less than the magic glow from within. . . . Gidean fervor . . . is simply the recognition that merely being alive is a voluptuous pleasure.

The doctrine contained in *The Fruits of the Earth* was so new, so startling in French letters in the mid-nineties that few readers realized how almost incidentally it grew, as things in nature grow, from the dithyrambic, lyrical tone of the book. Certainly the original intention was to celebrate the five senses and the manifold joys they bring. The title is, after all, *The Fruits of the Earth*—which enter the body through the senses; consequently Gide emphasizes hunger and thirst, symbolic of all desires. *Marshlands* . . . reeks appropriately of stagnant, scummy water. *The Fruits of the Earth*, on the contrary, flows with living water, trickling, bubbling, lapping, dripping, cascading through its pages.

Justin O'Brien. *Portrait of André Gide: A Critical Biography* (New York, McGraw-Hill, 1953), pp. 129–31

There is something immensely humbling in this last document [*Et Nunc Manet in Te*] from the hand of a writer whose elaborately graceful fiction very often impressed me as simply cold, solemn and irritatingly pious, and whose precise memoirs made me accuse him of the most exasperating egocentricity. He does not, to be sure, emerge in *Et Nunc Manet in Te* as being less egocentric; but one is compelled to see this egocentricity as one of the conditions of his life and one of the elements of his pain. . . .

The great problem is how to be—in the best sense of that kaleidoscopic word—a man. This problem was at the heart of all Gide's anguish, and it proved itself, like most real problems, to be insoluble. He died, as it were, with the teeth of this problem still buried in his throat. What one learns from *Et Nunc Manet in Te* is what it cost him, in terms of unceasing agony, to live with this problem at all. Of what it cost her, his wife [Madeleine], it is scarcely possible to conjecture. But she was not so much a victim of Gide's sexual nature . . . as she was a victim of his overwhelming guilt, which connected, it would seem, and most unluckily, with her own guilt and shame. . . .

Her most definite and also most desperate act is the burning of his letters—and the anguish this cost her, and the fact that in this burning she expressed what surely must have seemed to her life's monumental failure and waste—Gide characteristically . . . cannot enter into and cannot understand. . . . He had entrusted, as it were, to her his purity, that part of him that was not carnal; and it is quite clear that, though he suspected it, he could not face the fact that her life could begin, that the key to her liberation was in his hands.

But if he had ever turned that key madness and despair would have followed for him, his world would have turned completely dark, the string connecting him to heaven would have been cut. And this is because then he could no longer have loved Madeleine as an ideal, as Emmanuèle, God-with-us, but would have been compelled to love her as a woman, which he could not have done except physically. And then he would have had to hate her, and at that moment those gates which, as it seemed to him, held him back from utter corruption would have been opened. He loved her as a woman, indeed, only in the sense that no man could have held the place in Gide's dark sky which was held by Madeleine. She was his Heaven who would forgive him for his Hell and help him endure it.

James Baldwin. *NLr.* Dec. 13, 1954, pp. 18–20

[By 1895] Gide had found his way, and understood that his originality would consist in remaining faithful to the ambivalence that had been his weakness and would be his strength, if he could manage to bring out all his contradictions in the work of art, with the sole objective of expressing them with order and beauty. Through patience, tact, and revision, he did in fact succeed in completing an extraordinary portrait of the ambivalent man, which perhaps has no equal in all literature.

In that sense, it is true that he remained "faithful" to his youth and prolonged it indefinitely, making every effort to attain a serenity within his ambivalence. Everything happened as though he had wanted to settle into a state of crisis and sustained it to the end. His essentially divided personality, whose inconstancy could have passed for inconsistency, was —like Édouard's in *The Counterfeiters*—to take on consistency only through the practice of literature. . . .

Gide did not think that the word "maturity" had the same meaning for the man as for the artist, especially one who chose to make his works an expression of his youth, with everything that implies of irreducible antagonisms and profound irresolution. One might say that he meant to remain permanently attached to the age of life in which the future still seems completely open, in which the undefined being feels unbounded and enjoys an availability that is so pure it gives the illusion of freedom. [1957]

Jean Delay. The Youth of André Gide (Chicago,
University of Chicago Press, 1963), pp. 491–92

[Gide's work] is among the most significant of our time. . . . For me, *The Fruits of the Earth, The Immoralist, Amyntas* can never wholly lose the charm with which the fervour of my twentieth year endowed them. But Gide, like Jean-Jacques [Rousseau] and Chateaubriand, was one of those writers whose lives are a great deal more interesting than their works. They are at the very opposite pole from Shakespeare and Racine who vanish from sight in the radiance of their created characters. Like Rousseau's *Confessions* and Chateaubriand's *Memoirs from Beyond the Grave*, and for the same reason, it seems to me that Gide's *If the Grain Die...* and his *Journal* will long keep active that ferment in the dough of humanity which it was their mission to provoke. . . .

It is a rare occurrence for culture and taste to reach so high a level in one man, who, moreover, was free of all ideological shackles. I have said that Gide, like Jean-Jacques and Chateaubriand, will live on only in those of his books which treat directly of himself: *If the Grain Die...* and the *Journal*, because it is he who interests us, and not the creatures of his invention. But I was forgetting that he remains the one and only subject of his imaginative books: *The Immoralist* is he; *The Narrow Gate* describes the cerebral love on which he built the painful ambiguity of his life. All through *The Counterfeiters* which, taken by and large, is a failure, runs the pulsating vein of Édouard's Journal. His presence in everything he wrote gives a lasting quality to his work.

Gide, the virtuoso of dialogue: with his friends, with his adversaries, with himself, with Christ. He was the only one of our elders who had this remarkable gift. [1959]

François Mauriac. Mémoires Intérieurs (New York,
Farrar, Straus and Cudahy, 1960), pp. 173–74, 177

Michel's "rights" to his "crime" pose a paradoxical moral question of judgment which each reader must answer for himself. With *The Immoralist* Gide calls upon the reader to give the novel its moral extensions. Far from being a novel of psychological analysis, as critics have often said, *The Immoralist* breaks abruptly with the techniques of psychological analysis. Michel describes facts and moods; he does not, he cannot explain them, hence the anguish he feels and his friends' dismay.

His story reveals a state of mind which is itself as thoroughly enigmatic as the tone he assumes throughout. . . . The "strange feeling of uneasiness" into which Michel plunges his friends is accentuated when, at the end of his tragic story, Michel, the man without a purpose —who in his distress spends his time cooling his hands with pebbles soaking in water—suddenly speaks with heightened excitement of that young "rascal" Ali, his boyservant. A rather disturbing future seems to be opening up before him. . . . Gide's own personal preoccupation with sexual inversion in those early years tends to limit and to mask the originality and force of his conception. All seems to lead merely to Ali, a disappointing end. Yet, until that end, Gide had succeeded in giving his subject much broader implications. Michel's real drama is not caused by his latent homosexuality. . . .

Homosexuality is in fact only one among a number of Michel's hidden "demons." Michel is not the "immoralist" because he is a potential homosexual; but that potentiality is the hidden and dynamic force through which his immoralism is revealed. Each episode in Michel's evolution revolves around the figure of an adolescent: Bachir, Moktir, Charles, Heurtevent, Ali. Each of the boys corresponds to one of Michel's inner impulses that Michel does not immediately discern. Bachir represents health and joy; Moktir, freedom from the restraints of ethics; Charles, the pleasure of the orderly exploitation of one's resources; Heurtevent, the return to barbarism; Ali, pure sensuality. With a remarkable foreknowledge of the discoveries Freud was to make, Gide deliberately exploited in *The Immoralist* the ambiguities of his character's subconscious life and its equivocal power. The dynamic principle in Michel's evolution is latent and subconscious so that his life is rather like a game of chess played against a baffling, elusive partner, informed beforehand of all his moves and countermoves.

Germaine Brée. Gide (New Brunswick, N.J.,
Rutgers University Press, 1963), pp. 126–28

Although *The Vatican Cellars* has some traits in common with *Marshlands* and *Prometheus Misbound*, it is unique in the literary career of Gide. Its strong comic vein, its tone of an irreverent hoax, places it in a very special lineage with Rabelais, Boccaccio, Defoe and Voltaire. It stands apart from the central tradition of European fiction, which from Prévost to Stendhal, Tolstoi to Proust, is characterized by extreme seriousness. Gide takes great care not to call his book a novel. In the letter to [Jacques] Copeau he explains that he calls it a *sotie* [satire] and his three preceding books *récits* [short narratives], in order to make it clear that they are not novels.

In the fourteenth and fifteenth centuries, a *sotie* was a parody or satirical play put on by law students and clerks of the Paris law courts. One of the themes was the election of a Pope of fools. In *The Vatican Cellars*, Gide will mock the Roman clergy and pious believers as vigorously as he will mock the materialists among the freethinkers and freemasons. A newspaper article became the pretext for one of Gide's most skillful and elaborately devised compositions. Even in the authentic *soties* of the Middle Ages, there was the attempt to demonstrate the madness of the real world by showing it capsized and led by fools. In *The Vatican Cellars*, likewise, several problems are grafted on the complicated plot: the free-thinker Anthime and his ludicrous conversion, for example, and especially the problem of the gratuitous act and human freedom as exemplified in Protos, the chief fool and bandit, and his pupil Lafcadio.

Wallace Fowlie. *André Gide: His Life and Art*
(New York, Macmillan, 1965), p. 69

Protean as André Gide undoubtedly was in both his private life and his published works, the themes which preoccupied him remain surprisingly constant. His works are readily recognizable for their insistence on the sincerity or authenticity of the individual in a world which is ironically full of counterfeit values and actions. They are obsessed with man's constant quest for happiness in a world where there seems to be little place for a person attracted by both spiritual fulfillment and sensual pleasure. They often stress the role of the artist who is constantly at grips with the task of transposing life into a disciplined and didactic yet palatable and permanent aesthetic form. At intervals they suggest a dichotomy between passionless love and a loveless passion.

Gide's principal fictional and dramatic figures from *The Notebooks of André Walter* to *Theseus* are all grappling with moral problems which often lead to an ironically inconclusive dénouement. Doubtless influenced by his own love of travel, he liked to set his characters on voyages which were sometimes literally trips from one identifiable place to another, sometimes figurative trips through the character's conscious past or present. During these voyages, Gide would often raise his characters to heights of glowing expectation, only to release them into depths of disappointment, disillusionment, or tragedy. Surely among all of Gide's themes, that of unfulfilled expectation is his most ironical and recurrent. "Expectation" is an abstract noun. The other aforementioned themes can also be succinctly expressed by abstract nouns: sincerity, hypocrisy, happiness, and love.

C. D. E. Tolton. In W. M. Frohock, ed., *Image and Theme: Studies in Modern French Fiction* (Cambridge, Mass., Harvard University Press, 1969), p. 99

The last period of Gide's work is dominated by the book with which it begins. He worked on *The Counterfeiters* from 1919 to 1925. It was the summary work of his mature years, just as *The Notebooks of André Walter* had been that of his adolescence. This great novel—the only one of his books to which he finally accorded the title of "novel"—is in some respects his greatest achievement in prose fiction. In other respects, it marks very clearly his decline as a poet. . . .

The subject of sexuality and erotic relations is a very large one in *The Counterfeiters*. It is presented in a manner quite unlike that of Gide's psychological novels. In those stories the erotic theme was developed logically and dramatically; here it is disclosed episodically. Édouard's history, it is true, exhibits the two essential motifs of Gide's work, the refusal of heterosexual relations and the formation of a homosexual alliance; but they are not shown in contention, and they are not related in a causal or sequential manner. Gide's design is as clear as it was in the conflict strategies of his earlier books. The erotic relations of men and women are everywhere a failure. The old La Pérouse couple are estranged to the point of no longer speaking to each other. The Moliniers and the Profitendieus are divided by infidelities past and present. Laura's history is one of repeated insuccess. Bernard, seeing the sad concern of Rachel over his intimacy with Sarah, is seized with disgust and quits the pension. The only heterosexual loves that have value are those of Boris for Bronja and of Bernard for Laura; both are symbolic expressions of the Oedipus complex. Bernard confesses to Olivier that since he has known Laura he "has no desires at all." Thanks to her his "instincts have been sublimated."

Thomas Cordle. *André Gide* (New York, Twayne,
1969), pp. 120, 131

GIONO, JEAN (1895–1970)

The Prix Brentano, which annually assures translation and American publication to some book chosen as an illustration of what the donor calls "the French cultural ideals," has this year fallen to M. Jean Giono's *Hill*. The author is a young clerk, still employed in his native town, Manosque in Provence. Just why his excellent first novel should have been chosen under the conditions is a little doubtful, since it is not in the traditional Gallic manner, and is wholly lacking in anything so deliberately artificial as a "cultural ideal."

It recalls, in fact, some recent Scandinavian novels more than anything French. In substance it is merely a strongly drawn study of peasant life, in which all the characters are inhabitants of a tiny hamlet under the shadow of a great hill. They are involved in a continual desperate struggle with nature. Their crops fail, disease attacks their ranks, their water supply gives out, and finally a forest fire all but reduces them to ashes along with their houses and possessions. . . .

Nothing in the book is improbable, yet an air of mystery (which is the author's chief contribution) lies over it. Neither narrative, well conducted as it is, nor the atmosphere, which is accurate with the unconscious precision possible only to a man writing of his own region and his own people, make the book unusual. M. Giono's particular distinction lies in the emphasis which he puts on the unknown element, the hidden malice which accompanies every event of his story. In the minds of his country folk the hill takes on an actual evil personality, carrying on an unending warfare with mankind which is half revenge and half sheer pleasure in doing all that can be done to hinder the reclamation of the land. The power of the soil, the trees, and the beasts of the field—"even the small ones," M. Giono adds—over the blindly struggling peasant has seldom been more eloquently stated. M. Giono's manner is simple and unaffected, since he has not yet acquired academic airs and graces.

Theodore Purdy, Jr. SR. Feb. 15, 1930, p. 738

When Giono sheds his proselytizing style and simply surrenders to his love of the land, when he captures the sound of a herd or a forest, the mating of the beasts, the walk or sleep of a peasant, the rebirth of day and night, then his lyricism surpasses all oratory and reaches greatness. And it will undoubtedly be a long time before Giono is equaled in this. The lyrical elements constitute the best part of his new book [*May My Joy Remain*]. Read, for example, the fifty pages in which he describes slowly, fact by fact, moment by moment—yet an amazing lightness runs through these pages—the dinner of a dozen peasants, who have gathered together one Sunday without knowing exactly why. These fifty pages compensate for the arbitrary and confusing aspects of the book, for the lack of progression and diversity in its episodes.

You might as well accept it all as a whole, good points and weaknesses, metal and slag. One is reminded of Hugo, in whose works the most surprising beauties exist side by side with the worst failures, and one cannot even say that the two are of a different nature. Perhaps Giono sometimes confuses abundance and power. It doesn't matter; he achieves power, and that is not so common.

Marcel Arland. NRF. June, 1935, p. 939†

Beside the overwhelming simplicity of Jean Giono's tales of peasant life, all similar novels that come from France are frankly negligible. In the high-perched village of Manosque in the French Basses-Alpes, Giono writes of the life which he sees about him and which he himself has led. He is one of those rare "naturals" like our own Steinbeck, who effortlessly reproduce the direct accents of a primitive life. When his novels run to any length, the reader, surfeited with simplicity, is likely to lay them down unfinished. But when, as in the case of *Harvest*, they do not exceed 200 pages, they are as refreshing as a Cézanne still life after a gallery full of surrealism.

The natural decay and equally natural regeneration of Aubignane, as witnessed by its one surviving inhabitant, the inarticulate Panturle, form the story of *Harvest*. Panturle is a party to that transformation of his village; in fact, he and Aubignane are one. It is only after he finds a woman, mysteriously guided toward him by the aged crone Mamèche, who has set out to find him a mate, that he and the earth and his goat Caroline awaken and become productive again. If the blood of the fox he flays, Arsule's breasts, old Gaubert's anvil, the goat's dry teats, and Panturle's fall into the river are so many symbols, they all symbolize substantially the same thing: the need for fecundation and its fulfillment. With *Hill . . . Harvest* is Jean Giono's best work.

Justin O'Brien. Nation. June 3, 1939, pp. 652–53

For Giono, man is exclusively weak and insignificant, a wretched instrument. Giono apparently scorns everything that approaches human grandeur and nobility. Rebellion itself is weak and spineless. And from this weakness of character there arises a strong, coherent system, a system that had to lead Giono where the Liberation now finds him: in the arms of the Germans. . . .

[In Giono's works] now . . . it is no longer passion detached from man, that dominates man, but nature. And so we no longer see anything of that queer being that was man except for his reflection; he is no longer anything but an insect that grazes in the grass of uselessness, a poor cog crushed in the apocalyptic whirlwind of the universe. And the more active and corrosive nature is, the more man is diminished and degraded. . . .

In the pre-Nazi era of Giono's evolution, there was a point at which man's cowardice—which, all things considered, is nothing but that of Giono himself—was transformed into dishonesty. Giono practiced a true intellectual swindle. He began to preach. And a herd of weak people, sincere men in other respects, whose vague and uneasy feeling of disturbance was manifested in an eternal dissatisfaction—this mob of the lost and disinherited of the century gathered together at Contadour. This abandoned village near Manosque witnessed a strange crowd of admirers grouped together to adore their master.

What did he teach? Vague and childish anarchist theories, total
pacifism, scorn for the values of this world, for money, a life of poverty,
a new sort of saintliness. But the sly Giono did not deprive himself of
the contemptible goods of this world. Films, the wide circulation of his
books, and clever publicity brought him—together with new adherents
—new contracts, new schemes, and new business deals. We do not find
a trace of this in *Cahiers du Contadour*, in which Giono published the
discussions of the "master" and his disciples. In them the overriding
issue is the return to the earth. We know what the old man of Vichy
with the quavering voice [Pétain] meant by that idea. Its aim was to
transform France into a nation of serfs within the Nazi Europe of the
future.

Tristan Tzara. LetF. Oct. 7, 1944, pp. 1, 5†

[Giono] feeds the writer, instructs the writer, inspires the writer. In
Jean the Blue he gives us the genesis of a writer, telling it with the
consummate art of a practiced writer. One feels that he is a "born
writer." One feels that he might also be a painter, a musician (despite
what he says). It is the "Storyteller's Story," *l'histoire de l'histoire*. It
peels away the wrappings in which we mummify writers and reveals the
embryonic being. It gives us the physiology, the chemistry, the physics,
the biology of that curious animal, the writer. It is a textbook dipped in
the magic fluid of the medium it expounds. It connects us with the
sources of all creative activity. It breathes, it palpitates, it renews the
blood stream. It is the kind of book which every man who thinks he has
at least one story to tell could write but which he never does, alas. It is
the story which authors are telling over and over again in myriad disguises. Seldom does it come straight from the delivery room. Usually it
is washed and dressed first. Usually it is given a name which is not its
true name.

His sensuousness, the development of which Giono attributes to his
father's delicate nurturing, is without question one of the cardinal features of his art. "Let us refine our finger tips, our points of contact with
the world. . . ." Giono has done just this. The result is that we detect in
his music the use of an instrument which has undergone the same ripening process as the player. In Giono the music and the instrument are
one. That is his special gift. If he did not become a musician because, as
he says, he thought it more important to be a good listener, he has
become a writer who has raised listening to such an art that we follow
his melodies as if we had written them ourselves. [1952]

Henry Miller. The Books in My Life (New York,
New Directions, 1969), pp. 108–9

Giono makes me a better person; not better than he, alas, but better than myself, which is easier to do. He is powerful and good. He has the kind of goodness that delights us Frenchmen as soon as we have crossed the frontier and are amazed to discover—in Italy, Spain, Germany, England, or America—a goodness only a few traces of which are left in our overly urbanized civilization. It is this quality in Giono that makes me feel that he comes from far away, beyond the mountains, like Jean-Jacques [Rousseau]. . . .

He teaches me the mysteries; this Giono knows everything. Where did he learn it all? He is never off the track. As a sedentary man, he sniffed, explored, and turned everything around; as a traveler, he knows Venice down to the treasures hidden in the mud of the canals. He can speak of a horseman like a squire, of happiness like a fakir, of aperitifs like a bartender, of English pastures like a gentleman, of colors like a painter, of fried food like a cordon bleu, of juniper trees like an horticulturist, of the care to give to an old lady like a nurse, of the sky like an astronomer, of the Cabala like a magus. . . . Giono is a seer, that is the only possible explanation; he is a visionary like Balzac, an interpreter of fate who knows destiny and who perhaps even forges destiny by naming it.

Paul Morand. Preface to Jacques Pugnet, Jean Giono
(Paris, Éditions Universitaires, 1955), pp. 6–7†

With The Song of the World Giono enlarges his canvas. The story here is less simple [than in his earlier novels] and appears to carry some symbolic significance. Each character seems to embody a theme, and the subject is less man himself than a full orchestration of various conflicting elements, their blending into a harmonious whole. . . .

The first part of the story develops with epic proportions, suggesting all the while that Giono is creating a myth—a myth analogous to that of the adolescent sun god who disappears with winter to be resurrected with the coming of spring. But Giono fails to give dramatic power and symbolic significance to the long period of waiting imposed by the winter months, and from this point on the plot becomes banal. The red-headed twin and Maudru, these two antagonists whose appearances have been so well prepared, are weak and insignificant. . . .

The themes of death and love are woven into the tale and connected with the wildness of the Maudru country, where Matelot [the father] dies at the end of winter. With the victory of the flame-like twin over the brute strength of the bull, order is re-established and harmony reigns. The story has somehow lost its power, and the artificially simple pronouncements of Toussaint and Antonio on love, death and evil are inadequate. Neither love nor death is so simple as Giono would have them be.

Giono's next two novels, written before 1940, *May My Joy Re-main* and *Battles in the Mountain*, show more clearly than *The Song of the World* where Giono's weakness lies. The intellectual armature of his work is too elementary to sustain his tremendous mythical structures. His portrayal of human feelings is rudimentary, perhaps voluntarily so, overly sentimental and slightly vulgar. A righteous naïveté informs his moral judgments and his stories. Dynamic in their outer movement, they are inwardly static.

Germaine Brée and Margaret Guiton. *An Age of Fiction: The French Novel from Gide to Camus* (New Brunswick, N.J., Rutgers University Press, 1957), pp. 111–13

Giono wanted to mingle with men, to excite a village, to found "an establishment through joy," to turn the French away from war, to spread conscientious objection. He did so well that, without being able to put anything into action, he succeeded very easily in having himself imprisoned twice, first during the "phony war," then during the happy and excessive times of the Liberation.

Fabrice [the hero of Stendhal's *The Charterhouse of Parma*], after he escaped from the citadel of Parma, still remained Fabrice. But when we read the novels published by Giono during the past ten years, it seems that we are dealing with a different Giono. Of course, this is not entirely true—never did a man succeed in shedding his first skin—but appearances can be disturbing. His spirit changed; his confidence in humanity disappeared. He discovered that the world is made up of "bad guys." And the wickedness of small towns, insipid gossip, and a caval-cade of base deeds, both small and great, comprise the background of *The Mill of Poland*. As for the style, it is no longer completely Giono's; it is quite often Stendhal's. I wonder if there is another example of an original creative artist, having possessed his own tone and themes, who went so far into the universe of another artist and appropriated his style and rhythm. No critic . . . has failed to pin the adjective "Stendhalian" on Giono's latest writings.

Why this choice? Why Stendhal? Undoubtedly because, however disgusted he was with men, Giono the writer had to rediscover the feeling of profound joy, the *impetus* of youth that was essential to his life. And Stendhal can communicate this feeling. . . . In literature, Stendhal is the master of happiness.

Marcel Thiébaut. *RdP*. June, 1957, pp. 144–45†

One of [Giono's] most endearing [characters], Angelo Pardi, whose adventures during an epidemic of cholera that laid waste the Haute-Provence in 1838 (*The Hussar on the Roof*) or during the ups and downs of a revolution in Italy in 1848 (*Mad Happiness*) [are related to us], aspires to being a spiritual grandson of Stendhal and is closely related to Fabrice del Dongo. He has Fabrice's youth, his generosity of feeling, a love of personal glory and the same lust for happiness. When he sets out on an adventure, it is to test his strength, his courage, his virility and will-power. The characters that succeed him possess the same simple tension: Giono is not concerned with psychological subtleties. Created to the same pattern, they all seem to be charged with a "mission," into which they throw themselves wholeheartedly, determined to destroy everything that comes in their way. They pursue their courses as if they were on rails, irrespective of whether, from a moral point of view, their objective is right or wrong. Giono's works are peopled by the "strong," some destined for good, and others destined for evil; what is important is that they should be "strong."

Giono is little concerned with verisimilitude and the situations he described are often scarcely credible. He could even be accused of falling into melodrama. What he is really aiming at is tragedy, classical tragedy with its choruses and recitatives. The old Giono, who tried to raise ordinary events of village life to the grandeur of epic, has not entirely been effaced. But this grandeur is now provided more by history than by folklore and the old poet of the earth and the stars turns more and more to historical reconstruction. This escape into the past saves Giono from having to take sides in the controversies of our time and allows him even more than before to turn away from a world that has disappointed him and which he totally rejects. [1963]

Maurice Nadeau. *The French Novel since the War*
(London, Methuen, 1967), p. 47

[Giono] the man is far from being one-dimensional. What is undoubtedly most striking in Giono is "this anarchistic and pitiful humanity of the men of 1848" to whom he seems so close, as if he had been born under their star. But while his instinctive rebellions, his hatred of war, of society, of the vices of the modern world, and his generosity recall his grandfather, the *carbonaro*, he also possesses a wisdom, a realism, and even a cynicism, which connect him to Machiavelli—the Machiavelli whom he read and commented on and with whom he shares tenacious observation—the art of not being duped.

A constant assertion dominates Giono's works and his life—that of happiness. "If there exists a happy man, it is I," he told me on my first visit. "And I repeat to myself, like Napoleon's mother: provided it lasts!"

This happiness has many facets. It was initially the joy of living in a region in which the air is pure and which is illuminated by the sun, even in the heart of winter. It was next the freedom achieved by an artistic career that brought its own reward. In short, for twenty or thirty years, Giono has been conscious of having been happy "totally, constantly, minute by minute."

Pierre de Boisdeffre. Giono (Paris, Gallimard, 1965),
p. 39†

Giono's numerous weaknesses as a novelist stem primarily from . . . prolixity and proliferation. In most of [his novels] there is great unevenness, resulting in majestic peaks worthy of an anthology that alternate with dreary wasteland and monotonous marshes in which the reader is bogged down. In the earlier period Giono's verbosity keeps him from resting until he has almost smothered the reader with adjectival synonyms and breathless metaphors. On other occasions his quest for naturalness led him into the artifice of elementary dialogue, replete with irregular syntax and repetition. His absorption with natural forces sometimes tended to diminish his human figures until they were scarcely distinguishable from plant or animal creation.

Until he reached the sophistication of his later manner, Giono showed himself to be occasionally a trifle clumsy and awkward in his technique. . . . Like Balzac, Giono sometimes has difficulty plunging *in medias re*s; and in many novels, such as *Battles in the Mountain, Strong Souls*, and *Mad Happiness*, the reader becomes discouraged by the confusion and tedium of the exposition before he reaches the truly dramatic scenes in which the plot unfolds. In all fairness to Giono, however, it should be said that he would be the first to agree with this criticism.

But, if Giono has several faults, they are more than redeemed by virtues which in many cases are merely the obverse of the medal and spring from the same source. Thus his prolixity is only the price he pays for verve and intensity—a richness of the creative imagination which few writers have exceeded.

Maxwell A. Smith. Jean Giono (New York, Twayne,
1966), pp. 174–75

Giono suggested that life itself can be lived every minute with the excitement and marvel of a great adventure, mysterious, unforeseeable, and unique for each human being. Thus, Giono's novels generally commence and close with departures. They commonly figure a circle and a road bisecting it, involve a tangential stranger and peripheral groups encountered by chance and rapidly spun out centrifugally. . . .

The great ironic novels of Jean Giono appeal, then, not only because he succeeded in clothing his vision in aesthetically admirable and identifiable forms, which allow the reader the pleasure of placing the works severally into familiar and rich literary traditions; they also afford shelter and comfort by reminding the modern reader, with whom the world is much too much, that beyond his routine and narrow horizons lies a vast, adventuresome universe of freedom and pure delight. They thrill some readers with their portraits of brave men and magnificent women, who trust the earth and their own bodies. Last of all, they delight eye and ear and bring joy to many hearts because, more than most authors, Giono possessed what Aristotle considered the surest mark of a born genius: the gift of abundant metaphor. There lies his waspish humor, and there also the reader's enjoyment.

> Norma L. Goodrich. *Giono, Master of Fictional Modes* (Princeton, N.J., Princeton University Press, 1973), pp. 22–23

GIRAUDOUX, JEAN (1882–1944)

Some would like to have us believe that all young people of today are only frenzied pleasure-seekers, wonderfully lacking any scruples, and are also aimless and hurried, capable of going anywhere at all, as long as they get there quickly. The example of Jean Giraudoux is reassuring. Nothing could be both more modern or more youthful than [*Provincial Women*] and more leisurely. I like to surrender to Giraudoux without knowing exactly where he is leading me; what does it matter, since we are on a path around which everything invites us to roam about? We linger; he gathers and gleans everywhere, chats with everything, lends everything his smile, and turns the entire creation into a pleasure. . . .

The power of invention bursts forth throughout the book in a continual gush and sustains, from image to image, the tender, quivering, loving, and delicately calculated *poetic airiness* of which Giraudoux has become the master immediately, with his first attempt. . . .

I think that the four tales that comprise the book, or at least the last three, could have met the requirements for what are usually called "masterpieces" if Giraudoux, without adding anything to them, would have simply passed them through a sieve a little more; or, more precisely, he should have insisted that the mesh of his sieve be a little more closely woven.

> André Gide. *NRF*. June, 1909, pp. 463–65†

In content, *Suzanne and the Pacific* is thoroughly dada. There is in it that "howling of irritated colors, interweaving of contraries and of all the contradictions, of grotesques, of inconsequences" that M. Tristan Tzara has emphasized, though M. Giraudoux does less underscoring. His book is full of spontaneity, of irrationalities, unexpected relationships, fancies and fantasies. Logic, in his subject-matter at least, is abolished.

But M. Giraudoux does manifest a logic in his form, and it is his care for the technical functions of the narrative, for the manipulation of the elements in his plot, that differentiates him from the pure dadaist. . . .

M. Giraudoux is a man of fancy, fantasy and humor. His aesthetic is built upon unexpectedness and disproportion, and leaves us with the minor feeling Poe noted—a sense of difficulties happily surmounted. It moves in the direction of romanticism, not realism, of entertainment, not experience. The heart of his mental machinery is contained in the following sentence: his whole book is a dilation of that heart. "I tasted large scarlet mushrooms: in France I would have had spotted fever, numb fingers, twitching eyelids; but solitude vaccinated me against all these ills." One who believes that the function of literary art is to give a proportioned heightened representation of the actual cannot follow in the direction of M. Giraudoux.

But to such a one the principal overtone of *Suzanne and the Pacific* may be valuable. Suzanne is adorably attached to modern civilization. Pitched on a desert island, she hunts for rice powders, perfumes, tobacco, feather dresses: she yearns for railway stations, daily newspapers, moving-pictures, metropolitan crowds; she finally makes her island a fragment of France. . . . M. Giraudoux is adept at turning the texture of modern sensations into literature, and in the exploitation of these new undigested materials, he is a comrade of the dadaists.

Gorham B. Munson. *NR*. April 18, 1923, pp. 219–20

Giraudoux restores freedom to the French stage [in *Siegfried*]. He demands nothing either of the ballet, the cinema, or the music-hall. He asks everything of words, style, expression. His theater is a literary theater, a poetic theater, a return to dramatic literature; in the very heart of dramatic literature, he succeeds in asserting his originality.

This originality consists of starting off neither with characters nor a plot to develop, but with poetic themes. Each of the characters of *Siegfried* incarnates a poetic reality of France or Germany—a poetic reality of major or minor importance, pathetic or humorous—a symbol, so to speak, and the whole is animated by the idea of human brotherhood. . . .

Siegfried marks a date, a point of departure, a new hope. It marks the theater's escape from naturalism, from too much psychology, through poetry (not expressionism or futurism). It marks the renaissance of style in the theater, the resurrection of drama in which each character has the right to finish his sentences, to utter monologues or even long declamations, the resurrection of theater from which intellectual ideology, verbal magic have not been banished, theater which allows ecstasy, expansiveness, enthusiasm, theater big enough to house the world, great enough to contain the struggle between modern consciences and the most burning questions.

Since Musset, no French author has approached the stage with so much ease and grace. With fewer paradoxes and less vehemence, the *Siegfried* of Giraudoux introduces into our theater the freedom and diversity which the English stage owes to Bernard Shaw. [June, 1928]

Benjamin Crémieux. In Justin O'Brien, ed., *From the N.R.F.* (New York, Farrar, Straus and Cudahy, 1958), pp. 167–68

The role in Jean Giraudoux's universe delegated to Isabelle [in *Intermezzo*] is the one that the entire Middle Ages delegated to the young girl, that of the interpreter of the supernatural world. It is she who is tempted to exceed the limits of the earth—but not to betray the world. What she desires is not so much to die as to annex a new kingdom for life—and this kingdom happens to be the kingdom of the dead. . . . Although the wise supervisor reprimands her, dangerous tasks are always undertaken by young girls, and it is right that they should: thanks to these young girls, our vision is expanded, our dreams find some foundation, and the most ambitious extravagances acquire some sort of real substance. Are the dead not ready to reenter the world of the living? . . .

Only young girls can suppose so, and perhaps they can even find proof. Isabelle is our Parsifal, declares the sentimental yet ironic supervisor. But as soon as a potential husband appears for Isabelle, the whole beautiful supernatural world she has seen will disappear: Isabelle will become like Geneviève [in *Siegfried*], like Alkmena [Amphitryon's wife]. Her vision will become limited to the two towns of Gap and Bressuire, to the French provinces, to human life on earth—the life that is so brief and yet is the only life possible. She will be converted to the limited wisdom of the supervisor, and since she will no longer be able to know anything else, she will finally consent, with courageous calm, to turn her back upon the charms of ghosts and gods in order to rejoin humanity. It is a shame, no doubt—but that is the price of living.

Robert Brasillach. *Portraits* (Paris, Plon, 1935), pp. 145–47†

What troubles me in *Electra* and hampers my satisfaction is perhaps the fact that one cannot make a theatrical work out of intellectual games. I was seeking in *Electra* what we gratefully discovered in *The Trojan War Will Not Take Place*, that moment choked with emotion, subdued, religious. But this response to *The Trojan War Will Not Take Place* derives from the characters themselves, not from the mere skillfulness of the lines; thus, the emotions reach us easily across the footlights. But in *Electra* Giraudoux does not seek, seems to have given up seeking, to escape from himself; on the contrary, he indulges himself almost intentionally—as a child fixes himself in front of a mirror and tries different expressions so as to resemble more closely the image he has created of himself. As an escape from Giraudoux's glaring lights and poems with a thousand different facets, I am tempted to seek refuge in the great darkness of Claudel, in his vast nocturnal forest.

Ultimately, I envision many dangers for the dramatist in so completely casting off all straightforwardness. An obligatory simplicity of means, including the text itself, is a joyous humiliation to which the real man of the theater instinctively consents (granted that such simplicity is indeed a great artifice). But Giraudoux refuses to abandon his delicate touch, his silky paws. Will he get annoyed with me if I say that he is to the playwright what the essayist is to the novelist? There are, thank God, essayists of genius. [May 23, 1937]

Colette. La jumelle noire (Paris, Ferenczi, 1938),
Vol. IV, pp. 192–93†

In [*Judith* Giraudoux] was measuring himself against his true adversary, and he did not name him Jupiter but called him by his real name. He danced his terrible dance around the God of Abraham, Isaac, and Jacob—the gentle, consoling God to whom the Psalmist appealed on such an un-Giraudoux-like note: "My sacrifice, O God, is a contrite spirit; a contrite and humbled heart, O God, thou wilt not despise."

All the graceful slaps that Giraudoux lavishes elsewhere on Jupiter, are they not actually aimed at Him whom he just once (and without meanness or hate, needless to say) attacked head-on? Giraudoux's work is conceived in the spirit of the eighteenth century battling with the Angel, but in him this spirit is purified and decanted. What progress! Our latter-day Voltaire would be incapable of thinking, much less writing, "Let us crush this infamy!" We no longer find the smile hideous but charming, this smile of Jean Giraudoux.

No party in France can exploit his rich resources for their own purposes. Giraudoux is the single flower of what our pious instructors used to call the "godless" school. In its fifty-year-long search for a morality, this group has been counting on Sorbonne professors and school inspectors to discover one. Why doesn't it turn instead to this graduate of the Lycée of Châteauroux who amuses himself in the playground by shooting beribboned arrows at heaven? Must I tip them off to the fact that the work—the plays especially—of Giraudoux contain a magnificent little catechism for humanists?

It is a small, earthly catechism, naturally, and one which through time and use would find itself utterly demolished. The cutting edge of Giraudoux's mind collides with a hard stone against which Greek thought before him blunted itself, the stone that we call original sin; he puts his trust in Nature and does not know that she is flawed. All the same, the little Giraudoux catechism would be a miracle. Even when pulverized by the other, its débris would be precious and useful to the sons of men. [1940]

François Mauriac. *Second Thoughts* (Cleveland, World, 1961), pp. 127–28

In order to enter fully into the universe of *Choice of the Elect*, we must first forget the world in which we live. I therefore pretended that I knew nothing at all about this soft, pasty substance traversed by waves whose cause and purpose are exterior to themselves, this world without a future, in which things are always meeting, in which the present creeps up like a thief, in which events have a natural resistance to thought and language, this world in which individuals are accidents, mere pebbles, for which the mind subsequently fabricates general categories.

I was not wrong. In the America of Edmée, Claudie and Pierre, rest and order come first. They are the goal of change and its only justification. These clear little states of rest struck me from the very beginning of the book. The book is composed of rests. A jar of pickles is not the fortuitous aspect assumed by a dance of atoms; it is a state of rest, a form closed in upon itself. A scientist's head, filled with laws and calculations, is another such rest, as is the painter's head which lies lightly on the lap of a beautiful, motionless woman, as is a landscape, a park, and even a fleeting morning light. . . .

It would be a mistake, however, to regard M. Giraudoux as a Platonist. His forms are not in the heaven of ideas, but among us, inseparable from the matter whose movements they govern. They are stamped on our skin like seals in glass. Nor are they to be confused with simple concepts. A concept contains barely more than a handful of the traits common to all the individuals of a given group. Actually, M. Giraudoux's forms contain no more, but the features that compose them are all perfect. They are norms and canons rather than general ideas. [March, 1940]

Jean-Paul Sartre. *Literary and Philosophical Essays* (New York, Criterion, 1955), pp. 43–44

I still know *Siegfried* by heart, dear Giraudoux. . . . As a consequence [of seeing it] I was to enter into a long night from which I have not yet completely emerged, from which, perhaps, I shall never emerge, but it is because of those spring evenings in 1928 when I, the only spectator, wept, even at the amusing dialogue, that I have been able to move somewhat out of myself.

Then came *Amphitryon 38, Intermezzo*, both farther from me; then, irritated with the man who produced them and intransigent as innocence is wont to be, I no longer saw your plays performed. I would read them, overwhelmed, without opera *décor*, without glitter, without excess of magic tricks, without that imposing air of gala which your *premières* always managed to take on somewhat too lavishly. I would talk about them with [Georges] Pitoëff—my other master, but with whom I was on familiar terms—who regretted so much your admirable *Electra* and then, finally, I experienced that tender despair a last time with *Ondine*. . . .

It was not only too beautiful, it not only made ridiculous everything I had wanted to do, it was tender, solemn, and definitive like a farewell. I had a very certain feeling about it: the farewell of Hans to Ondine took on the meaning of another farewell which wrenched my heart. It was the time of the phony war and we dreamed about lives in danger. I believed, naïvely, that this mysterious farewell concerned me.

Dear Giraudoux, it was you whom I was leaving, owing you so much without ever having told you, having known you so little and so well. [Feb., 1944]

Jean Anouilh. *TDR*. May, 1959, pp. 4–5

The metaphysical ambiguity of Giraudoux's universe undoubtedly explains the place in his works, and especially in his plays, occupied by the theme of mistaken identity—extending from the very construction of the plots to the minutest details. At least two plays fundamentally revolve around an ambiguity: *Amphitryon 38*, that metaphysical light comedy, completely contrived so that Alkmena never knows that she has been possessed by Jupiter; and *Judith*. Moreover, the characters, even the secondary ones, spend their time putting on disguises: one could even say that they take pleasure in doing so. Jupiter's disguises in *Amphitryon 38* are indispensable to the play's economy; but what can be said about Egon, in *Judith*, who at one point passes himself off as Holophernes, or about Suzanne, who claims to be Judith and does actually resemble her?

We cannot help feeling that there is a meaning behind these games. Similarly [in *Ondine*], the supposed parents of Ondine are the real parents of Bertha, and Orestes first appears before his sister [in *Elec-*

tra] as a stranger. Even the ghost in *Intermezzo* tries to pass himself off as a man, and what character could be more disguised than Siegfried [in *Siegfried*], who has forgotten his own identity—unless it be the beggar in *Electra*: we never do find out exactly whether he is a real beggar or Jupiter himself. Earlier, in Giraudoux's novels, objects played at disguising themselves as if they had been touched by the wand of the illusionist in *Ondine*. . . . It is because of this use of disguise, more than anything else, that I call Giraudoux précieux.

For Giraudoux, the entire universe is an immense masked ball. The masquerade is not an amusement, however, but rather the expression of a profound metaphysical truth: it is impossible for us to know the definitive truth about anything.

Claude-Edmonde Magny. *Précieux Giraudoux* (Paris, Éditions du Seuil, 1945), pp. 101–3†

The theme of destiny is found almost everywhere [in Giraudoux's plays]. This theme seems natural in those plays whose subjects are drawn from classical Greek literature. The very choice of these subjects and the central position the problem of destiny has in his other plays show us that Giraudoux was strongly drawn to this theme, which tells us something about the man as well as the writer and his style. . . .

The Trojan War Will Not Take Place is completely dominated by the theme of destiny. Cassandra, the clairvoyant and bitter woman, is intimately familiar with the very essence of destiny. She knows that destiny is not interested in "negative statements," and she is able to explain the meaning of "destiny" to Andromache: "It is simply an accelerated form of time." She knows that destiny uses everything and everybody. . . . Helen, too, realizes that destiny cannot be tricked; she knows that Hector's efforts will be fruitless. . . . Andromache, for her part, would strongly like to believe that destiny will not triumph over passionate love . . . but her efforts to ward off the inevitable, by invoking Helen's love for Paris, are vain. The harsh Ulysses, on the contrary, is experienced enough to know that the most elaborate political activities can never hinder the fatal development of events, and his monologues on destiny develop this viewpoint. He is thoroughly familiar with the obstacles that prevent human beings from understanding the twisting paths of fate. . . . He also knows the implacable nature of this blind force. . . . Yet he does try to arrange a reconciliation with Hector, knowing all the while that their common adversary [fate] is the absolute master: "I am using my cunning right now against destiny, not against you. It is my first attempt, and I am all the more worthy for that reason." However great the talents of the diplomat Ulysses may be during the course of the international conference, and despite Hector's valiant plea to safeguard peace, destiny continues on its way without wavering: the Trojan War will take place.

Hans Sørensen. *Le théâtre de Jean Giraudoux: Technique et style* (Copenhagen, Universitetsforlaget i Aarhus, 1950), pp. 202, 205–6†

Seated on a bench at the Place de l'Alma, in front of the Café Francis, Countess Aurélie, the Madwoman of Chaillot, describes to a desperate young man, and the audience at the same time, one of her days in detail. "All the living are lucky," she says. This assertion suffices; there is no need for explanations or commentaries.

It is not necessary for us to explain dramatic works, to analyze them, to attempt to reveal their meaning, to discover anything about the author that is not in the text: his methods of creation, his sources, his influences. We should instead be discovering ourselves on hearing and coming into contact with these works. It is of little importance whether we know or discover that Giraudoux had a model for Countess Aurélie in Aunt Bijou, a colorful old madwoman whose photograph was published in all the newspapers after the première of *The Madwoman of Chaillot*.

Dramatic creation is a true revelation; it comes into being from an inner state, an inspiration. It resists the explanations of logic or psychology: it is not a fabrication and it is not a carbon copy of reality. Aunt Bijou has only been of interest since Giraudoux created Countess Aurélie. The author's invention is first, total, sovereign, and impossible to equal. Each of us innocently and artlessly "reinvents" this play when we attend a performance.

To understand this play we must suppress all sense of superiority, all critical faculties, and surrender and lose ourselves in the diversion it brings and the happiness it contains. This is exactly what Countess Aurélie suggests to us. The art of living, like the art of the theater, lies in one's attitude.

Louis Jouvet. *Témoignages sur le théâtre* (Paris, Ernest Flammarion, 1952), p. 213†

One year before his death, Giraudoux was quite logically led to tackle the myth of Sodom and Gomorrah [in *Sodom and Gomorrah*], which was so peculiarly well suited to serve as a vehicle for his persistent belief in the eminent dignity of the human couple. He significantly decided to modify it, in much the same way as he modified the story of Amphitryon and Alkmena [in *Amphitryon 38*], and to rehabilitate the human protagonists in their full nobility. In *Genesis* (Chap. 18), the Lord tells Abraham that the city of Sodom will be spared provided there can be found among its inhabitants fifty (and later ten) who are just. In Giraudoux's play the Lord requires only the presence of one happily married couple. So, at the end of the last act, the city is destroyed not because of the immorality of its citizens, but because its husbands and wives have been unable to give happiness to each other. Thus Giraudoux, who claims all through his works that man alone is capable of love, also asserts that love seldom suffices to generate happiness. . . .

The two opposite forms of disappointment experienced by Ruth and Lia [the two wives in *Sodom and Gomorrah*] point toward the same conclusion: once love is actualized, made concrete and, so to speak, incarnated in marriage, it vanishes. Any alleged reason for this frustrating phenomenon is an illusive one. The real reason, the only one, is that love does not lend itself to any kind of practical and material realization, because it is a pure ideal. Nearly all of Giraudoux's books relate this disappointment of life, this monotony of monogamy. In *Electra*, Clytemnestra confesses that the reason why she killed her husband Agamemnon was that she could no longer endure his unalterable immutability exemplified by his beard which remained curly even in the most violent rainstorms, and by his little finger which he constantly kept curled, even when he embraced his wife, even when he clutched the dagger for Iphigenia's sacrifice. . . .

Love is motion, marriage is stability. Love is ideal, marriage a practice. Love is change, marriage is uniformity. The harsher Giraudoux's indictment of marriage, the more eloquent his praise of love.

Georges May. YFS. No. 11, 1953, pp. 107–8, 111–12

Ondine [in *Ondine*] is a dramatic character of great complexity. She is both sprite and woman, both a symbol of nature and a symbol of love. . . . This little girl found on the beach has the limpidity and the freshness of water; she also has its mystery and power. Eternal and forever young, as is nature itself, such is Ondine. . . .

To declare, with Bertha [Hans's fiancée and Ondine's rival] and with some critics, that Ondine killed Hans is to commit a grave error in interpretation. If Hans had been faithful to Ondine and to nature, he could have basked in the favors and kindnesses of nature. But since Hans is unfaithful, the effects of his infidelity will turn against him. . . .

Giraudoux wanted to show that man, in the presence of nature personified by the delightful Ondine, should not feel any anxiety. Let him come out of his preoccupation with himself! Let him learn how to respond to nature! Far from being an amalgam of foreign and hostile forces, nature constitutes his best ally and should inspire confidence in him. The world of nature in *Ondine* is ruled not by anxiety or fear but by harmony. As the best of the humanist tradition has always asserted, the world is the right size for man, at least as long as Hans and man, whom he represents, have the necessary respect for nature. Far from "killing" Hans, Ondine made him live. Hans, and Hans alone, is responsible for his unhappy fate.

Marianne Mercier-Campiche. *Le théâtre de Giraudoux et la condition humaine* (Paris, Éditions Domat, 1954), pp. 129–30, 137–38†

Why, during his lifetime, did we so sorely neglect the author of *Ondine*? If we picture European drama between the wars as a house, Jean Giraudoux was the decorator, and he did it up so imposingly that only Shaw, Brecht, Pirandello, and O'Casey could live in it without feeling dwarfed. We travel through his plays as through a luminous grotto, glimpsing murals of time-suspending wit and loveliness; and it would be churlish, after such a journey, to complain that the labyrinth seemed shapeless, that there were too many blind alleys, or that every picture did not tell a story. As well might one condemn the Uffizi Gallery for lacking narrative impact. . . .

As a prose architect he easily eclipsed Shaw in the art, now forgotten but once obligatory, of providing long speeches for crucial moments. Not for him the clipped, chopped scurry of most modern dialogue. At regular intervals Giraudoux feels a set-piece coming on, and the plot must pause while it blazes; when this occurs, we get marvels like the Madwoman's account of her daily ritual in *The Madwoman of Chaillot*, or the Judge's speech in [*Ondine*], which describes the unearthly calm that hung over the world one summer afternoon when all the attendant spirits, celestial and infernal alike, ran off for a few hours and left mankind to its solitude.

A playwright is a man who can forget himself long enough to be other people; and a poet is a man who can forget other people long enough to be himself. In Giraudoux, as in few others, the two vocations are fused like Siamese twins. The playwright sets the scene, and in the *tirades* the poet takes over; and by a miracle of collaboration the poet's eloquence nearly always crowns an arch which the playwright has built. So it is with the Judge's speech in *Ondine*. The play has been making one of Giraudoux's pet points, that once humanity acquires knowledge of the supernatural it is lost. A brave but doltish knight-errant has married a water-sprite, unaware that if he is unfaithful to her he must die. We have squandered much time in the second act on glittering trivialities, Giraudoux in his rhinestone vein; but now, in the third, we return to the main theme. The loyal Ondine is on trial; but it is the disloyal knight who will die. One thinks of the warning delivered to the heroine of *Intermezzo*: "Don't touch the boundaries of life, its limits."

We have to live in the same universe as the agents of the supernatural; but we must beware of trying to live on the same plane. [1955]

Kenneth Tynan. Curtains (New York, Atheneum,
1961), pp. 106–7

The desire to restore the primitive communion between man and nature through poetic language led Giraudoux to an animist aesthetic. In adopting this aesthetic he was simply following the German romantics, who had inspired him. . . .

Things in nature are given human feelings. . . . It is a constant approach for Giraudoux to consider the smallest object as human, and to impart to it intentions that are most often alien to its essence. . . . This tendency would lead to affectation if the device were not so often enhanced by a fuller image, whose purpose is to connect the human and earthly microcosm to the universal macrocosm through a hidden analogy: "On the horizon a chariot is grating, unless it is the moon rolling over the stars and pulverizing another Milky Way" [*Provincial Women*]. These images, which are sometimes forced, contribute to the depiction of an harmonious world in which Giraudoux discovers secret intentions. . . .

Through the introduction of a will hidden in the natural elements, Giraudoux expresses the need to penetrate the universe by using a magic light. Although he does not create a supernatural world distinct from the readily visible universe, he constantly injects animism into the visible universe. The air, the mountains, the forests operate by following animal or human reactions. . . .

Always observant of the external world, Giraudoux, however, does not see it as a reality distinct from the human imagination. He does not describe the cosmos as a separate, nonhuman entity. His animism itself indicates that he locates reality midway between what common sense calls the internal world and what for him is the external world. Giraudoux's aesthetic can be defined as an effort to achieve unity.

René Marill Albérès. Esthétique et morale chez
Jean Giraudoux (Paris, Nizet, 1957), pp. 116–19†

[Giraudoux's novel] *Siegfried and Limousin* was conceived as a sort of pamphlet. But in its fictional form, despite its [winning the Prix Balzac] and the success it obtained, it did not reach the public Giraudoux could have hoped for. . . . For this author with a message, whose success as a novelist was not entirely gratifying, a try at the theater was exactly what one might anticipate.

In 1927, Louis Jouvet, having left the Théâtre du Vieux-Colombier three years before and trying his own wings at the Comédie des Champs-

Elysées, was on the lookout for new authors. He had already enlisted Jules Romains and Marcel Achard when the kind gods arranged that he should come across Giraudoux with the freshly written stage version of *Siegfried* in his brief case. . . .

The presentation of *Siegfried* was an electrifying event. . . . Overnight Giraudoux became an object of public discussion. Connoisseurs delighted at what they termed the return of letters to the theater. They recalled that the theater is basically one form of poetry, and that it is under no obligation to imitate life. There was no more question for the moment of Giraudoux's art being unadaptable to the theater. Rather did it seem to be the means whereby the theater could again affirm its true nature.

Yet the transformation of Giraudoux, precious and whimsical improviser, into the leading dramatic author of the between-wars period was not accomplished easily or alone. Between the manuscript of July, 1927, and the play presented on May 3, 1928, there was an enormous amount of rewriting. At least seven times Giraudoux did the play over, with Jouvet at his elbow to indicate what would and what would not get beyond the footlights. It may seem remarkable that Giraudoux did not fold up his manuscript and go home. It is to his credit and to the glory of the French theater that he did not. He heeded Jouvet's counsels, and he assiduously followed the rehearsals. . . . The friendly collaboration begun on the script of *Siegfried* lasted throughout the ten years preceding World War II, years made more brilliant for the lights of the Comédie des Champs-Elysées and the Théâtre de l'Athénée.

Laurent LeSage. *Jean Giraudoux: His Life and Works*
(University Park, Pennsylvania State University
Press, 1959), pp. 65–68

Siegfried, under its wise irony, is presented as a last appeal for compromise and peace between France and Germany. *The Trojan War Will Not Take Place* was premiered in 1935, four years before the outbreak of the actual conflict, yet at the end of the play the Gates of War open and the struggle begins. This is more than happenstance prophecy; it indicates the presence of an analytical mind which had discovered the vital patterns of behavior at all levels of politics and society, and made informed conclusions regarding the future. By 1935, Giraudoux had discovered the all but inevitable course of events which was to lead to war, and this is his subject in *The Trojan War Will Not Take Place*.

As with *Siegfried*, the broad political panorama prevents the drama from wallowing in seriousness. Giraudoux delighted in wit, wordplay, and theatrical legerdemain as before—concluding the play with an extraordinary device in which the curtain begins to fall and then rises again. The theatricalism enforces an objectivity over the crucial issue of war, and prevents the play from rigidly taking a side and becoming propagandistic instead of analytic, which it remains. . . .

The Trojan War Will Not Take Place is a play about war and against it. It is not mere pacifism—an oversimplification which Giraudoux would have abhorred, and it is far from one-sided. But the message is clear, and when the brilliance of the dialogue, the theatricalism of the setting, and the complex progression of the plot have receded in our minds, the bitterness at war's irrationality remains. Easily comprehensible in its major theme, The Trojan War Will Not Take Place is Giraudoux's final despairing cry for peace, and it has become one of the rare masterpieces of the century.

Robert Cohen. <i>Giraudoux: Three Faces of Destiny</i>
(Chicago, University of Chicago Press, 1968),
pp. 103–4

As Giraudoux advanced in age, his characters seemed to acquire more and more the value of pure symbols. Andromache was still in many respects warmly human, but the savage thirst for total justice often appeared inhuman in Electra. Then the preternaturally pure Lucile [the heroine of *For Lucretia*] hardly seems to belong to our world. Simultaneously, a definite deterioration takes place in the characters representing the real. Helen of Troy, although guilty of unleashing a catastrophic war, retains in [*The Trojan War Will Not Take Place*] a certain innocence and a winning personal charm. Clytemnestra herself [in *Electra*], in spite of her crimes, appears as pitifully pathetic and even at times truly loving and moving. Paola [in *For Lucretia*], on the other hand, is almost constantly vicious and odious.

This progressive degradation of the characters representing passionate reality seems to parallel the change for the worse that took place in Giraudoux's personal views of the real itself. In the last years of his life Giraudoux was evidently overwhelmed by a feeling of disgust for the world in which we live. Although he fought as best as he could against that feeling in such works as *The Apollo of Bellac* and *The Madwoman of Chaillot*, his final outlook remained grim. A few of the "elect"—of whom Lucile is the last example in his plays—may be personally exempt from the taint of almost universal corruption, but they can escape defilement at the contact of the world and retain their essence of purity only by moving out of this world altogether.

During his youth, a happy Giraudoux had fondly believed that the ideal and reality could meet. In his mature age, he had toyed with the hundred possibilities of interplay between them. When he grew old, he reached the disconsolate conclusion that they are incompatible. Rather than debase the ideal, rather than submit to the loathsome claims of reality, he chose to retain the ideal intact—in death. This is the fundamental meaning of *For Lucretia* and the last message of Giraudoux himself before his own end.

Georges Lemaitre. *Jean Giraudoux:*
The Writer and His Work (New York,
Frederick Ungar, 1971), p. 145

GRACQ, JULIEN (1909–   )

Surrealism is, in fact, the only organized intellectual movement which has succeeded in spanning the distance which separates [World War I and World War II]. It began in 1919 with the publication in the review *Littérature* of the first chapters of *Magnetic Fields*, a work written in collaboration by Soupault and myself and in which automatic writing as an avowed method is given free play for the first time; to result, twenty years later, in the appearance of *The Castle of Argol* of Julien Gracq, in which surrealism returns freely upon itself to confront the great feeling-experiences of the past and to evaluate, as much from the viewpoint of emotion as from that of clairvoyance, the extent of its conquest. [1942]

André Breton. *YFS.* Fall–Winter, 1948, p. 67

The signpost placed by the Goncourt jury in front of *The Shore of the Syrtes* without Gracq's consent [he refused the Prix Goncourt awarded him in 1951] has brought the book a great influx of visitors. But there has been no change in the distance that separates his singular oeuvre from the mass of literature.

We are always in a "region of castles" whose secrets are not easily penetrated. Yet although it is true that the castle setting dominates Gracq's writing, this setting is not what makes Gracq's writing so difficult to approach. This setting, as everyone knows, is one of the great favorites in the sort of books written by Gaston Leroux and Pierre Benoît, and these books have always sold well to average readers.

It could not even be said that Gracq's language creates great obstacles, either. Although it may be true that Gracq's style is dense, and occasionally overloaded, it is no more difficult than that of some of the literary classics. Gracq's style is not at all similar to the unusual outbursts of modern poetry.

Thus, the surrealist nature could pass almost unnoticed, and Gracq's books could be read like any others, if a few details—particularly the frequent use of italics—did not give his descriptions an uncommon depth. . . .

By taking up the myth of the Grail again, Gracq has sought to rediscover a pre-Christian yet sacred theme. This myth has been haunting him for a long time, it seems, because traces of it can be found in *The Castle of Argol* and *A Dark Stranger* [as well as in *The Shore of the Syrtes*]. It is particularly remarkable that, although the indifference of the surrealists in general to music is well known, Gracq, referring to the Grail myth, often underlines his admiration for Wagner, especially for the Wagner of *Parsifal* and *Lohengrin*—even though Gracq objects to the tone that Wagner gives to the quest for the Grail, an overly Christian tone in Gracq's opinion.

Michel Carrouges. Preuves. Jan., 1952, pp. 58–59†

Gracq is an explorer in the childlike realms of dream. Consequently he is not easy reading: whoever continues beyond the first chapter feels like an initiate of mysteries reserved for the elect. For Gracq habitually applies the art of the lapidary to an already sumptuously complex adventure. His dazzling style is made up of long, involved sentences, multiple epithets, archaisms, incantatory repetitions, and frequent use of italics for emphasis.

The haunting and suspense-laden spiritual adventure in which the three exceptional characters of *The Castle of Argol* are engaged is inspired by *Parsifal*; in fact, Gracq himself sees his narrative as a "demoniac version" of the Grail legend. But an even more direct antecedent than the mighty Wagner can be found in the early Symbolist dramatist and novelist, [Philippe] Villiers de l'Isle-Adam. The nature of the protagonists (all strangely beautiful, both physically and spiritually, educated on Hegel and "qualified to penetrate life's subtlest arcanas, to embrace its most exhilarating realities"), the romantic properties of desolate landscape, enchanted castle, secret passage, abandoned graveyard by the sea, and riderless horses combine with the persistent note of anxiety and the obsession of death to mark Gracq as a close descendant of Villiers de l'Isle-Adam, who stamped his mark also upon Maeterlinck.

Gracq's extraordinarily conscious art has already been likened more to the painter's than to that of the writer. And, indeed, Heide and Albert walking down the geometrically traced avenue of trees that closes behind them give one the illusion of an animated Dali.

Justin O'Brien. NYT. Jan. 20, 1952, pp. 5, 18

It is undoubtedly of secondary importance to decide whether Gracq is a surrealist or not. He is a writer who has always kept himself aloof from every movement and every literary fashion, who has always wished to stay "unattached"—and, more than that, to stay isolated. . . . The patterns he favors are drawn from romantic literature, and in particular from a special kind of romantic literature—to be blunt about it, from decadent literature. . . .

Gracq's novels are purely mythical creations. They do not refer to any other reality than the one they create in its entirety by their verbal magic, by what Baudelaire called the "witchcraft of words." Undoubtedly, imagination can only function when it has its source in reality. But it is also true that imagination transfigures reality. And the author of *The Shore of the Syrtes* emphasizes this transfiguration, to the point of retaining nothing else. . . .

Gracq tries to make language coincide not only with sensation, but with the most internal, the most subtle, and the most inexpressible part of each sensation. In short, his language is meant not only to speak and to describe but to *have an existence* as well. . . . And first of all, it is meant to have an existence for its author. It is as if, in this desire for language to have a life of its own, Gracq were pursuing something that keeps escaping him; it is as if he demanded from language a treasure he cannot find in reality.

Jean Pfeiffer. DV. April, 1953, pp. 61–63†

Balcony in the Forest, M. Gracq's first novel since *The Shore of the Syrtes* won the Prix Goncourt in 1951, certainly reads as if it has been long brooded over. A heavily anagogic account of a claustrophobic situation, it takes us back to autumn 1939. Young Lieutenant Grange, a Poe-lover caught between heroic pretensions and a more fundamental sense of self-preservation, commands an isolated, ill-equipped blockhouse on the Belgian frontier. . . .

Anyone with a taste for archetypes will have a feast here. With fey, atavistic fervour M. Gracq elaborates his blockhouse in terms of a "Red Riding Hood Hut," Verne's floating island and the Islands of the Blessed. The four men are now stranded fish, now unicorns; the forest is Arden. Grange, the most thoughtful of lieutenants, having too little to do, attends voraciously to everything. Consequently his perceptions are intense to the point of nausea; I can see this, and why he fills the void with his racing lavish mind. But when M. Gracq not only underlines his own Wagnerian-Jungian allegories but even thickens up every impression with snarled images and softly wadded repetitions, the reading becomes tedious. He also catalogues a good deal, perhaps intending an antithesis of hard objects (in rooms, bags, pockets) to the whimsy and soft degeneration of the isolated men. All he achieves, however, is a crammed fable, brisk and pappy by turns, but almost redeemed by an exciting, austere account of the German advance that surrounds Grange long before touching him.

Paul West. *NS*. July 23, 1960, p. 132

The Castle of Argol can be read as a poem—a poem of a lofty beauty and one that is difficult to read, without direct or indirect dialogue, without even a thought recorded for us and with italicized words that are so many look-out stations to serve as a guide through the darkness. The settings—and the metaphysic of the settings—reveal the inner feelings of the three protagonists, and the settings are perilous, like those in Arthurian romances: the cemetery, the forest path, the chapel in the abyss, the underground vault, and especially the castle of Argol. . . .

   The Castle of Argol, in which the fantasy is intellectual and frozen, is sustained by an oratorical and repetitive style that resembles Wagner's orchestration. No breath of air crosses the book: the storm may be raging, but the forest surrounding Argol remains motionless. Frenetic and torturing passions may indeed stir Albert, Heide, and Herminien, but we feel we are seeing them through a plate of glass. Their gesticulations are in another world. We experience nothing of the ardor that is consuming them.

Marcel Schneider. *La littérature fantastique en France* (Paris, Fayard, 1964), pp. 365–66†

The personages of *The Castle of Argol* have not withdrawn to this place of privilege simply to escape. They have done so to experience life more keenly, safe from encroachment by extraneous and irrelevant distractions. Time is both present and absent, and Albert and his companions are sensitive to this fact. . . . Despite their isolation from the rest of mankind, none of them can know a permanent sense of release. Fatality in this narrative is too closely linked with elements unexplained and inexplicable, borrowed from the Gothic novels and functioning beyond rational interpretation. The foreknowledge of fate makes its effect all the more upon Albert, Heide, and Herminien because they do nothing to resist it. On the contrary, they deliberately make themselves available to it. . . .

   In the purified atmosphere in which his personages are placed, remote from the petty concerns of day-to-day existence, Gracq explores potentialities and examines consequences in complete indifference to the "psychology" of the people he presents. . . . Despite the fact that he places his novel in a timeless world far from our own, guarding its inviolability within the walls of a Gothic castle, the author of *The Castle of Argol* displays his fidelity to surrealism in a narrative which refuses to reassure or to placate and which, on the contrary, assumes the value of an act of incitement.

J. H. Matthews. *Surrealism and the Novel*
(Ann Arbor, University of Michigan Press, 1966),
pp. 97–99, 104, 106

The state of idleness in which most of Gracq's characters find themselves can lead to boredom—and, at the same time, to a greater attention to the external world. Since he does not know what he should do, Gracq's man looks for signs, to feed his expectations. In this kind of situation the external world takes on an exceptional importance. Not only should the man immobilized in expectation be endowed with a refined sensitivity, but nature must be ready to oblige him. . . .

Recurring like a leitmotif in Gracq's work is the immensely troubling scene of the intrusion into an empty room. Whoever penetrates this room has come to search for something like a revelation, pushed by the temptation to seize the secret of another being through everyday objects, but objects that consequently are endowed with magical powers. The first impression he receives is one of vast dimensions and blinding light. The one who is curious enters a universe where the air blows more freely. But every object, careful to preserve its mystery, seems to fold back on itself; the impression becomes one of hostility. . . . While the feeling of uneasiness grows, the incongruity of some of the details or the feeling that things have been abnormally arranged in the room sharpens the curiosity of the visitor. The discovery of an object that provides evidence—even if the discovery slightly raises the veil off the unknown —completes the disorientation.

J.-L. Leutrat. *Julien Gracq* (Paris, Éditions
Universitaires, 1967), pp. 34, 47†

[*The Shore of the Syrtes*] was primarily meant to become a poetic novel, and its elevated style appears to have the function of subliminal evocation. One might dub the procedure magic realism. On another plane, however, the book is a novel with a political structure. The fictitious Mediterranean State of Orsenna vegetates in the haughty jadedness of political lethargy with which young Aldo suffers more than any of his peers. He has himself transferred as "observer of the forces in the sea of the Syrtans." Here mythical forces of the landscape arouse him to increased political activity. In addition, there is his encounter with Vanessa, who appears as the embodiment of the forces of danger and of the forces instigating to war—the age-old role of woman, the incitress from the time of the Icelandic epics on. Ultimately war flares up again on the shores of the Syrtan Sea after three centuries of seeming calm. What is it that Aldo has triggered? And how are we to understand this novel, anyway? This work, as well as the later *Balcony in the Forest*, must be taken as a structural representation—i.e., a representation not concerned with being historically documented—of the "phony war" of 1940. Both works reflect an attitude of waiting which impresses us as negative in the case of Orsenna and as positive in that of Vanessa, while it triggers in Aldo an "obsession with the possible."

It seems highly unlikely that Gracq meant to describe here the relationship between Germany and France in the form of an allegorical novel. What is certain is that the experience of the Second World War made him ask the question as to how wars are really caused and as to how the young soldier sees the State and the adventure lying beyond the borders. But the work also contains an unromantic component in the form of Fate, for super-personal powers—embodied essentially, it is true, in Vanessa—as well as mythical emanations of the landscape lead Aldo in his will and in his wishing. But do they relieve him of his responsibility? The question remains open.

> Winfried Engler. *The French Novel from Eighteen Hundred to the Present* (New York, Frederick Ungar, 1969), p. 148

Of the three stories that make up *The Peninsula*, the first, "The Road," is the shortest. It is also the most fanciful—or, if you prefer, the most mythical. . . . The work of Gracq's this story most resembles is *The Shores of the Syrtes*.

The second story, which gives the collection its title, is much more developed. "The Peninsula" takes place in a space and time that are our own, and is told somewhat realistically, because the story describes (in 145 pages) a day of wandering by a man who greatly resembles Gracq and who is awaiting his mistress, a young German woman, on the coast of Brittany.

My favorite story of the trio is the last one, "King Cophetua." . . . The story's eroticism is no less disturbing and the atmosphere no less highly charged than in [Jules] Barbey d'Aurevilly's *The She-Devils*. Rarely, I believe, has Gracq been more in control of his magical spells, writing with so much ease and perfection, as in this story, which will tempt many film-makers; rarely has Gracq dared to describe sexuality in the shadow of death with such penetrating acuity.

> André Pieyre de Mandiargues. *Le monde*. May 16, 1970, p. iv†

Dreams are at the heart of [Gracq's] mythical universe—dreams, or in other words, expectation. Expectation is in fact the only subject of his books, a subject taken up time after time. Nothing happens in this world of mist. A small group of men are waiting in a place from which there is no escape, waiting for an event that they both dread and hope for—war, death, or simply *something else*. This is how we dream when we are young, and Gracq's novels rediscover all the themes of youthful dreams: *forbidden* places, off-limits frontiers, hidden and secret places in which one can take refuge from the threatening Outside, the anticipation of things more than their realization, and war as an infinite game in which one never dies. There are also, less importantly, haunted castles and ghosts in the night. This is how I believe Julien Gracq should be read— like Poe, Jules Verne, and a few others, without worrying too much about what literary landscape Gracq should be placed in (there is always time for that), about what movement he belongs to, or about any other academic categories. Certainly, surrealism made his work *possible* —and that is important—but the essential quality of Gracq lies elsewhere. He cannot be classified; he is like [Robert Louis] Stevenson or Jules Verne, a little like the adventure stories of our childhood, in which we set off for forbidden lands, as Aldo [in *The Shore of the Syrtes*] sets off for Farghestan.

Does that mean that Gracq has no connection with our modern world? It would be too easy to brush aside his work by calling it untimely and minor. . . . But Gracq's themes, almost in spite of himself, place his books at the heart of our contemporary concerns: decadence, the end of the world (of a world), expectation (forgetfulness?), the things which cannot be expressed but which we must nevertheless attempt to express.

Ariel Denis. NL. Feb. 26–March 4, 1973, p. 4†

GREEN, JULIEN (1900–   )

It seems that the author of *Mont-Cinère* is a young man. His merit is all the greater because he chose to write about a human passion that is perhaps the most mysterious, the most guarded, and in any case the most resistant to simple cures. It is possible to experience many other sicknesses of the soul, and to rid oneself of them enough to be able to describe them; I think it would be necessary to enter avarice as completely as one enters death, because anyone, once having tasted its bitter delights would keep its secret forever. This is the secret that must be pried open.

Whatever mediocre people may think, youth can succeed in such enterprises. . . . Green has just proven that. One can try to armor oneself in order to escape the power of his book, a book cruel and calculated— but there is no escape. One must submit to this book, must let one's heart be devoured by shame, because this is one of those books that reveal our misery and humiliate the soul to the depths. . . .

Perfect innocence exists only in the gestation preceding conscious life. There is no vice or virtue of which we are unaware, and which does not awaken a mysterious recollection in the deepest recesses of our hereditary memories. But to perceive this recollection, a writer must possess powerful attention, a scorn for facileness, and especially a fearless love of the truth. Green has these virtues; they are worth more than diplomas [Green did not complete his schooling]. Courage, Green! Your book is good. The romantics blamed the universe to justify man. But it is man, man who has fallen.

Georges Bernanos. NL. Aug. 28, 1926, p. 1†

The bad parts of Green's latest novel [*Leviathan*] . . . are numerous. . . . It would seem that it matters little to him, he is so eager to go ahead, to go on, to reach the parts where his power is clearly marked and that sort of somber genius which relates him to the greatest. A certain evenness of flow in the course of the narrative bothers me more; I should prefer it more like a torrent, with pauses, windings, disappearances, cascades. Doubtless he conforms a little too closely, for my taste at least, to the tradition of the well-made novel. But otherwise he would have to be willing often to dissatisfy his public, and this calls for a sort of courage of which very few are capable. . . .

Yesterday spent almost three hours with Green. How I should have been attached to him if I had met him in my youth! I like everything in him; he is one of those for whom one would demand the best of oneself. Without beating about the bush I was able to tell him everything I have written above regarding *Leviathan*; but adding at once that I considered as a proof of value the very shortcomings of his book, and not having spent time or effort in trying to correct them.

He told me again that he had begun this book without a plan, without a definite outline, without at all knowing how his characters were going to act; that they surprised him and that, as soon as they began to live in him, he ceased to feel himself their master and could not foresee the outcome of the drama into which their passions hurled them. . . . He speaks of all this with simplicity and one feels him to be utterly sincere. That subconscious logic on which the automatism of his characters depends eludes him, and I believe that it is better so. But, from the point of view of Freud, here is something of the greatest interest. The characters of *Leviathan*, the plot of the novel, everything is of the same stuff as our dreams and the projection on a black background of everything that does not come to light in life. . . .

That evenness of flow of which I spoke to Green is explained by his method of work and the fear he has, if he drops his characters for a moment, of not being able to find them very readily. He dares not and cannot leave them. But that is why the reader cannot leave them either. [April 12, 1929]

André Gide. *The Journals of André Gide* (New
York, Alfred A. Knopf, 1947–51), Vol. III,
pp. 49–50

Julien Green's case is infinitely strange. . . . He takes characters who do not do anything real, who are not localized at all in any recognizable society, who moreover never say anything to one another, and who finally do not think anything at all, at least in terms of what people ordinarily think. He puts them into situations which are tragic or which resemble a magazine serial, and to justify their perpetual deficiency in words, gestures, and thoughts, he maintains that they are prey to "unknown forces." In this way he achieves an easy pathos but one that nobody could ever reproach for being vulgar. And yet... And yet nothing would be easier to parody than Green's tales. . . .

I would bet that in a very few years Green, who (unless I am badly mistaken) will have produced masterpieces by then, will consider those of his novels published to date as very imperfect works, bearing the marks of youth. . . .

Perhaps Green, like so many others, like Bernanos even, suffers from the modern attitude that condemns every writer to write great novels, and consequently to attempt to handle great subjects, whereas true pathos and grandeur reside perhaps in more limited designs. Imagine reading just the beginning of *Leviathan*, the news item. It would leave an unforgettable impression. Yet the complete book, with its complications and sudden surprises, resembles buildings which are very well constructed but which can only be seen and understood as a whole by their architect, on his drawing board.

André Thérive. *Galerie de ce temps* (Paris,
Éditions de la Nouvelle Revue Critique, 1931),
pp. 129, 132, 141†

Green has a somber imagination, and believes that happy people have no story, that the ugly offers greater interest than the beautiful. At first this attitude might have been attributed to his youth, for many a young author, fresh from Baudelaire and the Realists, adopts a morbid point of view. But since Green is now thirty-four and still sees black, it must be assumed that his point of view is adult and natural to him. If it were only a question of settings, his are neutral enough. Unfortunately, he must people these backgrounds, and he too frequently peoples them with monsters. Placing his characters in the most commonplace surroundings, he excels in endowing them with an abnormality of feeling and a violence of passion all the more dramatic because of their everyday background. . . .

The contemplation of so much suffering would be a greater emotional experience were it not apparent that for most of it Julien Green and not life itself is responsible. The failure of these ill-starred destinies to move us more deeply is due to our realization that though fate may be cruel, it is not so immutably perverse. Green has no desire to arouse sympathy for his characters; his ambition is rather to make us say: "How true, how real that is!" but he has a far greater chance of capturing our pity than gaining our credulity. His weakness as a psychologist lies in not having masked his own sinister intentions in the cataclysms he lets loose. It is his own ruthless hand which adds the touch of salt to every wound; which shoves these luckless people over their tragic precipice. Like Zola before him, he resembles a scientist injecting a helpless specimen with malignant bacteria in order to study the disease thus artificially induced. The poison once in circulation, Green gives a magnificent demonstration of its deadly course; but the fact remains that all this had to be concocted in a laboratory, and no amount of skilful chemistry can make of it the stuff of life. . . .

And yet, so great is Green's talent, that we forget at times the test tubes. The landscape seems so trustworthy, small wonder if we are thrown off our guard. For in the creation of his pictorial background he has adhered with the strictest fidelity to truth.

Milton H. Stansbury. *French Novelists of Today*
(Philadelphia, University of Pennsylvania Press,
1935), pp. 148, 153–54

With *The Dreamer* M. Green took a first step in the right direction, away from the over-emphatic chiaroscuro of his early novels, into a system of fantasy in which his peculiar mind is far more at home. *Midnight* marks a further, and in some ways more important, step in the same direction. The world which M. Green has discovered is essentially that of Lewis Carroll and Kafka—a world where terror and wild laughter follow hard on the steps of one another, where the humour is terrible because it is a last resort and the terror is relieved from sordidness (as in *Leviathan* it was not) by the composed lights of beauty.

Such a world presupposes allegory, a perfectly legitimate form of art which abuse has brought into ill-repute. All that one need remember is that allegory is quite permissible so long as the symbols are in themselves as interesting as the thing symbolised. Here M. Green—like Lewis Carroll and Kafka before him—is brilliantly successful. The adventures of the child, Elizabeth—from the moment at which she escapes from the house of her sinister aunt, to that at which she leaps from the window of Fontfroide at the bidding of the beautiful and essentially destructive Serge—are firmly rooted in both worlds. The passage from one to the other, in the reader's mind, is achieved by a skilful balance of terror and humour. . . . It is stupid to shy away from the book on the supposition that it is "mad"—i.e., divorced from reality—a mere wanton toying with reverie. In it reality is approached from the opposite direction; that is all.

Edward Sackville-West. *NSN*. Oct. 10, 1936, p. 522

Julian Green's diaries, which ten years ago or even five years ago might have seemed comparatively commonplace, are at this moment of the greatest interest. What they really record is the twilight of the aesthetic age, the last gasp of the cultivated second-generation *rentier* [upper middle class]. With his extreme sensitiveness and his almost effeminate manner of writing, Mr. Green is a figure peculiarly representative of the nineteen-twenties, of the period when simply to preserve your aesthetic integrity seemed a sufficient return for living on inherited money. Although the *Diary* records visits to London, to various parts of Europe, and to America (Mr. Green is of American origin though he writes in French), one has the feeling of being all the while in Paris, the Paris of old yellow-faced houses and green plane trees, and also of first nights, private views and interminable literary conversations with Gide, Gertrude Stein and Madame de Noailles. Everything is recorded with the restless sensitiveness of the writer, who translates his experience into literature almost as automatically as a cow turns grass into milk. . . .

He writes much of his work, and his difficulties with his work (like the majority of writers he never feels in the mood for writing, and yet his books somehow get finished), of his dreams, which seem to affect his waking life considerably, and of his remembered childhood in the golden age "before the war." Nearly all his thoughts have a nostalgic tinge. But what gives them their special interest is that he is far too intelligent to imagine that his way of life or his scheme of values will last for ever. Totally uninterested in politics, he is nevertheless able to see, even as early as the nineteen-twenties, that the age of liberalism is ending and that wars, revolutions and dictatorships are just round the corner. . . . But what is attractive in this diary is its complete impenitence, its refusal to move with the times. It is the diary of a civilised man who realises that barbarism is bound to triumph, but who is unable to stop being civilised. A new world is coming to birth, a world in which there will be no room for him. He has too much vision to fight against it; on the other hand, he makes no pretence of liking it.

George Orwell. *TT*. April 13, 1940, pp. 404–5

One may well wonder whether Green the writer of his *Diary* does not harm Green the novelist. I am not only thinking of the time and effort which are taken away from the writing of novels (Green's novels *have* been appearing less frequently). It seems to me, moreover—and more significantly—that the very material used by the writer in his diary is, at least in part, material his novels are being deprived of. It seems to me that Julien Green's novels have lost something in vivacity, in completeness, and in resonance.

Moïra is certainly a good novel, even an excellent novel. One can read it from beginning to end with interest, with an interest that constantly increases. Once again Green has been able to create an atmosphere which corresponds to his characters, which is an extension of them, and which is indistinguishable from them. He knows how to fill this atmosphere with anxiety and menace. As always, he knows how to give the smallest detail novelistic importance. He organizes the plot skillfully and displays a sure sense of dramatic progression. . . . *Moïra* is therefore a very successful work. But a comparison with *Adrienne Mesurat*, *Leviathan*, or *Midnight* will reveal its limitations. It lacks the freedom, the inner resonance, the sense of anguish and vulnerability, the poetic quality that we recognize in the best works of Green. *Moïra* is a novel that seems to have been conceived and written on the margin of the *Diary*. [1950]

Marcel Arland. *Lettres de France* (Paris, Albin Michel, 1951), pp. 223–24†

Without Jesus Christ, said Pascal, we really know nothing either of God or of ourselves. And indeed, Green's characters have only a debased conception of God. In their eyes God has become a malignant power once again, has become the evil spirit who, in the eyes of primitive peoples, controlled the entire zone of mystery and plunged their lives into fear. Baudelaire represented the Creator as a torturer who was never satiated by his tormentings, and Baudelaire wavered between revolt and cowardly submission. Malraux and Camus, saturated with the same pessimistic concept of existence, opted for revolt: If God really created such a world, how could he be absolved of such a crime? Green's characters do not revolt, but some of them think of Destiny in horrible terms that remind us of Aztec divinities. Green's characters crawl gropingly through a nightmarish darkness, watching for "signs," flirting with magic, occultism, and necromancy. Green's presentation of them is of great interest for us: today many of our contemporaries take refuge in the very same depths of their souls. . . .

Each in His Darkness seems to mark an advance for Green the novelist. More substantial than *Moïra*, and written in a style less clear but also less dry, this new novel is rich in life and swarming with characters; but the thread of the plot never gets lost, as sometimes happens in Green's earlier novels. . . . Moreover, we are spared the uncontrolled reflexes of the unconscious, the insane illogic and the dreamlike confusion. Thus, the greater literary mastery is only the sign of a better-controlled spiritual viewpoint. . . . *Each in His Darkness* is Green's most complex and best-constructed novel, his darkest and yet most luminous novel—one of the three or four great Christian novels in French literature.

André Blanchet. La littérature et le spirituel (Paris,
Éditions Montaigne, 1960), Vol. II,
pp. 200–201, 207–8†

[François] Mauriac, defending *South* against its baffled critics, said . . . that only a novelist could have written it. Precisely. If we study Green's plays in the context of both the generic requirements and his fictional practice, we find that he is attempting to translate novels into plays. . . .

[In his novels] Green ensnares the unwary reader in common-sense reality and propels him through a sequence of progressively unreal scenes until he is left with the central character, helpless in the bleak teleology of the Greenian universe. To effect the transition Green concentrates on the mental state of the central character, who is too young, too disturbed, or too abnormal to keep a grip on reality. The perspective of childhood and adolescence adds a dimension of mystery and wonder to objects, actions, and words. . . . With his introspective characters the difference between dreaming and being awake is often slight. He introduces the dream as the character experiences it so that the reader will accept it as part of "real" experience. . . .

Obviously, if Green converts this method to the stage, he must leave out point of view, prose rhythm, and imagery. That leaves only fragmentary, enigmatic drawing room conversations. The dialogues of the plays *are* the same in kind as his other prose. With reference to *South* Green writes in his *Diary*, February 15, 1952, that God alone knows what characters mean when they speak. The spectator, consequently, does not.

Marilyn Gaddis Rose. MD. Sept., 1963,
pp. 195, 197–98

Whether the narration in Green's novels is in the first or third person, the main character has considerable dimensions, which also partly explains why the reader's attention is almost exclusively focused on a single individual in the story. Jacques Maritain was struck by this fact: "When all the interest is concentrated on one character, as in some of Green's and Bernanos's novels, his portrait is thrown into such relief, and the world of his inner life takes on such amplitude, that he seems to fill the whole earth."

One character for each novel, and at least one strong passion for each character. In other words, the character-minotaur is formed by the personal dramas of the writer. The writer thinks he perhaps would not have completely kept his balance if he had not been delivered by his work. Objectivity is an illusion, and the novelist discovers himself in all—or almost all—of his characters. That is to say, he discovers his great resemblance to these unknown creatures who suddenly rise up before him like housebreakers (Joseph Day's "appearing," after weeks during which Green had no inspiration, to dictate *Moïra*) and make him obey them without a protest. More precisely—and more simply—the character is sometimes prey to a very active spiritual force (the anxiety over salvation) and sometimes victim of carnal desires. These two giant waves collide in him, breaking against each other. . . .

If it were necessary to sum up Green's works in a few words, one should stress their originality and the violence of the contrasts within them.

Robert de Saint Jean. *Julien Green par lui-même*
(Paris, Éditions du Seuil, 1967), pp. 160, 162, 177†

Green's works have earned the respect and admiration of European readers. His plots are central to much human experience; his characters are powerfully drawn; his settings and atmosphere are most compelling in their uncanny blending of reality and hallucination; his penetration into the dark sources of human motivation is illuminating and convincing; and, to put it most simply, he knows how to tell a story. Why, then, has he failed to catch on in America? Perhaps one reason . . . may be that Green's religious anguish with its body-soul, purity-impurity obsession is simply too alien to contemporary American experience, whereas Catholic France, seeing Green in a great tradition from Pascal through Baudelaire to Bernanos, finds his themes more familiar. Perhaps the American reader is disturbed by novels which begin on familiar solid ground and then proceed unexpectedly to dissolve into fantasy and the supernatural. We accept this in nineteenth-century Gothic fiction but perhaps not in a twentieth-century writer. Green has been criticized . . . on two other grounds: first, although he lived through two world wars, a depression, and any number of social crises, there is no reflection what-soever, no apparent awareness, of what is going on of crucial impor-tance in the contemporary world; second, he is solely concerned with his personal vision—personal conflicts which he erects into universal prob-lems. Some critics have admitted the power of his works but say that they are merely case studies of individual neuroses. . . .

But even Green's negative critics grant him an impressive talent, admitting that much of his power comes from his rendering his charac-ters' thoughts and actions in terms of intense immediacy, of total in-volvement. He rarely indulges in the authorial prerogative of wandering outside the immediate context of his character's experience. Distinction between author and novel disappears, and this complete absorption is carried over to the reader.

Glenn S. Burne. Julian Green (New York, Twayne,
1972), pp. 140–41

GUILLEVIC, EUGÈNE (1907–   )

Guillevic's poetry is not meant for those readers who expect a text to dazzle them through images and to entrance them through subtle or powerful music. Here they will find little music and still less of the euphoria they are seeking. This rustic lyricism cannot be used as a drug. . . .

In *Terraqueous*, his first important collection of poetry, Guillevic takes an entirely personal position, one that differs profoundly from that of most young poets. He has nothing to do with either the escapism or the exploration of the unconscious mind that were fashionable not long ago. Moreover, he by-passes the sincere (or not-so-sincere) commitment and all the confused metaphysics of current poetry. Guillevic's attitude is cerebral rather than emotional, but without thereby being intellectual. His attitude is of a totally different nature, in my view closer to what Paul Valéry once called "extreme attention." In Guillevic's case, atten-tion, instead of being directed toward states of consciousness or budding images, is concentrated on concrete objects. One has the impression that Guillevic has incarnated himself in the object of each poem, making himself now vegetable, now mineral. This is poetry whose culmination, a true act of witchcraft, would be to animate the inanimate. . . .

Guillevic speaks of a stone, and we see it in our hands; he speaks of a bird, and suddenly a song wells up. When Guillevic sets an immense Breton chest of drawers down at the threshold of his book, a chest of drawers full of threats and riches, we know perfectly well that the chest is not symbolic, and we will take care not to open it to find out what it contains. Any presence is possible, and the presence of objects is as disturbing after years of familiarity as it was at a first meeting. This is because the experience contained by objects has nothing in common with the experience that enriches men.

Léon-Gabriel Gros. CS. June, 1943, pp. 460–64†

Guillevic won critical esteem in the Paris of the 1940s. He was praised for his reserve, his elliptical and precise language, his complete absence of rhyme, and his respect for recent tradition. When he recently ventured to engage in the well-defined game of the alexandrine sonnet, that was acceptable insofar as it could be taken as a game, a sort of challenge, a mockery—to put it simply, insofar as *he did not believe in what he was doing*. But if he believed in it, he was disgracing himself. Such is the current *morality*. . . .

Guillevic did believe in what he was doing. It was the opposite of a game. What was at stake, when he took the risk of writing a sonnet, was his life, his reputation. The meaning of the word "game" varies with the seriousness of the stakes, one must admit. In the domain of literature you cannot imagine what the "specialists" are prepared to do to a man without thinking twice. You can believe me; I have felt their teeth or their knives often enough. They are assassins with clear eyes. But they are still assassins. . . .

I do not know if those who refuse to attach importance to Guillevic as a writer of sonnets hear the real sound of his sonnets and understand that their content completely dismisses any notion of a game. Read Guillevic's sonnets; I shall not go into detail. They are about very serious things. Whoever understands what is said will clearly see that the man whom people were ready to dismiss lightly carves his work out of some of the flesh of his heart. Guillevic must therefore be accepted or rejected. There is no third alternative.

Aragon. Preface to Guillevic, Trente et un sonnets
(Paris, Librairie Gallimard, 1954), pp. 13–15†

It cannot be said of Guillevic that he actually "sides with things" like Ponge, although both poets turn their eyes toward objects in the same manner—and both poets similarly turn away from the kind of poetry that preceded them. But for both men, what has considerable importance is the outside world. Ponge, indeed, deliberately sides with things by bestowing on them qualities that may be useful and even exemplary —and his *Siding with Things*, a warning to those who are so arrogant that they forget the limitations of the human mind, largely records the lessons taught by objects. Guillevic, however, especially in *Terraqueous*, approaches objects as if to free them from what makes them foreigners and even potentially enemies. In Ponge, the object in question contains a lesson. . . . This lesson pertains to language. In Guillevic, on the contrary, objects begin in their own darkness, in their own impurity. If they affect language, if they establish a certain primordial silence, it is because objects are too threatening in their heaviness and their shapelessness not to make language afraid to have to name them. For Ponge, objects must be named before their true qualities can be revealed. For both poets, there is something to be conquered: Ponge must conquer language, but Guillevic must conquer the object itself.

> Jean Tortel. *Guillevic* (Paris, Pierre Seghers, 1962),
>
> pp. 37–38†

Guillevic reaches an almost Hugo-like position: "There is something terrifying in the world." What is terrifying, we understand perfectly well, is ontological in nature. . . . But this terror can also recur on other psychic levels of experience—the level, for example, of a less personal mythology, of a folklore. There is no doubt that the soil of Brittany, traditionally fertile in supernatural characters—goblins, ghouls, demons, vampires—has provided Guillevic's intimate anguish with abundant imaginative material. Moreover, the mere invocation of legend could give rise to anguish, because, as we know, in its structure legend is nothing other than the return of the "other time," the prehistoric time, the "time that is not the present," the time that, after having been stored in the depths of things, springs out now to curse or devour us, like the god Saturn, "turning his hungry jaws" around us [all quotations are from Guillevic's works].

There is another movement of anxiety in Guillevic's poetry, this one situating us in our own century and in the horror of a very real period: the years between 1940 and 1945, in a France occupied by the Nazis; and, less violent but also disturbing, the years after the Liberation, marked by a struggle against social oppression. In short, our whole era exists, for Guillevic, as a feared assault, as a blockade that may be fatal. The same danger exists for men and for things. But the ego feels equally threatened by objects and by history, both of which elicit the same sort of resistance, enabling us to make a preliminary connection (there are others) between tangible experiences and political issues. [1963]

> Jean-Pierre Richard. *Onze études sur la poésie*
> *moderne* (Paris, Éditions du Seuil, 1964), p. 192†

[Guillevic's] Communism, and perhaps the poverty of his own youth, sometimes seem to make him divide mankind rather too sharply into the oppressors . . . and the oppressed. . . . However, anyone who supposes an avowed Communist will write only social-realist or propagandistic poetry will find themselves confuted by the ambiguity and even mysticism of Guillevic's writing. When I said to him that he was a religious poet he replied, "Of course. But mine is a religion of earth, not of heaven."

There seems to have been a crisis in his development in the middle 1950's, when *Thirty-one Sonnets* appeared, with a preface by Aragon. These are by no means his only "political" or overtly "engaged" poems (*Writ of Execution* and *To Win*, in particular, contain many), but in these he seems—in the adoption of the sonnet form itself, as if to give to the common reader an absolutely familiar point of entry—to have been making a deliberate effort to write a kind of poem he felt (or had by external pressures, from the intellectual milieu in which he at that time found himself, been made to feel) he *ought* to be writing: which he owed to the social struggle.

A number of the sonnets . . . seem to me admirable works in their way. But Guillevic himself seems to have felt it was not *his* way, for after a lapse of [seven] years the next work he published was *Carnac*, a major sequence in which he reverted to, and further refined, the distinctive voice, the condensed and usually unrhymed forms, that characterized his earlier volumes. . . . In *Carnac* Guillevic has created a sustained and profound book-length poem, but formally his method in it remains the sequence of short poems, each paradoxically autonomous yet closely related to one another.

> Denise Levertov. Introduction to Guillevic, *Selected Poems* (New York, New Directions, 1969), pp. xi–xiii

One expects such a poet, with [Guillevic's] precise, almost mechanical viewpoint, to be lacking in compassion, in feeling, in empathy with *man's* world. Our perplexity is caused by our traditional view of nature; there is no contradiction between Guillevic's observation of nature—sympathetic rather than detached—and his compassion for the suffering of mankind. But one feels that his poems, and there are many, inspired by World War II, by revolution or any tragedies stemming from man's inhumanity to man are equalled by those in which his mission is to describe nature to itself, in which he uses his poetic tools to redescribe to us man's longing. The result is a curious understatement of our situation, with analytical descriptions of corpses, blood, rotting flesh, death, torture. . . .

The appeal of Guillevic must, as far as analysis of his work goes, remain mysterious. Only through the poems themselves can we attempt to understand his many facets, his unique philosophy. He is enjoyable and shocking, obtuse and aggravating, humane and unhuman. But it takes no time at all for us to begin to inhabit his world. And, as he begins to be translated into more and more languages, admiration for his skill as an artist, his poetic ability, becomes international.

Our difficulty, after reading his work, is to return to our former viewpoints, our previous focus on the world of cause and effect, of apathy and self-interest. Guillevic's ultimate artistry transcends that of either content or aesthetics: in that integrated fourth dimension within which he lives and writes, he has reconciled political and social concerns with an almost mathematical dissection of nature. And through reading his poetry, we are led toward a reconciliation, inward and outward, ourselves.

Teo Savory. *BA*. Winter, 1971, pp. 44–45

GUILLOUX, LOUIS (1899–   )

The two Andrés, Gide and Malraux, plus a formidable battalion of American writers—Waldo Frank, Malcolm Cowley, Matthew Josephson, and Samuel Putnam, its very capable translator—are heavily sold on *The Black Blood*. For Mr. Putnam it is "a very great novel," and for Mr. Cowley "the most effective anti-war novel" that he has read.

Now, Monsieur Guilloux has undeniable talent. He has written an interesting book, containing a half-dozen scenes powerful enough to stick in your memory and a half-dozen characters disagreeable enough to ditto. But I don't think he has written a very great novel. And I especially do not think that he has written more than a mildly successful anti-war novel. . . .

Guilloux does some of the following things better than he does others, but he tries to do them all, and that is his undoing. First, in the well-worn tradition of Balzac and Flaubert, he wishes to paint a contemptuous picture of French provincial life and manners—Alphonse Daudet with acid substituted for molasses. Second, he wishes to shove into his story as many tormented, eccentric, half-mad characters as possible. Third, he wishes, in the character of Cripure, a crippled, bitter, deluded, run-down intellectual, to project a kind of modern Don Quixote. Fourth, he wishes to satirize one-hundred-per-cent patriotism and to show up the brutality and mental callousness underlying the jusqu'auboutisme [refusal to compromise] of the average "respectable" French civilian during the direful spring of 1917. No doubt there is some magic formula to make all these elements jell, but Guilloux hasn't found it. A superficial unity is obtained by having all the events crowded into a single day and night, yet in the end this gives an effect of confusion rather than of neatness. . . .

There rises from this book, as from its literary blood relation, [Céline's] *Journey to the End of the Night*, an effluvium, a miasma of disgust, hatred, almost of nihilism. Cripure, with his morbid self-contempt and self-pity, his pathetic cowardice, his scorn for his respectable colleagues, and his genuine superiority, which has never had a chance to express itself sanely, is the symbol of this Swiftian misanthropy. Cripure is a remarkable character, but, unlike Don Quixote, he has little symbolic value. His bitterness is unreasoned and eccentric, he is a diseased personality, and though Guilloux's study of him is clever, it remains, when all is said and done, a study in abnormal psychology.

Clifton Fadiman. *NY*. Nov. 14, 1936, p. 138

Indignation, disgust, and a passionate desire for renewal and purity are the mainsprings of Guilloux's writing. His books are entirely dedicated to a powerful effort toward liberation. It may seem to the reader of *The House of the Common People*, Guilloux's first novel, that the writer has limited himself to somewhat hastily preaching the class struggle, the revolt of the proletariat against an oppressive and unjust social order. His second book, *Confidential Dossier*, shows that the debate is really on a much higher level. The novel deals not with abolishing one institution or another, or with changing the direction of a political party, but with freeing men from what prevents them from loving one another and being happy—money. The generous hero of *Confidential Dossier* dreams of building his house, of sowing his wheat, and of baking his bread—until the day that he comes to the poignant realization that here on earth there is no scrap of ground that does not already belong to someone. As one might imagine, aspirations such as this man's must end in complete failure. And I am not so sure that the clever reader, who can shrug his shoulders at similar utopias, will not refuse even to consider these novels, because the defeats that conclude them are obvious from their first pages.

Nobody, however, can remain unmoved by *The Black Blood*. The immense tentacles of this formidable book do not let any reader brush it aside.

Jean Fougère. *NRF*. Nov., 1942, pp. 617–18†

I do not claim that Louis Guilloux fully carried out his plans [in *The Jigsaw Puzzle*]. Whatever meaning he intended to give—or actually gave—to the confusion of his novel, it nonetheless appears to be an essentially confused novel. A game of patience for the writer, it requires even more than that from the reader. It requires an attention and clear-mindedness that the public of today is not usually willing to grant novels. I fear that the difficulty of the game will put off many readers before they even begin. What a pity! I would gladly advise these readers to give up trying to play the game, to abandon any effort to put the puzzle together. They should simply accept the pleasure of one episode, then another, and another. Little by little, without their awareness, the book will take root in them with all its inner relationships intact.

In addition, the richness of the book is such that everyone can find something in it to please him. It was written for the most part during the war, and so, needless to say, there are plenty of dramatic scenes. They are moving in themselves, but they also combine with our memories of those more violent and more heartbreaking scenes which we remember and which so many novels and personal accounts have described for us since the Liberation. The Spanish refugees, whose story Guilloux tells us, also played an important part: for the author they represent heroism and a passion for liberty, then defeat and exile, but always hope and faith. They embody Guilloux's romanticism—a generous romanticism, although somewhat too susceptible to exoticism and imagery. Opposed to the refugees is the evocation of a "prehistoric" world and time, the high society of the town of Saint-Brieuc around 1914, its holidays and receptions, the social chronicle of Mr. Rouletabille—in short, a reconstruction in the manner of René Clair, but sometimes overly emphasized, too complacent, I think, and in any case somewhat facile.

But finally, between drama and farce, Guilloux finds his rightful domain. Here are the characters who belong only to him, whom he both observes and identifies with, whom he smiles at but loves, characters he can exaggerate without deforming them. [1949]

Marcel Arland. Lettres de France (Paris,
Albin Michel, 1951), pp. 123–25†

The beginning of [*The Jigsaw Puzzle*] places us in the ambiguous zone between memory and artistic re-creation. The author is writing a chronicle that begins in February, 1912. But he has not begun writing until long after that date. While he is working—during the time he is writing his book—he meets characters whose fate he is in the process of describing with the insight given him by the passing of time. So he sees them through a double perspective: that of creation—a perspective frozen into document and at the same time subject to the actions and reactions of the imagination—and that of present life, "here and now," a perspective that contradicts or reinforces the first one. Guilloux lives and moves in this decomposition of time. A *marvelous* reality is born from this conjunction. . . .

The Jigsaw Puzzle is the work of a "pure" writer, a born rebel, a mind both resolute and ironic, without illusions and without weaknesses. It is a book by a witness to human misery, a man who is wise, without vanity and without fear, unyielding yet tender. If I may abandon the voice of the critic for a moment, this is a book I wish I had been worthy of writing myself.

Gilbert Sigaux. TR. Dec., 1949, pp. 1905–7†

In 1927 . . . Louis Guilloux published his first novel. It was called *The House of the Common People* and it related very simply the struggles and misfortunes of a poor shoemaker and his family, ending with the outbreak of war in 1914 and the father's departure for the army. Since then M. Guilloux has published some six or seven other novels, the early ones being as short and straightforward in treatment as the last, *The Jigsaw Puzzle*, is long and almost bewilderingly complex. But if Guilloux has constantly widened his angle of vision, with a corresponding elaboration of technical methods, his basic theme and setting have scarcely changed. Inevitably, one thinks of Joyce and Dublin. In the same way, Guilloux has made Saint-Brieuc [in Brittany] both his parish and microcosm of the greater world outside. . . .

At the heart of Guilloux's world, then, lies a poor childhood, with its dreams and revolts; and poverty—whether it is lack of brute resources or any one of the more subtle forms of spiritual deprivation—remains his theme. It is a difficult theme, since, for obvious reasons, most writers know very little about it: and certainly the world that Guilloux re-creates is poles apart from the sentimental slumming of many ostentatiously "proletarian" novels. It is, for the most part, a world of monotonous routine. . . .

Where M. Guilloux's novels transcend their local setting and serve as signposts to a whole chapter of French history is in their portrayal of social struggles among the working masses, and the reiterated impact of war. Nearly all the main characters in the early novels are in some degree militant socialists, trying to organize their fellow workmen, and at once entering into conflict with the local powers. But although M. Guilloux leaves no doubt as to where his own sympathies lie, he also knows the torturing suspicion that, in revolution as in war, the people always lose in the long run.

TLS. Mar. 26, 1954, p. xii

When Mme Bourcier [in *The Black Blood*] curses the "abominable" influence Cripure has exerted on her son Lucien and thinks of him as a "Professor of Discord," an enemy of the family and of society, a "public menace"—she obviously expresses the age-old view of the intellectual as a subversive. Guilloux unquestionably wishes to raise his characters and his situation to a symbolic level. The small town, enemy of all intelligence, becomes a microcosm in which the clumsy giant-thinker is slowly asphyxiated. *The Black Blood* describes the ache of awareness, the pain of being alive beyond mere physical existence. The very walk and stature of Cripure are pathetically meaningful. The brain and the limbs, utterly unsynchronized, are out of gear. The feet do not obey: heavy, invalid, they keep the philosopher rooted in the mire. For the difficulty lies not only in the clash with the outside world of which Nabucet, Cripure's private enemy and symbol of all turpitude, is the incarnation. The enemy is also within, an invading, corrupting, paralyzing Fifth Column of doubt and disgust. . . .

And yet, in spite of all the reprobation, pathos and ridicule, Cripure does emerge as a character endowed with dignity and even with grandeur. Beyond the tenderness, beyond the pity, there is an unmistakable note of admiration. Neither his grotesque appearance nor his extravagant manners prove to be incompatible with a certain fierce nobility.

Victor Brombert. *The Intellectual Hero: Studies in the French Novel, 1880–1955* (Philadelphia, J. B. Lippincott, 1961), pp. 125–26, 132

Anyone of my generation who read Guilloux and failed to take his writing to his heart would not, I fear, have gained very much awareness —not only of literature but also of life. . . . I came from the same milieu as Guilloux, but one generation later. My grandfather, like Guilloux's father, was the secretary of a socialist group, a job that landed him in prison for a while. I received a hundred firsthand accounts of the great strikes at the beginning of the century and of their effects on individual families. I spent enough time with my grandparents during my childhood so that nothing said by Guilloux could astonish me, neither about misery nor about becoming accustomed to misery. I think that what amazed me was that such things could be said, and that they could be said in a unified and pure tone, confidentially, without any straining of the voice. . . .

To tell the truth, I had the idea—a very natural one, I think, for my age and for the period—that the common people could not enter a book just as they were, that they had to be dressed up with a little literature for the sake of their greater glory. Guilloux taught me the opposite. The words of Camus on this subject cannot be improved upon: "I love and admire the work of Louis Guilloux, who neither flatters nor despises the common people and who restores to them the

only grandeur that they can never lose, that of the truth." Precisely:
Guilloux always tells the truth.

Georges Conchon. NL. Dec. 7, 1967, p. 3†

GUITRY, SACHA (1885–1957)

At the Aldwych we had a French season. Slices from the biography of
Pasteur [*Pasteur*], superbly acted by M. Lucien Guitry, one serious
comedy, *Jean de la Fontaine*, and three light comedies. . . .

One of the most entertaining of the plays was *My Father Was
Right*, and it had the advantage of containing parts for M. Lucien Guitry
and for his son Sacha as well. This play, written like all the rest by M.
Sacha Guitry, reveals all the qualities and all the limitations of its high-
spirited author. It is witty, extraordinarily lifelike at moments, revealing
a gift of acute and penetrative observation and tailing off into farce at
the end. M. Sacha Guitry has not yet by the writing of a masterpiece
entered the first class of French writers of comedy, but his work is
always irresistible and sometimes moving. [1920]

Maurice Baring. Punch and Judy (London,
William Heinemann, 1924), pp. 352–54

The gift Sacha Guitry possessed even as a young man was the ability to
put words in the right places, to make the audience wait for them, to
prepare the way for the best lines with ones not as good, to capture the
spectator's attention, to guess at what second he would be most impatient, and then to toss out a phrase that would dazzle him. In two hours,
he wrote the first act of *Nono*. Thirty years later, he could not change a
word of it. . . .

Nono brought the first appearance of a character Guitry would
never cease returning to, developing, and modifying in the course of his
career. His plays put a singular male character on stage. Women, who
are less fully drawn than he, gravitate around the male character. They
are sketched with a light hand—certainly not an indifferent one, and
even less a scornful one, but always something of a condescending one.
There are all sorts of minor characters to provide straight lines for the
main character, or rather for whom the main character provides straight
lines. There are friends who are in sad straits usually, but are likable.
Finally, there are servants, who are faithful and never stupid, never
stupid enough to do anything vulgar.

An egoist? If all that Guitry had created was the egoist type, he would not be so attractive. If he himself were an egoist, he would not think of the public. But he charms it. He even charms the people who start by telling you that he infuriates them and that he always writes the same play. His plays must not all be the same, however, because audiences keep paying attention to them and go into ecstasy as soon as they hear the first lines.

Maurice Martin du Gard. *Mon ami Sacha Guitry*
(Paris, Éditions de la Nouvelle Revue Critique,
1941), pp. 56–57†

When one considers the place that Guitry occupied in the "typically Parisian" theater before World War II, and that in spite of his enemies who envy him, his name will live in histories of the drama (where he should appear as the Scribe of our time), one wonders what has been the cause of such an astonishing fall [in *The Limping Devil*]. Scribe, after all, who like Guitry provided agreeable and hollow plays, dead as soon as they were born, for a segment of the bourgeoisie of his time— Scribe never fell to the level of inconsistency that Guitry has in *The Limping Devil*. What could be the cause of this decline? I would like to propose an explanation alien to dramatic art, but which I do not hesitate to offer, because it honors Guitry. My explanation is that Guitry, consciously or not, feels some embarrassment for his conduct during the Occupation. . . . The ardor that he uses to justify himself, under the mask of Talleyrand, takes precedence in *The Limping Devil* over the play itself. This is why the play is so disappointing, for although he is gifted as an entertainer, Guitry is not at all gifted as a moralist. . . .

It is laughable that some people, taking Guitry for a serious writer and possibly for a thinker, held some of his attitudes and friendships against him. All they gained was that Guitry was not there to greet the victorious allies after the Liberation. He would have saluted them with such a lovely remark, so timely and so sincere! Furthermore, during the Occupation he did not denounce anyone or have anyone executed, as far as I know. So what more does anyone want? Guitry has never had any other concern or any other importance than to divert us for an evening. By persecuting this frivolous and aging spoiled child, people have succeeded in persuading him to write a political play. What an error for him, and what a loss for us! "Shoemaker, look no higher than at your shoe." [Jan., 1948]

Francis Ambrière. *La galerie dramatique* (Paris,
Éditions Corrêa, 1949), pp. 259–60†

Sacha should not be accused of ingratitude. He proclaimed that *My Father Was Right* and allowed his father to exhibit his talents in plays like *Pasteur* and *Béranger*. He was lavish at improvising so that, although he reserved the leading role for himself, he gave an opportunity to each of his successive wives. He wrote countless sketches in which he displayed—either openly or under the transparent disguise of some great man—the paltry complexities of his Self. As long as he was on stage, it did not matter very much to him whether it was before dozing capitalists, his fellow members of the Académie Goncourt, or German generals who had just executed his countrymen. Let us sadly remember the hopes raised by the champagne bubbles of his early plays, *The Night Watchman* or *The Capture of Berg-op-Zoom*. Then let us throw a cloak over this Noah who became intoxicated by his own lamentable self-satisfaction.

René Lalou. *Le théâtre en France depuis 1900*
(Paris, Presses Universitaires de France, 1951), p. 37†

Cahiers: Guitry claimed that he was not interested in [film] technique. Did he look in the viewfinder of the camera?

Lamy [editor of many of Guitry's films]: Yes, he always did. He wanted to make sure of the way the actors were framed, because he had great respect and esteem for the actors who performed with him. It was very important to him to know how they were framed for a particular line in the dialogue. Because even though he loved films and visual images a great deal, what was obviously most important to Guitry was the text he had written.

Cahiers: What were his reactions when he watched the rushes?

Lamy: He did not say very much. I remember one incident, however. One day he was watching the rushes of a battle scene in *Napoleon*. There was one very fine shot; if I remember correctly, it showed a bayonet charge. Since the scene had naturally been filmed with several cameras, using panning shots, the camera filming this particular shot also picked up another camera at the edge of the screen, which nobody had noticed before. Someone said, while we were showing the scene, "Isn't that a shame! In this shot you can see another camera!" Guitry interrupted, "But my dear friend, the audience is certainly not going to think that we made a movie without using any cameras." And that was the end of the incident.

Raymond Lamy. Interviewed in *CdC*.
Dec., 1965, p. 100†

[After the war Guitry] returned to his previous custom of filming a play as soon as he had produced it in the theater. In the next ten years he wrote and directed no less than sixteen films, sometimes at a rate of three a year. The best of them were conceived directly for the medium.

By contrast, the plays he wrote after *The Limping Devil* were carelessly thrown together and often fell back on reminiscences of his earlier work. With his doubtful health he no longer felt able to make the effort needed to dominate an audience afresh every night, for a serious stomach operation in 1951 left him weakened. . . .

In Paris he made his last stage appearance in *Palsambleu* [1953]. He tackled the problem with ingenuity. The part he wrote for himself was that of a centenarian, hard of hearing and condemned to a bathchair. Since his colleagues had to keep repeating their speeches to him he had thus guarded against possible lapses of memory; and the bathchair spared him undue physical exertion. After writing the first act he did not feel at all well, so he cut himself out of the second. He did the same with the third act. Then, a few days later, he suddenly felt better and wrote a fourth act in which he was again on the stage. Still, he could not ignore that this was the end of a career that had for half a century given him his happiest moments. He rang down the curtain firmly and without sentimentality. As a sign of retirement he grew a large beard. The very nature of an actor's profession, in which he has to wear a variety of different make-ups, forbids this indulgence, and no famous performer has ever permanently worn a beard. The gesture was irrevocable. . . .

He could look back on a sustained period of activity rivaled only by such prolific dramatists as Goldoni or Lope de Vega. He had no thought for posterity and wrote simply to please himself and the audience of an evening. It was obvious that not all of his production would survive. It was just as clear that much of it would continue to live, as revivals of his plays and films have already shown.

James Harding. *Sacha Guitry: The Last Boulevardier*
(New York, Charles Scribner's Sons, 1968),
pp. 235–36, 249

HÉBERT, ANNE (1916–   )

CANADA

Miss Hébert is essentially a poet and [the short stories in *The Torrent*] are distinguished from poetry only by their form; the poetic experience, resulting from the duality of the poetic personality, expresses itself here less abstractly, as symbolic characters who incarnate the two opposing forces which create the anguish. A poet, who is aware of his life as a surge of impulses within him, is irked by routine, every-day existence, which appears stagnant, paralysing, and seeks to free himself from it. If he cannot free himself physically he frees himself imaginatively and this separation of dream from reality is tragic.

On the one hand, "house"—as it does in "The House on the Esplanade"—might come to symbolize the bondage of tradition and custom; on the other, "water" symbolically expresses the essential life of the poet, his super-reality. First there is a torrent, a rush and roar of falling water. François [in "The Torrent"] comes to it by looking into himself. And, as his mother had forbidden him to look into himself, he saw a raging gulf and heard accusing voices. His fate, the poet's fate, is to become one with the torrent, to lose himself in his lonely, frightful, rich adventure. This story is notable for its luminous examination of the poet's consciousness of his fate.

One of her most beautiful creations, "Dominique's Angel," is the story of an invalid who is visited—when her aunt is not about—by a cabin-boy who charms her with his dancing, for he is the dancing spirit of the sea. In the end Dominique's spirit, a dancing spirit, dances into the water. The exquisite beauty of Miss Hébert's tragic irony is created by the play of her intelligence on these structural symbols.

W. E. Collin. *UTQ*. July, 1951, pp. 397–98

Anne Hébert's novel [*The Wood-Paneled Rooms*] indisputably reveals a writer of quality, but one whose poetic nature, I think, takes precedence over novelistic temperament.

Not, of course, that there is a clearly defined frontier between poetry and the novel. Gérard de Nerval, George Sand, and Alain-Fournier created magical narratives in which atmosphere was more important than plot, and in which the undefinable musical vibration of souls had a richer essence than the careful analysis of characters and passions.

Nevertheless, a novel needs a minimal base in the perceptible and physical world of realities; the development of the theme requires a minimal amount of depth and intensity, to make up for the lack of anything unexpected. What I would reproach Hébert for is not for having almost completely excluded Canadian local color and poetic folklore from her novel. . . . What strikes me as rather disappointing in her free form of writing is that she does not arrive at anything genuinely new. Her experiments, although often successful, could be placed somewhere between [Philippe] Villiers de l'Isle-Adam, for the exploration of painful neuroses, and Maeterlinck, for the idealization of a pale and thin heroine surrounded by white light.

P. Henri Simon. *RdP*. Dec., 1958, p. 178†

[*The Tomb of the Kings*] is a book closely unified by its constant introspection, by its atmosphere of profound melancholy, by its recurrent themes of a dead childhood, a living death cut off from love and beauty, suicide, the theme of introspection itself. Such a book would seem to be of more interest clinically than poetically, but the miracle occurs and these materials are transmuted by the remarkable force of Mlle. Hébert's imagery, the simplicity and directness of her diction, and the restrained lyric sound of her free verse. . . .

When these poems are weak, it is because the imagery becomes too elaborate, turns into machinery, and begins to echo that naturalized French citizen, Edgar Poe. The title poem has this fault (although the similarity of the title to Mallarmé's is, I think, accidental), as do a few others, but they are far outnumbered by the poems in which this most difficult subject is given the strange grace of art.

Samuel Moon. *Poetry*. June, 1968, p. 201

"The Mystery of the Word" is a title whose meaning is derived from liturgy; this meaning is confirmed by a poetic language whose hieratic nature has often been stressed by critics in Quebec. This language is nevertheless one of total communication. Its hieratic nature, which should be a property of all poetic expression, is not sufficient to define the full significance of Anne Hébert's work. This "mystery of the word," which enters into the world of man, has the power to enable man to regain possession of his wealth and his own identity—gifts of which he has been dispossessed. . . .

"The Mystery of the Word" situates poetic expression in a spiritual and social climate in which the word permits the exiled man to return to the world, and his return is like a new creation of the world. Poetic language has powers that are organized by the poet, powers whose nature the poet alone has determined, but powers whose action the poet does not control; in the reader's consciousness poetic language provokes shocks and illuminations that modify, enrich, and unsettle his personal universe. . . .

I need not insist on the fact that Hébert's inspiration, which moves me very deeply, has its sources in life in Quebec. More fundamentally than any other work, "The Mystery of the Word" helps us understand the soul and the life of a people from whom we have been separated not only by the distance of an ocean but much more by our illusion that their origin and language ought to make them altogether similar to us.

René Lacôte. Anne Hébert (Paris, Éditions
Seghers, 1969), pp. 84, 86–87

[*Kamouraska*] is striking and holds one's attention. This is not an ephemeral work, dependent on fashions, a slave to circumstances—but a profound and enduring achievement. *Kamouraska*, whose density of language is astonishing, opens onto the mysteries of the heart and the body: one can see the frenzy of possession and abandonment appear and grow in intensity. We are firmly placed in a universe in which reason has abdicated some of its constricting powers, in which despair seizes on living tissue and bites down hard on it, in which love is lacerating, and in which time and dreams are joined together. This novel is a dazzling descent into man's darkness, with fantastic images that work perfectly. . . .

The value of such a book is clearly separate from the story it tells. This book is the work of a poet. . . . The inspiration for *Kamouraska* was a real event, a "news item" that took place in Canada toward the middle of the nineteenth century: a story of love and murder, set against a background of blood and snow. Naturally, if a writer of Hébert's quality selects such an episode, we can assume that her choice of material is meaningful. But what does it mean? Perhaps the story was one she had heard, undoubtedly with a shudder of fear, during her childhood. And this story could have later become, in the course of many days and nights, a dream—or more precisely, an instrument for building dreams. The organization of dreams is such, we know, that real people who find a place in dreams are altered, metamorphosed, freed of their dross, and in the end transformed into creatures totally imaginary in

[Huysmans] took all [artistic] aspirations and exaggerated them, in a spirit I can find only one precedent for in French literature—Rabelais. . . . Both had more learning than most of their contemporaries, and this learning was accompanied by a very keen critical spirit that prevented them from totally adhering to the innovations of their periods. . . .

Huysmans spoke the language he wrote; it was spoken in artistic circles. His wit was the kind that flourished in Paris at the end of the last century; it flooded the magazines, reigned in the cabarets and on the boulevards . . . and can be found in the epigrams of Count Robert de Montesquiou, in Jules Renard, in Willy, to name a few.

One of Huysmans's originalities was to incorporate this special language, this superargot, into literary language, to incorporate this wit into the novel. The risk he ran was great: there is nothing as ephemeral as the language fabricated artificially in a restricted milieu . . . and nothing as frail as a special kind of wit. But there is a profound closeness between Huysmans's linguistic ardor and his very temperament, and this accord gives books like his their unity.

> Marcel Cressot. *La phrase et le vocabulaire*
> *de J.-K. Huysmans* (Paris, Librairie
> E. Droz, 1938), pp. 557–58†

The centenary of Huysmans, which fell on February 5, recalls something more than a novelist of unusual talent; it suggests a train of reflection which makes him singularly topical. To writers, especially, his case is sympathetically familiar: in brief, he shares very evidently their experience that with all the talent and all the opportunity in the world it has nevertheless become extremely hard to find anything worth writing about.

Even superficially, his circumstances have a familiar ring. Huysmans made his debut in 1874, at a time when (as Gustave Kahn summed it up later) it was fashionable to consider that Paris, under the German invasion, had suffered like Rome or Byzantium at the hands of the barbarians. The decadents—among whom Huysmans liked at first to consider himself a leader—thus acquired in the intellectual world some of the glamour attached in 1944 and afterwards to the members of the Resistance; their exaggerations were readily taken as a proof of vitality; their promises, to a startled and disillusioned society, appeared all the more alluring for their strangeness. And when Huysmans began to write, equipped with large erudition, a brilliantly personal style and an eye for detail as quickening as that of a Flemish master—although it lacks the affectionate warmth of Terborch or Vermeer—he found in the established naturalism of Zola an immediate affinity. What he did not find, however, was a subject. For the aim of Huysmans was constant in one respect: he was never able to discover an appropriate sanction for his creative gift, yet it was this sanction uniquely which he sought. And so, like others in the same dilemma, he spent a lifetime projecting his own disquiets on to paper, assembling, as it were a perpetual dossier with the anxious thoroughness of one who is never perfectly sure before what authority he will at last be called.

TLS. Feb. 14, 1948, p. 93

[Huysmans'] life revolved around two central ideas, both of which are strange to many of us. One was that it is possible and in fact desirable for the human spirit to pay the same kind of attention to ugliness as it does to beauty—that the aesthetic sense can be exercised both by a painting of the grave, calm, majestic river Seine at sunrise, and by an etching of a miserable degraded little stream, half canal and half sewer, full of dead cats and floating abominations, winding its slow way between the backs of slum houses and the noisome yards of tanneries; both by the contemplation of the cathedral of Notre Dame, superb and saintly, and by the spectacle of a cheap saloon, garishly lit, hideously noisy, full of vulgar decorations, repulsive smells, and the faces of coarse and swinish men and women.

His other idea (allied to the first) was the conception that a truly sensitive soul can be as happy in suffering pain as in enjoying perfect physical and spiritual bliss, simply because the two intensities approach one another, and both are far clearer and far nobler than any mild, half-numb, half-blind perception of the commonplace. He was a man of really exceptional sensibility. One of his friends said he had been born "with one skin too few." It was not an accident of birth, but rather poverty and early squalor that flayed him alive. Until you read Huysmans' own works you cannot credit how far his masochistic sensibility can go. For instance, one of the most individual qualities of the French people is their economy in soap and water; even apart from the garlic breaths, the smell of a Parisian crowd in a hot music hall or in the stifling Métro is quite unforgettable. Well, Huysmans (unlike most Frenchmen) perceived this: he saw it was inescapable, and he rhapsodized on it. He wrote a prose poem about the sweaty odor of imperfectly bathed Parisian girls, and he claimed to be able to distinguish, with his eyes shut, between brunettes, blondes, and redheads. [1954]

Gilbert Highet. *Talents and Geniuses* (New York,
Oxford University Press, 1957), pp. 97–98

Besides their interest and importance as "human documents," Huysmans' novels have considerable historical significance, since each of his major works epitomizes some vital phase of the aesthetic, spiritual, or intellectual life of late nineteenth-century France. Thus *Down Stream*, the "missal of minor misfortunes," is permeated with the pessimistic spirit of the post-war [Franco-Prussian] years, and impregnated with the ideas of that period's favourite philosopher, Arthur Schopenhauer. *Against the Grain*, which [Arthur] Symons aptly called "the breviary of the Decadence," expresses the tastes and aspirations of an entire generation of writers and artists, and its hero, as Gustave Geoffroy observed, "embodies part of the soul of the dying century." *Down There* tells of the occultist and spiritualist revival which took place in France in the eighties, and reflects the state of mind of a generation which, in its revulsion from materialism and determinism, sought comfort in spiritualism, theosophy, and even satanism, before repairing at last to the Church. And finally, *En Route*, a story of conversion written in an era of notable conversions, in the time of [Ernest] Dowson and [John] Gray, Claudel and Jammes, epitomizes the Catholic revival of the last decade of the nineteenth century.

Robert Baldick. *The Life of J.-K. Huysmans*
(Oxford, Oxford University
Press, 1955), p. 354

Of all the Catholic writers of [his] period it was to Huysmans that the epithet "dilettante" was most often applied; and yet when one examines his work one finds a gradual change of approach resulting from his conversion which makes his religious belief interdependent with his literary creation. Despite the fact that he retains many characteristics of his pre-conversion way of thinking and writing, these have become metamorphosed by the change of emphasis which is given to him by his firm religious belief. . . .

Huysmans's is a hard religion, a religion of suffering, far from the aesthetic delights of a *fin de siècle* dilettante. In Christian art, too, he comes to look for a depiction of that suffering, in a conception of beauty far from that of the conventional church art of his day. The twisted forms of a [Mathis] Grünewald crucifixion contain more impact and meaning for him than any religious art created since. Huysmans's religion was no aesthetic game; he still loved beauty in Church art when it was compatible with his beliefs, but for him the main thing was the meaning of this art in religious terms.

It was nevertheless Huysmans who became the target for all those who wished to criticise aesthetic Catholicism. Seeing religious art as the attraction which originally drew him to Catholicism, and perceiving so much of his work to be still devoted to this question, his critics classed him as a shallow believer of aesthetic leanings. Léon Bloy, in a furious attack on this attitude in his novel *The Woman Who Was Poor*, contrasts his own character Léopold (in whom there is much of Bloy himself) with a thinly disguised Huysmans, who is given the name of Folantin (a character in one of Huysmans's early novels). . . .

Bloy's attack is violent and unimaginative. He does not credit Huysmans with any of that solid belief which characterises his work. The false emphases in Huysmans's beliefs may at times have been extreme; but it is difficult, in the face of his later writings and of his attitude to his own sufferings, to class them as "purely aesthetic" Christianity.

> Richard Griffiths. *The Reactionary Revolution*
> (New York, Frederick Ungar,
> 1965), pp. 104, 109

Doubtlessly it is in Huysmans' Decadent worldview that most contemporary readers take their interest and from which they derive a lasting understanding and appreciation of the human condition. . . .

Against the Grain, of course, is his masterpiece. Undoubtedly it will be read as the great work of Decadence so long as the Decadent school holds any interest whatsoever in the history of French literature. This is natural. For here Huysmans develops the entire psychology, or, better still, religion, of the Decadent movement. Aspects of this religious orientation toward life, the so-called "decadent worldview," are present throughout all his other writing, including the earlier Naturalistic works; and they are especially present and apparent in the later spiritual period. But in this one work, *Against the Grain*, the Decadent worldview is revealed, described, stated, summarized, and expounded, as it has never been developed before or since.

> George Ross Ridge. *Joris-Karl Huysmans*
> (New York, Twayne, 1968), pp. 111–12

What [Des Esseintes in *Against the Grain*] takes from Huysmans are fragile nerves and a shaky—indeed, disastrous—state of health. That is not very much; for Huysmans, that is everything, precisely because the celebrated neurosis he senses in Flaubert is, in Huysmans's opinion, expressed in just this way, through gastric troubles and an imbalance of the senses. And for the rest of Des Esseintes? There is Robert de Montesquiou, of course, whose habits and habitat were described to Huysmans by Mallarmé. . . . Once again, that is not very much. . . . Huysmans told Zola: Des Esseintes is not I, and he is not (strictly speaking) Montesquiou either. Also to Zola: Besides, you know perfectly well that his tastes are not mine at all. From these remarks of Huysmans's, one might think that as a true naturalist he simply chose to describe a special case, and that he did so patiently and meticulously.

He did add, however, that his work made him ill, that this neurosis he wrote about at such length reawakened his own. Moreover, when *Against the Grain* was concluded, Huysmans was a different person. . . .

Against the Grain is a book that changed minds. It altered Huysmans; it also profoundly altered the views and goals of the era. It made Verlaine and Mallarmé more popular. It gave Maeterlinck . . . the theme and the mystical tone of his *Hothouses*. Rémy de Gourmont was inspired by it to write a book that became a Bible for several symbolists—*Mystic Latin*. Even Paul Claudel, during his years of experimentation, was far from indifferent to it. A segment of the age contemplated itself in the mirror held to it by Des Esseintes.

Hubert Juin. MagL. Oct., 1972, p. 50†

IONESCO, EUGÈNE (1912–   )

That Ionesco makes us laugh is undeniable; it can even be said that what is best in each play is very often the part that made us laugh the most. But it is impossible, nevertheless, to put those passages precisely into the following, still very respectable categories: the *comic*, the *humorous*, and the *odd*. Perhaps, however, for Ionesco, laughter is only a means: a means to make us come out of our intellectual habits, which are reasonable and *Cartesian* (an adjective that frequently recurs in his texts, at the most unexpected times), and to enable us to reach a richer world in which a week contains two Tuesdays, in which one must avoid confusing "a fountain" and "a fountain," and in which the lady of the house in all earnestness sets fifty cups on the table to serve tea to three people. . . .

The most disturbing thing remains the possibility of expansion lying under every word, leaving us at the mercy not only of uncomfortable doublings but of such rapid multiplications that we are tempted to cry for help. In the course of a conversation [in *The Bald Soprano*] we get to know one Bobby Watson, then his wife who is also named Bobby Watson, then immediately afterward children—Bobby and Bobby—and finally uncles, aunts, grandparents, and so on—about ten individuals within a few lines, all of whom are named Bobby Watson and who, in addition, are *all traveling salesmen*. Mr. and Mrs. Smith's clock, which at first chimes from time to time, soon begins to strike without stop; this is, we are told, because it indicates the opposite of the real time.

Without any doubt, it is the function of the spoken *word* that is most explicitly being brought into suspicion in all of this. . . . It is the word, which has been set free, which surprises us unexpectedly at each line, in mix-ups that can take your breath away in their mistakes, contaminated words, examples from grammar books and *absurd* sentences such as are found in bilingual conversational phrase books. We ought to be gripped with panic, but all we can do is laugh.

Alain Robbe-Grillet. Critique. June, 1953, pp. 564–65

Ionesco represents, in the eyes of a small, a very small group, a *Libertador*, a kind of Bolívar of the theater. Let him hold onto this flattering illusion. He is a minor "curiosity" of today's theater. . . . If he seriously applied his sure talents as a writer he would produce things that count. But *The Picture* and *Jacques; or, The Submission,* which I have just seen, are flies for fly-catchers.

Nothing is more trite than the first half of *The Picture.* . . . The dialogue is vulgar, for whatever it is worth. It is a second cut, as the butcher would say. . . .

I did like *Jacques; or, The Submission* a little better, since it is pure and simple madness. Everyone in Jacques's family is frightened, yelps, waves his arms around a rebellious son. What did the outcast do? We do not know. He is obstinate. Fits of anger turn into ecstasy when he agrees to say that he likes potatoes cooked in lard. . . . Then it comes to marrying him off, and they handle the bride the way people touch a heifer at the cattle market. But Jacques does not want anything to do with her. She is not ugly enough. He wants a fiancée with three noses. Why didn't he say so? Here she is. It becomes slightly repulsive. But suddenly strange and charming words, grating and voluptuous words, come from one of her three mouths. . . . This is the flash of Ionesco's talent for the evening. But a flash only lasts as long as a flash. And that is all. . . .

I like to please people, but not enough to tell Ionesco that his double-bill is good.

Robert Kemp. Le monde. Oct. 18, 1955, p. 8†

Many good plays, as James Agate used to say, are built in two storeys—a ground floor of realism and a first floor of symbolism. Ionesco goes further than that: farcical at street level, he is tragic one flight up. *Amédée* is a perfect example of this unique architectural audacity.

On the ground floor the play is a macabre farcical anecdote about a married couple with an unusual problem. There is a corpse in their flat. Neither of them can recall how it got there or who killed it, but its presence has kept them indoors for the best part of fifteen years. . . .

The *dénouement,* never Ionesco's strongest point, is a messy phantasmagoria. . . . The upshot of it is that Amédée pulls the house down and plunges to his death, in which condition he takes on the appearance of the corpse he was trying to extricate.

And now, if you will just step upstairs to the symbolic level, watching out for the dustbins that Mr. Beckett has carelessly left on the landing, we will examine the meaning of what we have just been laughing at; for up here sits Ionesco the puppet-master, inscrutably pulling the strings. Something, in the bourgeois marriage whose last hours we have witnessed, died long ago. Neither partner will take the blame for it; but the wife protests her innocence a thought too shrilly; and this, coupled with the fact that the victimized male is a pet Ionesco figure, is enough to convince me that she is the principal culprit. But what has she killed? What is the dead thing that won't lie down, that so hilariously tumesces? A tableau from the play springs to mind: Amédée, the writer unable to communicate, vainly repeating the two lines which represent fifteen years' work, while his wife sits at the switchboard, communicating like mad in glad contrapuntal cries of: "I'm putting you through! I'm putting you through!" What has died is the creative spark that was the real Amédée, and the tragedy is that he doesn't know it. In the loveless hot-house of his marriage the dead tissue has flowered into a cancerous life of its own, which eventually destroys him. Only as he dies does he realize that the corpse in the bedroom was himself. [1957]

Kenneth Tynan. *Curtains* (New York,
Atheneum, 1961), pp. 167–68

If [Ionesco] is proposing to an intellectual audience a condemnation of contemporary vices, he is not conceiving a new theater, but giving instead to a conventional genre a new form that defeats his purpose. If, on the other hand, he proposes a nonsense pattern that will be suggestive of a particular aura, then he is proposing a theater somewhat in the manner of Jean Cocteau: a poetry of the stage. This is presumably the dream-like (*onirique*) quality of which Nicolas d'Eu speaks [in *Victims of Duty*] when he tentatively accepts surrealism as the form of his drama. The intellectual concerns of Ionesco will show at first glance that he is failing at least to the extent that Cocteau succeeded. In Cocteau's felicitous moments, his stage people are able to blend in a harmonious ballet with the remarkably fluid objects around them. The salvation of the Cocteau object derived . . . from its human quality. The Ionesco object cannot assume human grace for the people on Ionesco's stage are as wooden and as angular as those of Jarry. . . .

Like Jean Genet's theater (*The Maids*), this is a cruel theater, one of physical torture and degrading death (in *Victims of Duty*, Nicolas kills the detective who had been torturing Choubert only to start torturing him in turn; in *The Lesson*, the professor kills the student who had come to him for tutorial guidance, just as he has killed thirty-nine others and just as he will kill the forty-first that is about to enter as the curtain falls; etc.).

If [in Ionesco's plays] the object momentarily acts without ex-pressing an intellectual statement, it is apparent that it is responding, like the meaningless puns and the nonsense repartee, to the perceptible ill temper of the author. Its motion that should have been allowed to develop freely in surrealistic fashion is hampered, as was once the Dada experiment, by a single expression of destruction and scorn.

Indeed, the drama of Ionesco is monochromatic. Not only does it reflect too consistently a single one of the author's moods (and drama is poor in proportion to its refusal to exploit its many modulations), but it is poor as well in its subject matter.

David I. Grossvogel. The Self-Conscious Stage
in Modern French Drama (New York,
Columbia University Press,
1958), pp. 315–17

[Certain works of art] are entirely unaccountable at first glance, but after a while they become more unaccountable. The more you try to figure them out, the more you settle for being delighted that they are there at all.

Of the plays of this sort, those of Eugène Ionesco bewilder, delight, annoy, astonish, amaze and amuse me the most. How did they ever come to pass in the first place? Why didn't he write the way the rest of the kids are writing? Who told him to transform lunacy into a thing of greater beauty than mathematics itself, and probably more meaningful and useful than science itself? What triggered this Rumanian in Paris, at the age of forty-five or fifty or whenever it was he started rolling the hoop straight through the maternity ward to the last headstone in the cemetery? . . .

Ionesco seems to find the world entirely laughable, Beckett weepable, although Beckett is fiercely funny in the midst of perhaps the most abysmal anguish ever put into a play or performed upon a stage—pure, inconsolable, bleak anguish. Ionesco laughs steadily, and the ache of absurdity, failure and despair is felt, if it is felt at all, in the midst of a kind of hyena laughter, a voiceless laughter, a laughter that is noisy only in the lungs and mouth of the astonished spirit. . . . Ionesco himself most likely would prefer people to laugh. Laugh all you like, but just try to forget what you saw and how it made you feel. You can't.

It was art. It was new art.

It is the beginning of something possibly as important as anything lately achieved in science. If as much creative energy were put after what Ionesco has discovered, or revealed or hit upon by accident, as the governments of the world have put after the things they put men and energy after, if billions of dollars and hours were put after Ionesco's fission, not one single solitary weapon of use would come out of it, and very likely not even one little play of real worth. This makes our gratitude to Ionesco greater than ever.

William Saroyan. TA. July, 1958, p. 25

I went to the Théâtre Recamier to see Ionesco's *Killer without Wages*, without any particular enthusiasm. And my spirits caught fire there!

It is as if everything that I had seen or read by Ionesco up to now had only been a stylistic exercise preparing for this play, scales he practiced to be able to write this play with virtuosity and, forgive me, feeling. Here nothing is gratuitous, and the peeling away of common-places is indispensable because they surround a pit, a fruit, a heart, flesh: a man, that great commonplace, a man like many others.

Bérenger is an average middle-aged citizen; he's a pleasant, gentle man. The bad words he uses are "scatterbrain," "nincompoop," nothing more—not that he never gets angry or is devoid of temperament, but he takes hold of himself and controls himself so as not to hurt anybody. He is sensitive, emotional; he easily becomes lyrical and displays his enthu-siasms and indignations without restraint. He has normal reflexes when faced with beauty or crime; he is afraid of the police like everybody else, and he cannot "remain indifferent." In short, he is a man like any other. Not only an average citizen but also an average intellectual, judging from his endless chatter. He is also, like most men, slightly childish and completely gullible, and he does not see evil at all. . . .

It is very good that this naïve, kindly, and ridiculous man is not a coward. He is even a hero, in his way. It is difficult to be able to die when one could still remain alive. To die because one cannot tolerate evil, to die rather than live with it, is a very noble despair. This ridicu-lous chatterbox, this naïve, weak individual is a Man; he does not merely cling to his own life.

Elsa Triolet. LetF. March 5, 1959, p. 1, 7†

The horror of proliferation—the invasion of the stage by ever-growing masses of people or things—which appears in *The Future Is in Eggs* is one of the most characteristic images we find in Ionesco's plays. It expresses the individual's horror at being confronted with the over-whelming task of coping with the world, his solitude in the face of its monstrous size and duration.

This is also the theme of *The Chairs* . . . often considered one of Ionesco's greatest achievements. In a circular tower on an island (very similar to that of Beckett's *Endgame*) live two old people, man and wife, aged 95 and 94 respectively. . . . The couple is expecting the visit of a crowd of distinguished people who have been invited to listen to the message that, at the end of his life, the old man wants to pass on to posterity—the fruit of a long lifetime's experience. . . .

A play like *The Chairs* is a poetic image brought to life—complex, ambiguous, multi-dimensional. The beauty and depth of the image, as symbol and myth, transcends any search for interpretations. Of course it contains the theme of the incommunicability of a lifetime's experience; of course it dramatizes the futility and failure of human existence, made bearable only by self-delusion and the admiration of a doting, uncritical wife; of course it satirizes the emptiness of polite conversation, the mechanical exchange of platitudes that might as well be spoken into the wind. There is also a strong element of the author's own tragedy in the play—the rows of chairs resemble a theatre; the professional orator who is to deliver the message, dressed in the romantic costume of the mid-nineteenth century, is the interpretative artist who imposes his personality between that of the playwright and the audience. But the message is meaningless, the audience consists of rows of empty chairs—surely this is a powerful image of the absurdity of the artist's, the playwright's, own situation.

Martin Esslin. *The Theatre of the Absurd*
(Garden City, N.Y., Doubleday,
1961), pp. 99–100

The form [Ionesco] selected [for *Rhinoceros*] is social parable, whereby a simple idea is embodied in a complex poetic metaphor. As the central character (an alcoholic, unkempt anti-hero named Bérenger) watches in shocked horror, the inhabitants of a small provincial town are gradually turning into rhinos. First to go are those most fully committed to Society or System. . . . The rhino pack symbolizes "community spirit triumphing over anarchic impulses"—in other words, a kind of collective insanity, similar to the total conformity of Nazism, by which the mildest rationalists are transformed into raging, violent, thundering, trumpeting beasts. . . .

Since *Rhinoceros* contains a number of delightful scenes, and dramatizes an idea which, with a little less paranoiac tenacity, I hold myself, I feel almost churlish in adding that there is not enough nourishment here for a full length play. In a short farce like *The Bald Soprano*, Ionesco could hold our attention with his deft annihilation of language, logic, and cliché, for he possesses a unique gift for manipulating the absurd which makes him an uncanny comedian. In his longer works, however, his farcical gifts are suppressed in favor of expanded intellectual allegories, designed for social commentary rather than comic invention. Ionesco obviously thinks a great deal, mostly about the futility of conceptual thought, but his intellect strikes me as the weakest of his faculties. I suspect he was once, like the old Groucho Marx, an instinctual anarchist; then read Antonin Artaud and the French Existentialists who converted him to the *philosophy* of the absurd, a far different thing.

. . . *Rhinoceros*, for all its intermittent power, finally suffers from a certain impoverishment of mind.

Robert Brustein. NR. Jan. 30, 1961, pp. 22–23

What was being displayed to those tiny audiences who attended the first performances of *The Bald Soprano* and *The Lesson* was, as Jean Vannier has written, "a drama of language, wherein human speech is put on exhibition." The clichés of the first play, which Ionesco was inspired to write by his dizzying encounter with an English phrase-book, and the deadly logical flights of the second, were the dramas themselves, not simply means of advancing some anteriorly conceived "action" or of illustrating character or even, as the chief dignified misreading of Ionesco would have it, of mocking the orderly processes of social existence and celebrating an absurd counterpart. . . .

Ionesco, however, had a future, and it was to go beyond the exigencies and fatalities of language, although they were always to remain a condition of his work. His later plays are richer and more complex; in them new lyrical and philosophic modes develop, humor becomes less a matter of linguistic sport than of the tension between appearance and reality, the dramatic consciousness spreads to include fuller states of being and more inclusive attitudes toward the horrifying, the banal, the metaphysically unjustifiable. In his greatest plays—*Amédée, Victims of Duty, Killer without Wages*—Ionesco has written works of the same solidity, fullness and permanence as his predecessors in the dramatic revolution that began with Ibsen and is still going on. . . .

The Bald Soprano and *The Lesson*, for all their durability in comparison with the bulk of recent theatre, are not durable enough. They are not so much dated as superseded, their achievements have been absorbed into the larger accomplishment of the stage in our time, and they appear to us now, only a decade after their arrival, to distill a faint but growing air of remoteness and historical curiosity. In these plays Ionesco buried himself in the falseness and absurdity of language and shocked us into recognition; they provided a central, necessary moment in the reeducation of the contemporary sensibility, but the moment, perfect and inimitable, has passed. [1963]

Richard Gilman. Common and Uncommon Masks:
Writings on Theatre—1961–1970 (New York,
Random House, 1971), pp. 87–89

[*Thirst and Hunger*] is a cry for help, the story of a wandering, of a quest. Jean travels around the world to satisfy [his] needs; he is mistaken, however, about both the roads to take and his desires. He does not gain anything. He continues to be thirsty and hungry. No thirst can be quenched, no hunger satisfied for him. Why this dissatisfaction? Because every man has a need for the absolute and the infinite and seeks answers in precisely those things that are relative and temporary. He cannot find anything, since everything is wind and ashes. . . . The nourishment offered to Jean is insufficient because it is precarious, because it deteriorates and is only an illusion. . . .

Jean has condemned himself never to love except absolutely. All earthly love is insufficient to satisfy him. He has refused love because he claims that he has to be free; is there not deceit in such a statement? Since all human love implies death, he cannot bear the very idea of death through the image of love. He is afraid of suffering; thus, he carries a greater nostalgia. To love absolutely is to be freed from death, and this freedom is not granted to him.

Simone Benmussa. Eugène Ionesco (Paris,
Éditions Seghers, 1966), pp. 9, 28†

The Bérenger of *Killer without Wages* and the Bérenger of *Rhinoceros*, except for their final decisions, are much the same man. They both initially experience the winter of the soul; they next encounter those forces which would deprive them of the individuality that distinguishes one man from another and would rob them of life itself; then finally they use much the same arguments against their assailants, seeking to reaffirm those values which have traditionally been viewed as the life-giving sustenance of their culture. Yet one capitulates to the Killer, and the other holds out against rhinoceritis.

Herbert Bérenger [in *The Pedestrian in the Air*] sees the horror beyond physical death; King Bérenger [in *The King Is Dying*] makes his exit with death. That Ionesco seems or is inconsistent matters little, for he is not intent upon defining the ultimate fate of sick men in a sick society. . . . Ionesco . . . presents the problems but does not try to offer definitive solutions.

It is thus not surprising that, in his two most stunning and probing plays, *Killer without Wages* and *Rhinoceros*, he gives his protagonists the same name, similar characteristics, and similar dilemmas and antagonists, and yet he provides each with a different outcome; nor is it susprising that *Pedestrian in the Air* and *The King Is Dying* play still other variations on the same basic theme. Even with such variations, however, it is possible to make some general observations about Ionesco's view of man and society. To take into consideration his whole work is to conclude that he is hardly optimistic about our chances of regaining paradise. . . .

Yet there is implicit in his works a thin ray of light. At the least Ionesco is saying that we must learn to accept the inevitability of death with dignity and manliness. . . . At the most Ionesco intimates that, if there is the possibility of man's working his way out of this world's present foggy thicket, it lies in a stubborn, persistent, courageous conviction that he is different from the beasts of the field—and from every other man as well.

Josephine Jacobsen and William R. Mueller.
Ionesco and Genet: Playwrights of Silence
(New York, Hill and Wang,
1968), pp. 71–72

Ionesco's importance no longer needs to be demonstrated. His plays compel recognition because they create a substantial body of work. They compel recognition through their audience and their success: they are read, performed, translated, and published in all languages. They compel recognition above all by their originality.

Ionesco has succeeded at what Alfred Jarry and Antonin Artaud attempted in vain. He has discredited, if not destroyed, the "Boulevard" theater, a degraded development of naturalism. He has created new dramatic forms and put new techniques of expression into practice. He has captured the absurdity of the world and has unveiled a surreality. He has changed the public's sensitivity. . . .

If Ionesco's plays became less polemical after 1956, if he is considered to be more "classical," it is because he developed a new way of seeing and feeling things. It is no longer possible to write for the stage, today, without taking account of everything he has brought to it.

Along the path he opened up, experiments in writing and staging must lead us farther, must go more deeply into his view of surreality, must give more pregnancy to verbal expression, must further accentuate the "cruelty" (in the sense in which Artaud uses that word) of his dramas. Ionesco is one of those who "found schools."

Claude Abastado. *Eugène Ionesco* (Paris,
Bordas, 1971), pp. 253–54†

A world in which pedestrians fly, corpses grow, and Roberte's noses multiply while Jacques, standing before the three-nosed girl, is transformed into a neighing horse, is not, you will agree, a logical world. It is a magical world, close to dreams or nightmares, in which imagination takes control and plays with the laws of nature as with the categories of our understanding.

A man who dreams escapes the well-learned rules that have made the rest of mankind accept the inevitable; he returns to the childhood of humanity, to the life of fables, to the sources of anxiety and wonder.

This dreamlike quality gives its unity to the collection of short stories that you [Ionesco] entitled *The Colonel's Photograph*. As soon as you awaken, at the moment that your mind reenters reality, you note down the fantasies of your nocturnal dreams, a source of future scenarios that will develop into dialogues those proofs born in the darkroom. In opposition to realistic drama, which you hate, you have created surrealistic drama.

It is not surprising that André Breton declared after seeing one of your first plays: "That is the theater that we [the surrealists] would have liked to create." You have done it. You have dislocated the real, you have disconnected it with so much precision in your imprecision, so much naturalness in your ridiculousness, that the sensible spectator, who discovers Ionesco for the first time, has the same impression of false vision that the untrained eye experiences when seeing one of the paintings of "purgatory" that were dear to our friend Jean Paulhan. One needs an initial provocation in order to enter the celebration of fantasy. . . .

From your first anti-plays to your latest plays you have followed your natural inclination but have elevated it. You could easily have limited yourself to burlesque, but your comic vision of the absurd is accompanied by a tragic feeling for life, which is more and more evident as your characters come to express your own anxiety in the face of destiny. A counterpoint of black humor and metaphysical lyricism characterizes your new style. To keep a balance between such contrasting tendencies, between the comic and the pathetic, is like walking on a tightrope, but it is a fine, courageous act to pursue (at your own risk and danger) ends that are more and more difficult to achieve. Your previous work is only the springboard for your future work.

Jean Delay. NL. Feb. 25, 1971, p. 1†

A very strange event took place in Paris on the afternoon of Feb. 25, 1971: Eugène Ionesco, the world-famous avant-garde playwright, was received into the bosom of the Académie Française. This celebrated institution is normally looked upon as a bastion of cultural conservatism; since its formal organization in the 17th century by Cardinal Richelieu, it has almost always set its face against new ideas, except for one period during the 18th century when it was taken over by supporters of the Enlightenment. . . .

A few years ago, Ionesco himself wrote a charming one-act play, *The Oversight*, which poked gentle fun at the Académie by presenting a venerable Academician as an endearing idiot, incapable of passing an elementary examination. And yet there Ionesco was, on that Thursday afternoon, dressed up in the comic-opera green uniform which has been the ceremonial dress of Academicians since the Napoleonic period, delivering his speech of thanks, for all the world like Charlie Chaplin entering the House of Lords or the Marx Brothers solemnly officiating at the White House. . . .

There is something profoundly satisfying for the Absurd sense of humor in the idea of Ionesco, the one-time failure, the half-Rumanian, the deflator of the bourgeois commonplace, ending up in that ultra-French, ultra-conventional institution, with a laurel-embroidered uniform, a gilded sword and a cocked hat. . . .

The Western world is so confused that there is no cultural orthodoxy for the Académie to defend, and so it can elect Ionesco and he can allow himself to be elected.

John Weightman. NYT. April 4, 1971, p. 8

One of the main reasons why Ionesco has devoted so much attention to the theatre is clearly because it has offered him a medium in which he could best explore his own most fundamental concerns in ways quite distinct from those of conceptual thought and discursive language. By creating a highly individual form of theatre in which the surprising, the fantastic, the irrational and the paradoxical play a large part, and in which dream sequences, and visual, as well as verbal, images also figure prominently, he has been able to express aspects of existence (and particularly of the inner life of man) that, in purely rational terms, might appear difficult to reconcile, even totally contradictory. Ionesco has said that many of his plays were created at times when there was the least semblance of equilibrium and coherence in his thought and feelings, at times indeed when he came nearest to a state of inner chaos. And yet the dramatic world which results from the materialisation and exteriorisation of these conflicts and contradictions possesses a much greater degree of internal coherence and unity than might at first appear to be the case. . . .

His plays are artistically most successful when the broad lines of his dramatic construction are at their simplest and most economical, as, for instance, in *The Lesson, The Chairs*, or *The King Is Dying*. In a play like *The Pedestrian in the Air*, on the other hand, the themes of euphoric dream, inner yearnings, disillusionment and regret, fear of age, loneliness and death are set in a subtle, ironic counterpoint that makes the play too complex to be wholly successful in the theatre. . . . Ionesco is at his best when he avoids the over-explicit, allowing his extremely resonant visual and verbal imagery to affect the spectator directly. . . . By using words as instruments of shock, scenic effects as visual metaphors, and dreams to illuminate reality, Ionesco has created a dense and highly personal form of "total theatre" that has provided a practical demonstration of controlled freedom and has played a most important part in freeing the theatre from an ossified traditionalism of form.

James R. Knowlson. In John Fletcher, ed.,
Forces in Modern French Drama
(New York, Frederick Ungar,
1972), pp. 168, 186–87

JACOB, MAX (1876–1944)

Max Jacob is an attractive and enchanting figure. It would be hard to find a mind more liberated or more trained in games of the imagination. His flexibility would have made him a first-rate journalist, but he would have felt some remorse if he had followed the path of an easy success. He preferred to follow the arduous road of the "pure man"—or, if one prefers, the poet. . . .

Before this new book [*The Dice Box*] Jacob had scarcely published anything but sumptuous books aimed at a few collectors loaded with money. A collection of Celtic songs, however, entitled *The Coast*, had spread this writer's name in various circles and gave it a grace that can never be lost. Jacob's public reputation dates from that time (1911), although even then he had been famous for a long time in the vicinity of Sacré-Coeur.

Jacob wrote many prose poems and read them to a few friends for their greater aesthetic edification. These poems had all seven colors of the rainbow, and listeners passed under their starlike arch to breathe the orchids of the Impalpable and the Mysterious. And Jacob favored his listeners with commentaries that were nothing less than *new* prose poems. . . .

The prose poems in *The Dice Box* are varied—allegorical, often anecdotal, adroit and lively—and written in a precise style, but they do not illustrate Jacob's theory of the prose poem in every respect, because the theory did not find its definitive form until *after the fact*.

Louis de Gonzague-Frick. *Sic.* Dec., 1917, p. 3†

Max Jacob's astonishing and angelic power of creation draws its strength from the most secret recesses of this kind man who is tightly closed as is a church to those who lack faith. This figure of light, who shines at the very center of so much profound writing, is more human than so many others who look on humanity as the outline for a book. . . .

Jacob's writing forms one of the most powerful oeuvres at the moment constituting the essential literature of Europe. It would be very difficult to compare Jacob's writing to anyone else's. His writing is a secret force that idealizes the elements of contemporary society, almost without anyone's being aware of it and almost without those elements' being aware of it themselves. There is the small provincial businessman, the bad son, the good nephew, the concierge and the grocer from a little street in Paris, in a neighborhood that has already been spoiled by a shoddy artistic reputation. When one includes the traffic jams in a big city, the idle talk crackling in the twilight like electric sparks, the memories of a young bourgeois, the violence of drunken soldiers, their helmets thrown back on their necks, and the presence of the little pink-skinned shepherd guarding the mystical doves, one obtains, mixing all this together, an elixir—only a few drops of which, incorporated into the writing of anyone else, would give that other author considerable quality. And it would not be an error to use Jacob's art in that way. But it should not be forgotten that Jacob is the one who makes the elixir.

Pierre Mac Orlan. DV. Nov., 1923, pp. 17–18†

In Jarry humor preserved a certain logic in the absurd, a "professional" continuity; with Jacob it assumes such equivocal appearances, it has so many facets that it becomes extremely difficult to catch the poet in the act of being ironical, to define his attitude toward his work, and the position of the work itself. It may seem for a moment that the smile of the "stage director" will be revealed in a dark corner and gradually illumine the poem as a whole, but suddenly everything is blurred. Ariel, gleaming and dancing in the rainy dawn, suddenly changes into a grimacing demon scoffing at himself and destroying his own work. At other times Max Jacob makes use of the equipment of a magician, and handles mirror effects in such a way that his refuge becomes impenetrable. . . .

In Jacob there is almost always an intention to mystify, that is, a need for gratuitous invention without reference to reality, or (more often) with a seeming realism that is only a lure; and the finished poem is meant to deceive, for it is never what it seems to be, either in its literary or moral aspect. What is it actually? "We are holding in our hands an unnamed object, endowed with some kind of monstrous and diabolic life," says Jean Cassou. We, and no doubt the author, as well, will never know its identity, what it represents. We are similarly deceived by the universe, we never know what it "means." The irony here is like a defensive reflex of the mind, which refuses to believe in anything or to be "anything whatsoever." [1933]

Marcel Raymond. From Baudelaire to Surrealism
(London, Methuen, 1970), pp. 230–32

Max Jacob's novels leave an impression of malaise. One senses that the author, torn between his artistic concepts and his concern for the public, has partly renounced the ideals he dreamed of. The novelist, he admits, would have no readers if he did not make a few concessions to their taste—for the simple reason that he would have no publisher. Because everyone expects to find characters joined together by a plot, Jacob does not dare to free himself from that convention. But the plots of his novels are always very weak. . . .

What always holds the reader's attention in Jacob's novels is the depiction of characters. A picturesque and swarming crowd moves before our eyes and, even more, before our ears. Everyone, even characters who play the most minor roles in brief episodes, is shockingly true. . . .

Jacob's prose masterpiece is incontestably the brilliant *Cinematoma*, a "collection of characters" in which the writer has his characters speak in short monologues that reproduce, with astonishing naturalness, each individual voice and accent. Jacob truly has the genius of imitation; he would undoubtedly have been an admirable actor. While reading this book, one can almost imagine the physical appearance and posture of those who complain, brag, or lose their tempers. . . .

Although Jacob did not at all succeed, as did Jarry with his Father Ubu, in giving the public one immortal character, in his prose works he at the very least gave life to a whole world of picturesque characters who, in spite of the writer's tendency toward caricature, retain the unforgettable accent of truth. And the reader of future centuries who will pick up a Jacob book to discover, as in the *Contemporaries* by Restif [de la Bretonne, an eighteenth-century novelist], a curious image of the society of the time, will certainly not miss the fascinating comic verve of the writer. This reader will sometimes pause for a long time, surprised and charmed, at a sentence whose pathos suddenly reveals the great heart of this extraordinarily paradoxical man.

Hubert Fabureau. Max Jacob (Paris, Éditions de la
Nouvelle Revue Critique, 1935), pp. 79–82, 90–91†

[In 1926] I found a perfect friend in Max Jacob. . . . No man's character was more difficult to circumscribe. His was in a continual ferment, a fluid in constant ebullition, and sometimes the loveliest flowers and plants were brought to the surface, while at others the most loathsome creatures appeared. He was both Cinderella and her sisters, the ogre, the wolf, and all seven dwarfs. . . .

Just as he saw enemies everywhere, he believed he once saw God, Who commanded him to convert to Catholicism.

If nothing was closer to his mind than casuistry, nothing was further from his temperament than Christian rigor. He had such difficulties abiding by it, the poor man, that he awakened both tears and laughter in those around him. Sin on a broomstick and virtue on a white horse joined in a wild witches' sabbath. Communion, sin, penitence, the sacraments, sin, and remorse, this was the daily chain that warped his soul, struggling between the love of God, the lure of the devil, and the fear of hell.

This showed in all his remarks, in his whole life, and made him one of the most evidently human men of the period. And one of the only true poets of our times, as much of a poet as Claudel, and even wilder, with more prepossessing demons as inhabitants, incomparably superior to Cocteau, his temperament much richer than that of Francis Jammes; all Max Jacob lacked was a little lucidity and a little order to equal Apollinaire.

But oh his loquacious and chaotic pen! That handwriting which traced so firm a line produced poems with contours, wildly gossiping novels whose genius was to open unlimited poetic vistas yet which could never accept limits to shore them up. [1939]

Maurice Sachs. Witches' Sabbath (New York,
Stein and Day, 1964), pp. 143–46

In 1917 [Jacob] published *The Dice Box*, a work conceived as the expression of his unconscious mind, and therefore a work that makes him one of the precursors of surrealism. He was also of the opinion that he had, in those pages, created a kind of poetry in which the subject itself and picturesqueness have no importance: all that counts are the connections between words and images. If a word or a sentence contributes to the effect of the whole, the poet is concerned neither about their own intrinsic value nor about their connection with the action. Only the poetry matters. From now on the "new spirit" can annex anything that can be used for beauty—and above all, the most variegated associations of syllables and ideas.

Is this madness? Jacob immediately protests, since he considers the thesis that genius is close to madness to be absurd; or, more accurately, he admits to feeling a desire for harmonious madness, for a lyricism that is delirious and never satisfied. But is this anything other than poetry itself, which liberates thoughts and objects? Max Jacob is by inclination an elegiac poet, but—and herein appears the conflict in his personality —his avowed need for excessive lyricism collides with his critical spirit. Does he wish to give free rein to his inspiration? His irony slows down every flight. A desire for mortification impels him to destroy, or at least to repress, his true personality under various masks. . . .

From the moment the Catholic faith lit up the poet's soul, however, his thoughts became more human, and his sensitivity, slowly encroaching on his irony, gave his poetry more and more of a real unity. . . . Above the airy dance performed by the clouds of his imagination, the eternal sun has just appeared; it will not dissipate those clouds but will henceforth cover them with its spiritual gold.

> Emmanuel Aegerter and Pierre Labracherie.
> *Au temps de Guillaume Apollinaire* (Paris,
> René Julliard, 1945), pp. 108–10†

In an early letter of Max Jacob's there is the prescience of a little phrase which will become fatally attached to his name: "I don't want to be known to posterity," he wrote, "as the friend of Picasso." How is he remembered to-day? As Picasso's friend and fellow-tenant of the *Bateau Lavoir*, the laboratory of Cubism. As the clown. As the Breton Jew who became a Christian because he had seen an apparition of Christ on the studio wall. As the ascetic who fled from Paris [in 1921] for the solitude of Saint-Benoît-sur-Loire. As the volatile, enchanting, exasperating creature who was arrested by the Gestapo in the last months of the war and died in the camp for Jews at Drancy.

But as a poet? Perhaps, but one whom few trouble to read. He is in the anthologies, but he is not always represented by his best poems. It is assumed that he belonged to a period that has lost its significance. . . .

The Abbé Garnier [who edited Jacob's *Correspondence*] speaks of "the extraordinary and unfortunately impossible dialogue between Max Jacob and his epoch" and indeed this dialogue can be traced in all the correspondence. But this dialogue concealed another dialogue which was fully explicit only in the meditations he scattered through the post. Max Jacob's conversion has been both underplayed and overplayed. For those who were unable to take it seriously and saw it as yet another facet of the clown, it was proof of his fundamental insincerity. For those who saw it as something which might be used to sectarian advantage, it had a disconcerting inability to conform to type. Max was both too complicated and too simple; he was a Jew and he was Breton. There is no indication that he was beguiled by the historical grandeur of the Church or that he rallied to it, as did many at that time, for the defence of the West. . . . He was converted because the "apparition" on the studio wall had issued a command. As for sincerity, it took him five years to convince a priest who would baptize him.

> *TLS*. Oct. 9, 1959, p. 576

In order to appreciate fully Jacob's contribution to recent literary productions, one must first sight back down the line of his poetic techniques. The fragmented images with which he habitually works piece together into a cogent whole as one applies knowledge of the source, Baudelairean decadence in this case. But if one looks forward in time, and loses sight temporarily of the identifications afforded by the Baudelaire-decadence-cubism *rapprochement*, the image undergoes increasing fragmentation. It becomes correspondingly difficult for the reader to isolate the rational, real-life referent of any given subject, or even to distinguish with any certainty the ideological implication.

If we glance back to Jacob's intellectual beginnings in Montmartre before 1900, we find a worldly fop, a dandy gotten up in superannuated finery, engaged in writing elegant art criticism. Few authors of his generation were more imbued with the values of late romanticism, few more a slave to what he himself considered its preposterously contradictory premises. At the same time, probably no young writer was more caustically lucid about what he understood as the falsifications fundamental to and inherent in all the works of the romantic *Zeitgeist*, nor did any young writer exert a more corrosive influence on what were, for him, its hackneyed conventions.

In this sense Jacob was a master of both centuries, taking much from the one, giving much to the other. In addition to his annihilation of the sacred cows, he forged an entire new literary vocabulary, as witness the fact . . . that it is difficult to cite a modern French writer whose work (or elements of it) cannot be traced back to similar procedures in Jacob. His was a prophetic voice announcing the dissolution of the esthetic resources of a century, and it is precisely by his uncanny ability to show us in 1903 what the future—our present—was to be like that he imposes himself as a true herald of the new art.

Gerald Kamber. *Max Jacob and the Poetics of Cubism* (Baltimore, Johns Hopkins University Press, 1971), p. 170

JAMMES, FRANCIS (1868–1938)

I remember, in 1892, Hubert Crackanthorpe sending me a tiny, privately printed book of verses, dedicated to himself, which he wished me to read. It was by Francis Jammes, an unknown name, and the verses were of so unparalleled a naïveté that I imagined, for a moment, some mystification. Since then my French friends have often spoken to me of Francis Jammes, but I was not tempted to read any more of his works until, the other day, I received this volume of collected poems [*From the Morning Prayer to the Evening Prayer*]. Reading them in the country idly, among the scenes in which they pass, I find that they have a genuine savour of the soil, and that it is possible to find an almost illicit pleasure in their halting verse, their deliberate air of being improvised.

A tired soul, for which happiness is to be found only among the fields, in rest, seems to speak out of these pages with an almost pathetic outspokenness. They give one a particular sensation of the country, of its tranquil pleasures, its limited lives, the solace of its grass and space and leisure. All its colours and sounds and odours are known by heart, like friends; there is not a page which does not call up some definite picture or mood, the mood being always indeed implicit in the picture. The word picture gives too formal a notion of these accidental meditations, in which there is nothing of the painter, but a good deal of the peasant; of what the peasant would be, that is, if he had the faculty of ready feeling and sharp sensation. And in the form of the verses, so languid, so incorrect, often so childish, there is something of that revolt against mere "literature" which is being so generally divined as one of the present necessities of art.

Arthur Symons. SR (London). Oct. 15, 1898, p. 510

To appreciate Francis Jammes's poetry, the reader should forget all the habits, all the conventions, all the traditions, and all the "beauties" of other kinds of poetry. Above all, he must forget one rule that the French somehow usually impose on a writer as a criterion: "Write in such a way that your style can be held up as a universal model." Jammes's individual style can be a model only for itself; it is unnecessary to wonder what would happen if his style were imitated, if every other poet began to write the same way. With all this in mind, we can enjoy the very sweet and sometimes very powerful charm in the poetic images he offers.

"Jean de Noarrieu" [in *The Triumph of Life*] is a very simple idyll ("idyll" is the word that always comes to mind when one writes about Jammes) in which the almost childlike style creates the energetic and healthy atmosphere of the good rustic life. This kind of simplicity is pleasing, and objects are isolated and depicted so sharply and distinctly that we are made to see them as clearly as if they had been described by the most refined art.

The other poem [in *The Triumph of Life*], "Existences," is more disconcerting: it is like a series of snapshots that reveal the life of a small town, its vulgarities, its meannesses, its patches of both misery and innocence, the humble joys and resignations of its creatures and objects. Everything is here, from the most disagreeably raw realities to the wildest fantasies.

Gustave Lanson. RU. No. 2, 1902, p. 88†

It is of the essence of [Jammes's] religious sentiment to feel that nothing is too humble for art, there being none of God's creatures which he must not approach with reverential wonder. He mentions in verse plants, animals, and objects in general, humble, forgotten things, or things despised, which seemed forever excluded from the language of poetry, although Chaucer and Villon might serve as reminders of an earlier, pre-Victorian order of things. We were still under the spell—not long since—of the neoclassics, still bowing more or less to their injunction not to mention in verse any "base" objects, such as animals of the lower kind, and in any case to prefer the general to the particular, as more refined. . . .

Jammes has undertaken in French poetry what Wordsworth undertook, with considerable success in English—to do away with the tradition of "poetical" subjects. As with Wordsworth, too, this breadth in the choice of subject-matter is associated with, is perhaps rooted in, a religious mysticism; but in both cases it shows itself in many observations little connected with religious feeling, and in his claim to freedom in this matter the modern poet makes no appeal to other principles than those of poetic naturalism. This poet writes of fish and fishing with distinctions as precise as those of Izaak Walton himself. . . .

More direct and obvious is the reading of nature in religious terms, once more after the fashion of Wordsworth, but with a greater naïveté of anthropomorphic realism. The sense of natural objects as living in the breath of God is present throughout all his work, even the most secular.

Joseph Warren Beach and Gustave van Roosbroeck.
SwR. April–June, 1920, pp. 175–77

What is Jammism? A doctrine, a method of thinking and feeling? Certainly not! Quite simply an attitude toward nature and life, an attitude which is Francis Jammes's alone and which, astonishingly enough, has never been contrasted to Baudelaire's satanism. "Jammism" is "angelism." Jammes is the anti-Baudelaire. Jammism is ingenuousness, innocence, and all the middle-class family virtues; the attachment to the native soil; the adoration of the Good Lord and the love of all His creatures; humility and saintliness, at least a secular saintliness. . . .

Jammes has the great distinction of never having descended into writing confectionary or sugary poetry. But he has not remained all that aloof from the foolish and the juvenile. The fervor with which educated readers used to admire Jammes has diminished somewhat as the poet has grown older and has affected a lofty manner and played the role of thinker and moralist, a role for which he is not suited. It is the poet of *Primroses in Mourning* and *Christian Georgics*, the creator of *Clara d'Ellébeuse* and *Almaïde d'Étremont*, who will carve his name in the history of literature that glorifies nature. Jammes has been compared to Vergil, Theocritus, Rutebeuf, Clément Marot, La Fontaine, and Mistral. Mystical and bourgeois, unsophisticated and fond of practical jokes, gothic and classical—he reconciles many opposites into a harmony that, although it lacks power, always has grace and often has purity.

> André Billy. *La littérature française contemporaine*
> (Paris, Librairie Armand Colin, 1927), pp. 5–7†

Jammes's mystic feeling toward nature finds its most complete expression in *Romance of the Rabbit*. This story is like a delicate poem in prose; but it is truly impossible to make distinctions between Jammes's poetry and his prose, except perhaps that when he writes in prose he is less concerned with creating an original form and more spontaneous, allowing his language be more supple and reflect more closely the feeling he is trying to convey.

What makes this delicate story so admirable is its perfect stylistic unity. And unity of style, which implies the exclusion of all elements extraneous to the artistic intuition—even lofty elements—means unity of vision and therefore a successful work of art. . . .

The beautiful effect of the story's final repetition [of the opening scene] is a primarily musical inspiration; it is as if, in the return of phrases and rhythms, we were experiencing the conclusion of a piece of music, in which the principal themes are repeated. . . . The artistic value of *Romance of the Rabbit*, I think, lies precisely in its exquisite musicality, which gives coherence and coordinates elements that in other works remain isolated fragments, mere ingredients awaiting the breath of life.

> Augusta Guidetti. *Francis Jammes* (Torino,
> Fratelli Bocca, 1931), pp. 42, 46–47†

From the Morning Prayer to the Evening Prayer is Francis Jammes's densest work; it is enough to know it to know Jammes. It contains all the elements of Jammism. Each of his subsequent books emphasizes one element or another; none of them reveals any new elements. . . .

The verse line Jammes uses in this book has a varying number of syllables, despite the promise of classicism implied by the impeccable alexandrine of the title. The verse is not like the free verse of [Francis] Vielé-Griffin, Régnier, or Verhaeren—which, although it seems very loose, actually takes into consideration the rhythmic effects obtained by the succession of long and short lines. Jammes has almost totally freed himself from the preoccupation with melody to which the so-called free-verse poets were enslaved. . . . His goal is to charm not through meter but through the simplicity of the tone. Others *sing*, but Jammes *speaks*; he compensates for the loss of musical appeal by the appeal of the images and the natural tone of the words. . . .

[After 1898] his name became known in all the intellectual circles, sometimes engendering lively controversies. Praised as a restorer, attacked as a revolutionary; praised for his originality; attacked for his strangeness. His simplicity enchanted those who did not consider it ingenuousness. His sincerity was moving except to those who saw it as the worst of calculated tricks. As an improviser, Jammes astonished or disturbed, fascinated or shocked. The extent and intensity of the arguments Jammes provoked indicated that, as controversial as he was, he had made his mark. The literature of the new century had to take Jammes into consideration. [1946]

Robert Mallet. *Francis Jammes: Sa vie, son œuvre*
(Paris, Mercure de France, 1961), pp. 128, 137, 143†

What struck me most—and I would almost say edified me—about Francis Jammes, during the few days I spent with him, was his gift of sympathizing with his fellow men. . . . The people who lived [in his town in the region of Béarn] were not passers-by or shadows to him as they were to me. . . . They *existed*; and, indeed, the title of one of his most unusual poems, which I only understood when I recently reread it, is "Existences" [in *The Triumph of Life*]. For two whole hours I was half-dead with impatience and boredom while I listened to him have a discussion with two old ladies about the events of his small town—all the aspects, origins, and consequences of those events, in detail and in depth. And I said to myself: Well, Saint-Simon was also like that! . . .

This ability to sympathize, this interest of the man and the artist in his neighbor, Jammes was able to express in a whole group of prose works, some full of good-natured and comic verve, some slightly bitter. . . .

Jammes did not embark, like the *conquistadors* of the romantic period, for exotic lands, far removed either in space or in time, to discover new stars. Unlike Baudelaire (who, however, was also, with Boileau and Balzac, the best painter of Paris), he did not dream of plunging "to the depths of the unknown to find something new."

Jammes stayed at home, and he made it seem as if, before him, there had been no Pyrenees, no Béarn, no small town called Orthez, which he elevated to the importance of a capital, no young girls, no mountain torrent speaking loudly and clearly about the Holy Virgin! . . . Jammes does not criticize; he does not have any grievances against the Almighty. He is too busy looking around, breathing in deeply this mag-

nificent creation—the work of God and man. He looks at it, and he finds
it beautiful. He finds it beautiful, and he says so.

Paul Claudel. *RdP*. April, 1946, pp. 4, 7–8†

Francis Jammes was on the periphery of all schools of poetry at the turn
of the century, but he had a greater effect on French poetry than is
usually believed. Jammes himself was not very good about knowing
where he belonged, and was very wrong about the people he thought
were his models. He felt he owed a lot, if not everything, to François
Coppée and Sully-Prudhomme. Nothing of the kind: with his first poems
Jammes broke the iron yoke of Parnassianism. Simultaneously, he
turned his back on the elaborate and learned structures of many of the
symbolists. Verlaine did not need to have existed for Jammes to choose
"uneven" verse. His guide was the imperfect alexandrine and the constant rejection of metaphor. . . .

Jammes's work, so eager to open itself to light and the rays of the
sun, also has its shadowy side: salons with drawn shutters, the twilight
suffusing the garden and the rooms. . . .

In Jammes's work, as in Charles van Lerberghe's, there is a dual,
ambiguous approach to virginity and erotic passion. In Jammes the girl,
the young woman—virgin or lover—is always "drawn" in the nude. . . .
This subject is a constant in his poetry, and can be clearly seen everywhere—at least, until Paul Claudel made Jammes fall down gasping at
the feet of a God with a patriarchal beard, who would become more
and more of an encumbrance.

Hubert Juin. *Écrivains de l'avant-siècle* (Paris,
Éditions Seghers, 1972), pp. 267, 270–71†

JARRY, ALFRED (1873–1907)

The performance of *King Ubu*: *a guignolesque comedy* by M. Alfred
Jarry, at the Théâtre de l'Œuvre, if of little importance in itself, is of
considerable importance as a symptom of tendencies now agitating the
minds of the younger generation in France. The play is the first Symbolist farce; it has the crudity of a schoolboy or a savage; what is, after all,
most remarkable about it is the insolence with which a young writer
mocks at civilisation itself, sweeping all art, along with all humanity,
into the same inglorious slop-pail. That it should ever have been written
is sufficiently surprising; but it has been praised by Catulle Mendès, by
Anatole France; the book has gone through several editions, and now

[December, 1896] the play has been mounted by [Aurélien] Lugné-Poë (whose mainly Symbolist Théâtre de l'Œuvre has so significantly taken the place of the mainly Naturalist Théâtre Libre) and it has been given, twice over, before a crowded house, howling but dominated, a house buffeted into sheer bewilderment by the wooden lath of a gross, undiscriminating, infantile Philosopher-Pantaloon.

M. Jarry's idea, in this symbolical buffoonery, was to satirise humanity by setting human beings to play the part of marionettes, hiding their faces behind cardboard masks, tuning their voices to the howl and squeak which tradition has considerably assigned to the voices of that wooden world, and mimicking the rigid inflexibility and spasmodic life of puppets by a hopping and reeling gait. . . .

King Ubu is the gesticulation of a young savage of the woods, and it is his manner of expressing his disapproval of civilisation. Satire which is without distinctions becomes obvious, and M. Jarry's present conception of satire is very much that of the schoolboy to whom a practical joke is the most efficacious form of humour, and bad words scrawled on a slate the most salient kind of wit. These jerking and hopping, these filthy, fighting, swearing "gamins" of wood bring us back, let us admit, and may legitimately bring us back, to what is primitively animal in humanity. Ubu . . . is not invented with sufficient profundity, nor set in motion with a sufficiently comic invention. He does not quite attain to the true dignity of the marionette. He remains a monkey on a stick.

Yet, after all, Ubu has his interest, his value; and that strange experiment of the Rue Blanche its importance as a step in the movement of minds. For it shows us that the artificial, when it has gone the full circle, comes back to the primitive; [Huysmans's] Des Esseintes relapses into the Red Indian. [1896]

Arthur Symons. *Studies in Seven Arts* (New York,
E. P. Dutton, 1906), pp. 371–72, 375–76

Alfred Jarry was a man of letters, which few men are. His slightest gestures, his pranks—they were all literature. He had been formed by literature and by nothing else. But in what an admirable way! I once heard someone say that Jarry was the last writer of burlesques. This is a mistake! One might as well say that most of the writers of the fifteenth century, and a good number of those of the sixteenth, were merely writers of burlesques—a word that cannot refer to the rarest products of humanist culture. There is no word that could be applied to this particular sort of lightness, in which lyricism becomes satirical and in which satire, aimed at reality, goes so far beyond its object that the object is destroyed—in which satire soars so high that most poetry would have a hard time reaching it. At the same time triviality emerges as good taste itself and, by some inconceivable phenomenon, becomes a necessity. Only the Renaissance permitted writers to indulge in the debauches of the intelligence, in which the emotions have no place, and Jarry, by a miracle, was the last of these sublime debauchees.

Guillaume Apollinaire. *Les marges.* Nov., 1909, pp. 167–68†

I go to the first performance of Alfred Jarry's *King Ubu*, at the Théâtre de L'Œuvre. . . . The audience shake their fists at one another, and [my companion] whispers to me, "There are often duels after these performances," and he explains to me what is happening on the stage. The players are supposed to be dolls, toys, marionettes, and now they are all hopping like wooden frogs, and I can see for myself that the chief personage, who is some kind of King, carries for Sceptre a brush of the kind that we use to clean a closet. Feeling bound to support the most spirited party, we have shouted for the play, but that night at the Hotel Corneille I am very sad, for comedy, objectivity, has displayed its growing power once more. I say, "After Stephane Mallarmé, after Paul Verlaine, after Gustave Moreau, after Puvis de Chavannes, after our own verse, after all our subtle colour and nervous rhythm, after the faint mixed tints of Conder, what more is possible? After us the Savage God." [1922]

William Butler Yeats. *Autobiographies* (New York, Macmillan, 1927), p. 430

People relentlessly hissed *King Ubu*, a simple satire of every form of polite behavior and especially of war, of the Great War that was to come. It was an impressive uproar. . . .

Nevertheless, the impartial critics still saw, through the overwhelming racket, the vision of a new character, although an external one: a Guignol-tyrant and also a frightened bourgeois, cruel in a cowardly way, miserly, genially philosophical, related to Shakespeare's characters by his grandiloquence and to those of Rabelais by his primitive humanity. . . .

Despite all the condemnation and the scandal he provoked, this Father Ubu was to enter our heritage and make a permanent place there for himself. The sagacious Catulle Mendès, a disciple of Hugo, remained enough of a romantic to have understood fully the import of that unforgettable evening. . . . In his review Mendès wrote: ". . . Father Ubu exists. . . . As of now, he exists, unforgettable. You will be unable to get rid of him; he will haunt you; he will constantly force you to remember that he was, that he is; he will become a popular legend of the base, greedy, and filthy instincts, and Jarry, who I hope is destined for more delicate glories, will have created an infamous mask."

Mendès . . . did not forgive Jarry for his indifference to all glory and profit. . . . Jarry did not make a single move to thank Mendès, on the evening of his pseudo-triumph, for having sent him the proofs of his article. "I can't believe it," said Mendès, bewildered by the disdain of the triumphant Jarry. "Does he have bad manners, *too*?"

Rachilde. *Alfred Jarry; ou, Le surmâle de lettres*
(Paris, Bernard Grasset, 1928), pp. 79, 81–82, 84–87†

Jarry . . . signifies the eruption into life of humor, the supreme value of "those who know": that humor which he managed to exude with even his last breath. Ubu, "admirable creation for which I would give all Shakespeare and a Rabelais" (Breton), is the bourgeois of his time, and still more of ours. He coagulates in himself the cowardice, the ferocity, the cynicism, the disdain for the mind and its values, the omnipotence of *la gidouille* (the belly). He is the prototype of a class of tyrants and parasites the extent of whose misdeeds Jarry, dead too soon, was unable to contemplate.

The answer to Father Ubu is Doctor Faustroll [in *Deeds and Opinions of Doctor Faustroll, Pataphysician*], *savant pataphysicien*, imperturbable logician, carrying to their ultimate consequences the "speculations" of the geometricians, physicists, and philosophers, and quite at ease in a world grown utterly absurd. For even more than the types created, it is the atmosphere of Jarry's work which is unique and inimitable. Humor is the fourth dimension of this world, without it futile and unlivable. It seems to sum up Jarry's testament. A secret conquered at the cost of long suffering, humor is the answer of superior minds to this world in which they feel themselves alien. More than a natural secretion, as it has too often been regarded, humor manifests, on the contrary, the heroic attitude of those who are unwilling to compromise. It is as far from the famous "romantic irony" that considers with a detached expression and from a supraterrestrial world the unimportant events of this one, as from the cubist and futurist fantasies, diversions of aesthetes or bohemians who still imagine they have a part to play. Jarry never played a part, any more, than he lived his life. He made himself another life, a marginal one which he fulfilled perfectly. [1945]

Maurice Nadeau. *The History of Surrealism*
(New York, Macmillan, 1965), pp. 72–73

The literary group that found a home at the *Mercure de France* certainly had a considerable importance. I can bear witness to that, but I feel that I am not very well qualified to discuss the matter, since I only belonged to the group by the tip of my pen. I also spent very little time at the receptions held by Rachilde [who was married to Alfred Vallette, the magazine's founder and director]. All the same, I have lively memories of the rare appearances I made at her very hospitable salon. That was during the heyday of Alfred Jarry, an unimaginable figure whom I also met at Marcel Schwob's home and elsewhere. He was always a source of extremely keen amusement, until he sank horribly into attacks of delirium tremens. This kobold with a plaster face, dressed as a circus clown and playing a role that was whimsical and resolutely artificial, outside of which nothing human in him could be seen, exerted a strange sort of fascination at the *Mercure de France* (at that time). Almost everyone around him forced himself, some more successfully than others, to imitate and adopt his humor—and especially his manner of speaking, which was bizarre, rigid, without inflection or nuance and with every syllable given equal stress, including silent vowels. If a nutcracker could have spoken, it would not have spoken any differently.

Jarry declared his views without any embarrassment, with a perfect disdain for conventions. The surrealists, who followed him, never invented anything better, and there is good reason for them to recognize and salute him as a precursor. It would be impossible to push negation any farther than he did. . . . I consider some passages from his very uneven *Minutes of Memorial Sand*—the dialogue between Ubu and Professor Achras, and then Ubu's ensuing debate with his conscience—to constitute an extraordinary, incomparable, and perfect masterpiece, more so than *King Ubu*. [1946]

André Gide. *MdF*. July, 1940–Dec., 1946, p. 168†

I asked Jarry to have dinner with me in the little bistro on the Rue de Seine I had spoken so much about. I used to share a table there with several friends. The owner, a hefty man from Auvergne, was used to our behavior and was no longer amazed by anything. Nevertheless, the eating habits of Father Ubu surprised our good host more than the worst eccentricities of the "youth of today."

With a great deal of authority, and without deigning to take any notice of the growing bewilderment of the owner, Jarry ordered and consumed, in turn: a glass of cognac, a cup of coffee, a piece of gruyère, a fruit compote, a half-chicken, a plate of macaroni, a rib steak, a radish, and a bowl of soup—precisely in the fine order I have given. When Jarry got to the point of calling for a pernod—a five-star pernod, the drink of generals—the owner, who was sincerely sorry for him, placed an enormous paw on Jarry's shoulder and said: "Young man, you're going to harm yourself."

Father Ubu was naturally annoyed! The small restaurant took precedence over Literature! Jarry grimaced as well as he could, although his features were so delicate that he never really succeeded in making himself look as hideous as he would have liked. He ordered: "Bring me some red ink and a small glass!" The heroic and ingenuous hoaxer then courageously dipped a piece of sugar into the unusual liqueur and munched the sugar, filled with the pleasure of revenge.

Poor Jarry! Having invented the odious and sublime Ubu that we all admire, Jarry forced himself—without realizing how inferior he was to his own creation—first to eat backward and then to poison himself for the joy of astonishing an innocent wine-merchant. . . .

The memory of Jarry is precious to me. I have a very high opinion of the poet of *King Ubu* and the creator of *Love on a Visit*, this latter work not so well known as a less worthy book, *Supermale*, which drew screeching cries of joy from Rachilde, who reviewed novels for the *Mercure de France* then and did so detestably. I avow that the treasure trove of the human spirit has been increased by *Speculations* and *Deeds and Opinions of Doctor Faustroll, Pataphysician*. I believe that the proof of Jarry's genius is the fact that he has succeeded in surviving until the present time by influencing many people without, however, having any specific disciple.

André Salmon. *Souvenirs sans fin* (Paris, Gallimard, 1955), Vol. I, pp. 153–54†

Jarry's literary work . . . may appear on first examination to break in half. The extreme points seem to lie so far apart that one end will not lift the other. At one extreme, occupied principally by the enormity of Ubu, one finds scandal and coarse humor; at the other one finds a very personal manner of lyric and hermetic writing. A random sampling of his poetry may easily disclose texts that seem to come from two different authors, two different countries of the mind. Yet both in the idiom of popular balladry and in a style of contorted symbolism, Jarry used internal rhyme, alliteration, and refrain to build up a monotonous rhythm. The lullaby effect serves to throw into relief the boldness of certain images and to prepare the way for comic effects. With its roots deep in a childhood spent in the French countryside, Jarry's "symbolist" poetry never departs far from the aural, jocose, yet moving manner of the popular ditty. Not versatility but singleness of vision produced the variety of his writings.

Because of the contradictions in his work, however, critics have tended to recognize Jarry either as an important and influential poet who later squandered his gifts on novels and farces, or as a humorist on a new level of seriousness, or as a talented psychotic. None of these estimates is entirely wrong; they are partial. Jarry remains a humorist who surpassed laughter, a poet with a double feeling for symbolist tracery and argot, and a visionary in the tradition of Poe, Lautréamont, and Rimbaud. Nevertheless, his work must be taken whole despite its disparity at first glance. Carefully read with an open mind, his writings do not break in half. On the contrary, they turn and turn constantly away from a straight line, modulating from grossness to subtle irony to sentiment to metaphysical speculation to blasphemy to anarchism—and come full circle back to grossness. His work shows the circular structuring of a ring which can be held at any point to test its strength. There is no "end" beyond which one falls off into vacancy. For Jarry, truculent indecorum reaches round by visible paths to lyric intensity. The unity, the center, is the same as for his life: hallucination accepted as reality. In that vividly lit universe all products, base and elevated, of his fertile mind demand equal standing. His writings elude criticism as stubbornly as his life confounds biography.

Roger Shattuck. *The Banquet Years* (New York,
Harcourt, Brace, 1958), pp. 174–75

In 1894, a month before Jarry's twenty-first birthday, Éditions du Mercure de France brought out his first book, *Minutes of Memorial Sand.* . . . *Minutes of Memorial Sand* is essential to an understanding of all Jarry's later work, since within a framework of ultra-symbolism (almost a *reductio ad absurdum* of symbolist preoccupations with the ambiguity of meaning and the magic of sound) the author carefully introduces and blends the subtle intrusion of the concept of pataphysics and the gross intrusion of Monsieur Ubu. . . . The manifest imposture of Ubu is equivalent to, and inseparable from, the magnificent posture of pataphysics.

Betweeen 1894 and 1898 Jarry worked steadily on the development of this Universal Science which was to supersede what he summed up succinctly in a later text as "la Science avec une grande Scie" (*scie* is a slang expression for anything tedious), and his original concept of a theoretical exposition of pataphysics gave way to the more grandiose scheme of a Rabelaisian narrative, not only incorporating this theoretical apparatus, but applying it to the literary, artistic and scientific achievements of his era, within the context of a journey undertaken by the hero from one highly symbolic (and symbolist) island to another, and through the supplementary universe called Ethernity. This densely allusive "neo-scientific novel" (Jarry's own sub-title) describes *Deeds and Opinions of Doctor Faustroll, Pataphysician.*

The misunderstandings about Jarry's intentions that pursued him during his life, and continued to haunt him long after his death, resulted from the arbitrary separation, in the mind of the reader, the critic, the playgoer, of the person of Ubu, the Master of Phynances, from the spiritual nutrition of the force that motivated him—pataphysics, the

"science of imaginary solutions," which "will examine the laws govern-
ing exceptions, and will explain the universe supplementary to this one."
Simon Watson Taylor. *TLS*. Oct. 3, 1968, p. 1132

JOUHANDEAU, MARCEL (1888–   )

Jouhandeau's [characters] hold deep within themselves, and not inspired from without, the possibilities of a magnificent gesture or a great
decision. By that movement, and in that instant, the humblest or the
most wretched of creatures reaches the climax of life, is exalted and is
justified, whether like the insignificant Major [in *Tite-le-Long*] he sees
himself at the moment of death on the throne of God, or like the poor
hairdresser [in *The Hairdresser's Diary*] is enabled to feel that he has
dared to be a murderer. "O miracle of my heart!" the feeblest of them
may exclaim, "which has its root deep in Eternity."

Jouhandeau's most typical narratives are of this pattern: the story
of the failure in life of a maimed or sordid nature, suddenly lighted up at
the end by a flash from a source latent all the time, and so revealing
rather than contradicting all that went before. It is a pattern of life
which an Adlerian psychoanalyst might well invoke for his vindication:
the constitution of organic inferiority leading up to the reaction of a
triumphant masculine protest. For Jouhandeau, however, who is not
concerned with theories, that culmination may sometimes take on the
shape of solemn buffoonery—not easily to be imagined in an English
presentation—which would hardly be approved by the worthy Dr.
Adler. But Jouhandeau is not tied to this pattern.

Havelock Ellis. *LL*. March, 1933, p. 32

Jouhandeau's thought is always haunted by the same obsession, that of
the sin of his heart and of his body, "for which women have disgraced
themselves." His mysticism stems from his painful awareness of his
abnormality; he constantly returns to his vice: to explain himself, to
lessen his sin in the eyes of those who think of it as something odious,
and even to boast about it. Homosexuality is an incessant leitmotif; it
accompanies his entire work and is never silent; while it never bursts
forth in a victorious fanfare, rest assured that with a little attentiveness
you would constantly detect the low rumble of its music.

That is why this profound moralist does not always reach universality; that is why this first-rate psychologist sometimes seems a little

limited to us. But it is also because of this limitation that as a philosopher Jouhandeau reaches an unlimited perspective: his whole mind, bent in only one direction, discovers what an intellect that is normal—and therefore subject to continual distractions—would never have been able to grasp. . . .

Satan possesses him at the same time as God, and for the same reason. To the degree that he hates his nature, God rises before him; but whenever he allows himself to defend his vice, Lucifer appears. Some of Jouhandeau's words reveal the divine presence so intensely that we are seized by a holy terror; other times Jouhandeau gives the impression of having written at the command of the Evil One. Because of this occult duality, each of his works possesses a terrifying grandeur.

Claude Mauriac. *Introduction à une mystique de l'enfer* (Paris, Éditions Bernard Grasset, 1938), pp. 65–67†

No oeuvre is, in appearance, harder than Jouhandeau's to classify as belonging to any particular literary genre. Certainly, he has his masters, but he has no immediate predecessor. The name of Jules Renard has often been mentioned, but how can Renard's dryness be compared to Jouhandeau's richness? How can Renard's fastidiousness be compared to Jouhandeau's full, vivid, strongly accented style? No, Jouhandeau remains alone; the masters who taught him to think are far removed from those who taught him to write, and Jouhandeau seeks to join the two extremes—to impose Bossuet's tone on Pascal's anguish, Saint-Simon's cold violence on the malicious curiosity of a Princess Palatine, Saint John of the Cross's rigor on the adulterated elegance of the decadent symbolists. And Jouhandeau's work, far from suffering from such strange mixtures, is all the more enriched for them. The reason is that his work, instead of taking shape according to a continuous philosophy or style, is organized, somewhat concentrically, around a man—Marcel Jouhandeau himself. Jouhandeau is at the same time a real and fictitious figure who is able to draw both his existence and his style from these varied elements.

Undoubtedly, this is why Jouhandeau's work can be thought of as *novelistic*—as an immense novel of which Marcel Jouhandeau is simultaneously the writer and the central character. It is as if Gide's *The Counterfeiters* and *Journal of "The Counterfeiters"* were rolled up into one and multiplied to infinity. . . .

Nevertheless, there is no trace in Jouhandeau of the diarist who, in the manner of Gide, for example—conscientiously strives to speak sincerely about his own life. Jouhandeau is not concerned at all with that kind of sincerity, which results from successive revaluations. Jouhandeau invents his own sincerity. More than that—he invents *himself*. The way he invents his own character is the essence of novelistic creation.

Bernard Dort. Critique. Feb., 1954, pp. 106–7, 109†

[Jouhandeau's] adult experience is not fully transmuted into art. He is, of course, a Catholic homosexual, but more genuinely homosexual, I suspect, than Catholic. At the core of his writing lie masturbation, sodomy and guilt, the usual dreary trinity. Élise, his flamboyant, unpredictable wife, provides him with a good "subject," but she is really on the fringe of his attention. He gives various reasons for having married her; to escape from "freedom," to try to cure his homosexuality, in order to suffer. Perhaps the salutary irritation of Elise, together with the hygiene of writing, prevented him from going mad. If so, his marriage is genuine in its way. But the way is not ordinary enough to be representative. I am mildly amused by Élise's tantrums, but she does not become present to me as an interesting but shoddy person—like, say, Proust's Odette. In the long run, she is a bore, because she is just part of M. Jouhandeau's set-up. He does not really love her, in the intervals of hating her (which would be the usual conjugal situation); he is using her as a sheet-anchor or as an Aunt Sally. This is perhaps why, when he comes to what should be a major issue, the struggle between homosexual and heterosexual love, in *Chronicle of a Passion*, his writing fails. Élise is not a worthy enough object to set against his other interests. . . .

Moreover, philosophical or theological meditation, which he goes in for a good deal, is not his forte, although Claude Mauriac has published a rather pompous book, *Introduction to a Mysticism of Hell*, about Jouhandeau the sinner-saint. Jouhandeau writes well, but he wrangles self-importantly with God and he has no gift for organizing his experience. To give a simple example; at one moment he is all for sexual indulgence; at another he stresses the beauties of chastity; this is human enough, but it does not amount to a thought, and it is futile as literature, unless the reader is carried along some aesthetic curve from one attitude to the other.

The earlier works, *Chaminadour* in particular, are aesthetically satisfying in a traditional way; they show many signs of careful rewriting and are unclouded by argument. Perhaps Jouhandeau's psychological stresses later became too great for him to control, or perhaps he grew careless and self-satisfied and expected his readers to nibble experience raw out of his hand. Some certainly like to do so. For me, however, the greater part of his output is a confused psychological document, spangled with particles of literature.

J. G. Weightman. NSN. Oct. 29, 1955, pp. 547–48

The adventures [of Jouhandeau's character] Élise have entertained newspaper readers: their somewhat sensational glare has left other works by Jouhandeau in the shadow, works that are almost unknown but into which he put perhaps the best of himself. Jouhandeau is still misunderstood, but he has become famous—in the eyes of most people —as "Élise's husband." A recent literary survey states that the "essential part" of his work "is his analysis of married life," a statement that betrays ignorance of three-fourths of Jouhandeau's writing. Others who are better-informed recognize Jouhandeau's merits, but their praise is accompanied by astonishing misinterpretations: "I sought in vain [writes Maurice Nadeau] what prevented me from liking this writer of genius, what made me close his books every time I tried to read one. *Essay about Myself*, which *can* be read and reread, opened my eyes: what I object to is his sarcastic and icy inhumanity." After reaching such a conclusion, this critic had no need to confess to having closed Jouhandeau's books after only a few pages.

"Élise's husband"—certainly Jouhandeau cannot refuse that title, and that honor. But he has many others. "Sarcastic"—he is sometimes sarcastic, but more often he is as sensitive as someone whose skin has been flailed. Who could be less inhuman and icy than Jouhandeau, who is interested in, astonished at, and moved by everything? . . . Many of his books stem from the insatiable curiosity he has about others, and the power of sympathy that enables him to identify with them.

José Cabanis. *Jouhandeau* (Paris, Librairie Gallimard, 1959), pp. 36–37†

The scale of Jouhandeau's reputation in France is comparable with that of Ivy Compton-Burnett here. He is an author of addiction and something of a writer's writer. His genius was early recognised by Jacques Rivière, Gide, Paul Léautaud, Philippe Soupault (the Catholics other than Rivière and Charles du Bos found him a bit of a worry). Before the war, the pages of *La nouvelle revue française* were open to him (at the outbreak, one was delightedly reading *My Own* in instalments). The period immediately after the war was difficult. During the "purification," a communist-dominated trades-unionism flourished among writers in France. M. Jouhandeau was among those who were considered to have compromised themselves obscurely with the Germans, and nothing written by him was published for several years. . . . [Yet] Jouhandeau was the least politically minded of writers. Then matters eased, and for the first time he began to reach a wider audience. . . .

The value we place upon reticence seems to imply a belief that to be too candid is only too easy. I take this belief to be false. It seems to me that human beings are generally confused in purpose and lacking both in simplicity of manner and in true self-consciousness. . . .

All too rarely, there appears a man in whom unclouded introspection is accompanied by a vivid eye and a penetrating tongue. He must be cherished, and it is foolish to require of him either that he shall deploy all the contrivances of a novelist or that he shall refrain from using any such little tricks of presentation as his modesty or his self-regard may suggest. He may not be at his best when all contrivances have been shed. It would be difficult to say whether Jouhandeau's masterpiece is *Mr. Godeau in Private* or *Mr. Godeau Married*. In the face of such a writer, all one's notions of sincerity break down, if only because his malice may still be important to him.

Rayner Heppenstall. *The Fourfold Tradition*
(London, Barrie and Rockliff, 1961), p. 171–72, 175

[Jouhandeau's] "difference" is much deeper, much more fundamental, than that of the greatest "different" writers. We can much more easily assimilate Gide, Genet, Valéry, Proust, and Breton, no matter how personal their messages may be. Despite the lofty contempt of Montherlant and Bernanos when faced with eternal mediocrity, they can be classed with one group of thinkers or another. At the very least, their attitude toward us can be defined. The enigma of Jouhandeau is more unusual, almost unique. . . . After a solitary labor lasting half a century, standing apart from all writers of his generation, Jouhandeau reminds us of those vanilla plants that live in full luxuriance, totally detached from the soil.

Jouhandeau's egocentricity has made him many enemies. Many people open his books only out of curiosity or for the originality and admirable qualities of his style. Because Jouhandeau is thought to be an eccentric, he is not liked; yet other eccentrics, proud of being eccentric— Paul Léautaud, for example—are sought out for their very eccentricity. This paradox is not inexplicable. One must know all of Jouhandeau's work to evaluate individual volumes and place them in the ensemble. One soon perceives that there is no disorder in his work, if one goes back to his youth and follows the rigorous effort Jouhandeau has constantly made to perfect himself. His merit is that he has never refused to investigate his own abysses, has never allowed himself refuge in the shadow of self-deception, concealment, or lies. While he may have pushed self-esteem to its limits, one can quickly see that he is no less capable of charity, of compassion, and of passion.

Henri Rode. *Marcel Jouhandeau: Son œuvre et ses personnages* (Paris, Éditions de la Tête de Feuilles,
1972), pp. 10–11†

JOUVE, PIERRE JEAN (1887–1976)

[*Paulina 1880*] is a very strange and very interesting novel. Its merits rightly attracted the attention of the members of the Académie Goncourt, who might just as well have awarded their prize to this novel as to [Maurice Genevoix's] *Raboliot*. Paulina Pandolfini lives under her father's strict surveillance in Milan. She is beautiful, passionate, and mystical, and she is just as impatient to intoxicate the man who has been destined for her on this earth as she is concerned about being worthy of heaven. Nothing could be more Italian than this duality; and the manner in which Jouve accentuates it—by having his heroine make boldly ingenuous remarks about the agitation and pleasures of her body, while having her speak burning words of faith at the same time—would have delighted Stendhal. . . .

Such a creature is certainly unusual! Yet the evolution of the moral crisis that drives her to commit murder seems to follow an irreproachable logic. Jouve masterfully handles his drama, and he pursues the conflict that devastates his heroine's soul to its ultimate consequences with the understanding of a reliable psychologist. I admit, nevertheless, that I was not thrilled with the novel's form, even while conceding that the form suits Jouve's subject. Perhaps there is something artificial in the way in which Jouve divides his narrative into short chapters in which he moves rapidly from a personal to an impersonal style. His method, which consists of mixing his characters' words or thoughts into his narration, is disconcerting and becomes ultimately tiring or irritating. While aiming at concision, or cinematographic speed, Jouve forces the reader to stop and go back over what he has just read, since he has not been warned by any kind of sign that the style was changing. I believe that transition—which is one of the most difficult arts to acquire—makes the greatest contribution to the development of a narrative. In *Paulina 1880* that art clearly is totally absent. And this disturbs me, because Jouve has admirable virtues.

John Charpentier. *MdF*. March 1, 1926,
pp. 399–400†

In *The Marriage* . . . we see Jouve tragically disentangling himself from the earth and from accursed mankind, to soar backward through time toward the Garden of Eden, toward a naked Adam and Eve, toward the world's first awakening. *The Marriage* closes with this elation, with this dawning light. . . . The world is ordered. Chaos has disappeared from history. But Chaos is not dead. It has only been repressed. It is still within us, in the shadowy depths of our souls. . . .

Modern myths will arise from the memories pushed into the darkness of crypts. Poetry's power of incantation will conjure up those myths. Certainly, as Jung has shown us, the individual's subconscious is always deeply rooted in the collective unconscious. The primitive pagan myths that Christian magic turned to stone with a wave of the cross have not been completely exorcised; the old gods are still crouching within us, ready to leap to life in the madness of a nightmare or the intoxication of poetry. Jouve's [*Sweat of Blood*] brings back some of the old gods. But they will not return the way the bards embellished them, wearing the hypocritical veils of fiction; instead, they will return in all their savage truth, just as they burst forth in the clouded minds of primitive men.

Renaissance writers wanted to rediscover the freshness of paganism; Ronsard, for example, tried to re-create the soul of the ancient Greeks. But this kind of paganism was artificial, a purely rational construct. Instead of relying on their intelligence and will, Renaissance writers should have let themselves be carried away by their secret desires; they should have descended into the deepest part of themselves. And it is precisely by doing so that Jouve has succeeded where a writer like Ronsard failed.

Roger Bastide. CS. April, 1936, pp. 293, 296–97†

Pierre Jean Jouve and Marcel Jouhandeau both deal with the relationship between man and God. This relationship occupies the most important place in their work, taking precedence over the relationship between man and the world. In Jouhandeau the central concern is the problem of freedom; in Jouve, the problem of sin. The problem of liberty and the problem of sin are not part of the same concern. The first is a metaphysical issue, the second a moral one. The difference is more clearly perceptible if I add that Godeau, Jouhandeau's recurring protagonist, craves absolute liberty; Paulina, Jouve's central character, is tormented by carnal sin. . . .

Her anguish is even deeper than it appears. Not only is she dual—simultaneously pure and impure; but God is only revealed to her as a result of her dual nature. If she abandons sin, she has to abandon God. . . .

For Jouve, the only sin is carnal sin. In Paulina's diary we read this humiliating confession, this almost irrevocable condemnation: "What is monstrous is the nature of my sin. Not its circumstance, but its nature, and that will be true forever. God does not like the carnal act, and at the very least he imposes his law upon it; thus, the act is purified by his hands. But I have engaged in the carnal act against God. In other words, with the devil."

Almost everything written by Jouve is a commentary on these words.

René Micha. *L'œuvre de Pierre Jean Jouve* (Brussels, Cahiers du Journal des Poètes, 1940), pp. 8, 14–15†

It is easy to produce art, or at least a work which bears all the appearances of art, while leaving in shadow those energies of the soul which are most distressing and least admitted, yet which total art cannot ignore. Jouve made these energies his starting-point: the conversion of man to himself, the beginning and end of his art, would have been vitiated from the start, had he not taken as his poetic material this unstable and restless mixture of matter and spirit which constitutes the clay of being. The more terrible was the brutal nudity of the words, the stronger was the symbolic virtue of the universe of *Sweat of Blood*. Its sexuality was neither disguised nor indulged: it was not veiled in an air of complicity, but neither was it exhibited. It appeared in its own form, its ineluctable reality. Taken in its proper sense, no word struck Jouve as impermissible. He might have thought otherwise, had he judged the beautiful from the outside, by the texture and sound of the words: but the beautiful, in his mind, was clearly the expression of a certain knowledge; it would have been to destroy its essence to conceal what ought to be said.

But although the sexual aspect was important, it never became an obsession. If, in *Sweat of Blood*, it reappeared on almost every page, it was, after all, the primitive form of the anguish of man faced with himself, and as such the first which demanded elucidation. The eroticism of Jouve (as the preface clearly stated) could not be taken in any narrow sense: to seek in these images the diffused expression of sexuality alone, would have been a grave mistake. Now that this early book may be judged in relation to Jouve's work as a whole, it is easy to see that the *great Eros* whose divine action it sings, is universal creative energy, which consciousness has the role of integrating in extent and depth. [1947]

Pierre Emmanuel. *The Universal Singular* (London, Greywalls, 1950), p. 115

In 1935 [Jouve] published *The Principal Scene* and gloriously justified his previous labours in prose. His earlier novels became at once intelligible, not indeed as successful works of art—no retrospective judgment could make them that—but as necessary preliminaries, as directed and instructive enterprises, however unsuccessful. It is an unusual case: so many stutters before the statement is made, and then to find a statement of such astonishing confidence! M. Jouve has told the present writer that this will be his last novel, and indeed its title has a ring of finality which seems to refer to more than the contents of the book. Writers often break such resolutions as this, and even the *Last Poems* of the resolute [A. E.] Housman were not, as it was posthumously shown, final. But if ever such a resolution was intelligible it was this one. It is possible that M. Jouve will change his whole direction, turn aside into some new and unfamiliar path, but if he continues the exploration which he has followed until now, it is difficult to see how he can write another novel. In his poems there will always be new visions and apprehensions, new aspects of the truth he has discovered; prose, however, is a more explicit and therefore a more conclusive vehicle.

The Principal Scene consists of two stories, intimately related in theme, though differing widely in environment and in key. They are more than variations on a theme; rather they are the two sides of a coin, the two antithetical outcomes of a similar situation. . . . Each story is held together, integrated, by the controlling mind and purpose of the writer. Nothing in these stories is accidental or haphazard; nothing is added simply for extraneous effect. . . .

Guilt is the spur, love is the catharsis, death is the penalty for an inadequate love. Thus we might present the philosophy of Pierre Jean Jouve in bare and platitudinous form. It is a token, not of the occasional and almost inevitable ambiguity of his terms, but of his rich profundity that an exegesis of his great book could be made on many different levels. M. Jouve is a Freudian (Madame Jouve is a prominent psychoanalyst) and on one level Freudian terms can unravel nearly all the mysteries of his philosophy. Thus to have accepted the discoveries of Freud and to have transmuted them for his high creative purpose is by no means the least of his achievements.

TLS. April 24, 1948, pp. 225–27

Pierre Jean Jouve's greatness lies in his constant desire to reproduce, through his fiction and poetry, an obscurity that is never merely a verbal obscurity but has its roots in existence, in life. Words can seem obscure to us—but actually enlighten us if they delve into the secret of existence and life, a secret whose mythical resonance is reflected in words when they reach what we call the state of poetry. . . .

Jouve warns us: "I do not feel that my poetry depends on my childhood. I can only think of myself as an adult." Elsewhere he has written: "Art for me, you might say, does not have a local origin; it is a matter of *blood*, of heredity." Or: "To find a *religious* perspective in the act of writing poetry is the only answer to the annihilation of Time."

Jouve's is therefore a poetry deeply rooted in an adult civilization —a too-adult civilization. Jouve's is a poetry that the reader can only hope to discover—through meditation rather than illumination—by obstinately going back to that poetry's relationship with its sources, or rather with its principal theme. . . . And Jouve's works, his novels and poems, cannot have any theme other than love. [1957]

Giuseppe Ungaretti. *NRF.* March, 1968, pp. 385–86†

Post-war France was bound to disappoint Jouve, who had seen in the Resistance and Liberation a potential national "vita nuova." After 1948 his poetry returned to its private meditation. However, his poetic universe was never again as narrow as before the war. The climate of the soul for Jouve had been associated with the very few places in Europe that offered to him "a very powerful model of our interior life"—the Italian Alps, Salzburg, certain parts of a ravaged France. Now the scene became larger; seas, islands, deserts revolve in the wider and more flexible rhythms of a verset like that of Claudel, and a mysterious Oriental note recalls [Victor] Segalen or Saint-John Perse. The poetry also appears less purely personal because it approaches the problem of the nature of language. Jouve is by no means the advocate of uncontrolled inspiration, but he is able to describe one of his war-time poems as being written "apparently under dictation." He regards poetry as a mystery, and is impelled to penetrate it more deeply. Hence we find in *Language* and other books the repercussions of a battle to create a language that will faithfully translate the unknown. . . .

Jouve's excursions into novel and essay writing, his criticism and his occasional pieces, are all part of a remarkably consistent artistic vision, but it is as a poet that his stature must be measured. *Celestial Matter, The Virgin of Paris, Language*—with a special place for *The Marriage*—these are the most unified and beautiful of his books, and, taken all together, his poetry represents a unique investigation of man's spiritual problems in the twentieth century.

Margaret Callander. *The Poetry of Pierre Jean Jouve*
(Manchester, Manchester University Press, 1965),
pp. 7–8

It is our right and our good fortune to see Pierre Jean Jouve's complete works—his narrative works as much as his poetic works—as a successful attempt to construct a mystico-priapic temple in which the old god Pan unites with Christ above the abyss where ancient Rome once crumbled. Jouve's temple is a theater and an amphitheater as well, through the grace of Baudelaire and Freud. In Jouve's temple sexual joy, sublimated through the filter of ancestral guilt, is both the vehicle of the initiation and the principle of the drama. . . .

If Jouve's three great novels, *Paulina 1880, The Deserted World,* and *Adventure of Catherine Crachat,* and his shorter tales, *Bloody Stories* and *The Principal Scene,* had appeared between 1950 and 1960 instead of between 1925 and 1935 (according to the dates on the original editions), what a triumph they would have had! What an important influence they would have exerted on contemporary literature, and what fame they would have brought their author! Everything that fascinates contemporary minds is in these magnificent books, and the prose from which they are built is exemplary of the new narrative styles that modern writers, devoted to the difficult task of telling a story in an original way, are seeking, more or less successfully, to perfect. "These 'novels' are the tales of a poet," they said at the time and undoubtedly would still say today, in a country in which being called a "poet" is pejorative, in which readers do not take the work of a writer seriously when the word "poet" is applied to him.

Nevertheless, I take pleasure in saying that these novels are among the very best written in the narrative genre in France in the interwar period, along with Malraux's and Jouhandeau's early novels. Jouve's novels can be set apart from Malraux's and Jouhandeau's by the primordial and sovereign role played in Jouve's by love considered in its sexual aspect. . . . In Jouve's novels sex is human, too human, and superhuman; it raises man and woman to glory while simultaneously remaining devastating. The poems of *Sweat of Blood,* coming immediately after the narrative works, constitute for this idea a defense and illustration without parallel in any literature to which I have had access.

Jouve's church is built to defy time, because its basis, the radical element of man, can only be destroyed by the disappearance of the species. And I would like to contribute, as much as I am able, to directing the faithful toward that church.

André Pieyre de Mandiargues. L'Herne. No. 19,
1972, pp. 77–78†

Jouve's struggle has not ceased, nor his memory of the original darkness faded. Jouve's latest poems do not tell about man conquering death through the glory of the word, of the immortal memory of the world snatched up in an instant into eternity. On the contrary, they describe the poet's impulse to escape from darkness, seeking a light that continually evades his grasp. Day has dawned, but so, too, has the battle—the day's battle.

Jouve has condensed the alexandrine and has used the *verset* (a biblical verse form) in controlled patterns of musical expression: strophe, antistrophe, epode. But this music is full of harsh cries. His poetry is quite different from the surrealist's poetry of instant experience (that of sensory data or of automatic writing); in Jouve, poetry and experience are grounded in and justify each other. Each moment is the gauge, the measure of a life in progress. This poetry of time and toil has no facile charm to attract the reader; for its essence is not to be found in the places in which it glitters most brightly, but rather in the dark laborious path of its progress and development.

Though of impressive breadth and variety, Jouve's work has been too hermetic, too difficult, and too frequently intractable to appeal to a wide audience. Nonetheless, he has greatly influenced such younger poets as Pierre Emmanuel and Yves Bonnefoy, and he seems today to be one of the few modern writers who has fulfilled all the requirements of the word "poet."

Gaëtan Picon. *Contemporary French Literature*
(New York, Frederick Ungar, 1974), pp. 120–21

WORKS MENTIONED

Listed here, author by author, are all works mentioned in the critical selections. Each writer's works are arranged alphabetically by the literal translation used uniformly throughout the book. Following each literal translation in parentheses are the French title and the date of original publication. If a published translation of a full-length work or an essay exists, its title, together with the city and year of first publication, is given after a colon. (Translations of individual poems and stories, often available in numerous anthologies, are not listed.) When more than one translation of a work exists, the most recent American translation has been chosen. Collections in English of an author's poems, essays, or stories that do not correspond to a French collection are listed at the end of the author's works.

ACHARD, MARCEL

Do You Want to Play with Me? (*Voulez-vous jouer avec moâ?*, 1924): *Let Me Play with You* (London, 1933)

Jean from the Moon (*Jean de la lune*, 1929)

Malborough Goes to War! (*Malborough s'en va-t'en guerre!*, 1924)

Next to My Blonde (*Auprès de ma blonde*, 1946): *I Know My Love* (New York, 1952)

The Stupid Girl (*L'idiote*, 1961): *A Shot in the Dark* (New York, 1962)

Sweet Potato (*Patate*, 1957): *Rollo* (New York, 1956)

ADAMOV, ARTHUR

All against All (*Tous contre tous*, 1953)

The Confession (*L'aveu*, 1946)

The Direction of the March (*Le sens de la marche*, 1955)

The Great and Small Maneuver (*La grande et la petite manœuvre*, 1953)

The Invasion (*L'invasion*, 1950)

Paolo Paoli (*Paolo Paoli*, 1957): *Paolo Paoli* (New York, 1959)

Parody (*La parodie*, 1950)

Ping Pong (*Le ping-pong*, 1955): *Ping Pong* in *Two Plays* (New York, 1962)

The Politics of Garbage (*La politique des restes*, 1966)

Professor Taranne (*Le professeur Taranne*, 1953): *Professor Taranne* in *Two Plays* (New York, 1962)

ALAIN

History of My Thoughts (*Histoire de mes pensées*, 1936)

Mars; or, The Truth about War (*Mars; ou, La guerre jugée*, 1921): *Mars; or, The Truth about War* (New York, 1930)

Propos on Education (*Propos sur l'éducation*, 1932)

Propos on Happiness (*Propos sur le bonheur*, 1928): *Alain on Happiness* (New York, 1973)

Propos on Literature (*Propos de littérature*, 1933)

System of the Fine Arts (*Système des beaux-arts*, 1920)

ALAIN-FOURNIER

Big Meaulnes (*Le grand Meaulnes*, 1913): *The Lost Domain* (New York, 1959)

Correspondence between Jacques Rivière and Alain-Fournier (*Correspondance de Jacques Rivière et Alain-Fournier*, 1926)

Miracles (*Miracles*, 1924)

ALEXIS, JACQUES-STEPHEN

Comrade General Sun (*Compère Général Soleil*, 1955)

In the Blink of an Eye (*L'espace d'un cillement*, 1959)

The Musical Trees (*Les arbres musiciens*, 1957)

Romancero in the Stars (*Romancero aux étoiles*, 1960)

ANOUILH, JEAN

Antigone (*Antigone*, 1946): *Antigone* (New York, 1946)

Becket; or, God's Honor (*Becket; ou, L'honneur de Dieu*, 1959): *Becket* (New York, 1960)

Dear Antoine; or, The Love that Failed (*Cher Antoine; ou, L'amour raté*, 1969): *Dear Antoine; or, The Love that Failed* (New York, 1971)

Don't Wake the Lady (*Ne réveillez pas madame*, 1970)

The Ermine (*L'hermine*, 1934): *The Ermine* in *Five Plays*, Vol. I (New York, 1958)

Eurydice (*Eurydice*, 1945): *Legend of Lovers* (New York, 1952)

The Goldfish (*Les poissons rouges*, 1970)

Invitation to the Chateau (*L'invitation au château*, 1948): *Ring Round the Moon* (New York, 1950)

Jezebel (*Jézabel*, 1946)

The Lark (*L'alouette*, 1953): *The Lark* (New York, 1956)

Poor Bitos; or, The Masquerade Dinner-Party (*Pauvre Bitos; ou, Le dîner de têtes*, 1956): *Poor Bitos* (New York, 1964)

Rendezvous at Senlis (*Le rendez-vous de Senlis*, 1942): *Dinner with the Family* (London, 1958)

Romeo and Jeannette (*Roméo et Jeannette*, 1946): *Romeo and Jeannette* in *Five Plays*, Vol. I (New York, 1958)

There Was a Prisoner (*Y'avait un prisonnier*, 1935)

Thieves' Carnival (*Le bal des voleurs*, 1938): *Thieves' Carnival* in *The Modern Theatre* (New York, 1955)

Traveler without Luggage (*Le voyageur sans bagage*, 1937): *Traveler without Luggage* in *Seven Plays*, Vol. III (New York, 1967)

The Untamed Girl (*La sauvage*, 1938): *Restless Heart* in *Five Plays*, Vol. II (New York, 1959)

The Waltz of the Toreadors (*La valse des toréadors*, 1952): *The Waltz of the Toreadors* (New York, 1957)

APOLLINAIRE, GUILLAUME

Alcohols (*Alcools*, 1913): *Alcools* (Berkeley, Cal., 1965)

Anecdotal Life ("La vie anecdotique," 1911–18)

The Breasts of Tiresias (*Les mamelles de Tirésias*, 1918): *The Breasts of Tiresias* in *Modern French Theatre* (New York, 1964)

Calligrams (*Calligrammes*, 1918): *Calligrams* (Santa Barbara, Cal., 1970)

The Cubist Painters: Aesthetic Meditations (*Les peintres cubistes: Méditations esthétiques*, 1913): *The Cubist Painters: Aesthetic Meditations* (New York, 1944)

The Heresiarch and Co. (*L'hérésiarque et Cie*, 1910): *The Heresiarch and Co.* (Garden City, N.Y., 1965)

Honoré Subrac's Disappearance ("La disparition d'Honoré Subrac," 1910)

The Musician of Saint-Merry ("Le musicien de Saint-Merry," 1914)

The New Spirit and the Poets ("L'esprit nouveau et les poètes," 1918): "The New Spirit and the Poets" in *Selected Writings*

The Night of April 1915 ("La nuit d'avril 1915," 1916)

Onirocritique ("Onirocritique," 1908)

The Poet Assassinated (*Le poète assassiné*, 1916): *The Poet Assassinated* (New York, 1968)

The Sailor from Amsterdam ("Le matelot d'Amsterdam," 1910)

The Song of the Badly Loved ("La Chanson du Mal-Aimé," 1909)
Zone ("Zone," 1912)

Selected Writings (New York, 1950)

ARAGON, LOUIS

Anicet; or, The Panorama (*Anicet; ou, Le panorama*, 1921)
Blanche; or, Forgetfulness (*Blanche; ou, L'oubli*, 1967)
Elsa at the Mirror ("Elsa au miroir," 1945)
Elsa's Eyes (*Les yeux d'Elsa*, 1942)
Heartbreak (*Le crève-cœur*, 1941)
Holy Week (*La semaine sainte*, 1958): *Holy Week* (New York, 1961)
The Moment of Truth (*La mise à mort*, 1965)
The Peasant of Paris (*Le paysan de Paris*, 1926): *Nightwalker* (Englewood Cliffs, N.J., 1970)
Persecuted Persecutor (*Persécuté persécuteur*, 1931)
The Real World (*Le monde réel*, 9 vols., 1934–51):
   The Bells of Basel (*Les cloches de Bâle*, 1934): *The Bells of Basel* (New York, 1936)
   The Good Neighborhoods (*Les beaux quartiers*, 1936): *Residential Quarter* (New York, 1938)
   Those Who Ride Outside the Bus (*Les voyageurs de l'impériale*, 1942, 1947, 1965): *The Century Was Young* (New York, 1941)
   Aurélien (*Aurélien*, 1944): *Aurélien* (New York, 1947)
   The Communists (*Les communistes*, 5 volumes, 1949–51)
The Rooms (*Les chambres*, 1969)

Aragon: Poet of the French Resistance (New York, 1945)

ARLAND, MARCEL

Antares (*Antarès*, 1932)
The Gift of Writing (*La grâce d'écrire*, 1955)
The Great Pardon (*Le grand pardon*, 1965)
The Most Beautiful of Our Days (*Les plus beaux de nos jours*, 1937)
Order (*L'ordre*, 1929)
The Souls in Purgatory (*Les âmes en peine*, 1927)
Where the Heart Is Divided (*Où le cœur se partage*, 1927)

ARRABAL, FERNANDO

And They Put Handcuffs on the Flowers (*Et ils passèrent des menottes aux fleurs*, 1969): *And They Put Handcuffs on the Flowers* (New York, 1973)

The Architect and the Emperor of Assyria (*L'architecte et l'empereur d'Assyrie*, 1967): *The Architect and the Emperor of Assyria* (New York, 1969)

The Automobile Graveyard (*Le cimetière des voitures*, 1958): *The Automobile Graveyard* in *The Automobile Graveyard, and The Two Executioners* (New York, 1960)

The Condemned Man's Bicycle (*La bicyclette du condamné*, 1961): *The Condemned Man's Bicycle* in *Plays* (London, 1967)

The Coronation (*Le couronnement*, 1965)

Fando and Lis (*Fando et Lis*, 1958): *Fando and Lis* in *Four Plays* (London, 1962)

The Labyrinth (*Le labyrinthe*, 1961): *The Labyrinth* in *Guernica, and Other Plays* (New York, 1969)

Long Live Death (*Viva la muerte*, 1971)

Orison (*Oraison*, 1958): *Orison* in *Four Plays* (London, 1962)

Picnic on the Battlefield (*Pique-nique en campagne*, 1961): *Picnic on the Battlefield* in *Guernica, and Other Plays* (New York, 1969)

The Tricycle (*Le tricycle*, 1961): *The Tricycle* in *Guernica, and Other Plays* (New York, 1969)

ARTAUD, ANTONIN

The Cenci (*Les Cenci*, 1964): *The Cenci* (New York, 1970)

The Theater and Its Double (*Le théâtre et son double*, 1938): *The Theater and Its Double* (New York, 1958)

The Theater and the Plague ("Le théâtre et la peste," 1934): "The Theater and the Plague" in *The Theater and Its Double* (New York, 1958)

The Theater of Cruelty (First Manifesto) ("Le théâtre de la cruauté [Premier manifeste]," 1932): "The Theater of Cruelty (First Manifesto)" in *The Theater and Its Double* (New York, 1958)

AUDIBERTI, JACQUES

The Ant in the Body (*La fourmi dans le corps*, 1961)

The Black Feast (*La fête noire*, 1948)

Carnage (*Carnage*, 1942)

Evil Is in the Air (*Le mal court*, 1947)

The Falcon (*La hoberaute*, 1959)

The Gardens and the Rivers (*Les jardins et les fleuves*, 1954)

"Monument with Words" ("Stèle aux mots," 1943)

The New Origin (*La nouvelle origine*, 1942)

Race of Men (*Race des hommes*, 1937)

AYMÉ, MARCEL

Clérambard (*Clérambard*, 1950): *Clérambard* in *Four Modern French Comedies* (New York, 1960)

The Green Mare (*La jument verte*, 1933): *The Green Mare* (New York, 1955)

The Heads of Others (*La tête des autres*, 1952)

Intellectual Comfort (*Le confort intellectuel*, 1949)

The Road of the Students (*Le chemin des écoliers*, 1946): *The Transient Hour* (New York, 1948)

The Tales of the Perched Cat (*Les contes du chat perché*, 1934): *The Wonderful Farm* (New York, 1951)

Travelingue (*Travelingue*, 1941): *The Miraculous Barber* (New York, 1950)

Uranus (*Uranus*, 1948): *The Barkeep of Blémont* (New York, 1950)

The Walker-through-Walls ("Le passe-muraille," 1943)

Across Paris, and Other Stories (New York, 1958)
The Proverb, and Other Stories (New York, 1961)

BARBUSSE, HENRI

Fire (*Le feu*, 1916): *Under Fire* (New York, 1917)

The Inferno (*L'enfer*, 1908): *The Inferno* (New York, 1918)

Light (*La clarté*, 1919): *Light* (New York, 1919)

The Supplicants (*Les suppliants*, 1903)

We Others (*Nous autres*, 1914): *We Others: Stories of Fate, Love and Pity* (New York, 1918)

BARRÈS, MAURICE

Colette Baudoche (*Colette Baudoche*, 1909): *Colette Baudoche* (New York, 1918)

A Free Man (*Un homme libre*, 1889)

The Garden of Bérénice (*Le jardin de Bérénice*, 1891)

A Garden on the Orontes (*Un jardin sur l'Oronte*, 1922)

In the Service of Germany (*Au service de l'Allemagne*, 1905)

The Sacred Hill (*La colline inspirée*, 1913): *The Sacred Hill* (New York, 1929)

Under the Eyes of the Barbarians (*Sous l'œil des barbares*, 1888)

BARTHES, ROLAND

Critical Essays (*Essais critiques*, 1964): *Critical Essays* (Evanston, Ill., 1972)
Criticism and Truth (*Critique et vérité*, 1966)
The Empire of Signs (*L'empire de signes*, 1970)
Myth Today ("Le mythe aujourd'hui," 1957)
Mythologies (*Mythologies*, 1957): *Mythologies* (New York, 1972)
On Racine (*Sur Racine*, 1963): *On Racine* (New York, 1964)
Writing Degree Zero (*Le degré zéro de l'écriture*, 1953): *Writing Degree Zero* (New York, 1968)

BATAILLE, GEORGES

Hatred of Poetry (*La haine de la poésie*, 1947)
Inner Experience (*L'expérience intérieure*, 1943)
Story of the Eye (*Histoire de l'œil*, 1928)

BAZIN, HERVÉ

The Cry of the Screech Owl (*Le cri de la chouette*, 1972)
The Death of the Little Horse (*La mort du petit cheval*, 1950)
In the Name of the Son (*Au nom du fils*, 1960): *In the Name of the Son* (New York, 1962)
Matrimony (*Le matrimoine*, 1967)
Stand Up and Walk (*Lève-toi et marche*, 1952): *Constance* (New York, 1955)
Viper in the Fist (*Vipère au poing*, 1948): *Viper in the Fist* (New York, 1951)
Whom I Dare Love (*Qui j'ose aimer*, 1956): *A Tribe of Women* (New York, 1958)

BEAUVOIR, SIMONE DE

All Men Are Mortal (*Tous les hommes sont mortels*, 1946): *All Men Are Mortal* (Cleveland, 1955)
All Said and Done (*Tout compte fait*, 1972): *All Said and Done* (New York, 1974)
The Blood of Others (*Le sang des autres*, 1945): *The Blood of Others* (New York, 1948)
The Force of Things (*La force des choses*, 1963): *Force of Circumstance* (New York, 1965)
The Guest (*L'invitée*, 1943): *She Came to Stay* (Cleveland, 1954)

The Mandarins (*Les mandarins*, 1954): *The Mandarins* (Cleveland, 1956)

Memoirs of a Dutiful Daughter (*Mémoires d'une jeune fille rangée*, 1958): *Memoirs of a Dutiful Daughter* (Cleveland, 1959)

Old Age (*La vieillesse*, 1970): *The Coming of Age* (New York, 1972)

The Prime of Life (*La force de l'âge*, 1960): *The Prime of Life* (Cleveland, 1962)

The Second Sex (*Le deuxième sexe*, 1949): *The Second Sex* (New York, 1953)

A Very Easy Death (*Une mort très douce*, 1964): *A Very Easy Death* (New York, 1966)

BECKETT, SAMUEL

All that Fall (*Tous ceux qui tombent*, 1957): *All that Fall* in *Krapp's Last Tape, and Other Dramatic Pieces* (New York, 1960)

Endgame (*Fin de partie*, 1957): *Endgame* (New York, 1958)

Film (not published in French): *Film* (New York, 1969)

Happy Days (*Oh les beaux jours*, 1963): *Happy Days* (New York, 1961)

How It Is (*Comment c'est*, 1961): *How It Is* (New York, 1964)

Krapp's Last Tape (*La dernière bande*, 1959): *Krapp's Last Tape* in *Krapp's Last Tape, and Other Dramatic Pieces* (New York, 1960)

Lessness (*Sans*, 1969): *Lessness* (London, 1970)

Malone Dies (*Malone meurt*, 1951): *Malone Dies* (New York, 1956)

Molloy (*Molloy*, 1951): *Molloy* (New York, 1955)

More Pricks than Kicks (not published in French): *More Pricks than Kicks* (London, 1934; New York, 1970)

Murphy (*Murphy*, 1947): *Murphy* (London, 1938; New York, 1957)

The Unnamable (*L'innommable*, 1953): *The Unnamable* (New York, 1958)

Waiting for Godot (*En attendant Godot*, 1952): *Waiting for Godot* (New York, 1954)

Watt (*Watt*, 1968): *Watt* (Paris, 1953 [in English]; New York, 1959)

BENDA, JULIEN

Attempt at a Coherent Discourse on the Relationships between God and the World (*Essai d'un discours cohérent sur les rapports de Dieu et du monde*, 1931)

Belphegor (*Belphégor*, 1918): *Belphegor* (New York, 1929)

Byzantine France (*La France byzantine*, 1945)

The Ordination (*L'ordination*, 1912): *The Yoke of Pity* (New York, 1913)

The Treason of the Intellectuals (*La trahison des clercs*, 1927): *The Treason of the Intellectuals* (New York, 1928)

The Youth of an Intellectual (*La jeunesse d'un clerc*, 1936)

BERGSON, HENRI

Creative Evolution (*L'évolution créatrice*, 1907): *Creative Evolution* (New York, 1911)

The Two Sources of Morality and Religion (*Les deux sources de la morale et de la religion*, 1932): *The Two Sources of Morality and Religion* (New York, 1935)

BERNANOS, GEORGES

A Bad Dream (*Un mauvais rêve*, 1950): *Night is Darkest* (London, 1953)

A Crime (*Un crime*, 1935): *A Crime* (New York, 1936)

Dialogues of the Carmelites (*Dialogues des Carmélites*, 1949): *The Carmelites* (London, 1961)

The Diary of a Country Priest (*Journal d'un curé de campagne*, 1936): *The Diary of a Country Priest* (New York, 1937)

The Imposture (*L'imposture*, 1927)

Joy (*La joie*, 1929): *Joy* (New York, 1946)

Mr. Ouine (*Monsieur Ouine*, 1943, 1955): *The Open Mind* (London, 1945)

Under the Sun of Satan (*Sous le soleil de Satan*, 1926): *Under the Sun of Satan* (New York, 1949)

The Vast Cemeteries in the Moonlight (*Les grands cimetières sous la lune*, 1938): *A Diary of My Times* (New York, 1938)

BERNARD, JEAN-JACQUES

Invitation to a Voyage (*L'invitation au voyage*, 1924): *Invitation to a Voyage* in *Continental Plays* (Boston, 1935)

Martine (*Martine*, 1922): *Martine* in *The Sulky Fire: Five Plays* (London, 1935)

National 6 (*Nationale 6*, 1935)

The Springtime of Others (*Le printemps des autres*, 1924): *The Springtime of Others* in *The Sulky Fire: Five Plays* (London, 1935)

The Sulky Fire (*Le feu qui reprend mal*, 1921): *The Sulky Fire* in *The Sulky Fire: Five Plays* (London, 1935)

The Unquiet Spirit (*L'âme en peine*, 1927): *The Unquiet Spirit* in *The Sulky Fire: Five Plays* (London, 1935)

BETI, MONGO

Cruel Town (*Ville cruelle*, 1954)
The King Miraculously Healed (*Le roi miraculé*, 1958): *King Lazarus* (New York, 1971)
Mission Accomplished (*Mission terminée*, 1957): *Mission to Kala* (New York, 1971)
The Poor Christ of Bomba (*Le pauvre Christ de Bomba*, 1956): *The Poor Christ of Bomba* (London, 1971)
Tumultuous Cameroon ("Tumultueux Cameroun," 1959)

BHÊLY-QUÉNUM, OLYMPE

An Endless Trap (*Un piège sans fin*, 1960)
The Song of the Lake (*Le chant du lac*, 1965)

BILLETDOUX, FRANÇOIS

How Is the World, Mister? It's Turning, Mister! (*Comment va le monde, môssieu? Il tourne, môssieu!*, 1964)
Rintru Pa Trou Tar, Hin! (*Rintru pa trou tar, hin!*, 1971)
Silence, the Tree Is Still Moving (*Silence, l'arbre remue encore*, unpublished)
Tchin-Tchin (*Tchin-tchin*, 1959): *Tchin-Tchin* in *Two Plays* (New York, 1964)
Well, Go Along to Törpe's Place (*Va donc chez Törpe*, 1961): *Chez Torpe* in *Two Plays* (New York, 1964)
You Must Pass through the Clouds (*Il faut passer par les nuages*, 1965)

BLAIS, MARIE-CLAIRE

The Beautiful Beast (*La belle bête*, 1959): *Mad Shadows* (Boston, 1960)
David Sterne (*David Sterne*, 1967): *David Sterne* (Toronto, 1973)
The Day Is Dark (*Le jour est noir*, 1962): *The Day Is Dark* (New York, 1967)
A Joualonais, His Joualonie (*Un Joualonais, sa joualonie*, 1973): *St. Lawrence Blues* (New York, 1974)
The Manuscripts of Pauline Archange (*Manuscrits de Pauline Archange*, 1968): in *The Manuscripts of Pauline Archange* (New York, 1970)
The Sacred Travelers (*Les voyageurs sacrés*, 1963): *Three Travelers* (New York, 1967)

A Season in the Life of Emmanuel (*Une saison dans la vie d'Emmanuel*, 1965): A Season in the Life of Emmanuel (New York, 1966)

To Live! To Live! (*Vivre! Vivre!*, 1969): in *The Manuscripts of Pauline Archange* (New York, 1970)

The Unsubmissive Woman (*L'insoumise*, 1966)

BLANCHOT, MAURICE

The Almighty (*Le Très-Haut*, 1948)

Aminadab (*Aminadab*, 1942)

Death Sentence (*L'arrêt de mort*, 1948)

The Fire's Share (*La part du feu*, 1949)

Infinite Conversation (*L'entretien infini*, 1969)

The Last Man (*Le dernier homme*, 1957)

Literary Space (*L'espace littéraire*, 1955)

The One Who Did Not Accompany Me (*Celui qui ne m'accompagnait pas*, 1953)

Thomas the Obscure (*Thomas l'obscur*, 1941, 1950): *Thomas the Obscure* (New York, 1974)

Waiting, Forgetting (*L'attente L'oubli*, 1962)

BLOY, LÉON

The Desperate Man (*Le désespéré*, 1886)

The Diary of Léon Bloy (*Le journal de Léon Bloy*, 8 vols., 1897–1920)

Exegesis of Commonplaces (*Exégèse des lieux communs*, 1902)

The Man Who Revealed the Globe (*Le révélateur du globe*, 1884)

Napoleon's Soul (*L'âme de Napoléon*, 1912)

Salvation through the Jews (*Le salut par les Juifs*, 1892)

The Thankless Mendicant (*Le mendiant ingrat*, 1898)

The Woman Who Was Poor (*La femme pauvre*, 1897): *The Woman Who Was Poor* (New York, 1939)

Pilgrim of the Absolute (New York, 1947)

BONNEFOY, YVES

The Improbable (*L'improbable*, 1959)

On the Motion and Immobility of Douve (*Du mouvement et de l'immobilité de Douve*, 1953): *On the Motion and Immobility of Douve* (Athens, Ohio, 1968)

The Second Simplicity (*La seconde simplicité*, 1961)

Written Stone (*Pierre écrite*, 1959, 1965)
Yesterday Reigning Desert (*Hier régnant désert*, 1958)

Selected Poems (London, 1968)

BRETON, ANDRÉ

Anthology of Black Humor (*Anthologie de l'humour noir*, 1940)
Arcanum 17 (*Arcane 17*, 1944)
The Communicating Vessels (*Les vases communicants*, 1932)
Interviews (*Entretiens*, 1952)
The Lost Steps (*Les pas perdus*, 1924)
Mad Love (*L'amour fou*, 1937)
Magnetic Fields (*Les champs magnétiques*, 1920, with Philippe Soupault)
Manifesto of Surrealism (*Manifeste du surréalisme*, 1924): *Manifesto of Surrealism* in *Manifesto of Surrealism* (Ann Arbor, Mich., 1969)
Nadja (*Nadja*, 1928): *Nadja* (New York, 1960)
Poems (*Poèmes*, 1948)
The White-Haired Revolver (*Le revolver à cheveux blancs*, 1932)

Young Cherry Trees Secured against Hares (New York, 1946)
Selected Poems (London, 1969)

BRIEUX, EUGÈNE

Blanchette (*Blanchette*, 1892): *Blanchette* in *Blanchette, and The Escape* (Boston, 1913)
Damaged Goods (*Les avariés*, 1901): *Damaged Goods* in *Three Plays by Brieux* (New York, 1911)
The Escape (*L'évasion*, 1897): *The Escape* in *Blanchette, and The Escape* (Boston, 1913)
Faith (*La foi*, 1912): *False Gods* in *Woman on Her Own, False Gods, and The Red Robe* (New York, 1916)
The Machine (*L'engrenage*, 1894)
Maternity (*Maternité*, 1904): *Maternity* in *Three Plays by Brieux* (New York, 1911)
The Philanthropists (*Les bienfaiteurs*, 1897)
The Red Robe (*La robe rouge*, 1900): *The Red Robe* in *Woman on Her Own, False Gods, and The Red Robe* (New York, 1916)
The Substitutes (*Les remplaçants*, 1901)
The Three Daughters of Mr. Dupont (*Les trois filles de M. Dupont*, 1899): *The Three Daughters of M. Dupont* in *Three Plays by Brieux* (New York, 1911)

BUTOR, MICHEL

Degrees (*Degrés*, 1960): *Degrees* (New York, 1961)

Inventory (*Répertoire*, 2 vols., 1960–64): selections from both volumes in *Inventory* (New York, 1968)

Mobile: Study for a Representation of the United States (*Mobile: Étude pour une représentation des États-Unis*, 1962): *Mobile: Study for a Representation of the United States* (New York, 1963)

The Modification (*La modification*, 1957): *A Change of Heart* (New York, 1959)

Où: The Spirit of the Place, II (*Où: Le génie du lieu, II*, 1971)

Passage de Milan (*Passage de Milan*, 1954)

Passing Time (*L'emploi du temps*, 1956): *Passing Time* (New York, 1960)

Portrait of the Artist as a Young Monkey (*Portrait de l'artiste en jeune singe*, 1967)

6,810,000 Liters of Water per Second (*6,810,000 litres d'eau par seconde*, 1965): *Niagara* (Chicago, 1969)

The Spirit of the Place (*Le génie du lieu*, 1958)

Your Faust (*Votre Faust*, 1962)

CAMARA, LAYE

The Black Child (*L'enfant noir*, 1953): *The Dark Child* (New York, 1954)

Dramouss (*Dramouss*, 1966): *A Dream of Africa* (London, 1968)

The Gaze of the King (*Le regard du roi*, 1954): *The Radiance of the King* (London, 1956)

CAMUS, ALBERT

Caligula (*Caligula*, 1944): *Caligula* in *Caligula, and Three Other Plays* (New York, 1958)

Essays of Current Interest (*Actuelles*, 3 vols., 1950–58): selections in *Resistance, Rebellion, and Death* (New York, 1961)

The Fall (*La chute*, 1956): *The Fall* (New York, 1957)

A Happy Death (*La mort heureuse*, 1971): *A Happy Death* (New York, 1972)

The Just (*Les justes*, 1950): *The Just Assassins* in *Caligula, and Three Other Plays* (New York, 1958)

Letters to a German Friend (*Lettres à un ami allemand*, 1945): *Letters to a German Friend* in *Resistance, Rebellion, and Death* (New York, 1961)

The Misunderstanding (*Le malentendu*, 1944): *The Misunderstanding* in *Caligula, and Three Other Plays* (New York, 1958)

The Myth of Sisyphus (*Le mythe de Sisyphe*, 1942): *The Myth of Sisyphus* in *The Myth of Sisyphus, and Other Essays* (New York, 1955)

Notebooks, May, 1935–February, 1942 (*Carnets, mai 1935–février 1942*, 1962): *Notebooks, 1935–1942* (New York, 1961)

Observation on Rebellion ("Remarque sur la révolte," 1945)

The Plague (*La peste*, 1947): *The Plague* (New York, 1948)

The Rebel (*L'homme révolté*, 1951): *The Rebel: An Essay on Man in Revolt* (New York, 1954)

The Renegade ("Le rénégat," 1957)

The Stranger (L'étranger, 1942): *The Stranger* (New York, 1946)

CAYROL, JEAN

All in a Night (*L'espace d'une nuit*, 1954): *All in a Night* (London, 1957)

Foreign Bodies (*Les corps étrangers*, 1959): *Foreign Bodies* (New York, 1960)

I Shall Live the Love of Others (*Je vivrai l'amour des autres*, 3 vols., 1947–50):

Someone Speaks to You (*On vous parle*, 1947)

The First Days (*Les premiers jours*, 1947)

The Fire that Breaks Out (*Le feu qui prend*, 1950)

Poems of Night and Fog (*Poèmes de la nuit et du brouillard*, 1946)

CÉLINE, LOUIS-FERDINAND

Bagatelles for a Massacre (*Bagatelles pour un massacre*, 1937)

Castle to Castle (*D'un château l'autre*, 1957): *Castle to Castle* (New York, 1968)

Death on the Installment Plan (*Mort à crédit*, 1936): *Death on the Installment Plan* (New York, 1966)

Fairyland for Another Time, I (*Féerie pour une autre fois, I*, 1952)

Guignol's Band (*Guignol's Band*, 1944): *Guignol's Band* (New York, 1954)

Journey to the End of the Night (*Voyage au bout de la nuit*, 1932): *Journey to the End of the Night* (New York, 1934)

Normance: Fairyland for Another Time, II (*Normance: Féerie pour une autre fois, II*, 1954)

North (*Nord*, 1960): *North* (New York, 1972)

Rigadoon (*Rigadon*, 1969): *Rigadoon* (New York, 1974)

Shooting Gallery (*Casse-pipe*, 1949)

CENDRARS, BLAISE

Blaise Cendrars Speaks to You (*Blaise Cendrars vous parle*, 1952)
Easter in New York (*Les Pâques à New York*, 1912): *Easter in New York* in *Selected Writings* (New York, 1966)
Gold (*L'or*, 1925): *Sutter's Gold* (New York, 1926)
Negro Anthology (*Anthologie nègre*, 1921): *The African Saga* (New York, 1927)
Panama; or, The Adventures of My Seven Uncles (*Le Panama; ou, Les aventures de mes sept oncles*, 1918): *Panama; or, The Adventures of My Seven Uncles* (New York, 1931)
The Prose of the Trans-Siberian and of Little Jehanne of France (*La prose du Transsibérien et de la petite Jehanne de France*, 1913): *Prose of the Transsiberian and of Little Jeanne of France* in *Selected Writings* (New York, 1966)

CÉSAIRE, AIMÉ

And the Dogs Were Silent (*Et les chiens se taisaient*, 1956)
Discourse on Colonialism (*Discours sur le colonialisme*, 1950): *Discourse on Colonialism* (New York, 1972)
Notebook on a Return to My Native Land (*Cahier d'un retour au pays natal*, 1939): *Return to My Native Land* (Baltimore, 1969)
A Season in the Congo (*Une saison au Congo*, 1966): *A Season in the Congo* (New York, 1969)
A Tempest (*Une tempête*, 1969)
The Tragedy of King Christophe (*La tragédie du roi Christophe*, 1963): *The Tragedy of King Christophe* (New York, 1970)

CHAR, RENÉ

The Action of Justice Is Extinguished (*L'action de la justice est éteinte*, 1931)
Arsenal (*Arsenal*, 1929)
Artine (*Artine*, 1930)
First Mill (*Moulin premier*, 1936)
The Hammer with No Master (*Le marteau sans maître*, 1934)
Leaves of Hypnos (*Feuillets d'Hypnos*, 1946): *Leaves of Hypnos* (New York, 1973)
The Library Is Burning ("La bibliothèque est en feu," 1956)
The Pulverized Poem (*Le poème pulvérisé*, 1947)
Selected Poems and Prose (*Poèmes et prose choisis*, 1957)

Hypnos Waking (New York, 1956)
Poems of René Char (Princeton, N.J., 1976)

CLAUDEL, PAUL

Agamemnon (*L'Agamemnon*, 1896)

Break of Noon (*Partage de midi*, 1906): *Break of Noon* in *Two Dramas* (Chicago, 1960)

The City (*La ville*, 1893): *The City* (New Haven, Conn., 1920)

The East I Know (*Connaissance de l'Est*, 1900): *The East I Know* (New Haven, Conn., 1914)

The Exchange (*L'échange*, 1901)

Five Great Odes (*Cinq grandes odes*, 1910): *Five Great Odes* (Chester Springs, Pa., 1967)

The Hard Bread (*Le pain dur*, 1918): *Crusts* in *Three Plays* (Boston, 1945)

The Hostage (*L'otage*, 1911): *The Hostage* in *Three Plays* (Boston, 1945)

The Humiliation of the Father (*Le père humilié*, 1920): *The Humiliation of the Father* in *Three Plays* (Boston, 1945)

Magnificat ("Magnificat," 1910)

The Maiden Violaine (*La jeune fille Violaine*, 1901)

Poetic Art (*Art poétique*, 1907): *Poetic Art* (New York, 1948)

The Satin Slipper (*Le soulier de satin*, 1929): *The Satin Slipper; or, The Worst Is Not the Surest* (New Haven, Conn., 1931)

The Seventh Day's Rest (*Le repos du septième jour*, 1901)

The Sleeping Girl (*L'endormie*, 1925)

Tête d'Or (*Tête d'Or*, 1890): *Tête d'Or* (New Haven, Conn., 1919)

The Tidings Brought to Mary (*L'annonce faite à Marie*, 1912): *The Tidings Brought to Mary* in *Two Dramas* (Chicago, 1960)

Words for the Marshall ("Paroles au Maréchal," 1941)

COCTEAU, JEAN

Bacchus (*Bacchus*, 1952): *Bacchus* in *The Infernal Machine, and Other Plays* (New York, 1963)

Beauty and the Beast (*La belle et la bête*, 1973): *Beauty and the Beast* in *Three Screenplays* (New York, 1972)

The Blood of a Poet (*Le sang d'un poète*, 1948): *The Blood of a Poet* in *Two Screenplays* (New York, 1968)

A Call to Order (*Le rappel à l'ordre*, 1926): *A Call to Order* (New York, 1927)

Cock and Harlequin (*Le coq et l'arlequin*, 1918): *Cock and Harlequin* in *A Call to Order* (New York, 1927)

The Dance of Sophocles (*La danse de Sophocle*, 1912)

The Enfants Terribles (*Les enfants terribles*, 1929): *The Holy Terrors* (New York, 1957)

The Infernal Machine (*La machine infernale*, 1934): *The Infernal Machine* in *The Infernal Machine, and Other Plays* (New York, 1963)

Memory-Portraits (*Portraits-souvenir*, 1935): *Paris Album* (London, 1956)

Oedipus Rex (*Œdipe-Roi*, 1928): *Oedipus Rex* in *The Infernal Machine, and Other Plays* (New York, 1963)

Opera (*Opéra*, 1927)

Orpheus [play] (*Orphée*, 1927): *Orpheus* in *The Infernal Machine, and Other Plays* (New York, 1963)

Orpheus [film] (*Orphée*, 1951): *Orpheus* in *Three Screenplays* (New York, 1972)

The Parents Terribles (*Les parents terribles*, 1938): *Intimate Relations* in *Five Plays* (New York, 1961)

Plain-Song (*Plain-chant*, 1923)

Professional Secrets (*Le secret professionel*, 1922): *Professional Secrets* in *A Call to Order* (New York, 1927)

Thomas the Impostor (*Thomas l'imposteur*, 1923): *The Impostor* (New York, 1957)

The Wedding on the Eiffel Tower (*Les mariés de la Tour Eiffel*, 1923): *The Wedding on the Eiffel Tower* in *Modern French Theatre* (New York, 1964)

COLETTE, SIDONIE GABRIELLE

The Blue Lantern (*Le fanal bleu*, 1949): *The Blue Lantern* (New York, 1963)

Break of Day (*La naissance du jour*, 1928): *Break of Day* (New York, 1961)

Chéri (*Chéri*, 1920): *Chéri* in *Chéri, and The Last of Chéri* (New York, 1953)

Claudine at School (*Claudine à l'école*, 1900): *Claudine at School* (New York, 1957)

Claudine's House (*La maison de Claudine*, 1922): *My Mother's House* in *My Mother's House, and Sido* (New York, 1953)

Gigi (*Gigi*, 1944): *Gigi* (New York, 1952)

The Last of Chéri (*La fin de Chéri*, 1926): *The Last of Chéri* in *Chéri, and The Last of Chéri* (New York, 1953)

Mitsou (*Mitsou*, 1919): *Mitsou* (New York, 1958)

Retreat from Love (*La retraite sentimentale*, 1907): *Retreat from Love* (New York, 1974)

The Ripening Seed (*Le blé en herbe*, 1923): *The Ripening Seed* (New York, 1956)

Seven Animal Dialogues (*Sept dialogues de bêtes*, 1905): *Creature Conversations* in *Creatures Great and Small* (New York, 1957)

Sido (*Sido*, 1929): *Sido* in *My Mother's House, and Sido* (New York, 1953)

The Vagabond (*La vagabonde*, 1910): *The Vagabond* in *7 by Colette* (New York, 1955)

COURTELINE, GEORGES

Boubouroche (*Boubouroche*, 1893): *Boubouroche* in *The Plays of Georges Courteline* (London, 1961)

The Boulingrins (Les Boulingrin, 1898): *These Cornfields* in *Let's Get a Divorce!, and Other Plays* (New York, 1958)

The Commissioner Has a Big Heart (*Le commissaire est bon enfant*, 1900): *The Commissioner Has a Big Heart* in *Three Popular French Comedies* (New York, 1975)

The Conversion of Alceste (*La conversion d'Alceste*, 1905)

The 8:47 Train (*Le train de 8h.47*, 1888)

The Philosophy of Georges Courteline (*La philosophie de Georges Courteline*, 1917)

CROMMELYNCK, FERNAND

Carine; or, The Girl in Love With Her Soul (*Carine; ou, La jeune fille folle de son âme*, 1930)

The Childish Lovers (*Les amants puérils*, 1921)

Golden Guts (*Tripes d'or*, 1930)

Hot and Cold; or, Monsieur Dom's Idea (*Chaud et froid; ou, L'idée de Monsieur Dom*, 1936)

The Magnificent Cuckold (*Le cocu magnifique*, 1930): *The Magnificent Cuckold* (New York, 1966)

CUREL, FRANÇOIS DE

The Comedy of Genius (*La comédie du génie*, 1918)

The Fossils (*Les fossiles*, 1892): *The Fossils* in *Four Plays of the Free Theater* (Cincinnati, 1915)

The Guest (*L'invitée*, 1893)

Inhuman Land (*Terre inhumaine*, 1922)

The New Idol (*La nouvelle idole*, 1899)

The Lion's Meal (*Le repas du lion*, 1897)

The Reverse of a Saint (*L'envers d'une sainte*, 1892): *A False Saint* (New York, 1916)

The Soul Gone Mad (*L'âme en folie*, 1920)

DADIÉ, BERNARD BINLIN

The Black Skirt (*Le pagne noir*, 1955)

Boss of New York (*Patron de New York*, 1964)

The Circle of Days (*La ronde des jours*, 1956)

Climbié (*Climbié*, 1956): *Climbié* (New York, 1971)
A Negro in Paris (*Un Nègre à Paris*, 1959)

DAMAS, LÉON-GONTRAN

Black Label (*Black-Label*, 1956)
Et Cetera ("Et cætera," 1937)
Graffiti (*Graffiti*, 1952)
Pigments (*Pigments*, 1937)

African Songs of Love, War, Grief, and Abuse (Evanston, Ill., 1963)

DESNOS, ROBERT

Body and Belongings (*Corps et biens*, 1930)
Fortunes (*Fortunes*, 1942)
Rrose Sélavy ("Rrose Sélavy," 1922–23)
Saint-Merri Quarter ("Quartier Saint-Merri," 1936)
The Shadows ("Les ténèbres," 1927)
The Spaces inside Sleep ("Les espaces du sommeil," 1926)
30 Fable-Songs for Well-Behaved Children (*30 chantefables pour les enfants sages*, 1944)

---

22 Poems (Santa Cruz, Cal., 1971)
The Voice (New York, 1972)

DIB, MOHAMMED

Algeria (*L'Algérie*, 3 vols., 1952–57):
   The Big House (*La grande maison*, 1952)
   The Fire (*L'incendie*, 1954)
   The Loom (*Le métier à tisser*, 1957)
God in Barbary (*Dieu en Barbarie*, 1970)
Guardian Shadow (*Ombre gardienne*, 1961)
He Who Remembers the Sea (*Qui se souvient de la mer*, 1962)

DIOP, BIRAGO

The Bone ("L'os," 1958)
An Errand ("Une commission," 1947)
The Excuse ("Le prétexte," 1958)
The Inheritance ("L'héritage," 1947)
Little-Husband ("Petit-mari," 1947)

Lures and Lights (*Leurres et lueurs,* 1960)

New Tales of Amadou Koumba (*Les nouveaux contes d'Amadou Koumba,* 1958)

Tales of Amadou Koumba (*Les contes d'Amadou Koumba,* 1947)

Tales of Amadou Koumba [selections from both *Les contes* and *Les nouveaux contes*] (London, 1966)

DIOP, DAVID

Hammer Blows (*Coups de pilon, 1956*): *Hammer Blows* in *Hammer Blows, and Other Writings* (Bloomington, Ind., 1973)

Negro Tramp ("Nègre clochard," 1956)

To a Black Child ("À un enfant noir," 1956)

The Vultures ("Les vautours," 1956)

DRIEU LA ROCHELLE, PIERRE

The Comedy of Charleroi (*La comédie de Charleroi,* 1934)

Dreamy Bourgeoisie (*Rêveuse bourgeoisie,* 1937)

Gilles (*Gilles,* 1939)

Interrogation (*Interrogation,* 1917)

The Man Covered with Women (*L'homme couvert de femmes,* 1925)

Measure of France (*Mesure de la France,* 1922)

A Strange Kind of Journey (*Drôle de voyage,* 1933)

The Will-o'-the-Wisp (*Le feu follet,* 1931): *The Fire Within* (New York, 1965)

The Young European (*Le jeune Européen,* 1927)

Secret Journal, and Other Writings (New York, 1974)

DUHAMEL, GEORGES

The Chronicle of the Pasquiers (*Chronique des Pasquier,* 10 vols., 1933–45): *The Pasquier Chronicles* (New York, 1938) [vols. 1–5]; *Cecile Pasquier* (New York, 1940) [vols. 6–8]; *Two Novels from the Pasquier Chronicles: Suzanne, and Joseph Pasquier* (New York, 1949) [vols. 9–10]

Civilization (*Civilisation,* 1918): *Civilization* (New York, 1919)

Conversations in the Turmoil (*Entretiens dans le tumulte,* 1919)

Life and Adventures of Salavin (*Vie et aventures de Salavin,* 5 vols., 1920–32): *Salavin* [includes all but the second vol.] (New York, 1936)

The Light (*La lumière,* 1911): *The Light* in *Poet Lore* (25, 1914)

Life of the Martyrs (*Vie des martyrs*, 1917): *The New Book of Martyrs* (New York, 1918)
The Possession of the World (*La possession du monde*, 1919): *The Heart's Domain* (New York, 1919)
Scenes of the Future Life (*Scènes de la vie future*, 1930): *America: The Menace* (Boston, 1931)

DURAS, MARGUERITE

The Afternoon of Mr. Andesmas (*L'après-midi de Monsieur Andesmas*, 1962): *The Afternoon of Mr. Andesmas* in *Four Novels* (New York, 1965)
A Dam against the Pacific (*Un barrage contre le Pacifique*, 1950): *The Sea Wall* (New York, 1952)
Hiroshima, My Love (*Hiroshima, mon amour*, 1960): *Hiroshima, Mon Amour* (New York, 1961)
Love (*L'amour*, 1972)
Moderato Cantabile (*Moderato cantabile*, 1958): *Moderato Cantabile* in *Four Novels* (New York, 1965)
La Musica (*La musica*, 1965)
The Sailor from Gibraltar (*Le marin de Gibraltar*, 1952): *The Sailor from Gibraltar* (New York, 1967)
The Square (*Le square*, 1955): *The Square* in *Four Novels* (New York, 1965)
Suzanna Andler (*Suzanna Andler*, 1968)
The Vice-Consul (*Le vice-consul*, 1966): *The Vice-Consul* (London, 1968)
Whole Days in the Trees (*Des journées entières dans les arbres*, 1954)

ÉLUARD, PAUL

Capital of Pain (*Capitale de la douleur*, 1926): *Capital of Pain* (New York, 1973)
Immediate Life (*La vie immédiate*, 1932)
A Lesson in Morality (*Une leçon de morale*, 1949)
Pablo Picasso ("Pablo Picasso," 1926)
Poetry and Truth 1942 (*Poésie et vérité 1942*, 1942, 1943): *Poetry and Truth 1942* (London, 1944)
Uninterrupted Poetry (*Poésie ininterrompue*, 1946)

Thorns of Thunder (London, 1936)
Selected Writings (Norfolk, Conn., 1951)

EMMANUEL, PIERRE

Abraham's Prayer (*Prière d'Abraham*, 1943)
Babel (*Babel*, 1951)
Christ in the Tomb ("Christ au tombeau," 1942)
Day of Anger (*Jour de colère*, 1942)
Evangeliary (*Évangéliaire*, 1961)
Fight with Your Defenders (*Combats avec tes défenseurs*, 1942)
Golgotha ("Golgotha," 1942)
Orpheus' Tomb (*Tombeau d'Orphée*, 1941)
The Poet and His Christ (*Le poète et son Christ*, 1942)
Sodom (*Sodome*, 1944)
XX Cantos (*XX Cantos*, 1942)
Who Is This Man? (*Qui est cet homme?*, 1947): *The Universal Singular* (London, 1950)

FARGUE, LÉON-PAUL

After Paris (*D'après Paris*, 1931)
The Parisian Pedestrian (*Le piéton de Paris*, 1939)
Poems (*Poèmes*, 1912)
The Shipwrecker's Second Tale ("Second récit du naufrageur," 1927)
Spaces (*Espaces*, 1929)
Tancrède (*Tancrède*, 1911)
Total Solitude (*Haute solitude*, 1941)
Under the Lamp (*Sous la lampe*, 1930)

FAYE, JEAN-PIERRE

Analogues (*Analogues*, 1964)
Between the Streets (*Entre les rues*, 1958)
The Break (*La cassure*, 1961)
The Canal Lock (*L'écluse*, 1964)
The People of Troyes (*Les Troyens*, 1970)
Pulsation (*Battement*, 1962)

FERAOUN, MOULOUD

The Climbing Roads (*Les chemins qui montent*, 1957)
Days of Kabylia (*Jours de Kabylie*, 1954)
Diary (*Journal*, 1962)
Earth and Blood (*La terre et le sang*, 1953)
The Poor Man's Son (*Le fils du pauvre*, 1950)

FEYDEAU, GEORGES

Champignol in Spite of Himself (*Champignol malgré lui*, 1925 [with Maurice Desvallières]): *A Close Shave* (London, 1974)

A Flea in Her Ear (*La puce à l'oreille*, 1909): *A Flea in Her Ear* (Chicago, 1968)

The Hotel of Free Trade (*L'Hôtel du Libre-Échange*, 1928 [with Maurice Desvallières]): *Hotel Paradiso* (New York, 1957)

I Don't Cheat on My Husband (*Je ne trompe pas mon mari*, 1921 [with René Peter])

Keep an Eye on Amélie (*Occupe-toi d'Amélie*, 1911): *Keep an Eye on Amélie!* in *Let's Get a Divorce!, and Other Plays* (New York, 1958)

The Lady from Maxim's (*La dame de chez Maxim*, 1914): *The Lady from Maxim's* (New York, 1971)

The Master Goes Hunting! (*Monsieur chasse!*, 1896): *The Happy Hunter* (New York, 1972)

The Sucker (*Le dindon*, 1949)

Your Deal Next (*La main passe*, 1907): *Chemin de Fer* (New York, 1968)

FRANCE, ANATOLE

Contemporary History (*Histoire contemporaine*, 4 vols., 1897–1901):
The Elm-Tree on the Mall (*L'orme du mail*, 1897): *The Elm-Tree on the Mall* (New York, 1910)
The Wicker Work Woman (*Le mannequin d'osier*, 1897): *The Wicker Work Woman* (New York, 1910)
The Amethyst Ring (*L'anneau d'améthyste*, 1899): *The Amethyst Ring* (New York, 1919)
Monsieur Bergeret in Paris (*Monsieur Bergeret à Paris*, 1901): *Monsieur Bergeret in Paris* (New York, 1922)

The Crime of Sylvestre Bonnard (*Le crime de Sylvestre Bonnard*, 1881): *The Crime of Sylvestre Bonnard* (New York, 1890)

The Crainquebille Affair (*L'affaire Crainquebille*, 1901): *Crainquebille* (New York, 1949)

The Gods Are Athirst (*Les dieux ont soif*, 1912): *The Gods Are Athirst* (New York, 1953)

Golden Poems (*Les poèmes dorés*, 1873)

The Life of Joan of Arc (*Vie de Jeanne d'Arc*, 1908): *The Life of Joan of Arc* (New York, 1909)

My Friend's Book (*Le livre de mon ami*, 1885): *My Friend's Book* (New York, 1913)

Penguin Island (*L'île des Pingouins*, 1908): *Penguin Island* (New York, 1909)

The "Queen Pédauque" Grill (*La rôtisserie de la Reine Pédauque*, 1893): *At the Sign of the Queen Pédauque* (Chicago, 1933)

The Red Lily (*Le lys rouge*, 1894): *The Red Lily* (New York, 1908)

The Revolt of the Angels (*La révolte des anges*, 1914): *The Revolt of the Angels* (New York, 1914)

Thaïs (*Thaïs*, 1891): *Thaïs* (New York, 1929)

GARY, ROMAIN

A European Education (*Éducation européenne*, 1945): *A European Education* (New York, 1960)

Lady L. (*Lady L.*, 1963): *Lady L.* (New York, 1958)

Promise at Dawn (*La promesse de l'aube*, 1960): *Promise at Dawn* (New York, 1961)

The Roots of Heaven (*Les racines du ciel*, 1956): *The Roots of Heaven* (New York, 1958)

White Dog (*Chien Blanc*, 1970): *White Dog* (New York, 1970)

GASCAR, PIERRE

The Ark (*L'arche*, 1971)

Beasts (*Les bêtes*, 1953): in *Beasts and Men* (Boston, 1956)

The Chimeras (*Les chimères*, 1969)

The Season of the Dead (*Le temps des morts*, 1953): in *Beasts and Men* (Boston, 1956)

Suns (*Soleils*, 1960): in *Women and the Sun* (Boston, 1965)

Women (*Les femmes*, 1955): in *Women and the Sun* (Boston, 1965)

GATTI, ARMAND

The Imaginary Life of the Street Cleaner Auguste G. (*La vie imaginaire de l'éboueur Auguste Geai*, 1962): *The Imaginary Life of the Street Cleaner August G.* in *The Contemporary French Theater* (New York, 1973)

Public Hymn before Two Electric Chairs (*Chant public devant deux chaises électriques*, 1964)

The Second Life of the Tattenberg Camp (*La deuxième existence du camp de Tattenberg*, 1962)

The Toad-Buffalo (*Le crapaud-buffle*, 1959)

GENET, JEAN

The Balcony (*Le balcon*, 1956): *The Balcony* (New York, 1958)

The Blacks (*Les Nègres*, 1958): *The Blacks* (New York, 1960)

Complete Works (*Œuvres complètes*, 3 vols., 1951–53)

The Criminal Child (*L'enfant criminel*, 1949)

Deathwatch (*Haute surveillance*, 1947): *Deathwatch* in *The Maids, and Deathwatch* (New York, 1954)

The Maids (*Les bonnes*, 1947, 1954): *The Maids* in *The Maids, and Deathwatch* (New York, 1954)

Miracle of the Rose (*Miracle de la rose*, 1946): *Miracle of the Rose* (New York, 1966)

Our Lady of the Flowers (*Notre-Dame-des-Fleurs*, 1948, 1951): *Our Lady of the Flowers* (New York, 1963)

The Screens (*Les paravents*, 1961): *The Screens* (New York, 1962)

The Thief's Journal (*Journal du voleur*, 1949): *The Thief's Journal* (New York, 1964)

GHELDERODE, MICHEL DE

Barabbas (*Barabbas*, 1932): *Barabbas* in *Seven Plays*, Vol. I (New York, 1960)

The Blind Men (*Les aveugles*, 1949): *The Blind Men* in *Seven Plays*, Vol. I (New York, 1960)

Christopher Columbus (*Christophe Colomb*, 1928): *Christopher Columbus* in *Seven Plays*, Vol. II (New York, 1964)

Exit of the Actor (*Sortie de l'acteur*, 1941)

Hop Signor! (*Hop Signor!*, 1938): *Hop Signor!* in *Seven Plays*, Vol. II (New York, 1964)

The Ostend Interviews (*Les entretiens d'Ostende* [with R. Iglesis and A. Trutat], 1956): *The Ostend Interviews* in *Seven Plays*, Vol. I (New York, 1960)

Pantagleize (*Pantagleize*, 1934): *Pantagleize* in *Seven Plays*, Vol. I (New York, 1960)

GIDE, ANDRÉ

Amyntas (*Amyntas*, 1906): *Amyntas* (New York, 1958)

Back from the Chad (*Le retour du Tchad*, 1928): *Back from the Chad* in *Travels in the Congo* (New York, 1929)

Corydon (*Corydon*, 1924): *Corydon* (New York, 1950)

The Counterfeiters (*Les faux-monnayeurs*, 1926): *The Counterfeiters* (New York, 1927)

Et Nunc Manet in Te (*Et nunc manet in te*, 1951): *Madeleine* (New York, 1952)

The Fruits of the Earth (*Les nourritures terrestres*, 1897): *The Fruits of the Earth* in *The Fruits of the Earth* (New York, 1949)

If the Grain Die... (*Si le grain ne meurt...*, 1924): *If It Die...* (New York, 1935)

The Immoralist (*L'immoraliste*, 1902): *The Immoralist* (New York, 1970)

Journal (*Journal, 1889–1939*, 1939; *Journal, 1939–42*, 1946; *Journal 1942–49*, 1950): *The Journals of André Gide* (New York, 4 vols. 1947–51)

Journal of "The Counterfeiters" (*Journal des "Faux-monnayeurs,"* 1927): *Journal of "The Counterfeiters"* in *The Counterfeiters* (New York, 1959)

Journey to the Congo (*Voyage au Congo*, 1927): As *To the Congo* in *Travels in the Congo* (New York, 1929)

Marshlands (*Paludes*, 1895): *Marshlands* in *Marshlands, and Prometheus Misbound* (New York, 1953)

The Narrow Gate (*La porte étroite*, 1909): *Strait Is the Gate* (New York, 1924)

The New Fruits (*Les nouvelles nourritures*, 1935): *The New Fruits* in *The Fruits of the Earth* (New York, 1949)

The Notebooks of André Walter (*Les cahiers d'André Walter*, 1891): *The Notebooks of André Walter* (New York, 1968)

The Pastoral Symphony (*La symphonie pastorale*, 1919): *La Symphonie Pastorale* in *Two Symphonies* (New York, 1931)

Prometheus Misbound (*Le Prométhée mal enchaîné*, 1899): *Prometheus Misbound* in *Marshlands, and Prometheus Misbound* (New York, 1953)

Theseus (*Thésée*, 1946): *Theseus* in *Two Legends: Oedipus, and Theseus* (New York, 1950)

The Vatican Cellars (*Les caves du Vatican*, 1914): *The Vatican Swindle* (New York, 1925)

GIONO, JEAN

Battles in the Mountain (*Batailles dans la montagne*, 1937)

Harvest (*Regain*, 1930): *Harvest* (New York, 1939)

Hill (*Colline*, 1929): *Hill of Destiny* (New York, 1929)

The Hussar on the Roof (*Le hussard sur le toit*, 1951): *The Horseman on the Roof* (New York, 1954)

Jean the Blue (*Jean le Bleu*, 1932): *Blue Boy* (New York, 1946)

Mad Happiness (*Le bonheur fou*, 1957): *The Straw Man* (New York, 1959)

May My Joy Remain (*Que ma joie demeure*, 1935): *Joy of Man's Destiny* (New York, 1940)

The Mill of Poland (*Le moulin de Pologne*, 1952): *The Malediction* (New York, 1955)

The Song of the World (*Le chant du monde*, 1934): *The Song of the World* (New York, 1937)

Strong Souls (*Les âmes fortes*, 1949)